SLAVERY RACE AND THE AMERICAN LEGAL SYSTEM 1700-1872

A SIXTEEN VOLUME FACSIMILE SERIES REPRODUCING OVER ONE HUNDRED AND SEVENTY RARE AND IMPORTANT PAMPHLETS

Edited by Paul Finkelman
President William McKinley Distinguished
Professor of Law and Public Policy
and Senior Fellow, Government Law Center,
Albany Law School

THE LAWBOOK EXCHANGE, LTD.
Clark, New Jersey

CONTENTS OF THE SET

Series I
SOUTHERN SLAVES IN FREE STATE COURTS
The Pamphlet Literature
three volumes

Series II
FUGITIVE SLAVES AND AMERICAN COURTS
The Pamphlet Literature
four volumes

Series III
ABOLITIONISTS IN NORTHERN COURTS
The Pamphlet Literature
one volume

Series IV
SLAVE REBELS, ABOLITIONISTS, AND SOUTHERN COURTS
The Pamphlet Literature
two volumes

Series V
THE AFRICAN SLAVE TRADE AND AMERICAN COURTS
The Pamphlet Literature
two volumes

Series VI
FREE BLACKS, SLAVES, AND SLAVE OWNERS IN CIVIL AND CRIMINAL COURTS
The Pamphlet Literature
two volumes

Series VII
STATUTES ON SLAVERY
The Pamphlet Literature
two volumes

ABOLITIONISTS IN NORTHERN COURTS

THE PAMPHLET LITERATURE

SERIES III

Edited with an Introduction by

Paul Finkelman

THE LAWBOOK EXCHANGE, LTD.
Clark, New Jersey

ISBN 9781584777397 (Series III)
ISBN 9781584778127 (Slavery, Race and the American Legal System 1700–1872 set)

Lawbook Exchange edition 2007, 2012

The quality of this reprint is equivalent to the quality of the original work.

THE LAWBOOK EXCHANGE, LTD.
33 Terminal Avenue
Clark, New Jersey 07066-1321

Please see our website for a selection of our other publications and fine facsimile reprints of classic works of legal history:
www.lawbookexchange.com

Library of Congress Cataloging-in-Publication Data

Abolitionists in northern courts : the pamphlet literature / [edited with an introduction by] Paul Finkelman.
p. cm.
Originally published: New York : Garland Pub., 1988. (Slavery, race, and the American legal system, 1700-1872 ; ser. 3).
Includes bibliographical references.
ISBN-13: 978-1-58477-739-7 (acid-free paper)
ISBN-10: 1-58477-739-7 (acid-free paper)
1. Slavery--Law and legislation--United States--Cases. 2. African Americans--Legal status, laws, etc.--Cases. 3. Abolitionists--Legal status, laws, etc.--United States--Cases. 4. Criminal law--United States--Cases. 5. Criminal justice, Administration of--United States--Cases. I. Finkelman, Paul, 1949- II. Series: Slavery, race, and the American legal system, 1700-1872 ; ser. 3.
KF4545.S5 A5 1988 ser. 3 2007
342.7308'7--dc22 2006017313

Printed in the United States of America on acid-free paper

Slavery, Race and the American Legal System 1700–1872

Series Preface

In 1980 while holding the J. Franklin Jameson Fellowship at the Library of Congress I discovered a number of mostly unknown primary sources on slavery and law. Many were contained in the law library's huge "trials collection." At the time most of the materials in the trials collection were catalogued only by the names of litigants. Only if a researcher knew the names of litigants would it be possible to easily find materials on a case or a genre of cases. There was no subject access to the ten thousand or so items in the collection. These items ranged in size from a few pages to multi-volume sets. Some of the items in the trial collection were not even catalogued. To find the materials on slavery and law, I looked at about 30,000 cards in the trials collection catalog. If the cards mentioned slavery then I had the item pulled. Where the cards gave no indication of the content of the pamphlet, I pulled and ordered the item to examine it.

In the end I found about 150 primary sources—pamphlets and books—on the law of slavery. Some were a few pages long; others were substantial volumes. This foray into the LC's trial collections led to *Slavery in the Courtroom,* first published by the Government Printing Office in 1985 and reprinted by the Lawbook Exchange in 1998.

Slavery in the Courtroom provided a guide and a roadmap to the LC's primary source material on the law of slavery. These included briefs, oral arguments, transcripts of cases, pamphlet editions of judicial opinions, and collections of statutes. After the publication of *Slavery in the Courtroom,* Ralph Carlson, then at Garland Publishing Co., proposed that I gather these materials as well as items not in the holdings of the Library of Congress for a full reprint collection, which Garland published in 1988. This sixteen volume series had a very small print run, and quickly sold out. This Lawbook

PREFACE

Exchange reprint allows libraries and scholars an opportunity to acquire this set.

When I first began working on this project there had been relatively little published scholarship on the law of slavery. Thomas D. Morris's *Free Men All* (1974) provided a solid history of the northern opposition to the Fugitive Slave Laws. Stanley Campbell's *The Slave Catchers* (1970) gave us a reasonably good overview of the political and institutional enforcement of the Fugitive Slave Law of 1850, but did not offer much analysis of the legal history of the law. Robert M. Cover's *Justice Accused: Antislavery and the Judicial Process* (1974), a brilliant meditation on the way law and morality intersect, showed us how slavery might teach us about law, but did not provide a legal history of slavery. A few other books, such as Leonard W. Levy's *The Law of the Commonwealth and Chief Justice Shaw* (1957) or David Brion Davis's *The Problem of Slavery in the Age of Revolution* (1974) contained chapters about the law of slavery, but were not essentially about that subject. A number of law reviews had begun to publish articles on slave law that seriously examined the nature of the legal system designed to maintain total dominance over a large class of people.

Starting in 1977 scholars began to study slave law in earnest. A spate of books put the study of slave law at the center of historical debate and knowledge. These included William M. Wiecek, *The Sources of Antislavery Constitutionalism in America, 1765 TO 1848* (1977); Don Fehrenbacher's *The Dred Scott Case* (1978); A. Leon Higginbotham, *In the Matter of Color* (1978); Michael S. Hindus, *Prison and Plantation* (1980); Paul Finkelman, *An Imperfect Union: Slavery, Federalism and Comity* (1981) and Mark Tushnet, *The American Law of Slavery* (1981). In the next quarter century historians, law professors, and scholars in such diverse fields as literature, rhetoric, economics, and political science published books and articles on slavery and law. Entire issues of law reviews were devoted to slavery and the law. Some scholars focused on particular cases, others on the laws of specific states, and still others on comparative slave law in the Americas. In 1996 Thomas D. Morris published his massive study: *Southern Slavery and the Law.*

The interest in the law of slavery continues. Courses on the subject are taught at a number of law schools. Scholars continue to write about the subject. Mainstream history classes assign books on slave law as supplemental readings. Law reviews regularly publish articles and even entire issues on the law of slavery. Conferences on slavery and the law bring law professors into contact with scholars from a wide variety of disciplines to contemplate the nature of law and bondage. The on-going interest in reparations for slavery raises new interest in how the legal system created, perpetuated, and helped undermine bondage.

The pamphlets in this collection illuminate how the legal system supported slavery. The sixteen volumes of this collection are divided into seven separate series. Each series deals with a particular legal issue connected to slavery. Some raise major constitutional issues; others illustrate the day-to-day nature of slavery and the law. The materials here include the only known reports of some cases, lawyers arguments in others, and pamphlet editions of judicial opinions. The materials illustrate the way both supporters and opponents of slavery used the legal system – and print media – to support their position on human bondage. Some were published as part of the on-going debate over slavery. Some of the briefs and arguments of attorneys were printed and distributed by lawyers trying to enhance their reputation or gain support for their legal position. In that way, they are the eighteenth and nineteenth century equivalents of scholarly reprints, sent from one expert to another. Other materials included here were produced by entrepreneurs, convinced that the report of an exciting slave case would sell. Taken together, this material helps us better understand the intersection between bondage and liberty, between law and slavery.

Paul Finkelman

President William McKinley Distinguished Professor of Law and Public Policy, Albany Law School

November 2006

ABOLITIONISTS IN NORTHERN COURTS

THE PAMPHLET LITERATURE

SERIES III

Edited with an Introduction by

Paul Finkelman

GARLAND PUBLISHING, INC.
NEW YORK & LONDON 1988

Design by Renata Gomes

Library of Congress Cataloging-in-Publication Data

Main entry under title:

Abolitionists in northern courts.

(Slavery, race and the American legal system, 1700-1872)
1. Slavery—Law and legislation—United States—Cases. 2. Afro-Americans—Legal status, laws, etc.—Cases. 3. Abolitionists—Legal status, laws, etc.—United States—Cases. 4. Criminal law—United States—Cases. 5. Criminal justice, Administration of—United States—Cases. I. Finkelman, Paul, 1949- . II. Series.
KF4545.S5A5 1988b 342.75'0872 87-35731
347.502872

ISBN 0-8240-6720-7

All volumes in this series are printed on acid-free, 250-year-life paper.

Printed in the United States of America

CONTENTS

INTRODUCTION

American antislavery was primarily a northern movement. In 1688 the *Germantown Friends Protest Against Slavery* became the first attack on slavery published in America. It was followed by a few other antislavery publications, including Samuel Sewall's *The Selling of Joseph* (Boston: 1700), John Woolman's *Some Considerations on the Keeping of Negroes* (Philadelphia: 1754), and Anthony Benezet's *A Short Account of that Part of Africa Inhabited by the Negroes* (Philadelphia: 1762). Despite these early protests, at the time of the American Revolution slavery was legal in all of the northern colonies as well as the southern ones. However, during the Revolution and its aftermath slavery was abolished through constitutional provisions and supreme court decisions in Massachusetts and New Hampshire, and by gradual emancipation statutes in the rest of the North. Gradual emancipation statutes provided that all existing slaves would remain in lifetime bondage, unless manumitted by their owners, but that the children of such slaves would be born as indentured servants, and would become free at ages ranging from eighteen to twenty-eight. In addition, these statutes prohibited the introduction of any new slaves to a state. These statutes were designed to gradually end slavery through the death of living slaves. Eventually every northern state but New Jersey accelerated this process by emancipating all existing slaves. New York did this as early as 1827 and Pennsylvania did so as late as 1847.

Pamphlet 1 contains the first published record of the abolition of slavery in Massachusetts. This case was, oddly enough, not published until 1874. Another version of this decision, which was not discovered until the middle of the twentieth century, is reprinted in Paul Finkelman, *The Law of Freedom and Bondage* (New York: 1986). Even before the northern states had abolished slavery many citizens had taken steps to emancipate their own slaves. The New Jersey Society for Promoting the Abolition of Slavery often litigated to insure that slaves freed in that state retained their liberty. Many of these cases appear in pamphlets 2 and 3.

While the North took the lead in ending slavery, much of that region was intolerant towards both free blacks and their abolitionist allies. Pamphlets 4–8 detail the case of Prudence Crandall, a Quaker prosecuted for running a school for out-of-state black children in violation of a Connecticut statute. In 1832 Crandall opened a private school in Canterbury, Connecticut for girls whose families could afford the modest tuition. Encouraged by community leaders, Crandall invested all of her own funds and borrowed additional money to purchase a large house to serve as the school.

A few months after the school opened she admitted a black girl who was a graduate of the Canterbury schools and a member of the local church. A number of parents threatened to withdraw their daughters if the school remained integrated. Crandall responded by advertising that the following year she would admit black students, as well as any whites who might apply. When in fact a dozen or more black students came to Canterbury the following year, Crandall faced harassment and intimidation, as well as threats of vagrancy prosecutions. Town officials meanwhile convinced the state legislature to enact a law prohibiting the maintenance of schools which taught black children from other states. Crandall was soon convicted under this law, but the Connecticut Supreme Court overturned her conviction on a technicality. Five years later Connecticut repealed the law under which Crandall was convicted.

Crandall was not the only New England abolitionist to face prosecution for opposing slavery and supporting the rights of free blacks. Pamphlet 9 tells the story of George Storrs, a New Hampshire minister who was tried for vagrancy after he came to Northfield, New Hampshire to give a lecture on slavery. Although speaking in a church, at the invitation of that church, Storrs was arrested by a sheriff on charges of being "an idle person and disorderly person, and wanton and lascivious in speech and behavior, a common railer and brawler." After a short trial, described in Pamphlet 9, he was acquitted.

Abolitionists in the midwest faced more dangerous opposition than their eastern counterparts, as pamphlets 10 and 11 describe. In 1836 rioters in Cincinnati destroyed the printing presses of the antislavery newspaper, *The Philanthropist.* The owner of the paper retained Salmon P. Chase, who successfully sued the leaders of the mob for the value of the press. Less fortunate was Elijah P. Lovejoy, the editor of the antislavery *Alton Observer*. Lovejoy, a Presbyterian minister, had initially published his paper in St. Louis, where he was only mildy critical of slavery. However, even mild criticism was too much for that slaveholding community, and Lovejoy prudently moved across the river to Alton, Illinois. There his antislavery position became increasingly strident. Twice mobs from St. Louis, joined by Lovejoy's opponents in Alton, destroyed his press. In 1837 Lovejoy was killed while attempting to defend a third press from a proslavery mob. Lovejoy thus became the first white northerner to be a martyr to the cause of antislavery. Those who helped Lovejoy defend his press, as well as some of those who attacked the press, were later tried for riot. All the defendants were acquitted. Pamphlet 11 contains the details of these trials.

By the 1840s abolitionists in the North no longer faced mobs and riots. They no longer needed lawyers to defend them on specious charges. Instead, they could use lawyers to attack slavery and racial discrimination. Many of the pamphlets in Series I of this collection, *Southern Slaves in Free State Courts*, report cases brought by abolitionists to free slaves taken into the North. Pamphlets 12 and 13 in this Series contain reports of cases initiated by northern abolitionists to change conditions in the North.

Although New Jersey passed a gradual emancipation statute in 1804, by 1845 there were still more than four thousand slaves and indentured blacks in the state. In 1844 New Jersey adopted a new constitution, which declared: "All men are by nature free and independent, and have certain natural rights, among which are those of enjoying and defending life and liberty, acquiring, possessing, and protecting property, and of pursuing and obtaining safety and happiness." Alvan Stewart, an abolitionist attorney and theorist from New York, used this clause as a basis to sue for an immediate end to all slavery in New Jersey. In a three to one decision the New Jersey Supreme Court rejected Stewart's arguments in the case of *State* v. *Post*, 1 Spencer (20 N. J. Law) 368 (1845). The dissenting judge in this case was Joseph Hornblower, who had opposed slavery from the bench throughout his life (see Series II, pamphlet 3 of this collection). In 1846 New Jersey passed legislation declaring that all remaining slaves in the state would become indentured servants for life. As servants they had numerous rights that they did not have as slaves, but their masters were still responsible for their maintenance. By this time the youngest slaves in New Jersey were forty-two, while most were much older.

Charles Sumner, a Massachusetts lawyer and future United States Senator, was equally unsuccessful before the

Massachusetts Supreme Judicial Court in his attempt to have segregated schools declared unconstitutional in an 1849 case. Sumner's arguments are found in pamphlet 13 of this Series. In *Roberts* v. *The City of Boston*, 5 Cushing (Mass.) 198 (1849), Chief Justice Lemuel Shaw ruled that the city of Boston did not violate the Massachusetts Constitution by maintaining separate schools for blacks, as long as they were "as well conducted in all respects, and as well fitted, in point of capacity and qualification of instructors . . . as the other primary schools." This was the first use of the "separate but equal" doctrine in American law. This case, however, was decided a dozen years before the Civil War began, and two decades before the adoption of the Fourteenth Amendment. Therefore, it can hardly be seen as a legitimate precedent for the segregation of later periods of American history.

Although Sumner lost the battle against segregated schools in Shaw's court, he ultimately won the war. In 1855 the Massachusetts legislature prohibited segregated education in the state. Moreover, in the aftermath of the Civil War Sumner had an important role in shaping the civil rights legislation and the three Constitutional amendments that ultimately dismantled slavery and made segregation illegal. Sumner's argument in the *Roberts* case helps Americans today understand the intention of Sumner and his allies when they adopted the Thirteenth and Fourteenth Amendments after the Civil War.

THE CASE

OF

NATHANIEL JENNISON.

THE CASE

OF

NATHANIEL JENNISON

FOR

ATTEMPTING TO HOLD A NEGRO AS A SLAVE
IN MASSACHUSETTS IN 1781

FROM THE MINUTES OF

CHIEF JUSTICE CUSHING

WITH REFERENCES TO CONTEMPORANEOUS RECORDS

Communicated to the Massachusetts Historical Society
April 16, 1874

BOSTON
PRESS OF JOHN WILSON AND SON
1874

THE CASE OF NATHANIEL JENNISON.

1781–83.

At a social meeting of the Massachusetts Historical Society, at the house of the President, on the evening of the 16th of April, 1874, Chief Justice Gray submitted for the inspection of the members of the Society Chief Justice Cushing's original note-book of the trials before the Supreme Judicial Court of Massachusetts at the terms held in the County of Worcester in 1783, (which had been intrusted to him for the purpose by Mr. William Cushing Paine, the namesake and great grand-nephew of Chief Justice Cushing), and read therefrom the minutes of the trial at April Term 1783 of the case of *The Commonwealth* v. *Nathaniel Jennison*, in which it was established that slavery was wholly abolished in this Commonwealth by the Declaration of Rights prefixed to the Constitution of 1780.

These minutes, now printed for the first time, and copied *verbatim* from the note-book of the Chief Justice, altering nothing but the abbreviations and errors in spelling incident to memoranda of this kind, and adding in brackets what is necessary to render them easily understood, are as follows: —

'INDICTMENT, found September, 1781, *vs.* NATHANIEL JENNISON of Barre, for an assault on Quack Walker, and beat with a stick 1st May, 1781, and imprisoned two hours.

[*Opening of the Attorney-General.*]

"Born in Caldwell's house, who engaged he should have his freedom at 25 — his widow, who married defendant, promised the same when he was *28* — dismissed — and defendant attempted [to retake him?]

[*Testimony for the Government.*]

"*Mr. Caldwell.* The negro came to my house about a week before the warrant. He was at work in my field with a team working — heard a screaming — got upon a knoll 5 or 6 rods from Jennison and several others, who had got the negro down, young fellow upon the negro, I took him off — bruised his fingers — carried him off — went to a saw-mill — and told Jennison his master had freed him — and Winslow let him go — wounds in his hands and arms. My brother said always he should be free at 25 — Mrs. Caldwell [that he should be free at 21?]

"*Quack.* I was harrowing. 10 years old when master Caldwell died. Mrs. lived a number of years before she married again. I lived with Dr. Jennison 7 years and ½ after I was *21.* My old master said I should be free at 24 or 25. Mistress told me I should be free at *21* — said so to Jennison, before and after marriage.

"*Defence.*

"From Zachariah Stone to Caldwell, deceased — Bill of Sale of Mingo and Dinah, 1754, and Quaco, 9 months old.

"*Charles Baker.* I was divider of Caldwell's estate. (About 20 years ago he died.) 2 or 3 years after, the widow received Quaco as part of her dividend.

"*Mr. Jones.* Quaco lived with Caldwell till he died — appraised at £40 — set off to his Mrs. as part of her personal estate. She married Jennison about 1770, and died about 3 years after.

"*Joshua Winslow.* I was desired by defendant to help him reclaim Quaco.

[*Charge of the Chief Justice.*

" *Fact proved.*

"Justification that Quack is a slave — and to prove it 'tis said that Quack, when a child about 9 months old, with his father and mother was sold by bill of sale in 1754, about 29 years ago, to Mr. Caldwell, now deceased; that, when he died, Quack was appraised as part of the personal estate, and set off to the widow in her share of the personal estate; that Mr. Jennison, marrying her, was entitled to Quack as his property; and therefore that he had a right to bring him home when he ran away; and that the defendant only took proper measures for that purpose. And the defendant's counsel also rely on some former laws of the Province, which give countenance to slavery.

"To this it is answered that, if he ever was a slave, he was liberated both by his master Caldwell, and by the widow after his death, the first of whom promised and engaged he should be free at 25, the other at 21.

"As to the doctrine of slavery and the right of Christians to hold Africans in perpetual servitude, and sell and treat them as we do our horses and cattle, that (it is true) has been heretofore countenanced by the Province Laws formerly, but nowhere is it expressly enacted or established. It has been a usage — a usage which took its origin from the practice of some of the European nations, and the regulations of British government respecting the then Colonies, for the benefit of trade and wealth. But whatever sentiments have formerly prevailed in this particular or slid in upon us by the example of others, a different idea has taken place with the people of America, more favorable to the natural rights of mankind, and to that natural, innate desire of Liberty, with which Heaven (without regard to color, complexion, or shape of noses) features) has inspired all the human race. And upon this ground our Constitution of Government, by which the people of this Commonwealth have solemnly bound themselves, sets out with declaring that all men are born free and equal — and that every subject is entitled to liberty, and to have it guarded by the laws, as well as life and property — and in short is totally repugnant to the idea of being born slaves. This being the case, I think the idea of slavery is inconsistent with our own conduct and Constitution; and there can be no such thing as perpetual servitude of a rational creature, unless his liberty is forfeited by some criminal conduct or given up by personal consent or contract.

" *Verdict guilty.*"

NOTE BY CHIEF JUSTICE GRAY.

The original indictment in this case is preserved, with such other records and papers of the Superior Court of Judicature and the Supreme Judicial Court before August 1797, as have come down to us, in the clerk's office in Boston, and is as follows: —

"Worcester, ss. At the Supreme Judicial Court begun and holden at Worcester within and for the County of Worcester on the third Tuesday of September in the year of our Lord one thousand and seven hundred and eighty-one.

"The Jurors for the Commonwealth of Massachusetts upon their oath present that Nathaniel Jennison, of Barre in the County of Worcester aforesaid, yeoman, on the first day of May last past at Barre in the said County of Worcester in and upon one Qock Walker, then and there in the peace of GOD and of this Commonwealth being, with force and arms an assault did make, and then and there, with force as aforesaid, with his the said Nathaniel's fist and a large stick which the said Nathaniel then and there held in his hand, the said Qock did beat, bruise, and evilly entreat, and him the said Qock, with force as aforesaid, without warrant, just cause, or lawful authority, did imprison during the space of two hours, in evil example to others to offend in like case, to the damage of the said Qock, against the peace of the Commonwealth aforesaid and dignity of the same. A true bill,

"OLIVER WHITNEY, *Foreman*."

"R. T. PAINE, *Att'y pr. Repub.*"

The record of April Term 1783 sets forth the indictment in full, and proceeds as follows: — "This indictment was found September Term A.D. 1781. And now in this present term the said Nathaniel Jennison comes into court and has this indictment read to him, he says that thereof he is not guilty and thereof for tryal puts &c. A jury thereupon is impannelled and sworn to try the issue, viz: Jonas How, foreman, and fellows, viz: William McFarland, Isaac Choate, Joseph Bigelow, John White, Daniel Bullard, Ebenezer Lovell, Phillip Goodridge, John Lyon, Johnathan Woodbury, Thomas White and John Town, who after hearing all matters and things concerning the same return their verdict and upon their oath do say that the said Nathaniel Jennison is guilty. It is therefore considered by the Court that the said Nathaniel Jennison pay a fine to the Commonwealth of Forty Shillings, pay cost of prosecution, and stand committed till sentence be performed. — Cost taxed at £ ."

This term appears by the record to have been held by the whole court, consisting of William Cushing, Chief Justice, and Nathaniel Peaslee Sargeant, David Sewall, and Increase Sumner, Justices.

William Cushing was born in 1732, graduated at Harvard College in 1751, and was appointed in 1772 a Justice of the Superior Court of Judicature. Upon the breaking out of the Revolution, and the removal by the General Court of all officers holding commissions under the King, the Council, exercising the executive power, in 1775 appointed him a Justice, and in 1777 (John Adams having declined the office) Chief Justice of the Superior

Court of Judicature. After the adoption of the Constitution of the Commonwealth in 1780, he was recommissioned by Governor Hancock as Chief Justice of the Supreme Judicial Court. In 1788 he was Vice-President of the Convention of the Commonwealth of Massachusetts which ratified the Constitution of the United States. After the adoption of that Constitution, he was appointed by President Washington the first Associate Justice of the Supreme Court of the United States, and in 1796 Chief Justice, but declined that office, and continued to be an Associate Justice until his death in 1810.

Nathaniel Peaslee Sargeant was born in 1731, graduated at Harvard College in 1750, was appointed in 1775 a Justice of the Superior Court of Judicature, recommissioned in 1781 as a Justice of the Supreme Judicial Court, appointed Chief Justice in 1789, and died in 1791.

David Sewall was born in 1735, graduated at Harvard College in 1755, was appointed in 1777 a Justice of the Superior Court of Judicature, recommissioned in 1781 as a Justice of the Supreme Judicial Court, appointed in 1789 the first District Judge of the United States for the District of Maine, and died in 1825.

Increase Sumner was born in 1746, graduated at Harvard College in 1767, was appointed a Justice of the Supreme Judicial Court in 1782, elected Governor of the Commonwealth in 1797, and continued in that office until his death in 1799.

The doctrine laid down by the Chief Justice upon the trial of the indictment against Nathaniel Jennison had previously been discussed and approved in the civil suits arising out of the same transaction, the following statement of which is taken from the records and files of the Court of Common Pleas remaining in the custody of the clerk of the courts in Worcester, and from those of the Supreme Judicial Court which are preserved in the office of the clerk of this court in Boston: —

On May 1, 1781, Quork Walker brought an action of trespass against Nathaniel Jennison, returnable at June term of the Court of Common Pleas, and alleging that the defendant on April 30, 1781, at Barre, "with force and arms on him the said Quork, then in our peace being, did make an assault, and then and there with force as aforesaid seized the said Quork and threw him down and struck him several violent blows upon his back and arm with the handle of a whip, and did and then and there imprison, and other enormities to him the said Nathaniel Jennison then and there did, against the peace and the law." To that action Jennison pleaded that, long before the date of the writ, "one Caldwell, being seised of the said Quork as of her own proper negro slave, was duly married to and became the lawful wife of the said Nathaniel, by means whereof the said Nathaniel, being the lawful husband of the said [Caldwell], became possessed of the said Quork as of his own proper negro slave, and so the said Nathaniel says that the said Quork, at the time of suing out the said writ and long before, and ever since, was the proper negro slave of him the said Nathaniel." The plaintiff replied "that he the said Quork is a free man, and not the proper negro slave of the said Nathaniel," and tendered an issue to the jury, which was joined by the defendant. The jury returned a verdict for the plaintiff for £50 damages, upon which judgment was rendered in the Court of Common Pleas. The defendant appealed to September term 1781 of the Supreme Judicial Court, but, failing to appear there, was defaulted, and the judgment below affirmed.

On May 28, 1781, Jennison brought an action of trespass on the case against John Caldwell and Seth Caldwell, alleging that, on April 2, 1781, at Barre, "a certain negro man named Quarko" was the plaintiff's servant, and was kept, retained, and employed by him as his servant in and about his proper affairs and business; yet the defendants, well knowing the premises, but maliciously contriving to injure the plaintiff and deprive him of the benefit and service of his said servant, unlawfully solicited and seduced the said negro man from the business and service of the plaintiff, and caused and procured him to absent himself from his said master's service; by means whereof said servant did absent himself from such business and service; and the defendants unlawfully kept, retained, and employed the said negro with them in their own proper business for six weeks, against the will and without the consent of the plaintiff, and did unlawfully take and rescue out of the plaintiff's hands and possession his said servant, and did hinder, prevent, and molest him in claiming and reducing his said servant to his business and service, the defendants during all the time well knowing that the said negro was the plaintiff's servant; whereby the affairs and business of the plaintiff was very much neglected, and he lost the benefit of the service of his said servant during all the time aforesaid. This writ was returnable at the same June term of the Court of Common Pleas, and was entered before the writ of Walker *v.* Jennison. The Caldwells severally pleaded not guilty, and tendered an issue to the jury, which Jennison joined, and upon a trial in the Court of Common Pleas he obtained a verdict and judgment for £25. The defendants appealed to September term 1781 of the Supreme Judicial Court, and upon a trial there were found not guilty, and had judgment for costs against the plaintiff.

The Judges present at September term 1781 of the Supreme Judicial Court appear by the record to have been Justices Sargeant and Sewall, and James Sullivan, who resigned his office in 1782, and was afterwards Attorney-General and Governor of the Commonwealth.

Among the papers on file in the case of Jennison *v.* Caldwell is the bill of sale mentioned in Chief Justice Cushing's minutes, which is as follows: —

"Rutland District, May 4, 1754. Sold this day to Mr. James Caldwell, of said District in the County of Worcester and Province of the Massachusetts Bay: a certain negro man named Mingo, about twenty years of age, and also one negro wench named Dinah, about nineteen years of age, with her child Quaco, about nine months old: all sound and well: for the sum of one hundred and eight pounds lawful money, received to my full satisfaction, which negroes I the subscriber do warrant and defend against all claims whatsoever. As witness my hand.

"In presence of ZEDEKIAH STONE.
"JNO. MORRAY,
"JOHN CALDWELL."

The abstract made by Professor Washburn, and heretofore printed by the Society, of the brief of the counsel for the defendants in the case of Jennison *v.* Caldwell, shows that they took the position that slavery was abolished by the Constitution of the Commonwealth. (34 Mass. Hist. Soc. Coll. 337, 341–344; Proceedings, 1855–58, pp. 193, 197–201.)

On June 18, 1782, Jennison presented a petition to the House of Representatives, "setting forth that he was deprived of ten negro servants by a judgment of the Supreme Judicial Court, on the following clause of the Constitution, 'that all men are born free and equal,' and praying that, if said judgment is approved of, he may be freed from his obligations to support said negroes." (3 Journal of the House of Representatives, 99.)

It can hardly be doubted that the case of Jennison *v.* Caldwell is the one to which Chief Justice Parsons, in 1808, referred in these words: "In the first action involving the right of the master, which came before the Supreme Judicial Court, after the establishment of the Constitution, the judges declared that, by virtue of the first article of the Declaration of Rights, slavery in this State was no more." (Winchendon *v.* Hatfield, 4 Massachusetts Reports, 123, 128.)

On February 8, 1783, the House of Representatives appointed a committee "to bring in a bill upon the following principles: 1st. Declaring that there never were legal slaves in this Government; 2d. Indemnifying all masters who have held slaves in fact; 3d. To make such provisions for the support of negroes and mulattoes as the committee may find most expedient." A bill was brought in, and passed through its several stages in the House, and read a first time in the Senate, and then appears no further in the records of the legislature. (3 Journal of the House of Representatives, 444, 529, 537. 3 Journal of the Senate, 413 *& seq.*)

It should not be overlooked that the Constitution of 1780 gave the right of suffrage to "every male person, being twenty-one years of age," and having a certain amount of property, and omitted the words "being free" and "excepting negroes, Indians, and mulattoes," which had been inserted in the Constitution rejected by the people in 1778; and that Chief Justice Cushing, Justices Sargeant, Sewall, Sullivan, and Sumner, as well as Levi Lincoln and Caleb Strong (the counsel of the Caldwells in the action brought against them by Jennison) and Attorney-General Paine (who tried the indictment against Jennison) had all been members of the Convention which framed the Constitution of 1780, and all of them, except Justices Sargeant and Sumner and Mr. Lincoln, members of the committee which framed the Declaration of Rights. (Journal of the Convention of 1780, as printed in 1832, pp. 8, 10, 11, 12, 14, 15, 16, 28, 29, 30, 234, 257.)

All subsequent investigation of the subject of the abolition of slavery in Massachusetts has confirmed the accuracy of the statement drawn up by our founder, Dr. Jeremy Belknap, April 21, 1795, in answer to the queries of Judge Tucker, of Virginia, and printed in the fourth volume of our Collections. Dr. Belknap says: —

"The present Constitution of Massachusetts was established in 1780. The first article of the Declaration of Rights asserts that 'all men are born free and equal.' This was inserted not merely as a moral or political truth, but with a particular view to establish the liberation of the negroes on a general principle, and so it was understood by the people at large; but some doubted whether this was sufficient."

"In 1781, at the court in Worcester County, an indictment was found against a white man for assaulting, beating, and imprisoning a black. He was tried at the Supreme Judicial Court in 1783. His defence was, that the black was his slave, and that the beating, &c., was the necessary restraint and correction of the master. This was answered by citing the aforesaid clause in the Declaration of Rights. The judges and jury were of opinion that he had no right to beat or imprison the negro. He was found guilty, and fined forty shillings. This decision was a mortal wound to slavery in Massachusetts." (4 Mass. Hist. Soc. Coll. 203.)

And again, as a result of his previous statements: "The complete abolition of slavery may be fixed at the year 1783." (Ibid., 206.)

The source of the information condensed in the second paragraph above quoted was evidently a letter, dated April 9, 1795, to Dr. Belknap from James Sullivan (himself one of the Judges that took part in the decision of the civil action of Jennison *v.* Caldwell, and who resigned before the trial of Commonwealth *v.* Jennison), as will appear by comparing it with the following extract, now first printed from the original letter found among Dr. Belknap's papers in the possession of the Society: —

"In the year 1781, an indictment was found in the County of Worcester against Nathaniel Jennison of Barre, yeoman, for assaulting, beating and imprisoning Quock Walker. He was tried at the Supreme Judicial Court in April, 1783. The defence was, that the said Quock was a slave brought from Africa, and sold to some person who many years before had sold him to the defendant, and that the assaulting, beating and imprisonment was done by the defendant as the restraint and necessary correction of the master on the servant. This was answered by the Declaration of Rights, declaring all men free, equal, &c. The judges and jury were of opinion that Jennison has not right to beat or imprison the negro. He was found guilty, and fined 40*s*. This decision put an end to the idea of slavery in this State."

The reasonable conclusion seems to be, that the doctrine that slavery was abolished in this Commonwealth by the Declaration of Rights was declared in 1781 by the three Associate Justices, in the absence of the Chief Justice, upon the trial of the civil action brought by Jennison against the Caldwells; but, not being universally assented to throughout the State, the indictment against Jennison was brought to trial in 1783 before the whole court, and the same doctrine, being then distinctly affirmed by the Chief Justice, and the jury instructed accordingly, was thereby conclusively established as the law of the Commonwealth, further legislation on the subject was deemed unnecessary, and the bill pending before the legislature was therefore suffered to drop. Dr. Belknap notes the fact that in the first census of the United States, taken in 1790, no slaves are set down to Massachusetts. (4 Mass. Hist. Soc. Coll. 199, 204.) And the law of Massachusetts has ever since been recognized by all legal authorities, in this Commonwealth and elsewhere, to be as stated by Chief Justice Cushing in the charge printed in the text. (Winchendon *v.* Hatfield, 4 Massachusetts Reports, 123, 128. Commonwealth *v.* Aves, 18 Pickering's Reports, 193, 208–210, 217. Parsons *v.* Trask, 7 Gray's Reports, 473, 478. Jackson *v.* Phillips, 14 Allen's Reports, 539, 563. 2 Kent's Commentaries, 252. Betty *v.* Horton, 5 Leigh's Virginia Reports, 615, 623.)

CASES

ADJUDGED

IN THE

SUPREME COURT

OF

NEW JERSEY.

RELATIVE TO THE

MANUMISSION OF NEGROES

AND OTHERS HOLDEN IN BONDAGE.

COLLECTED AND PUBLISHED BY THE LATE

GOVERNOR JOSEPH BLOOMFIELD.

SECOND EDITION.

PRINTED FOR JOSIAH HARRISON

COUNSELLOR AT LAW.

BY FRANKLIN FERGUSON,

CAMDEN, N. J.

1843

At a general meeting of the *New Jersey Society for promoting the Abolition of Slavery*, September 2, 1793.

RESOLVED,

That the *President* of this Society collect and have printed, the 'Decisions of the Supreme Court in this State, relative to the Manumission of Negroes and others, unlawfully holden in Bondage.'

Extract from the Minutes,

ROBERT SMITH, JUN.

Secretary.

On the application of JOSEPH BLOOMFIELD, Esquire, President of the *New Jersey Society for promoting the Abolition of Slavery*, I have carefully examined the following cases with the original entries thereof, in the Minutes of the Supreme Court of New Jersey; and I do hereby certify, that the same are truly taken from the said minutes,

GERSHOM CRAFT, for the Clerk
of the Supreme Court.

November 20, 1793.

JUSTICES OF THE SUPREME COURT,

AND ATTORNEY GENERALS

OF NEW JERSEY, SINCE 1774.

1774 to May Term 1776 inclusive.	Frederick Smyth, Chief Justice. David Ogden, } Richard Stockton, } Cortland Skinner, Atty. General.
1776 September 4.	William Paterson, Atty. General.
1777 February 5.	Robert Morris, Chief Justice.
15.	Isaac Smith, } Justices. John Cleves Symmes, }
1779 June 10.	David Brearly, Chief Justice.
1783 June 13.	Joseph Bloomfield, Atty. General.
1788 September 4.	John Chetwood, Third Justice.
1789 November 20.	James Kinsey, Chief Justice.
1792 May 23.	Aaron D. Woodruff, Atty. General.

TABLE OF THE NAMES OF THE CASES.

CASES

ADJUDGED

IN THE

SUPREME COURT

OF

NEW JERSEY.

I NOVEMBER TERM, 1775.

(Minutes, p. 44, 142.)

The KING *against* ESTHER BARBER and others.

On Habeas Corpus *to bring the body of* Beulah, *a Negro Girl.*

By the admission of the Counsel, it appeared that Beulah the Negro Girl, brought up by the Habeas Corpus, and now before the Court, is the daughter of a Negro Man and Negro Woman, the first named David, and the other named Dinah, both of whom formerly belonged to Caleb Haines, of the City of Burlington, which said Negroes David and Dinah, were set free by the said Caleb Haines in his lifetime, and before the birth of the said Girl Beulah, without having given any Bond pursuant to the Act of Assembly, passed in the twelfth and thirteenth years of her late Majesty Queen Ann; for which reason the said manumission was alledged to be void.

The Court having heard the arguments of Counsel, as well for the said Esther Barber and others, as for the said Beulah, at the Term of May last, and now again at this present Term, and

2

haying fully considered thereof *are of Opinion*, That the said manumission by the said Caleb Haines, of the said David and Dinah, the parents of the said Beulah, was good in law against the said Caleb Haines and those claiming under him, notwithstanding the not giving bond as aforesaid; and that the same Beulah is entitled to her freedom under the said manumission against the said Caleb Haines, and all claiming under him; and do order her the said Beulah to be delivered up from out of the custody of the said Esther Barber and others, in which she hath been illegally detained.

Kinsey, Elias Boudinot and Skinner, for Negro.
Sergeant and Paterson, for Defendant.

II APRIL TERM, 1782.

The STATE *against* JACOBUS VANHUYS.

On Habeas Corpus *for Negro* Will *claiming his freedom.*

The Court having heard the arguments of Counsel on the part of Negro Will, and the reasons assigned for and against his freedem, and the evidence in support thereof: It is ordered by the court that the said negro *Will* be, and he is hereby discharged and set free from the said Jacobus Vanhuys, on motion of Mr. Deare.

III SEPTEMBER TERM, 1782.

(p. 36.)

The STATE *against* EDMUND BAINBRIDGE.

On Habeas Corpus *of Negro* Nelly.

It appearing to the Court, and the said *Edmund Bainbridge* conceding, that the said Negro Nelly was formerly the property of Edmund Bainbridge, the elder, of Maidenhead, deceased, who let his daughter Abigail, (late wife of Thomas Biles, of Bucks county in Pennsylvania, deceased,) have her when very young; that many years afterwards he made his will and bequeathed her to his said daughter Abigail, during the life of his said daughter, and to her issue, and did further order, that if she should die childless, then the said negro Nelly should be sold, and the money appropriated as mentioned in his said will; that the said Abigail Biles who survived her husband and her father, did by her will dated 30th April 1779, set forth and declare, that the said negro Nelly had by her said father been presented to her on a New-Years Day, when she was a child, and therefore, both from that gift and from bringing her up, she had a better right to dispose of her than any other person, and did therein order and direct, that the said negro Nelly should be manumitted and set free, a thing which she had very much at heart; that the said negro Nelly resided in the state of Pennsylvania at the time of the passing of the Act for the gradual Abolition of Slavery, 1st March, 1780, and until the first of Nouember in the same year, the term and period allowed and fixed in the said Act for registering Slaves and for some time afterwards: that she was not registered as the said act requires, and that she is not within the exceptions specified therein.

The Court having fully considered the premises, *are unanimously of Opinion*, that the manumission of the said negro Nelly by the said Abigail Biles, daughter of the aforesaid Edmund Bainbridge, is good in law against all persons claiming under either of them; the said Edmund Bainbridge, having given her to his said daughter, when she the said negro Nelly was a child, and his said daughter having directed by her will that she should be manumitted; and further that the said negro Nelly, not having been registered as the above mentioned Act of the state of Pennsylvania requires, and therefore entitled to Freedom in that State, is not by law put in a worse situation here: It is therefore *Ordered*, That the said negro Nelly be discharged and set at liberty from the said Edmund Bainbridge. On motion of Mr. *Morris* for Mr. *Houston.*

IN THE SAME TERM OF

IV SEPTEMBER, 1782.

(p. 48.)

The STATE *against* LEWIS Mc KNIGHT.

On Habeas Corpus *to bring the Body of Negro* Cæsar Tite.

The defendant having returned the habeas corpus, and brought up the body of the said negro Cæsar Tite, It is ordered that the defendant enter into security in the sum of two hundred pounds to bring up the body of the said negro Cæsar on the second Tuesday in November next, and abide the judgment of the Court respecting the said Negro, and that in case the said Negro should be adjudged by this Court free, that the said Lewis M'Knight shall pay for the service of the said negro from this time.

Recognizance accordingly.

V SEPTEMBER TERM, 1782.

(p. 49.)

The STATE *against* ENLOES PHILPOT.

Whereas it hath appeared to this Court, upon the affidavit of Jack Tappen, that the defendant holds a certain Anthony Tappen in bondage and slavery, without lawful authority for the same as the said Jack alledgeth: therefore, *Ordered*, on motion of Mr. Leake for the said Anthony, that a writ of *habeas corpus ad faciendum, subjiciendum et recipiendum* do issue, returnable to this Court at the next term.

VI NOVEMBER TERM, 1782.

(p. 59.)

The STATE *against* LEWIS Mc KNIGHT.

On Habeas Corpus *of Negro* Cæsar Tite. See ante p. 10

Agreeably to the command of the within writ, I have here in Court the body of the within mentioned Cæsar Tite, and do say that the said negro Tite is my property, being bought of Kenneth Hankinson, Esquire, for valuable consideration, and he is not a free man;* but I am willing and desirous to contest that property by a jury of the country, agreeably to the laws of this State, and pray that it may not be taken from me without a trial by jury, &c.* LEWIS Mc KNIGHT.

*S. P. 28, 29.

IN THE SAME TERM OF

VII NOVEMBER, 1782.

(p. 76.)

IN THE SAME CASE OF

The STATE *against* LEWIS Mc KNIGHT.

It appearing to the Court, that the said negro Cæsar Tite, brought up by *habeas corpus*, and now before the Court, heretofore belonged to Grace Tite, of the county of Monmouth, who by her last will and testament ordered that he should be free when he attained the age of twenty-one years, till which period he was to serve Thomas Leonard of the said county of Monmouth; that the said Thomas Leonard joined the enemy some time before the expiration of the said service, and the said negro Cæsar Tite was sold at public vendue, with other confiscated personal property of the said Thomas Leonard, by the Commissioners of forfeited estates for the county of Monmouth, and bought by David Forman, Esq. who afterwards sold him to Kenneth Hankinson, Esq. and he to the said Lewis M'Knight the defendant; that no bond was given by the said Grace Tite, pursuant to the Act of Assembly, passed in the twelfth and thirteenth years of the late Queen Ann: And that the said negro Cæsar Tite is now above twenty-one years old, *to wit*, of the age of about twenty-four or twenty-five.

The Court having heard the argument of counsel on both sides, and fully considered thereof, *are unanimously of Opinion*, That the said Manumission is good in law against all persons claiming under the said Grace Tite, notwithstanding bond was not given as aforesaid; *and do order*, on motion of Mr. Bloomfield for the Attorney General, that the negro Cæsar Tite be discharged and set at liberty from the said Lewis M'Knight.*

* Ante I and post 32.

VIII SEPTEMBER TERM, 1783.

(p. 252, 270)

MERCY HILL *against* WILLIAM LEDDELL.

On Habeas Corpus *for Manumission.*

It being alledged by the counsel for the said Mercy Hill the plaintiff, that she is the daughter of a certain Jupiter Lee, a negro slave, heretofore belonging to Samuel Lee of the town of Swansey in the colony of Massachusetts Bay, now commonwealth of Massachusetts, and Deliverence Hill, a free-born native Indian woman; that in her infancy she was put apprentice to James Power of that place, with whom, or his assigns she served many years, and then labored for her livelihood in different places as other free persons usually do; that long afterwards she was by some means sold as a slave, and by sundry transfers and sales came at length into the possession of the defendant William Leddell.

The Court having heard the testimony, with sundry affidavits offered and read, to prove the truth of the foregoing allegations, and having also heard the arguments of counsel on both sides, and maturely considered thereof, *are unanimously of Opinion*, that the said Mercy Hill is entitled to her freedom, and ought not to be held in slavery; and do accordingly adjudge and order that the said Mercy Hill be discharged and set at liberty from the said William Leddell, on motion of Mr. Morris in behalf of Mercy Hill.

IN THE SAME TERM OF

IX SEPTEMBER, 1783.

(p. 286, 295.)

The STATE *against* TIERCK TENBROECK.

On Habeas Corpus *of Negro* Philip *for Manumission.*

The Court having fully considered the evidence, and the argument of counsel in this cause, *are unanimously of Opinion,* and do adjudge, that the said negro *Philip* be discharged and set at liberty from the said Tierck Tenbroeck, and also from John Vanhorne of Rocky-Hill, in the county of Somerset, who hath appeared and claimed the said negro Philip, on motion of Mr. Paterson for the State.

X MAY TERM, 1784.

(p. 33)

The STATE *against* ADRIAN POST

On Habeas Corpus *of Negro* Charles *and* Wife.

In November Term, 1781. (p. 467)

On the hearing of this case, the Court adjudged in favor of the discharge of the negroes, and ordered the defendant to deliver them to the Sheriff of Bergen, to remain in his custody, until the further orders of the Court.

And now, on motion of Mr. Elias Boudinot for Nicholas Covenhoven, master of the said negroes, it is ordered by the Court, that the Sheriff of Bergen, do on service of this rule, deliver to the said Nicholas Covenhoven, or his order, the said negro Charles and Wife.

XI APRIL TERM, 1785.

(p. 300)

The STATE *against* BENJAMIN APPLEGATE.

On Habeas Corpus *of Negro* Peter Ridley, *claiming to be manumitted.*

The said negro Peter being brought into Court by habeas corpus, and it appearing to the Court on testimony, that the said negro Peter is the son of a certain William Ridley, a free negro and his wife Diana, a negro woman sometime the property of Dollans Hegeman, and who became free before the birth of the said negro Peter, and that the said parents of the said negro Peter have ever since lived and been reputed as free.

The Court *are of Opinion* and *do adjudge*, that the said negro Peter was free-born, and is entitled to be discharged as a free man; and do order that he be discharged accordingly, on motion of Mr. Paterson for the State.

XII MAY TERM, 1785.

(p. 358)

The STATE *against* JOHN VANHORNE.

On Habeas Corpus *of Negro* Prime, *claiming his Freedom.*

The Court in *September Term,* 1784, (*p.* 125) on return of the *habeas corpus,* obliged defendant to enter into recognizance with security in £140, conditioned for the appearance of the said negro Prime at the next term, to abide &c. and not depart &c.

November Term, 1784, (*p.* 195) Recognizance continued.

April Term, 1785, (*p.* 299) Argument postponed, and Recognizance continued.

And now (*May Term,* 1785,) *Moore Furman,* Esquire, agent of forfeited estates for the county of Hunterdon, having applied to the Court, and represented that the State hath a claim to the said negro Prime; it is ordered by the Court that the said negro Prime be delivered into the custody of John Anderson, Esquire, Sheriff of Hunterdon, until a trial of the property can be had, and until the further order of the Court.

AFTERWARDS IN THE

XIII TERM OF MAY, 1786,

(p. 128)

MOORE FURMAN, ESQ. Agent of Forfeitures for the County of Hunterdon *against* JOHN VANHORNE, *In Detinue.*

This action having been brought by agreement of parties under the direction of the Court, to try the property of a certain negro Prime, and a verdict and judgment having passed in favor of the plaintiff, *It is ordered* by the Court, on motion of Mr. Houston for the plaintiff, that the said negro Prime now in the custody of the Sheriff of Hunterdon, agreeably to an order of this Court of May term last, be delivered to the said Moore Furman, Esq. agent of forfeitures for the county of Hunterdon.*

XIV NOVEMBER TERM, 1785.

(p. 519 and 472.)

Negro GEORGE *against* BARNT DE KLYN.

On Habeas Corpus *and complaint of cruel Treatment.*

The hearing of this cause came on, and the evidence being gone through, Mr. Elias Boudinot on behalf of the Negro, prayed that Mr. De Klyn should oblige himself not to send the said negro George out of the State, and the Court having considered thereof, required Mr. De Klyn so to do, which he accordingly did in open Court.*

*S. P. 18.

---

*NOTE. *The Legislature by Act dated* 21 *November*, 1786, *declaring themselves "to be desirous of extending the Blessings of Liberty," generously manumitted Prime from Slavery. He had been enlisted and served in the Army in the late War.*

IN THE SAME TERM OF

XV NOVEMBER, 1785.

(p. 525)

Negro QUAMINI *against* WILLIAM LEDDEL, Esquire.

On Habeas Corpus *for Manumission.*

It being alleged on the part of the said negro Quamini, that several years ago he belonged to Dr. Samuel Tuthill, of Morris county, from whom he was purchased by Captain Augustine

Bayles of the same County, that the said Captain Bayles, divers times in his lifetime promised the said negro Quamini, that if he would be honest, faithful, and industrious, he never should serve any other master, but should be free at his the said Captain Bayles's decease; that the said Captain Bayles on his death-bed, considering that his wife would be left very destitute of help, directed that the said negro Quamini should continue in her service during her widowhood, and that then he should be free; that the said Captain Bayles died in the year 1781, or 1782, and that about two years ago, Keziah Bayles his widow intermarried with one Thomas Faircloth.

The Court having heard the testimony for establishing the several facts aforesaid, and having duly considered the same, *do order*, on motion of Mr. William De Hart, that the said negro Quamini be discharged, and set at liberty from the said William Leddel, Esquire.

XVI MAY TERM, 1787.

(p. 449)

The STATE *against* JACOB PHILLIPS.

On Habeas Corpus *of Negro* Obadiah Gale.

The Court having heard the evidence and argument of counsel in this cause, *do order* that the said Jacob Phillips enter into recognizance in the sum of one hundred pounds, conditioned, that the said Jacob Phillips on the twenty-fifth day of June next, liberate and discharge from his service the said Obadiah Gale, and the Court do further adjudge and order, that on the twenty-sixth day of June next, the said Obadiah Gale shall be set at Liberty, and go thereof free without day, and that the said Obadiah Gale be in custody of the Sheriff of Hunterdon till the said twenty-sixth day of June next, unless the recognizance is entered into by the said Jacob Phillips before one of the Justices of the Supreme Court, on motion of Mr. Elias Boudinot.

XVII SEPTEMBER TERM, 1787.

(p. 36, 39)

The STATE *against* JOHN B. OLIVER *and his* Wife.

On Habeas Corpus *of Negro* Kate.

The Court after hearing the arguments of counsel, *are of Opinion*, that the said John B. Oliver enter into recognizance in five hundred pounds, conditioned that he do not send or suffer to be sent, the negro Kate mentioned in the said habeas corpus, out of this State, till the Court shall take further order therein at the next term. Recognizance entered into accordingly by the said John B. Oliver.*

S. P. 16.

The Attorney General and Elisha Boudinot for State.
Elias Boudinot and Aaron Ogden for defendants.

* NOTE. *The counsel for the defendants in this case, contended that they ought not to be compelled to answer the allegation of Abuse, because, as the habeas corpus, was in common form to bring the Body, and no cause in particular alledged, they could not be presumed to come prepared to answer any thing but the illegal detainer of the Negro as a Slave, and insisted that they ought not to be compelled to answer this until a sufficient prosecutor should be indorsed on the habeas corpus, and security given for the costs: All this the Court over ruled. The counsel for the defendants undertook that the Negro should not be ill-treated, and the dispute was afterwards settled and the Court heard nothing further of the affair.*

XVIII SEPTEMBER TERM, 1788.

(p. 356)

The STATE *against* DANIEL TAYLOR, Junior.

On Habeas Corpus for bringing up a Negro Man named Harry.

The habeas corpus being returned, the Court proceeded to consider the same, and counsel both in favor of the Negro, and on behalf of the said Daniel Taylor, Jun. being heard; *It is ordered*, that the said negro man be discharged from being a slave, and that he serve the said Daniel Taylor, Jun. his master as a servant for the space of six years, from the first day of September instant, and that from thenceforward he be entirely discharged and free from servitude.

XIX APRIL TERM, 1789.

(p. 437)

The STATE *against* DAVID LYON.

On Habeas Corpus of Negro Margaret Reap, claiming her Freedom.

Upon the hearing before the Court, it appeared, that Zacheus Mayhew, of Massachusetts, by deed of gift, dated the first day of March, 1750, did give a certain negro girl called Flora, unto his daughter, Lucy Little, then the wife of   Little. That the said Lucy Little afterwards being a widow, and having one son called William Little, intermarried in Massachusetts with a Dr. Joseph Eaton, who came from thence with his wife to Shrewsbury in New Jersey, and at the same time brought the said negro Flora with them. That on the 31st day of August, 1752, the said Dr. Eaton sold the said negro Flora with a child she then had called Rose, unto one John Worthley. That the said John Worthley by bill of sale, dated 27th September, 1753, sold the said negro Flora to one John Williams. That John Williams the 8th of May, 1754, sold the said negro Flora to the aforesaid Dr. Eaton for the sum of sixty pounds York money. That the said Dr. Eaton upwards of twenty years ago, and about five days after one Jacob Dennis had purchased the aforesaid negro girl Rose, daughter of the said Flora, of the said John Worthley, he the said Dr. Eaton informed the said Jacob Dennis, he was collecting those Negroes for William Little (his son-in-law)—that they should return to him again as they belonged to him; and at that time and often afterwards declared that he was principled against Slavery, and that he never intended the said Flora should belong to his estate, nor should any of his children be benefited by having her as their property—It also appeared that the said Lucy Eaton survived her said husband, the said Dr. Eaton. That shortly after the death of the said Dr. Eaton (*to wit*, about seventeen years ago) one Thomas White applied to the said Lucy Eaton to purchase and did purchase at private sale, a small Spinning wheel, which she then said she had not any further use for, as she had given Flora free who used to spin on the said wheel. That since that time the said Flora has passed for, and been esteemed a free woman, and for a considerable time worked about in the neighborhood of the said widow Eaton, and in the house of the said widow, and for the wife of John Eaton the eldest son of the said Dr. Eaton, and always received her wages as well from the said John Eaton's wife, as the neighbors; and the said widow Eaton herself promised to compensate her therefor. And it further appeared that whilst the said Flora worked about for herself as aforesaid, she intermarried with a certain Joseph Reap, a free negro, with whom the said Flora has ever since lived unmolested and as a free woman, and still continues so to live. That after the marriage of the said Flora with the said Joseph Reap, she had two children called Lydia, and *Margaret* (the present claimant,) that these children lived with their said father and mother, who brought them up by their own industry without any expense or trouble to any other person whatsoever, until last Fall, when they were taken away from their said parents without their consent. That since the said taking, it appears by a certain instrument of writing, bearing date the 8th day of Janury, 1789, executed under the hand and seal of the aforesaid William Little, (the son-in-law of the said Dr. Eaton, and for whom the said Dr. Eaton declared as aforesaid, he was collecting the negroes.) That the said William Little hath manumitted and set at liberty the said Flora and her said two children, Lydia and Margaret; whereupon

The Court having considered this state of facts, and the arguments of counsel on both sides thereupon, *are of Opinion*, That, permitting the said negro woman Flora to remain at liberty for so long a time, and to work for herself, and having intermarried with the said Joseph Reap a free man, with whom she has ever since lived as a free woman, is such evidence of freedom, both of the said negro woman Flora, and consequently of her children, as to entitle the said negro Margaret Reap to her discharge; and the Court do therefore accordingly *order* the said negro Margaret Reap to be discharged and set at liberty from the said David Lyon; on motion of the Attorney General.

Bloomfield, Attorney General, and R. Stockton for the State.
M. Williamson, and Aaron Ogden for defendant.

IN THE SAME TERM OF

XX APRIL, 1789.

(p. 438.)

The STATE *against* JOHN LEIGHTON.

On Habeas Corpus *of Negro* Lydia Reap, *returnable the first day of this Term.*

The Court order an attachment against the said John Leighton, for contempt in not returning the said writ of *habeas corpus*, agreeably to the command thereof, and for divers expressions made use of by him reflecting on the authority of this Court and its process, on motion of Mr. Attorney General.

XXI APRIL TERM, 1790.

(p. 42)

The STATE *against* LEWIS PRALL *and* ROBERT ROSS *Administrators of* ISAAC PRALL, *deceased.*

On Habeas Corpus *of Negro* Thomas *claiming his Freedom.*

[Habeas Corpus returned and filed.]

RETURN,

"We have the negro in the above writ named, at the day and place as by the said writ we are commanded, *and we do certify*, that we as administrators of all and singular the goods and chattels, rights and credits which were of Isaac Prall, deceased, took possession of said negro as part of the personal property of the said Isaac Prall, and that there is no other cause of detaining him.

LEWIS PRALL,
ROBERT ROSS, JUN. } Administrators."

Upon the hearing in this cause, it appeared to the Court, that the said negro Thomas belonged to the said Isaac Prall, deceased. That the intestate, about three years before his death, and frequently afterwards, declared that Tom should never have another master. That he had been a faithful servant to him. That they had been born under one roof, that they had received sustenance from one breast, and had broke up the ground, and always lived together; and continued to show great affection and regard for the negro until his last sickness, and during that sickness whilst he had his senses. That in his last illness, on the Friday before he died, he requested a person might be sent for to make his will, at which time his sister being present, she asked him what he intended to do with his negroes, he replied they should all be sold but Tom, and he should be free; which declaration he also made the same day to several others, with this, further, that Tom should not serve any other master. The person sent for to write his will, did not come 'till the next day, when the intestate was so deranged in his mind as to be incapable of making his will, and continued so until he died, which was on the Wednesday following; that the said intestate, after he was in some measure deranged, continued to show strong and evident marks of affection for the said negro, and of the continuance of his design and intention to make him free; It also appeared to the Court that the said negro had always before the death of the intestate, and till that event took place, been much attached to his master, had shown a great affection for him, and had behaved himself well and faithfully.

The Court having considered of the whole, case, and the arguments of counsel for and against the manumission of the negro, *are unanimously of Opinion*, That the frequent and full declarations of the intestate, amounted to more than a bare intention of doing something in future; that even if these declarations were taken in the sense of a promise to do something in future, the good behaviour of the negro which was admitted on all hands, the evident continuation of the affection of the master as long as he had his senses, and even when in some measure deprived of them, afforded a strong ground of presumption of a contract between the negro and master for his freedom, conditionally on his behaving well, which having performed on his part, the negro was entitled to his liberty, and that the performance of the condition on the part of the master and his representatives, might be effected on this habeas corpus, *do therefore adjudge*, That the said negro Tom being entitled to his freedom, be discharged from the custody of the said administrators, and all the representatives of the said Isaac Prall, deceased. On the motion of Mr. Bloomfield, Attorney General.

The Attorney General and Elisha Boudinot for State.

Frelinghuysen and Aaron Ogden, for defendants.

3*

XXII MAY TERM, 1790.

(p. 85)

The STATE *against* TOBIAS HENDRICKSON.

On Habeas Corpus *of Negro* Jack *claiming his Freedom.*

The Court having considered this case under all its circumstances, and it appearing that John Coward the former master, under whom Tobias Hendrickson claims title to the negro, antecedent to the year 1785, actually entered into an agreement with Jack for his freedom, the terms of which have been fully complied with; *The Court are therefore of Opinion,* and *do order,* the said negro Jack to be liberated from the custody of the said Tobias Hendrickson. But as John Coward the former master is not before the Court, und of course not heard, and his interest may be materially concerned, this judgment for the liberation of the said Jack is not to affect any present or future claim of the said John Coward.

XXIII SEPTEMBER TERM, 1790.

(p. 119.)

The STATE *against* JOHN WARE.

On Habeas Corpus *of Negro* Jethro *(son of Charity Briggs) claiming his Freedom.*

It appearing to the Court that the said Negro Jethro was born on the eighth day cf September, 1763, in the county of Cape May in this State; that his mother Charity Briggs a (Mulatto woman) was free at the time of his birth. That the said Charity was by indenture bound by the justices and overseers of the poor of the Lower Precinct of Cape May to one Nathaniel Foster, in order to bear the expenses of her having had the Small-pox.— That in the said year of 1768, the said Charity was purchased by a certain John Connell, she then having the said Jethro an infant at her breast. That afterwards the time of service of the said Charity was sold by Connel to Captain Jonathan Jenkins, and that she the said Charity took her said son with her. That the said Jethro her son, was brought up by Jenkins until he was fit for business, and then was sold unto Christopher Leaming of the said county of Cape May, who kept the said Jethro a number of years, and within two years last past sold the said Jethro unto John Ware of Cumberland, the defendant now in Court, for the term of twelve years and eight months, and by bill of sale engaged to warrant the service of the said negro Jethro for the said term.

And the Court having taken the said case into consideration, *are unanimously of Opinion*, That the said Jethro being the son of a free woman, and of the age of twenty-one years, is now entitled to his freedom, and do therefore adjudge, that the said negro Jethro (otherwise called Jethro Briggs,) be discharged from the custody of the said John Ware, on the motion of Joseph Bloomfield, Attorney General.

IN THE SAME TERM OF

XXIV SEPTEMBER, 1790.

(p. 141.)

The STATE *against* JAMES ANDERSON.

On Habeas Corpus *of Negro* Silas *claiming his Freedom.*

Returnable Saturday 11th September, and returned accordingly.

The defendant appears with the negro, to do and receive, &c. pursuant to Recognizance.

Vide post 31, two cases decided upon the authority of this case

The case stated by counsel for the Opinion of the Court is as follows:

That on the fourth day of December, 1761, John Horsfield was entitled to two negro girls, named Betty and Nelly as slaves, and on the said fourth day of December by his last will and testament, (then dated) made the following devise, "Item, my two negro girls named Betty and Nelly, I leave to be sold by my executors, hereafter named, for the term of fifteen years, and at the end of that time to be free, and the money arising thereby, to be equally divided amongst my four youngest daughters, and they that buy the said negro girls, if the said girls or either of them misbehave, or become chargeable, it must be at the risk or cost of the buyer." That the said executors sold the said negro girls to one Covenhoven, who sold them to the present defendant Anderson, for the term mentioned in the will. That Betty had a child (the negro Silas) now of full age, which child was not born in matrimony.

The Court having considered the above state of facts, are *unanimously of Opinion,* That on the death of John Horsfield the testator, Betty ceased to be a slave, that she ceasing to be a slave, no child born of her body can be deemed so by the birth of such child during the fifteen years, and that the claim of James Anderson to hold the said negro Silas as a slave, is not warranted by law: *Wherefore it is ordered,* That the same Silas be liberated from the illegal detention of the same James Anderson, and he is hereby liberated accordingly, *ex-motione* J. Bloomfield, Attorney General.

The Attorney General, Fisher, Howell and Todd for the negro.
R. Stockton and Frelinghuysen for defendant.

NOTE.

Chief Justice Kinsey, in giving the Opinion of the Court said,

By the words of the will taken together, it appears that the testator intended to increase the daughters' portions, to effect this purpose, he ordered the mother of the negro now before the Court, and another, to be sold by his executors for the term of fifteen years, and every construction which will not detract from this intention should be made in a case of this nature. It is also evident that the testator foreseeing probably, that some means might, after his death, be made use of to frustrate his benevolent design, took care to guard against it, by ordering that whoever should purchase these negroes, the purchasers should run all risks, and be at all the expense which should arise from their misbehaviour, the most probable ground on which that attempt might be made. The Chief Justice was of Opinion, that these words take in the fact which has happened, and the purchaser ought not to avail himself of it by making a slave of the child.

IN THE SAME TERM OF

XXV SEPTEMBER, 1790.

(p. 120)

The STATE *against* JOSHUA FARLEY.

Ordered that a habeas corpus do issue, directed to the said

NOTE CONTINUED.

He thought this might be sufficient to say on the present occasion, but he would go further, and say that in his opinion, at the death of the testator, the two negro women were not slaves, no body at that time had that absolute property in either, which distinguishes the slave from what we call a servant, and the retention of the temporary interest excludes that supposition entirely. The argument made use of by the counsel for the claimant, from the word *fell*, might have had some weight if it had not been coupled with and explained by the particular time to which it applies, but taken together, it is of no kind of consequence, neither could he give his assent to the idea suggested that both were slaves until the expiration of the fifteen years: Indeed the thought in his opinion was absurd, for he had no other idea of a slave but where the servitude is perpetual, or in other words for life. Neither did he see the impropriety of supposing, that the right to freedom subject to the temporary servitude, might vest in the negro at the death of the testator. If this be so, and if the misbehaviour of the mothers were not to affect themselves, he could not bring himself to entertain an opinion that it should affect their innocent offspring and make them slaves: all that Anderson bought was the service of the mother for a term of years, and that too subject to all risks: As the party buying, had nothing else in contemplation, no construction can be unjust which gives that right in the fullest extent to him, and if he suffers by his bargain, it is no more than he undertook to subject himself to; and a construction of this nature appeared much more rational than one which subjects a human creature to be a slave for no fault of his own. For these reasons the Court were unanimously of Opinion that the claim of James Anderson is unfounded and the negro boy should be liberated from his custody.

Joshua Farley for the body of negro Joseph here on the first day of the next term, ex-mo-Linn.

XXVI NOVEMBER TERM, 1790.

(p. 165.)

The STATE *against* JOSHUA FARLEY.

On Habeas Corpus *of Negro* Joe, *claiming his Freedom.*

The said Joshua Farley having returned that the said negro Joe in the writ named, before the coming of the said writ, was and still is, the negro slave of him the said Joshua Farley, and that he had, and still has right and title to hold the said Joe a slave during life; and thereof tendered an issue to the country, and prayed the Court that the said issue so tendered might be tried by a jury of his country; whereupon, the Court having heard counsel, and taking the matter into consideration, are of Opinion that a jury in this case is improper, and therefore do refuse the same.

The evidence both for and against the claim of the said negro Joe to be set at liberty, being fully heard, and counsel thereupon on both sides,

The Court do adjudge that the said negro Joe is illegally detained in the custody of the said Joshua Farley, and therefore do order him to be discharged from the said custody and illegal detention of him the said Joshua Farley, on the motion of Elisha Boudinot.

XXVII MAY TERM, 1791.

(p. 248)

The STATE *against* JOSEPH BEAVERS, JOHN CLIFFORD, and JOHN MARTIN, *Administrators of* EDWARD CLIFFORD, *dec.*

On Habeas Corpus *ad subjiciendum, for the liberation of Negro* Abraham Solomons, *and Negro* Dolly *his Wife.*

The Attorney General, Elisha Boudinot, and Linn, counsel for the Negroes. Leake and Richard Stockton, counsel for the said Administrators.

The defendants having returned the bodies with the cause &c. "That they are the negro slaves of the said defendants of the estate of their intestate, and that they have right to hold them as such, during life," and thereof having tendered an issue to the country, and prayed that the same might be tried by a jury of the country.

The court considering that this point was fully argued and determined by them in the case of the State *against* Joshua Farley, *November term* last,* do refuse to hear any argument thereupon, and do direct that the cause be opened and heard before the Court in the usual manner; whereupon,

The Court having heard the return filed and evidence and allegations of the parties, *do order*, on motion of Mr. Leake, Attorney for the said Administrators, that the said Abraham and Dolley be remanded into the custody of the said Administrators.

* Ante 28.

IN THE SAME TERM OF

XXVIII MAY, 1791. (p. 257)

The State *against* Abraham Probasco.

On Habeas Corpus *of Negro* Hagar, *wife of* Cornelius Wilson, *and* Cornelius, Lydia *and* Anna *their children, praying their Freedom, detained by the defendant, claiming their service for life.*

[Habeas Corpus returned this Term and filed]

The Court have fully heard the allegations and proofs of all parties, and the arguments of counsel thereon; it appeared to the Court, that the said negroes brought up on the said writ, were in the year 1776, the slaves of William Winds, Esq. of the county of Morris;—That the said William Winds, in consideration of the good behaviour of the said negro Cornelius Wilson the father, in the said year 1776, did manumit and set free the said Cornelius, his wife Hagar, and all the said children. That the said Cornelius and his family built a house on the lands of the said William Winds by his assistance, and with his permission, and lived thereon as free citizens for the term of three years, when the said Cornelius Wilson and wife were taken sick; on which the said William Winds removed them to a house near his own, and took care of them till they recovered, when he employed them and paid them wages for their labor as free persons;

that the said William Winds, fearing they might become a burthen on his estate, urged them to obtain security to indemnify him from any expense in case of their becoming a charge. That thereupon the said William Winds gave to the said negro Cornelius Wilson a Pass to go into the county of Monmouth to obtain such security. That the said Cornelius accordingly went to the said county of Monmouth, and agreed with Abraham Probasco the defendant, that in consideration of his becoming security to the said William Winds, he and his family would serve him five years. That the said Abraham Probasco in consequence thereof, came to the said William Winds and agreed with him accordingly, and in order to secure the said William Winds, the said Abraham Probasco proposed, that the said William Winds should give to the said Abraham a bill of sale for the said negroes, and at the end of five years, the said Abraham would release the said negroes and set them free: That a bill of sale for the consideration of five shillings, without any condition or reservation was drawn up accordingly by the said Abraham, and executed by the said William, and a receipt given by the said Abraham to the said William therefor, calling it a deed of gift. That at the execution of the said instrument or bill of sale, the said William Winds mentioned his fear lest the said Abraham should claim the said negroes as slaves by virtue of the said bill of sale, when he and the witnesses should be dead, and declared that although he could get two hundred pounds for the said negroes, yet he had given the said bill of sale for five shillings in order that they might be free. That the said negroes have faithfully served the said Abraham for more than six years under the said agreement, and are still detained by the said Abraham who claims their service for life by virtue of the said bill of sale.

The Court therefore having maturely considered the premises, *are unanimously of Opinion*, that the said negroes and every of them, be discharged from the custody of the said Abraham Probasco as free citizens, and they are hereby discharged accordingly, on motion of Mr. Attorney-General, Bloomfield.

The Attorney General, and R. Stockton for the negroes.
Kirkpatrick for defendant.

XXIX SEPTEMBER TERM, 1792.

(p. 471)

The STATE *against* WILLIAM LAIRD.

On Habeas Corpus *of Negro* Rachel, *claiming her Freedom.*

[The Writ returned and filed.]

The Court taking into consideration this case, and it appearing to depend on the decision, in the case of the State *against* James Anderson, on the habeas corpus of negro Silas, September term, 1790, ordered, that the said negro Rachel be discharged and entirely liberated from the custody of the said William Laird, on the motion of the Attorney General.

XXX APRIL TERM, 1793.

The STATE *against* BENJAMIN COVENHOVEN.

On Habeas Corpus *of Negro* Agnus, *claiming her Freedom.*

[The Writ returned and filed]

The Court having considered this case, and it appearing that the same depends on the decisions in the case of the State *against* James Anderson, on the habeas corpus of negro Silas, September term, 1790, ordered that the said negro Agnus be discharged and entirely liberated from the custody of the said Benjamin Covenhoven, on motion of the Attorney General.

XXXI MAY TERM, 1793.

The STATE *against* JAMES PITNEY of the county of Morris.

On Habeas Corpus *of Negro* James, *a boy about thirteen years of age, claiming his Freedom.*

The case upon the *habeas corpus* and return, coming before the Court appeared to be as follows,

Jasper Smith of the township of Maidenhead, in the county of Hunterdon, by will bearing date the 29th day of *November*, 1769, (among others) made the following devise, "And as for all my negroes, Jack, old Juddy, and Young Juddy, with all her

4*

children, and with all their cloathes, Chests, Beds, and bedding, after my decease, I do hereby order that they are all by me forever freed from all servitude from me or any of mine, and from all others whatsoever at my decease, and that they may go and work for their living with whomsoever they please." That the said Jasper Smith afterwards died. That notwithstanding the said will, the said negroes, and in particular the said young Juddy were detained by Joshua Smith, son of the said Jasper, and one of the devisees named in the said will, that during such detention and before the death of the said Joshua, the negro James in the present habeas corpus named, was born of the body of the said Juddy. That the said Joshua Smith died, leaving Keziah Smith and John Biles his executors, and the said negro Juddy and her son James in their possession. That on the 9th day of March, 1790, the said Keziah Smith and John Biles, as executors of the said Joshua Smith, by bill of sale of that date, conveyed the said negro James to James Pitney the defendant in the habeas corpus named; but that no bond or other security whatsoever was given by the said Jasper Smith, the master of the said young Juddy and testator in the will above named, pursuant to the act of assembly passed 16th November, 1769, whereupon,

The Court having taken due consideration, *are unanimously of Opinion*, That the said negro Juddy the mother of the said James, was a free woman by the will of the said Jasper Smith, the want of security pursuant to the said act of assembly notwithstanding, and that consequently the said James her son is entitled to his freedom; and do therefore *order*, that the said James be discharged from the illegal detention of the said James Pitney, and he is discharged accordingly, on the motion of Mr. Bloomfield for the State.

INDEX

OF THE

POINTS OF LAW &c.

ADUJUDGED IN THE FOREGOING CASES.

THE END.

C A S E S
A D J U D G E D
IN THE
SUPREME COURT
OF
N E W J E R S E Y;
RELATIVE TO THE
M A N U M I S S I O N
OF
N E G R O E S
AND OTHERS HOLDEN IN BONDAGE.

—"GOD has created men of all nations, of all languages, of ALL COLOURS, EQUALLY FREE:

"SLAVERY, in all its forms, in all its degrees, is a violation of the divine laws, and a degradation of human nature."

B U R L I N G T O N,
PRINTED FOR "THE NEW-JERSEY SOCIETY FOR PROMOTING THE ABOLITION OF SLAVERY,"
BY ISAAC NEALE,—M,DCC,XCIV.

AT a general Meeting of the NEW-JERSEY SOCIETY FOR PROMOTING THE ABOLITION OF SLAVERY, *September* 2, 1793,

RESOLVED,

That the *Preſident* of this Society collect and have printed, the ' Deciſions of the Su-' preme Court in this State, relative to the ' Manumiſſion of Negroes and others, un-' lawfully holden in Bondage.'

EXTRACT FROM THE MINUTES,

ROBERT SMITH, JUN.

SECRETARY.

ON the Application of Joſeph Bloomfield, Eſquire, Preſident of the *New-Jerſey Society for promoting the Abolition of Slavery*, I have carefully examined the following Caſes with the original Entries thereof, in the Minutes of the Supreme Court of New-Jerſey; and I do hereby certify, that the ſame are truly taken from the ſaid Minutes,

GERSHEM CRAFT, for the Clerk
of the Supreme Court.

November 20, 1793.

JUSTICES OF THE SUPREME COURT,

AND

ATTORNEY GENERALS

OF THE STATE OF NEW-JERSEY, SINCE 1774.

1774 to May Term 1776 inclufive.	Frederick Smyth, Chief Juftice. David Ogden, } Juftices Richard Stockton, } Cortland Skinner, Atty. General.
1776 September 4.	William Paterfon, Atty. General.
1777 February 5.	Robert Morris, Chief Juftice.
15.	Ifaac Smith, } Juftices. John Cleves Symmes, }
1779 June 10.	David Brearly, Chief Juftice.
1783 June 13.	Jofeph Bloomfield, Atty. General.
1788 September 4.	John Chetwood, Third Juftice.
1789 November 20.	James Kinfey, Chief Juftice.
1792 May 23.	Aaron D. Woodruff, Atty. General.

CASES ADJUDGED IN THE SUPREME COURT OF *NEW JERSEY.*

November Term, 1775.

(Minutes, p. 44, 142.)

The KING *againſt* ESTHER BARBER and others.

On Habeas Corpus *for to bring the Body of* Beulah, *a Negro Girl.*

BY the Admiſſion of the Counſel, it appeared that Beulah the Negro Girl, brought up by the Habeas Corpus, and now before the Court, is the Daughter of a Negro Man and Negro Woman, the firſt named David, and the other named Dinah, both of whom formerly belonged to Caleb Haines, of the City of Burlington, which ſaid Negroes David and Dinah, were ſet free by the ſaid Caleb Haines in his life time, and before the Birth of the ſaid Girl Beulah, without having given any Bond purſuant to the Act of Aſſembly, paſſed in the twelfth and thirteenth Years of her late Majeſty Queen Ann; for which Reaſon the ſaid Manumiſſion was alledged to be void.

The Court having heard the Arguments of Counſel, as well for the ſaid Eſther Barber and others, as for the ſaid Beulah, at the Term of May laſt, and now again at this preſent Term, and having fully conſidered thereof *are of Opinion,* That the ſaid Manumiſſion by the ſaid Caleb Haines, of the ſaid David and Dinah, the Parents of the ſaid Beulah, was good in Law againſt the ſaid Caleb

Haines and thoſe claiming under him, notwithſtanding the not giving Bond as aforeſaid; and that the ſame Beulah is entitled to her Freedom under the ſaid Manumiſſion againſt the ſaid Caled Haines, and all claiming under him; and do order her the ſaid Beulah to be delivered up from out of the Cuſtody of the ſaid Eſther Barber and others, in which ſhe hath been illegally detained.

April Term, 1782.

The STATE *againſt* JACOBUS VANHUYS.

On Habeas Corpus *for Negro* Will *Claiming his Freedom.*

THE Court having heard the Arguments of Counſel on the Part of Negro Will, and the Reaſons aſſigned for and againſt his Freedom, and the Evidence in Support thereof: It is ordered by the Court that the ſaid Negro *Will* be, and he is hereby diſcharged and ſet Free from the ſaid Jacobus Vanhuys, on Motion of Mr Deare.

Kinſey, Elias Boudinot, and the Attorney General for the Negro.

Sergeant, and Paterſon, for Defendant.

September Term, 1782.

(p. 36.)

The STATE *againſt* EDMUND BAINBRIDGE.

On Habeas Corpus *of Negro* Nelly.

IT appearing to the Court, and the ſaid *Edmund Bainbridge* conceding, that the ſaid Negro Nelly was formerly the Property of Edmund Bainbridge, the elder, of Maidenhead, deceaſed, who let his Daughter Abigail, late the Wife of Thomas Biles, of Bucks County in Pennſylvania, deceaſed, gave her when very young; that many Years afterwards he made his Will and bequeathed her to his ſaid Daughter Abigail, during the Life of his ſaid Daughter, and to her Iſſue, and did further order, that if ſhe ſhould die childleſs, then the ſaid Negro Nelly ſhould be ſold, and the Money appropriated as mentioned in his ſaid Will; that the ſaid Abigail Biles who ſurvived her Huſband and her Father, did by her Will dated 30th April 1779, ſet forth and declare, that the ſaid Negro Nelly had by her ſaid Father been preſented to her on a New-Year's Day, when ſhe was a Child, and therefore, both from that Gift and from bringing her up, ſhe had a better Right to diſpoſe of her than any other Perſon, and did therein order and direct, that the ſaid Negro Nelly ſhould be manumitted and ſet free, a thing which ſhe had very much at Heart; that the ſaid Negro Nelly reſided in the State of Pennſylvania at the Time of the paſſing of the Act for the gradual Abolition of Slavery, 1ſt March, 1780, and until the firſt of November in the ſame Year, the Term and Period allowed and fixed in the ſaid Act for regiſtering Slaves and for ſome Time afterwards; that ſhe was not regiſtered as the ſaid Act requires, and that ſhe is not within the Exceptions ſpecified therein.

The Court having fully conſidered the Premiſes, *are unanimouſly of Opinion*, That the Manumiſſion of the ſaid Negro Nelly by the ſaid Abigail Biles, Daughter of the aforeſaid Edmund Bainbridge, is good in Law againſt all Perſons claiming under either of them; the ſaid Edmund Bainbridge, having given her to his ſaid Daughter, when ſhe the ſaid Negro Nelly was a Child, and his ſaid Daughter having directed by her Will that ſhe ſhould be manumitted; and further that the ſaid Negro Nelly, not having been regiſtered as the above mentioned Act of the State of Pennſylvania requires, and therefore entitled to Freedom in that State, is not by Law put in a worſe Situation here: It is therefore *Ordered*, That the ſaid Negro Nelly be diſcharged and ſet at Liberty from the ſaid Edmund Bainbridge. On Motion of Mr. *Morris* for Mr. *Houſton*.

B

IN THE SAME TERM OF

September, 1782.

(p. 48.)

The STATE *againſt* LEWIS Mc. KNIGHT.

On Habeas Corpus *to bring the Body of Negro* Cæſar Tite.

THE Defendant having returned the Habeas Corpus, and brought up the Body of the ſaid Negro Cæſar Tite, It is ordered that the Defendant enter into Security in the Sum of Two Hundred Pounds to bring up the Body of the ſaid Negro Cæſar on the ſecond Tueſday in November next, and abide the Judgment of the Court reſpecting the ſaid Negro, and that in Caſe the ſaid Negro ſhould be adjudged by this Court free, that the ſaid Lewis M'Knight ſhall pay for the Service of the ſaid Negro from this Time.

Recognizance accordingly.

September Term, 1782.

(p. 49.)

The STATE *againſt* ENLOES PHILPOT.

WHEREAS, it hath appeared to this Court, upon the Affidavit of Jack Tappen, that the Defendant holds a certain Anthony Tappen in Bondage and Slavery, without lawful Authority for the ſame as the ſaid Jack alledgeth: therefore, *Ordered*, on Motion of Mr. Leake for the ſaid Anthony, that a Writ of *Habeas Corpus ad faciendum ſubjiciendum et Recipiendum* do iſſue, returnable to this Court at the next Term.

November Term, 1782.

(p. 59.)

The STATE *against* LEWIS Mc. KNIGHT.

On Habeas Corpus *of Negro* Cæſar Tite.

AGREEABLY to the Command of the within Writ, I have here in Court the Body of the within mentioned Cæſar Tite, and do ſay that the ſaid Negro Tite is my Property, being bought of Kenneth Hankinſon, Eſquire, for valuable Conſideration, and he is not a free Man; but I am willing and deſirous to conteſt that Property by a Jury of the Country, agreeably to the Laws of this State, and pray that it may not be taken from me without a Trial by Jury, &c.

LEWIS Mc. KNIGHT.

IN THE SAME TERM OF *November*, 1782.

(p. 76.)

IN THE SAME CAUSE OF

The STATE *against* LEWIS Mc. KNIGHT.

IT appearing to the Court, that the ſaid Negro Cæſar Tite, brought up by *Habeas Corpus*, and now before the Court, heretofore belonged to Grace Tite, of the County of Monmouth, who by her laſt Will and Teſtament ordered that he ſhould be free when he attained the Age of Twenty-one Years, till which period he was to ſerve Thomas Leonard of the ſaid County of Monmouth; that the ſaid Thomas Leonard joined the Enemy ſome Time before the Expiration of the ſaid Service, and the ſaid Negro Cæſar Tite was ſold at Public Vendue, with other confiſcated perſonal Property of the ſaid

Thomas Leonard, by the Commiſſioners of forfeited Eſtates for the County of Monmouth, and bought by David Forman, Eſq. who afterwards ſold him to Kenneth Hankinſon, Eſq. and he to the ſaid Lewis M'Knight the Defendant; that no Bond was given by the ſaid Grace Tite, purſuant to the Act of Aſſembly, paſſed in the twelfth and thirteenth Years of the late Queen Ann: And that the ſaid Negro Cæſar Tite is now above Twenty-one Years old, *to wit,* of the Age of about Twenty-four or Twenty-five.

The Court having heard the Arguments of Counſel on both ſides, and fully conſidered thereof, *are unanimouſly of Opinion,* That the ſaid Manumiſſion is good in Law againſt all Perſons claiming under the ſaid Grace Tite, notwithſtanding Bond was not given as aforeſaid; *and do order,* on Motion of Mr. Bloomfield for the Attorney-General, that the Negro Cæſar Tite be diſcharged and ſet at Liberty from the ſaid Lewis M'Knight.

September Term, 1783.

(p. 252. 270.)

Mercy Hill *againſt* William Leddell.

On Habeas Corpus *for Manumiſſion.*

IT being alledged by the Counſel for the ſaid Mercy Hill the Plaintiff, that ſhe is the Daughter of a certain Jupiter Lee, a Negro Slave, heretofore belonging to Samuel Lee of the Town of Swanſey in the Colony of Maſſachuſetts Bay, now Commonwealth of Maſſachuſetts, and Deliverence Hill, a free-born native Indian Woman; that in her Infancy ſhe was put apprentice to James Power of that Place, with whom, or his Aſſigns ſhe ſerved many Years, and then laboured for her Livelihood in different Places as other free Perſons uſually do; that long afterwards ſhe was by ſome Means ſold as a Slave, and by ſundry Transfers and Sales came at length into the Poſſeſſion of the Defendant William Leddell.

The Court having heard the Teſtimony, with ſundry Affidavits offered and read, to prove the Truth of the foregoing Allegations, and having alſo heard the Arguments of Counſel on both Sides, and maturely conſidered thereof, *are unanimouſly of Opinion*, That the ſaid Mercy Hill is entitled to her Freedom; and ought not to be held in Slavery; and do accordingly adjudge and order that the ſaid Mercy Hill be diſcharged and ſet at Liberty from the ſaid William Leddell, on Motion of Mr. Morris in behalf of Mercy Hill.

IN THE SAME TERM OF

September, 1783.

(p. 286. 295.)

The STATE *againſt* TIERCK TENBROECK.

On Habeas Corpus *of Negro* Philip *for Manumiſſion.*

THE Court having fully conſidered the Evidence, and the Arguments of Counſel in this Cauſe, *are unanimouſly of Opinion*, and do adjudge, that the ſaid Negro *Philip* be diſcharged and ſet at Liberty from the ſaid Tierck Tenbroeck, and alſo from John Vanhorne of Rocky-Hill, in the County of Somerſet, who hath appeared and claimed the ſaid Negro Philip, On Motion of Mr. Paterſon for the State.

May Term, 1784.

(p. 33.)

The STATE againſt ADRIAN POST.

On Habeas Corpus *of Negro* Charles *and* Wife.

In November Term, 1781. (p. 467.)

ON the hearing of this Caſe, the Court adjudged in favor of the diſcharge of the Negroes, and ordered the Defendant to deliver them to the Sheriff of Bergen, to remain in his Cuſtody, until the further Order of the Court.

And now, on Motion of Mr. Elias Boudinot for Nicholas Covenhoven, Maſter of the ſaid Negroes, it is ordered by the Court, that the Sheriff of Bergen, do on ſervice of this Rule, deliver to the ſaid Nicholas Covenhoven, or his Order, the ſaid Negro Charles and Wife.

April Term, 1785.

(p. 300.)

The STATE againſt BENJAMIN APPLEGATE.

On Habeas Corpus *of Negro* Peter Ridley, *claiming to be manumitted.*

THE ſaid Negro *Peter* being brought into Court by Habeas Corpus, and it appearing to the Court on Teſtimony, that the ſaid Negro Peter is the Son of a certain William Ridley, a free Negro and his Wife Dianna, a Negro Woman ſometime the Property of Dollans Hegeman, and who became free before the Birth of the ſaid Negro Peter, and that the ſaid Parents of the ſaid Negro Peter have ever ſince lived and been reputed as free.

The Court *are of Opinion* and *do adjudge*, that the ſaid Negro Peter was free-born, and is entitled to be diſcharged as a free Man; and do order that he be diſcharged accordingly, on Motion of Mr. Paterſon for the State.

May Term, 1785.

(p. 358.)

The STATE *against* JOHN VANHORNE.

On Habeas Corpus *of Negro* Prime, *claiming his Freedom.*

THE Court in *September Term*, 1784. *(p.* 125.) on return of the *Habeas Corpus*, obliged Defendant to enter into Recognizance with Security in £140. conditioned for the Appearance of the said Negro *Prime* at the next Term, to abide &c. and not depart &c.

November Term, 1784, (*p.* 195.) Recognizance continued.

April Term, 1785, (p. 299.) Argument postponed, and Recognizance continued.

And now *(May Term,* 1785.*) Moore Furman*, Esquire, Agent of forfeited Estates for the County of Hunterdon, having applied to the Court, and represented that the State hath a Claim to the said Negro Prime; it is ordered by the Court that the said Negro Prime be delivered into the Custody of John Anderson, Esquire, Sheriff of Hunterdon, until a Trial of the Property can be had, and until the further Order of the Court.

AFTERWARDS IN THE

Term of May, 1786, (p. 128.)

Moore Furman, Esq. Agent of Forfeitures for the County of Hunterdon—*against*

John Eauhouse, In Detinue.

This action having been brought by Agreement of Parties under the Direction of the Court, to try the Property of a certain Negro Prime, and a Verdict and Judgment having passed in favor of the Plaintiff, *It is ordered* by the Court, on the Motion of Mr. Houston for the Plaintiff, that the said Negro Prime now in the Custody of the Sheriff of Hunterdon, agreeably to an Order of this Court of May Term last, be delivered to the said Moore Furman, Esq. Agent of Forfeitures for the County of Hunterdon.*

November Term, 1785.

(p. 519 and 472.)

Negro GEORGE against BARNT DE KLYN.

On Habeas Corpus *and complaint of cruel Treatment.*

THE hearing of this Cause coming on, and the Evidence being gone through, Mr. Elias Boudinot on behalf of the Negro, prayed that Mr. De Klyn should oblige himself not to send the said Negro George out of the State, and the Court having considered thereof, required Mr. De Klyn so to do, which he accordingly did in open Court.

IN THE SAME TERM OF *November*, 1785.

(p. 525.)

Negro QUAMINI *against* WILLIAM LEDDEL, *Esquire.*

On Habeas Corpus *for Manumission.*

IT being alledged on the Part of the said Negro Quamini, that several Years ago he belonged to Dr. Samuel Tuthill, of Morris County, from whom he was pur-

* Note. *The Legislature by an Act dated 21 November, 1786, declaring themselves "to be desirous of extending the Blessings of Liberty," generously manumitted Prime from Slavery. He had been enlisted and served in the Army in the late War.*

chased by Captain Augustine Bayles of the same County, that the said Captain Bayles, divers Times in his Life-time promised the said Negro Quamini, that if he would be honest, faithful, and industrious, he never should serve any other Master, but should be free at his the said Captain Bayles's decease; that the said Captain Bayles on his Death-Bed, considering that his Wife would be left very destitute of Help, directed that the said Negro Quamini should continue in her Service during her Widowhood, and that then he should be free; that the said Captain Bayles died in the Year 1781, or 1782, and that about Two Years ago, Keziah Bayles his Widow intermarried with one Thomas Faircloth.

The Court having heard the Testimony for establishing the several Facts aforesaid, and having duly considered the same, *do order*, on Motion of Mr. William De Hart, that the said Negro Quamini be discharged, and set at Liberty from the said William Leddel, Esquire.

May Term 1787.

(p. 449.)

The STATE *against* JACOB PHILLIPS.

On Habeas Corpus *of Negro* Obadiah Gale.

THE Court having heard the Evidence and Argument of Counsel in this Cause, *do order* that the said Jacob Phillips enter into Recognizance in the Sum of One Hundred Pounds, conditioned, that the said Jacob Phillips on the Twenty-sixth Day of June next, liberate and discharge from his Service the said Obadiah Gale, and the Court do further adjudge and order, that on the Twenty-sixth Day of June next, the said Obadiah Gale shall be set at Liberty, and go thereof free without Day, and that the said Obediah Gale be in Custody of the Sheriff of Hunterdon till the said Twenty-sixth Day of June next, unless the Recognizance is entered into by the said

C

Jacob Phillips before one of the Juſtices of the Supreme Court, on Motion of Mr. Elias Boudinot.

September Term, 1787.

(p. 36,—39.)

The STATE *againſt* JOHN B. OLIVER *and his* Wife.

On Habeas Corpus *of Negro* Kate.

THE Court after hearing the Arguments of Counſel, *are of Opinion*, that the ſaid John B. Oliver enter into Recognizance in Five Hundred Pounds, conditioned that he do not ſend or ſuffer to be ſent, the Negro Kate mentioned in the ſaid Habeas Corpus, out of this State, till the Court ſhall take further Order therein at the next Term. Recognizance entered into accordingly by the ſaid John B. Oliver.

The Attorney General and Eliſha Boudinot for State.

Elias Boudinot and Aaron Ogden for Defendants.

Note, *The Counſel for the Defendants in this Caſe, contended that they ought not to be compelled to anſwer the Allegation of Abuſe, becauſe, as the Habeas Corpus, was in common form to bring the Body, and no Cauſe in particular alledged, they could not be preſumed to come prepared to anſwer any thing but the illegal Detainer of the Negro as a Slave, and inſiſted that they ought not to be compelled to anſwer this until a ſufficient Proſecutor ſhould be indorſed on the Habeas Corpus, and Security given for the Coſts: All this the Court over ruled. The Counſel for the Defendants undertook that the Negro ſhould not be ill-treated, and the diſpute was afterwards ſettled and the Court heard nothing further of the Affair.*

September Term, 1788.

(p. 356.)

The STATE *against* DANIEL TAYLOR, Junior.

On Habeas Corpus *for the bringing up a Negro Man named* Harry.

THE Habeas Corpus being returned, the Court proceeded to consider the same, and Counsel both in favor of the Negro, and on behalf of the said Daniel Taylor, Jun. being heard; *It is ordered,* that the said Negro Man be discharged from being a Slave, and that he serve the said Daniel Taylor, Jun. his Master as a Servant for the Space of Six Years, from the First Day of September instant, and that from thenceforward he be entirely discharged and free from Servitude.

April Term, 1789.

(p. 437.)

The STATE *against* DAVID LYON.

On Habeas Corpus *of Negro* Margaret Reap, *claiming her Freedom.*

UPON the hearing before the Court, it appeared, that Zacheus Mayhew, of Massachusetts, by Deed of Gift, dated the first Day of *March*, 1750, did give a certain Negro Girl called Flora, unto his Daughter, Lucy Little, then the Wife of   Little—That the said Lucy Little afterwards being a Widow, and having One Son called William Little, intermarried in Massachusetts with a Dr. Joseph Eaton, who came from thence with his Wife to Shrewsberry in *New-Jersey*, and at the same Time brought the said Negro Flora with them—That on the 31st Day of *August*, 1752, the said Dr. Eaton sold the said Negro Flora with a Child she then had called

Rose, unto one John Worthley—That the said John Worthley by Bill of Sale, dated 27th *September*, 1753, sold the said Negro Flora to one John Williams—That John Williams the 8th of *May*, 1754, sold the said Negro Flora to the aforesaid Dr. Eaton for the Sum of Sixty-Pounds York-Money—That the said Dr. Eaton upwards of Twenty Years ago, and about Five Days after one Jacob Dennis had purchased the aforesaid Negro Girl Rose, Daughter of the said Flora, of the said John Worthley, he the said Dr. Eaton informed the said Jacob Dennis, he was collecting those Negroes for William Little (his Son-in-Law)—that they should return to him again as they belonged to him; and at that Time and often afterwards declared that he was principled against Slavery, and that he never intended the said Flora should belong to his Estate, nor should any of his Children be benefited by having her as their Property—It also appeared that the said Lucy Eaton survived her said Husband, the said Dr. Eaton—That shortly after the Death of the said Dr. Eaton (*to wit*, about Seventeen Years ago) one Thomas White applied to the said Lucy Eaton to purchase and did purchase at private Sale, a small Spinning Wheel, which she then said she had not any further Use for, as she had given Flora free who used to spin on the said Wheel—That since that Time the said Flora has passed for, and been esteemed a free Woman, and for a considerable Time worked about in the Neighborhood of the said Widow Eaton, and in the House of the said Widow, and for the Wife of John Eaton the eldest Son of the said Dr. Eaton, and always received her Wages as well from the said John Eaton's Wife, as the Neighbours; and the said Widow Eaton herself promised to compensate her therefor—And it further appeared that whilst the said Flora worked about for herself as aforesaid, she intermarried with a certain Joseph Reap, a free Negro, with whom the said Flora has ever since lived unmolested and as a free Woman, and still continues so to live—That after the marriage of the said Flora with the said Joseph Reap, she had Two Children called Lydia, and *Margaret* (the present Claimant), that these Children lived with their said Father and Mother, who brought them up by their own Industry without any Expence or Trouble to any other Person whatsoever, until laſt Fall, when they were taken away from their ſaid Parents without their Conſent—That ſince the ſaid taking, it appears by a certain Inſtrument of Writing, bearing date the 8th Day of *January*, 1789, executed under the Hand and Seal of the aforeſaid William Little, (the Son-in-Law of the ſaid Dr. Eaton, and for whom the ſaid Dr. Eaton declared as aforeſaid, he was collecting the Negroes)—That the ſaid William Little hath manumitted and ſet at Liberty the ſaid Flora and her ſaid Two Children, Lydia and Margaret; whereupon

The Court having conſidered this ſtate of Facts, and the arguments of Counſel on both Sides thereupon, *are of Opinion*, That, permitting the ſaid Negro Woman Flora to remain at Liberty for ſo long a Time, and to work for herſelf, and having intermarried with the ſaid Joſeph Reap a free Man, with whom ſhe has ever ſince lived as a free Woman, is ſuch Evidence of Freedom, both of the ſaid Negro Woman Flora, and conſequently of her Children, as to entitle the ſaid Negro Margaret Reap to her Diſcharge; and the Court do therefore accordingly *order* the ſaid Negro Margaret Reap to be diſcharged and ſet at Liberty from the ſaid David Lyon; on Motion of the Attorney General.

Bloomfield, Attorney General, and R. Stockton for the State.—

M. Williamſon, and Aaron Ogden for Defendant.

IN THE SAME TERM OF *April*, 1789,

(p. 438.)

The STATE *againſt* JOHN LEIGHTON.

On Habeas Corpus *of Negro* Lydia Reap, *returnable the firſt Day of this Term.*

THE Court order an Attachment againſt the ſaid John Leighton, for contempt in not returning the ſaid Writ of *Habeas Corpus*, agreeably to the Command thereof, and for divers Expreſſions made uſe of by him reflecting on the Authority of this Court and its proceſs, on Motion of Mr. Attorney-General.

April Term, 1790.

(p. 42.)

The STATE *against* LEWIS PRALL *and* ROBERT ROSS *Administrators of* ISAAC PRALL, *deceased*.

On Habeas Corpus *of Negro* Thomas *claiming his Freedom*.

[Habeas Corpus returned and filed.]

RETURN,

" WE have the Negro in the above Writ named, at the Day and Place as by the said Writ we are commanded, *and we do certify*, that we as Administrators of all and singular the Goods and Chattels, Rights and Credits which were of Isaac Prall, deceased, took Possession of said Negro as part of the personal Property of the said Isaac Prall, and that there is no other Cause of detaining him.

LEWIS PRALL,
ROBERT ROSS, JUN. } Administrators."

Upon the hearing in this Cause, it appeared to the Court that the said Negro Thomas belonged to the said Isaac Prall, deceased—That the Intestate, about Three Years before his Death, and frequently afterwards, declared that Tom should never have another Master—That he had been a faithful Servant to him—That they had been born under one Roof, that they had received Sustenance from one Breast, and had broke up the Ground, and always lived together; and continued to shew great Affection and Regard for the Negro until his last Sickness, and during that Sickness whilst he had his Senses—That in his last Illness, on the Friday before he died, he requested a Person might be sent for to make his Will, at which Time his Sister being present, she asked him what he intended to do with his Negroes, he replied they should all be sold but Tom, and he should be free; which Declaration he also made the same Day to several others, with this, further, that Tom should not serve any other Master—The Person sent for to write his Will, did not come 'till the next Day, when the Inteſtate was ſo deranged in his Mind as to be incapable of making his Will, and continued ſo until he died, which was on the Wedneſday following; that the ſaid Inteſtate, after he was in ſome meaſure deranged, continued to ſhew ſtrong and evident Marks of Affection for the ſaid Negro, and of the Continuance of his Deſign and Intention to make him free: It alſo appeared to the Court that the ſaid Negro had always before the Death of the Inteſtate, and till that Event took place, been much attached to his Maſter, had ſhewn a great Affection for him, and had behaved himſelf well and faithfully.

The Court having conſidered of the whole Caſe, and the Arguments of Counſel for and againſt the Manumiſſion of the Negro, *are unanimouſly of Opinion*, That the frequent and full Declarations of the Inteſtate, amounted to more than a bare Intention of doing ſomething in future; that even if theſe Declarations were taken in the Senſe of a Promiſe to do ſomething in future, the good Behaviour of the Negro which was admitted on all Hands, the evident Continuation of the Affection of the Maſter as long as he had his Senſes, and even when in ſome Meaſure deprived of them, afforded a ſtrong Ground of Preſumption of a Contract between the Negro and Maſter for his Freedom, conditionally on his behaving well, which having performed on his Part, the Negro was entitled to his Liberty, and that the Performance of the Condition on the Part of the Maſter and his Repreſentatives, might be effected on this Habeas Corpus, *do therefore adjudge*, That the ſaid Negro Tom being entitled to his Freedom, be diſcharged from the Cuſtody of the ſaid Adminiſtrators, and all the Repreſentatives of the ſaid Iſaac Prall, deceaſed. On the Motion of Mr. Bloomfield, Attorney-General.

Attorney-General, and Eliſha Boudinot, for the State.

Freelinghuyſen and Aaron Ogden, for Defendants.

May Term, 1790.

(p. 85.)

The STATE *against* TOBIAS HENDRICKSON.

On Habeas Corpus *of Negro* Jack *claiming his Freedom.*

THE Court having considered this Case under all its Circumstances, and it appearing that John Coward the former Master, under whom Tobias Hendrickson claims Title to the Negro, antecedent to the Year 1785, actually entered into an Agreement with Jack for his Freedom, the Terms of which have been fully complied with; *The Court are therefore of Opinion,* and *do order,* the said Negro Jack to be liberated from the Custody of the said Tobias Hendrickson—But as John Coward the former Master is not before the Court, and of Course not heard, and his Interest may be materially concerned, this Judgment for the Liberation of the said Jack is not to affect any present or future Claim of the said John Coward.

September Term, 1790.

(p. 119.)

The STATE *against* JOHN WARE.

On Habeas Corpus *of Negro* Jethro *(Son of Charity Briggs) claiming his Freedom.*

IT appearing to the Court that the said Negro Jethro was born on the eighth Day of *September,* 1768, in the County of Cape-May in this State; that his Mother Charity Briggs a (Mulatto Woman) was free at the Time of his Birth—That the said Charity was by Indenture bound by the Justices and Overseers of the Poor of the Lower Precinct of Cape-May to one Nathaniel Foster, in order to bear the Expences of her having had the Small-Pox—That in the said Year of 1768, the said Charity was purchased by a certain John Connel, she then having the ſaid Jethro an Infant at her Breaſt—That afterwards the Time of Service of the ſaid Charity was ſold by Connel to Captain Jonathan Jenkins, and that ſhe the ſaid Charity took her ſaid Son with her—That the ſaid Jethro her Son, was brought up by Jenkins until he was fit for Buſineſs, and then was ſold unto Chriſtopher Leaming of the ſaid County of Cape-May, who kept the ſaid Jethro a number of Years, and within Two Years laſt paſt ſold the ſaid Jethro unto John Ware of Cumberland, the Defendant now in Court, for the Term of Twelve Years and Eight Months, and by Bill of Sale engaged to warrant the Service of the ſaid Negro Jethro for the ſaid Term.

And the Court having taken the ſaid Caſe into Conſideration, *are unanimouſly of Opinion,* That the ſaid Jethro being the Son of a free Woman, and of the Age of Twenty-one Years, is now entitled to his Freedom, and do therefore adjudge, that the ſaid Negro Jethro (otherwiſe called *Jethro Briggs)* be diſcharged from the Cuſtody of the ſaid John Ware, on the Motion of Joſeph Bloomfield, Attorney General.

IN THE SAME TERM OF *September*, 1790.

(p. 141.)

The STATE *againſt* JAMES ANDERSON.

On Habeas Corpus *of Negro* Silas *claiming his Freedom.*

Returnable Saturday 11*th September, and returned accordingly.*

The Defendant appears with the Negro, to do and receive, &c. purſuant to Recognizance.

THE Caſe ſtated by Counſel for, the Opinion of the Court is as follows,

That on the fourth Day of December, 1761, John Horsfield was entitled to Two Negro Girls, named Betty and Nelly as Slaves; and on the ſaid fourth Day of December by his laſt Will and Teſtament, (then dated) made the following Deviſe, "Item, my Two Negro Girls named Betty and Nelly, I leave to be ſold by my Executors, hereafter named, for the Term of Fifteen Years, and at the end of that Time to be free, and

D

" the Money arising thereby, to be equally divided a-
" mongst my Four youngest Daughters, and they that buy
" the said Negro Girls, if the said Girls or either of them
" Misbehave, or become chargeable, it must be at the
" Risque or Cost of the Buyer." That the said Executors sold the said Negro Girls to one Covenhoven, who sold them to the present Defendant Anderson, for the Term mentioned in the Will—That Betty had a Child (the Negro Silas) now of full Age, which Child was not born in Matrimony.

The Court having considered the above State of Facts, are *are unanimously of Opinion*, That on the Death of John Horsfield the Testator, Betty ceased to be a Slave, that she ceasing to be a Slave, no Child born of her Body can be deemed so by the Birth of such Child during the Fifteen Years, and that the Claim of James Anderson to hold the said Negro Silas as a Slave, is not warranted by Law: *Wherefore it is ordered*, That the same Silas be liberated from the illegal Detention of the same James Anderson, and he is hereby liberated accordingly, *ex motione* J. Bloomfield, Attorney-General.

The Attorney-General, Fisher, Howell and Todd for the negro.—R. Stockton and Frelinghuysen for defendant.

NOTE.

Chief Justice Kinsey, in giving the Opinion of the Court said,

BY the words of the Will taken together, It appears that the Testator intended to increase the Daughters' Portions, to effect this Purpose, he ordered the Mother of the Negro now before the Court, and another, to be sold by his Executors for the Term of Fifteen Years, and every Construction which will not detract from this Intention should be made in a Case of this Nature—It is also evident that the Testator foreseeing probably, that some Means might, after his Death, be made use of to frustrate his benevolent Design, took care to guard against it, by ordering that whoever should purchase these Negroes, the Purchasers should run all Risques, and be at all the Expence which should arise from their Misbehaviour, the most probable Grounds on which that Attempt might be made—The Chief Justice was of Opinion, that these words take in the Fact which has happened, and the Purchaser ought not to avail himself of it by making a Slave of the Child—

IN THE SAME TERM OF *September*, 1790.

(p. 120.)

The STATE *against* JOSHUA FARLEY.

ORDERED, that a Habeas Corpus do iſſue, directed to the ſaid Joſhua Farley for the Body of Negro

---

He thought this might be ſufficient to ſay on the preſent Occaſion, but he would go further, and ſay that in his Opinion, at the Death of the Teſtator, the two Negro Women were not Slaves, no body at that Time had that abſolute Property in either, which diſtinguiſhes the Slave from what we call a Servant, and the Retention of the temporary Intereſt excludes that Suppoſition intirely—The Argument made uſe of by the Counſel for the Claimant, from the Word *ſell*, might have had ſome Weight if it had not been coupled with and explained by the particular Time to which it applies, but taken together, it is of no kind of Conſequence, neither could he give his aſſent to the Idea ſuggeſted that both were Slaves until the Expiration of the Fifteen Years: Indeed the thought in his Opinion was abſurd, for he had no other Idea of a Slave but where, the Servitude is perpetual, or in other Words for Life—Neither did he ſee the Impropriety of ſuppoſing, that the Right to Freedom ſubject to the Temporary ſervitude, might veſt in the Negro at the Death of the Teſtator—If this be ſo, and if the Miſbehaviour of the Mothers were not to affect themſelves, he could not bring himſelf to entertain an Opinion that it ſhould affect their innocent offspring and make them Slaves: all that Anderſon bought was the Service of the Mother for a Term of Years, and that too ſubject to all Riſques: As the Party buying, had nothing elſe in Contemplation, no Conſtruction can be unjuſt which gives that Right in the fulleſt extent to him, and if he ſuffers by his Bargain, it is no more than he undertook to ſubject himſelf to, and a Conſtruction of this Nature appeared much more Rational than one which ſubjects a human Creature to be a Slave for no Fault of his own. For theſe Reaſons the Court were unanimouſly of Opinion that the Claim of James Anderſon is unfounded and the Negro Boy ſhould be liberated from his Cuſtody.

Joſeph here on the firſt Day of the next Term, *ex mo. Linn.*

November Term, 1790.

(p. 165.)

The STATE *againſt* JOSHUA FARLEY.

On Habeas Corpus, *of Negro* Joe *claiming his Freedom.*

THE ſaid Joſhua Farley having returned that the ſaid Negro Joe in the Writ named; before the coming of the ſaid Writ, was and ſtill is, the Negro Slave of him the ſaid Joſhua Farley, and that he had, and ſtill hath Right and Title to hold the ſaid Joe a Slave during Life; and thereof tendered an Iſſue to the Country, and prayed the Court that the ſaid Iſſue ſo tendered might be tried by a Jury of his Country; whereupon, The Court having heard Counſel, and taking the Matter into Conſideration, are of Opinion that a Jury in this Caſe is improper, and therefore do refuſe the ſame.

The Evidence both for and againſt the Claim of the ſaid Negro Joe to be ſet at Liberty, being fully heard, and Counſel thereupon on both ſides.

The Court do adjudge that the ſaid Negro Joe is illegally detained in the Cuſtody of the ſaid Joſhua Farley, and therefore do order him to be diſcharged from the ſaid Cuſtody and illegal Detention of him the ſaid Joſhua Farley, on the Motion of Eliſha Boudinot.

May Term, 1791.

(p. 248.)

The STATE *againſt* JOSEPH BEAVERS, JOHN CLIFFORD, *and* JOHN MARTIN, *Adminiſtrators of* EDWARD CLIFFORD, *deceaſed.*

On Habeas Corpus *ad ſubjiciendum, for the Liberation of Negro* Abraham Solomons, *and Negro* Dolly *his Wife.*

The Attorney-General, Eliſha Boudinot, and Linn, Counſel for the Negroes.—Leake and Richard Stockton, Counſel for the ſaid Adminiſtrators.

THE Defendants having returned the Bodies with the Cauſe &c. " That they are the Negro Slaves of

" the ſaid Defendants of the Eſtate of their Inteſtate, " and that they have Right to hold them as ſuch, during " Life," and thereof having tendered an Iſſue to the Country, and prayed that the ſame might be tried by a Jury of the Country.

The Court conſidering that this Point was fully argued and determined by them in the Caſe of the State againſt Joſhua Farley, *November Term* laſt, do refuſe to hear any Argument thereupon, and do direct that the Cauſe be opened and heard before the Court in the uſual Manner; whereupon,

The Court having heard the Return filed and Evidence and Allegations of the Parties, *do order*, on Motion of Mr. Leake, Attorney for the ſaid Adminiſtrators, that the ſaid Abraham and Dolley be remanded into the Cuſtody of the ſaid Adminiſtrators.

IN THE SAME TERM OF *May*, 1791. (p. 257.)

The STATE *againſt* ABRAHAM PROBASCO.

On Habeas Corpus *of Negro* Hagar, *Wife of* Cornelius Wilſon, *and* Cornelius, Lydia *and* Anna *their Children, praying their Freedom, detained by the Defendant, claiming their Service for Life.*

[Habeas Corpus returned this Term and filed.]

THE Court having fully heard the Allegations and Proofs of all Parties, and the Arguments of Counſel thereon; it appeared to the Court, that the ſaid Negroes brought up on the ſaid Writ, were in the Year 1776, the Slaves of William Winds, Eſq. of the County of Morris;—That the ſaid William Winds, in conſideration of the good Behaviour of the ſaid Negro Cornelius Wilſon the Father, in the ſaid Year 1776, did manumit and ſet free the ſaid Cornelius, his Wife Hagar, and all the ſaid Children—That the ſaid Cornelius and his Family built a Houſe on the Lands of the ſaid William Winds by his Aſſiſtance, and with his Permiſſion, and lived thereon as Free Citizens for the Term of Three Years, when the ſaid Cornelius Wilſon and Wife were taken ſick; on which the ſaid William Winds removed them to a Houſe near his own, and took care of them till they recovered, when he employed them and paid them

Wages for their Labor as free Persons; That the said William Winds, fearing they might become a burthen on his Estate, urged them to obtain security to indemnify him from any Expence in Case of their becoming a Charge—That thereupon the said William Winds gave to the said Negro Cornelus Wilson a Pass to go into the County of Monmouth to obtain such Security—That the said Cornelius accordingly went to the said County of Monmouth, and agreed with Abraham Probasco the Defendant, that in Consideration of his becoming Security to the said William Winds, he and his Family would serve him Five Years—That the said Abraham Probasco in Consequence thereof, came to the said William Winds and agreed with him accordingly, and in order to secure the said William Winds, the said Abraham Probasco proposed, that the said William Winds should give to the said Abraham a Bill of Sale for the said Negroes, and at the end of Five Years, the said Abraham would release the said Negroes and set them free: That a Bill of Sale for the Consideration of Five Shillings, without any Condition or Reservation was drawn up accordingly by the said Abraham, and executed by the said William, and a Receipt given by the said Abraham to the said William therefor, calling it a Deed of Gift—That at the Execution of the said Instrument or Bill of Sale, the said William Winds mentioned his Fear least the said Abraham should claim the said Negroes as Slaves by virtue of the said Bill of Sale, when he and the Witnesses should be dead, and declared that altho' he could get Two Hundred Pounds for the said Negroes, yet he had given the said Bill of Sale for Five Shillings in order that they might be free—That the said Negroes have faithfully served the said Abraham for more than Six Years under the said Agreement, and are still detained by the said Abraham who claims their Service for Life by Virtue of the said Bill of Sale.

The Court therefore having maturely considered the Premises, *are unanimously of Opinion*; That the said Negroes and every of them, be discharged from the Custody of the said Abraham Probasco as free Citizens, and they are hereby discharged accordingly, on Motion of Mr. Attorney-General, Bloomfield.

The Attorney General, and R. Stockton for the Negroes.
Kirkpatrick for Defendant.

September Term, 1792.

(p. 471.)

The STATE *against* WILLIAM LAIRD.

On Habeas Corpus *of Negro* Rachel *claiming her Freedom.* [*The Writ returned and filed.*]

THE Court taking into Consideration this Case, and it appearing to depend on the Decision, in the Case of the State against James Anderson, on the Habeas Corpus of Negro Silas, *September Term*, 1790, ordered, That the said Negro Rachel be discharged and entirely liberated from the Custody of the said William Laird, on the Motion of the Attorney-General.

April Term, 1793.

The STATE *against* BENJAMIN COVENHOVEN.

On Habeas Corpus *of Negro* Agnus, *claiming her Freedom.* [*The Writ returned and filed.*]

THE Court having considered this Case, and it appearing that the same depends on the Decisions in the Case of the State against James Anderson, on the Habeas Corpus of Negro Silas, *September Term*, 1790, ordered that the said Negro Agnus be discharged, and entirely liberated from the Custody of the said Benjamin Covenhoven, on Motion of the Attorney-General.

May Term, 1793.

The STATE *against* JAMES PITNEY *of the County of Morris.*

On Habeas Corpus *of Negro* James, *a Boy about Thirteen Years of Age, claiming his Freedom.*

THE Case upon the *Habeas Corpus* and Return, coming before the Court appeared to be as follows,

Jasper Smith of the Township of Maidenhead, in the County of Hunterdon, by Will bearing Date the 29th Day of *November*, 1769, (amongst others) made the following Devise, " And as for all my Negroes, Jack, old " Juddy, and young Juddy, with all her Children, and " with all their Cloaths, Chests, Beds, and Bedding, af- " ter my Decease, I do hereby order that they are all

" by me for ever freed from all Servitude from me or " any of mine, and from all others whatſoever at my " Deceaſe, and that they may go and work for their " Living with whomſoever they pleaſe"—That the ſaid Jaſper Smith afterwards died—That notwithſtanding the ſaid Will, the ſaid Negroes, and in particular the ſaid young Juddy were detained by Joſhua Smith, Son of the ſaid Jaſper, and one of the Deviſees named in the ſaid Will, that during ſuch Detention and before the Death of the ſaid Joſhua, the Negro James in the preſent Habeas Corpus named, was born of the Body of the ſaid Juddy—That the ſaid Joſhua Smith died, leaving Keziah Smith and John Biles his Executors, and the ſaid Negro Juddy and her Son James in their Poſſeſſion—That on the 9th Day of March, 1790, the ſaid Keziah Smith and John Biles, as Executors of the ſaid Joſhua Smith, by Bill of Sale of that Date, conveyed the ſaid Negro James to James Pitney the Defendant in the Habeas Corpus named; but that no Bond or other Security whatſoever was given by the ſaid Jaſper Smith, the Maſter of the ſaid young Juddy and Teſtator in the Will above named, purſuant to the Act of Aſſembly paſſed 16th *November*, 1769; whereupon,

The Court having taken due Conſideration, *are unanimouſly of Opinion*, That the ſaid Negro Juddy the Mother of the ſaid James, was a free Woman by the Will of the ſaid Jaſper Smith, the want of Security purſuant to the ſaid Act of Aſſembly notwithſtanding, and that conſequently the ſaid James her Son is entitled to his Freedom, and do therefore *order*, that the ſaid James be diſcharged from the illegal Detention of the ſaid James Pitney, and he is diſcharged accordingly, on the Motion of Mr. Bloomfield for the State.

F I N I S.

ERRATA.

Page 5, line 4, dele *of the State*.
Page 8, after line 7, read *Kinſey*, *Elias Boudinot*, *and Skinner Attorney-General*, *for the Negro*.
Sergeant and Paterſon for Defendant.
Same page, after line 16, dele the names of Counſel.
Page 15, line 24, for *Eauhouſe* read *Vanhorne*.

ANDREW T. JUDSON'S

REMARKS,

To the Jury, on the trial of the Case,

STATE v. P. CRANDALL.

Superior Court, Oct. Term, 1833.

WINDHAM COUNTY, Ct.

HARTFORD:
JOHN RUSSELL, PRINTER.

The information, State *vs.* Prudence Crandall, was filed in the Superior Court, Oct. Term, 1833, held by the Hon. DAVID DAGGETT, Chief Justice.

The facts charged against the defendant were harboring and boarding colored persons, not inhabitants of the State of Connecticut, in violation of the *act* of the last Session of the General Assembly.

Plea—Not Guilty.

After the evidence closed, the case was opened on the part of the State, as follows.

GENTLEMEN OF THE JURY:

The subject matter of this cause, has been much misunderstood by some, who were honest, and so much perverted by others, less entitled to that appellation, you will allow me for the purpose of preventing all future misapprehension, and staying the current of unjustifiable reproach, attempted to be cast upon our native State, to say, that the legislators who enacted this law, and the people who support it, are not opposed to the *education* of the black population, as you may have so often heard reiterated by those who love to put darkness for light. The law rests upon no such basis, and will not be supported upon any such principle.

The people of Connecticut have done more for the *education* of the blacks. than has been done in any other portion of the civilized world. It is a matter of congratulation with us, that *all the black* children have the same and equal privileges, at all our common schools, with the *white* children. Nay more, they are admitted to all our district schools, nearly 1500 in number, supported entirely by the school fund, which exceeds one million eight hundred thousand dollars. They are indeed admitted upon better terms than the white children. The white inhabitants are taxed for *school houses—they* board the instructors—*they* furnish the wood, while the colored population are exempt from all these burthens, and then participate equally in all the benefits and blessings of the shcool fund. No other State in this Union has done any thing like this, yet some of them are quite liberal in abusing us. I wish you particularly to understand, that in supporting *this* cause, and *this* law, I do not oppose the *education* of the people of color, but I do oppose the importation of blacks from other countries, for any purpose. There is also one other topic, to which I would advert for one moment, and upon that too, I desire not to be misunderstood, and for the purpose of placing it out of the power of any one, to put a false construction upon my sentiments or my opinions, I deem it my duty to remark, that I am no advocate or apologist for slavery. I lament its existence, and regret its evils as much as you can. It was the policy of our fathers to rid the State of the evils of slavery, and as early as 1784, they began this great work, and long since, by wise and salutary laws, this State took its rank as a "free state," among her sister States. This work was done by State legislation. In its own sovereign capacity, freedom was given to the slave. Those who may be acquainted with the history of events know, that the States south of the Potomac came not here to prevent this philanthropic reformation within *our* State. The constitution of the United States *does* recognize slavery, and leaves it with every state to continue, regulate, or abolish it, at their pleasure. One State cannot interfere with another State, in this matter, any more than she can in the election of its state officers. To admit the proposition that we can authorize an interference with Virginia because she does not see fit to liberate her slaves, will be giving Virginia the same power to come hither and say to Connecticut, you shall be a slave state! To instruct and educate missionaries, to go there for the purpose of disturbing their tranquility, and teaching the massacre of their inhabitants, would prove a sad business for us. If there are any among us, who feel it their duty to alleviate the condition of the slave, let them go where that slave is, and address the master. Let them go to that government where laws tolerate slavery, and read to that government, their moral lessons. If too cool or cowardly to do this, their philanthropy is not worth possessing.

There are indeed a few individuals in New England, who "*would prefer to see the constitution torn into a thousand atoms, rather than live under it, so long as it tolerates slavery.*" But these mistaken men, should be informed, that by dissolving the Union, they cannot abolish slavery—they would only make it perpetual. There are now twelve free, and twelve slave states, in the Union, and as the Constitution cannot be amended except by the consent of three quarters of the States, it is evident this matter must be left, where the framers of the Constitution left it, *with each State*, or *force* must be the resort. If the time has indeed arrived, when the citizens of New England are to go deliberately at the work of dissolving the Union of the States and a Jury of the County of Windham is to begin that work, then we will so understand it. For one, I will enter my protest at the outset, and call upon you, as a branch of that government under which we have enjoyed so much prosperity, to do the same, by your verdict. The law in question is not made to promote the interest of slave holders, for we have none in our State. It is not made to perpetuate the evils of slavery, for there is not a man in the State of Connecticut who is in favor of slavery. I admit there are many, and that I am of that number, who would not break up the union of the States, as an experiment to abolish slavery at the South. I would prefer to leave this matter to the moral sense of that portion of the Union who now deem it their right to hold slaves. New England has nobly discharged its own debt, and she ought not to incur another, by dissolving the Union, for then slavery would be perpetuated for ages to come, where it now exists.

Having made these preliminary remarks, I will now invite the attention of the Jury to the case in question.

The *information* filed by the Attorney for the State, charges Prudence Crandall, the defendant, with the violation of a law passed at the last session, entitled "An Act in addition to an Act, entitled an Act for the admission and settlement of inhabitants in Towns." The particular facts charged in this case, are, that the defendant, wilfully and knowingly did harbor and board, for the purposes of instruction, within a school by her set up, in the town of Canterbury, certain *colored persons not inhabitants of this State*, and that the defendant did so harbor and board them after the 22d day of August, 1833, to wit: On the 24th day of September, 1833, for the purposes mentioned in said Act. The first question relates to the facts in the case. It is incumbent on the State, to prove beyond reasonable doubt, that the defendant has done the acts charged in this information. Unless *this* is proved, it is your duty to acquit the defendant.

On the part of the State it is claimed, that these facts are proved, beyond doubt, or contradiction. You learn from the evidence, that a school has been set up in the town of Canterbury, by the defendant, for the purpose of instructing colored persons, who are not inhabitants of this State: or in other words. for colored persons from other States, and other countries, and that in point of fact, since the 22d day of August last, she has admitted into that school, and instructed therein, the following persons, all of whom are not inhabitants of this State, viz: M. E. Carter, Sarah Hammond, A. E. Hammond, C. A. Weldon, Emila Willson, Eliza Weldon, C. G. Marshal, Maria Robinson and Elizabeth Henly. One is from Pennsylvania, some from New York, and the residue from Rhode Island.

The colored girls who have been sworn, testify that they have been members of the school, at all times since the 22d of August, and on the day specified in this information, and that the above named *foreign persons of color*, have been harbored and boarded by Miss Crandall, and have been instructed by her in the school. They also tell you where these girls belong. In addition to this, Asael Bacon and Ebenezer Sanger, Esquires, two of the select men of the town of

Canterbury, tell you that the defendant gave the names of these girls to them, with the place to which each belonged.—One girl has testified that the defendant went to New York and Philadelphia, and some of the girls by her named, returned with her. This evidence is proper to show you, that the defendant has *knowingly* harbored these foreigners, against the provisions of this act. The defendant has introduced no evidence, and of course, the testimony offered by the State, stands uncontradicted. You are therefore to decide upon its weight, and if on considering this testimony, you entertain any reasonable doubt, you will say the defendant is not guilty, and the State must abide by your verdict. If you should believe from this evidence, that the facts are proved, as charged, then another duty will be suggested by the learned and ingenious counsel for the defendant. They have intimated to us, that their defence will rest on the *unconstitutionality* of the law. They have told us, on a former trial, and will tell you now, that the Legislature of this State do not possess the power to make this law. And as we have had this defence so fully developed, it will become my duty, even in the opening of this case, to present to the jury, the honest convictions of my own mind, on this important question, and then leave it with their intelligence to pronounce such verdict, as shall be deemed proper.

I shall have no hesitation to admit, that a law made by any State in the Union, in *violation* of the Constitution of the United States is a dead letter, and must be so declared by that judicial tribunal having cognizance of the matter.

I shall admit also, that in a case called criminal, and in prosecutions on penal statutes, like the present, the jury are the judges of both law and fact. In criminal cases the court can advise the jury, but cannot direct them how to find. As the Constitution of the United States is the supreme law, I shall admit again, that the jury may decide upon the constitutionality of this law. I have made these admissions frankly, so that the real question between us, may stand upon its own merits, and if the law is indeed inconsistent with the Constitution, I would not have it executed, upon any individual. Let me ask your attention to the law itself which reads as follows.

"An act in addition to an act, entitled an act for the admission and settlement of inhabitants in towns.

Whereas attempts have been made to establish literary institutions in this State for the instruction of colored persons belonging to other States and countries, which would tend to the great increase of the colored population of the State, and thereby to the injury of the people: Therefore.

Sec. 1. *Be it enacted by the Senate and House of Representatives, in General Assembly convened*, That no person shall set up or establish in this State any school, academy, or literary institution, for the instruction or education of colored persons who are not inhabitants of this State, nor instruct or teach in any school, academy, or other literary institution whatsoever in this State, or harbor or board, for the purpose of attending or being taught or instructed in any such school, academy, or literary institution, any colored person who is not an inhabitant of any town in this State, without the consent, in writing, first obtained of a majority of the civil authority, and also of the select men of the town in which such school, academy or literary institution is situated; and each and every person who shall knowingly do any act forbidden as aforesaid, or shall be aiding or assisting therein, shall, for the first offence, forfeit and pay to the treasurer of this State. a fine of one hundred dollars, and for the second offence shall forfeit and pay a fine of two hundred dollars, and so double for every offence of which he or she shall be convicted. And all informing officers are required to make due presentment of all breaches of this act. *Provided*, That nothing in this act shall extend to any district school established in any school society, under the laws of this State, or to any school established by any school society under the laws of this State, or to any incorporated academy or incorporated school for instruction in this State.

Sec. 2. *Be it further enacted*, That any colored person, not an inhabitant of this State, who shall reside in any town therein for the purpose of being instructed as aforesaid, may be removed in the manner prescribed in the sixth and seventh sections of the act to which this is an addition.

Sec. 3. *Be it further enacted*, That any person not an inhabitant of this State, who shall reside in any town therein, for the purpose of being instructed as aforesaid, shall be an admissable witness in all prosecutions under the first section of this act, and may be compelled to give testimony therein, notwithstanding any thing contained in this act, or the act last aforesaid.

Sec. 4. *Be it further enacted*, That so much of the seventh section of the act to which this is an addition, as may provide for the infliction of corporeal punishment, be, and the same is hereby repealed."

There are several provisions of this law, which have been entirely misunderstood, to say the least. Upon the face of this statute, *you* will readily see, that it has no relation whatever to those colored persons who *belong* to Connecticut. It leaves all those precisely where they were before the passage of the act. All negroes, molattoes or other colored persons born in Connecticut, or who have gained a settlement in Connecticut, in any way, are not subject to the provisions of the act, and any person may set up a school for *them*, because they *belong* to this state, and we are not only bound, but are willing to educate them, let the tax be what it may. If other states would do as much, *all* the blacks might be educated.

In the next place, the jury will notice, that all *district schools, all schools established by school societies—all academies and colleges incorporated by this State*, are exempt from the provisions of this act, so that all colored persons whereever they may belong, foreigners, as well as natives—those coming from other States and other countries, as well as all those who were born in this state, have free access, under this law, to all district schools, academies and colleges within the State.

The only operative provision of the law complained of by the defendant, is, that a penalty is imposed on those of our own citizens, who may harbor, board and instruct foreign blacks *without first obtaining from the civil authority and Select Men of the town, their consent in writing*.

It may be added, if that consent is obtained, then the penalty is removed, and the schools for *foreign* blacks may be kept in any town. This in effect leaves the matter of harboring *foreign* blacks, to the towns themselves. And the subject is left under their control, where it should be. In substance then, this law merely provides, that schools for *foreign blacks*, shall be under the control of a board of visitors, and that board is the civil authority and Select Men. Other schools are to be visited and examined, and why not this?—If persons from abroad are to be brought into our State, under the pretence of education, what harm can there be, in creating a board of visitors for that school, as well as for a common district school for the instruction of the children, whose parents live within the State? It is a *regulation* of the school, and it will be found at some future day, to be a regulation essential to the existence of the State.

This is the law upon which this information is founded, the alleged breach of which, has been proved against this defendant. The defendant by her counsel now tells you, this law is unconstitutional, and therefore void. To sustain this defence the 2d section of the 4th article of the Constitution of the United States is to be brought before you. I will so far anticipate that defence, as to read you this section. It is as follows, viz.

"The *citizens* of each State, shall be entitled to all privileges and immunities of *citizens* in the several States."

To shew you that this law of Connecticut does not violate this section of the Constitution, I shall have occasion to call the attention of the jury to three propositions.

I. It is believed by some, that the section just read, has a special reference to the action of the General Government and none whatever, to the laws of a particular State.— That by the laws of Congress, equal and exact justice should be measured out alike to the citizens of all the States, because those citizens are all equally bound to sustain that government, and therefore have equal claims to the distribution of its favors and blessings. Not so with the States. They are sovereign and also distinct governments, having retained all power, not expressly given and imparted to the General Government.

In support of this proposition I can refer you to what was said concerning this section, in the 52d No. of the Federalist, page 267, written by *Mr. Madison*, one of the framers of this Constitution From his exposition of this section, it would seem that this was a substitute for the 4th article of the *Confederation*, and relates solely to the matters of naturalization which is committed to the Congress of the United States and taken away from the State governments, by the Constitution. But upon this point I will not dwell, because there are other claims which may be presented with more confidence, to your consideration.

II. This law is not unconstitutional, because the State of Connecticut has never surrendered to the General Government its power to regulate schools within its own limits. The same distinguished author, just quoted, page 292, same volume, makes the following just comment upon the powers surrendered, and the powers retained. "The powers delegated by the proposed Constitution, to the federal government, are few and defined. Those which are to remain in the State governments are numerous and indefinite. The former will be exercised principally on external objects, as war, peace, negociation, and foreign commerce; with which last, the power of taxation, will for the most part be connected. The powers reserved to the several States, will extend to all the objects, which in the ordinary course of affairs, concern the lives, liberties, and properties of the people: and the *internal order*, improvement and *prosperity* of the State."

The *internal order* of a State depends much on *schools* and *education*. Its *internal* prosperity too, may be said to depend mainly upon the regulation of schools. The whole subject requires minute and special care, and would in its details be impracticable by the General Government. It never was imparted to that government. This State, in particular, may boast of its care over education, and its superintendence of schools. It belongs to our early history, and is the foundation of all our glory, that our schools have been under the watchful eye, and faithful guardianship of legislative action, and visatorial power of the State. When Yale College, which has been the pride of our State, and from whence have issued so many annual streams of mental brightness, was established, the visatorial power was committed to a board of trustees, a part of whom were composed of legislators annually elected. The two succeeding colleges, and every incorporated academy, has a board instituted to have a direct power over instructors. Should any of the instructors in these high schools or colleges, attempt to disseminate the principles of immorality, or equally dangerous principles of treason against our government, such men, and such instructors would feel, as they should do, the power of these boards of visitors. The common district schools in every town are required to be visited, and the instructors must be approved of by a board of visitors. And why let me ask, should a school for foreign colored persons, be free from visitation, and subject to no restraint? It would seem to me, of all others, most to require it. Is it not a little remarkable that as early as 1717 the General Assembly of this State passed an act in the following words, regarding schools. "The civil authority, together with the Select Men, in every town, or the major part of them, shall inspect, and they are hereby empowered and directed, as visitors to inspect the state of all such schools, as are by this act appointed to be kept, within said towns from time to time, and particularly once in each quarter of a year, and inquire into the qualifications of masters. And they are to give such directions, as they shall find needful, to render such schools most serviceable for the increase of knowledge, religion and good manners. And if said inspectors or visitors observe any such *disorders*, or misapplications of money, allowed for the support of such schools, as will be likely to defeat the good ends proposed, they shall lay the same before the General Assembly, that proper orders therein may be given." By that act, which continued in force about 80 years, the select men and civil authority were continued a board of visitors, and as we all know, for mere convenience, in the year 1799, visitors elected by school societies were substituted, and now possess the same powers.—The act of last session very properly selects the *ancient board*, for this obvious reason, that there is a two fold interest involved, the existence of schools, and the introduction of foreigners. The select men and civil authority were supposed to be the better board, because the interest of the whole town might be concerned, and as the school societies were often composed of parts of towns, and different towns, the *visitors* would not become as suitable as the *ancient board*. It was their duty under the old law to observe any such *disorders*, as might be likely to defeat the good end proposed, so under this law, if they should observe any such *disorders*, as would tend to disturb the union—the inculcation of any such wicked principles as might hazard the peace of community, the select men and civil authority might withdraw their licence, and leave the person thus treating the government under which they live, to the penalties of the law. Every State in the union has with an uninterrupted course of legislation regulated *their* schools, and this is surely the first instance of calling in question the validity of *school laws*, whatever they may have been. This long course of legislation is to my mind, high evidence, that the subject of schools and education was left entirely to the States.

I will lay before you the laws of Massachusetts on this subject. These laws are collected by Dr. Dwight, and you will find them in the 4th volume of his travels, page 503, with very appropriate comments. " All instructors of the university, colleges, academies, and schools, *and all private instructors* are required to take dilligent care, and exert their best endeavours to impress on the mind, of the children and youth, the principles of piety, justice, and a sacred regard to truth, *love to their country*, humanity and universal benevolence, sobriety, industry and frugality, chastity, moderation and temperance, and all other virtues, and to shew them the tendency of these virtues to secure the blessings of liberty, and the tendency of the opposite vices to slavery and ruin. The select men were to determine the qualification of masters and also those which fit children to enter into the grammar schools. Districts to forfeit from 10*l* to 30*l* if they did not comply. With respect to other schools [private] not contemplated in these provisions, it is enacted that no person shall be a master or mistress of any school, and keep the same without obtaining a certificate, as in other cases, under a penalty of 20 shillings. The duty of every master and mistress of every private school is made the same as the public schools. It is further enacted, "if a person who is not a *citizen*, shall keep a school in the Commonwealth for one month, he shall be subjected to a fine of 20*l*." Grand jurors are diligently to inquire and presentment make of all breaches and neglect of the act.

By these laws you will perceive, that it has been the policy of Massachusetts to put all her schools, both public and private, under the superintendence of the board of select men. And they go so far as not to allow any but *citizens* to instruct their schools.

In Connecticut, education has been our pride and boast. We are small in territory but rich in science. All our strength and glory consists in the superior advantages of education to our inhabitants. We have a school fund, provided by the wisdom of the State, amounting to one million eight hundred thousand dollars, the annual interest of which, is distributed to all classes, rich and poor—black and white, *belonging to our State.* We have colleges, and academies scattered over the State, in greater perfection than any other State, or country on the earth. And why is it, that Connecticut has been so distinguished for education? The answer may be found in your Statute Books, from the earliest settlement of the colony. *Connecticut has kept her schools under strict visatorial power.* Why is it that our inhabitants are peaceable and moral? It is because our *schools* are under strict discipline, and when *disorders*—or bad sentiments are promulged—or treasonable doctrines are attempted to be thrown into the minds of youth, to poison and destroy them, then the visatorial power is put in requisition, and all is made right. What necessity is there, that *colored persons* from the West Indias, or Slave States, should be educated here and not have their instructors subject to the same care and inspection as the children of those who inhabit the State? If there be any such necessity, let it be shown to us.

In closing what I have to say on this topic, I do claim, that Connecticut, or any other State in the Union may enact such laws regarding education as their wisdom and prudence may dictate, and their laws will be binding upon the people.

III. There is yet a more important consideration. Should either or both the preceding propositions which I have presumed to advance, in support of this cause, be held untenable, then I have another, upon which I can look with great confidence, and which I feel justified in submitting to an enlightened Court and an honest Jury, whose love of our common country, and the honour of our native State, will secure to me a patient and candid hearing.

You will perceive that this law is assailed, because there is another law above it, in these words—"The *citizens* of each State shall be entitled to all privileges and immunities of *citizens* in the several States."

We are told on this trial, and you are called upon to decide, that persons of color are *American citizens*, within the meaning of this section of the Constitution, and therefore a law of Connecticut, which requires that schools set up for *coloured persons*, not inhabitants of this State, without the consent of the board named in that act, is a violation of this Constitution. I am willing to meet this argument at the threshold, and, without evasion, answer it in such manner as shall be satisfactory to the court and jury.

Coloured persons are not citizens, within the meaning of that term, as technically used in the Constitution. The gentlemen bring us to the construction of this section, and this single term *citizen*, and would have the case turn upon that point. I am content that it should be so, and will now proceed to show you why I shall ask you to come to a different result. We must go back to the period when the Constitution was framed, and take into consideration the circumstances and condition of the country, the different races of men, and their conditions, and looking through the whole instrument, call to our aid also, such other cotemporaneous acts, as might have existed, then we may derive the true construction, and the only construction to be given to the term. It is quite immaterial how that term may have been used upon other occasions, or how it may be understood in common parlance at the present day. The real question is, what did the framers of the Constitution mean, when they said in such concise and emphatic language, "the *citizens* of each State shall be entitled to equal privileges and immunities of citizens of the several States"?

From a thorough examination of this question, I am brought to the irresistable conclusion, that at the time when the Constitution was formed, it was very far from the intention of those members of the Convention to include *blacks* under the term *citizen*. This may be proved by the *acts of Congress*—by the *Constitutions of most of the States*—by the *course of legislation* adopted and uninterruptedly pursued by the States, since the adoption of the Constitution, and by *judicial decisions*.

Soon after the government was formed, under the new Constitution, Congress began to legislate, and in 1790, that Congress being composed of several of those who framed the Constitution, in carrying into full effect that provision which directs Congress to "establish a uniform rule of naturalization," passed their first act on this subject, to make *American citizens out of aliens*. This precise and technical language is there used—"Any alien, being a free *white person* may become a *citizen* by complying with the requirements after named." In the law of 1795, the same language is used. "A free *white person* may become a *citizen*." Similar laws were passed in 1798—in 1802, 1813, and in 1824, without the least variation of phraseology. It will be a given point, that a *foreign* black person cannot be naturalized, so as to become a *citizen*; and let him reside in what state he may, such person can never enjoy equal privileges and immunities with the white citizens. Any *white* person coming from a foreign country, can be made a citizen by naturalization, but a *black one cannot*. Here is clearly and undeniably a distinction of colour; but here the argument on the other side will present to the understanding of every man this gross absurdity. A black person arrives from Cuba, and makes application for naturalization, for *he* wishes to become a *citizen*. He is denied this right on account of his color. The law is so, and he never can become a *citizen*. This person has a child born here, of the same colour, and according to the claims on the other side, this black child is a *citizen* of the United States, because of his birth! Congress were however not mistaken when they supposed the spirit of the Constitution gave to *white* persons alone the right of citizenship.

In all subsequent laws of Congress, no colored person can be in any way engaged in transporting the mail, or in the management of the post office concerns. Many consider it a privilege and an immunity too, to transport the U. S. mail. It gives employment to many persons—it supports many families, and yet a person of colour, however honest or capable, is cut off from all these employments, and upon what ground? Because of his color. Surely Congress ought to make laws giving equal privileges to all American citizens. Upon the ground claimed in opposition to the Connecticut law, these laws of Congress are unconstitutional, and notwithstanding their provisions, a black man may maintain his rights to these privileges before a court of justice!!!

Chancellor Kent settles this question beyond cavil. Vol. 2, page 72. "The act of Congress confines the description of aliens capable of naturalization to 'free white persons.' I presume that this excludes the inhabitants of Africa and their descendants; and it may become a question, to what extent persons of mixed blood, as mulattoes, are excluded, and what shades or degrees of mixture of color disqualify an alien from application for the benefits of the act of naturalization. Perhaps there might be difficulties also as to the copper-colored natives of America, or the yellow or tawny race of Asiatics, though I should doubt whether any of those were 'white persons,' within the purview of the law. It is the declared law of New-York that Indians are not *citizens*, but distinct tribes, being under the protection of the government, and consequently never can be made citizens under the act of Congress."

The Indians of America were born upon the soil we now possess—they are *native men*—they were the proprietors of this whole country, now occupied by white men—and of all others, if birth alone made and constituted *citizenship*, it ought to be yielded to the Indian. If we owe a debt to the Africans, how is that obligation swelled to the Indians, when we view the remnants of those mighty nations, who have been driven away by the power of civilization and arms?

And yet, the defendant's counsel must admit that Indians are not citizens. They are not such within the meaning of that term, in the Constitntion. and as Chancellor Kent says, they cannot be made such. And why? The answer is obvious; they are *persons of color*. This term "citizen" was adopted by the Americans, because they used to be denominated *King's subjects*, and when they declared themselves free of the King's power, they adopted the Roman appellation *American* "*citizen*." That proud term means something more than a slave—it means a white man who can enjoy the highest honors of a republic, the privilege of choosing his rulers, and being one himself.

I prove my position also, by the Constitutions of the several States, enacted by the highest tribunal, the sovereign people. In many of these Constitutions it will be found that a difference of color is maintained. I am not now on the question of whether this is morally right or morally wrong, but only proving by these *facts*, what has been the uniform Construction of the term "*citizen*" since its use in the constitution.

This evidence will be so satisfactory, that you cannot fail to see, when you have nullified the law of Connecticut, as the defendant claims you should, your work is but just commenced. Your own State Constitution must be the subject of destruction. You must put your hand upon that also, and tear out of it so much as shall prevent colored persons from enjoying equal privileges and immunities with you. We shall all admit that the elective franchise is an "immunity and privilege," of the highest grade—it is *one* which all seek for, and find it necessary to attain in a free government, before its honors can be enjoyed.

By the Constitution of Connecticut, none but a *white male citizen* of the U. S. can be admitted an elector. This is the language of the Constitution. It is further provided in our Constitution that "no person who is not an elector of this State shall be eligible to the office of Governor. Should any one tell you, as we heard boastingly on the former trial, that "a black man had the same right to be Governor of the State as the white man," I would say in reply, this must be an assumption against the Constitution. Members of the House of Representatives must be *Electors*, and therefore colored men cannot be representatives.

I will call your attention to the provisions of other Constitutions.

Delaware. The Constitution of this State, is that in "elections every free *white* male citizen shall vote."

Maryland. "Every free *white* male *citizen* shall vote."

Virginia. "Every *white* male *citizen* of the Commonwealth, resident therein, shall vote."

South-Carolina. Every free *white man* may vote, &c.

Ohio. "All *white* male inhabitants" shall vote.

Louisiana. " Every free *white* male *citizen* of the United States" shall have right to vote.

Mississippi. "Every free *white* male person" shall vote, &c.

Illinois. " All *white* male inhabitants" shall vote. And " all *white* male inhabitants, resident at the adoption of the Constitution of Illinois, had right to vote on that question.

Alabama. " Every *white* male person" shall vote.

Indiana. " Every *white* male citizen of the U. S." may vote.

In all these States, and perhaps some others, constitutional provisions have cut off the black man from all participation in the affairs of government.

Rhode-Island, has defined the qualifications of *freemen*, and among those qualifications, a man must be *white* to become an *elector.*

In the State of New-York, a singular distinction of this matter of color is maintained. A *white* man is admitted to vote, without property, while the colored man is excluded, unless he shall have in real estate actually taxed, the value of $250.

From this mass of evidence, it must be manifest, that every one of these constitutional provisions is *void*, if colored persons are " *citizens*" within the 2d section of the 4th article of the Constitution of the U. S. And in that event every black man, and every mulatto would have a right to call them up for adjudication, on a writ of mandamus, that he might be made an *elector*, and so be in the way to be made a Governor or Judge, or Representative or Senator.

Gentlemen of the Jury—Your verdict is to do more than might be supposed in the first instance. You would not only nullify the law of Connecticut, and its sacred Constitution, but you would also afford an example for other States ; nay, you would teach them by *your* solemn decision, that their laws and Constitutions were only dead letters. Do you regard the institutions of government, and the stability of those institutions as blessings, then I would conjure you to begin no such work—set no such example—presume to walk on no such dangerous ground, least its foundation sink beneath your feet, and plunge your country in inevitable ruin.

I will now endeavour to shew that the Legislatures of the several States, have by *their* solemn acts, put the same construction on the *section* in question, as I claim to be just. Some of these will relate to persons of color, others will relate to white persons who belong to *other States*, and come to participate in State privileges, and others still, will apply to distinct classes of unquestionable *citizens.* I shall consider these at the same time, for the purpose of shewing that distinctions are, and ever have been made, between *citizens* of that State and those of another State, as well as between white persons and persons of color.

If persons come from other States into this, they shall enjoy equal privileges with us, *subject, nevertheless, to such limitations, as the good of the whole may require.*

In Connecticut persons who come from other States, and who are not inhabitants of this State, may be warned to depart, and may be *removed.* Persons entertaining them, or leasing property to them, incur a penalty.

By an antient law of the State now in force, and re-enacted since the Constitution, if a person comes here *from any other State*, and seeks to recover a debt or maintain an action to recover his rights or redress his wrongs, *he* cannot do it, nor step into any court of justice, until he shall persuade some *inhabitant of this State to be his bonds-man.*

A person coming from another State, cannot maintain a petition for divorce, until a residence of three years shall have been had in this State. A person not born here, and coming from any other State, can never become an elector or vote in town meetings, except on entire different qualifications required of citizens of our own State. A citizen of Connecticut may become an elector, in the town where he lives, the next day after he shall be 21, having performed military duty, or having paid a State tax on a single article of property of the smallest value, while a person from any other State must have owned, and actually possessed $335 dollars value in real estate, and have resided within this State one year. Here is a vast difference, but public good requires it should be made. These laws are upon the same principle as the laws of licences to physicians, lawyers, taverners, surveyors and retailers. All men have natural rights to pursue such business as their own ingenuity may suggest, but public policy requires that guards be thrown around them for public good—that restrictions be laid upon them for the general welfare.

The foreman of this jury, an eminent man in his profession, has a natural right to practice physic, but the law is so, without a licence, he can never recover his debt. A man may be well informed in the profession of the law, and may have the same natural right to pursue that business, as one of these foreign blacks has to go to the defendant's school, yet he cannot do it. Public policy requires that the Court should give him licence.

This is the case with regard to numerous articles of commerce, which you cannot send to market without an inspection. Although by the Constitution, Congress has power to regulate *commerce*, yet every State in the Union has its inspection laws, upon these very articles of commerce, for he general good of the whole. By the laws of Rhode-Island, persons who have gained no settlement there, may be removed. So also in Massachusetts. The instances have not been unfrequent, of the removal of persons from one State to another, by process of law.

In the State of Rhode-Island I have noticed that *unsuitable* persons shall not gain a settlement, cannot hold real estate without *licence* from the Town Council, and these persons may be removed, leaving it to the Town Council to say who are "unsuitable" persons.

Bad houses shall not be kept by free negroes—they may be broken up, and the owners bound out, by the laws of Rhode-Island. According to the modern doctrines of equality, this law would be unconstitutional, for there is no such law for the "white citizen."

By the same laws intermarriages between white people and negroes are declared void, and the person celebrating any such marriage, shall forfeit $200.

The laws of Massachusetts also render void such marriages. If a citizen of Connecticut, being a white man, should go to Rhode Island, and fall in love with a black woman, and take her before a magistrate, and claim his "*privilege*" or insist upon his "immunity," on being denied, I see not but this minister might be brought up before the U. States Court, and compeled to marry the loving pair notwithstanding this law of Rhode Island.

There are numerous other legislative enactments, emanating from the States, which I might bring before you, but I have already trespassed too much upon your patience.

I have said that the position we assume, could also be maintained by a judicial decision. Allow me to refer you to that case.

It is reported in the 4th of Washington's Reports, page 371. *Corfield* vs. *Coryel*. It is a case in principle exactly similar to the one on trial. Indeed the Connecticut law is almost a copy of the law upon which that case proceeded. You will allow me to be minute in the report of this case. The Legislature of New Jersey passed the following Act. "That it shall not be lawful, for any person, who is not, at the time, an actual inhabitant, and resident in the State of New Jersey, to take or gather clams, oysters, or shells in any of the rivers, bays or waters, in this State, on board of any canoe, flat, scow or other vessel, not wholly owned by some person, inhabitant of, and actually residing in" [New Jersey.] Every such person offending herein, shall forfeit the sum of $10, and shall also forfeit the vessel.

The next section provides for the condemnation and sale of the vessel.

After this law of New Jersey was enacted, *Corfield*, the

Plaintiff, an inhabitant of New-York, sailed his vessel into one of the bays of New Jersey, and was there found, taking oysters. The defendant seized the vessel, and sold it under the act of New Jersey, as forfeited, and the plaintiff brought his action before the Circuit Court, of Pennsylvania, for damages. On the trial of that case, the plaintiff claimed the law to be in violation of the 2d section of the 4th article of the Constitution, in the same manner as will be claimed here. Judge Washington pronounced the opinion of the Court as follows.

"The 2d section of the 4th article declares, that the citizens of each State shall be entitled to all privileges and immunities of citizens in the several States. The enquiry is, what are the privileges and immunities of citizens in the several States? We feel no hesitation in confining these expressions to those privileges and immunities which are in their nature fundamental, and which have at all times, been enjoyed by the citizens of the several States, which compose this Union, from the time of their becoming free, independent, and sovereign. What those fundamental principles are, it perhaps would be more tedious, than difficult, to enumerate. They may however be all comprehended under the following general heads; protection by the government; the enjoyment of life and liberty; with the right to acquire and possess property of every kind; and to pursue and to obtain happiness and safety; *subject, nevertheless, to such restraints as the government may justly prescribe for the general good of the whole.*

"The right of a citizen of one State to pass through, or to reside in any other State for the purpose of trade, agriculture, professional pursuits, or otherwise; to claim the benefit of the writ of habeas corpus; to institute and maintain actions of any kind in the Courts of the State; to take, hold, and dispose of property, real and personal; and an exemption from higher taxes or impositions, than are paid by other citizens of the State: may be maintained as some of the particular privileges and immunities of citizens which are clearly embraced by the general description of privileges deemed to be fundamental. to which may be added, the elective franchise, as regulated and established by the laws or Constitution of the State in which it is to be examined. *But we cannot accede to the proposition, which was insisted on by the counsel, that under this provision of the Constitution the citizens of the several States are permitted to participate in all the rights which belong exclusively to the citizens of any other State, merely on the ground that they are enjoyed by those citizens.* Much less, that in regulating the common property of the citizens of such State, the Legislature is bound to extend to the citizens of all the other States, the same advantages as are secured to their own citizens."

This decision is made by a very learned Judge, and it is entitled to great weight. I think it determines this case. Even if we were to yield one strong point here, that colored persons are not citizens, we then have the authority of this case, that the section will not warrant the construction claimed by the other side.

Judge Washington says, that he cannot accede to the proposition, that under this provision of the Constitution the *citizens* of the several States, are permitted to participate in *all* the rights which belong to the citizens of particular States, merely on the ground that they are enjoyed by those citizens. And so you will say, should it be claimed otherwise. These privileges and immunities may be enjoyed, but this learned Judge adds, "they must nevertheless be subject to such restraints as the government may justly prescribe for the *general good of the whole.*

Now all the restraint imposed in this case, is for the instructor setting up the school. *first to obtain in writing, the consent of the civil authority and select-men of the town.* This surely is for the general good of the whole, and is indeed a provision which in a very few years may be necessary to our political existence.

Sure I am, if the establishment of a school embraces any *good* object. the licencing board provided by the act, will readily give their consent—but if it be for a bad object—a dangerous scheme, then the board ought to deny its licence, and thus check the progress of immorality. This restriction is no more unjust than the restriction imposed upon an ordinary district school. It places both within the power of the visitors in the one case, and the select-men and civil authority in the other. Let it be remembered, that no individual can instruct a district school in Connecticut, according to the law long established, unless he shall obtain a certificate in writing from the board of visitors. Is this law unconstitutional? Let this question be answered.

Should it be pressed upon you, that the defendant in this case must not be convicted, because black men, the sons of Africa, served in the war of the revolution, and many of them are now receiving at the pension office, the bounty of the government, you will allow me to say. this is fallacious indeed, and would never be urged for any other purpose than to mislead and deceive the honest and unsuspecting. It is a mere finesse. True, some of the black men were soldiers —they served with fidelity—but you well remember that there is no State in the Union which does or can subject a black man to military duty. They are, and ever have been exempt. By the law of Congress of 1792, they are exempts, ecause they were not citizens. By all the colony laws, it was the white man alone, who was compelled to perform military duty—who was compelled to defend his country. Those were volunteers in that war, but *that* never made them citizens. The Hessians, the French, as well as the Africans were volunteers in that glorious cause, but who ever before supposed, that services of this sort made them *citizens*. I "*scout the idea*," and send it back to him who gave it utterance.

The *Declaration of Independence* has been quoted to sustain the argument, but go back with me, and see whether that declaration will not disprove the proposition. *When* was that declaration made—by *whom* was it signed—and against *whom* did it speak? It does say that "*all men are created equal.*" But who does not know, that on the 4th of July, 1776, every Colony or State tolerated slavery—they had laws to hold their slaves in bondage. Still more, perhaps every signer of that declaration, was himself a *slave-holder*, and that declaration did not dissolve those bonds, nor break up the fetters of slavery. The *object* of that declaration was a dissolution of their connection with a *foreign government*.—The tyranny of Great-Britain—the misrule of a king, and the oppression of a corrupt ministry, were to be thrown off.—*These* were the evils complained of, and the declaration of Independence applied to *those evils*, and those alone.—Hence you see, that there ever has been in this country, a marked difference between the black and the wite men. There is still that difference, and it is impossible to do it away. Those who claim to be the *exclusive philanthropists* of the day, will tell you this is prejudice. I give it no such name. It is entitled to no such appellation. It is *national pride* and *national honour* which mark this distinction. The white men were oppressed and taxed by the king—they assembled in Convention, and at the peril of their lives declared this *white nation* free and independent. It was a nation of *white men*, who formed and have administered our government, and every American should indulge that *pride* and *honor*, which is falsely called prejudice, and teach it to his children. Nothing else will preserve the *American name*, or the *American character*. Who of you would like to see the glory of this nation stripped away, and given to another race of men? Give up this distinction, and you part with all which makes the name of an American our pride and boast. Injured Africa, it is said, calls for your verdict of acquittal in this case.—Those who make this appeal, seek only to move your passions. This is not the way to heal the wounds which have been inflicted on Africa. This is not the method to redeem Africa. There is a better mode. As patriots you are not called upon to abandon your own country for Africa. Let your brethren of the South return their slaves to their own native land. Nothing is wanting but the means, and if the abolitionists would take half the pains to obtain the means they now do to retard the progress of benevolence, much would be done. Instead of aiding in this mighty work of preservation—of saving our own country, and redeeming Africa, there is a class of men, even in New-England, who would prefer to have the slaves loosed from their chains and brought to Connecticut, in such manner as to overwhelm our own inhabitants. We deserve no such visitation, and shall never submit to it, so long as we are free. Connecticut was the second State in the Union to rid itself of slaves, and now shall she lay down, and quietly behold the flood of emigration which must pour in upon us, when the gates are thrown open? The present is a scheme, cunningly devised, to destroy the rich inheritance left by your fathers. The *professed* object is to *educate* the blacks, but the *real* object is, to make the people yield their assent by degrees. to this universal amalgamation of the two races, and have the African race placed on the footing of perfect equality with the Americans. If this be not so, why are the leaders of this scheme so anxious to withdraw their black scholars from excellent schools in the city of New-York, where they belong, and force them upon Connecticut, in violation of our law, placing them at the same time, at a school inferior in every respect to those in their own city? This small cord is first to be sounded, a larger one will next vibrate. There are now seven valuable schools in the city of New-York, located at convenient places—provided with able teachers—books and apparatus of every kind, and at this moment vacant places for more than three hundred scholars—where they can be educated *free*, if they choose, if *education* be their object. But this does not serve the purpose. There is something else needed beside an education. This, they can have at home.

Those men with their millions, are willing to withdraw pupils from such schools, and send them here, perhaps, because their own particular tenets can be the better inculcated here. This is but an experiment, and should it succeed, then every town in this State will be liable to be visited in the same way. This is not the case of the town of Canterbury alone, against Prudence Crandall, the mere nominal defendant, put forward by others, whose machinations would disturb the tranquility of this whole nation, but it is *the case* of the State of Connecticut, and every town, however remote, and every citizen, however unconcerned, has involved in it, a deep interest. Let the law be pronounced unconstitutional, by this high tribunal, and a corresponding school for males will be immediately established in some other town. This will compel the white children of these towns to be sent abroad for education, and, in the end, it will drive from these towns their valuable inhabitants. In a very few years the evil will be spread over the State. The law in question is made for the preservation of the State. Public policy demands it. The existence of the State requires its faithful execution. Its resistance is only for the purpose of sowing the seeds of disquiet at the South, and let it not be said, that a Jury in Windham county, commenced the work of dissolving the Union. I leave this case in your hands, trusting that you will return a verdict which shall do honor to yourselves and your country.

CHARGE.

"This is an information filed by the Attorney for the State for the alledged violation of a Statute law, passed by the General Assembly, at their last session, relating to inhabitants; the preamble to the act, embracing the reasons for the law. It reads thus:

"Whereas attempts have been made to establish literary institutions in this State, for the instruction of colored persons belonging to other States and countries, which would tend to the great increase of the colored population of the State, and thereby to the injury of the people; Therefore it is enacted that no person shall set up or establish, in this State, any school, academy, or literary institution, for the instruction or educatiou of colored persons who are not inhabitants of this State, nor instruct or teach in any school, academy, or literary institution, or harbor or board, for the purpose of attending or being taught, or instructed in any such school, any colored person not an inhabitant of any town in this State, without the consent, in writing, first obtained of a majority of the civil authority and select men of the town where such sohool is situated, on penalty," &c.

It is alleged in this information, that since the 22d day of August last, to wit, on the 24th day of September 1833, the defendant has wilfully and knowingly, harbored and boarded colored persons not inhabitants of the State, for the purposes mentioned in said act, without having obtained in writing, the consent of the civil authority and select men of the town of Canterbury, where the school had been set up.—As to the facts in this case, there seems to be but little controversy. It has scarcely been denied, that colored persons have been harbored and boarded by the defendant, for the objects alleged, within the time set forth in this information. You, Gentlemen of the Jury, have heard the evidence, and as it is your exclusive business to pass upon these facts, you will say whether or not they are true.

If these facts are not proved to your satisfaction then you may dismiss the case, for in that event, you have no further duty to perform. If however, you find the *facts* true, then another duty equally important, develoves upon the jury. It is an undeniable proposition, that the jury are judges of both law and fact, in all cases of this nature. It is, however, equally true, that the Court is to state *its* opinion to the jury, upon all questions of law, arising in the trial of a criminal cause, and to submit to their consideration, both law and fact, without any direction how to find their verdict.

The counsel for the defendant, have rested her defence upon a provision of the Constitution of the United States, claiming that the statute law of this State, upon which this information is founded, is inconsistent with that provision, and therefore void. This is the great question involved in this case,. and it is about to be submitted to your consideration.

It is admitted that there are no provisions in the Constitution of this State, which conflict with this act.—It may be remarked here, that the Constitution of the United States, is above all other law,—it is emphatically the supreme law of the land, and the judges are so to declare it. From the highest Court to the lowest, even that of a Justice of the Peace, all laws, whether made by Congress or State Legislatures, are subject to examination, and when brought to the test of the Constitution, may be declared utterly void. But in order to do this, the Court should first find the law contrary, and plainly contrary to the Constitution. Although this may be done, and done, to, by the humblest Court, yet it never should be done but upon a full conviction that the law in question is unconsitutional.

Many things said upon this trial, may be laid out of the case. The consideration of Slavery, with all its evils and degrading consequences, may be dismissed, with the consideration that it is a degradiug evil. The benefits, blessings and advantages of instruction and education, may also cease to claim your attention, except you may well consider that education is a 'fundamental privilege,' for this is the basis of all free governments.

Having read this law, the question comes to us with peculiar force, does it clearly violate the Constitution of the United States? The section claimed to have been violated, reads as follows, to wit: Art. 4—sec. 2. 'The citizens of each State, shall be entitled to all privileges and immunities of citizens in the several States.' It has been urged that this section was made to direct, exclusively, the action of the General Government, and therefore can never be applied to State laws. This is not the opinion of the Court. The plain and obvious meaning of this provision, is, to secure to the *citizens* of all the States, the same privileges as are secured to our own, by our own State laws. Should a citizen of Connecticut purchase a farm in Massachusetts, and the Legislature of Massachusetts tax the owner of that farm, four times as much as they would tax a citizen of Massachusetts because the one resided in Connecticut and the other in Massachusetts; or should a law be passed by either of those States, that no citizen of the other, should reside or trade in that other, this would undoubtedly be an unconstitutional law, and should be so declared.

The second section was provided as a substitute for the 4th article of the *Confederation.* That article has also been read, and by comparing them, you can perceive the object intended by the substitute.

The act in question, provides that colored persons, who are not inhabitants of this State, shall not be harbored and boarded for the purposes therein mentioned, within this State, without the consent of the civil authority and select men of the town. We are then brought to the great question, are they *citizens* within the provisions of this section of the Constitution? The law extends to all persons of color not inhabitants of this State, whether they live in the State of New York, or in the West Indias, or in any other foreign couutry.

In deciding this question, I am very happy that my opinion can be revised by the Supreme Court of this State and of United States, should you return a verdict against the defendant.

The persons contemplated in this act are *not citizens* within the obvious meaning of that section of the Constitution of the United States, which I have just read. Let me begin by putting this plain question. Are *slaves* citizens? At the adoption of the Constitution of the United States, every State was a slave State. Massachusetts had begun the work of emancipation within her own borders. And Connecticut, as early as 1784, had also enacted laws making all those free at the age of 25, who might be born within the State, after that time. We all know that slavery is recognized in that Constitution, and it is the duty of this Court to take that Constitution as it is, for we have sworn to support it. Although the term 'slavery' cannot be found written out in the Constitution, yet no one can mistake the object of the 3d section of the 4th article :—'No person held to service or labor in one State, under the laws thereof, escaping into another, shall in consequence of any law or regulation therein, be discharged from such service or labor, but shall be delivered upon claim of the party to whom such service or labor may be due.'

The 2d section of the 1st article, reads as follows :— Representatives and direct taxes, shall be apportioned among the several states which may be included in this Union, according to their respective numbers, which shall be determined by adding to the whole number of free persons, including those bound to service for a term of years, and excluding Indians not taxed, three fifths of *all other persons.*' The 'other persons' are slaves, and they became the basis of representation, by adding them to the white population in that proportion. Then slaves were not considered citizens by the framers o the Constitution.

A *citizen* means a *freeman*. By referring to Dr. Webster, one of the most learned men of this or any other country, we have the following definition of the term—'Citizen: 1st, a native of a city, or an inhabitant who enjoys the freedom and privileges of the city in which he resides. 2. A townsman, a man of trade, not a gentleman. 3. An inhabitant; a dweller in any city, town or country. 5. In the United States, it means a person native or naturalized, who has the privilege of exercising the elective franchise, and of purchasing and holding real estate.'

Are Indians citizens? It is admitted in the argument that they are not, but it is said they belong to distinct tribes. This cannot be true, because all Indians do not belong to a tribe. It may be now added, that by the declared law of New York, Indians are not citizens, and the learned Chancellor Kent, says 'they never can be made citizens.' Indians were literally natives of our soil,—they were born here, and yet they are not citizens.

The Mohegans were once a mighty tribe, powerful and valiant; and who among us ever saw one of them performing military duty, or exercising, with the white men, the privilege of the elective franchise, or holding an office? And what is the reason? I answer, they are not citizens, according to the acceptation of the term in the United States.

Are *free blacks*, citizens? It has been ingeniously said, that vessels may be owned and navigated by free blacks, and the American flag will protect them; but you will remember that the Statute which makes that provision, is an act of Congress, and not the Constitution. Admit, if you please, that Mr. Cuffee, a respectable merchant, has owned vessels, and sailed them under the American flag, yet this does not prove him to be such a citizen as the Constitution contemplates. But that question stands undecided by any legal tribunal within my knowledge. For thepurposes of this case it is not necessary to determine that question.

It has been also urged, that as colored persons may commit treason, they must be considered citizens. Every person born in the United States, as well as every person who may reside here, owes allegiance of some sort, to the government, because the government affords him protection. Treason against this government, consists in levying war against the government of the United States, or aiding its enemy in time of war. Treason may be committed by persons who are not entitled to the elective franchise. For if they reside under the protection of the government, it would be treason to levy war against that government, as much as if he were a citizen.

I think Chancellor Kent, whose authority it gives me pleasure to quote, determines this question by fair implication. Had this authority considered free blacks citizens, he had an ample opportunity to say so. But what he has said, excludes that idea.

Kent's Commentaries, vol. 2d, p. 258. "In most of the United States, there is a distinction in respect to political privileges, between free white persons and free colored persons of African blood; and in no part of the country do the latter, in point of fact, participate equally with the whites, in the exercise of civil and political rights. The African race are essentially a degraded caste, of inferior rank and condition in society. Marriages are forbidden between them and whites in some of the states, and when not absolutely contrary to law, they are revolting, and regarded as an offence against public decorum. By the revised statutes of Illinois, published in 1829, marriages between whites and negroes, or mulattos, are declared void, and the persons so married are liable to be whipped, fined and imprisòned. By an old Statute of Massachusettss, of 1705, such marriages were declared void and are so still. A similar statute provision exists in Virginia and North Carolina. Such connexions in France and Germany, constitute the degraded state of concubinage, which is known in the civil law. But they are not legal marriages, because the parties want that equality of statues or condition, which is essential to the contract."

I go further back still. When the Constitution of the United States was adopted, every state, (Massachusetts excepted) tolerated slavery. And in some of the states, down to a late period, severe laws have been kept in force regarding slaves. With respect to New-York, at that time her laws and penalties were severe indeed, and it was not until July 4th, 1827, that this great state was ranked among the free states.

To my mind, it would be a perversion of terms, and the well known rule of construction, to say, that slaves, free blacks, or Indians, were citizens, within the meaning of that term, as used in the Constitution. God forbid that I should add to the degradation of this race of men, but I am bound by my duty to say, they are not citizens.

I have thus shown you that this law is not contrary to the 2d section of the 4th Art. of the Constitution of the United States, for that embraces only citizens.

But there is still another consideration. If they were citizens, I am not sure this law would then be unconstitutional. The Legislature may regulate schools. I am free to say, that education is a fundamental privilege; but this law does not prohibit schools. It places them under the care of the civil authority and select men, and why is not this a very suitable regulation? I am not sure but the Legislature might make a law like this, extending to the white inhabitants of other states, who are unquestionably citizens, placing all schools for them under suitable boards of examination, for the public good, and I can see no objection to the board created by this act.

What can the Legislature of this State do? It can make any law, which any Legislature can make, unless it shall violate the Constitution of the United States, or the Constitution of its own State, and in my opinion *this* law is not inconsistent with either.

The Jury have nothing to do with the popularity or unpopularity of this or any other law, which may come before them for adjudication. They have nothing to do with its policy or impolicy. Your only enquiry is, whether it is constitutional.

I may say with truth, that there is no disposition in the judicial tribunals of this State, nor among the people, to nullify the laws of the State, but if constitutional, to submit to them, and carry them into full effect, as good citizens. If individuals do not like the laws enacted by one Legislature, their remedy is at the ballot boxes. It often occurs, on subjects of taxation, that laws are supposed by some, to be unjust and oppressive. Nearly every session of the Assembly, attempts have been made to alter and change such laws, but as long as they exist, they must have effect.

You will now take this case into your consideration, and notwithstanding my opinion of the law, you will return your verdict according to law and evidence. I have done my duty, and you will do yours."

The jury returned a verdict against the defendant.

The Joint Committee of the General Assembly made the following report, May Session, 1833, and thereupon the law passed:

REPORT.

To the General Assembly:—The Committee to whom was referred the petition of the town of Canterbury, and others, respectfully report, that they have attended to the subjects submitted to their consideration.

The condition of the colored population throughout the United States, and its influence on society, ought to command the attention of every Legislature. The slave trade commenced centuries ago, and about eighty millions of the human race have been its victims. They have suffered death in various and cruel forms, or have been left to drag out a miserable existence in the most abject slavery. Nations and individuals have been engaged in the horrid traffic, and our own country has participated deeply in its guilt; but the trade is now forbidden by the general government, under the penalty of death, and nations are leagued together for its suppression. However effectual these measures may prove, it will be long before we cease to suffer from the evils entailed upon us by the slave trade.

That every prudent and wise means for their mitigation should be anxiously sought and adopted, is not less enjoined by a regard to the welfare of society, than by the duties of humanity and justice.

It is about half a century since the Legislature of this State commenced a system for gradual abolition of slavery, and the great object has been consummated, still the unhappy class of beings, whose race has been degraded by unjust bondage, are among us, and justly demand at our hands, all which is consistent with the common safety, and their own best interest, for the amelioration of their state and character.

Our obligations as a *State*, acting in its sovereign capacity are limited to the people of our *own territory*. *Our* whole population of color, born within the last century, are already restored to the blessings of freedom. The Constitution and laws of the State have secured to them all the rights and privileges of other citizens, except that of elective franchise, and those to which it is essential. It is not contemplated for the Legislature to judge of the wisdom of that provision of the Constitution which denies that franchise to the people of color; but your Committee are not advised that it ever has been a subject of complaint. In every other point the white and colored population of *this State* are entitled by law to equal privileges. The latter, not less than the former, are within all the provisions which relate to education—they are alike protected in their persons and property, and in the exercise of every occupation and profession. They also enjoy a special exemption from the poll tax and military duty. In regard to the education of all those of that unfortunate class of beings who belong to this State, the Legislature ought not to impede, but so far a may be within their province, and consistent with the best interest of the people, to foster and sustain the benevolent efforts of individuals directed to that end. Here our *duties* terminate. The colored people of *other States* and *other countries*, are under the laws and guardianship of their respective sovereignties, and *we* are not entrusted with the powers of enquiring into the expediency or justice of their local regulations, except to acquire wisdom in regard to *our own*. Here are the boundaries of our Legislative rights and *duties*. We are under no obligation, moral or political, to incur the incalculable evils, of bringing into *our own State*, colored emigrants from abroad. For this we have the example of other members of our confederacy by whom slavery is tolerated. It is a fact confirmed by painful and long experience and one that results from the condition of the colored people, in the midst of a white population, in all States and countries, that they are an appalling source of crime and pauperism. As this, in our own State, proceeds from degradation to which their ancestors have been wrongfully subjected, it imposes on us an imperious duty, to advance their morals and usefulness, and preserve them so far as possible from the evils which they have been obliged to inherit, but at the same time, the duty is not less imperative, to protect *our own citizens*, against that host of colored emigrants, which would rush in from every quarter, when invited to our colleges and schools.

The memorials which have been referred to your Committee are signed by great numbers of respectable citizens who reside in different towns in this State. They have been occasioned by repeated efforts made to establish literary institutions, embracing in their objects, the colored people from *other* States and Countries.

The citizens of those places, where the establishment of those seminaries has been attempted, have manifested toward them a united and very ardent opposition, grounded as your Committee believe, on most reasonable apprehensions of their effects, especially on the places of their injurious location.

Although the introduction of colored persons for the purpose of education merely, would seem to contemplate but a temporary residence, yet that class of people have seldom any settled establishment in their own States, or other inducements to return, after the period of instruction has expired; and as their last associations and attachments would be here;—a great portion of the whole number would make this State their permanent resiednce. The immense evils with such a mass of colored population, as would gather within this State, when it has become their place of resort from *other States* and from other countries would impose on our own people burthens which would admit of no future remedy, and can be avoided only by timely prevention.

The records of criminal courts, prisons and asylums for the poor where great numbers prevail among a white population, admonish us of the dangers to which we are exposed, and evince the necessity, in the present crisis, of effectual legislative interposition.

Particular instances may occur in which the admission of a colored person belonging to any other State, to the privileges of a school, might be justified from peculiar circumstances. The several towns in which schools are located, must be the first and greatest sufferers from too liberal indulgence. It would seem both safe and just to place the subject under the direction of their own *civil authority and select men*. With a view to these objects, your Committee respectfully report the accompaning bill for a public act.

Respectfully submitted, per order of the Committee.

PHILIP PEARL, Jr. Chairman.

REPORT

OF THE

TRIAL

OF

MISS PRUDENCE CRANDALL.

BEFORE THE COUNTY COURT FOR WINDHAM COUNTY,

August Term 1833.

ON AN INFORMATION

CHARGING HER WITH TEACHING COLORED PERSONS NOT INHABITANTS OF THIS STATE.

BROOKLYN:
Unionist Press, C. Webber, Printer.
1833.

TRIAL.

Windham County ss. County Court August term A. D 1833.

State of Connecticut vs. Prudence Crandall. } information on the Statute, &c

Miss Crandall was originally brought before Rufus Adams, Esq. a Justice of the Peace for Windham County, by a warrant issued by him on a complaint by the Grand Juror of the town of Canterbury, charging her with violating a statute law of the State of Connecticut passed at the last session of the Legislature in regard to teaching, boarding, harboring &c. persons of color, not inhabitants of the State. She entered a demurrer to the complaint, the Court judged the complaint sufficient and thereupon ordered Miss Crandall to give bond with surety in the sum of $150. for her appearance before the next County Court to be tried on said complaint, and abide the judgment of said court thereon. Failing to procure bonds, she was committed to prison. The cause came on for trial before the County Court on Friday August 23d: C. F. Cleaveland, Esq. the Attorney for the State, being absent from indisposition, the Court appointed Jonathan A. Welch, Esq. special attorney to conduct the prosecution. A. T. Judson and I. Bulkley, Esqs. were associate counsel. Hon. Calvin Goddard, Hon. W. W. Ellsworth and Henry Strong, Esq. appeared for the defence. The jury being empannelled and sworn, the counsel for the defence objected to one of the jurors from Canterbury on the ground that he had signed petitions &c. in respect to Miss Crandall's School and taken active measures to put it down.—The Court sustained the objection, and the juror was excused. They also objected to another of the jurors on the ground that he was a member of the Legislature which passed the law, was one of those who voted for it, and had, of course, formed an opinion with respect to its constitutionality. The Court decided that the juror was competent to sit. (He got excused, however, on account of sickness.) The information against Miss Crandall consisted of two counts. The first charged "that the said Prudence "Crandall, on the 24th day of June last, with force "and arms, in a certain school which before that time "had been and then was set up in said Canterbury, "for the instruction and teaching of colored persons, "to wit, Theodosia De Grasse, Ann Peterson, Amelia "Elizabeth Wildes, Ann Eliza Hammond and others "whose names are unknown, who at the time so "taught and instructed were not inhabitants of any "town in this state, which said acts were done, by "the said Prudence Crandall, without the consent, in "writing, first had and obtained of a majority of the "civil authority and select men of the said town of "Canterbury, within which said school was then in-"structed, against the peace of this state, and con-"trary to the form and effect of the statute in such "case made and provided."

The second count charged "that the defendant, with "force and arms did wilfully and knowingly harbor "and board, and aid and assist in harboring and "boarding certain colored persons (named above,) "who when so harbored and boarded were not inhab-"itants of any town in this State—without the con-"sent in writing of the civil authority and select men "&c."

Plea, Not Guilty.

The following witnesses were then called on the part of the prosecution.

Ashel Bacon, called at Miss Crandall's last June, accompanied by Capt. Sanger, saw several of the colored scholars, and was informed by Miss C. that they were from New York.

George Cady, went to Miss Crandall's last Friday to summon some of her pupils as witnesses, Miss C. said she saw no need of witnesses, as she should confess having broken the law.

Ann Peterson, This witness was a colored girl, said to be a pupil of Miss Crandall, and was one of those named in the information to whom Miss C. had given instruction. Mr Ellsworth objected to the examination of the witness on the ground that she could not testify without implicating herself. Mr Welch read the clause of the statute under which this prosecution was sustained, in which it was enacted that the pupils in a school kept contrary to the act, might be compelled to testify. Mr Ellsworth said that he denied, altogether, the competency of the Legislature to compel a witness to testify, or answer questions that might implicate him, even to render himself liable in debt—otherwise a witness might be compelled to testify to what would charge him with the crime of murder. He alluded to the State Constitution and Bill of Rights which he claimed protected every person from criminating himself by being compelled to give testimony. It was contrary to fundamental principles. In this case the witness might make herself an aider and abettor, and subject herself to the penalties imposed by the statute. Mr Judson claimed that the witness would not by her testimony implicate herself. The law was penal, and must be construed strictly. Even if she swore that she was instructed by Miss Crandall, it would not charge herself with any crime. Mr Judson read at length from Starkie on evidence to show that the witness ought, on common law principles, to be examined, and was bound to answer quetions as to what she knew of Miss C.'s school. At all events he claimed that, in this instance, such must be the case as the Legislature had expressly enacted that the pupils should be witnesses. Mr. Ellsworth, in reply, said he apprehended the question to be whether the Legislature possessed the power to compel a witness to convict himself. He read from the opinion of Chief Justice Hosmer, in the 8th Con. Rep. and also from the case of the people vs. Mather, in 4th Wendell's Reps. on the subject of examining witnesses. By the principles which decided these cases, which were the settled law of the land, he claimed that the witness was not compelled to answer any questions in relation to her knowledge of this school. The court decided that the witness, under the circumstances, was not protected, but must be examined. The examination was about to proceed when Mr Ellsworth rose and stated to the court that the witness had been advised not to answer interrogatories in regard to her knowledge of this school. He felt it to be his duty now to repeat this advice. He wished the Court, however, distinctly to understand that the counsel for the accused had taken this course not with a view to embarrass the trial, but solely from a sense of duty. He conscientiously believe that the legal rights of the witness were such that she could not be compelled to testify. The counsel for the prosecution, asked the witness when she came to Canterbury, but she declined answering the question. A number of other questions were then proposed to the witness the principal of which were—"Has Miss Crandall kept a school for colored girls not inhabitants of this state?" "Will you say whether the defendant has or has not instructed any person of color other than yourself since the 10th of June last, or boarded and instructed colored persons not inhabitants of this State?" To all these and other questions of similar character, the witness declined giving an answer, on the ground that she could not do so without criminating herself.

The counsel for the prosecution then called Catherine Ann Weldon and Ann Eliza Hammond both girls of color, and charged with being pupils of Miss Crandall, and propounded to them the same questions as above; but they for the same reason,and by the advice of counsel, declined answering. The prosecuting Attorney reserved to himself, though he waived for the present, the right of moving for an order that these witnesses be committed for a contempt of court.

Jacob C. Gould, Knows Ann E. Hammond. She belongs in Providence, R. I. where her mother now lives.

Levi Kneeland, Is pastor of the church to which Miss Crandall belongs. Has seen several of the colored girls at his church during the summer. Has been in Miss C's. school twice—has taken meals at her house—has prayed in the school, and conversed with the pupils on religious subjects. Thinks some of the girls present, were among those he saw at Miss Crandall's and that Miss C. has told him some of them were from New York.

Eliza Glasko, This witness was a colored girl belonging to the school but an inhabitant of this state. The same objection was made to examining her as was before made in respect to the others, but the objection was overruled by the Court, She however declined answering the questions propounded to her. The prosecuting attorney moved the court for a mittimus to commit the witness for contempt of court. The court granted the motion and ordered the clerk to make out a mittimus.

Hezekiah Crandall, (affirmed) Knows A. E. Hammond,and has often seen her at his sister's. Supposes she boards there and is instructed by his sister with others. Has never been in the school.

Mary Benson, (affirmed) Has been at Miss Crandall's school and found it very interesting. Saw Miss Hammond there. She is from Providence—is one of the scholars and boards with Miss C. Recognises several of those present, as among those seen at Miss Crandall's—one of them is from New York. Has heard Miss C. instruct the girls in Geography and Arithmetic.

Several other witnesses were examined, but their testimony was unimportant.

The sheriff having served his process on Eliza Glasko was about committing her to prison, when Mr Ellsworth interposed and stated to the court that rather than have the girl committed he should advise her to testify—again repeating that the course of the defendants counsel in relation to the testimony of these girls, was dictated by an imperious sense of professional duty.

Eliza Glasko then testified. Is a member of Miss Crandall's school, and the girls near her, are also members. The ordinary branches—reading, writing, grammar, &c. are taught by Miss C. The school is usually opened and closed with prayer—the scriptures are read and explained in the school daily—portions are committed to memory by the pupils and considered part of their education.

Mr Judson then opened the case on the part of the prosecution.

He first stated the case and read the Act of the Legislature which he claimed that Miss Crandall had violated. He said that this act did not prevent any black from attending the district schools in the state, or any higher schools—that they had all the benefits of the school fund, and might attend the academies, high schools, or colleges, and that too whether they were citizens of this state, of other states or of any part of the world. The sole intention and provision of the act was, that colored persons, from another jurisdiction, should not be intruded into any town in this state, without a written permission from the select men and civil authority of the town in which they proposed to reside. This was all, and this was perfectly lawful. The whole tenor and effect of the law was to place a school for colored persons under the care and supervision of the select men and civil authority of each town. He should ask the attention of the Court to the fact that the legislature had exercised a controlling power over schools within the limits of the state since 1717. (Mr Judson here read from an old edition of the statutes, in respect to the power which the Legislature had exercised over schools in respect to preventing disorders and the application of the public money.) These said Mr. Judson, were schools for the instruction of all classes and the acts which he had read showed that the Legislature thought proper to exercise care over these schools. Such was the ancient policy of the state, and this new law was no change of policy. The state owed its present honors, its present glories, to pursuing this policy of keeping its schools under a supervising power.—Nor was there anything in the Constitution of the United States to prevent it. Towns, he claimed, had a right to say who should be allowed to become inhabitants by residence in their limits and this law gave them no more power than was necessary for the exercise of that right. That the law was illiberal and reflected disgrace on the state, on the Legislature which enacted it, he denied. On the contrary, said Mr J., there are now more than 15,00 schools in the state, supported by our fund of $1,800,000, to which blacks may go without the payment of a cent. Small as the state was, smaller than single counties in some other states, these facts were true concerning it.—For himself he was proud of it. Where could a parallel be found in the Universe?

Public policy, continued Mr. J., absolutely demands that a law of this description should be maintained. It was claimed to be unconstitutional because exclusive in its operation on a particular class. Other laws of the state were liable to the same objection. Physicians and lawyers were instances of the operation of our exclusive law. Tanners, Taverners, Surveyors, &c. must all be licensed. Manufactories were liable to be visited by the selectmen and civil authority for the purpose of seeing that the children employed in them were properly educated. If persons came here from other states and set up manufacturing establishments they were equally liable to be visited in this way though no such provisions existed in the laws of the states from whence they come.—Lawyers in this state could not purchase choses in action. All these laws, with many similar ones, were passed in derogation of rights originally common to all; public policy however required the enactment of them, as it did of the one in question, and in his opinion they all stood on similar grounds, and were, without question, in accordance with the Constitution.

Mr J. next referred to the course which other states had pursued in legislating on the subject of the blacks. He remarked on the law of

Ohio. Our law is not, said Mr J., an act of exclusion, nor an act of prohibition. It does not pretend to send away those who belong here, nor does it prohibit any from coming, but only makes it necessary that permission be first obtained. The laws of Georgia and North Carolina went so far as to authorise the imprisonment of blacks who came within their limits, even though they came in the capacity of cooks and stewards of vessels. In Tennessee blacks could not come from other states and remain within the state above twelve days without incurring penalties. In Maryland a man could not manumit his slave without his leaving the state. Even in Pennsylvania, "the land of Penn," no free negro could remain without giving bonds for his support. All these laws Mr J. claimed to be obnoxious to equal, and indeed to greater constitutional objections than the one in question. The article in the constitution of the United States with which this law was supposed to conflict, he understood to be the 2d section of the 4th article: "The citizens of each state shall be entitled to all the privileges and immunities of citizens in the several states." Mr J. claimed that the term "citizens" in this place, and throughout the constitution, had a technical signification—a legal meaning—that it did not include colored persons—that they were not by the constitution recognized as citizens. A certain class of colored persons, (slaves) were in it considered as property.

Mr J. here referred to the laws of the United States on the subject of naturalization, reading from Ingersoll's Digest, the several acts of Congress, and insisted that from them all, the language being precise, technical, and certain, none other than white persons could be naturalized citizens of the United States. He also read from the 2d Kent's Com. 78, 71, 72. by which he further illustrated these views.

There have been, continued Mr J., concurrent acts of the State of Connecticut which give the same construction to the constitution. If "citizen" do not mean a white person only —if it be claimed that a black is a citizen, then is the constitution of our own State a nullity, for it allows "free white males" alone to be electors. The privilege of being a freeman, he claimed to be a higher one than the right of being educated. Why should a man be educated who could not be a freeman? A person who pays a single cent State tax, or who does military duty, is entitled to the privilege of voting. In Massachusetts these qualifications were not sufficient. Each state in the Union has these local laws and customs peculiar to itself—these must all be abrogated at a blow, by deciding the law in question to be unconstitutional. Full effect however might be given to the clause in the constitution, referred to without producing this result, and that was, by construing the term "citizen" in the manner he had before pointed out.

The first act in our own statute would be nullified by a decision that this law was unconstitutional—a citizen of another state cannot maintain an action in our courts for any cause unless a substantial inhabitant of the State give bond for him. No one has doubted the constitutionality of this law, and the law in question, with respect to constitutionality, could not be distinguished from it.

Mr J. said he should conclude his remarks on this subject by alluding merely to one other argument in suppost of this law, and that was, that the public safety of this State, the preservation of its true interests, required this law to be enforced. The southern states might emancipate their slaves and send them all to Connecticut instead of Liberia. The influx of that species of population might be so great as to be overwhelming. (Mr. J. proceeded to remark on the effect which recent measures of the British Parliament, on the subject of slavery, might have on this question, when he was interrupted by the court, who remarked that though far from inclined to restrain all the limits of the discussion, yet it did not seem pertinent to the issue to argue the policy or expediency of the laws. Mr J. said he would not press the point.) Mr J. hoped that he had not been misunderstood in the remarks he had made. He wished not to oppress any class of population. He heartily wished that every slave might be emancipated that very day. But if it could not be done without destruction to our constitutions, and desolating our land, he could not desire it.

He would only add to the Jury that though it was true they were at liberty to consider what the court said to them on the subject of the law, as advice, still he hoped they would pay it such respect as advice from the bench was properly entitled to. A single word as to the facts. The information charged the defendant with boarding and instructing, in different counts. It was sufficient if they found her guilty on either. The day was immaterial. If they found her guilty of doing the act charged on any day, since the passage of the law, and before the filling of the information 'twas sufficient. It was not necessary that they should find that she had boarded or instructed each of the persons named in the information; to instruct or board one was a transgression of the law.

As to the proof it was abundant and conclusive.

Mr. Ellsworth then followed for the defence.

Gentlemen of the Jury

The statute law of this state on which this prosecution is founded, prohibits three things; under the extraordinary penalty of $100 for the first transgression, $200 for the second and so on, for each subsequent offence. It prohibits the *setting* up a school for colored persons not inhabitants of this state—*boarding* persons attending such schools—and *teaching* them in any school not licensed by the select men or the incorporated schools excepted in the latter part of the 1st section of the law. The last prohibitory clause is the one on which the prosecutor must rely, for it is certain the school of Miss Crandall has not been set up since the passage of this law. Miss Crandall is accused of teaching certain persons, named in this information, who are it is admitted, citizens of other states, provided people of color can be citizens, in this country. The crime charged, consists in *teaching* and not in the instuction given; indeed, so far as the trial discloses, it appears that nothing but the usual fundamental branches of knowledge are taught. Were it in point, or within the range of this inquiry, we would gladly examine the manner of conducting this school and every thing done in it.

Gentlemen—I will not occupy your time, in relation to the facts in the case; the testimony is fresh in your recollection. I would have advised the pupils of my client, to testify at once, but it was proper, exposed as thoy are to the most vigilant and relentless opposition, that it should be known they will assert their rights, and cannot be compelled to criminate themselves. And it was meet, the public should know, how cheap the personal rights of the pupils of this school are held, in the estimation of certain persons.

True it is, my client has kept this school, but whether this is a *crime*, is for you to determine. In order to convict, you gentlemen must find, on your oaths, that she has committed a *crime*. You may find that she has violated an act of the Legislature of this state; but if you also find that she is protected by a higher power, it will be your duty to acquit. I trust that the Court will inform you that the law is unconstitutional and void; but should they be of a different opinion, after all it belongs to you, taken immediately from the people, to determine whether one of that people has been guilty of a crime. This ultimate right, this high responsibility resting with a jury to pass, in criminal cases, as is the language of the oath administered to you, "between the State of Connecticut and the prisoner at the bar" is peculiar to free governments, and is one of the last rights to be surrendered by a jury. The constitution may be, it has been, violated; Legislators are not without human infirmities; passion, prejudice, error, and even corruption have been known to sway the decisions of the Legislative Hall.—Judges have decided their laws to be no laws, and jurors may do the same. While the people retain this power they are safe; but yield it and they are not safe. The existence of a constitution, proves that laws may be passed, beyond the power of the Legislature. In such a case your duty is plain. Each one of you, must be satisfied, both upon the law and the fact, beyond every *reasonable doubt*, that a *crime* has been committed. I flatter myself, that I shall be able to load you to the conclusion that the law in question is a violation of the constitution of the United States. The constitution of the United States, where it controls, is the highest power in our land: beyond this no Legislature can go; and if you find that this law conflicts with that, you will by your verdict, say so.

There are two positions, that I shall endeavor to establish, which if true, will entitle my client to a verdict.

1st. The persons named in the information as having been taught by Miss Crandall are citizens of one of the states of this Union.

2d. As such, they are protected against this law by the 2d sec. of the 4th art. of the constitution of the United States, which is in these words: "*The citizens of each state shall be entitled to all privileges & immunities of citizens in the several states.*" The assertion on the other side that, people of color are not citizens, is the only apology I offer for feeling it necessary to say one word upon the first branch of the argument.

But first, let us see what is the question to be settled—then, we will settle it.

The true question is this, can the Legislature of Connecticut prohibit the citizens of other states in this Union, from residing here, to pursue those avocations, which are open and lawful to our own citizens; or more exactly, can our Legislature prohibit a citizen of New York or Rhode Island from residing here, to pursue the acquisition of knowledge, open to all the citizens of this state. Can the place of *birth*, merely, be made the criterion of the rights of citizens of these states. This is the precise question; and it reaches deep and wide; deeper and wider than is perhaps imagined. It is not a question of *color*, as it might seem to be, at first thought; but of state supremacy. If a state may exclude a colored citizen of another state, it may exclude a *white* citizen, unless their political rights are different.—There must be some admitted distinction, some qualification of right, growing out of color, or it is quite certain, a prohibition to-day, extending to a colored man, may to-morrow be extended to others. If today we may expel from Canterbury, people of color, tomorrow we may expel from New Haven, every youth who was not born in the state. Will any one contend that such an exclusive and sovereign power rests in the state Legislatures of these United States? This doctrine is akin to nullification itself. No such barrier can be erected against the citizens of this Union. An absurdity so manifest, must strike every mind. Nothing but a state of high excitement could ever have caused the enactment of such a law as the present. The good citizens of Canterbury, I doubt not will perceive that their course is precipitate and indefensible; and in my opinion, as bad in policy as in law.

Let us then, gentlemen, proceed to the 1st inquiry, "Are the persons named in the information, *citizens.*" The criterion of citizenship in the view of my friend from Canterbury is complexion; in mine, it is *birth* and *naturalization*. Admitting that under the Constitution and laws of the United States, none but free white persons born abroad, can be naturalized, and thus made citizens, not of any state, but only of the United States; this does not touch the question of citizenship by birth. This is not a subject belonging to the general government; and even legislation upon it in relation to aliens, by the alien & sedition law, of Congress, made a revolution of parties in the government.—Is it so that a person born on our own soil is not a citizen of our soil? In the days which tried men's souls, did not men of color stand side by side with our fathers and shed their blood for this country, which was THEIR country? The country to which they owed indefeasible allegiance? Are not their names inscribed on the pension rolls of the government? and are they not now receiving the honorable testimonies of the services they rendered? Can they not be guilty of treason? Where does the gentleman get the doctrine, that the rights of man depend on his complexion, and above all, where does he learn to make a distinction, among *free born citizens*, on such gronnd? A colored man can appeal to the laws for the protection of his rights in every free state in the Union—as a citizen, technically and exactly he can sue and be sued in the courts of the United States; in those cases too where citizenship is the sole ground of jurisdiction,—but can all this be true, and yet the man be no citizen? I am so much of a republican, that I love to refer, now and then to that immortal instrument which our republican fathers put forth, as the ground work of all true government, viz. the Declaration of Independence. There, gentlemen, we read, "we hold these truths to be self-evident, that all men are created *equal*, that they are endowed by their creator with certain *unalienable* rights; that among these are life, liberty, and the *pursuit of happiness*;" but the gentleman would read, "people of color excepted." So too we read in the declaration of rights, at the head of the constitution of this state (and the like we find in the constitution of each of the free states,) "all men when they form the social compact are equal in rights; and that no man or set of men are entitled to exclusive public emoluments or privileges from the community," "colored people excepted" the gentleman would add. Gentlemen, I had hoped better things of the republicanism of my friend from Canterbury. I am not ashamed of these great land marks of free government, as they *are;* and will not give my consent to have them interpolated as is done to day. I hope I shall not live long enough to see such qualifications of the rights of man go forth, under the judicial sanction of any court in this state. Such sentiments may comport with slave owners & slave drivers; but they are abhorrent to the feelings of freemen and republicans, and they cannot receive countenance in this community.—The free colored population has, and is justly entitled to equal representation in the Congress of the United States with the white population. Indians "not taxed" alone are unrepresented, and even slaves are represented in the proportion of three fifths. I have here before me, the constitution of each of these states; and so far as I have looked, in every free state, excepting Connecticut, color is no disqualification in voting, and how this strange anomaly ever found its way into our constitution, is, to me matter of astonishment. But it cannot effect the question now under consideration; and besides, free colored persons can vote in New York and Rhode Island, from whence these particular pupils came.

The gentleman has gravely read from 2d Kent's Commentaries, pages 70, 71, 72, to show that, that learned commentator sustains the doctrine of citizenship now advanced—but I appeal to you, to the gentleman himself, if the book contains *one* sentence of the kind; the very parts read disprove it. Chancellor Kent speaks only of the persons who may be *naturalized* and says expressly that all who are *born* here are citizens, except Indians living in tribes; he classes all persons, as *aliens* or *natives*, as does Blackstone, Swift and every other elementary writer or expounder of international law.

The gentleman next contended that only white persons can be electors, by our constitution, and therefore, they only are citizens. But what then becomes of all white females and minors under age? are they denationalised because the constitution does not allow them to vote?—Is the wife of my friend an alien? And what is the condition of all those white males, who were born here, but have not the necessary qualifications of electors, such as property, paying taxes &c? Right or qualification to vote is no criterion of citizenship; either by birth or naturalization. There are distinctions established for another purpose, and are altogether arbitrary; differing from time to time in the same state; and always, in different states. But it must be remembered that in New York and Rhode Island, where these pupils belong, male citizens without distinction of color, are electors, and it must further be remembered, that we are not now contending about the right to vote; which is not allowed to our own blacks, but to seek knowledge which is allowed to them. The law of naturalization and the inability for the blacks to vote, in Connecticut, are the only arguments urged against us; if these prove that persons *born* on our soil are aliens, I give up the point.

Now gentlemen, before we go to the second position of my argument, having as I trust established the first, I wish to dispose of some considerations, confidently urged on the other side, as saving this law from the condemning sentence of the constitution. And first, it is said, the law excepts, in a subsequent section, from its operation, all colleges, incorporated schools and district schools, and here says the prosecutor, is opportunity enough; what more can blacks ask for—our noble school fund is all open to them. But, if the state has power to *limit* a citizen of another state, to such schools as are enumerated, has it not power to make the limit much narrower? If it may confine to several schools may it not to one? and finally to one of a particular religious denomination? If *birth* in another state, can be made the sole ground of limitation, why may not that limitation be carried to an extreme, even to total exclusion? The power is of the same nature and not more supreme. The exceptions then amount to nothing; absolutely nothing As to district schools, these pupils being foreign citizens, cannot be enumerated nor strictly can they be entitled to the benefit of the school fund; but if they could *enter* these schools, and if these schools should be kept all the year, as they are not; what would it avail persons of their age from 10 to 20? Of every age and in every district school, they are to the other pupils, but hewers of wood and drawers of water; literally in many instances the objects of taunt, contempt and ridicule. In the town of Hartford, so sensible of the utter inutility of the common school to black children, have the people become, that that the people of color have obtained from the Legislature power to form a district school of their own, and they draw the public money by themselves. And into what college or high school can these persons find access? Let the gentleman tell me where, *where* in this state the doors are not barred against pupils of color. The law declares it is *dangerous* to have them in this state, and why then talk of the liberality extended to them in the exceptions of certain schools? The law means nothing else, it was designed for nothing else, but to drive this school from Canterbury: its professions are one thing and its objects another.

If people of color are to be educated, it is necessary that they should have schools of their own; public sentiment, at present demands it; they cannot enter our schools without being made the cause of excitement—unless therefore their minds are to be sealed up in darkness, they must be permitted, according to their circumstances to form schools of their own.

Again, gentlemen; it is said, that this law permits private schools, if the consent of the selectmen is first obtained.—Now does not the gentleman see, that a power to license is a power to refuse; and that a delegation of this power to the selectmen does not alter it, in view of the constitution. The argument then comes to this, that the Legislature or their agents have the power to limit, suspend, or flatly refuse, and yet the right thus affected is not narrowed or destroyed by the Legislature. Every right we hold, under such circumstances, we hold at the pleasure of of the Legislature. It is then no right, but a favor. *And when think you, will this favor be extended to Miss Crandall's school?*

But it is again urged, that the Legislature has the power of regulating schools and that it has ever exercised this power, it regulates trades, taverners, professional men, pedlers &c. &c. Now, gentlemen, I do not deny that the Legislature, may for the good of the people, supervise, schools, trades and professions. Our public schools are regulated by law, because they are supported by public money, and although private schools never have been controled by the Legislature as is now attempted to be done, I do not say they may not be, if the law be general; but the true difficulty is, you make one law for the citizens of Connecticut and a different one for citizens of New York—you make citizenship or the place of birth the test of right. All the people of Connecticut both white and black may institute private schools, or such instruction as they please, but if they come here from New York, they shall have no such right. Let us follow out this principle—while every citizen of Connecticut may pursue his trade, profession, or business, with or without a license, you say, if he *comes in from another state*, he shall be placed on a different ground; shall obtain a license where none is required of our own citizens, or if any, then a different and more onerous one; thus making the place of birth or legal inhabitancy, the criterion of right, when this is the very thing the constitution prohibits.

It has been further said, that such laws as this have been passed in several of the states, and that our law authorising selectmen to remove out of the state, those who have no settlement in it, is just like it. I am aware that the preamble of this offensive law, classes it with our laws respecting settlements; and while this profession is as discreditable and insincere as the provisions of the law are oppressive and illegal, it does not relieve the difficulty in the least. We are to test the constitutionality of this law, by the constitution and not by the laws of our own statute book or that of any other state. Our law, authorising the removal of certain persons, was passed when we were a separate and not a federal State, and had of course a right to say no person, not born in Connecticut, should live in it; and this law has been continued since, without any examination whether it might not conflict, in some cases with the 2d sec. of the 4th art. of the Constitution of the United States. The state may undoubtedly guard itself against pauperism; but that it can, under such a pretence, raise a barrier on its limits, so that no one who is not born in it, can enter it, I deny. As well it may be said that the people of South Carolina could constitutionally remove the army of the United States who were sent to Charleston last winter, to compel obedience to the law.—The constitution secures to the citizens of our state a residence in another. And as for the laws of other states what have we to do with them, on this occasion? Most of the states referred to by the gentleman, are slave states, where the owners of slaves are the law makers; but even in Georgia, where a law was passed forbidding any free negro from entering the state, a decision was had in the federal court that the law was unconstitutional and no law. The gentleman is in an error when he says such a law exists in Pennsylvania, the state of Penn. And although such a law has lately passed in Ohio, yet I am not aware it has ever received judicial sanction, and I trust it never will. The truth is there is nothing in the settled and practiced law of any free state in the Union, to countenance the provisions of our law. Enough however may be found in the statutes of the slave states. The gentleman will pardon me for reading some of the authorities on which he relies, but did not *read*; in doing which he showed his judgement. The Legislature of Louisiana have enacted "that whosoever shall make use of language, in any public discourse, from the bar, the bench, the pulpit, the stage or in any other place whatsoever, shall make use of language, in any private discourses, or shall make use of signs or actions having a tendency to produce discontent among the colored population, shall suffer imprisonment at hard labor, not less than three years, nor more than twenty-one years or *death* at the *discretion* of the Court." It has also prohibited the instruction of blacks in sabbath schools, $500 for the first offence, *death* for the second. *Our law*, gentlemen, imposes a penalty of $100 for teaching a black, not born in this state, in a *sabbath* school and $200 for the second offence. In Virginia all meetings of free negroes, at any school house or *meeting* house for teaching them writing or reading, are declared an unlawful assembly. Georgia and North Carolina have made it criminal, subject to fine or imprisonment for free persons of color to enter their ports as cooks, stewards or seamen—these, gentlemen, are a specimen of the disgusting, and unrighteous authority, to which the gentleman from Canterbury refers, to sanction this law. I regret, most deeply, that either he or the good people of Canterbury, and above all that the Legislature of Connecticut should give any countenance to such laws and such notions. The truth is, the passage of the law in question, in Connecticut, so distinguished for her republican feeling and her attachment to universal education, has been a matter of astonishment, and unfeigned sorrow throughout this country; and it has not escaped the notice and regret of the people in England. And what makes it still worse, is, that there was not the least necessity for such a law. It was an unlucky hour when it was devised and passed;—passed inconsiderately I doubt not—time will never efface the stigma, though I do trust, if the law is not virtually repealed by a refusal on the part of jurors to sustain it, it will be repealed by the people, in the next Legislature. The law *cannot* remain, though the school of Miss Crandall will remain. It has been made permanent, through the indiscretion, violence and persecution of those who made the law. Friends have been raised up on every side and sympathy will secure it patronage, from those, who would otherwise never have heard of it.

The moral sentiment of this community will not sanction the idea that a man of color shall not direct, according to his ability, the education of his child. Mr. Wilberforce, aided by several benevolent individuals established a seminary for colored people at Clapham, a few leagues from London. Miss Crandall need not be ashamed to imitate his example. The people of this country forced the ancestors of these pupils from Africa; they have since kept their descendants in bonds, and darkness, and now talk of right and prejudice founded on slavery and the degradation of the negro, as a justification for our continued wrong, and the deprivations, this day, attempted to be maintained on principle and morality. Gentlemen, need I tell you, we owe a debt to the colored population of this country, which we can never pay—no, *never*, NEVER, unless we can call back oceans of tears, and all the groans and agonies of the middle passage, and the thousands and millions of human beings, whom we have sent and are now sending, ignorant, debased and undone, to eternity. Let this law perish. Be *you* the executioners. It's object is to extinguish the light of knowledge; to fasten chains and ignorance upon those, whom the God of all has made equal with ourselves; whose future destiny is as high; whose hopes are as dear as ours. For Heavens sake, let us not, by legislative enactments and the solemn forms of judicial sanction, add to the prejudice which already exists against the descendants of the negro. Let us not verify the declaration of Montesquieu, "that we must not allow negroes to be *men*, lest we ourselves should be suspected of not being *christians*.

Gentlemen, we come now to the very question in hand, to wit, "can our Legislature prohibit the citizens of other states from residing here to pursue the acquisition of knowledge, as all our citizens may do?

In the early period of these colonies, it was seen, that so intimate were their relations, and so intermingled their interests and connexions, that the disabilities of alienage, among the inhabitants of the several colonies, could not be endured; we find therefore in the 4th art. of the Articles of Confederation this language, "The better to secure and perpetuate mutual friendship and intercourse among the people of the different states in this Union, the free inhabitants of each of these states, paupers, vagabonds and fugitives from justice excepted, shall be entitled to all privileges and immunities of free citizens in the several states; and the people of each state shall have free ingress and egress to and from any other state, and shall enjoy all the privileges of trade &c."

In the Constitution of the United States, the provision is general, "that citizens of each state shall be entitled to all privileges and immunities of citizens of the several states."

Every one must see, the necessity of such a provision—even the Courts of the different states are placed upon the footing of domestic Courts, and their judgments are equally conclusive, throughout the Union. The constitution itself would lose its excellence and be ineffectual in preserving a united Nation, if its parts were *alien* to each other. The wall of partition is broken down—the place of birth is unimportant—one measure of justice and one system of laws, is not to be given to one citizen, and another, to another. All other things bring equal, *mere place of birth* shall make no difference.

The first thing that strikes us in the provisions of the article of Confederation and the Constitution, is that citizens may remove into and *reside in* each state;—but what does this mean, and what does it amount to, if when a foreign citizen is here, he cannot engage, as others do, if he must ask permission of the select men—or live and act under limitations extending to him alone. Why, if the immunities and privileges of all are the same, then a law founded on such a distinction is in the very teeth of the constitution. May not a citizen of Connecticut remove to Ohio and there live and act as other citizens do?—Could the Ohio Legislature say to him, "you are an alien, we will prescribe the size of your farm, the manner of its cultivation, and the way of teaching your children." Can we raise a barrier against the people of Massachusetts, because they are people of Massachusetts, and may they not come in and settle among us and pursue husbandry, merchandize, manufactures, the arts or acquisition of knowledge without getting license from the selectmen? The law must be general and alike for all, or else there is an end of equal privileges and immunities.

Will it be asserted that education is not one of the fundamental rights, included in the broad words "privileges" and "immunities?" The Pope of Rome and the Despots of Turkey may say this, but an enlighted jury of Connecticut will not say it. What right so valued by us? What so much applauded by us? It is the peculiar honor of our state? Education, is the first and fundamental pillar on which our free institutions rest,—*the last privilege we will give up*. For ourselves, the books we may read and the teachers we may resort to is not so important; for our mature judgments may secure us against error, but for our children, who will not insist on the right of parents to select their books, their teachers and their schools. The restrictions of this law are exceedingly onerous and distressing to the parents of these people; shut out as they are virtually from the schools of white children, they have retired to a place by themselves, in deference to the prevailing prejudice against them—here, they have sought out a virtuous and competent teacher, to instruct their children—in the common branches of education, spelling, reading, arithmetic, geography and the like—these parents are able to do this, many of them are wealthy—they feel that by education, their daughters will be happier and better and fitted for higher usefulness, among their depressed fellows, either here or in Liberia. And who, *who* will rise up to oppose this effort? Let our opponents act openly—let them pass a law to immure in like ignorance the blacks of our own state, and not attempt the same thing, by selecting the blacks of other states, under the miserable pretence, that educating them here will fill our state with a vicious and pauper population.

Gentlemen, we believe that we are not without high authority, if we needed any, to support our views. In the 4th Wash. Ci. Ct. page 380, Corfield *vs* Corgell, we have the following remarks of the Circuit Ct. although the case was finally decided on another ground. "The next question is whether this act (a law of New Jersey) infringes that section of the Constitution which declares that the citizens of each state shall be entitled to all the privileges and immunities of citizens in the several states?" "The enquiry is, what are the privileges and immunities of citizens in the several states. We feel no hesitation in confining these expressions to those privileges and immunities which are in their nature fundamental, which belong of right to the citizens of all free governments; and which have at all times been enjoyed by the citizens of the seveal states which compose this Union, from the time of their becoming free, independent and sovereign. What these fundamental principles are, it would perhaps be more tedious than difficult to enumerate." "The right of a citizen of one state to pass through, or *to reside* in any other state, for purposes of trade, agriculture, professional pursuits or otherwise are among the rights secured." "These and many others which might be mentioned are, strictly speaking, privileges and immunities, and the enjoyment of them by the citizen of each state, in every other state, was manifestly calculated (to use the expressions of the preamble of the corresponding provision in the articles of confederation) 'the better to secure and perpetuate mutual friendship and intercourse among the people of the different states of the Union." 3d Story's Com. chap 81, page 674. sec. 1800. "The provision in the constitution is plain and simple in its language and its object is not easily to be misunderstood.—Connected with the exclusive power of naturalization in the National Government, it puts at rest many of the difficulties which affected the construction of the articles of confederation. It is obvious that if the citizens of each state were to be deemed aliens to each other, they could not take or hold real estate, or other privileges, except as other aliens. The intention of this clause was, to confer on them if one may so say, a general citizenship, and communicate all the privileges and immunities which the citizens of the same state would be entitled to under the like circumstances."

By the resolution of Congress providing for the admission of Missouri into the Union, it was declared to be a condition, that a particular clause in her constitution should not be construed to authorize the passage of any law, and that no law should be passed in conformity thereto, by which any citizen of either of the states in the Union, should be excluded from the enjoyment of any of the privileges and immunities to which such citizen was entitled under the constitution of the United States. The clause in the constitution of Missouri referred to, directed the Legislature to pass laws to prevent free negroes and mulattoes from coming to and settling in the State." This resolution of Congress looks as if in their view, free blacks were citizens and entitled to the privileges and immunities of citizens.

It cannot be claimed that the Connecticut law is not against the constitution, because it only forbids teaching blacks from abroad, but says nothing to criminate such blacks themselves; because if the constitution secures to these pupils the right of instruction. it secures to them the proper means of obtaining it; and how can they be taught without a teacher? To say no one may teach them, is to say, they shall not be taught. Besides, if soliciting and receiving instruction is aiding and abetting the act of giving instruction, then this very law makes them equally criminal with Miss Crandall and the prohibitions and penalties of the law reach the pupils as much as any others.

The general policy of this law as well as its connection with the subject of slavery, that greatest curse and blight upon our country, tho' matters of deep and everlasting interest to us, to our children, to our free institutions, cannot, I am sorry to say, properly be discussed here: the law is not denied for its impolicy, but for its *unconstitutionality*. Had I been a member of the Legislature who enacted the law, with my present views, I should have raised my voice against it. It is a most wanton and uncalled for attack upon our black population,—it opens wounds not easily healed, it exasperates to madness many who live among us; it strengthens the unreasonable prejudice already pervading the community against blacks, and in short, it rivets the chains of bondage and makes our own state an ally in the unholy cause of slavery itself. Deep, deep, are the fears and feelings at this moment pervading the slave states. The moral example of England, in her late act of Emancipation—the practical effects of the emancipation of her slaves in the West Indies, the injustice and high offence against heaven, of slavery itself, are spreading a gloom over the south, more awful and foreboding than nullification ten times told. Slavery is a volcano, whose fires cannot be quenched, and whose ravages cannot be controlled. We already feel its convulsions—and if we sit idly gazing upon its flames, as they rise higher and higher, our happy republic, will be buried in ruin, beneath its overwhelming energies.

I thank you gentlemen, for the attention you have given me; my thoughts are not equal to the merits of my cause and quite unsatisfactory to myself. I trust you will see your way clear before you convict my client of a crime, for teaching children of color, what is daily taught to your children —for endeavoring to elevate and enlighten an unfortunate portion of our race. Are you, gentlemen, prepared to say, *that teaching the word of God is a crime*? The Court, I trust, will pronounce the law unconstitutional and void; but if they should not, my appeal is to the PEOPLE, who you are, and WITH THE PEOPLE I LEAVE MY CLIENT AND MY CAUSE.

MR STRONG said that after the very full, and eloquent, and conclusive argument of his brother Ellsworth, it would be more grateful to his feelings to leave the case in the hands of the jury without adding a word. He feared that he should rather diminish than add to the force of that argument. He however found an apology for occupying a short time, in the magnitude of the case under consideration. It involves the liberties of the people.

Those who advocate the cause of the defendant, said Mr S., are charged with endeavoring to nullify the laws. What is nullification? An attempt by the Legislature of a state, to destroy a power higher than itself.—South Carolina had done this to the fullest extent—our own state had made some progress, but the right of trial by jury was still left us.—A culprit is here arraigned—a female—by the courtsey of the court she had not been called upon to hold up her hand, and plead to the information against her, but she nevertheless stood there as a criminal. She was charged with giving instruction, but there was no pretence that she inculcated bad principles. He had heard of a land where this might be criminal, but it was a land where despots reigned. Her crime consisted in this, that she had given light to those who were in mental darkness—had taught those who were ignorant, to read the bible. It was true that the persons to whom she had given instruction were descendants of that unfortunate race, who were even in a state of slavery in this country. He said this not to their reproach, but to our own. He rejoiced that public sentiment had changed on the subject—but one feeling now exists and that was not peculiar to our own country. The Legislature of Great Britain was engaged in passing a law of a very different character from the one now in question, at the very time our Legislature passed this. Even in a country where a king and nobles constituted one branch of the legislature, a law had been passed, almost simultaneously with our own, strikingly dissimilar in its provisions. We complained that this class of persons were low, degraded, and addicted to crime. Has God made them so, or have they been made so by ignorance? 'Twas a little boon to give them liberty, and keep them in ignorance. Better rivet the chains of slavery, than break those and rivet again the chains of ignorance. But one sentiment now pervaded the people of this country, with respect to educating these people—there was a difference as to the way. Some were for colonizing them, others had different views, but all agreed they ought to be instructed in some way. If they were carried out of the country in ignorance, was it not carrying them away that they might destroy themselves.

Unless education accompanied them all was in vain. What, asked Mr S., has been the course pursued by the defendant? He rejoiced that her pupils had been before the jury, and that they had had opportunities of seeing them.—Were they not worthy of being instructed? Had not the defendant entirely deferred to public sentiment, in relation to keeping the races separate? What more feasible course for educating these people could be pointed out, than the one she had adopted? The colored race could not educate themselves—unless some person would step forward and overcome these prejudices, whether rightful or not, he should not decide, they must ever live in ignorance.

Mr Strong, next proceeded to remark on the law.

He read the preamble and said it put him in mind of the painter, who affixed a label to his pictures, lest the spectators might not otherwise be able to determine what animal he intended to delineate. The question, continued Mr S., is often asked, "would you be willing to have a school of this description in your own neighborhood?" What if we should not, could we put it down by passing an unconstitutional law? What if I did not wish my neighbor to keep a large number of dogs, could I of course compel him to put them away? This law does not prevent colored persons from coming to this State. They may come and be idle, and welcome—they may come for any earthly purpose except education. That, they are told they must get in the district schools. In these schools, the colored class sit on the lowest bench. They cannot go to these schools—as soon as their minds become a little expanded, they must retire from them. He wished to have an instance pointed out where any black had continued to attend, for any length of time, and derived benefit. It was impossible that such should be the case as things now were. What they desired was a school by themselves, where & only where, they could acquire an education. They asked of us bread, but we gave them a stone—they asked a fish, but we gave them a scorpion—there was the sting of reproach in it. We place our foot on the black, and hold him down in the dust, and then complain that he does not grow to the perfect stature of a man. There was but one Academy in the State where they could be admitted at all, and this was by the munificence of a private individual—he alluded to the late Mr Bacon of Colchester.—He should have supposed by the argument of the gentleman who opened the case for the prosecution, that the new act would open the doors of every academy and college in the State. The proviso in the law amounted to nothing—it might as well have provided that nothing in that act should be construed to prevent colored persons from holding all the Bank stock in the State. The act exposed one to penalties who should instruct a colored person, from another state, in a sabbath school. It compelled us to obtain a license to seek out the poor, the ignorant, the destitute, and the benighted.

It is claimed, said Mr S., that the legislature have the power to regulate schools—be it so. He asked however to be pointed to an instance where the regulation depended on the character of the scholar. This law excluded those whom it pronounced bad. He would say, let all be instructed, particularly the bad that they might be made better. He spoke however with confidence, when he said, that no law had ever existed, in this State, to regulate private schools. (Mr S. then read from some of the ancient statutes, regulating schools, appointing inspectors, &c.) The legislature, continued Mr S., regulated these schools because they had established them, and they undoubtedly might do so. Was this power claimed in order to prevent bad principles from being taught? He did not perceive that the defendant had offended in this respect. There was nothing bad in teaching arithmetic, geography, grammar, and the bible. If this however was the object of the law, whom did it protect? Our own citizens? No—we might teach them every thing naughty that we chose, but were restrained from doing so to those who came from abroad. This, said Mr S., is really the most *diffusive* kind of benevolence I ever heard of. Most of our criminal laws, continued Mr S., give the court some discretionary power in imposing punishment, in this law the penalty is fixed, if the law itself be not fixed—if it be not pierced by the spear which emanate from the constitution. All public officers are sworn to support the constitution of the United States, and if any law interferes with that, it must be disregarded—otherwise they would incur the guilt of perjury. Whether any of the jury had taken this oath, he knew not, nor was it material to his argument. The Constitution of the United States was the supreme law, and must be so regarded by all citizens, whether public officers or not. He meant to speak with all respect of the opinion of the Court, and though in civil matters the jury were bound to take the law as given from the Bench, it was otherwise in criminal questions. Here the Court advise, and the jury decide.

He intended no disrespect to the legislature which enacted this law, by the animadversions which he made concerning it. It was notorious that public feeling frequently exercised a strong influence in regard to the passage of laws. As an instance of this, he would refer to a law passed a few years since in this State, called the Steam-boat law. In this law, we cut off many of our privileges for the sake of retaliating on the State of New-York. The law was passed by acclamation. Gov. Wolcott sent a sensible well written message to the legislature, suggesting its impolicy and unconstitutionality, but it was no more regarded than if he had sent a page of the spelling book—it did not change a vote. The Dartmouth College case was another instance of the passage of a State law in time of high excitement. Again and again had our sacred constitution been called to exert its conservative principle.

Mr. S. said that it was with some surprise that he had listened to the statement of the opening Counsel for the prosecution, as to the law of Pennsylvania, relating to the residence of blacks in their limits. What the gentleman asserted to be the law of that State, which he had so properly styled "the land of Penn," was a bill reported to the legislature, but never passed into a law. Other bills had been framed and prepared to pass, in other legislatures, which Mr. S. apprehended would form a miscellaneous collection. It would greatly gratify his curiosity, could he get a sight of some of them. It was no reflection on the character of our State, that under excitement, it had passed an unconstitutional law—other States had done the same. Mr. S. here referred to the second section of the 4th Article of the constitution, on which he said he relied to prove the unconstitutionality of the law. He also read from the articles of confederation, which he claimed to contain a similar provision. By the adoption of the constitution, we were, said Mr. S. made one people. 'Twas necessary—'twas the principle of the proclamation of Gen. Jackson, so deservedly popular throughout this section of the Country. If this principle was impugned, it destroyed that which alone made our government worth anything. (Mr. S. also read from Judge Story what had before been quoted by Mr. Ellsworth.) A citizen of the United States was entitled to one no less proud—I am an American citizen. We were not to say that we were citizens of Connecticut, but that we were American citizens. A portion of our countrymen might wish to raise the Palmetto banner, but the eagle and the stripes were our badge.—The attorney for the prosecution would improve upon the Nullification of South Carolina. That State had only to pass an act excluding the standing army of the United States from her territory, and the principles of the old General's proclamation were all nullified, or Mr S. was greatly mistaken. Were blacks citizens? The term "citizen" was to have a technical sense. He had listened with pleasure to this remark from the gentleman who opened the case, for when a word has a technical signification, it was always easy to get its precise meaning. All the technics however which seemed to attach to this word were that a citizen must not be colored. If colored persons were not citizens, Mr. S. claimed that they were not inhabitants, which conclusion was manifestly absurd. Color had no connection with the question of citizenship by birth, though it had in respect to naturalization. In deference to southern views, the Militia laws of the nation, passed in 1792, did not include colored persons—the words were, "every free white male citizen"—was not this an express recognition that persons other than whites were citizens? If "citizens" meant a white person only, why was this language used? (Mr. S. here read from Ingersoll's digest 745, relative to the protections granted to American seamen, which, he said were always given to blacks as well as whites.) The war of 1812 was caused, in no small degree, by the impressment of our seamen who had the protections in their pockets. Our government considered the impressment of blacks who had these protections, as standing on the same ground with the impressment of the whites, and the war was declared and fought as much on their account as on account of the whites. The law in relation to American shipping required that in order to be entitled to discriminating duties at the custom house, it must be owned in whole or in part, by American Citizens. Colored persons frequently owned ships which were uniformly regarded as the property of American citizens.

Mr S. named Paul Cuffee as an instance.

The courts of the United States were open to citizens and also to aliens—aliens, however, must describe themselves as such, in order to maintain an action. The uniform practice was for blacks to sue as citizens, never as aliens. Mr S. here read from Kent's Com. and claimed from the doctrine there advanced that a black might go from one State to another, and enjoy in that other, the same privileges that a person of the same class enjoyed who belonged to that other state, I do not claim, said Mr S., that a citizen of an other State coming into this State, brings all privileges with him which he before enjoyed—he brings with him however the character of a citizen of the United States, and that entitles him to enjoy here, the same privileges with our citizens under circumstances similar to his own.

Gen. Jackson, said Mr S., in his proclamation at New Orleans, addressed the blacks as "fellow citizens." Did he mean to insult them? No, he meant to recognize them as citizen and the law so recognized them. They could purchase and hold real estate, could gain a settlement, and could, in fact, do what citizen could, and what aliens could not do. It would be an insult to talk of naturalizing a man born here. The constitution of our State had been alluded to, in order to prove that blacks were not citizens, because it did not allow them to vote. Voting was no test of citizenship. If it was then by the showing of the gentleman, blacks were citizens, for in New York they were allowed to vote, and were therefore, according to the gentleman, citizens of the United States in New York; of course they were citizens here.

Mr Strong here replied to the arguments which had been drawn from the course of legation pursued by other States in respect to the blacks—the law of Ohio, &c. He read the law of Louisiana, which affixed a penalty of $500 for the first offence of instructing a black in the Sabbath Schools, death for the second. The jury, he said, were not to regard the laws of other States as necessarily giving the true construction to the Constitution.—These laws, if unconstitutional, did not support our law, and it was their province to decide their constitutionality. He also referred to a late opinion of Judge Baldwin, given in the Circuit Court of the United States, and also to the opinion of Judge Washington before referred to, with respect to rights of citizens of the U. States in the several states.

Our ancient law, said Mr S., which allowed persons to be carried out of the State, who were not citizens, was restrained from operating on apprentices, because they came for the acquisition of knowledge. While minors were prevented from contracting for any thing but necessaries, they were allowed in express terms, to contract for the purpose of education.—Was education, he asked, a fundamental right? Ferdinand of Spain, he presumed did not believe that it was, neither did that king who was now chased through Portugal—and why? because education was the basis of liberty. Should such however be the doctrine of this free land? If our law had said that blacks in this State should not be educated at all, though inhuman and unchristian, it would not be liable to the same objections that it now is. The case seemed to him as plain as any he had ever submitted to a jury. The conclusion followed on the heel of the premises. If a school was opened to blacks who belonged to this state, it was certain it must be open to those who came from other states, under the same circumstances, for by the Constitution of the United States, they were entitled to a community of rights.

As it regarded the license, which, under this law, might be obtained of the select men and civil authority, 'twas nothing at all,—it would not be given, but, if it would, we were not bound to ask it.—As well might we be told that we should not eat without their permission. That would merely starve the body—this starved the mind—it kept on husks that which conferred on man his immortality.

It was claimed that we had other laws of a similar character. 'Twas no matter—it made this law no better—doing wrong once was no apology for doing it again, much less did it create a right to do it. Make the law equal as to its application and he would find no fault.

He took the case of Eliza Glasko.—She was an inhabitant of the state, and Ann Eliza Hammond was not. What difference could the legislature make in relation to these persons as to the right to attend what school they chose? As to the law requiring citizens of other states to give bonds before they could maintain an action in our Courts, it operated equally—citizens of our state, if they resided out, were subject to the law—it depended simply on residence. The law providing against the settlement of paupers would not sustain this law. That required bonds for the support of those likely to become chargeable. Bonds were not sought here, except the bonds which tie the mind, and fetter the man—not bonds of security, but bonds of vassalage. It cannot, said Mr S. be sustained. The people would not endure the alien law of '98—'twas abhorrent to the principles of our government, and drove from power the man that made it. This law has features even more odious than that. The people will not and ought not to endure it. By santioning this law, he said the jury would sanction a principle which would prevent them or their sons from emigrating to the western states.

He trusted he need spend no more time—he believed they would do their duty. He should ask the court to charge them that the law was obnoxious to the charges he has made against it, but should the court do otherwise, his appeal was to them. It was their prerogative to pass upon this law which owed its creation to an excited state of feeling. To them he looked for a verdict which would maintain civil liberty.

Mr Welch regretted the duty that had devolved upon him, his state of health,* and his recent connexion with the case, would, he said, perhaps prevent him from doing to the case even that justice which might have been in his power to do under other circumstances. Besides the eloquence and ingenuity of the defendant's counsel might have diverted the mind of the jury from the real issue. He should discharge his duty without personal feeling. If he had before harbored any, he should strive to banish it from his mind now. He wished the right of the state of Connecticut to be fairly, impartially, and dispassionately examined. The government asked no conviction but upon principles which could be consistently reconciled with justice and the constitution. The government asked no conviction but upon principles which could be consistently reconciled with justice and the constitution. The fact that the defendant was a female had been alluded to, but this altered not her rights. She had the same and none other rights, than every citizen. He hoped the jury would not be misled by the impassioned flashes of eloquence which they had heard from her counsel. He would have them pause and examine. The rights of the judge and the beggar were the same at the bar of justice. Rights there, were common, but artificial rights in society were different. The rights of citizens had been pressed upon their attention—the rights of states must not be forgotten.

Was the law Constitutional? Possibly it was not. Laws had been passed which undoubtedly were unconstitutional, and if this was, he asked no conviction under it. They had but one course to pursue. If the law was contrary to the constitution they were bound to acquit—no one, if such was the character of the law, would acquiesce in the decision more cheerfully than himself. The gentlemen opposed to him had said, very emphatically, that they appealed to the people if the court decided the law to be constitutional. The jury, he said, were the people. It was no doubt true that in criminal cases the jury could decide in spite of the court, but, was it enviable? Would they desire to do it? Rights were at stake, the rights of the state as well as the rights of the party.—He would have the jury look at the result of their verdict as it respected the effects it would have on these right. They might take the law into their own hands and acquit the defendant. They sacrificed the rights of the state beyond remedy by doing so—their verdict against the state was final. If, however, they found a verdict against the defendant, it had no such effect on her. The case could be carried to another tribunal where she could have perfect justice, and where her rights would not be at all prejudiced by a conviction here. 'Twas no hardship to her, and a contrary conrse might do an irremediable wrong to the state.

They had been told that they had, that day, to decide a great question---an exciting one. It was true. Why then had they been called so loudly to take the case from the court? If they decided the law to be unconstitutional 'twould be no evidence except between the same parties as a matter of fact. Another jury might decide the law to be constitutional, and thus what was a crime at one time would be no crime at another, though tried under the same law. He had no idea that they had any motive but to discharge impartially their duties as jurors.

Mr W. said, that as the defendant, by her plea, had put all the facts necessary to her conviction in issue, he should now examine the proof. The counsel for the defence had seemed tacitly to admit the facts charged to be true, but as he did not mean to desert any part of the case which the gentlemen opposed to him had not distinctly admitted to be in favor of the prosecution, he should recapitulate the evidence, and see if a case had been made out. (Mr W. here examined the testimony, commented upon it at length, and claimed that it was perfectly conclusive.)

The gentlemen who had argued for the defence, said Mr W., never meant to make the constitutionality of this law a point in the case. They thought they had thrown a barrier around their client by closing the mouths of witnesses. It was the object of the gentlemen to go out of court in triumph for want of proof to convict, but the grating doors of a certain building, though it did not unstop deaf ears, did open dumb mouths. The witnesses then spoke, notwithstanding the gentleman had hoped to apply to them the gag law. Their efforts had proved ineffectual—their flag was furled, and when he saw the quivering step of a retreating army he believed they anticipated defeat

Mr W. rejoiced that a spirit was going abroad to improve the colored race. 'Twas one thing however to produce a reformation by proper and legal means and another by improper and illegal ones. He would refrain no longer from considering the constitutional question in the case. The law was called unconstitutional because it was said to prohibit free persons of color from coming into this state, from other states, to be educated. Mr W. said that he knew no better way of testing the constitutionality of a law, than a comparison of the law with the provisions of the constitution. Whenever they came in collision, it was easy to decide which must stand.—By this test then, by a comparison of the letter of the law with the letter of the constitution, he perceived no discrepancy. (Mr W. here read the second section of the fourth article of the constitution and then read the law.) Now, continued Mr W. this law does not prohibit any one from coming here for any purpose, if permission be obtained. If it is on the prohibition that gentlemen claim the law to be unconstitutional. But if permission be granted in all cases when asked, as possibly it may be, where is the unconstitutionality of the law? The gentlemen claim that it is prohibitory and therefore unconstitutional—it may never be prohibitory; how then is it unconstitutial? In order, gentlemen, said Mr W., to determine that this law is unconstitutional, you must look through the vista of coming time, and with a keen prophetic vision, foresee that the civil authority will never grant their license. You must settle a question of fact which you cannot settle. If you can find this fact, put it in your verdict—render this libel on your understandings along with it—such a principle as this ought not to be contended for—the tears of contrition should blot it out, and the blush of shame should light a fire to consume it.

In respect to the meaning of the term "citizen" in the constitution, Mr. W. claimed that the ground taken by Mr Judson, in opening the case, was tenable —that the term was used in a technical sense. He denied that it meant all persons who lived and moved within certain limits, as he understood the gentleman to claim. (Mr. W. here read from the articles of confederation, to support his construction of the term "citizen.") He said that his brother Strong had read this quotation on a long trot, as though he feared the jury would understand it, and perceive the falacy of his argument. Mr W. claimed that there was a distinction between the term "people" or "inhabitants," in the article of confederation, and the term "citizens" in the constitution He also read from Dr. Webster's dictionary the definition of "citizen," and insisted that blacks do not come within it.—

Mr W. also read and commented on the subject of naturalization, and claimed that Congress had never treated blacks as capable of becoming citizens. It was not the policy of the government. The Missouri question had been alluded to, but the whole of it was one continued act of political juggling—he should not think of appealing to it as authority for any thing.

Mr. W. said that he derived a strong argument in construction which he gave the constitution from the usages and legislation of other states. He then went on to remark at length upon the statutes of many of the states, in relation to the black population. If blacks were citizens he said the legislatures of many of the states must be called worse than Turkish tyrants —He dwelt with much emphasis and ability on the laws of Massachusetts and Rhode Island, prohibiting the intermarriage of whites and blacks. These laws said Mr W., could only be reconciled with the constitution on the ground that blacks were not citizens. The right of education had been called a fundamental right. He was not disposed to contest the truth of this position. The right of selecting the partner of one's joys and sorrows was however a right no less dear, no less sacred, than the right of selecting those whom we will have to educate our children. If our law was unconstitutional it was clear that all these laws to which he had alluded were also unconstitutional. He did not believe they were—the fact that they had been acquiesced in so long was evidence conclusive to his mind that they were not.

The case had been so fully gone into by his associate who opened the case, that he would not detain the jury longer. He put the rights of the state into their hands, and also the rights of the defendant, under direction of the court as to the law. They were not to inquire whether their verdict would advance the power of one party or another—whether it would feed or allay the excitement which existed. They shoutd forget all that did not legitimately belong to the case—even the eloquence of the gentlemen who had argued for the defence should be forgotten, so far as it was not relevant. Duties were theirs—consequences devolved elsewhere.

His Honor Judge Eaton then charged the Jury in substance as follows.

GENTLEMEN OF THE JURY.

Prudence Crandall is charged in the information before you, with a violation of a certain statute law of this state, forbidding the setting up of a school for the instruction of colored persons, not inhabitants of this state, boarding or harboring them for the purpose of instruction. Provided the acts charged are proved to be done, the day is not material, if since the passage of the law, and before the filing of the information. Neither are the names nor the number of the persons instructed material. The facts must be proved to your satisfaction, gentlemen, and whether they are so or not you are the sole judges—it is not the duty of the court even to advise in relation to the measure of proof.

As to the law of the case, this also belongs to you decide, but the Court has a duty to perform in regard to it. That duty is, to advise you as to its validity and constitutionality. It has been claimed at the Bar that the law is unconstitutional, and that the state legislature had no power to pass it. It is gratifying to the court, gentlemen, that its opinion is not final—that it can be revised by a higher tribunal, and corrected if erroneous. The opinion of the Court is, that the law is constitutional and obligatory on the people of this state. You will take the case into consideration, gentlemen, and render a verdict of guilty or not guilty, as to you shall seem just and proper.

The JURY then retired, and after an absence of several hours, returned into Court not having agreed on a verdict. They were again ordered out, and again returned not having agreed. The third time they stated to the court that there was no probability that they should ever agree.—The court then discharged them. This operates as a continuance of the case to the next term of the County Court to be holden on the second Tuesday of December next.

The testimony in the foregoing report has been somewhat abridged from the original report but every thing essential to the issue is preserved. It was thought of less importance to give all the particulars of the evidence than to present the arguments of counsel, because the whole question of conviction or acquittal turned upon the constitutionality or unconstitutionality of the law, a point on which the testimony could of course have no bearing. The arguments of Messrs. Judson, Strong and Welch are but imperfect sketches taken by the reporter—as perfect, it is true, and as faithful a statement of the positions taken and the arguments advanced, as could be expected—but still from the necessity of the case imperfect. The argument of Mr. Ellsworth is given as written out by himself.

A BRIEF HISTORY

OF MISS CRANDALL'S SCHOOL.

It is thought to be well to give, in connection with the report of Miss Crandall's trial, a brief account of the establishment of her school, for colored females as well as of some of the various events which have transpired in consequence of its establishment and continuance. Though most of the facts which will be here related, have been published in several of the periodicals of the day, yet as they have scattered through pages of miscellaneous reading, and have appeared at different dates, it seems proper briefly to state them again in a connected form.

Miss Crandall's employment has been for several years, imparting instruction to the youth of her own sex, and in this business she had been engaged in the village of Canterbury for about fifteen months before she announced her intention of opening her school for colored females. As an instructress she has sustained a high reputation, and has received very favorable testimoniols of her qualifications, from those who have patronized her.

Her reasons for "changing the complexion of her school," (as has been expressed,) she has herself given to the public, through the columns of the Windham County Advertiser. About a year ago, a respectable, pious colored girl, a resident in Canterbury and a member of the Congregationol church, wishing to qualify herself to become a teacher among those of her own complexion, requested admission into Miss C's school. Miss C. at first hesitated, but at length on a repetition of the request, urged with more earnestness than before, she admitted the colored girl.—The excitement which ensued was such as seemed to leave her no alternative but the loss of her school, or the dismission of the new pupil. After much anxiety and deliberation on the subject, she came to the conclusion that it was not her duty to do the latter, and formed the design of devoting herself to the instruction of colored females exclusively. Having for some time wished to visit the schools of New-York or some other of our cities, and also to buy school apparatus for the benefit of her scholars, she united with these—as another and principal object of her journey—the purpose of consulting Mr. Garrison, the well known friend of the colored people, respecting the propriety of opening such a school as she contemplated, and the prospect of success should she open one, and with these intentions visited Boston. She subsequently went to New-York and New Haven to consult with the friends of the colored people in those cities, and the encouragement she received was such that on her return she dismissed her white school, and made arrangements to receive colored pupils.

The annunciation of her intention immediately aroused the people of the village, and four of the principal inhabitants waited on her the next day as a committee to disuade her from her design. The attempt was unsuccessful, as was also a second attempt made on the first of March by the same persons under the sanction of a larger body of the town's people.

After the second failure a town meeting was called to consider the subject. The citizens assembled on the 9th of March, when resolutions were offered strongly disapproving Miss Crandall's design, and naming the Select men and civil authority of the town, a committee to wait on her and endeavor to induce her to relinquish the project. Several persons addressed the meeting with much warmth in favor of the resolutions, but the only man who attempted to oppose them was frequently interrupted by calls to order. A written request from Miss Crandall that the Rev. Mr. May of Brooklyn and Mr. Buffum might be permitted to speak in her behalf was refused, and language unnecessarily harsh and indignant was used in reference to it. The resolutions passed unanimously, and the meeting was dissolved. Messrs. May and Buffum then attempted to address such of the people as were willing to stay and hear them, but were directed to leave the house, which they accordingly did, the whole proceedings of this meeting were characterized by an apparent disposition to carry matters with a strong hand and without giving the people an opportunity to hear what could be said in Miss Crandall's defence, a fact which considering the strong excitement that prevails, was more to be regretted than wondered at. Mr. May had come to the meeting with instructions from Miss C. to propose some terms of compromise with a view to changing the obnoxious locality of the school, but he not being able to obtain a hearing, his proposition of course could not be made. Mr. White of Canterbury however did recommend the purchase of Miss Crandall's house, and offered to bear his proportion of the expense. The proposal was not acceded to by any other person. A few days after the meeting, the committee attended to the duty assigned to them, but met with no better success than the former committee.

This attempt having failed, petitions to the legislature, praying for a law against the establishment of such schools as that of Miss Crandall, were drawn up and circulated through Canterbury and several other towns. A considerable number of signatures having been obtained, the petitions were sent to the legislature, who granted the prayer to the petitioners by passing an act, prohibiting the instruction of colored persons from other states, in any schools except the common free schools and incorporated academies, with the consent of the town in which such school should be situated. In the mean time Miss Crandall's school commenced, according to her advertisement, on the first day of April, and has continued to the present time. The passage of the law, (which took place nearly two months after,) was celebrated in Canterbury by ringing the bell and the firing of cannon.

Miss C. soon found that the step she had taken, had not only cut her off from all neighborly intercourse* with the villages, but had exposed her to insults and injuries, which if not approved and countenanced by the more respectable inhabitants, were at least suffered to pass with an impunity that would hardly have attended them, had any other person been the injured party. While walking with her pupils for exercise, she has repeatedly been surrounded by a collection of young men and boys, drumming firing guns, blowing horns and ringing bells. Insulting labels have been placed on her front yard fence, her gate and doors have been besmeared with filthy substances and in one instance a stone was thrown through her window in the night time.

Her examination before Esquire Adams, mentioned in the preceding "Report," was on the 27th of June between 2 and 3 weeks after the rising of the legislature which passed the law. It resulted in her commitment to prison for want of bail, but she remained in confinement only one day before Mr. George Benson of Brooklyn gave the requisite bond for her appearance at the next session of the County Court and she was released. Since that time the bitterness of opposition has continued unaltered, and has appeared in the various annoyances to which it has subjected Miss Crandall. She has been in effect prohibited from attending meeting with her scholars at the meeting house, a few rods distant from her door,—the only place of public worship within less than three miles of her residence. Manure from the barn yard has been thrown into her well, rendering the water unfit for use, and the neighbors steadfastly refuse to give her water from their wells, thus compelling her to have water for the use in her family, brought from a very inconvenient distance.

On Friday of last week, [Sept. 20th,] while Miss C. and her pupils were assembled in the school room for the purpose of holding a religious meeting, (Rev. Mr. Potter of Pawtucket, R. I. having accepted her invitation to preach to them,) near the close of the services a clamorous rabble, without, assailed the house a volley of rotten eggs and other missiles were thrown at the window, breaking the glass and lodging part of the filth on the curtain. The pupils, regardless of the assault, commenced singing the hymn which had just been read and went through without interruption.

On Thursday last [Sept. 26th] Miss Crandall was again brought before Esquire Adams for examination on two separate complaints, one for instructing and the other for boarding and harboring colored persons from abroad. She was bound over to the Superior Court which holds its next session in Brooklyn on Thursday the first day of October next.

*Not long after the commencement of the school, it is believed most- - of the residents in and near the village combined together with the resolution that they would sell Miss Crandall nothing which she might wish to buy.

A

STATEMENT OF FACTS,

RESPECTING THE

SCHOOL FOR COLORED FEMALES,

IN CANTERBURY, CT.

TOGETHER WITH

A REPORT OF THE LATE TRIAL

OF

Miss Prudence Crandall.

BROOKLYN, CT: 1833.

[Advertiser Press.]

PUBLISHER'S NOTICE.

In the history of the far famed "Canterbury Affair," the publisher has aimed at nothing so much as *truth* and *impartiality*. It was deemed advisable that the principal *facts* of this transaction,—subjected as they have been, to distortion and misrepresentation—should be collected together, and in a connected view, presented to the public. The reputation of Miss Crandall—the motives of the citizens of Canterbury—the honor of the State of Connecticut—and the great principles of justice itself, have all become involved in this singular "affair."

Convinced that the public is the best and only judge in the case, bona fide materials are now laid before it, from whence to draw just inferences, and make up a correct judgement.

The drawing of the Village of Canterbury, and the engraving attached to this work, are remarkably accurate, and highly creditable to the young artists who prepared them.

Brooklyn, Sept. 1833.

SOUTH VIEW OF THE VILLAGE OF CANTERBURY.

A.——MissCrandall's School.

STATEMENT OF FACTS.

After having gained a very respectable reputation, as a female Teacher, by her labors in Plainfield, Ct., Miss Prudence Crandall went to Canterbury, an adjoining town, about the 1st of November, 1831, and made known her desire to many of the leading individuals of the place, to open a "Boarding School" in their Village, for the instruction of Young Ladies. Her proposal was very favorably received by every individual who could be expected to take any interest in such an Institution as was proposed, and every assistance was readily extended to her, in carrying her project into immediate effect. The School was opened some time in the month of November, 1831. The people of Canterbury continued to befriend Miss Crandall, in every possible manner,—patronizing her school by sending their own children, and procuring scholars from abroad, by favorable recommendations, &c.

An advertisement of Miss C.'s "Boarding School," appeared in the several papers, accompanied by a flattering notice of recommendation over the signatures of the following gentlemen, who constituted a Board of Visitors:—Rev. Dennis Platt, Rufus Adams, Wm. Kinne, Andrew T. Judson, Andrew Harris, Daniel Packer, Daniel Frost, Jr. Samuel L. Hough. The school continued to prosper, and to sustain a reputation of the first order, both on account of the connection of its pupils with families of great respectability in Canterbury and elsewhere, and on account of its management, so long as Miss C. continued to fulfil her engagements as an Instructress of white Young Ladies. Some time during the month of September 1832, (according to Miss Crandall's own statement of the case,) a respectable colored girl called on her, and expressed a wish to be admitted into her Boarding School. This girl did not, at that time, receive a definite answer, whether she could or could not be received. Upon a second and more earnest application, and after considerable reflection, Miss Crandall yielded to her solicitations, and the colored girl, in the words of the Instructress, "entered as one of my pupils." Miss C. further states, (in her letter, which has been given to the public,) that the girl had not long been under her instruction, when some complaint arose on the part of her original patrons, accompanied by an expression of the belief, that she [the colored girl] must be removed or the Boarding School would be greatly injured. Miss C., however, retained the objectionable scholar, notwithstanding this advice; and after having perused several publications, professing to be devoted to the elevation of the colored population in this country, her feelings, as she says, "began to awaken." By her statement, it appears that she had for some time, contemplated a journey to New York or Boston, for the purpose of visiting schools, and procuring apparatus* for the benefit of her own school, then in operation in Canterbury; "while at the same time, [in her own language,] the most prominent object of my visit was, to see Wm. Lloyd Garrison,—to obtain his opinion respecting the propriety of establishing a school for colored females, and the prospect of success, should I attempt it."

[COMMENT. Was or was not the course of Miss Crandall, justifiable, in making a journey to Boston, to consult Mr Garrison, who was an entire stranger to her, when at the same time, the object of her visit, was kept from those kind and able advisers with whom she was surrounded in Canterbury,—and whom she had often eulogised for their warmth of friendship, and the interest they had manifested in her welfare? The public must judge.]

Soon after her visit to Boston, Miss C. went to New York, and found those who were friendly to the contemplated school for colored females, from whom she received great encouragement, with the advice to abandon the school to which she was then under engagements, and open one exclusively for colored pupils, who were chiefly to be obtained from New York, Philadelphia, Boston and Providence. She then returned to Canterbury, under an engagement to receive twenty or more colored girls, and soon after, not far from the 20th of February, 1833, went about executing her new designs, by dismissing her white scholars. This was the first knowledge of the change, which was given to the parents of her scholars, or to those who had aided her in the establishment of her original school. The house in which the school had been kept, was then fitted up, newly furnished, &c. and put in readiness for the reception of the colored girls.

An advertisement soon appeared in the papers, announcing to the public, that on the first day of April 1833, her school would be opened for "Young Ladies and little Misses of color." At the close of this notice, reference was directed to be made to Arthur Tappan, Rev. Peter Williams, Rev. Theodore Raymond, Theodore Wright, Rev. Samuel C. Cornish, Rev. George Bourne, Rev. Mr. Heyborn, James Forten, Joseph Cassey, Rev. S. J. May, Wm. Lloyd Garrison, Ar-

* In Miss Crandall's Letter, recently published, she makes the procuring of apparatus for her white School, one of the objects of her visit to Boston, and in the same letter, states that the only reason why she did not make the intended purchase, was the want of money. Does not the necessity of funds, naturally occur to one, before starting on a journey to make a purchase? The public must judge.

nold Buffum, George Benson.* This advertisement has doubtless met the eye of the reader, as its publication is yet continued.

On the day after the white scholars were dismissed, a Committee, composed of Rufus Adams, Daniel Frost, Jr. A. Harris, R. Fenner, (all of whom, were among her most efficient friends in establishing her former school,) visited her for the purpose of "persuading her, if possible, to give up her project, so far as Canterbury was concerned."—The propriety of the conduct of this committee, and the manner in which they presented to the lady, the objections which existed, to the course she was pursuing, has been spoken of in every instance, as highly creditable. It did not however, produce any visible effect, and consequently the same gentlemen were delegated from a larger body of the citizens of the town, to wait on Miss Crandall, on the 1st day of the following month. At this interview, every argumentative effort was made to convince her of the impropriety and injustice of her proposed measure. Daniel Frost, Jr., was appointed by the committee, to address Miss C., which was done, says one of the gentlemen, in a kind and affecting manner. In the course of his remarks, he alluded to the danger of the levelling principles, and intermarriage between the whites and blacks; when Miss C. made him the following reply,—"Moses had a black wife." This is not stated for the purpose of bringing censure upon the lady, but because her reply to the Com. seems to have been made in justification of the course she had adopted. The public must decide whether the amalgamation of the whites and blacks is a profitable or safe doctrine. The lady is not here charged with teaching that doctrine. The above reply was made by her to the committee, and every reader must decide its meaning, for himself.

Thus far, Miss Crandall had made no offers of compromise, to those who had been appointed from time to time, to reason with her. She had made no allowances for the feelings and wishes [prejudices if you choose] of her former friends and patrons. She had gone on with a firmness of design, and a decision of action, worthy the holiest cause.

On the 9th of March, a Town Meeting was held,† for the purpose of taking this subject into consideration, townwise, when the follow-

* All Abolitionists, and with a few exceptions, residents of other States.

† It is allowed on all sides, that the proceedings of this meeting, were marked with unusual spirit and unanimity. The object which had called together the people of the town, was of a peculiar nature. *All* those proceedings, however, are not justifiable. There was *one* step taken, which cannot be accounted for in any other way than by charging it to the exciting circumstances of the occasion. The step here referred to, is that of refusing to listen, after the town meeting had been dissolved, to those whom Miss Crandall had engaged to speak for her. True, her Agents had no right to interfere with, or disturb that meeting, because they were not citizens of Canterbury, and had nothing to do with its concerns. But after the meeting had been broken up, a proper sense of justice would seem to secure for them the privilege of speaking to the people, if they were disposed to hear. Those who had charge of the meetinghouse, it will be remembered, directed the gentlemen to retire, that the house might be closed.

ing Resolutions were submitted, and after proper consideration, unanimously adopted:—

"Whereas it hath been publicly announced, that a school is to be opened in this town, on the 1st Monday of April next, using the language of the advertisement, 'for young ladies and little misses of color,' or in other words, for the people of color, the obvious tendency of which would be, to collect within the town of Canterbury, large numbers of persons from other States, whose characters and habits might be various, and unknown to us, thereby rendering insecure, the persons, property and reputations of our citizens. Under such circumstances, our silence might be construed into an approbation of the project—

"*Thereupon Resolved*,—That the localities of a school, for the people of color, at any place within the limits of this town, for the admission of persons from foreign jurisdictions, meets with our unqualified disapprobation, and it is to be understood, that the inhabitants of Canterbury protest against it, in the most earnest manner.

Resolved,—That a Committee be now appointed, to be composed of the Civil Authority and Selectmen, who shall make known to the person contemplating the establishment of said school, the sentiments and objections entertained by this meeting, in reference to said school—pointing out to her, the injurious effects, and incalculable evils, resulting from such an establishment within this town, and persuade her to abandon the project."

On the 14th, the above resolutions were communicated to Miss C., by the Civil Authority and Select Men, in a formal and becoming manner. She was urged to consider the impropriety of persisting in her new plan, against "all their wishes." That she might not be the loser, in consequence of the original purchase of her house, which was made for her former school, responsible individuals offered and urged upon her, the sum she had paid for the house, upon condition that she would abandon the proposed school. This she declined. Nothing could overcome her determination to go on.

The people soon became satisfied that any further attempts, by the employment of Committees, &c., would prove unavailing. The only source to which they could now look for protection, against what they considered an evil of the greatest magnitude, was to the civil arm,—to the Legislature of the State, composed of the Representatives of the People. Petitions were accordingly sent up from the citizens of Canterbury, as well as from many other towns in the State, praying the General Assembly (soon to be convened) to enact some law by which the introduction of foreign blacks, might be regulated in a proper degree, by the feelings and wishes of the inhabitants of the towns. This petition came up for consideration, in its turn. The subject was referred to a Committee, who made the following

REPORT.

To the General Assembly:—The Committee to whom was referred the petition of the town of Canterbury, and others, respectfully report, that they have attended to the subjects submitted to their consideration.

The condition of the colored population throughout the United

States, and its influence on society, ought to command the attention of every Legislature. The slave trade commenced centuries ago, and about eighty millions of the human race have been its victims. They have suffered death in various and cruel forms, or have been left to drag out a miserable existence in the most abject slavery. Nations and individuals have been engaged in the horrid traffic, and our own country has participated deeply in its guilt; but the trade is now forbidden, by our federal government, under the penalty of death, and nations are leagued together for its suppression. However effectual these measures may prove, it will be long before we cease to suffer from the evils entailed upon us by the slave trade.

That every prudent and wise means for their mitigation should be anxiously sought and adopted, is not less enjoined by a regard to the welfare of society, than by the duties of humanity and justice.

It is about half a century since the Legislature of this State commenced a system for gradual abolition of slavery, and the great object has been consummated, still the unhappy class of beings, whose race has been degraded by unjust bondage, are among us, and justly demand at our hands all which is consistent with the common safety, and their own best interest, for the amelioration of their state and character.

Our obligations as a *State*, acting in its sovereign capacity, are limited to the people of our *own territory*. *Our* whole population of color, born within the last century, are already restored to the blessings of freedom. The constitution and laws of the State have secured to them all the rights and privileges of other citizens, except that of the elective franchise, and those to which it is essential. It is not contemplated for the Legislature to judge of the wisdom of that provision of the constitution which denies that franchise to the people of color; but your committee are not advised that it ever has been a subject of complaint. In every other point the white and colored population of *this State* are entitled by law to equal privileges. The latter, not less than the former, are within all the provisions which relate to education—they are alike protected in their persons and property, and in the exercise of every occupation and profession. They also enjoy a special exemption from the poll tax and military duty. In regard to the education of all those of that unfortunate class of beings who belong to this State, the Legislature ought not to impede, but so far as may be within their province, and consistent with the best interest of the people, to foster and sustain the benevolent efforts of individuals directed to that end. Here our *duties* terminate. The colored people of *other States*, and *other countries*, are under the laws and guardianship of their respective sovereignties, and *we* are not entrusted with the powers of enquiring into the expediency or justice of their local regulations, except to acquire wisdom in regard to *our own*. Here are the boundaries of our Legislative rights and *duties*. We are under no obligation, moral or political, to incur the incalculable evils, of bringing into *our own State*, colored emigrants from abroad. For this we have the example of other members of our confederacy by whom slavery is tolerated. It is a fact confirmed by painful and long experience, and one that results from the condition of the colored people, in the midst of a white population, in all States and countries, that they are an appalling source of crime and pauperism. As this, in our own State, proceeds from the degradation to which their ancestors have been wrongfully subjected, it imposes on us an imperious duty, to advance their morals and usefulness, and preserve them so far as possible from the evils which they have been obliged to inherit, but at the same time the duty is not less imperative, to protect *our own citizens*, against that host of colored emigrants, which would rush in from every quarter, when invited to our colleges and schools.

The memorials which have been referred to your Committee are signed by great numbers of respectable citizens who reside in different towns in this state. They have been occasioned by repeated efforts made to establish literary institutions, embracing in their objects, the colored people from *other* States and Countries.

The citizens of those places, where the establishment of those seminaries has been attempted, have manifested toward them a united and very ardent opposition, grounded as your committee believe, on most rersonable apprehensions of their effects, especially on the places of their injurious location.

Although the introduction of colored persons for the purpose of education merely, would seem to contemplate but a temporary residence, yet that class of people have seldom any settled establishments in their own States, or other inducements to return, after the period of instruction has expired; and as their last association and attachments would be here;— a great portion of the whole number would make this State their permanent residence. The immense evils which such a mass of colored population, as would gather within this State, when it has become their place of resort from *other States* and from other countries, would impose on our own people burthens which would admit of no future remedy, and can be avoided only by timely prevention.

The records of criminal courts, prison and assylums for the poor where great numbers prevail among a white population, admonish us of the dangers to which we are exposed, and evince the necessity, in the present crisis, of effectual legislative interposition.

Particular instances may occur in which the admission of a colored person belonging to any other State, to the privileges of a school, might be justified from peculiar circumstances. The several towns in which schools are located, must be the first and greatest sufferers from too liberal indulgence. It would seem both safe and just to place the subject under the direction of their own *civil authority and select men.* With a view to these objects, your committee respectfully report the accompanying bill for a public act.

Respectfully submitted per order of the Committee.

PHILIP PEARL, Jr. Chairman.

[As many erroneous opinions are yet in existence, in relation to the real character and provisions of the Law, on this subject, it will be well perhaps to lay it before the reader, that it may speak for itself. It follows:]

An act in addition to an Act entitled "An Act for the admission and settlement of Inhabitants of Towns."

WHEREAS, attempts have been made to establish literary institutions in this State for the instruction of colored persous belonging to other states and countries, which would tend to the great increase of the colored population of the State, and thereby to the injury of the people: Therefore,

Sec. 1. Be it enacted by the Senate and House of Representatives, in General Assembly convened, That no person shall set up or establish in this State, any school, academy, or literary institution, for the instruction or education of colored persons who are not inhabitants of this State, nor instruct or teach in any school, academy, or literary institution whatsoever in this State, or harbor or board, for the purpose of attending or being taught or instructed in any such school, academy or literary institution, any colored person who is not an inhabitant of any town in this state, without the consent, in writing, first obtained of a majority of the civil authority, and also of the select men of the town in which such school, academy, or literary institution is situated; and each and every person who shall knowingly do any act forbidden as aforesaid, or shall be aiding or assisting therein; shall, for the first offence, forfeit and pay to the treasurer of state, a fine of one hundred dollars, and for the second offence shall forfeit and pay a fine of two hundred dollars, and so double for every offence of which he or she shall be convicted. And all informing officers are required to make due presentment of all breaches of this act. *Provided*, That nothing in this act shall extend to any district school established in any school society, under the laws of this state, or to any incorporated academy or incorporated school for instruction in this state.

Sec. 2. *Be it further enacted*, That any colored person, not an inhabitant of this state, who shall reside in any town therein for the purpose of being instructed as aforesaid, may be removed in the manner prescribed in the sixth and seventh sections of the act to which this is in addition.

Sec. 3. *Be it further enacted*, That any person, not an inhabitant of this state, who shall reside in any town therein, for the purpose of being instructed as aforesaid, shall be an admissible witness in all prosecutions under the first section of this act, and may be compelled to give testimony therein, notwithstanding any thing contained in this act, or the act last aforesaid.

Sec. 4. *Be it further enacted*, That so much of the seventh section of the act to which this is an addition, as may provide for the infliction of corporeal punishment, be, and the same is hereby repealed.

SAMUEL INGHAM, Speaker of the House of Representatives.

EBENEZER STODDARD, President of the Senate.

Approved, May 24, 1833.

HENRY W. EDWARDS.

About six weeks after the passage of the above law, and nearly a month after the rising of the General Assembly, Miss C. was notified that a suit would be commenced against her, by the Grand Juror. Her first trial came on before Rufus Adams, Esq. on the 27th June, 1833. 'At the trial, her counsel gave in a demurrer to the complaint, admitting the facts true, and submitted to the finding of the Court, without argument.' The bonds required for her appearance at the next session of the County Court, (August,) were fixed at $150. No one appearing to give bonds for her, she was committed to the County Jail,* in Brooklyn, at about 8 o'clock, P. M. on the day of the trial. At about

*No circumstance in the legal proceedings of the State, in this case, has been more ungenerously perverted, than the manner in which she was committed to jail, and the treatment she received while there. The most astonishing statement of all is, that she was thrown into the cell of a murderer, when the truth is, she occupied the debtor's room, which no one will call uncomfortable in the least, who will take the trouble to examine it. The cell referred to, is located in the opposite corner of the building. This statement is the only one, on this point, that has any claim to truth. Miss C. ought to have given herself a little trouble to correct those misstatements, in a public manner, and more especially to express, in some way or other, her acknowledgements for the gratuitous favors which she received at the hands of the Jailor. This was not done, however.

3 o'clock on the following day, she was released, bonds having been given by George Benson, Esq. whose daughter had remained with Miss Crandall, for company, during the whole of her confinement. Nothing further, of much interest, transpired until the time of her trial before the County Court in August last. Of course the opposition to her school continued,* but without any decided action. It continues up to this time, and every one must judge for himself, how far that opposition is to be sustained.

Report of the Trial.

WINDHAM COUNTY, SS.
County Court, August Term, A. D. 1833.

Present, JUDGES EATON, GRIFFIN, and CHASE.

State of Connecticut, vs. Prudence Crandall. } Information on the Statute, &c.

This case came on for trial before the County Court, on Friday, August 23d. C. F. Cleveland, Esq. the Attorney for the State, being absent from indisposition, the Court appointed Jonathan A. Welch, Esq. special Attorney, to conduct the prosecution. A. T. Judson and I. Buckley, Esq's. were assistant counsel. Hon. Calvin Goddard, Hon. W. W. Ellsworth, and Henry Strong, Esq. appeared for the defence. The Jury being empanneled and sworn, the counsel for the defence objected to one of the Jurors from Canterbury, on the ground that he had signed petitions, &c. in respect to Miss Crandall's school, and taken active measures to put it down. The Court sustained the objection, and the Juror was excused. They also objected to another of the Jurors, on the ground that he was a member of the Legislature which passed the law—was one of those who voted for it, and had of course formed an opinion with respect to its constitutionality. The Court decided that the Juror was competent to sit. (He got excused however, on account of sickness.) The information against Miss Crandall consisted of two Counts. The first charged "that the said Prudence Crandall, on the 24th day of June last, with force and arms, in a certain School, which before that time had been, and then was, set up in said Canterbury, for the instruction and teaching of colored persons, not inhabitants of this State, to wit:—Theodosia Degrass, Ann Peterson, Ann Elizabeth Wilder, Ann Eliza Hammond and others whose names are unknown, who at the time when so taught and instructed, were not inhabitants of any town in this State, which said acts were done by the said Prudence Crandall, without the consent in writing first had and obtained of a majority of the Civil Authority and Selectmen of the said town of Canterbury, within which said School then was instructed, against the peace of this State, and contrary to the form and effect of the Statute, in such case made and provided."

The second Count charged "that the Defendant, with force and arms did wilfully and knowingly harbor, board, and aid, and assist, in

*It has been charged upon the people of Canterbury, that their excited and unjustifiable state of feeling, led them to indecorous measures against the school.—Such as disturbing the Instructress and her pupils in their walks,—encouraging improper assaults upon her house, &c. Such conduct, (it is stated upon the best authority,) never was sanctioned by her opponents. Whenever any thing of the kind was resorted to, it was the work of boyish folly, or is chargeable upon some of the blacks belonging to the neighborhood.

harboring and boarding certain colored persons, (named above,) who, when so harbored and boarded, were not inhabitants of any town in this State, without the consent in writing of the Civil Authority and Selectmen, &c.—Plea, NOT GUILTY.

The following witnesses were then called on the part of the prosecution:—

Asahel Bacon, said that he called at Miss Crandall's house in the month of June last, having heard that she had taken some scholars from abroad. Captain Sanger accompanied him—they were both Selectmen of the town. Miss Crandall invited them into her house, very politely. They asked her in relation to her scholars. She said she had four who were from New York, and one from Hartford. She called them in and introduced them. Theodosia Degrass, Ann Elizabeth Wilder and Catharine Ann Weldon, he thinks were the names of those called. Witness did not remember the day of the month that he called—thinks it was the day after the girls came—certainly soon after.

Ebenezer Sanger, coincided in the statement of Mr Bacon.

George Cady, has conversed with Miss Crandall. Went to her house on Friday last to summon as witnesses to support this prosecution, some of the girls who were attending her school. One of these named in his subpoena, said that she had been sent for home, on account of the sickness of her mother, and wished him to excuse her attendance at Court. Told her he could not, but would state the circumstance to the public prosecutor. Miss Crandall said that she did not see that there was any need of witnesses at all, for she should confess that she had broken the law.

Ann Peterson. This witness was a colored girl, said to be a pupil of Miss Crandall, and was one of those named in the information to whom Miss Crandall had given instruction. Mr Ellsworth objected to the witness, on the ground that she could not testify without implicating herself. Mr Welch read the clause of the Statute under which this prosecution was sustained, in which it was enacted that the pupils in a school kept contrary to the act might be compelled to testify. Mr Ellsworth said that he denied altogether, the competency of the Legislature to compel a witness to testify, or to answer a question that might implicate him, even to render him liable in debt—otherwise a witness might be compelled to testify to what would charge him with the crime of murder. He alluded to the State Constitution and Bill which, he claimed, protected every person from criminating himself, by being compelled to give testimony. It was contrary to fundamental principles. In this case the testimony of the witness might make her an aider and abettor, and subject her to the penalties imposed by Statute.

Mr Judson claimed that the witness could not by her testimony implicate herself. The law was penal, and must be construed strictly—even if she swore that she was instructed by Miss Crandall, it would not charge herself with any crime. Mr Judson read at length, from Starkie on evidence, to show that the witness ought, on common law principles, to be examined, and was bound to answer questions as to what she knew of Miss Crandall's school. At all events, he claimed that in this instance, such must be the case, as the Legislature had expressly enacted that the pupils should be witnesses. Mr Ellsworth in reply, said he apprehended the question to be whether the Legislature possess the power to compel a witness to convict himself. He read from the opinion of Chief Justice Hosmer, in the 8th Connecticut Reports, and also from the people, vs. Mather in 4th Kendals Reports, on the subject of examining witnesses. By the principles decided in these cases which were the settled law of the land, he claimed that the witness was not compelled to answer any question in relation to her knowledge of this school. The Court decided that the witness, under these circumstances, was not protected, but must be examined. The examination was about to proceed, when Mr Ellsworth rose and stated to the Court, that the witness had been advised not to answer interrogatories in regard to her knowledge of this School. He felt it his duty now to repeat this advice—he wished the Court distinctly to understand that the counsel for the accused had taken this course, not with a view to embarrass the trial, but solely from a sense of duty—he conscientiously believed that the legal rights of the witness were such that she could not be compelled to testify.—The counsel for the prosecution asked the witness when she came to Canterbury; but she declined answering the question. A number of other questions were then propounded to the witness, the principal of which were—'Has Miss Crandall kept a school for Colored Misses not inhabitants of the State?' 'Will you say whether the defendant has or has not instructed any person of color other than yourself, since the 10th of June last?' 'With whom do you board?' 'Has or has not Miss Crandall, since the 10th of June last, boarded and instructed colored persons not inhabitants of this State?' To all these and other questions of a similar character the witness declined giving an answer, on the ground that she could not do so without criminating herself.

The counsel for the prosecution then called Catharine Ann Weldon and Ann Eliza Hammond, both girls of color, and charged with being pupils of Miss C. and propounded to them the same questions as above, but they, for the same alledged reason, and by the advice of counsel declined answering. The prosecuting attorney reserved to himself, tho' he waived for the present the right of moving that these witnesses be committed for a contempt of Court.

Jacob C. Gould said he was acquainted with Ann Eliza Hammond. She belonged to Providence R. I.—had known her since she was a child—was the daughter of Thomas Hammond, who died in 1826.—Her mother now lives in Providence—the father at his death was worth from $1,500 to $2,000 in real estate.

Levi Kneeland. Was not connected with Miss Crandall's School except as an adviser in relation to it—was Pastor of the church to which Miss Crandall belonged—had seen several of the colored girls who were present at his church during the summer. In reply to a question whether he had seen one of them at Miss C's, declined answering—declined to answer whether he had advised Miss Crandall in relation to her school—declined answering whether or not he had been in Miss Crandall's school since the 10th of June last,—To a question from the prosecuting attorney whether or not he had eaten at Miss C's since the 10th of June last, he replied that he believed the Court had no business to know. The Court having decided that he was bound to answer the questions put to him, that the reasons he offered for refusing to do so, namely, that he might subject himself to a prosecution and entangle himself in difficulties, were insufficient, granted the motion for a mittimus to commit him to prison; and he was taken into custody by the Sheriff.

Eliza Parkis, (a woman of color.) was acquainted with Ann Eliza Hammond, one of the girls that Miss Crandall was charged with having instructed. Has seen her in Providence—has also seen her at Miss Crandall's—Miss Crandall has employed witness to wash for her and to do other work—has staid at Miss Crandall's and slept in a room with Miss Degrass, a colored girl from New York.—Miss C. employed witness to work for her because she said she did not wish to keep her scholars out of school to do work—never saw any of the girls in school—has seen them have books, and read them.

Roland Green (affirmed) has often heard that Miss Crandall keeps a school for colored girls in Canterbury—has been at her house often, was called as a physician—went there and saw several colored girls—heard some of them in grammar, geography, &c—some of the girls have been at his own house—has seen a little girl, said to be from N. York—has heard Miss Crandall talk concerning her scholars from abroad-does not remember to have heard her say that they were from New York.

Mr Kneeland was now placed at the bar by the Sheriff at his request and said that he intended no disrespect to the Court by declining to answer the questions put to him, and on being advised that he should not implicate himself by doing so—he was ready to answer. He proceeded to state that he had visited Miss Crandall's school twice—once it was under her charge, and once under the charge of another person—he had prayed in her school, and conversed with the girls on religious subjects—does not remember faces as well as people in general, could not therefore positively identify any of those present, as being the ones he had seen at Miss Crandall's—should think they were—his best belief on the subject would be a guess—had taken meals at Miss Crandall's, and eaten with her pupils—he heard them recite their lessons—thinks he has heard Miss Hammond spoken of, either by the defendant or her sister—Miss Crandall has conversed with him in relation to her scholars—thinks she has told him that some of them were from N. York, and some from Providence, and New Haven.

Albert Hinckley has been at Miss Crandall's several times since the month of June last—knows not whether he has been in her school room or not, as he knows not in which room the school was kept—has never seen her engaged in instructing—has not conversed with her on the subject of the residence of her scholars—called on her as a friend and conversed on various topics—has heard that she kept a school for colored persons—has heard her speak of scholars and school—has seen colored ladies at her house and taken tea with them—cannot say whether any of those present were the ones or not.

Eliza Glasco. This witness was a colored girl belonging to the school, but an inhabitant of this State. The same objection was made to examining her as was before made in respect to the others, but the objection was overruled by the court. She however declined answering the questions propounded to her. The prosecuting attorney moved the court for a mittimus to commit the witness for a contempt of court. The court granted the motion and ordered the clerk to make out a mittimus.

Hezekiah Crandall (affirmed) his sister Prudence keeps a school at Canterbury for colored girls—knows Ann Eliza Hammond—could not certainly recognize any other that was present except perhaps Ann Peterson—has never been in the school or heard the pupils recite—has seen Ann Eliza Hammond at his sisters often during June and July—supposed she was boarded there and instructed by his sister with others—knows by sight and name Amelia Wilder—does not know where she is now—has not heard his sister say anything on the subject of her school for some time—she has resided in Canterbury some portion of the time for twelve years past.

James B. Chandler said that he was at Miss Crandall's several times last spring.—(Not being able to say with certainty whether he had been there since the passage of the law, he was not interrogated further.)

George Roberts. Went to Miss Crandall's about five months ago and carried a Colored Girl, (Miss Hammond) to the school—Miss Hammond, it was said, belonged to Providence—has been at Miss Crandall's since that time, within ten weeks, and drank tea—then saw Miss Hammond—does not know whether she constantly boards there or not—has heard her and other colored girls recite in Miss Crardall's school—should think it was two or three months ago—has been at Miss C's within a week, but did not as he remembers, see any of the girls present there at that time.

Mary Benson. (affirmed) has been at Miss Crandall's school, found it very interesting—was never present but for a short time—'tis for colored persons—saw Ann Eliza Hammond there—she is one of the scholars and boards with Miss C.—witness recognized several of those present as among the number she had seen at Miss Crandall's—one of the pupils, Ann Wilder, was from New York—Miss Hammond was from Providence—witness was at Miss Crandall's about five weeks since and took tea—several colored girls were at the table—does not know where any of them belonged except by report—visited the school when it was near closing and heard Miss Crandall give the girls instruction in geography and arithmetic.—The prosecuting attorney here rested his evidence, and the Sheriff having served his process on Eliza Glasko, was about committing her to prison, when Mr Ellsworth interposed and stated to the court that rather than have the girl committed he should advise her to testify, again repeating that the course of the defendant's counsel in relation to the testimony of these girls, was dictated by an imperious sense of professional duty.

Eliza Glasko then proceeded to give her testimony.—She said she was a member of Miss Crandall's school and that the girls near her were also members—one of them was from Providence and the others were said to be from New York—the ordinary branches were taught them by Miss Crandall, reading, writing, grammar, geography, &c.—witness began to go on the 1st of April—the school was usually opened and closed with prayer—the scriptures were read and explained, daily, in her school—some portions were committed to memory by the pupils, and considered a part of their education.

[Not being able to procure full and accurate copies of all the arguments in this case, it is thought advisable not to lay any part of them before the public, at this time. And considering the result of the trial, it will not probably be expected. The counsel both on the part of the State, and in defence of Miss Crandall, manifested on this occasion, unusual ingenuity and ability. Immediately after the concluding plea, his Hon. Judge Eaton, proceeded to charge the Jury. Although the right of expressing his opinion, as to the constitutionality of the law, was fully exercised, the charge was nevertheless dignified and impartial.]

The Jury retired, and after an absence of several hours, returned into court, not having agreed on a verdict. They were again ordered out, and again returned, not having agreed. The third time they stated to the court that there was no probability they should agree. The court then discharged them. This operates as a continuance of the case to the next term of the County Court to be holden on the second Tuesday of December next.

THE RIGHT OF COLORED PEOPLE TO EDUCATION, VINDICATED.

LETTERS

TO

ANDREW T. JUDSON, ESQ.

AND OTHERS IN CANTERBURY,

REMONSTRATING WITH THEM ON THEIR UNJUST

AND

UNJUSTIFIABLE PROCEDURE RELATIVE

TO

MISS CRANDALL AND HER SCHOOL

FOR

COLORED FEMALES.

BY SAMUEL J. MAY,
Minister of the 1st Church in Brooklyn, (Conn.)

BROOKLYN:
ADVERTISER PRESS.
1833.

LETTER I.

BROOKLYN, MARCH 29, 1833.

ANDREW T. JUDSON, ESQ.

SIR:—I left Canterbury, after the town-meeting on the 9th ult. grieved that so large a number of persons could be so completely misled by the art and influence of a few individuals; and ashamed that in Connecticut (which claims to be the most enlightened and moral State in our Union,) a community of freemen could be found, who would thus yield themselves to be the instruments of such injustice and cruelty.

From your high official standing, Sir, both in the town and state, it was to have been expected that you would have endeavored to allay the popular excitement, and to persuade your fellow-citizens to act advisedly. So far from it, however, you were the prominent actor on the occasion; and exerted yourself beyond measure to heat the imaginations of your hearers, to enkindle their bitterest feelings against Miss Crandall and her friends, and to hurry them on to an immediate decision—a decision which can reflect no honor upon the town; and which, if it cannot be reversed, may indirectly affect the happiness of *millions* in our land.

I therefore take the liberty thus publicly to plead with you, and with your fellow-citizens. Nay—Sir, I have a right to claim from yourself, and from the people of Canterbury, and from the community at large, some attention to the defence I am about to offer of Miss Crandall's most benevolent project; of the part I have acted on her behalf; and of the sentiments and purposes of those Gentlemen, who with myself have encouraged her undertaking. I solemnly aver, that so far as I know any thing about that young lady, or her patrons, or my own intentions, we have all been grossly misrepresented and traduced.

It was not until about the time of Miss Crandall's return from New-York, that I received the first intimation of her design to open her School for the education of colored females. I expressed to my informant, my heartfelt satisfaction that there was one so near me, who would dare to brave the prejudices of the public, so far as to devote herself to that great "labor of love." The young lady was then an entire stranger to me. I had heard however of her good reputation as a teacher in Canterbury and Plainfield, and, better than that, of her great integrity of mind, benevolence of heart, and energy of purpose; and therefore I determined to hold myself in readiness to aid her, if my assistance should be needed by her in any way.

A few days afterwards, i. e. on the 27th of February, I was further informed that she had made her intention publicly known in your town, and that the people there, were, in consequence, filled with indignation at her, especially yourself and her immediate neighbors. Not having received from Miss Crandall any notice of her plan (though my deep interest in the melioration of the condition of our colored brethren must be well known in this vicinity,) I at first concluded, that she might prefer to avoid receiving any assistance from me, because perhaps of her strong objections to my religious opinions. On further reflection however, it seemed to be my duty to proffer her a helping hand, which she would be at liberty to accept or reject as she might choose. Accordingly on the 28th I wrote her a hasty letter, of which the following is an exact copy.

Brooklyn, Feb. 28, 1833.

MISS CRANDALL.

Although I am a stranger to you I shall offer no apology for addressing you.

The cause, which I hear you have espoused, is one which has long been deeply interesting to me. My situation and engagements have prevented my doing as much in behalf of our colored brethren, as I fain would have done. Last week I heard indirectly from Dr. Green that you proposed to open a boarding school for colored girls. The intelligence rejoiced my heart, and I determined to do all in my power to assist you. You are probably well aware that my religious sentiments have rendered me obnoxious to the suspicion, and ill-will of the Clergy, and a considerable proportion of the people in this vicinity. This may lessen very much my ability to serve you. But

I wish you would command my services in any way in which you think I can be useful to you.

Last evening, Chauncy Morse informed me that there was considerable excitement in Canterbury, in consequence of your proposal. This was to have been expected, so inveterate are the prejudices of the people against the Blacks. But it is disgraceful to any community pretending to be Christian. I would enlarge upon this topic, but I feel too deeply to write in a proper temper.

It has been intimated that there is to be even a town-meeting to prevent you from carrying your plan into operation. If there is, I shall endeavor to attend it. But how do they purpose to prevent you? It has occurred to me that your *conspicuous* residence in the village might render your plan more objectionable to those, who are so hostile to the blacks. Perhaps your removal to some more retired situation would at once allay the violence of your opponents, and be more favorable to your pupils, who would not be so exposed to insult as they might be where you now are.

I should be very happy to see you at my house—or I will come and see you, if a visit, from such a heretic as I am accounted, would not increase the ill-will of your neighbors towards you.

Yours in the cause of the oppressed.

S. J. MAY.

It was not until the following Monday (March 4th) that I received her reply, in which she assured me that I could be of service to her, and requested me to visit her as soon as might be convenient to myself. About the same moment, the Liberator for March 2d came to hand, in which I saw for the first time the Advertisement of her school, and my name in the list of those to whom she referred.—This satisfied me, that she had relied upon my co-operation. I therefore set off immediately for Canterbury, in company with a mutual friend.

Every thing we gathered from Miss Crandall, and from others with whom we conversed, satisfied us that a most determined effort would be made at the town meeting, then warned, to prevent the prosecution of her benevolent plan. Regarding it not, by any means as a local, town affair, but on the contrary as affecting indirectly the happiness of millions of the American people, we were deeply impressed with the importance of sustaining the school. Should a second attempt to provide for the better education of our colored people, be put down by the popular clamor in New-England, (the land of schools) discouragement we feared would enfeeble the efforts of many, who are now laboring to meliorate the condition of this immense body of the inhabitants of our land. The location of the school in your village was not indeed a matter, in itself considered, of any moment. But that the school should not be abandoned, we deemed a matter of the utmost consequence. As therefore it so happened, that Miss Crandall was already established in Canterbury, it was obviously right in our view, that she should be sustained there; at least until her opponents or her patrons should provide her with a suitable situation elsewhere. And such a situation we thought could not easily be obtained any where else, if she were first to relinquish the one she now has. For wherever we looked, we saw reason to believe, that there too would be found much of the same feeling of hostility to the people of color; added to which would be the disgrace that would follow her and her school, wherever she might go—the disgrace of having been expelled from your town as a nuisance.

We have long since perceived how deep and inveterate, even in New-England, are the prejudices of the whites against those of African descent. We have apprehended, that ere our colored brethren will have any chance to rise to that intellectual and moral elevation, which they may doubtless reach, there would need to be a conflict between those great republican principles, on which our civil institutions are based, and that aristocracy of color which has become hereditary among us. It seemed to us that, in the course of Providence we were called to take a part in this conflict. We did not dare to shrink from it; nor to advise Miss Crandall to withdraw, let the consequences to her or to ourselves be what they might. We therefore exhorted her to be steadfast—meekly to bear the injuries that might be heaped upon her; and in hope of the good she would be instrumental in doing, to despise the shame she would incur.—We also promised to afford her all the assistance in our power; and assured her she might rely upon those who had encouraged her undertaking; upon others who were doubtless watching with deepest interest the result; and above all upon Him who will prosper the cause that is right.

The injurious reports which were busily circulated respecting Miss Crandall, and the friends of her school, filled her and us with apprehension, that her sentiments and purposes would be sadly misrepresented at the approaching town meeting. Who would be there to speak in her behalf? A sense of propriety forbade her appearing in person. She knew of no one that would venture to breast the current of public sentiment, that was set against her. Fearing that the prejudices which prevail in your town against my religious opinions, might only aggravate the public odium if I should appear there in her stead,* I hesitated some time whether it would be advisable for me to undertake her defence. But as there was no one else, in the town or neighborhood, that she supposed would be willing to stand up for her, she strongly expressed her desire that I would do so. She agreed to give me a *written* request to the Moderator of the meeting, that I might be permitted to speak in explanation and defence of her sentiments and purposes.

When I went again to Canterbury on the 9th of March, I found at Miss Crandall's house, Arnold Buffum, the Agent of the New-England Anti-Slavery Society. Having heard that he was at Norwich, in the prosecution of his official duty, she had been to that city the day previous, and induced him to come to Canterbury to help her. I had had the pleasure of seeing that gentleman two or three times. I knew that he was an able advocate of the rights of the oppressed; and rejoiced that he was permitted to be there. It was at once determined, that he should be her principal attorney at the meeting. She however requested me also to speak on her behalf; and I had now become so deeply interested in the cause, that I longed for an opportunity to advocate it.

Mr. Buffum and myself accordingly proceeded to the house, where we found the meeting already organized. Asael Bacon, Esq. Moderator. Andrew T. Judson. Esq. Clerk. Looking about us, I perceived many persons present from neighboring towns, who came there, as I have reason to believe with no very friendly regard towards the proposed school. I assure you and the public, that I went to Canterbury not knowing that a single individual was to be at the meeting besides the inhabitants of the town, excepting only the young gentleman who accompanied me. I had not heard that Mr. Buffum was in the region; and I was equally surprised when I saw the two young men from Providence ("boisterous boys" as you have called them,) enter the house. In the gallery there were two or three decent looking colored men. Who they were I did not know, but at the time supposed them to belong to your town. I saw nothing in their deportment at all improper, though if they had manifested great displeasure at some of your remarks, I should not have wondered. I am thus particular, because you have endeavered through the Norwich papers to make the public believe, that the friends of Miss Crandall's school presented themselves at your "perfectly orderly meeting" in a most formidable array, as if to awe your

*Though I meant to be there as a *witness* of your proceedings.

citizens into a compliance with their wishes. Permit me to say Sir, if you or some of your coadjutors had adopted the precaution of "taking notes" at the time, (for which precaution you seem to be offended at one of the Providence young men,) you probably would have given as correct an account of the meeting as he has done in "the Liberator,"* and not have committed so many mistakes in your communications to the Norwich papers, as must be apparent to all who were witnesses of what you have therein attempted to describe.

After "the warning" had been read, the following Resolutions were laid before the meeting by Rufus Adams, Esq. viz:—

"Whereas, it hath been publicly avowed that a school is to be opened in this town, on the first Monday of April next, using the language of the advertisement, "for young ladies and little misses of color," or in other words, for the people of color, the obvious tendency of which, would be, to collect within the town of Canterbury large numbers of persons, from other States, whose characters and habits might be various and unknown to us, thereby rendering insecure the persons, property, and reputation of our citizens—

Under such circumstances our silence might be construed into an approbation of the project.

Therefore Resolved, That the location of a school for the people of color, at any place within the limits of this town, for the admission of persons from foreign jurisdictions, meets with our unequivocal disapprobbation, and it is to be understood that the inhabitants of Canterbury, protest against it, in the most earnest manner.

Resolved, That a Committee be now appointed, to be composed of the Civil Authority and Select Men, who shall make known to the person contemplating the establishment of said school, the sentiments and objections entertained by this meeting, in reference to said school, pointing out to her, the injurious effects, and the incalculable evils, resulting from such an establishment within this town, and persuade her, if possible, to abandon the project."

Mr. Adams accompanied the presentation of these resolves with a speech, in which he attempted to set forth the causes of complaint, which the town of Canterbury had against Miss Crandall. But, I am sorry to say, he sadly misrepresented her sentiments and purpo-

*I suspect no one will undertake to prove the statements, made by H. E. Benson, untrue in any one material point. But he is not, nor is any one but the Editor of the Liberator, responsible for the heading and the remarks prefixed to the Letter; nor for the black letter type, in which the names of certain individuals in Canterbury are signalized. I respect and love Mr. Garrison's fervent devotion to the cause of the oppressed, and his fearlessness in reproving the oppressors; but no one can disapprove, more than I do, the harshness of his epithets, and the bitterness of his invectives.

ses; and made several most ungenerous insinuations against her motives.

As soon as he sat down, you took the floor. I shall not pretend to repeat all that you said, nor to describe minutely the style of your address. It was a most inglorious exploit! And oh Sir! what a golden opportunity you lost, on that day, to act as a true patriot and genuine philanthropist should have done; ay, to illustrate the principles of a real *republican!* It is much more difficult, I grant, but how much more honorable is it to withstand public prejudice, and labor to enlighten and correct it, than it is to avail ourselves of its blindness and impetuosity to accomplish some selfish purpose, or gratify some private feelings! Who Sir, have ever been instrumental in the melioration of the human condition, or the advance of knowledge and virtue, but they who have dared to oppose public error, and even defy public odium? I deeply lament, Sir, that you did not perceive, or that you chose not to pursue the course, in which the principles of our civil institutions, as well as the precepts of the gospel would have guided and sustained you. To whom Sir, should they, who, condescending to men of low estate, would labor to instruct and raise them, to whom I ask should such look for encouragement, if not to those who profess to believe that all men are born with equal rights—that the King of Kings and Lord of Lords is no respecter of persons? But all such reliance upon you, Sir, it seems would have been misplaced. You vented yourself in a strain which evinced your reckless hostility to Miss Crandall, her school and her patrons; and your determination to do every thing in your power to thwart her project. You twanged every chord that could stir the coarser passions of the human heart; and with such sad success that your hearers seemed to have lost for the time their perception of right and wrong. The remarks that were made by yourself and by others, were adapted to make an impression of this sort upon the minds of your fellow-citizens,—that a great calamity was impending over your town, of which Miss Crandall was the author, or the instrument—that there were powerful conspirators combined with her in the plot—and that the people of Canterbury should be roused by every consideration of self-respect and self-preservation, to prevent the accomplishment of the design, defying the wealth and influence of all who were abettors of it.

When I supposed you were done, though it appears from the account in the Norwich paper I was mistaken—but certainly not until I thought you had drawn your remarks to a close—I whispered to

Mr. Buffum, it is now high time for us to present Miss Crandall's request to be heard. He therefore, being the one on whom her defence was chiefly to rest, first handed her respectful petition to the Moderator. I watched until he had read it, and passed it to you, and you had read it; and I then gave to the Moderator a similar billet from Miss Crandall, praying that I also might be permitted to speak on her behalf. For reasons however, known only to yourself and to Him who sees all hearts, you *reversed* the order of our certificates, when you read them to the meeting. But let this pass. It might have been accidental.

You instantly broke forth with even more violence than before, and accused us of insulting the town, and interfering in the management of its local concerns. Other gentlemen arose in high displeasure, (Mr. Solomon Payne in particular,) and opposed Miss Crandall's petition; and very roughly admonished us, that if we dared to interfere, we should suffer the penalty which the Law prescribes.— Of course we did not dare to interfere; and so we sat quietly until the dissolution of the meeting. But we dare now to appeal from your decision; and we do appeal in full confidence that it will be reversed by the opinion of the fair minded, and impartial, every where. It is necessary that I should dwell for a moment upon this point, because it has been made so prominent by yourself and your coadjutors. Not only has Rumor with her thousand tongues spread every where the slander, that Mr. Buffum and Mr. May thrust themselves into a peaceable town meeting in Canterbury, and interfered with the business of the town; but the same false accusation is brought against us in the public prints. It is not true that *we* asked leave to address the meeting. Miss Crandall asked leave to be heard *by us*, her sex forbidding her to advocate her own cause. We said not a word: but simply put into the hand of the Moderator a written request from Miss Crandall. We were silent, because we were not permitted to speak. How then did we interfere? The meeting was called for the sole purpose of opposing a project started by that young lady. Her sentiments and purposes were misrepresented, by you and others, and even her integrity called in question. And where Sir, was your sense of justice, where your honor, to say nothing of your gallantry, when you opposed, as you did with vehemence of passion, her being heard in reply? A young lady was accused by you and others before the assembly of the people, ay, and in the presence of her aged father, accused of entertaining sentiments and purposes which excited the public disgust, and no one was permitted to speak in her defence! Where will you find an upright man, who will say this was fair? You will not Sir, I hope pretend to justify it yourself. You have been so long accustomed to the proceedings of our Courts of Justice, in which no judgment is ever given, until both parties have been patiently heard, that you Sir, of all others, should have seen at a glance the propriety of Miss Crandall's claim to be heard; and should have had the honor to insist on her right to speak by those, whom she *chose* to represent her sentiments and purposes, and vindicate her character. I did expect as much as this from you, although I had been told of the violence of your opposition to the proposed school; for I would not suppose there was a Lawyer, of good standing in this community, that would claim at any tribunal a verdict in favor of the side he espoused, until after the opposite counsel had been heard. I am now compelled to believe, that you were afraid to submit the case in question to a fair investigation. You relied upon the prejudices of the people; and having excited them to the utmost, hurried on a decision which you plainly foresaw would gratify your wishes. If this be not the just inference, why were you so much offended at the presence of Mr. Buffum and myself? And why did you show so much passion when we presented Miss Crandall's request to be heard by us?

You sought to turn off the minds of your fellow-citizens, from the very proper request of that defenceless young lady, by holding *us* up as foreigners who had come there to interfere. And you have since pressed this accusation of *foreign interference* with so much urgency, that I am persuaded you rely, for the justification of your own conduct, upon the impression you may make on the public mind by this charge against us. Calling us foreigners (especially those of us who live in an adjoining town) would be only a ludicrous misnomer, if it had not been obviously applied by you for a sinister purpose.

Of course Sir, there are town rights, as well as state rights, which every individual is bound to respect, and every town competent to maintain. If I have violated those rights I shall be most anxious to make to the people of Canterbury a public apology. But surely the rights and interests of any town are not to be regarded as of equal, much less of paramount importance to the rights and interests of larger portions of the community. To maintain that they are, would be to maintain a wilder doctrine than our South Carolina brethren ever broached. Nor are the rights of any town to be considered as of equal, much less of paramount importance to the *eternal principles* of right, and truth, and justice. Whenever therefore any town is seen to be pursuing a measure that will be prejudicial to other portions of community, those not belonging to that particular town have a *right* to interfere. There can be nothing wrong in their going into that town, and asking leave of the town to remonstrate with them against the measure. If permission be not given, they are then left with the right to call the measure in question before a common tribunal. So too, if the procedure of a town is likely to be unnecessarily injurious to an individual, whether that individual be a resident in the town or not, he has a *right* to interfere—he has a right to present himself at the town meeting where such a procedure is to be determined on, and claim to be heard. If he be an inhabitant of the town he may speak without special permission; if not an inhabitant, he must obtain permission. In neither case however is he doing wrong. And if he cannot present himself in person, or is unable to speak, he obviously has a right to appoint an advocate; and the town would obviously do wrong if they refused to hear the advocate. Now, will you Sir, say that he must select for his advocate one who is an inhabitant of the town in which the meeting is convened? I trust not. How futile then was your objection to us that we were foreigners! and how false the accusation, which you have reiterated, that we interfered, or were disposed to interfere (in an improper manner at least,) with the business of your town meeting.* If the question, to be considered on that occasion, had been altogether local, still as it deeply involved the interests and character of one who could not with propriety be present, she had a right to delegate one or more to appear for her. And as she knew of no one in the town, who would be willing to undertake her defence, she was under the necessity of seeking assistance from some *foreigners*, as you are pleased to call those who do not live within the limits of Canterbury. I leave it for all honorable men to decide between us, whether on this supposition I should have done wrong to go to the meeting; and whether you would have done right to oppose my being heard at her request?

But Sir, the question at that meeting was not one of local interest

*A gentleman of Plainfield has assured me, that some years ago, Andrew T. Judson, Esq. himself, attended a town meeting in Plainfield, and asked permission to speak upon the subject under consideration; that permission was given him, and he did address the meeting. The gentleman did not recollect the subject. But it is a matter of no consequence what the subject was, in order to test the principle. If it were a less important one, than that at Canterbury, there was the less reason for the interference.

merely. It was intimately connected with the *greatest* question our nation is now called upon to decide—i. e. whether our immense colored population shall henceforth be permitted to rise among us, *as they may be able*, in intellectual and moral worth; or be kept down in hopeless degradation, until in the providence of a just God they may throw off the yoke of their oppressors, with vindictive violence. Such Sir, was the magnitude of the question agitated at Canterbury on the 9th of March. So momentous was it in my view, that I should have attended the discussion, even if Miss Crandall had not called on me to advocate her cause. And so deeply interesting is the question to our whole country, that I cannot think I should have been guilty of any great impropriety if, without her certificate, I had respectfully asked permission to address your fellow-citizens. Had leave been given me, I could have assured them, that there was no intention or wish on the part of those who will patronize the school, to injure your village or incommode an individual in it; but that they would be ready at any time to have it removed to any more retired spot, wherever such an institution could be suitably accommodated. And I should have plead with you and your neighbors Sir, with all the earnestness in my power, that, in view of the momentous connexions and dependencies of the question, you would so far forego your prepossessions and prejudices, as to decide that a School for the better education of those, who of all others in our land need it most, might be permitted to remain unmolested where it happens in the providence of God to have been located.

I will not detain you and the public longer Sir, with this direct exculpation of Mr. Buffum and myself. It might be easily shown that several other statements in the Norwich papers are untrue, and that the whole account of the meeting is highly discolored.* Our presence there evidently disturbed the feelings of yourself and those who were leagued with you against Miss Crandall's school. But we neither did nor said any thing to disturb the meeting. When we carried Miss Crandall's certificates to the Moderator, we did so as quietly as possible. And when we spake to each other, which we did but three or four times, it was in a whisper.

*It may not be improper here to inform the public that one of the Civil Authority, whose name appears in the Norwich Courier, was *not* at the meeting --that another has been since heard, by three witnesses, to say that some of the statements in that address to the American Colonization Society were not true; and also I believe that not more than two or three of the Authority remained after the meeting, to hear the remarks by Mr. Buffum and myself.

So soon as the meeting was *dissolved*, I called upon the people to hear us. Perhaps in this, I misjudged. But I thought, after what had been alleged against Miss Crandall, our absent friends and ourselves, that we ought to speak, when we could do so without impropriety. What we said, those who *heard* us can testify. I can only aver that neither Mr. Buffum's language nor my own was what it is represented to have been in the Norwich Republican.

I am Sir, not a foreigner, but
Your fellow-citizen,
SAMUEL J. MAY.

LETTER II.

BROOKLYN, APRIL 6, 1833.

ANDREW T. JUDSON, ESQ.

SIR;—I intend now to consider some of the charges brought by you and others against Miss Crandall; and some of the objections urged against her proposed school; correcting as I proceed, some of the many misrepresentations, which were given (and have been reiterated,) of the sentiments and purposes of those, who have encouraged her undertaking.

The first complaint or charge, if I remember correctly, which was alleged at the town meeting on the 9th, was that Miss Crandall had perverted her school from its original purpose. 'She was introduced here,' said one or more of her accusers, 'to instruct our children. We gave her our patronage and our confidence. She has set aside the one, and abused the other, and is now about to introduce into the town a class of persons whose presence will be offensive to us.' I do not give this as the precise language, but as the substance of the charge; and the same is repeated in the Norwich papers. It struck me at the time, that the tone of the complaint implied that you had conferred upon this young lady a much greater amount of favors, than she has in fact received. All that has been done for her, by the Ladies and Gentlemen of Canterbury, has been to encourage her opening a school there, which surely was as much for their own accommodation, as for her benefit. The favor was then at least mutual. But I am one Sir, who regard a capable and faithful Teacher of youth as a greater benefactor to the community, than the community is to her. Will you tell me she was furnished with money? Very true. But did she not give the lender good security for the repayment of the loan, with lawful interest? The house in which she resides was purchased by herself, and she is still indebted for it to a considerable amount. If the establishment had been bought and fitted up for her by her patrons, they would unquestionably have the right to insist that it should be still appropriated to its original purpose, or else given back into their hands. But they cannot pretend to so much as this. Unless therefore you and your neighbors have good reason to believe, that she had her present plan in contemplation when she came into your village; and that she availed herself of your patronage only that she might get herself established there, all the while intending to enter as soon as possible upon the course now proposed—I repeat, unless you have good reason to believe this, you have no reason to be offended with her. Now I have never heard this alleged. Nor do I suppose she ever thought of devoting herself to the instruction of colored females until last Fall, after she had been resident among you a year or more. She has not been bribed nor persuaded by others, to this undertaking. The circumstances which have led her to it, (as she relates them) seem to have been providential. How could she resist the convictions wrought in her mind? How could she refuse to obey them, without disregarding a higher obligation, than any she is under to her patrons? Some men may sneer if they will, at what is called a sense of duty. There is such a thing. And when it is awakened in the human breast it leads one to act with a determination, consistency and fearlessness, which is never to be seen in the conduct of the selfish, calculating and worldly.

The next charge was that Miss C. went off to Providence, Boston and New-York to make arrangements for her proposed school, without having apprised her neighbors of her intention, asked their advice, or consulted their wishes. Surely, Sir, it was not her fault that none of the people of Canterbury were known to feel so much commiseration for the colored people in our land, that she could hope for encouragement from them to pursue her intention to labor for their good.

But it has been repeatedly said of her since, if it was not alleged against her at the meeting, that she was guilty of falsehood or at least prevarication respecting the object of her journies. This is indeed a grave accusation. The untruth is said to have been this: when asked by some one or more, why she was going to the above named cities, she replied, to visit schools and procure school apparatus; whereas it now appears that she went to seek patrons and pupils for her school, under the new arrangement. Miss Crandall's reply to this accusation is, that she had for sometime previous contemplated a visit to the schools in the various parts of our country—that she had long felt the need of more apparatus, and that such a journey as she has lately made would have been ere long necessary, if she had not proposed the important alteration that has taken place in her school. She adds that when about to leave home, she was wholly unacquainted with the friends of the colored people, excepting by reputation; and did not know that they would approve of her design; and that she therefore felt herself justified in acquainting those of her neighbors who inquired, with only a part of the objects of her journey. She assures me, and is ready to prove to her opposers if they wish, that while absent from Canterbury she did visit *eight* different schools in Providence and Boston. If she had not met with so much encouragement to open her school for colored females she would have devoted more of her time to similar examinations; and this would then have become the principal purpose of her journey. But finding so many persons, where she went, deeply interested in her proposal; and so large a number of pupils ready to be placed under her care; this assumed that prominence among the purposes of her journey, which it doubtless had in her thoughts.—Now Sir, I am willing to leave this explanation with the public, as she has left it with me; and I have no doubt it would satisfy even yourself and her opposers, if you were in a state of mind that would permit you to judge impartially.

Again; it was, (by more than one of the Speakers at your town meeting,) objected to the school proposed by Miss Crandall, that it would greatly lessen the value of property in your village, by rendering it no longer a desirable place of residence. One gentleman, if not more, intimated that he should wish to sell out his property, and move off. If this depreciation of real estate will be consequent upon the establishment of her school, the effect should be attributed to its true cause; not to that benevolent institution, but to the prejudices of those who would crush it. If you and the other gentlemen who have become so unhappily conspicuous, had interested yourselves as much as all patriots and philanthropists in our county should have done long ago in the condition of that immense portion of the American people, which is held in degradation, you would have rejoiced to hear that an experiment was to be made so near you to benefit them; and would have watched its operation with increasing satisfaction. But if on the contrary, you have cherished your unrighteous prejudices against them—prejudices which have no deeper foundation than their skins, unless it be in that deep degradation itself, to which they have been consigned by our government, in despite of the principles on which our government rests,—I repeat Sir, if you and other gentlemen in Canterbury have cherished your prejudices against them to such an extent, that you cannot bear even to have a few of them resident among you—who is to blame? Who but yourselves? Although therefore, you may, through the influence of the same prejudices in the breasts of your earthly judges, escape utter condemnation at the bar of public opinion; can you expect a similar impunity at the tribunal of the Most High? He is no respecter of persons! He does not regard the rich and mighty, more than the poor, and the despised! The cause of truth and righteousness—the melioration of the human condition has never made any advance, but in opposition to the wishes of a certain sort of men. Ought the cause at any time to have been abandoned on their account? The preaching of Paul at Ephesus was very prejudicial to one Demetrius, and a few other silversmiths; and they succeeded in raising an uproar, and making it appear to be an affair of great consequence to *all* the Ephesians. But Sir, did you ever think Paul was to blame in that matter?

In a pecuniary point of view, such a seminary will doubtless be beneficial to the inhabitants of Canterbury. Thirty or forty temporary residents will be introduced among you to be clothed, fed and warmed, as well as instructed; thus making a considerable addition to the class of consumers. Some of them will be the daughters of men of wealth; and all of them supported there by their parents or relatives,* who are able and willing to pay all their expences.—However, to quiet the fears of those who are, or pretend to be, apprehensive that some of Miss Crandall's colored pupils may become chargeable to the town, the patrons of her school hold themselves in readiness to give bonds, in any amount that may be required, to secure the town from all such harm.

*There is a solitary exception among those who are now engaged, the very honorable exception of a young woman, now keeping a school in New-York, who by her own frugality has accumulated enough to defray her expenses for half of a year. She will be assisted by a gentleman of that city, to complete

Nothing, I am confident, could have been further from Miss Crandall's intention, than to do her neighbors any injury. And Sir, you may rest assured, the gentlemen referred to in her Advertisement would not uphold her a moment in violating any of your rights. The determination she has formed to devote herself to the education of colored females, we cannot but highly approve. Her residence in your village is altogether a providential circumstance.—We should encourage her benevolent enterprise, wherever it might be undertaken. And if a suitable situation can be provided for her, in some place where her neighbors would assist and cheer her, or where they would only not molest her, we should rejoice to have her remove thither.† But you declared, in the town meeting, that the school should not be located in any part of Canterbury—and also that there is not a town in the State which would admit such a seminary within its borders. It is therefore all the more necessary that she should be sustained where she now is. It is to be deeply regretted that yourself and others are opposed to her. We think you are doing yourselves no honor; and more than that, we are persuaded you are helping to perpetuate the great iniquity, and the deep disgrace of our country. The question between us is not simply whether thirty or forty colored girls shall be well educated at a school to be kept in Canterbury; but whether the people in any part of our land will recognize and generously protect the "inalienable rights of man," without distinction of color? If this be not done, in Connecticut, where else in our land can we expect it will be done, at least in our day? That it cannot be done even in this State without a struggle is now most shamefully obvious. A year or two since, some benevolent individuals proposed to erect an institution, at New Haven, for the education of colored young men. The design was defeated by violent opposition. If the citizens had opposed merely its location in that City, they might have escaped condemnation, for such a seminary there might have been very prejudicial to Yale College. But it was only too apparent, that their hostility to the institution was peculiarly embittered by their prejudices against the color of those, who were to be educated at it. So too in the case at Canterbury; no one pretends there would have been any opposition to Miss Crandall's school, if her pupils were to be white. The tincture of their skin then it is which has called out all the men of influence in array against her; and has even procured from the freemen of the town an expression of their "unqualified disapprobation" of her plan.

Here then, in Connecticut, we have had two recent instances of outrage committed upon "the inalienable rights of man." Among these rights, to use the language of the Declaration of Indepen-

---

a year with Miss Crandall.

†An offer may have been made to Miss Crandall by responsible individuals to purchase her house, as stated in the Courier; but we beg the public to take notice, that the offer implied an abandonment of the project. No proposal has been made to her to procure her some other suitable situation in lieu of the one she now has. Such a proposal would have been acceded to.

dence "are life, liberty, and the pursuit of happiness." Now Education has from the first, been regarded in this State highly conducive to the private happiness, and the public weal. Yet have our colored brethren been twice angrily denied permission to seek this blessing, to the extent that they have desired. Will the people of Connecticut generally, countenance these violations of our civil and religious principles? If they will, let them no longer claim to be a republican, much less a christian people!

The appeals, you have made in the public newspapers, are very similar to those you urged at the town meeting on the 9th. I trust however they may be shown to rest upon mistakes or prejudices.

Throughout your remarks it was continually implied, and sometimes offensively expressed, that Africans and their descendants are *naturally*, as well as actually, inferior to the white varieties of the human race. This notion has become so prevalent through our country, that I suppose it is generally received as resting upon an indubitable fact; and so few take pains to examine the ground of it. If there were room within the limits, to which I must restrict myself, I could easily lay before you enough of the results of those inquiries, which physiologists have pursued into this matter, to show you that the teaching of our Sacred Scriptures on this point is deserving of so much higher deference, than your prejudices have permitted you to pay to it. Causes enough have been in operation to produce all the varieties of men, which we now behold among the descendants of the primitive pair. I might also adduce many instances of Africans, who under the withering influences which have surrounded their race for the last three hundred years, have yet risen to a considerable elevation in science, literature, and moral excellence. But I shall leave their defence for the present in far abler hands. The Massachusetts Colonization Society at its last Annual Meeting, February 9, was addressed by Hon. Alexander H. Everett, one of the ripest scholars, and most distinguished civilians in our land. Having spoken at some length of the new hopes of Africa, which seem to be kindling in many bosoms, and having pointed out the benefits which may be conferred upon that benighted land by colonies planted there from this country and Europe, he said

"But, Sir, we are sometimes told that the African is a degraded member of the human family—that a man with a dark skin and curled hair is necessarily, as such, incapable of improvement and civilization, and condemned by the vice of his physical conformation to vegetate forever in a state of hopeless barbarism. Mr. President, I reject with contempt and indignation this miserable heresy. In replying to it, the friends of truth and humanity have not hitherto done justice to the argument. In order to prove that the blacks were capable of intellectual efforts, they have painfully collected a few imperfect specimens of what some of them have done in this way, even in the degraded condition which they occupy at present in Christendom. Sir, this is not the way to treat the subject. Go back to an earlier period in the history of our race. See what the blacks were, and what they did, three thousand years ago, in the period of their greatness and glory, when they occupied the fore front in the march of civilization—when they constituted, in fact, the whole civilized world of their time. Trace this very civilization, of which we are so proud, to its origin, and see where you will find it. We received it from our European ancestors:—they had it from the Greeks and Romans, and the Jews. But, Sir, where did the Greeks, the Romans, and the Jews get it? They derived it from Ethiopia and Egypt,—in one word—from Africa. Moses, we are told, was instructed in all the learning of the Egyptians. The founders of the principal Grecian cities—such as Athens, Thebes, and Delphi—came from Egypt, and for centuries afterwards, their descendants returned to that country, as the source and centre of civilization. There it was that the generous and stirring spirits of the time—Herodotus, Homer, Plato, Pythagoras, and the rest, made their noble voyages of intellectual and moral discovery, as ours now make them in England, France, Germany, and Italy. Sir, the Egyptians were the masters of the Greeks and Jews, and consequently of all the modern nations in civilization, and they had carried it very nearly as far—in some respects, perhaps, a good deal further than any subsequent people. The ruins of the Egyptian temples laugh to scorn the architectural monuments of any other part of the world. They will be, what they are now, the delight and admiration of travellers from all quarters, when the grass is growing on the sites of St. Peter's and St. Paul's,—the present pride of Rome and London.

Well, Sir, who were the Egyptians? They were Africans:—and of what race? It is sometimes pretended, that, though Africans, and of Ethiopian extraction, they were not black. But what says the father of history—who had travelled among them, and knew their appearance as well as we know that of our neighbors in Canada? Sir, Herodotus tells you that the Egyptians were blacks, with curled hair. Some writers have undertaken to dispute his authority, but I cannot bring myself to believe, that the father of history did not know black from white. It seems, therefore, for this very civilization of which we are so proud, and which is the only ground of our present claim of superiority, we are indebted to the ancestors of these very blacks, whom we are pleased to consider as naturally incapable of civilization.

So much for the supposed inferiority of the colored race, and their incapacity to make any progress in civilization and improvement.—And it is worth while, Mr. President, to remark, that the prejudice which is commonly entertained in this country, but which does not exist to any thing like the same extent in Europe, against the color of the blacks, seems to have grown out of the unnatural position which they occupy among us. At the period to which I just alluded, when the blacks took precedence of the whites in civilization, science and political power, no such prejudice appears to have existed. The early Greek writers speak of the Ethiopians and Egyptians as a superior variety of the species:—superior, not merely in intellectual and moral qualities, but what may seem to be much more remarkable, in outward appearance. The Ethiopians, says Herodotus, excel all other nations in longevity, stature, and personal beauty.—

The black prince, Memnon, who served among the Trojan auxiliaries at the siege of Troy, (probably an Egyptian prince,) is constantly spoken of by the Greek and Latin writers, as a person of extraordinary beauty, and is qualified as the son of Aurora, or the Morning. There are, in short, no traces of any prejudice whatever against the color of the blacks, like that which has grown up in modern times, and which is obviously the result of the relative condition of the two races. This prejudice forms at present, as was correctly observed by President Madison in one of his speeches in the late Virginia Convention, the chief obstacle to the practical improvement of the condition of that portion of them who reside in this country."

Coming as this testimony does, from a distinguished member of the Colonization Society, I trust it will make some impression upon your mind, and upon the minds of other gentlemen in Canterbury, who have all at once come to take such a deep interest in the operations of that Society.* I have however one word more to say before I leave this topic. If it were true, that the African members of the human family are naturally inferior to others, would not this be a very strong argument with correct reasoners, no less than with benevolent men, in favor of their being aided by peculiar assistance, ay, with every possible facility for improvement? Surely it would be, methinks, unless they can be shown to be *insusceptible* of improvement.

But Sir, that even you do not consider them thus incapable of improvement, is evident enough from what you have said may be done for them, on the other side of the Atlantic. It is then only their being improved in America that you object to. The thought of encouraging or even permitting colored men to rise, if they can, to an equality with us, even us! white ones (who have no doubt departed quite as much as they have from the original complexion of our race)—the thought, that they should ever be partakers with us, even us! in all the privileges of this land of *equal rights*, this is a thought, which seems to have maddened you and other gentlemen who have been preeminent in this region for their *republican* zeal! Surely the heart of man is deceitful above all things!

I shall leave with you what I should say on this point also, in the words of Mr. Everett, who has set forth what I believe to be true, far better than I could.

"I was not, Mr. President—if so humble an individual may be permitted to allude to his own private sentiments, upon a subject of so much interest—I was not, in the first instance, very favorably impressed in regard to the character of this institution. Looking at it as it has been sometimes represented, as intended chiefly to remove from this country the colored portion of the population, I was inclined to consider it as an inadequate instrument for effecting an ob-

---

*I have reason to believe that neither Andrew T. Judson, Esq., nor indeed any of the Civil Authority and Select Men of Canterbury were members of the Colonization Society, or expressed any interest in it, until the excitement against Miss Crandall.

ject in itself impracticable, and which, if it could be effected, would be, after all, of doubtful utility. The pecuniary means at the disposal of the Association never have been, and probably never will be, sufficient to pay the expenses of the transportation to Africa of a tenth part of the annual increase of the colored people. It is quite clear, therefore, that there could be no prospect of ever making any approach in this way, to a removal of the whole mass. And Sir, if this could be effected, why should we desire it? Is there not ample room and verge enough in our vast territory for the population of all colors, classes and descriptions? Is it not our true policy rather, as far as possible, to induce emigration from abroad, than to endeavor to remove two or three millions of our present inhabitants? Whatever may be the case in the crowded countries of the Old World, here at least, thank God, there is no pressure of population upon the means of subsistence. Sir, it is literally true in this country, that the harvest is many and the laborers few. And this being the case, shall the little accident of the different color which it has pleased Providence to give to their complexion, render an entire variety of our fellow-men so odious to us, that we cannot abide them in the same continent? Suppose, Sir, that you or I, or any individual, had it in his power, by a mere act of the will, to change the color of the whole black race to white, would it be a proof of good sense and good feeling to exercise the power? Suppose that an individual had it in his power by an act of the will, to change all the black eyes in this assembly to blue? Would he think it worth while to exercise it? Sir, one of these operations would be just as judicious as the other. The attempt to break down the beautiful variety that pervades all the works of Providence into a tame and monotonous sameness, is every way objectionable. To desire the removal of two millions of our population, merely because their complexion is different from that of the rest, would be inconsistent with any correct principles of taste, morals, or political economy. No Sir, I am quite willing that the colored people should remain with us. What we really ought to desire is, that their present political situation should be improved, that they should be, in the language of Curran, redeemed, regenerated, and disenthralled—that they should be placed, in short, on an equal footing in point of civil and political rights, with all the other inhabitants of our favored country.—This, Sir, is a change which ought to be effected—which must, at some time or other, be effected— which, I have no hesitation in saying, will, at no very distant period be effected."

That my own sentiments are perfectly accordant with Mr. Everett's, you may see in my published discourse, which was delivered July 3d 1831. No one surely will deny, that it is benevolent to provide a retreat on some far distant shore for any of our countrymen, who may wish to escape from oppression at home. But there are many who deny that it is right to make any, even the blackest, wish to emigrate by cherishing our wicked prejudices against them, or withholding from them any of the privileges which our country affords. And there are many too, who have satisfied themselves that it can never be in the power of the Colonization Society to transport so many of our colored brethren every year to the shores of Africa, as to make any sensible dimunition in their numbers; even if so many could be made willing to go. For my own part, I would as soon undertake to remove our Alleghany mountains across the great deep, in any given time, as I would to transport in the same time *two millions, five hundred thousand* human beings with their annual increase of *sixty-two thousand*, and prepare the wilds of Africa for their reception. Sir, there never will be fewer colored people in this land than there are now. They must then be admitted to the full exercise of all their rights, as men, here. The reason, and the only reason why the Colonization Society is losing favor with many true philanthropists in the land, is that sentiments are continually disseminated in its publications, which tend to perpetuate the degradation of our colored brethren, and put further off the day, when they will be permitted freely to enjoy with us the blessings of this favored portion of the earth. For six or eight years past I have been a member of this Society. But I have come to be so doubtful of the tendency of its operations, that I shall probably soon withdraw. Should the late procedure at Canterbury be accepted as promotive of its real objects, sure am I that the worst suspicions that have been awakened of it, would be confirmed in the bosom of every true friend to our colored brethren. But I cannot believe it will be.—Many Colonizationists at the South may perhaps applaud what you have done, and threaten still to do; but there are many in New England who will condemn your proceedings as heartily as I do. Others besides Mr. Everett acknowledge the rights of the colored people to a full participation in the privileges of American citizens; and insist that they ought to be educated. I would particularly refer you to the closing remarks of the review of "Mr. Garrison's Thoughts on Colonization" in the last No. of the Christian Spectator, supposed to have been written by Rev. Mr. Bacon of New-Haven, a zealous member of the Colonization Society.

Had I room I could easily bring forward other sentiments from other gentlemen who are members of the Colonization Society, very little in accordance with those uttered by yourself and others at the meeting, and since published in the Norwich papers. But I must hasten to notice one or two more of your allegations.

It has often been charged upon those, who advocate the abolition of Slavery, that they are aiming to amalgamate the blacks and the whites. This string was harped upon at the town meeting by all the opposers of Miss Crandall. It served to shock the prejudices of the people, and dupe their judgment. The same charge is repeated in the Norwich papers to the same effect, so that I am compelled to take some notice of it. And I now call upon you, and others who have brought this accusation to prove it, if you can. I know and am sure, that such is not one of the intentions or wishes of the Anti Slavery Society, nor of any Abolitionists that I am acquainted with. Of course we do not believe there are any barriers established by God between the two races. If there were any, the complexions of tens of thousands in our land show to our disgrace that those barriers are not impassable. Whether marriages shall or shall not take place between those of different colors, is a matter which time must be left to decide. We do not advocate them, we do not hope to see them, we only say that such connections would be incomparably more honorable to the whites, as well as more consistent with the laws of God, and the virtue of our nation, than that illicit intercourse which is now so common especially at the south.

As to your charge that we advocate the immediate emancipation of the slaves in our country, it is true. We do so from the deep conviction, that few if any sins can be more heinous, than holding fellow men in bondage and degradation; and in the assurance that men cannot leave off sinning too suddenly. So long as we believe there is a wise and good Being presiding over the affairs of men, so long we must believe that it will be safe for men to do right at any moment. Persons who are alarmed at the doctrine of immediate emancipation, forget that the same civil arm which now holds the slaves in bondage would still be stretched over them, when free laborers, to keep them in due subjection to righteous laws. And that when free they may be brought more effectually under the soothing and sanctifying influences of Religion. I am unwilling to pass from this topic without making all the remarks I intended. But I have not room to enlarge.*

By reiterating the charges, I have now been considering, you and your coadjutors succeeded in effecting your purpose. You procured from the inhabitants of Canterbury an expression of their unqualified disapprobation of Miss Crandall's project. But remember Sir, this does not prove that Miss Crandall's project is an unworthy one. Far otherwise. The purest and best undertakings have often been opposed. There are those, who, deeply persuaded of the importance of doing what we may to meliorate the condition of our colored people; and believing that Miss C. is actuated by right motives, will do all in their power (not to injure Canterbury) but to sustain her school. I sincerely hope Sir, that you and your neighbors will see your mistake, and by upholding instead of overthrowing this institution, secure to your town the high praise of being first in this great "labor of Love."

Yours,

SAMUEL J. MAY.

---

*My views are given at some length in my Discourse on "Slavery in the United States."

REPORT

OF THE ARGUMENTS OF COUNSEL,

IN THE CASE OF

PRUDENCE CRANDALL, PLFF. IN ERROR, VS. STATE OF CONNECTICUT,

BEFORE THE

SUPREME COURT OF ERRORS,

AT THEIR SESSION AT BROOKLYN, JULY TERM, 1834.

BY A MEMBER OF THE BAR.

BOSTON:
PUBLISHED BY GARRISON & KNAPP.
1834.

ADVERTISEMENT.

The Legislature of the State of Connecticut, at their annual session in May, 1833, passed an act entitled 'An Act in addition to an Act entitled "An Act for the admission and settlement of Inhabitants in Towns,"' to which was prefixed the following preamble :

'WHEREAS, attempts have been made to establish literary institutions in this State, for the instruction of colored persons belonging to other States and countries, which would tend to the great increase of the colored population of the State, and thereby to the injury of the people : Therefore,

Sec. 1. *Be it enacted by the Senate and House of Representatives, in General Assembly convened,* That no person shall set up or establish in this State any school, academy, or literary institution, for the instruction or education of colored persons, who are not inhabitants of this State, nor instruct or teach in any school, academy, or other literary institution whatsoever in this State, or harbor or board, for the purpose of attending or being taught or instructed in any such school, academy, or literary institution, any colored person who is not an inhabitant of any town in this State, without the consent, in writing, first obtained of a majority of the civil authority, and also of the select-men of the town in which such school, academy, or literary institution is situated ; and each and every person who shall knowingly do any act forbidden as aforesaid, or shall be aiding or assisting therein, shall, for the first offence, forfeit and pay to the treasurer of this State, a fine of one hundred dollars, and for the second offence shall forfeit and pay a fine of two hundred dollars, and so double for every offence of which he or she shall be convicted. And all informing officers are required to make due presentment of all breaches of this act. *Provided,* That nothing in this act shall extend to any district school established in any school society under the laws of this State, or to any school established by any school society under the laws of this State, or to any incorporated academy or incorporated school for instruction in this State.'

[The foregoing is the first Section of the Act referred to, and contains all which is applicable to the present case.]

Miss Crandall was informed against by the prosecuting attorney for the County of Windham for a violation of this Statute, and had her trial on the plea of *not guilty*, before the County Court, August Term, 1833. Her counsel rested the defence on the unconstitutionality of the law. The jury, not being able to agree on a verdict, were dismissed, and the cause was continued to the next Term.

At the following October term of the Superior Court, a new prosecution was commenced against Miss Crandall for a violation of the same Legislative act. She again pleaded *not guilty*, and her defence was rested on the same general grounds as in the County Court. His Honor Chief Justice Daggett, who held the Court, charged the jury that the law was constitutional; blacks not being citizens of the United States within the meaning of the Constitution. The jury rendered a verdict of *guilty*; the defendant's counsel, having tendered a bill of exceptions to the charge of the Judge, filed a motion in Error, and brought the legal questions arising on the record before the Supreme Court of Errors for revision.

REPORT, &c.

STATE OF CONNECTICUT, Windham County, ss. Brooklyn. Supreme Court of Errors, July Term, A. D. 1834.

Present,

Hon. DAVID DAGGETT, *Chief Justice.*
Hon. THOMAS S. WILLIAMS,
Hon. CLARK BISSELL,
Hon. SAMUEL CHURCH, } *Associate Judges.*

Prudence Crandall, plaintiff in error, *vs.* State of Connecticut. Counsel for Miss Crandall, Hon. Calvin Goddard, and Hon. William W. Ellsworth; for the State, Andrew T. Judson, Esq., and Chauncey F. Cleveland, Esq.

Argument of Wm. W. Ellsworth, in the case of the State of Connecticut *vs.* Prudence Crandall. Delivered before the Supreme Court of Errors of the State of Connecticut, July, 1834.

May it please the Court:—The statute on which this prosecution is founded, prohibits the *setting* up a school for persons of color, not inhabitants of this state—teaching them in *any* school, or boarding and harboring them, to attend a school, without first obtaining the consent, in writing, of the civil authority and selectmen of the town where said school is situated.

The record finds, that the pupils in this case were born in the states of Pennsylvania, New-York, and Rhode Island respectively, of free parents, and have recently come into Connecticut, to attend Miss Crandall's school, where they are taught the common and essential branches of knowledge.

The principle asserted in this law, and indeed such is its very language, is, that it is a crime for any individual to entertain a person of color, not having a legal settlement in any town in this state, (though he was born and has ever lived in these states,) having come here to pursue the acquisition of learning, in a manner *open, common*, and *lawful* to *all our* population, white or *colored.* The condition imposed by the law will be found not to alter the character of the law, as I have now asserted it to be. A power to license, implies a power to refuse—what one holds by *permission*, he does not hold by *right*. And if the Legislature can delegate the power to license, it can exercise it, itself; and hence, may impose conditions tantamount to exclusion or total denial. This statute, stripped of its appendages, makes the *place of birth* the criterion of the rights of citizens of these states; it is not a question of *color*, so much as of state *supremacy*; if a state may exclude a colored citizen of another state, it may exclude a white 'citizen.'

The defence of Miss Crandall will be rested upon the unconstitutionality of this statute law of Connecticut, and may be embraced under these two heads.

1. These pupils are *citizens* of their respective states.

2. As *citizens*, the constitution of the United States secures to them the right of *residing* in Connecticut, and pursuing the acquisition of knowledge, as people of color may do, who are settled here.

I would first remark, that if the constitution of the United States does indeed secure to these pupils this most valued right, it must secure the *means* necessary to enjoy the right: if the *pupils* may reside here—be entertained, and taught; it cannot be a crime in others to entertain or teach them. It is familiar law, that the specified powers in the constitution of the United States, contain a grant of all the powers necessary for their execution. A right that can be defeated at pleasure, is no right at all. The constitution of the United States secures to every man a right of trial by jury; but can the state legislatures defeat this object, by making it criminal for any person to act on the jury in the courts of the United States? The aid and co-operation of a teacher is a constituent part of the right secured to these people of color.

Again, if color, in a citizen of New-York, is made the ground, in Connecticut, of political inequality, degradation and deprivation; the principle run out, will justify, at the *pleasure* of our Assembly, a like deprivation among our blacks. If not citizens and protected as such, they are *aliens*—their property may be confiscated, and they be driven out from our borders as Turks or Chinese.

To the first position then.

Are these pupils citizens of their state respectively?

If they were white, it is conceded they would be.

1. A distinction founded in *color*, in fundamental rights, is *novel, inconvenient* and *impracticable.* Hitherto we have seen no such distinction; none in the ancient common law of England which justly boasts of her equal principles; none in that immortal instrument which our republican fathers put forth as the ground-work of all just government—the Declaration of our Independence. There, we read, 'we hold these truths to be self-evident, that all men are created *equal*, that they are endowed by their Creator with certain *unalienable* rights, that among these are life, *liberty*, and the pursuit of happiness.' The constitution of Connecticut too, which this honorable Court, let me now add, have sworn they will defend; declares '*all* men when they enter into the social compact are equal in rights, and that no man or set of men are entitled to exclusive public emoluments or *privileges* from the community.' Whatever difficulties may embarrass courts of justice and halls of legislation where slavery prevails, let *us* not be ashamed of these great land-marks of free government as they are. I trust this distinction of color will not receive a judicial sanction in Connecticut. The sentiments of this law may comport with notions entertained elsewhere, but they are abhorrent to the feelings of freemen and republicans, and they cannot receive countenance in this community.

2. Such were not the ideas of our fathers, when the colored soldier stood in the ranks of that army which achieved for us our liberty; nor when their names were enrolled on the pension list, as many of them were, the testimonial, that *they* had a country and had bled for it.

A declaration like that just now read from the constitution of this state, in the state of Massachusetts, where it is to be found in her constitution, *exterminated* at a blow every vestige of slavery, by the decision of her courts. The distinction of color would be found as *inconvenient* as it is novel. Who can tell the proportions and mixtures of blood? We shall want a scale for the ascertainment of citizenship. In Virginia, in the year 1785, they defined, by law, a mulatto to be a person having at least, *one quarter* negro blood in him. The least taint of it here will exclude from the rank of citizens.

3. These pupils are human beings, born in these states, and owe the *same obligation* to the state and the state's governments, as white citizens.

There is in all the writers of public or municipal law, one ancient and universal classification of the people of a country. Blackstone, Kent, Swift, Dane, Tucker and all others, without exception, Vattel, Martin, Ward, &c., agree in this proposition, 'that all who are born within the jurisdiction of a state are natives, and all others are aliens.' There is not to be found the least trace of any other distinction; no allusion to any as existing in fact, none in principle. It may be true that these writers had not their attention called to the distinction of color, but then, they declare the settled law on this subject, and the reasons of the law: and color no more than stature or age bears a relation to it. The distinction is not alluded to, because it did not exist; nor can it exist, in the nature of things.

The classification grows out of the doctrine of natural allegiance, a tie vacated by *birth*, giving rise to rights and duties between the government and the individual of the gravest importance and most permanent duration. All writers agree in the foundation of allegiance, and in its obligations, while it exists; some holding that it can never be thrown off, and some, that it can, under legislative enactments; but all agreeing that while the residence of the citizen continues, in the state of his birth, allegiance demands obedience from the citizen, and protection from the government. Allegiance is not peculiar to any one government or country; but is held to exist in every country and every government where there are any pretensions to social order and civil institutions. It reaches the man of one complexion as much as that of another: it is held to be the ordination of the great parent of all society, fairly inferrible from the nature and necessity of human governments. If allegiance is due from our colored population, its correlative is due from the government, viz. protection and equal laws. If allegiance is an ordination of heaven, it reaches, and binds and confers rights upon every man, within its range and rightful sway. Here, the free man of color may take his position, and upon the immutable principles of justice and truth demand his political rights, from that government which he is bound to aid and to defend: *he is not a citizen to obey, and an alien to demand protection.* Nor is he of an intermediate class; there is no trace of any such thing, in the history, the laws or institutions of this country. His relations to society are the same as others; his absolute and relative rights; his rights of person, and to things; his acquisitions of property by contract and by inheritance, even the soil, which no alien inherits, are the same: so every requisition of the law, in its civil and criminal provisions, reaches him: so his legal capabilities and his legal obligations are the same.—Every favor or right conferred on the citizens by general legislation reaches *him*;—so every requisition demands *his* obedience. To talk then of a class of non descript people among us, under these circumstances; to make a new classification, of half citizen and half alien, is equally against reason, justice, and policy.

This doctrine of natural allegiance has at various times received the attention of the courts in this country. In the case of Talbot vs. Jonson, 3 Dallas 133, the Supreme Court of the U. States in 1795 went far towards recognizing the doctrine in its fullest extent. So again in 1797, the late Chief Justice Ellsworth and Judge Low, in the case of Isaac Williams, held that their allegiance was *absolute*; their language is, 'the compact between the community and its members was, that the community should protect its members, and that the members should at all times be obedient to the laws of the community and faithful to its defence.'—Cited in 2 Cranch, 82, note. In the case of Murray vs. the Charming Betsey 2 Cranch 64, the Supreme Court of the U. States again pretty plainly intimated a like opinion. So again in 1822, in the case of the Santissima Trinidad, 7 Whea. 283. Chancellor Kent says, from the historical review of the principal discussions in the Federal Courts on this interesting subject, in American jurisprudence, the better opinion would seem to be, that a citizen cannot renounce his allegiance to the U. States without the permission of government, to be declared by law. The same doctrine has been laid down in 20 John. 188. Jackson ex dem Smith vs. Goodell.

We will now pass from the doctrine of natural allegiance, which embraces *all*, without distinction of color, to the constitutions of the native states of these pupils; for the question is, Are they citizens of *those States?* If I am correct thus far, and we do not find in their constitutions any deprivation of fundamental rights attached to color, we may justly say there is no distinction. The 9 art. of the constitution of Pennsylvania declares, 'That all men are born equally free and independent, and have certain inherent and indefeasible rights, among which are those of enjoying and defending life and liberty, of acquiring, possessing and protecting property and reputation, and of pursuing their own happiness.' No slavery nor distinction of color in fundamental rights exists in the land of Penn; not even in the matter of voting, as may be seen from the 1 sec. of art. 3. though as I shall hereafter shew, the right of suffrage and of citizenship, have no natural or necessary connection with each other.

The constitution of New-York contains no general declaration of the rights of the people, unless it may be the 1 sec. of 7 art. 'no *member* of this state shall be disfranchised or deprived of any of the rights or privileges secured to any citizen thereof, unless by the law of the land on the judgment of his peers.' In the matter of voting, the 2 art. declares, that *every* male citizen shall vote, though in the latter part of the same section, property and longer residence are required in the case of a '*colored citizen*,' so specifically called. The constitution of Rhode Island is the charter given them by Charles II. and embraces 'all the people that do or hereafter shall inhabit or be within the same.' I see no distinction in the *constitutional* rights of the people, and as to voting, I understand it is confined, by statute, to freeholders and the oldest sons of freeholders.

Again, there is nothing in the *constitution of the U. States*, nor in the legislation of Congress, to countenance the distinction of color. Let us go back to the articles of confederation: art. 4. sec. 1, is in these words: 'The better to secure and perpetuate mutual friendship and intercourse among the people of the different states in this union, the *free inhabitants* of each of these states, paupers, vagabonds and refugees from justice excepted, shall be entitled to all privileges and immunities of *free citizens* in the several states: and the people in each state shall have free ingress and egress, &c.' Here, then, *all free inhabitants* were included and secured, with the exception of paupers, &c., and secured too, in 'all the privileges and immunities of *free citizens*.' Can we suppose that when the constitution of the U. States was afterwards formed, for the same purpose as already expressed, to make more perfect the union of the states, and to do away more fully the idea of distinct nations here, and omitting too the excepted classes in the articles of confederation, paupers, &c., that the 4 art. 2 sec. of the constitution, which is in these words: 'The citizens of each state shall be entitled to all privileges and immunities of citizens in the several states;' narrowed the classes of the people to be protected from alienage and its consequences; and at once raised up a new species of human beings in these states. The provision of the constitution is very short, but it embraces all that its parent provision did, and more. It is worthy of remark, that after the articles of confederation were reported to the states for their approval, that the state of South Carolina instructed her delegates in Congress to propose an amendment, which was done as appears from the Journal, 25 June, 1778, where we find this entry: 'The delegates from South Carolina being called on, moved the following amendment, in behalf of their state—1st in article 4, between the words free inhabitants, insert, 'white,' passed in the negative, ayes 2; noes 8; divided 1. The colored population, who are free to pursue their interests, come within the salutary effect of this clause in the constitution. It was early discovered that so intimate and intermingled were the people and their interests in these states, separated only by an imaginary law, not unfrequently dividing the same farm and the same neighborhood, that alienage among them could not be endured; hence it was the design of the constitution to make one nation, to the extent of the general powers of the government; to declare a citizen of one state, to be a citizen of every state; and as such, to clothe him with the same fundamental rights, be he where he might, which he acquired by birth in a particular state; hence too we find, that judgments of the states are placed upon the ground of domestic proceedings. Do not our colored population need to be rescued from alienage in the prosecution and protection of their rights and interests, as much as others? They are in number, by the last census, 319,599. Some of them are possessed of property, and all of them of the same general rights with other citizens.

Again, by the constitution of the United States, color is no disqualification or impediment to naturalization. Congress can as well naturalize Asiatics, South Americans, Africans, as Europeans. There is no *constitutional* distinction — all aliens can be adopted; but if our own colored population are not already citizens, they cannot be made so by Congress, and are worse than foreigners.

Again, *all free* persons alike constitute the *representative* mass of the people. The language of the constitution is, 'Representatives and direct taxes shall be apportioned among the several states which may be included in this Union, according to their respective numbers, which shall be determined by adding to the whole number of *free persons*,' &c., art. 1. sec. 2. The represented mass is the true source of sovereignty; to them is due the allegiance and service of the citizens.

Again, Does not the judicial as well as the legislative power of the constitution extend to people of color? Among others, the judicial power is declared to extend to 'controversies between a state' and 'citizens of another state: between citizens of different states: between citizens of the same state claiming lands under grants from different states; and between a state or the citizens thereof, and foreign states, citizens or subjects.' Now, I ask if a man of color in New-York or Pennsylvania should sue a white citizen of Connecticut in their Federal Court, would it be a good plea in abatement that one of the parties is a man of color? Art. 3. sec. 2.

So the act of Feb. 21, 1799, granting patents for useful improvements, authorizes the issuing of a patent only to a 'citizen'—Cannot a man of color obtain one?—Such has been done, and he would be a bold officer, who should refuse one, on the ground of color. The act of 1831, on the subject of copy-right, is of the same character.

So the act of December 31, 1792, concerning the registering and recording of ships or vessels. It is enacted, that no vessel shall be considered or treated as an American vessel, unless she is *owned and commanded* by an 'American citizen;' — men of color have owned vessels, and they have always been considered American vessels.

So the act of Feb. 18, 1793, for enrolling and licensing vessels for the coasting trade and the fisheries, a like oath must be taken by the owner, before she can be permitted to engage in the same — a 'citizen' only, can do it; but cannot, and have not men of color?

So the militia law uses the words, *white* male citizens; implying that there are other citizens besides white ones; for else the word citizens would have been used. It is true colored people are exempt from military duty, but so are all persons under 18 or over 45, and all females; but, yet, Congress can call *all these* into the army or navy, or militia; and none will contend that exemption from military service proves political inferiority.

So the act of May 15, 1820, makes it criminal for a '*citizen*' to engage in the slave-trade. Can people of color do it? And yet penal laws are construed strictly.

So the act of May 28, 1796, for the relief

and protection of American seamen, declares that any '*citizen*' sailor can obtain from the custom house officer, a certificate of his citizenship; men of color have often done this, and can again.

So the act of July 20, 1790, for the regulation of seamen in the merchant's service, provides, that every ship or vessel belonging to a '*citizen* or *citizens*' of the U. States, of a certain burthen, on a foreign voyage, shall, under a severe penalty, be provided with a medicine chest. Are not men of color bound to comply with this law?

So all the intercourse laws with the Indians, where they forbid any '*citizen*,' from trading with the Indians without license, evidently reach people of color.

So it is worthy of remark that all our treaties with foreign nations, use the words *citizen of the United States*, as touching all our inhabitants, either in the imposition of new duties or the grant of new privileges.

These cases are enough to show that Congress, in its legislation, does not recognise the distinction of color; and I will venture to say that there is no case, where the word '*citizen*' is used in the laws of these states, but people of color are included, however penal and severe are its sanctions. Now all this would be inconsistent with the idea that people of color are not citizens, but constitute a new class of human beings, neither one thing nor another.

Again, when Missouri was admitted into the Union, there was a clause in her constitution *requiring* her legislature to pass a law to prohibit free negroes and mulattoes from coming into the state. Congress required, as a condition of her admission, that no law should be passed to keep out of the state any citizens of the U. States; this, though not decisive, is strong evidence of the sense of Congress, as to the character of people of color. Sarg. Con. Law. 385.

Looking, then, to the doctrine of natural allegiance—the articles of confederation—the constitution of the U. States—the legislative declarations of Congress—the treaties of the nation—the constitutions of the three states, in which these pupils were born, or the general sense of the country as to all free people; there is no reason to believe these pupils are not citizens in their birthplace—and, if citizens there, then by the constitution of the U. States they are entitled to 'all the immunities and privileges of the citizens of Connecticut,' under like circumstances. I might say, perhaps, *any* citizens, but I have no occasion to ask for more than is in this state allowed to our colored population; as by our constitution, colored people, born here, cannot vote; and hence, to that extent, we make a distinction founded on color. I have no occasion to put a colored citizen of New-York, on higher ground than our own, and therefore, I add, 'under like circumstances.'

If it were important to prove that colored people born in Connecticut are citizens, I should urge the same considerations as already stated; and further, I should urge some provisions in our constitution, viz. art. 1, sec. 1, 'that all men are equal in rights,' which is no fiction, but a solemn declaration, clear in its meaning, and to its full extent binding on this Court. I contend for equality in the political sense of the word, i. e. according to such circumstances as we have power to control. In theory we are all equal, and we must conform to that rule of action as far as we possibly can.

So in section 5th, 'Every *citizen* may freely speak with and publish his sentiments on all subjects, being responsible for the abuse of that liberty.

So in section 16th, The '*citizens* have a right in a peaceable manner to assemble for their common good, and to apply to those invested with the power of government for redress of grievances or other proper provisions by petition, address or remonstrance.'

So in section 17th, 'Every *citizen* has a right to bear arms in defence of himself and the state.'

Do not all these privileges and securities extend to the colored population? But they extend only to *citizens*, and not to any mongrel intermediate class, if there be any.

So in that part of the constitution, which speaks of the elective franchise; art. 6, sec. 2, the words are, 'every *white* male citizen,' the word white is superfluous, if there are none but white citizens.*

---

* In the state of New-York, in the convention held in 1821 to form a new constitution, the question was made, whether colored persons should not be denied the elective franchise; the determination was *on principle of right, to allow it to them.* In the progress of the discussion, we find the sentiments of some of the most distinguished citizens of that state. *Mr. Jay* says, 'Why, Sir, are these men to be excluded from rights which they possess in common with their countrymen? What crime have they committed, for which they should be punished? Why are they, who were born as free as ourselves, natives of the same country, and deriving from nature and our political institutions, the same rights and privileges which we have, now to be deprived of all those rights, and doomed to remain as aliens forever among us?' 'I would submit whether the proposition to withhold this right is not contrary to the constitution of the United States.' *Mr. Clarke* says, 'The people of color are capable of giving their consent, and ever since the formation of our government, they have constituted a portion of the people from whence your legislators have derived their 'just powers,' and by retaining that word, (i. e. white, the word of exclusion) you deprive a large and respectable number of the people of this state of privileges and rights which they have enjoyed in common with us, ever since the existence of our government, and to which they are justly entitled.

'In the war of the revolution these people helped to fight your battles by land and by sea. Some of

2

We will next consider the objections urged against us.

1st. Men of color cannot vote in Connecticut, and therefore they are not citizens of Connecticut.

Well, they can vote in Pennsylvania and New-York; if voting then is the criterion of citizenship, they are citizens there: besides, it appears from the constitutions of the states here before me, that colored people can vote in Maine, Massachusetts, Vermont, New Hampshire, New York, New Jersey, Pennsylvania, Delaware, Maryland, North Carolina, and Tennessee.

But again, voting is not the criterion of citizenship; it has no natural or necessary connection with it. Cases may occur where persons vote who are not citizens, and where persons are citizens and do not vote. Few men contend for universal and absolute suffrage. The right of choosing one's rulers is a valuable right; but perhaps it is not a natural so much as an artificial one, originating in, and regulated by, the sense of the community in which we live. Many considerations enter into its existence and enjoyment; such as age, property, residence, paying taxes, doing military duty. The right is founded in notions of internal police, varying and shifting every where, even in the same government; whereas citizenship grows out of allegiance which is every where the same, and is unchanging. Persons sometimes vote for one branch of the government only, as was lately the case in New York. *How much* of a citizen was such a voter? Once property was a necessary qualification in Connecticut. Were none but persons of property citizens? None but freeholders and the eldest sons of freeholders can vote in Rhode Island, at this time. Are they alone citizens? Suppose a voter in Connecticut should lose his right of suffrage by reason of criminal conduct, as the law declares he shall, does he cease to be a *citizen?* Does he become an *alien?* What is he? No female can vote, nor any minor, but are they not *citizens?*

2d. What confusion, if voting makes a citizen—the same *man*, in one state, is a full citizen; in another, half a citizen; in another, a non descript; in another, an alien. Now how absurd to create such distinctions in these states; and besides, of two colored men in New-York, one having property to vote, and one not, and otherwise just alike; one is a citizen and the other not—a father is a citizen, his son a non descript.

Again, if voting is the criterion of citizenship, then every person who has been naturalized, has a right to vote, for he is a citizen; but he cannot, of course, and must be qualified in other particulars. So the widow and children of a person who dies after he has applied for naturalization, but before he has obtained it, are declared citizens at once.

Suppose a state should allow a foreigner to vote who is not a citizen, he does not thereby become a citizen, for Congress only can make him such by a general law. The truth is, voting and citizenship have no natural relation to each other. If voters only are citizens, then we have twenty-four rules of citizenship in the U. States, and these are shifting from day to day, according to the notions of a dominant party, in every state.

I am by no means satisfied that the right of suffrage is one of the fundamental rights secured by the 4th art. of the constitution of the U. States. I will not say it is not, because if we qualify it, by giving it to the citizen of another state in *like circumstances with our own citizen*, we shall not be embarrassed by admitting that it is; but the rights of persons and of things do not seem to me necessarily to embrace the right of suffrage; and these are the privileges and immunities meant in the constitution.

On the trial below, the Chief Justice drew an argument against our idea of a 'citizen,'

---

your states were glad to turn out corps of colored men, and to stand shoulder to shoulder with them. In your late war, they contributed largely towards some of your most splendid victories. On lakes Erie and Champlain, where your fleets triumphed over a foe superior in numbers, and engines of death, they were manned in a large proportion with men of color. And in this very house, in the fall of 1814, a bill passed receiving the approbation of all the branches of your government, authorizing the governor to accept the services of a corps of 2000 free people of color.' *Chancellor Kent* says, 'We did not come to this convention to *disfranchise* any portion of the community, or to take away their rights. Suppose a negro owning a freehold, and entitled to vote in Vermont, removes to this state, can we constitutionally exclude him from enjoying that privilege?' 'There is much difficulty in the practical operation of such a principle—what shall be the criterion in deciding against the different shades of color? The Hindoo and Chinese are called yellow—the Indian red.—Shall these be excluded, should they come to reside among us? Great efforts were now making in the Christian world, to enlighten and improve their condition, and he thought it inexpedient to erect a barrier that should exclude them forever from the enjoyment of this important right.' *Mr. King* says, 'As certainly as the children of any white men are citizens, so certainly the children of the black men are citizens.' *Mr. Van Vechten* says, 'These electors are freemen, and have been recognized as *citizens* of the state, nearly half a century; have under the sanction of our laws and constitution duly acquired the legal qualifications of electors.' 'It seems that some gentlemen entertain doubts whether any of our own people of color are, in a legal sense, citizens, but those doubts were in his opinion unfounded. We are precluded from denying their citizenship, by our uniform recognition for more than forty years; nay, some of them were citizens when this state came into political existence, partook in our struggle for freedom and independence, and were incorporated into the body politic at its creation. As to their degradation, that had been produced by the injustice of white men, and it does not become those who have acted so unjustly towards them, to urge the result of that injustice as a reason for perpetuating their degradation.'

from Doctor Webster's dictionary. I do not believe it was the intention of Mr. Webster to use the word in any technical *legal sense*, as is most evident from all his definitions taken together. Gen. Jackson, at the battle of New Orleans, addressed the blacks as 'fellow citizens'; so the mayor of the city of New York, in his recent proclamation, called upon all the 'citizens' to aid in suppressing the mob; neither of them attached any *exact* meaning to the word. These are Webster's definitions, viz.

1st. The native of a City, or an inhabitant who enjoys the freedom and privileges of the City in which he resides. The freeman of a City, as distinguished from a foreigner, or one not entitled to its franchises.

2d. A Townsman; a man of trade, not a gentleman.

3d. An inhabitant; a dweller in a City, Town or place.

4th. In a general sense, a native or permanent resident in a City or Country.

5th. In the U. States, a person native or naturalized, who has the privilege of exercising the elective franchise, or the qualifications which enable him to vote for rulers, and to *purchase and hold real estate.*

'If the citizens of the U. States should not be free and happy, the fault will be entirely their own.' Washington.

This last definition, though it *excludes* these pupils, if voting and holding real estate, be the criterion, it excludes all white men, who are not voters—all minors and all women. Now, it is certain, General Washington did not use the word 'citizen,' in such a sense.

See Johnson and Walker's definitions.

1st. A freeman of a City.

2d. A Townsman.

3d. An Inhabitant.

Again, it is said Indians are not citizens, and hence an argument is drawn against us.

1st. These pupils are not Indians.

2d. Indians have hitherto been treated as members of national tribes, in alliance with the U. States, according to treaty stipulations and the intercourse law. They have been held to be without the *practical* jurisdiction of the states. But since Congress has withdrawn their ancient jurisdiction, and the states have extended theirs over these tribes, it is not certain what is the exact political character of an Indian born in these states. Even in New-York, before the late change in our Indian affairs, they were there decided to be 'citizens,' by a unanimous opinion of their Supreme Court, on the ground of the State having jurisdiction, and the Indians owing allegiance. 20 John. 191. 2. 3.

Again, it is said, slaves are not citizens.

These pupils are not slaves. The reason why slaves are not citizens is, because they are held to be '*property*,' and not men; and hence, have not freedom of choice or action. The reason does not reach these pupils. Color is not the difficulty.

It is said, that in some of the states, we find laws prohibiting the intermarriage of whites and blacks. The law is a wise one; but then it proves nothing. Which party does it declare is inferior? Marriage and citizenship have no relation to each other—they are founded upon and regulated by different considerations. The legislature have a right, (if they please to exercise it,) to regulate marriage according to age, or property, or profession, or color. Citizenship is founded in the tie of natural allegiance.

Chancellor Kent was cited against us, below. 2 Kent's Com. 39. 71. 2;—but there is nothing in his books to sanction the objection.

This is all I have to say upon the first point. I will next consider the second, viz.: That these pupils are, by the 4th art. of the constitution of the U. States secured in the right for which they are now contending. The language of the provision in the constitution is as follows:—'The citizens of each state shall be entitled to all privileges and immunities of citizens in the several states.' 4 art. 2 sec.

In the consideration of this question, we may lay out of the case, the matter of color; it is really a question of constitutional control, or the obligation of a state to abide by the constitution as the supreme law of the land. If we may *regulate* one citizen of another state out of our territory, we may another; making color or any other circumstances the rule, as it may please our legislature. If we may expel these colored citizens of New-York to-day, we may the white youth of New-York, in Yale College, tomorrow.

1st. The clear intent of this section is, to do away the character and consequences of *alienage*, among the citizens of these United States, to the extent of the reciprocity of the privileges and immunities secured, be they what they may. To *this* extent a citizen of any state, is a citizen of *every* state. In the language of Judge Story, (3 Story's Com. 674,) 'the intention of this clause is to confer on them, if one may so say, a *general citizenship*, and communicate all the privileges and immunities which the citizens of the same state would be entitled to under the like circumstances.' If citizenship in a particular state, secures immunities and privileges, so by the constitution a citizen of another state, may hold up the broad shield of this instrument to repel every attack founded upon *alienage*. All are, as it were, members of one government, one state. And now let it not be forgotten, that whatever these immunities and privileges are, they are solemnly *secured* and *guarantied* by the constitution; and let me add, it is the clear duty of this enlightened Court to see they are made so to these pupils, if citizens, as I have contended they are.

It was admitted, by the Court below, that the right of education is a *fundamental right;* and will it be questioned here? The Pope of Rome and the despots of Turkey may do it, but it will not be done in Connecticut. What right so justly valued by us? What so much applauded as the peculiar honor of our state, and so liberally secured and widely extended by the very constitution itself? How do the nations of the earth set in darkness for the want of it? and tyrants and despots and chieftains reign over mankind, through their ignorance and their superstition? *Education* is the first and fundamental pillar on which our free institutions rest, and it is the last privilege *we* will give up. And here let me add, that the restrictions of this law are exceedingly onerous and distressing to the parents of these pupils; shut out as these children are virtually from the schools of white persons, they have *retired* to a place by themselves, in deference to the prevailing prejudice against them—here they have sought out a virtuous and competent teacher to instruct them in the common branches of education, spelling, reading, arithmetic, geography and the like; —their parents are able to do this—many of them are wealthy, and they feel, that by education their children will be happier and better fitted for usefulness among their depressed fellows, either here, or in Liberia. And who, *who* will rise up to oppose this effort? Let our opponents act openly; let them pass a law to immure in like ignorance the colored population of our own state, and not attempt the same thing, by selecting the blacks of other states, under the pretence that educating them will fill our state with a vicious and pauper population. The moral sentiments of this community will not sanction the idea that a man of color shall not have, like others, the *right* to direct, according to his ability, the education of his children. Mr. Wilberforce, aided by several benevolent individuals, established a seminary for colored people at Clapham, a short distance from London. Miss Crandall need not be ashamed to imitate his example. The people of this country forced the ancestors of our colored population from Africa; they have since kept their descendants in bonds and darkness, and now talk of *right*, founded on the color and degradation of the negro, as a justification for continued wrong, and the deprivation, this day attempted, on principle and morality.

Need I tell this honorable Court, that we owe a debt to the colored population of this country, which we can never pay,—no, *never*, *never*, unless we can call back oceans of tears, and all the groans and agonies of the middle passage, and the thousands and millions of human beings, whom we have sent, and are sending, ignorant, debased and undone, to eternity.

In the 4 Wash. Ci. Ct. R. 380. Canfield *vs.* Cargell, we have the following remarks of the Court, delivered by Washington the presiding Judge, upon the clause of the constitution now in question.' 'The next question is, whether this act (a law of New Jersey) infringes that section of the constitution which declares, 'that the citizens of each state shall be entitled to all the privileges and immunities of citizens in the several states.' 'The inquiry is, what are the privileges and immunities, of citizens in the several states?' 'We feel no hesitation in confining these expressions to those privileges and immunities, which are in their nature fundamental, which belong of right to the citizens of all free governments; and which have at all times been enjoyed, by the citizens of the several states which compose this Union, from the time of their becoming free, independent and sovereign. What these fundamental principles are, it would, perhaps, be more tedious than difficult to enumerate. The right of a citizen of one state to pass through or *reside* in any other state, for purposes of *trade, agriculture, professional pursuits*, or *otherwise*, are among the rights secured.' These and many others which might be mentioned, are, strictly speaking, privileges and immunities, and the enjoyment of them by the citizen of each state, in every other state, was manifestly calculated, (to use the expressions of the preamble of the corresponding provision in the articles of confederation,) 'the better to secure and perpetuate mutual friendship and intercourse among the people of the different states of the Union.'

So in 3 Story's Com. 674, we read, 'The provision in the constitution is plain and simple in its language, and its object is not easily to be misunderstood. Connected with the exclusive power of naturalization in the general government, it puts at rest many of the difficulties which affected the construction of the articles of confederation. It is obvious if the citizens of each state were to be deemed aliens to each other, they could not take or hold real estate, or other privileges, except as other aliens. The intention of this clause was to confer on them, if one may so say, a general citizenship, and communicate all the privileges and immunities which the citizens of the same state would be entitled to under the like circumstances.'

Chancellor Kent, 2 Kent's Com. 61, says, 'If citizens of one state remove to another, they are entitled to the privileges that persons of the same description are entitled to in the state to which the removal is made, and to none other. If, therefore, for instance, free persons of color are not entitled to vote in Carolina; free persons of color emigrating there from a northern state, would not be entitled to vote. The laws of each state ought and must govern within its jurisdiction, and the laws and usages of our state cannot be permitted to prescribe qualifications for citizens, to be claimed and exercised in other states in contravention to their local policy.'

From a consideration of these authorities, and from a perusal of the clause in the constitution, we must admit—

1st. That a citizen of another state, may come here to *reside*, without being fined, whipped, or laid under peculiar exactions: this right is secured to him, if any thing is secured. He must have a right to do what our citizens may do, under like circumstances. But if he may come here to reside, it would seem to follow, that he may do as others may do, else why come at all? Like others, he may engage in agriculture, trade, or a profession, or bind himself out to learn a trade. Can he be compelled, merely because he is not *born here*, to obtain leave of the town, to come or remain here? If they may give leave, they may *withhold* it, and what becomes of the right? It is no *right*, but a *favor*. If he may not educate his children as others may do, it is no *right*, whatever else is allowed him. If immunities and privileges are the same, then a law founded on the distinction of birth in another state, is in the teeth of the constitution. May not a citizen remove to Ohio, and there live and act as other citizens do? Could the Ohio legislature say to him, you are an alien, we will prescribe the *size of your farm*, the *manner of its cultivation*, and *the mode of teaching your children*, while others are excepted? Can we raise a barrier against the people of Massachusetts because *they are people of Massachusetts*? and may they not come in and settle among us and pursue husbandry, merchandize, manufactures, the arts or acquisition of knowledge, without getting license from the town or legislature? The law must be alike and general, or there is an end of equal privileges and immunities.

Now, what is the law under consideration? It forbids a citizen of another state from coming here, to pursue education, as all others may do, *because* he has not a *legal settlement in the state*. It is a crime to feed him, to teach him, or entertain him, and it might be made equally so to sell a farm or rent a house to him, or in any way to aid a citizen of another state, who wished to establish himself in Connecticut. This power of regulating because of *alienage*, is virtually a power of *exclusion*, and in this case is, in effect, and was designed so to be. As well might the legislature, in order to raise up a more beautiful or vigorous generation of citizens, prohibit the harboring or entertaining of any citizen from the other states, who was not six feet high, or had not a well proportioned body, or black eyes, or a clear skin. In the case of M. Culloch *vs.* State of Maryland, the 4 Whea. 431. Chief Justice Marshall says, in giving the opinion of the Court, 'that the power to tax, involves the power to destroy; that the power to destroy may defeat and render useless the power to create; that there is a plain repugnance, in conferring on one government a power to control the constitutional measures of another, which other, with respect to those very measures, is declared to be supreme over that which exerts the control, are propositions not to be denied. But all inconsistencies are to be reconciled by the magic of the word *confidence*,' &c. If the power claimed does exist, then I say, the legislature has power to *regulate* every white youth at Yale College, being citizens of other states, out of our borders, as *aliens*. The question is not one of color, but of power, to be exercised according to the *pleasure* of the legislature. If indeed this power exists, such persons can just as well be prohibited all *entrance* into the state, as be removed or *regulated* away after they have come here.

But it is asked,—May we not keep out of Connecticut, paupers and vagabonds, and have we not such laws of long standing?

There is an excellent provision in our statute book, (to be found in the present edition, at page 281,) authorizing the civil authority of each town to issue a warrant for the removal, *out of the state*, of every person not a citizen of Connecticut, who comes to reside in it, and if need be, to follow up this order by whipping, nor shall any such person be here entertained, without the entertainer first gives security to the town, that the individual shall never become chargeable to the town. The present law contains a like provision for removing.

As to this ancient statute, my first remark is, that it was enacted before the adoption of the articles of confederation, or the present constitution of the United States; when this state had a right to exclude the citizens of other states or colonies, for they then stood in no other relation than *aliens*. I find these provisions in an edition of laws as early as 1750.

My second remark is, that this law is contrary to the constitution of the United States, and I am quite confident it cannot be sustained. If the 4 art. sec. 2, means any thing, it does secure to a citizen of New-York a right to come here, and *remain* here, if he offends against no general law: he cannot be whipped out nor carried out of the state because he has no legal settlement:

he may present the shield of the constitution, and as Paul claimed the immunity of a Roman citizen, he may claim the immunity of an *American* citizen. The legislature may declare that such an one shall not gain a legal settlement, nor can it be forced to burden the public treasury with the support of a foreign citizen; for indeed the whole matter of settlement, and supporting any paupers, is of mere municipal regulation; but it can go no further, and may leave whoever it pleases to private charity or public munificence. It cannot be, that every citizen of another state may be expelled from our territory, even though most excellent and desirable, because he or his posterity, in some *remote generation*, may become poor, and when they are so, the state may do as it pleases in supporting them: *this is a repeal of the constitution.* Neither present nor future poverty can strike out of the constitution the word 'citizen,' and a 'citizen' has a universal right, title and immunity, to a *residence*, and other fundamental rights. So the state may guard itself against thieves from without or within, by punishing them for crimes committed in our territory, or enacting *general* laws of prevention—but I deny that it can prohibit a '*citizen of the United States*' from entering this state and remaining in it, because he *has* offended elsewhere, or *may* offend again. If he has fled from justice and is demanded, *under the constitution*, he must be delivered up, but while he is here, unoffending, the state cannot drive him out, nor make it penal to supply his necessities *here:* it could, were it not for the constitution of the U. States: *he is a citizen, and that is his protection.*

We may learn much by looking at the articles of confederation, and the alteration of the same, in the particulars under consideration. In the articles, 'paupers, vagabonds and fugitives from justice,' are excepted, in the security of the immunities and privileges secured to other citizens; but in the constitution they are *all left out ;* and a provision is made for delivering up 'fugitives from justice;' the others are placed on the same footing with citizens, and so are fugitives, until they are demanded. Now, this power of state police, of expelling all citizens of other states, just according to the notions of our legislature in raising up a particular population, is a restoration to the constitution of the U. States the *very excepted classes in the articles of confederation ;* indeed, it is going much further, for it is making the entrance and residence of a citizen of another state, here, dependent upon the notions and pleasure of our own legislature.

The language of the constitution, art. 4. sec. 2, is *universal* and *unqualified :* it says *every* citizen. Apprehension of pauperism or crime, pretended or real, cannot be made the ground of *exclusion* or removal.

Indeed, the impracticability of carrying the exceptions, in the articles of confederation into effect, is reason enough for their relinquishment. Who is a pauper, or vagabond? What is the criterion of such a condition? At what exact time must it exist? Must the person be such when he comes, before, or after? And what are his rights in the mean time? Must he have made application to some public officer for relief? And as to refugees, suppose a person in South Carolina has broken a law which forbids him to teach his slaves to read, and flees here, but is not pursued, are we to mark him as an offender, and treat him as an alien? Were it not for the constitution, we would no more deliver him up, than we would one of the noble Poles, lately landed on our shores, fleeing from imperial resentment. Of all, *all* citizens, I say, they are in *their* country, be they in it where they will: they have one *common tie*, one *allegiance*, and one citizenship. But while it is urged that the state has power to pass the law now complained of, it should be remembered that it does not propose to keep paupers or colored citizens *out* of this state; this would have been too bold—hence they may come here, but they shall not be *educated*, for fear we shall have a dangerous and vicious population!

But it is asked, may not the legislature superintend our schools, and has not this always been done?

I do not doubt, but that the legislature may superintend public schools; for they are instituted by the legislature, and sustained by public money: nor do I doubt, but that the legislature may superintend and regulate private schools, as it does trades, professions, taverners, merchants, and may *all* the pursuits of the citizens; but then this must be done by a general and equal law. Mere *birth* in another state cannot be seized upon, as ground of distinction, discrimination and deprivation;—this is alienage, and is not consistent with the paramount authority, 'that the citizens of each state shall be entitled to all privileges and immunities of citizens in the several states.' Can we say that no man shall be a lawyer, or doctor, or farmer, *because* he was born in Massachusetts?

It is said a law like this has been in force in Ohio, for some years. The provisions of that law, I do not know, nor can I learn that they have ever received the sanction of judicial authority; and I trust they never will. There was a law like this in South Carolina, and the Circuit Court of the United States, there, held it unconstitutional and void; but as the colored persons there, were taken out of an English ship, I do not know but our treaty with England had some influence upon the decision, though I do not know that it had.

The truth is, there is nothing in the settled law of any free state in the Union to countenance the provisions of this obnoxious law. Enough, however, may be found in the statutes of the slave states. For instance, the legislature of Louisiana have enacted, 'that whosoever shall make use of language, in any public place, from the bar, the bench, the pulpit, the stage, or in any *other place whatsoever*, shall make use of language in any private discourses, or shall make use of *signs* or actions, having *a tendency* to produce *discontent* among the colored population, shall suffer imprisonment at hard labor, not less than *three years*, nor more than *twenty-one years*, or *death*, at the *discretion* of the Court.' It has also prohibited the instruction of blacks in *Sabbath Schools*, $5C0 for the *first* offence, *Death* for the second. Our law imposes a penalty of $100 for teaching a colored person in a *Sabbath School*, (having no legal settlement in this state) and $200 for the second offence. In Virginia, 'all meetings of free negroes, at any school house or *meeting house* for teaching them writing or *reading*,' are declared an unlawful assembly. These laws are all of a kindred character; they call for universal denunciation, and well may we fear, that a righteous God will not let them pass unheeded or unrevenged. And how, let me ask, can excitement be kept down, in the North, while such *bloody* and cruel laws are enforced against human beings like ourselves, of the same feelings, destiny, and hopes? I regret most deeply, that the legislature of Connecticut should give any countenance to such laws, and such notions, and add to the darkness that rests upon these neglected minds. The passage of the law in question, in Connecticut, so distinguished for her republican feeling, and her attachment to universal education, has been a matter of astonishment and unfeigned sorrow throughout this country: nor has it escaped the notice and regret of the people in England. It was an unlucky hour when it was devised and passed—passed inconsiderately, I doubt not.

The general policy of this law, as well as its connection with the subject of slavery,—that greatest curse and blight upon our country, and the greatest wrong ever done in our world,—though matters of deep and everlasting interest to us, to our children, to our free institutions, cannot, I am aware, be properly discussed here. The law is not denied for its impolicy, but for its *unconstitutionality*. Had I been a member of the legislature, I should have raised my voice against it. It is a most wanton and uncalled for attack upon our colored population; it opens wounds not easily healed; it exasperates to madness many who live among us; it strengthens the unreasonable prejudice already pervading the community against blacks;—and, in short, it rivets the chains of grinding bondage, and makes *our State* an ally in the unholy cause of slavery itself. Deep, deep, are the feelings this moment pervading the slave states. The moral example of England in her late act of emancipation,—the practical effects of the emancipation of her slaves in the West Indies; the injustice and high offence against heaven of slavery itself, are spreading a gloom over the South, more awful and foreboding than nullification ten times told. Nor do I see, I am pained to say, any serious movements for melioration or relief in *that* quarter. Slavery is a volcano, the fires of which cannot be quenched, nor its ravages controlled. We already feel its convulsions; and if we sit idly gazing upon its flames, as they rise higher and higher, our happy republic will be buried in ruin, beneath its overwhelming energies.

Mr. Judson commenced the argument for the State, in substance, as follows:—

At the trial of this cause, before the Hon. Chief Justice, in the Court below, the facts having been proved, the counsel for the defendant interposed a claim, that the Statute upon which the information was founded, was a violation of the constitution of the U. S. The Chief Justice in his charge, did not recognize this claimer, but instructed the jury that the law in question, was constitutional. The jury returned their verdict against the defendant, and for this cause, a *new trial* is sought, by the motion in error.

The original claim of the defendant is still maintained by her learned counsel, and we are referred to the first clause of the second section of the fourth article of the constitution of the U. S. as the ground of defence. It shall be my humble effort to maintain that the law in question is constitutional, and the magnitude of the question will assure to me a patient hearing. Although this question may be one of vital importance to the town of Canterbury, yet that interest is by no means confined to that town. Should this law be prostrated, this corporation may be prostrated too—the people may be driven away from their homes, and then the evils will but just commence. It is a question in which every town in *this State*, and every State in this Union, have an equal interest. Let the decision be against this law—let those principles so ingeniously urged by my worthy opponent, be once established by the judiciary, the consequences will inevitably destroy the government itself, and this *American Nation*—this nation of white men, may be taken from us, and given to the African race! In this question is involved the honor of the State—the dignity of its people—and the preservation of its name.

The law provides that no school shall be set up for the instruction of persons of color, who are not inhabitants of this State, without a license from the civil authority and selectmen of the town, and whosoever entertains any such persons, for that object, shall be subject to the penalty of the act. The objects of this law are plain. The first object of this law is, to regulate schools for colored persons, coming from other governments, and putting them under a *Board of Visitors;* and 2d, if the keepers of such schools will not submit to such regulations, then to exclude them as a dangerous and destructive population.

My first proposition is, that this State does possess the power to regulate its own schools, and pursue its own systems of education, in its own chosen way, independent of the question of citizenship. The matter of *education* was never given up to the General Government, because the structure, object, and end of that government were of a different character. The government has never attempted any control over *education*, in any one State in the Union, but only in the District of Columbia. The State governments have uninterruptedly exercised this power, and their capacities to do so will be found much more congenial, than that of the General Government. We ought to be satisfied that the State sovereignties maintain their internal police--their domestic arrangements, while the General Government moves on in its elevated sphere of action.

If the claims here set up are indeed to become the order of the day, we shall have a government of *consolidation* in good earnest.

It has ever been the policy of this State, to regulate all its *schools*, *academies*, and *colleges*, and subject them to a strict *visitorial power.* The seeds of morality and virtue are first sown in our schools, and if neglected, the seeds of vice and immorality soon spring up, and would undermine all that we hold dear, even the government itself. If in Connecticut we have any renown, it is because our fathers have watched over the education of youth with becoming solicitude. As early as the year 1717, a statute was passed by the General Assembly, establishing a *Board of Visitors*, such as this act contemplates. The act is in these words.

'The civil authority, together with the Selectmen, in every town, or the major part of them, shall inspect, and they are hereby empowered and directed as visitors, to inspect the state of all such schools as are, by this act, appointed to be kept within said town, from time to time, and particularly once in each quarter of a year, and enquire into the qualifications of masters. And they are to give such directions, as they shall find needful to render such schools most serviceable for the increase of knowledge, religion, and good manners. And if said inspectors or visitors observe any *such disorders*, or misapplication of money allowed for the support of such schools, as will be likely to defeat the good ends proposed, they shall lay the same before this Assembly that proper orders therein may be given.'

This law continued in force until 1795, when the present system was adopted, and a *new board* was instituted, less burthensome to the people. The law in question goes back to the early policy of the State, and takes the civil authority and Selectmen, as the proper board under this act. Every *college*, and every incorporated Academy in this State, have established a board of visitors, and this is not deemed a violation of the constitution. It is essential to good order, and the prosperity of these institutions, that it should be so. It may be presumed that every State in the Union has exercised the same unquestionable power.

The late President Dwight, in his *travels*, has taken pains to collect the laws of Massachusetts, on this subject, and by these laws it will be seen, that it has equally been the policy of that State to put all her schools, both *public* and *private*, under the superintendence of the *Selectmen*, and they go so far as not to allow any but *Citizens* to instruct their schools.

'All instructors of the universities, colleges, academies and schools, *and all private instructors* are required to take diligent care, and exert their best endeavors to impress on the mind of the children and youth, the principles of piety, justice, and a sacred regard to truth, *love to their country*, humanity and universal benevolence, sobriety, industry and frugality, chastity, moderation and temperance, and all other virtues, and to shew them the tendency of these virtues to secure the blessings of liberty, and the tendency of the opposite vices to slavery and ruin. The selectmen were to determine the qualifications of masters, and all those which fit children to enter into the grammar schools. Districts to forfeit from 10*l.* to 30*l.* if they did not comply. With respect to other schools [private] not contemplated in these provisions, it is enacted that no person shall be a master or mistress of any school, and keep the same without obtaining a certificate, as in other cases, under a penalty of 20 shillings. The duty of every master and mistress of every private school is made the same as the public schools. It is further enacted, 'if a person who is not a *citizen*, shall keep a school in the Commonwealth for one month, he shall be subjected to a fine of 20*l*.' Grand jurors are diligently to inquire and presentment make of all breaches and neglect of the act.'

The Legislature of Massachusetts became the guardians of all schools, that such schools may teach the 'principles of piety, justice, and *love of country*.'

These are objects worthy to be guarded, and are no less so now, than when Dr. Dwight wrote, or when the Legislature of Massachusetts enacted the laws he has enumerated. This 'love of country' ought to remind us, that the States have a great work to do, in regulating, and superintending their Schools, and as it has never been surrendered under the constitution, we should not, for the mere purpose of indulging the visionary fanatic, now construe it away.

It is incident to all these literary corporations, that students may be admitted or excluded at pleasure. Suppose the corporation of Yale College should, by solemn vote, prohibit students from South Carolina, would any constitutional question arise on that prohibition, or could they claim admission, as matter of right under the constitution? The answer is obvious. The corporation has that right of exclusion, and so has the State. Should the trustees of the Plainfield Academy pass an order that in future, no student from the State of Rhode Island should be admitted, is that a violation of the constitution of the United States? Surely not. The State created these corporations, and could not impart to them power it did not itself possess.

I leave *this question*, confidently believing that a State sovereignty does possess the power of regulating schools, and the exercise of that power is consistent with the provisions of the constitution of the United States.

Another question is here made by my learned opponents, who say these pupils are citizens, and as such, are entitled to all the privileges and immunities of others in our own State. To sustain this part of the defence, the 1st clause of the 2d section of the 4th Art. of the Constitution is read. '*The citizens of each State shall be entitled to all the privileges and immunities of citizens in the several States*.'

In deciding this question, every thing must depend upon the rules of construction, established by the common law. These rules are well understood, and as established in ages gone by, they will now be of infinite service in guiding to a correct result.

1st. The *intention* of the enacting power is to be sought for.

2d. The whole instrument or *act* must be taken together, so that its parts may be consistent with the whole—and

3d. The period of time when the enactment was made, embracing the language then in use, and the circumstances of the country, enter into the construction of the instrument and indicate its meaning.

In the administration of justice upon a *contract*—a deed, or a will, we go back to the period when the contract was made—the condition of the parties at the time when the deed was sealed—and all accompanying circumstances are taken into the account, to learn the extent of the obligation. In construing a legislative act, of a hundred years standing, the Court is not to be governed by the circumstances of the present day. To do so, would be to pervert, and not to construe. With these rules, we come to this question.

What *was* the *intention* of those who framed the constitution? Did they mean to place persons of color on the footing of equality with themselves, and did they mean to make them *citizens*?

In answering this question, it matters little what may be the opinion of a few madmen or enthusiasts now, but what was the intention of the people of the United States *at the time* when the constitution was adopted. Any *term*, like the term *inhabitant*, may be used in various senses. That term sometimes means a simple resident, or dweller, but when used in another sense, it means one who may have gained a settlement—one who has removed from another State, and complied with all the requirements of our Statute to constitute him a *legal inhabitant*. This is the technical use of that term. So also with the word *citizen*. That term may be used in diverse ways, and convey to the mind diverse meanings. It is quite immaterial how it may have been used in loose debate—in speeches—or in letters, but the question really is, how was it used in the Constitution? What was its meaning *then*, and for what purpose was it used there? Before this question can be properly answered, I may be allowed to enquire also, what was then meant by the term '*immunity*,' or '*privilege*?' Privilege then, as now, signified '*any particular benefit, advantage, right or immunity not common to others of the human race*.'

'Immunity,' as there used, is synonimous with privilege, so that *the* privileges and immunities to be enjoyed by *these citizens*, was something over and above what all the human race could enjoy. We must now advert to the condition of the country, and the circumstances of the human race, then upon the face of this country. The white men and the colored men composed the grand divisions of the human family. The *white* men then were entitled to particular privileges, above the colored men; civil and political rights belonged, by the laws of all the States, to the former, but not to the latter. The colored men were either natives, called Indians, or of African descent, called Negroes. From the *Indians* this whole country had but recently been conquered, and as in many of the States, they were still very numerous, it cannot even be pretended that *Indians* were embraced in this term *Citizen*. The African race, as a body, were then *slaves*, and held in bondage by those who made the constitution. It was then deemed fit and proper to hold slaves. All the States in the Union were slave States, and their laws tolerated slavery. Massachusetts and Connecticut had passed laws that colored persons born after a certain period should be free at 25, but they still held slaves. And can it be entertained for one moment, that those who framed the constitution should hold one portion of *a race of men* in bondage, while the other portion were made *citizens!* This would be strange inconsistency. Go back with me to the time when the constitution was made, and enquire after the condition of the country, and take into consideration all its circumstances, and all difficulties will be out of the way. *Then* it was not immoral to hold slaves. The *best men* bought and sold negroes, without a scruple. This impulse is of modern date, and however creditable to the heart, cannot alter the *constitution*. The immortal Washington who presided at the Convention, and who subscribed the instrument, under the laws of Virginia held more than one hundred slaves, as his property, on that day, and he was not thus inconsistent. He never intended to have you say, that the portion of the human race which were held in bondage were slaves, and the residue of that same color were *citizens*. This position is supported by the fact, that in the same article of the constitution, slavery is recognized. The 3d clause of the same section, is as follows: 'No *person* held to service or labor, in one State, under the laws thereof, escaping into another, shall in consequence of any law or regulation therein be discharged from such service, but shall be delivered up, on claim of the party, to whom such service or labor may be due.' Although the term 'slave' is not used in this clause, yet its meaning is perfectly obvious. It is as plain to our understandings, as if it had been written, 'No slave owned by any person in one State, escaping to any other State, shall, &c.' The term 'slave' also would carry with it the inseparable distinction of color. If *birth* alone gives *citizenship*, why is not this *slave* a *citizen?* Because the terms are contradictory. These slaves are called 'persons' in the constitution, and the white men are citizens. So that if we regard at all, the *whole instrument*, as we are bound to do, by the rules of construction, we must reject the use of the term *citizen* when applied to the colored race.

The counsel for the Defendant has told us, 'that the *distinction of color is novel, inconvenient and impracticable.*' The position thus assumed will embrace *Indians*, and if we add to this another proposition laid down in the defence, that *birth* and not *color* constitutes citizenship, the *Indians* are surely embraced. Can it be seriously contended, that the constitution does secure to Indians the right of citizens? Practically it has never been so. When the constitution was adopted, this country had but recently emerged from the Indian wars. These wars were wars of conquest, and the white men had driven the red men from their lands, and acquired a title to those lands by conquest and by force; and do you believe, that so soon, these conquered individuals would all be made *citizens?* There is another fact, which would repel this idea. In several of the States, when the constitution was adopted, there were more *Indians* than *white men*, and if citizens, the Indians would have had the supremacy. We need not go abroad for evidence on this point in the case. Connecticut has ever had within its limits numerous *Indians*, both tribes and others not belonging to tribes, and whoever saw one of these Indians, under our own laws, before or since the revolution, enjoying *one civil* or *political* privilege? If citizenship be a matter of favor, then surely the Indian stands far above the African. This is the Indian's home—it was once his soil, but it has passed into other hands. It is now the white man's country, and the white man is an American citizen.

Chancellor Kent adds his high authority to what I have said. 2 Kent's Com. p. 72. 'It is the declared law of New-York, that Indians are not citizens, but distinct tribes, being under the protection of government, and consequently never can be made citizens under the act of Congress.'

It has been remarked by the distinguished counsellor, 'that he can find no distinction of color: it is certainly novel.' It is not my fault, that my worthy opponent has not found this distinction of color, but I find it marked in numerous ways in our political system, and it becomes my duty to exhibit the evidence.

The *first Congress* after the constitution was adopted, was composed of many of those distinguished patriots who framed the constitution, and from that circumstance would be supposed to know what its spirit was. Some of the earliest work they performed for the country, was to establish by law a uniform rule of naturalization. The first law regarding naturalization was passed by Congress in 1790, and in it this precise and technical language is used. 'Any alien being a *free white person*, may become a *Citizen*, by complying with the requisites herein after named.' In the year 1795, a further regulation was made by law, when the same language is used. 'Any *free white* person may become a citizen,' &c. In 1798—1802—1813 and 1824, similar laws were passed on the same subject, and in each of those laws, the same technical language is used. These laws were carrying into effect the constitution itself, and if the constitution in any part of it embraced colored persons as citizens, then Congress mistook its duty, and early departed from its provisions. Congress have also marked this distinction of color in the Post-Office laws. 'No person of color can be engaged in the Post Office, or in the transportation of the mail.' This is a right open to all but persons of color. Chancellor Kent settles this question beyond cavil. 2 Kent. 72.

'The act of Congress confines the description of aliens capable of naturalization to 'free white persons.' I presume that this excludes the inhabitants of Africa and their descendants; and it may become a question, to what extent persons of mixed blood, as mulattoes, are excluded, and what shades or degrees of mixture of color disqualify an alien from application for the benefits of the act of naturalization. Perhaps there might be difficulties as to the copper-colored natives of America, or the yellow or tawny race of Asiatics, though I should doubt whether any of those were 'white persons,' within the purview of the law.'

Kent's Commentaries, vol. 2d. p. 258. 'In most of the United States, there is a distinction in respect to political privileges, between free white persons and free colored persons of African blood; and in no part of the country do the latter, in point of fact, participate equally with the whites, in the exercise of civil and political rights. The African race are essentially a degraded caste, of inferior rank and condition in society. Marriages are forbidden between them and whites in some of the states, and when not absolutely contrary to law, they are revolting, and regarded as an offence against public decorum. By the revised statutes of Illinois, published in 1829, marriages between whites and negroes, or mulattoes, are declared void, and the persons so married are liable to be whipped, fined, and imprisoned. By an old Statute of Massachusetts, of 1705, such marriages were declared void, and are so still. A similar statute provision exists in Virginia and North Carolina. Such connexions in France and Germany constitute the degraded state of concubinage, which is known in the civil law. But they are not legal marriages, because the parties want that equality of state or condition, which is essential to the contract.'

This distinguished author was in active life when the constitution was framed and knows its import, and has emphatically told us, that there ever has been, and still is, this distinction of color. Although not recognized by our worthy friends here, yet they have this high authority against them. To show that this is not 'novel,' we may refer to the constitutional provisions of many of the states. To begin with the constitution of our own State, we shall find this distinction of color is kept up throughout that instrument. No person can be elected to the office of Governor, Lieutenant Governor, or representative, unless he be an *Elector*, and none other than *white* male *citizens* can be made Electors.' These are the explicit provisions of the constitution of Connecticut, and now one branch of the government is solemnly called on to disregard the distinctions of color!

Let us mark the provisions of the constitutions of other States. *Delaware*—In all elections, none but free white male citizens can vote. In *Maryland*—Every free *white* male citizen shall vote. In *Virginia*—'Every white male citizen of the Commonwealth resident therein, shall vote.' In *South Carolina*—'Every free *white* man may vote.' In *Ohio*—'All *white* male inhabitants shall vote.' In *Louisiana*—'Every free *white* male citizen of the U. S.' shall have right to vote. In *Mississippi*—'Every free white male person shall have right to vote.' In *Illinois*—'All *white* male inhabitants, resident, have right to vote.' In *Alabama*—'Every *white* male person shall vote.' *Indiana*—'Every *white* male citizen of the U. S. may vote.' Rhode Island has defined the qualification of *freemen*, and among these qualifications, a man must be *white*, in order to enjoy the elective franchise. In all these States, constitutional provisions forever cut off the colored man from the enjoyment of the 'immunity' of voting for his rulers. By the constitution of the State of New-York, a singular disqualification exists. All white men who go into that State, can vote, after a residence of six months, but the colored man must have resided there three years, and possess, free from incumbrance, real estate to the value of $250. But it is said, that in relation to colored persons, that the constitution denominates them citizens: but a simple reading of the article will evince, that this term *there* signifies only the same as *residence*. It is used as synonimous with 'inhabitant' and 'resident.' All these constitutional provisions relate to the right of suffrage. These provisions exclude the black man from the enjoyment of this privilege, and this evidence is so strong that the learned advocate for the defendant is obliged to assume the ground, that this *elective franchise* is not an '*immunity* nor *privilege*'! I cannot assent to this proposition for one moment. It is indeed the legitimate consequence of the whole argument. It is an inevitable conclusion from the premises first advanced; but I have never heard any advocate of abolition doctrines before, frank enough to say that the right of voting was not a *privilege*. I admire this frankness of manner, but can never be induced to embrace the theory. The *right of suffrage* not a privilege! The whole structure of our government contradicts this proposition. We are distinguished from other nations, by this right of *electing our rulers*. It is the highest privilege which freemen can enjoy; it is an immunity at the very foundation of a republican government. Why was the revolution set in motion? Why was the declaration of Independence subscribed by those immortal patriots? Because the people said that *taxation* and *representation* should go together. This right of suffrage was denied, as a right, and the flames of the revolution burst forth, and taught those who denied the right, that it was one which freeman should enjoy. Take away this right, and American liberty will cease. It is an *immunity* which belongs to these States—one which they never will give up. It belongs to them as citizens, and as it has been denied to the colored race generally, it is evidence, that that race were not embraced by the framers of the constitution, in the term citizen. Did I need the aid of a judicial decision on this point, it may be found in the opinion of *Judge Washington*, given in a case, hereafter to be quoted at large. He says in that case, that the 'elective franchise is a fundamental privilege, secured by *this* article of the constitution.' We have therefore the authority of *Chancellor Kent* and *Judge Washington*—the laws of Congress and the constitutions of the several States, on the one side, and the opinions of our worthy opponent on the other, and the Court will decide who are right.

There is another part of the argument, addressed to your Honors, which requires an answer. My *brother Ellsworth* claims that all such State laws as may authorize the removal of paupers from one State, to that to which they belong, is an infringement of the constitution. A citizen of one State, although a *pauper*, may come here, and it is not in our power to remove him to his home. This doctrine, if true, would overturn half our State legislation. It would put down, as unconstitutional, our statute which directs that persons coming from another State, may be warned out, and if they refuse, may be removed. It is said this is an old law, and is now invalid. It will be recollected, that since the adoption of our State constitution, this law has been revised and re-enacted. In 1821, when the late eminent Chief Justice revised the Statutes, under the constitution, it did not occur to him, that it was unconstitutional. This is new doctrine indeed, and would be the result of a constitution wholly novel. Other States have a deep interest in this question. There is not a State in New-England, nor in the Union, but have laws of this character. These laws are made in self-defence—to preserve the State from the overwhelming effects of a bad population and from pauperism. These must all be swept from the Statute books, and the States must undo, what it has long been their policy to do. It is truly a startling doctrine, and would sweep into one general vortex all the State sovereignties.

When these States formed a Union, it never occurred to the people that all State legislation—all police laws—all pauper laws—and all education laws, were abrogated; and it cannot be apprehended that this Court will sanction such claims. The practical construction of the article in question will justify no such decision. There are indeed numerous other distinctions made by *State legislation*, between persons who are legal inhabitants of one State, and those coming into that State from another. If the position assumed on the other side be correct, then all these distinctions are invalid, and should be done away—are infractions of the constitution according to the claim set up, but according to the practical construction given to the constitution, they are good and wholesome laws. They are laws which never will be altered or repealed, until the State governments are wholly abandoned—until they are merged in the general government. I will notice some of these distinctions, resting not on color, but on inhabitancy or mere residence. The statute law of this State, title Inhabitants, provides that no person not an *inhabitant* of this State, shall be *entertained* or hired, unless he shall give security to the Selectmen, to save the town from expense. No person shall let any tenement to any such foreigner, unless such bonds of indemnity shall be given. No person shall 'bring into this State, any poor and indigent person, under the penalty of $67.' Inhabitants of other States, at the discretion of the civil authority, may be removed from this State, by warrant. Suppose these laws are unconstitutional, then any town in this State may, against the wishes of its inhabitants, be overrun with a bad population, or filled with paupers! This is a result to which the people never can be driven. It is a condition never before contemplated, 'novel, inconvenient and impracticable.' Among the distinctions of this class, many may be found in the constitutions of the States. In the constitution of Maine, all *students* from other States are prohibited the right of suffrage in the town where the college or seminary is situated. And all officers in the military, naval, or marine service of the United States are likewise prohibited from voting, when from another State, while one who belongs to that State may vote, and all others, with three months residence may vote. By the same constitution, no person can be a representative unless he shall have resided in the State one year, after he shall be 21, but an inhabitant of the State may vote in one day.

By the constitution of Massachusetts, a citizen of Connecticut removing there, must be a resident of that State 5 years, before he can be elected a Senator. To be elected Representative, and to become an elector of that State, he must have resided therein one year. To be elected Governor or Lieutenant Governor, he must have resided there seven years. Not so with one who is an inhabitant of that State.

By the constitution of New Hampshire, a citizen of Connecticut removing there, must reside in that State seven years, before he can be eligible to the office of Governor or Senator, while there is no such restriction upon the citizens of that State. A similar distinction in the constitution of Vermont may be found, differing only in the length of time.

By the constitution of New York, a native citizen of that State may be elected Governor, while a citizen of any other State, going there to reside, must have resided there five years.

By the constitution of Pennsylvania, a person to be a representative, must reside in that State three years next before the election. The Governor must have been an inhabitant of that State seven years, and electors must have resided in that State two years, but their own native citizens or inhabitants have no such restriction placed upon them.

In Delaware, when any person removes there from another State, he cannot enjoy the right of voting, until he has resided in the State two years—he cannot be a Senator until he shall have resided there three years —nor Governor until he shall have resided there six years. Similar restrictions are imposed by the constitution of every State in the Union, but I will not detain the Court longer with this class of restrictions. They are applied invariably to persons who go from one State to another; and if the position assumed on this defence be correct, then all these constitutions should be remodelled. These provisions are void! There can be no method of escape, except that which has been found, that the elective franchise is not a fundamental privilege!

In relation to these various restrictions, we have a judicial decision of high authority. It is reported in the 4th of Washington's Circuit Reports, page 371. *Corfield* vs. *Coryel.* It is a case in principle exactly similar to the one on trial. Indeed, the Connecticut law is almost a copy of the law upon which that case proceeded. You will allow me to be minute in the report of this case. The Legislature of New Jersey passed the following Act. 'That it shall not be lawful for any person, who is not, at the time, an actual inhabitant, and resident in the State of New Jersey, to take or gather clams, oysters, or shells in any of the rivers, bays or waters, in this State, on board of any canoe, flat, scow or other vessel, not wholly owned by some person, inhabitant of, and actually residing in' [New Jersey.] Every such person offending herein, shall forfeit the sum of $10, and shall also forfeit the vessel.

The next section provides for the condemnation and sale of the vessel.

After this law of New Jersey was enacted, *Corfield*, the Plaintiff, an inhabitant of New York, sailed his vessel into one of the bays of New Jersey, and was there found, taking oysters. The defendant seized the vessel, and sold it under the act of New Jersey, as forfeited, and the plaintiff brought his action before the Circuit Court of Pennsylvania, for damages. On the trial of that case, the plaintiff claimed the law to be in violation of the 2d section of the 4th article of the Constitution, in the same manner as will be claimed here. Judge Washington pronounced the opinion of the Court as follows.

'The 2d section of the 4th article declares, that the citizens of each State shall be entitled to all privileges and immunities of citizens in the several States. The enquiry is, what are the privileges and immunities of citizens in the several States? We feel no hesitation in confining these expressions to those privileges and immunities which are in their nature fundamental, and which have at all times been enjoyed by the citizens of the several States, which compose this Union, from the time of their becoming free, independent, and sovereign. What those fundamental principles are, it perhaps would be more tedious, than difficult, to enumerate. They may however be all comprehended under the following general heads: protection by the government; the enjoyment of life and liberty; with the right to acquire and possess property of every kind; and to pursue and to obtain happiness and safety; *subject, nevertheless, to such restraints as the government may justly prescribe for the general good of the whole.*

'The right of a citizen of one State to pass through, or to reside in any other State for the purpose of trade, agriculture, professional pursuits, or otherwise; to claim the benefit of the writ of habeas corpus; to institute and maintain actions of any kind in the Courts of the State; to take, hold, and dispose of property, real and personal; and an exemption from higher taxes or impositions, than are paid by other citizens of the State; may be maintained as some of the particular privileges and immunities of citizens which are clearly embraced by the general description of privileges deemed to be fundamental; to which may be added, the elective franchise, as regulated and established by the laws or Constitution of the State in which it is to be examined. *But we cannot accede to the proposition, which was insisted on by the counsel, that under this provision of the Constitution, the citizens of the several States are permitted to participate in all the rights which belong exclusively to the citizens of any other State, merely on the ground that they are enjoyed by those citizens.* Much less, that in regulating the common property of the citizens of such State, the Legislature is bound to extend to the citizens of all the other States, the same advantages as are secured to their own citizens.'

The law of Connecticut, in substance, is like the one upon which that action was founded, and in its execution I seek no other construction of the constitution, I claim no other power for the State, than what is here given. The counsel in *that* case, made the same argument that is here made—they urged an infringement of the 4th Article, but the learned Judge denied that claim. *Judge Washington* lived when the constitution was adopted—he had imbibed its true spirit, and when called upon to construe its provisions, he gave harmony to the whole, while at the same time he preserves the State governments. His language is emphatic. *These fundamental rights are secured to the citizens, subject, nevertheless, to such restraints as the government may justly prescribe for the general good of the whole.*

So we may say with equal propriety, and equal force, in this case, that the 'privileges and immunities' of education shall be subject to such restraints as the government may justly prescribe, for the general good of the whole. And who will not say it is for the general good of the whole to have all schools, academies and colleges, under the superintendence of some Board of Visiters, that the good ends of education may not be lost? Who will not say that these States must regulate education, or it never can be regulated? Who will not say that the whole system of education does not rest with the States? Who will not say that a State police, and the whole system of pauper laws, does not remain with the State governments? Who will say that Judge Washington was wrong in declaring that these fundamental privileges, whatever they may be, must be subject to restraints for the general good of the whole? May we not, under this wise decision, preserve our constitutions—our pauper laws—our police laws, and our school laws? Yes, we may exclude from our State a bad population—we may provide that pauperism shall not overwhelm the State, and we may provide for its safety, in doing so.

It has also been urged that Congress would not admit Missouri into the Union, until she expunged from her constitution, an article in the following words. 'It shall be the duty of the General Assembly to pass such laws as may be necessary to prevent free negroes and mulattoes from coming to, and settling in this State, under any pretext whatsoever.' And Sargeant's constitutional law is quoted as authority. This is no authority. The author of that work is wholly mistaken as to the progress of that matter, as well as in the main assertion of expunging the article. I have the constitution before me, and that provision is not '*expunged*,' and Missouri is in the Union. It is a part of the constitution. The law of Congress admitting Missouri into the Union, was approved March 6th, 1820, upon 5 distinct requisitions, this not being one, and afterwards on the 26th of February, 1821, the resolution alluded to by Sargeant was adopted. To show that this part of the argument is not justly entitled to weight, I read from the Journals of Congress as follows. 'The house after a short interval proceeded to the consideration of this resolution. It was advocated by Messrs. Clay and Brown, and opposed by Messrs. Adams and Allen of Massachusetts, on the grounds that Congress had no right to require of the Legislature of a State, *once admitted into the Union*, a compliance with the requisitions of this resolution.' In examining the journals of Congress further, it will be found that the resolution in question was adopted 89 to 81, the members of slave States voting for, and those from free States voting against, the resolution. Under these circumstances, nothing can be argued for the defendant, from that resolution.

There is an additional argument founded in patriotism and love of country. Are we now called upon to adopt such construction of the constitution, as shall surrender the country purchased by the blood of our fathers, up to another race of men? Then I would appeal to this Court—to every American citizen, and say that America is ours—it belongs to a race of white men, the descendants of those who first redeemed the wilderness. The American name and character have been handed down to this generation, and it is our duty to preserve that character, and perpetuate that name. Let not the determination of this case aid those who are plotting the destruction of our constitution. It rests with the Court to say, whether the country shall be preserved or lost, and I leave it to them to decide.

Mr. Cleveland* on the same side.

May it please your Honors:—The Legislature of the State has passed an Act in these words: [Mr. C. here read the first section of

* The argument of Mr. Cleveland is considerably abridged. He spoke without a brief, and without recurrence to any notes, which made it difficult to follow him very fully or very accurately.—*Reporter.*

the Act.] Upon this Act a prosecution has been had against the defendant in the Court below; the power of the Legislature to pass it was there contended and decided, and the question comes up here to be revised by your Honors. The question is, whether the State of Connecticut has the power to pass an Act to regulate the conduct of a citizen of their own State. The Act is not passed against citizens of other States; no penalty is affixed to them for disobeying it. The gentleman who opened the case appeared to be embarrassed by this view of it; he has labored to show that the Act affected citizens of other States indirectly, and that what a State cannot do directly, it cannot do indirectly. I submit the question, whether it is not entirely in relation to our own citizens. I proceed at once to examine the argument of the gentleman.

We shall have no controversy but that the Constitution of the United States is the Supreme law of the land—it has, however, no application here. I so claimed in the Court below, and so I claim here. The object of the Constitution was to regulate the general government rather than the state governments. There might be some little difficulty in the question, if the words of the Constitution are taken literally, but looking at its spirit, and the intention of the makers, there is none whatever.

Another position of the gentleman is, that there is no distinction in respect to color. I admire his candor—he has the sympathies of all. The Court cannot be called upon to act on their sympathies—they have nothing to do with the hardship of the case. I address four Judges who are white men. No black man can take the seat occupied by your Honors. In a moral view, there is no difference as to the color of the skin, but to carry out the assertion of the gentleman, will destroy a nation of free white Americans. Sound policy required those who have gone before us to make a distinction between these races—there ever has been, and there ever will be a distinction.

Citizenship, it is said, is founded on allegiance. What is that founded on? Protection from the government—every one owes it to the government—even the slave in South Carolina. The gentleman astonished me with his air of confidence, when he asked if a free black could not commit treason. At first, this argument might seem plausible, but apply it to a slave—one owned by a white man. He is killed—can punishment be inflicted for the act? Where then is the argument of the gentleman? A slave can commit treason, and the argument proves too much—does it not make a slave a citizen? What is the difference between a slave and a free negro?—Apply the doctrine to both—it is all bottomed on the broad principle of allegiance, and there is no distinction in this respect between a slave and a free negro.

Need I go further? Need I occupy more time? The framers of the Constitution made a distinction in color, and the entire argument on the other side was to show that there was no difference—no distinction in this respect.

The gentleman, with a frankness which I admire, says that he admits our pauper law to be unconstitutional. He seems aware that this law must be pronounced constitutional, if the pauper law is. SWIFT penned that law—our legislature adopted it, and I believe the Court will be slow to pronounce it unconstitutional. Unless, however, the gentleman makes out his proposition that there is no distinction founded in color, he entirely fails. If he makes that out, then a black man, coming here from New-York, has the same right as a white man. Does he dare carry out his principle? Where does he get the power to add 'under like circumstances?' Suppose a black man comes here from New-York, and offers himself to vote—we tell him that none but free white male citizens have that privileges by our laws. He replies, 'I know that, but I will teach you better—I'll teach your legislature that they have been groping in darkness.' Could the State resist if there is no distinction in color?

I leave the gentleman to get out of the dilemma as well as he is able. I care nothing about adding the words 'in the same condition'—this addition is unworthy of the high source from whence it came. It amounts to nothing to say that one coming here, under the circumstances supposed, is entitled to the privileges of a black man—he can claim, according to the gentleman, the privileges of a citizen of the United States.

We have been asked to define what 'colored persons' are—perhaps I ought to tell. I refer the gentleman to his client to find out what 'little misses of color' are.

The Court will excuse me for not referring to the authorities. Need I go over the ground so ably occupied by my associate counsel? Need I refer to Kent, and to the various acts of Congress? I ought perhaps to allude to arguments read from a little paper published within the sound of my voice—for aught I know, speeches of vile party men—made in a convention or legislature for political purposes. Opinions of this kind are of the least authority, and they come besides in too questionable a shape. Kent is named among them, but it is not very material whether he spoke so or not, as he wrote differently in his commentaries.

If I am right in the views I have taken, the constitution of the United States and the laws of Congress make a distinction in color. The legislature of this State certainly has a right to do the same. The legislature must possess the power to regulate the inhabitants of the State, and by the law in question nothing else is proposed to be done.

I ask if the Health laws are constitutional? Can the legislature pass an act that no citizen shall enter Yale College without the consent of the Corporation? If all inhabitants of other States have a right to come here for any purpose, may not New-York send an army of Indians to settle here? They were all born in the United States, and according to the gentleman, birth gives citizenship.—Indians can be prosecuted for crimes—may sue—hold lands—owe allegiance, but they are not citizens.

Black men are sold to eternal servitude, to slavery for life in this country. A white man cannot be a slave. The foundation of the distinction is color.

[Mr. Cleveland near the close of his argument alluded to 'Prudy Crandall and her school,' and also to the doctrine of nullification. He said, notwithstanding that doctrine was growing unpopular, the sovereign State of Connecticut stood as high as the sovereign State of South Carolina.]

Mr. Goddard closed the argument for the Plaintiff in error, substantially as follows:—

The questions involved in the decision of this case are of immense magnitude, and I regret, said he, that circumstances make it necessary to discuss them here, and particularly at this time. It is indeed singular, that occasion has never arisen, since the existence of our constitution, in which the question whether the free, native inhabitants of the United States were citizens, and entitled to the privileges of citizens, and been directly and judicially decided. The circumstance that no such question has arisen, is, to my mind, high evidence that their rights to the privileges of citizenship are unquestionable; for numerous occasions have arisen, in which those privileges have been exercised. I regret that this question should now come on for discussion and decision before the highest tribunal in this free and enlightened State, at a moment of great public excitement regarding our colored population, but I feel assured that this Court will experience none of its influence.

I do not come to advocate the claims of either of the great parties who are engaged in the business of emancipation, although the plan of educating free colored persons, and planting a colony on the shores of Africa; of sending thither free, intelligent, and virtuous instructors to diffuse through a continent the blessings of liberty, science, and religion; of commencing the work of renovating that continent, and in some measure repairing the wrongs which its colored inhabitants have suffered from the whites, is a plan, which I have always considered as grand in all its features; nor is it for me to say, whether its execution has been thus far equal to its conception. But whether the views of those who adopt this plan, be or be not more correct than the views of those who suppose that the cause of humanity as well as justice will be best promoted by the continuance of these people in the country of their birth, and elevating them to the condition of all other citizens, is, for the purposes of this argument, immaterial; as education lies at the foundation of both, and the adoption and execution of such laws as that against which we contend, will forever extinguish the benevolent exertions and hopes of all.

Nor do I come to disturb or agitate the question of slavery. That an evil of vast magnitude exists, and a stain remains upon our free republican institutions, which all good men would desire to wipe away, must be admitted by all such men.

But we come in behalf of *three hundred and twenty thousand* free, native inhabitants of this free country in which we live—under the free and happy Constitution of which we justly boast—we come to claim for them the privileges secured to us all—we come to claim instruction for those who alike with us are accountable to Him 'who made of one blood all nations of men for to dwell on the face of the earth'—we come in behalf of those, and the children of those, who, on the 4th of July, 1776, united in the self-evident truths then proclaimed to the world, and which very properly annually sound in our ears, 'That all men are created equal—that they are endowed by their Creator with certain unalienable rights—that among these are life, liberty, and the pursuit of happiness.' We come in behalf of those and the children of those who fought and shed their blood with our fathers to secure these blessings—we come to ask *to pursue* that happiness for which they fought, and to enjoy that life and liberty which they then secured. To learn to read—to read the word of God, and to pursue happiness temporal—happiness eternal!

We come to claim for those born free within the United States of America, the protection of the second section of the fourth Article of the Constitution of the United States, which provides 'That the citizens of each State shall be entitled to all the privileges and immunities of citizens in the several States.'

But we are told that this class of people have no such rights, privileges, or immunities, because they are not *citizens.* It becomes then our duty to show that the eight thousand free colored people in the State of Connecticut, part of the three hundred and twenty thousand which the last census showed as belonging to the United States, are *citizens of this State*—that they enjoy the privilege of being instructed, of being boarded for that purpose; and it will follow, as we think, that the free colored citizens of other States have secured to them the same privileges, and this without the license of any persons.

Are these eight thousand persons citizens of this State? What are citizens, generally? Lexicographers have been referred to, and their definitions are very various. In Rees's Cyclopedia, inhabitants of a city, vested with the freedom and rights thereof. It was a term used in the ancient republics to designate inhabitants of a republic with more or less privileges. The title and privileges were acquired in different ways: birth, however, conferred the title.

St. Paul, to prevent being scourged, in reply to the query of the centurion, said, 'But I was free born.'

In the American Encyclopedia, cities are spoken of as places where the democratic principle is most naturally developed—the firmest support of liberty—where the government, in the hands of citizens, affords nourishment to the spirit of freedom. Under the article Election, the qualifications of electors are considered, and it is said in *some* of the States it is required that they should possess property, and be free *white* citizens, implying not only that these are *citizens* who are not *white*, but that *such citizens*, in many of the States, are electors.

In the Classical Dictionary—a freeman of a city—a townsman—not a gentleman—an inhabitant—Walker's Dictionary not unlike this, and in some definitions a citizen is called a pert, low townsman. Some of these definitions our opponents will concede to those for whom we claim.

In some of Shakspeare's plays, citizens are introduced as performing low parts. Coriolanus Act 1st, Scene 1st, *2nd Cit.* says, 'One word, *good* citizen.' *1st Cit.* replies, 'We are accounted *poor* citizens—the patricians *good*—the leanness that affects us—the object of our misery, is an inventory to particularize their abundance. Our sufferance is a gain to them.' In answer to their claim to be fed with corn, Coriolanus tells them, 'Go, get you home, you *fragments*.'—In answer to the claim which is made in behalf of those whose interests we espouse, some Coriolanus may indeed call them '*fragments*,' which they are, if not citizens, but with no propriety may they be told to 'get home,' for home they have none. If not citizens, what are they? Not aliens—not denizens—not foreigners—not subjects—'*fragments*' of—we know not what.

The term, *citizen*, is, under a republican government, what the term *subject* is under a monarchy: it embraces high and low—rich and poor—male and female—white and colored—a general term which includes the whole republican family—all who are free and live under the same government, and owe to it permanent allegiance—subject to its duties—entitled to its privileges.

But whatever may be the import of the term *citizen* elsewhere, how is it used in the United States? in this State? in our constitution? in the constitution and laws of the United States? How are citizens *made* here?

In considering this question, I cheerfully adopt the rules laid down by the counsel on the other side (Col. Judson.) We are told that in construing laws and constitutions 'the intention of the enacting power, *at the time*, is to be sought for—the condition of the country and parties *then* is to be considered, and language is not to be construed according to any spirit of fanaticism which prevails at the present day.'

I concur in this, and am content to ascertain both with respect to the Constitution of the United States, and the law upon which this prosecution is founded, what was the intention of those who speak—of the law givers. If I do not much mistake, we shall be gainers by adopting this very rule. Unless I am deceived, language is held now and principles advanced, which the patriots of the revolution and the framers of our Constitution, would never have ventured to adopt or countenance. So impressed were they respecting the colored population, and so much had they talked, and so much did they feel on the subject of civil liberty for which they were struggling, that the term *slave* is not used in the constitution of the United States, but a periphrastic mode of expression adopted to attain that end. And I fear the further we recede from the point of time when we declared ourselves free and independent, the less do we feel the sentiments contained in the instrument by which the declaration was made.

But to the question—how were the citizens of the State of Connecticut made? I answer, *out of subjects of the king of Great Britain.*

Our ancestors fled from England to obtain and secure their liberties—liberty of conscience—to enjoy their religion. But they fled from a country where liberty was protected by law, and where, as is said in *Blac. Com. vol. I. page 125, Christian's notes*, 'every wanton or causeless restraint of the will of the subject, whether practised by a monarch, a nobility, or a *popular assembly*, is a degree of tyranny.' *Page* 127, 'This spirit of liberty is so deeply implanted in our constitution, that *a negro*, the moment he lands is under the protection of our laws, and becomes *a freeman*.' In a note to *page* 1[illegible] Christian combats the idea of Judge Blackstone, that this depends on either the soil or the air of Great Britain, *but ascribes it to writ of habeas corpus.* And in a note

4

page 425, he says, '*liberty*, by the English law, depends not on *complexion*.'

Our ancestors, when they came to this country, black or white, were subjects of the king of Great Britain—entitled to all the privileges of the *habeas corpus* act, which there made colored people FREEMEN. Let it not be forgotten that the people of Connecticut came to this country, and established for themselves a form of government which was sanctioned and contained in a charter, granted in the reign of Charles II., a reign in which the great writ of English liberties—the *habeas corpus*, was confirmed—that writ which secured to English subjects, black or white, their liberty. So confirmed and extended were the privileges secured by that writ in that reign, that some writers have considered it as having originated there. The historian Hume says of it that 'its principles had place in no other government, and this consideration alone may induce us to prefer our present constitution to every other.' He also adds that 'it makes atonement for the faction and violence into which the prejudices of parliament had in other respects betrayed them.'

But the principles of this great writ now have place in another government. Our ancestors in the same reign came to Connecticut with a charter in their hands, which is found in our edition of the Statutes of 1808, page 5.

'Our will and pleasure is, and we do, for us, our heirs, and successors, ordain, declare, and grant unto the said Governor and company, and their successors, that all and every the subjects of us, our heirs, or successors, which shall go to inhabit within the said colony, and every of their children which shall happen to be born there, or on the seas going thither, or returning from thence, shall have and enjoy all the liberties and immunities of free and natural subjects within any the dominions of us, our heirs, or successors, to all intents, constructions, and purposes whatever, as if they, and every of them were born within the realm of England.'

These privileges were not only secured to every *inhabitant* there, but to every such person as shall be *free* of said colony. It gave all power and authority, from time to time, to take, ship, and carry there, such of our loving subjects and *strangers* as shall or will accompany them into said colony;' and it was declared that 'those liberties and immunities shall be enjoyed by all who *shall happen to be born there*.'

The object also of establishing this colony is stated. After granting certain powers to be exercised, the reasons therefor are stated to be 'that our said people, inhabitants there, may be so religiously, peaceably, and civilly governed, as their good life and orderly conversation may win and invite the natives of the country to the knowledge and obedience of the only true GOD, and the Saviour of mankind, and the christian faith, which in our royal intentions, and the adventurers' free profession, is the only and principal end of this plantation.'

Is the law in question one of these laws?

Here then we find the *materials* from which citizens of Connecticut were made, and the purposes for which this free government was established. Let us next see whether in our struggle for liberty and independence we lost these principles,—whether they have been denied to those to whom they were granted.

This charter, granted in 1662, continued to contain the principles of the government of Connecticut, until after the Declaration of Independence, which severed the United States from the mother country. The first meeting of the Legislature of Connecticut, was held in the month of October following, (1776.) The same edition of the Statute, *page* 22, contains the Bill of Rights then adopted:

'The people of this State, being by the Providence of God free and independent, have the sole and exclusive right of governing themselves as a free, sovereign, and independent State; and having from their ancestors derived a free and excellent constitution of government, whereby the legislature depends on the free and annual election of the people, they have the best security for the preservation of their civil and religious rights and liberties. And forasmuch as the free fruition of such liberties and privileges as humanity, civility, and christianity call for, as is due to every man in his place and proportion, without impeachment and infringement, hath ever been, and will be the tranquillity and stability of churches and commonwealths; and the denial thereof, the disturbance, if not the ruin of both.'

It was declared after such a preamble, that the ancient form of civil government, contained in the charter from Charles II, king of England, *and adopted by the people of this State*, under the sole authority thereof, shall be and remain the tried constitution of this State:—not because it was derived from King Charles, but because it was *free*—because it was excellent—and because, more than all, *it was made and adopted by the people of the State*. If there ever was a written constitution adopted by the people themselves, it was this. Under this constitution the people of Connecticut lived till the adoption of the present constitution in 1818.

Has that constitution abandoned the rights and privileges for which we contend?

With one exception, it confirms them. The preamble begins with a grateful acknowledgment to God for having been permitted to enjoy a free government, and that the people do, in order more effectually to define, secure, and *perpetuate* the liberties, rights, and privileges, which they have derived from their *ancestors*,' &c.

Art. 1. Sect. 1, declares that 'all men, when they form the social compact, are *equal in rights*.' Will it be said that colored men did not *form* the social compact, because not voters, and therefore not citizens?

This will prove too much because it will exclude minors, females, and a great class of persons now, and many more then, who are and were not voters—qualifications in point of property being then here, as well as now in many of the States, necessary to the exercise of the elective franchise.

There were other citizens who were and are not voters, whose rights and privileges are secured by the constitution—they may be white, or black, or colored people.

Sec. 5. 'Every citizen may freely speak, write, and publish sentiments,' &c. May not blacks do so? If not, it may not be important that they should learn to read or write. *Sec.* 14 secures the writ of *habeas corpus*, to which Mr. Christian ascribes the liberty of colored people in England. This writ our ancestors brought with them to our soil, and it was one, not the least important, of those rights and privileges which this constitution professes 'to *secure* and *perpetuate*.' *Sec.* 16 *and* 17 secure to citizens the right of assembling for the common good, in a peaceable manner, and bearing arms in self-defence. Are colored people not citizens, and therefore excluded? *Art.* 6 provides for the qualifications of electors. This is arbitrary, and regulated in different States according to their views of the nature of their government, and is not employed in defining who are citizens. Its language is, 'Every *white* male citizen of the United States' who shall possess certain qualifications in point of property—done military duty—paid taxes, &c. shall be an elector. This article expressly recognizes the idea that there are *other* citizens than *white* ones—colored, of course. But if voting be the test of citizenship, it follows that all those who have not the requisite qualifications in point of property—do no military duty—pay no taxes, &c. are, by this very article, excluded from citizenship. So of females—the word *male* being much broader than *white*.

The rights of a free government—of conscience—of education and religion, are also professed to be secured to all by this constitution; and why not to Miss Crandall the right to follow the dictates of her conscience in devoting her time to the instruction, boarding, and educating human beings abandoned by others, and teaching them to pursue happiness?

If, as we believe, it has been shown that colored people are citizens of this State, in which instruction is given, then let us see how it is in New-York and other States from which the persons instructed come here to receive it.

To ascertain this, resort has been had to the opinions of distinguished men, politicians and jurists, and especially to that most distinguished jurist, Chancellor Kent. His opinions, though quoted against us, we think sustain the claim which we make. In *vol.* 2d of his Com. *page* 71, he says, 'The article in the constitution of the United States, declaring that citizens of each State were entitled to all the privileges and immunities of citizens in the several States, applies only to natural born or duly naturalized citizens, and if they remove from one State to another, they are entitled to the privileges that persons of the same description are entitled to in the State to which removal is made, and to none other. If, therefore, for instance, free persons of color are not entitled to vote in Carolina; free persons of color emigrating there from a northern State, would not be entitled to vote:' thus admitting that persons of color are citizens, but not entitled to vote in other States. It is said that in *page* 258 of the same volume, the learned author has advanced a different opinion, expressed as follows: 'In most of the United States there is a distinction in respect to political privileges, between free white persons, and free colored persons of African blood, and in no part of the country do the latter, in point of fact, participate equally with the whites in the exercise of civil and political rights. The African race are essentially a degraded caste of inferior rank and condition in society.' Has he so soon contradicted what he before advanced? Not so; he is now speaking of what the African race is *in point of fact*—how they have been treated in most of the United States. He says truly, 'the African race are essentially a degraded caste,' &c. Of this indeed there is lamentably abundant evidence. But does it follow that because by your laws they have been or may be degraded and deprived of *some* rights, that you have a right to deprive them of all? to deprive them of citizenship? That the learned author of the Commentaries did not consider it so, is evident from taking the whole together. It is also confirmed by the extract which has been read by my honorable associate from his speech made in the convention which formed the constitution of New-York, as well as by the extracts made from the speeches of Rufus King, De Witt Clinton, and other distinguished men in the same body. This is further confirmed by the fact that by that constitution, and the laws of the state, citizenship is recognized by the right of voting, which our opponents consider as the test of citizenship, but which we deny. Certificate of the right to vote of the fathers of some of these children, sent here for education, have been placed in our hands, but which it is unnecessary to read.

If colored persons are, as we think has been shown, citizens of Connecticut, New-York, and the individual States, let us consider whether they are not citizens of the United States, and how they became so.

The revolution produced a change in all the free inhabitants of the United States—all the citizens of the several States became citizens of the United States. They were *subjects* of Great Britain—they became *citizens* of the United States from the very nature of our government. In the case of *McIlvaine vs. Cox's lessees*, 2 *Cranch* 293, it is asserted without contradiction, 'it was therefore a political revolution, involving in the change *all the inhabitants* of America—rendering them all members of the new society—*citizens* of the new States.'

This doctrine was affirmed by the Supreme Court in the same case, 4 *Cranch* 212. In October, 1775, the Legislature of New Jersey, like that of Connecticut in the same month, met, and exercised their legislative powers under the new order of things. Daniel Cox was a tory, and adhered to the King of Great Britain, but continued to reside in New Jersey until June, 1777. In delivering the opinion of the Court, Cushing, J., says, 'The Court entertains no doubt that after the fourth of October, 1776, he (Cox) became a member of the new society, entitled to the protection of its government, and bound to that government by the ties of allegiance.' It was also claimed that by the treaty of peace, Cox was a subject of Great Britain. In answer to this the Court say, 'But the question who were at that period *citizens* of the United States is not decided or in the slightest degree alluded to in this instrument, but it was left necessarily to depend on the laws of the several States,' &c.

We are referred to the opinions entertained by our fathers, and those who achieved our independence. Let us look to the proceedings of Congress under the old confederation, and ascertain from it what was then decided. Were any such exceptions then made as are now claimed? No; they claimed the principles of liberty as we claim them, and did not hesitate to appeal to Heaven for their sincerity.

On the occasion of the adoption of the treaties with France in 1778, an address was made by Congress to the people of the U. States, which was recommended to be read by ministers of the gospel, immediately after divine service in the places of public worship. This address was drawn up by the late Judge Chase, one of the signers of the Declaration of Independence, and reiterated the sentiments of that instrument. All engaged in the conflict, without distinction of color, were exhorted 'to gird themselves for battle,' were assured in glowing language of the blessings for which they fought—were directed to look to heaven for assistance, and to conciliate that, 'by acts which heaven approves.'—'Thus shall the power and the happiness of these sovereign, free, and independent states, founded on the virtue of her citizens, increase, extend, and endure until the Almighty shall blot out all the empires of the earth.' *Pitkin's Hist. U. States*, vol. 2, p. 47. How durable would our opponents render the happiness of colored citizens, who united in obeying this address!!!

But a direct recurrence to the Journals of Congress will show this important subject was not left to conjecture, or inferred who citizens were, and how the term was used by that body, was repeatedly settled. In the 3d vol. of these Journals, page 366, on the debate respecting the articles of confederation, how and by whom they should be adopted, after the words, 'unless nine states shall assent to the same,'—it was moved to insert these words for the very purpose of excluding this class of population: 'provided that the nine states, so asserting, shall comprehend a majority of the people of the United States, excluding negroes and Indians, for which a true account shall be triennially taken,' &c. This passed in the negative, no state voting in favor of it except Virginia. This was on the 30th of October, 1777. On the 13th day of November following, the subject was resumed, and an article adopted without a division, in the following words: 'The better to secure and perpetuate mutual friendship and intercourse among the people of the different states in this Union, the *free inhabitants* of each of these states, paupers, vagabonds, and fugitives from justice excepted, shall be entitled to all privileges and immunities of free *citizens* in the respective states. And the people of each state shall have free *ingress* and regress to and from any state, and shall enjoy,' &c. Let it not be forgotten that only thirteen days before, the same Congress had refused to exclude persons of color. The Articles of confederation were then referred to a committee to be revised and arranged, and on the 15th of the same month adopted by Congress, containing in the 4th article the provision before recited. They were afterwards adopted by the States, and it is well known that many of the provisions of the present constitution were taken from that instrument.

The subject was not left here. Some of the provisions in the articles of confederation were objected to by some of the states, and on this subject I will take the liberty to read an extract from a letter which is put into my hand, and I do it with more pleasure, because it is in the hand writing of a son of one of the most distinguished citizens of the United States, and one of the purest patriots of which this or any other country can boast—JOHN JAY.—His son, to whom I allude, has conferred an obligation on his country by furnishing the life of his father, and I scarcely need to add that his own opinions are entitled to high credit:—He says,—

'It cannot with any decency be question-ed, that up to the moment when the federal constitution went into operation, a free ne-gro, of one state, was entitled by the national compact to all the rights and immunities of a free citizen in every state of the Union.'

'Little, certainly, did Sherman, Hunting-ton, Wolcott, and Hosmer,* anticipate the feelings on this subject, which now prevail in their native state, and still less the extra-ordinary means by which the gratification of those feelings is attempted.'

The delegates from Virginia who had voted to amend the article by the exclusion referred to on the 30th of October, informed Congress that they were instructed to vote for the articles as they stood.

Thus deliberately was the question now at issue settled, according to the views *then* entertained, as my opponents claim the con-struction should be *now*.

But, that no doubts may exist on this sub-ject, I refer to the 8th vol. of the Journals of Congress, page 71. On the 1st day of April, 1783, when another patriot of the revolu-tion, the father of my honorable associate, took his seat in Congress, a motion was made by Mr. Hamilton to amend the 8th ar-ticle of the confederation, which respected the mode of apportioning the expenses in-curred for the common defence, and provide 'that the treasury should be supplied by the several states in proportion to the whole number of white and *other free citizens*, and inhabitants of every age, sex, and condition, including,' &c.

It seems, then, that Alexander Hamilton thought these were '*free citizens*,' who were not *white*, and so thought Congress; for this amendment was adopted by all the states, with the exception of Rhode Island, which voted against it, and Massachusetts, which was divided.

On the 26th day of the same April, we find the report of an address to the people of the United States, prepared by a committee, consisting of Mr. Madison, Mr. Ellsworth, and Mr. Hamilton, on providing for the ex-penses incurred in achieving our Independ-ence.—These men, if any, understood what they wrote—and they assisted in framing and adopting the present constitution. In page 199, 8th vol. Jour. Cong., they speak of the difficulty of fixing the proper differ-ence between the labor and industry of *free inhabitants*, and *all other inhabitants*. They made two classes only. They exhort the state to provide for the public debt 'as ne-cessary to render the fruits of a revolution a full reward for the toils, the cares, and ca-lamities which have purchased it.' They speak of the meritorious nature of the debts due. 'Another class of creditors,' say they, 'is that illustrious and patriotic band of *fel-low citizens*, whose blood and whose bravery defended the liberties of *their country*.' They add: 'who even now ask for no more of their dues than such a portion as will enable them to retire from the field of victory and glory, into the bosom of peace and private citizen-ship.'

And who were 'that illustrious and patri-otic band' of our fellow citizens, whose 'toils, and cares, and calamities,' were to be re-warded? Were none of them colored? In looking at this subject recently in my of-fice, I could not but recur to a list of appli-cants for pensions, under the act of 1818, when I was clothed with authority to ex-amine the qualifications of applicants, and found within the little circle of my residence, nineteen colored persons whose claims, I believe, were well founded and successful. I cannot refrain from mention-ing one aged black man, Primus Babcock, who proudly presented to me an honorable discharge from service during the war, dated at the close of it, wholly in the hand writing of GEORGE WASHINGTON. Nor can I for-get the expression of his feelings when in-formed, after this discharge had been sent to the War Department, as a proof of his ser-vices, that it would not be returned. At his request it was written for, as he seemed in-clined to spurn the pension, and reclaim the discharge. Was not Primus a citizen? 'an illustrious citizen?'

But to return to this address of Madison, Ellsworth, and Hamilton. The people of the United States are reminded, that 'the rights for which they contended were the rights of human nature. By the blessing of the Author of these rights on the means ex-erted for their defence, they had prevailed.' They say, 'In this view the *citizens* of the U. States are responsible for the greatest trust ever confided to political society.' 'If vir-tue, &c. prevail,' say they, 'the cause of liberty will acquire a dignity and lustre which it has never yet enjoyed, and an ex-ample will be set which cannot but have the most favorable effect on the rights of man-kind.' If the reverse, they say, 'the last and fairest experiment in favor of the rights of human nature will be turned against them, and their patrons and friends exposed to be insulted and silenced by the votaries of tyranny and usurpation.'

At the close of this revolutionary struggle

* Delegates from Connecticut in the Congress of 1778.

in favor of civil liberty and the rights of *human nature*, and on which a government had been established, which from its very nature, as well as the express recognition of its distinguished friends, free inhabitants and subjects, had become free citizens, our pious ancestors, grateful to that Almighty Being, whose blessing they had so often implored, appointed a committee to prepare a Proclamation for a day of Thanksgiving.

If ever there was an occasion in which the actors in any scene were perfectly honest and upright, and would be cautious as to the language they used, one would suppose that this was that occasion.—This report was made Oct. 18th, 1783. Congress could survey the whole ground—they knew what they had done—for whom it was done, and by whom done. They were about to call upon the people of the United States to send up to the Supreme Ruler of all human events, their grateful acknowledgments for the success of the efforts which had been made, and crowned with success, in favor 'of the rights of *human nature*.' They say, 'And whereas in the progress of a contest on which the most essential rights of *human nature* depended, the interposition of Divine Providence in our favor has been most abundantly and most graciously manifested, and *the citizens of these United States* have every reason for praise and gratitude to the God of their salvation.' Alluding to the blessings for which those citizens are exhorted to be thankful, they say, 'and above all, that he hath been pleased to continue to us the light of the blessed Gospel, and secured to us in the *fullest extent*, the rights of conscience in faith and worship.' And among those things for which they are exhorted 'with hearts overflowing with gratitude to supplicate our great Creator'—'that it may please Him to pardon all our offences, to give wisdom and unanimity to our public councils—*to cement all our citizens in the bonds of affection*,' &c. 'To smile upon *our seminaries and means of education*, to cause pure religion and virtue to flourish, and to give peace to all nations, and fill the earth with his glory.'

Had the colored people, who had fought, and bled, and suffered to obtain these rights of 'human nature,' no part nor lot in this matter? Had they no cause for gratitude? Or were they turned out of the human family, not even 'fragments of citizens'? Did Primus keep this thanksgiving?

This proclamation was signed by Elias Boudinot, first President of a Society established for sending the Bible *to all people*—a book which modern colored people are forbidden to learn to read!

If then the Declaration of Independence, and the commencement of the war of the revolution, found these people citizens, or the events of that war, or the articles of confederation, or establishment of peace, made or continued them citizens, has any thing been done since, which deprives them of that character? The term *citizen*, occurs but a few times in the constitution of the U. States—which was adopted in about six years after the peace. The leading men of the old Congress made that constitution—the events to which reference has been made had not faded from their memories.

In the first and second article of the constitution, the word *citizen*, is employed in defining the qualifications of Representatives and President of the United States.

In article 3d, when provision comes to be made to secure the rights of the people generally—where the protection of the judicial powers thrown over them, and courts provided, where alone their rights are to be secured, language is used which is broad enough to extend to all—to secure all. The judicial power is made to extend to cases arising between citizens of a state and citizens of another state—between citizens of different states—between citizens of the state claiming lands under grants of different states—and between a state and the citizens thereof, and foreign states, citizens, or subjects.

Provision, broad provision is here made, for every body upon whom our laws might operate, whether citizens or subjects. A place to which an appeal may be made by every one whose rights may be violated—colored people excepted! They alone are not provided for by any term here used. Surely they are are not subjects nor citizens of any foreign state. Who will say that a colored man may not go into the courts of the United States to seek justice in any of the cases there provided for? If, however, he go there, unless it be alleged on the face of his writ, that he is A CITIZEN of some state, according to the established doctrine, first promulged in the case of *Bingham vs. Cabot.* 3 *Dal.* 382, often repeated since, his case will be dismissed. He is then *a citizen of the United States*.

Article 13, excludes any citizen from accepting any title of nobility or honor, from any king, prince, or foreign power, on forfeiture of his citizenship. And as I know of no colored man exposed to the operation of this provision, unless the colored gentleman who was married in Russian costume, under the auspices of the ambassador of the Emperor of Russia, may be in danger of becoming a count of the empire, I will consider the constitution of the United States no further on this point.

Is there any thing in the laws which have been passed under this constitution, which militates against our claim? These laws have been so fully considered by my associate counsel, that it will be unnecessary to trouble the Court with them—taking notice only of two or three which our opponents have attempted to use against us.

That regarding naturalization, is pressed into the service. It provides that 'any alien, being a *free white person*, may be admitted,' &c. The answer to this is obvious. The constitution of the United States authorized Congress to establish a uniform rule of naturalization; they may very properly exclude alien blacks from becoming citizens, but surely this decides nothing as to those born here—*free born*.

I would also refer to an early law, securing the copy right to authors, being citizens of the United States, and ask, could not a free black, born here, obtain that security under that law? If indeed the law of which we complain, and other similar laws, can be sanctioned, there will soon be no occasion for its use among colored people—they will indeed become, if they are not already, *a degraded people*.

The laws of Congress, *vol.* 3, *page* 529, which forbid importing or bringing any negro, mulatto, or other person of color, not being a native, or citizen, or registered seaman, into any port, &c., expressly recognize the existence of persons of color who are natives—who are citizens.

The Missouri case is urged against us—so far from its having any bearing against us, it will, if it produces any effect, support us. Under the old ordinance of Congress, which guarantied to every state in the Union, a republican form of government, they presented to Congress a constitution which contained a provision directing the legislature to pass laws to prevent free negroes and mulattoes from coming to a settling in the state. This subject was referred to a committee, and for the purposes of this argument, I cannot think it very important whether Col. Judson is right or wrong, as to the question whether the votes which passed were before or after the admission of that state into the Union. The committee consisted of the lamented Mr. Lowndes, for whose character I entertain very high respect, Mr. Sergeant, and Mr. Smith, of Maryland, I presume. This article of the constitution was under the consideration of that committee. Their report shows that they considered it not only a delicate, but very difficult subject. They consider it settled, that a discrimination may be made by the states between white and black men, though *both* be *citizens* of another state. They instance the right of voting and serving on juries. The former may be an important right, the latter is surely a burden, from which all may be willing to be exempt. Our juries are selected by the civil authority, selectmen, &c.; and I should surely never consider it any violation of a right not to be selected.

But we are not now considering what rights are secured by this clause in the constitution, but whether people of color are citizens, and entitled to any. That there may be colored citizens, this report expressly admits. In the vote of Congress, it is apparent that that body did not adopt the construction of this article of the constitution which our opponents claim, because, if they were of this opinion, it was idle at least to resolve that the article in the constitution of Missouri 'should never be construed so as to deprive any citizen of any state, of the privileges or immunities to which he is entitled as a citizen of the United States.' This surely cannot be claimed as a legislative opinion against us.

If, as we believe, it has been shown that the colored children, for the instruction of whom Miss Crandall has been prosecuted, are citizens of the state where they reside, and of course 'entitled to all the privileges and immunities of citizens in the several states,' it remains to be considered whether the statute law of this state infringes any of their rights.

Let it be borne in mind that whatever rights they have, those rights are secured to them by the Constitution. They enjoy them at the will of no man or men; they hold by a higher tenure, *by the Constitution*.

In a work written by one of the first jurists of this or of any conntry, one who has devoted great attention to the Constitution of our country, in the 3d volume of Judge Story's Constitutional Law, page 675, he says, 'The intention of this clause [2d section of the 4th article] was to confer on the citizens of each state, if one may so say, a general citizenship, and to communicate all the privileges and immunities which the citizens of the same state would be entitled to *under the like circumstances*.'

In the case of ——— ——— 9 *Johns*. 507, the Court say, 'the right of ingress to a state is unquestionable.'

In construing the statute of Connecticut, I again adopt the rule which the leading counsel on the other side claims; to construe it according to the *intention* of the law-makers at the time when the statute was enacted. Will the gentleman tell me that it was not the intention of the legislature to prevent colored people from coming into the state? from residing at Canterbury? to prohibit ingress? The preamble to a statute is said to be its key—that to the statute in question points to its object, which is to put down literary institutions for the instruction of colored people; to prevent their increase in this state, by preventing their introduction here from other states.

That you cannot do indirectly what you cannot do directly, is an axiom which may be safely adopted. This statute *prohibits their being instructed*—it takes away from them the privilege of being taught to read and write—it deprives them of all opportunity to acquire that knowledge and those habits which may render them good citizens, useful to each other and to *their* native country. It denies them all advantages for qualifying themselves for usefulness to the native country of their *ancestors*, by diffusing the light of civilization and christianity over that benighted and unfortunate country, from which those ancestors were taken by the cupidity of white men.

We are told that this law does not forbid them from coming *into* the state—the right of ingress is not taken away. Suppose the law should expressly allow citizens of another state to come into this state, but forbid their being fed when here. Would it be constitutional? And let me ask, is the mind of less value than the body? Is food for the mind of less value to the citizen in Connecticut than food for the body?

We are told that the law does not forbid colored people of other states from coming here and being educated—that all our common free schools are open to them—that they may enjoy the benefits of the funds which are here amply provided for the support of schools.

The evil then consists in being able to pay—in *paying* for their own education!

The low, the vicious, the miserable, may come and be educated freely. Those children whose parents are able to educate them, and qualify them for 'the pursuit of happiness,' intellectual happiness, are forbidden to come *for such purposes!!*—and is this a statute to prevent the introduction of a bad population?

The statute also contains a prohibition against setting up a school for the instruction of colored persons—forbids their being instructed or taught in any such school. It further forbids any person 'harboring or boarding such persons for the purpose of being taught or instructed.' Under this clause, the defendant is informed against. The statute also authorizes the removal from the state of all who shall reside in any town in the state for the purpose of being instructed. The third section provides that the persons who reside in this state for the purpose of being instructed, may be made witnesses and *compelled* to testify. They shall not come here to be instructed—they shall not reside here, they shall not be harbored or boarded here for that purpose, and they shall be *compelled* to be witnesses in prosecutions under this statute!

Let me now apply the rule of the opposing counsel, (Col. Judson) and ask what was the *intention* of the Legislature which made the law? Can any one hesitate to answer that it was to prevent the ingress of colored persons into the state? to forbid it? to do indirectly what they could not do directly, to break up the school at Canterbury?

But we are told that these persons may come and be instructed, provided the consent in writing of the civil authority and selectmen, is first obtained.

And is this the tenure by which constitutional rights are held and enjoyed? At the will of others? A right held by such a tenure is unworthy of the name. The gentlemen say,

> 'You shall be viceroy it is true,
> But I'll be viceroy over you.'

Obtain the leave of Esquire B. and others, and you shall enjoy the constitutional right of coming into Connecticut—of being instructed there—of being fed and harbored while instructed!

But this is all idle—all pretence. It was the intention of those who framed the law to put down the school, and if their intention had been directly expressed, in few words, it would have been entitled 'An act to prohibit Miss Crandall from setting up at Canterbury a school for colored citizens coming from other states—to prohibit her instructing them, boarding or harboring them, and to authorize those persons who come into the state for such purpose to be sent back.' Can this be done?

If we have succeeded in showing that colored persons are citizens, the prohibitions of this statute may be constitutionally extended to white citizens of other states. Its provisions may, upon the principles of this statute, be applied to students in Yale College and all our literary institutions, of which we so justly boast. And this in Connecticut, whose strength and respectability have been bottomed upon the information and intelligence of her citizens! And it is now debated before the highest judicial tribunal in the state, whether citizens of another state may come into this state *at all*—no, come they may, but not to be instructed—come they may, but not to be boarded or fed!

Suppose that distinguished citizen whose name and opinions have been referred to, should come into this state. Has he the right to do so? Yes. To reside here? Yes. To buy a farm or pursue a profession? Yes, but he may not be boarded, harbored, fed—the keepers of hotels shall not entertain him. Of what value, then, is the right of ingress into the state? To my mind it is absurd to talk of *securing* personal privileges and immunities, and yet have them depend on the will of others, or limit, embarrass, and control their enjoyment in such manner as to render them valueless.

That there are certain privileges and immunities secured by the constitution of the United States to citizens of any state, in each state, is clear. It may be difficult to define exactly what they are, or enumerate them all. They must be fundamental. It is said, 'the right of ingress to a state is unquestionable,' and indeed it scarcely requires an authority to prove this, for unless you can enter a state, you can enjoy no rights *there*. Is not the right to reside there, so long as you obey the laws, as unquestionable as your right of ingress? You may be boarded—harbored, but not instructed! If any one privilege can be supposed to be more important than another, I should suppose that it was this very right in question. It lies at the foundation of such a government as ours. Without instruction, of what value are citizens to themselves or others? But colored persons may not come to Connecticut for instruction. They are forbidden in many of the states, either to give or receive instruction under penalties of fine, imprisonment, whipping, and other most severe punishments. By a law of the free, enlightened, republican state of Connecticut, they are to be driven from our borders if they come here to seek instruction.

[Mr. Goddard here read extracts from the laws of several states imposing punishments for the instruction, &c. of colored persons.]

It is indeed to be deeply regretted, that a law should appear in our statute book which should occasion a debate, of the present description, before the highest judicial tribunal in the state, claiming, as it does, to be one of the most republican and enlightened of any in the union—made from a colony always free; grown up from a plantation whose principal end was 'to invite the natives of the country (colored people) to the knowledge and obedience of the only true God, and the Saviour of mankind, and the christian faith.' Driven from other states, they must now be forbidden by a law of Connecticut to learn to read the word of God, by which alone they can come to that knowledge. I trust that the clause in the constitution of the United States will protect these people, and also save this state from so foul an imputation.

In the passage already quoted, from Judge Story's Constitutional Law, the clause in question is said 'to communicate all the privileges and immunities which the citizens of the same state would be entitled to under the like circumstances.' Colored citizens of Connecticut are in all respects 'under the like circumstances,' and they may be taught, boarded, and educated in private schools or others. It follows of course, that colored citizens of other states may be taught, boarded, and educated in the same manner.

But the right of voting has been alluded to, and claimed as a test of citizenship. In connexion with that claim, a sentiment has been ascribed to my honorable associate which he never uttered, that the right of voting was no privilege. It is a privilege, and a high one, but not one that at all tests citizenship. If all citizens have a right to vote, a great portion of them, as has been already shown, are unjustly deprived of their privileges. Was it not for the authority of great names, I should venture to assert that the right of voting in another state is not one of the privileges secured to *any* person by this clause in the constitution.

Judge Washington in the New Jersey case which has been referred to does, indeed, speak of this as one of the fundamental privileges secured by this clause in the constitution. And the committee who reported on the Missouri question, (Mr. Lowndes and others) mention the right of voting and sitting on juries as cases in which a discrimination had been made in many states. The last is a burden and not a privilege, and that of voting not a privilege, as I contend, secured so as to be exercised in any other state than the one where the citizen is admitted. The error, as I apprehend, consists in this. The exercise of the right of voting is indeed fundamental *to the government*, because it is elective, but not to the individual citizen. This elective franchise is exercised in the different states according to the laws of each state. In Virginia, real estate is essential to entitle citizens to exercise this right. In Rhode Island, freeholders only, and the oldest sons of freeholders vote, and the different states make such regulations on this subject as they see fit. It is peculiarly an affair of each state to regulate at pleasure. Citizens are citizens of *the states* which for this purpose are *other* governments; and to use the language of Judge Story, this clause confers on them a sort of *general citizenship*. In the constitution of the United States, the term *voters* is not directly used. The states choose Electors for President, &c. in such manner as the legislature prescribe. It only provides that Representatives in Congress shall be chosen by those who vote for the most numerous branch of the state legislature. This recognises the right of the state to make distinctions as to the qualifications of voters in the different branches of the state legislature, and evinces that the constitution of the United States does not interfere at all on the subject.

But it has been shown that colored persons, possessing the qualifications necessary for electors, are entitled to vote in several of the states.

I may add another. The town of Alexandria, while it constituted a part of the state of Virginia, before the District of Columbia was ceded to the United States, had a charter, in which it was provided that all male citizens, who possessed the necessary qualifications in point of property, might vote. Sundry colored persons having those qualifications, for a long time, voted. Several years after the cession to the United States, application was made to Congress to amend that charter. A bill was reported for that purpose, and among other alterations, the word '*white*,' was introduced before the words 'male citizens.' A motion was made to amend the bill as reported, by erasing the word '*white*.' This did not prevail, but it shows that those persons were recognized as citizens, and permitted to vote until a direct prohibition was obtained.

That colored persons are not citizens is a doctrine of modern origin, as is the doctrine that they may not vote. If not citizens, they could never vote in any state. If citizens, voting is a privilege of which they may be deprived. It is a valuable privilege, but not essential to individual happiness. But far otherwise is it with the privilege of being instructed in the principles of our holy religion and of free government. The value of this privilege words cannot describe.

Having shown, as we trust, that the persons on whom this law are intended to operate are citizens of other states—that our citizens under the like circumstances have a right to enjoy the privileges forbidden them—that the privileges of which the law intends to deprive them are fundamental, we trust that this honorable Court will wipe away this stain upon our statute book, by declaring this law utterly void, because opposed to the constitution of the United States, the supreme law of the land.

The Court reversed the decision below, but did not decide either of the points presented by the counsel. The ground of the reversal was, the insufficiency of the Information, it omitting to allege that the school was set up without the license of the civil authority and selectmen. A copy of the Information is annexed; it was written at the commencement of the Report, as it then seemed unnecessary to insert it, the decision of the Court not having been made until after the printing of the trial commenced.

COPY OF THE INFORMATION.

To the Honorable Superior Court now in session in Brooklyn, within and for the county of Windham, Chauncey F. Cleaveland, attorney for the State of Connecticut, within the county of Windham aforesaid, on his office oath, informs that at Canterbury, in said county, after the twenty-second day of August, in the year of our Lord one thousand eight hundred and thirty-three, to wit: on the twenty-fourth day of September, in the year aforesaid, for the purpose of attending and being taught and instructed in a certain school, which before that time had been and then was set up in said town of Canterbury, for the instruction and education of colored persons, not inhabitants of this state, Prudence Crandall of said Canterbury, with force and arms, wilfully and knowingly did harbor and board certain colored persons, to wit:—Ann Eliza Hammond and others, whose names are to the attorney aforesaid unknown, and who when so harbored and boarded, were not inhabitants of any town in this state, all which acts and doings of the said Prudence Crandall were done and committed without the consent in writing first obtained of a majority of the civil authority, and also of the selectmen of said town of Canterbury, where said school was then situated, against the peace of this state, and contrary to the form and effect of the statute law of this state in such case made and provided.

Dated at Brooklyn this second day of October, A. D. 1833.

CHAUNCEY F. CLEVELAND, *Att'y.*

MOB, UNDER PRETENCE OF LAW,

OR, THE

ARREST AND TRIAL OF REV. GEORGE STORRS

at Northfield, N. H.;

WITH THE CIRCUMSTANCES CONNECTED WITH THAT AFFAIR AND REMARKS THEREON.

CONCORD:
ELBRIDGE G. CHASE....PRINTER.
1835.

REMARKS.

The case *reported* in the following pages, is believed to be without *precedent* in the law annals of New-Hampshire. That a minister of the gospel, of respectable character and standing in the community, having been invited to deliver an address before a philanthropic society, and being in the sacred desk, engaged in the solemn exercise of prayer, should be arrested in the name of the law as "an idler, a vagrant, a brawler," &c. &c., is probably without a parallel in the records of the Granite State. It reminds one of the scenes in by-gone days in Massachusetts,—about the middle and near the close of the seventeenth century, ere the fires of persecution had quite gone out, or at least while the spirit that enkindled them was yet in existence and in power. It is a melancholy proof that unhallowed opposition to moral good, to constitutional rights, may exist amidst the light of the nineteenth century, and in this boasted land of freedom. Yes, the rights so dearly purchased and so nobly maintained by our fathers, are now wrested from their sons by the hand of violence under the pretended sanction of law!

Has it come to this? That even while so many veterans of the revolution yet remain among us,—even while the last sun of these venerable men yet lingers above the horizon, the rich inheritance they have bequeathed to their country and their descendants, is trampled upon as a thing of little value? Must their gray hairs thus be brought down with sorrow to the grave?

But we are not yet a hopeless people. Abuses are often the occasion of their own remedy. Integrity and honor, and respect to the rights of man, are not wholly swept away in these days of anarchy. There is yet a redeeming power amongst us. There are Lo's and Abrahams within our borders. There are ten righteous men in the city. Our trust is in the God of our fathers,—Him who gave them wisdom to plan, and energy to establish our excellent institutions. And our prayers to Him is, that there may yet be virtue enough in the people to sustain those institutions, and transmit them unimpaired to the latest posterity.

The letter of invitation to Rev. Mr. Storrs to deliver an Address at Northfield, from the original.

Very dear Br. Storrs,

It is desired by your Anti-Slavery friends in this vicinity that you should give us an Anti-Slavery *Sermon* in Northfield Meeting House, as soon as will be convenient for you. We would prefer to have the Discourse in the *day time* that we may be less liable to disturbance from those who "choose darkness rather than light."

I hope you will find it consistent to favor us with an address. Make your own selection as to time. Please write soon, and let us know *whether* you *can come*, and if so, *when*.

Very respectfully, yours.
JAMES TEMPLETON,
In behalf of the Anti-Slavery
Society in Sandbornton and
Northfield.

Rev. George Storrs.
Sandbornton, Nov. 27th, 1835.

Answer of Mr. Storrs.

Concord, Dec. 7th, 1835

Dear Br. Templeton:

I have been from home three weeks past, and, of course, have but just received your letter.—If nothing in Providence prevent. I will give the Anti-Slavery Society at your place an address next Monday, viz. the 14th, at one o'clock, P. M. You can give notice accordingly. I think probable, I may spend the next Lord's day with you. The cause advances—the captives MUST go free. God is on our side. "The captive exile hasteneth that he may be loosed, and that he should not die in the pit." "God pleadeth the cause of his people: Behold I have taken out of their hand the cup of trembling—thou shalt drink it no more." See the whole of Isaiah LI. especially from the seventh verse.

Yours truly, in that Gospel which
proclaims liberty to the captive.
GEO. STORRS.

Extract from Mr. Storrs' Journal.

Dec. 12. Came to Sandbornton Bridge at the request of Northfield and Sandbornton Bridge Anti-Slavery Society. Received a cordial welcome from friends of the cause. Was entertained by Dearborn Sanborn, Secretary of the Anti-Slavery Society, a whole-hearted abolitionist.

Sunday, Dec. 13. Preached all day in the Methodist Meeting House, to a large congregation: endeavored to establish the *duty* of entire devotion to Christ and his cause, measuring that duty by God's word, and *not* by a corrupt *public sentiment*. I trust the word spoken was not in vain.

Dec. 14th. Had an appointment given out yesterday to preach this afternoon before the Anti-Slavery Society of this place.—There were some indications last evening that the mobocratic spirit was at work. This forenoon a few harmless guns were fired, upon the top of the hill that overlooks the village, by some boys, probably sent there by some larger sized *boys*—the *report* was not so loud as to indicate that very great *execution* was likely to follow.

About eleven o'clock, A. M. Nathan Wells and Joseph Smith, two of the Selectmen of Northfield, called upon me to know if my lecture could not be given up, as there was considerable excitement about the place. Mr. Wells thought that there would be trouble, and if so, *I* should be responsible for it. I told him I thought it very strange that I should be held responsible for the doings of a mob, while I was only in the exercise of a constitutional right: I remarked that if I did or said anything unconstitutional, the law was open, let me suffer for it. Mr Wells said he did not come to discuss the subject—but some of the people, viz. Samuel Tilton, Esq. and Judge Daniel C. Atkinson, advised them to come and see if the lecture could not be given up, for there *would be trouble*. I replied that I came here at the request of the Anti-Slavery Society, and for the time, I was their servant, if *they* chose *not* to have the lecture, I should acquiesce.

1*

I learn by a friend, who came in since the Selectmen left, that there are threats, by a man bound to keep the peace, that if I attempt to lecture this afternoon, I shall be sent to prison. Be it so, then! Our government have sanctioned by law sending a *colored* man, on suspicion of being a runaway slave, to the United States' prison, if he happen to be found in the Capital of this Republic without the evidence of his freedom! and to be sold a *slave* for life to pay his *jail fees* if he cannot prove his freedom!—and if he *can prove* his freedom, in that part of the District formerly belonging to Maryland, and refuses to pay his jail fees, he is still sold a slave for life to pay the fees of an unrighteous imprisonment!! No wonder that *fed* officers under such a government should threaten to send a *white* citizen to prison for asserting and exercising the right of FREE DISCUSSION.

Dec. 18th. Previous to attending the meeting at Northfield on Monday last, a friend sent me word that a warrant was being made out to apprehend me. It was intimated that Judge Atkinson was preparing said warrant and papers. Samuel Tilton, Esq. I learned was to serve the warrant. I left Mr. Sanborn's in Sandbornton about one o'clock, in company with Rev. J. Templeton and Joseph Clough, Jr.—proceeded to the Methodist Meeting House in Northfield—where having arrived I seated myself near the pulpit while the people were collecting. Esq. Tilton came in some time previous to my going into the pulpit. He had a large cane in his hand, I should judge about three feet and an half long, and an inch or an inch and a half in diameter.—After looking round the house, he seated himself in about the third or fourth pew from the pulpit, in front. Not long after this, Mr. Templeton and myself went into the pulpit—we sat a short time, and then I commenced the exercises by reading from the "Testimony of God against slavery," select portions of scripture. I then read a hymn, after which I knelt to pray—had proceeded some time in prayer—among other things, had prayed for the President of these United States and for both houses of Congress in their present session, for various classes of men:—at length I came to the slaves, for whom both "saints" and sinners have said "don't pray about them in public;" but I have not so learned Christ—therefore, I ventured to speak to God of their condition—*degraded*, bought and sold like beasts in the market—shut out from *mental* improvement—denied the Bible. and cut off from those religious privileges that we enjoy—that God would have mercy upon them—save them from avenging themselves—help them to be patient and quiet:—I was just about to pray for their *masters*, but it would almost seem as though heaven suffered it to be prevented, and hell was greedy of its prey, for near that point I heard a heavy rap upon the floor, made I supposed by the above described *cane*—and a voice gave loud utterance to something—I heard nothing that I recollect, except "Mr. Storrs." I still continued my prayer. I next heard a rushing from a pew in front of me towards the pulpit stairs, and some one rapidly ascend them—next I felt some one lay his hand strong upon my shoulder, and cry out, "You are a prisoner." I still kept on praying—my mind never more calm and stayed on God, for which I praise him. As I did not stop praying, the man next seized me by the collar, shook me. and uttered some expressions which I do not recollect. I now stopped praying *audibly*—my eyes still shut for a short time—I then opened them and beheld Samuel Tilton, Esq. a deputy sheriff, standing beside me with a paper in his hand, and heard him say, "I have a warrant to arrest this man as a *vagrant* and an *idler*," adding, "I now command assistance." I replied, (still upon my knees) you need call no assistance—I shall offer no resistance—allow me to put on my outside garment and I am ready to go with you. Esq. Tilton went down into the aisle of the house—at this moment. Samuel Forest, Esq. of Northfield, attempted to read the law relating to the disturbance of religious meetings. Mr. Sheriff Tilton cried out, "I care nothing about your law"—and added some other words, I do not remember what. In looking about for my surtout, I found that Mr. Sheriff, probably in his haste to get into the pulpit, for fear I should escape, had landed it safely in the bottom of the aisle, in the dirt. However, I soon recovered it, and having put it on, followed the sheriff, *remembering* "those in bonds as *bound* with them." As we passed out at the door the mob party followed—at a little distance from the house some of them *hissed* behind me, showing who their father was—a few harmless snow balls were discharged at my back, and some mirth followed. The sheriff ordered them to behave *civil*, and have all things done *orderly*.

Mr. Tilton said to me, as we passed along, "Mr. Storrs, this is very unpleasant, but there was no other way to prevent a mob —I have been trying ever since last Saturday to prevent a mob, and there was no other way to do it." It brought to mind an anecdote I read when a boy, of an Irishman who came to this country and landed in some of our cities—travelling upon the pavement, the dogs came out and barked at him—after several unsuccessful attempts to get up a stone to throw at them, he cried out, "A plague on such a country as this where the *dogs* are let *loose* and the stones *tied* down." The Mobites are left *loose*, but the men upon whom they would wreak their vengeance must be *bound!* And pray what is our *crime?* O, it is a *horrible* one! We believe and teach, that the Negro is a MAN!!! That he has "certain inalienable rights," among which our fathers "*fanatically*" included "LIBERTY." But as the discovery has lately been made by pro-slavery men that that was only a "rhetorical flourish of Mr. Jefferson's pen," it will not do for us to *repeat* it, for fear the people will have a mob!! However, as Mr. Sheriff Tilton was so exceedingly *kind* as to try *so hard* for two days to prevent a mob, with so *little success*, I would respectfully suggest to the High Sheriff, whether it might not be well for him to relieve his Deputy and appoint a man in his room who has more *influence*. I would also, with much respect, suggest to the High Sheriff, whether, if it is probable that many abolitionists are to be arrested, as they are *temperance* men, he cannot accommodate us with some Deputies whose *breath* is not so exceedingly offensive with RUM—especially if they are to be sent into the holy sanctuary to take us from our knees, while in the pulpit engaged in prayer. If he can we shall feel under great obligations to him.

But to return from this digression. I was taken before Nathan Wells, Justice of the Peace, one of the Selectmen, who visited me in the morning. The Court was opened. Judge Atkinson appeared as counsel for Rogers, the complainant. The complaint was read. I was interrogated, Guilty, or Not Guilty? I replied, *Not Guilty*. I was then asked if I was ready for trial. I requested the trial to be postponed until next Thursday. My request was granted. I gave bonds for my appearance in the sum of *twenty* dollars, and the Court adjourned to meet at ten o'clock on Thursday.

On Tuesday, one of the mobocrats was found dead in a horse barn, having drank, it is said, too freely of *brandy*. He was buried while the Court was in session on Thursday.

I felt happy that the complaint against me did not contain two charges, viz. that of being a *drunkard* nor *slaveholder*.

Previous to going into Court on Thursday, Judge Atkinson, counsel for Rogers, took me aside and said, that this complaint was not brought against me out of any bad feelings towards me, and now if I would come before the Court and say, that I did not think my coming to Northfield would produce excitement, he thought the matter might be stopped without proceeding any further. and that he would use his influence with the Justice for that purpose. I replied, as *they* had set out in the law, *I* wished it to be finished in, or by the law, and added, I am ready for trial.

We will now present our readers with the Complaint itself, and the doings of the Court on Thursday. I had no counsel on the occasion. The minutes of the testimony at the trial were taken by Rev. Samuel Hoyt of Concord.

To Nathan Wells, Esquire, one of the Justices of the Peace in and for the County of Merrimack and State of New-Hampshire— *Complains*—

In the name and behalf of said State, Benjamin Rogers of Northfield, in said County of Merrimack, husbandman, that George Storrs, now commorant in said Northfield, a transient person, complains and gives said Justice to understand and be informed that said George Storrs, at said Northfield, on the 12th day of December, 1835, and ever since has been an idle person and disorderly person, and wanton and lascivious in speech and behaviour, a common railer and brawler, and neglects any lawful employment, and mispends his time going about in said town * and County disturbing the public peace, contrary to the form

* I was not in the town of Northfield at all, except as I passed through. Saturday, the 12th. in my way to Sandbornton Bridge.

of the statute in such case made and provided. and against the peace and dignity of said State.—wherefore the said Benjamin Rogers prays that the said George Storrs may be apprehended and dealt with in the premises as law and justice shall require.

BENJAMIN ROGERS.

Merrimack, ss. December 14, 1835.

Then Benjamin Rogers personally appeared and made oath that the above complaint by him subscribed, is in his belief just and true. Before me—

NATHAN WELLS,* Justice of Peace.

NOTE. On this complaint a warrant was issued in the common form, signed by Mr. Justice Wells.

I put up in Sandbornton at Mr. Dearborn Sanborn's, where I spent both Saturday and Sunday night. I went into no other house in Sandbornton except Rev. Mr. Templeton's,—and I was in no house in Northfield, except Dr. Ladd's. where I went Sabbath noon to take some refreshment, and called a few minutes, on Saturday, in the south part of the town to warm me. I was not even so far from the house, where I put up, in Sandbornton, as to go into the street, on Monday, till I set out to go to the meeting in the afternoon. It will be seen then, that previous to this *complaint* being made out and sworn to, I had not been in Northfield at all except on the Sabbath to preach. My discourse throughout the day was on "*The duty of living to Christ.*"

G. S.

---

* Nathan Wells is one of the Selectmen of Northfield who visited me at Mr. Sanborn's. I was informed by a citizen of Northfield that he asked Mr. Wells if he was going to the lecture on Monday—Mr. Wells replied, "Yes, if they will find rotten eggs to throw at him."

TRIAL.

Northfield, Dec. 17, 1835.—Court met according to adjournment. Complaint read by Hon. DANIEL C. ATKINSON, Judge of Probate for Strafford County, who read the Statute and remarked as follows:

"So far as I understand it, the people think Mr. Storrs is an idler. I think he is an idler, and has taken up that which is not lawful. He is a beggar," &c.

Rev. *James Templeton*—affirmed.

Question by Judge Atkinson.—Where was the last Conference held? Answer. At Portsmouth. Q. Did you attend? A. Did not. Q. Did Mr. Storrs tell you that he was at the Conference? A. I do not know that we have had any conversation about it. I was informed that he was left without an appointment, by the Conference, to act as an Agent for the American Anti-Slavery Society. Q. Is there any such Society incorporated as the American Anti-Slavery Society? A. I do not know whether it is incorporated or not. Q. Did the Conference appoint him as an Agent? A. The Conference does not appoint preachers: the Superintendant does it. Q. Did the Superintendant approve of Mr. Storrs being appointed as an Agent? A. He did not. Q. Don't you know the Bishops have disapproved of the Abolition Society? A. Two of them advised the Trustees not to open their meeting-houses for lectures on Slavery. Q. How many Bishops have you? A. Five. Q. Have you seen any disapproval by the other Bishops? A. I have not. Q. Did Mr. Storrs have an appointment this year? A. He had. Q. Where was it? A. On Henniker Circuit. Q. Where does Mr. Storrs live? A. In Concord. Q. Is Concord in Henniker Circuit? A. I think not. Q. Has Mr. Storrs or not, spent his time on Henniker Circuit? A. He has not. Q. Does Henniker Circuit include Northfield or Sandbornton? A. It does not. Q. Did Mr. Storrs tell you that he had been to Dover or Portsmouth? A. I do not know that he did, but I have heard that he was there. Q. What did he tell you about his reception there?—did you hear that there was any disturbance? A. I think I have heard there was some. Q. What other places has Mr. Storrs lectured at? A. Plymouth, Newbury and Bristol. Q. What did he say about Newbury?—that they made any disturbance? A. I heard there was some through the influence of ardent spirits. Q. What did he say of Bristol? A. Nothing in particular. Q. Then you understood that disturbance has been made every where he has been? A. No,—I understood no such thing. Q. Was you *here* when this Anti-Slavery Society was formed? A. I was not. Q. What has Mr. Storrs told you his business was? A. I have understood that he was an Agent for the American Anti-Slavery Society. Q. Is there any such *legal* Society? A. I am not much of a *legalist*;—there is such a Society. Q. It is a Society of individuals then, is it, without any *lawful authority*? A. I do not know about their *authority* to form such a Society. Q. Did you know Mr. Storrs was requested not to speak upon that subject here? A. I did. Q. What is the name of the Society in *this* place? A. Northfield and Sandbornton Bridge Anti-Slavery Society. Judge Atkinson said—"Not Sandbornton, *we disclaim* all that." Not *all* of us, replied Mr. Templeton, I live there. Q. When did you give notice of Mr. Storrs' lecture? A. Sabbath day. Q. Was Mr. Storrs present? A. He was, and preached both in the forenoon and afternoon. Q. Who was it requested Mr. Storrs not to deliver the Anti-Slavery lecture? A. Two gentlemen came in to whom I was introduced, whom I learned to be Selectmen. Q. They told him not to deliver the address, did they? A. They did. Q. What did he say? A. That he was the servant of the Society by whom he was invited. Q. Did he lay it before the Society by which he was invited? A. The Officers were consulted. Q. Who were the Officers? [Mr. Templeton named them.] Q. He went on with the address, did he? A. He commenced the exercises by reading select portions of scripture, read a hymn, and then commenced praying. Q. Did he read a chapter in connection or did he pick out passages that related to slavery? A. I was of the opinion that the passages he read had a bearing on slavery. Q. Has he carried about papers and books with *niggers* on them for *children* and *women?* A. He has not: he has carried about papers and books, but not particularly for *children* and *women*. Q. Did he leave books and papers with you? A. He did. Q. What did he tell you to do with them? A. He gave no particular directions. Q. To whom have you given papers on this subject? Some persons were named by Mr. Templeton. Q. Has Mr. Storrs told you that his business was to circulate papers? A. He has not. Q. Has Mr. Storrs been on Henniker Circuit to preach? A. It is my impression he has not. I have seen a writing from the Presiding Elder of that District, authorizing him to act agreeably to the vote of the Conference on his case. Q. Was Mr. Storrs left superannuated? A. He was left supernumerary. Q. Mr. Storrs has been round delivering Anti-Slavery lectures, has he, and left his Circuit? A. I think he has. I saw the Presiding Elder and he told me he had given him permission to leave the Circuit; and brother Storrs showed me a writing to this amount. Q. Has any Presiding Elder called on Mr. Storrs to deliver an address here? A. None.

Cross-examined. Question by Mr. Storrs. Did the Selectmen of Northfield, when they called on me, say that they came by the advice of Judge Atkinson and Esq. Tilton? A. They said they were advised by them to come, and request you not to proceed.

Samuel Forrest, Esq.—sworn. Questioned by Judge Atkinson. Q. Mr. Forrest, are you President of this Society? A. I am. Q. When was this Society formed? A. In March. Q. By whom was this Society formed—had Mr. Storrs any hand in it? A. He was there and delivered an address. Q. Who wrote the Constitution? A. I do not know. Q. Was it in Mr. Storrs' hand writing? A. I am unacquainted with his hand writing. Q. What is the Society called? A. Northfield and Sandbornton Anti-Slavery Society. Q. How many belong to the Society? A. Over one hundred. Q. Men or *women?* A. About an equal number. Q. How many legal voters? A. I cannot tell. * Q. Was not three quarters women and children? A. I think

* It was ascertained at the close of the trial that there were fifty legal voters members of the Society.

1*

not—I never looked particularly. I know there was a respectable number of respectable men. Q. Has Mr. Storrs handed any of these little pamphlets and papers with *nigger pictures* on them to you? A. He gave me some Anti-Slavery publications. Q. Did he request you to give them to *women* and *children?* A. He made no particular request. Q. Did not Mr. Storrs know that people here were generally opposed to abolitionists? A. I heard him say nothing about it. The first I saw of him was Sabbath day in the pulpit. I did not see him again till at the meeting on Monday. Mr. Storrs commenced the meeting, on that day, by reading portions of scripture and a hymn—after which he knelt to pray: after praying awhile, I was disturbed by a noise that sounded like a cane brought down on the floor with considerable force, and some one called out, as I understood, "come on boys," * and a rush was made—I rose from my knees and beheld Esq. Tilton standing in the pulpit with his hand on Mr. Storrs shoulder, who was still kneeling with his eyes shut. Q. Is Mr. Storrs employed as a preacher on this Circuit? A. I do not know as he is. Q. Do you know of Mr. Storrs being employed as a preacher for the last six months? A. I heard him preach last Sabbath.

Dearborn Sanborn—sworn. Q. When did Mr. Storrs come to your house? A. Saturday evening. Q. Did he come to deliver an Anti-Slavery Address? A. He came to preach a sermon on slavery. Monday morning Mr. Wells and Mr. Smith came to my house—I introduced them to Mr. Storrs:—they wished he might postpone his lecture. He told them he was the servant of the Society and should do as they wished him to. The Officers were consulted and thought best to proceed. Q. These pamphlets,—have you any of them? A. I have some. Q.

* Sheriff Tilton manifested some *uneasiness* at this testimony, and it was finally admitted that Witness was mistaken as to Sheriff's saying "Come on, boys" in the pulpit, as he had supposed it was. But Esq. Forrest has no doubt, that Sheriff Tilton did say, "Come on boys," though it appears, by others, who say they are ready to testify to the same, that it was at the time Sheriff Tilton started from his pew, for the pulpit; there, he *did* say, "Come on boys."

What did he tell you to do with them? A. I do not know that he gave me any direction. Q. Were the books for *children* or whom? A. For any one who has a mind to read them. Q. Have you read them? A. I have. Q. Have they *pictures* on them? A. Some of them have. Q. Have you heard Mr. Storrs speak of the disturbance these papers have made at the South? A. I have not. Q. Have you read the Paesident's message and McDuffie's speech? A. I have not. Q. Have you heard Mr. Storrs speak of them? A. I have not. Q. How many books did Mr. Storrs leave with you? A. I do not know. Q. Can you tell within a hundred? A. I think there was not a hundred in the whole. Q. Did he leave all he had? A. I do not know. Q. Did you take them out of his sleigh box? A. I did not. Q. Q. Do you belong to the Anti-Slavery Society here? A. I do. Q. How many are there? A. About a hundred and thirty, I believe. Q. What proportion of males? A. I do not know. Q. Have any joined since March? A. I should think so. Q. How many—has five joined since that time? A. I should think there had, more than that. Q. Name some of them? A. I don't know who in particular has joined. [Some questions and answers passed here about Mr. Sanborn's child carrying Anti-Slavery books to the children at school.—Some questions were asked, also, with respect to what passed at Mr. Sanborn's between Mr. Storrs and the Selectmen. As this testimony was similar to that of Mr. Templeton's, it is not reported here.]

[*Cross-examined by Mr. Storrs,* in reference to what the Selectmen of Northfield said in regard to Judge Atkinson and Samuel Tilton, Esq. of Sanbornton, sending them to see him. Mr. Sanborn gave the same testimony, in substance, on this point with Mr. Templeton.]

Judge Atkinson now spoke and said, "I told them they had better go and see him and persuade him to give up his lecture."

Joseph Smith, * sworn. Examined by Judge Atkinson.—

* This witness was the other Selectman who visited me in company with Mr. Wells. I was told by a person who said he was ready to make oath to it, that this witness said, "Mr. Storrs ought to be tarred and feathered." What wonder if such "Selectmen" should think "there would be a riot," when, it seems, they were determined to help make one!! G. S.

Q. Mr. Smith, are you one of the Selectmen of Northfield? A. I am. Q. Did you call on Mr. Storrs and request him not to deliver his lecture? A. I did. Q. How came you to? A. By request of the people. Q. What did he say? A. He said he was the servant of the society and should do as they wished him to. Q. Did you tell him you feared there would be a riot? A. Yes. Q. You did it to prevent a riot, did you? A. Yes. Q. Whatever Mr. Rogers* did was for this purpose, was it not? A. Yes. Q. Where did you see Mr. Storrs? A. At Mr. Sanborn's. Q. Did you tell him you was Selectman? A. No: there was nothing said about it. Q. He said he should deliver it if the Society did not request him not to? A. Yes, that was the substance of it. Q. He said this after you told him of the excitement? A. Yes. Q. There was a great excitement was there? A. Yes.

Cross-examined by Mr. Storrs. Q. Who *first* came to request you to see me? A. [Witness hesitated.]—I don't recollect—a great many. Q. Can you name *any* of them? [Witness hesitated some time and gave no answer.] Q. Did Judge Atkinson? A. I talked with him about it. As I have been informed, it is a common thing for Selectmen to request you not to lecture. Q. Where has it been done? A. Have not the Selectmen of Concord requested you not to? [Mr. Storrs replied, *never*.] Q. What man in *Northfield* requested you to come to me? [Witness hesitated and then answered with considerable apparent irritation] Dolton was one—I don't recollect in particular—O—I don't say that all these come—I did not care whether they come or not.—Question by Judge Atkinson. You went because you thought it was right? A. Yes, so he need not go headlong.

Dr. Enos Hoyt—sworn. Examined by Judge Atkinson. Q. Will you tell what you know? A. Some time last week Capt. Hill called on me and named that they were going to have an ad-

---

* Of Rogers, it may be said, he was, probably, only the *tool* of others: a convenient one to employ, as he has no property, that is known of—had an illegitimate child some years since—and is a rum drinker. He is to be pitied. He *sweat* badly during the trial, though the coldest day we have probably had this winter. He had a hard time no doubt, notwithstanding Esquire Atkinson attended to all the business.

dress—and going to have it by day, so as to face the enemy, and requested me, as I was riding about town to give the friends notice. He likewise wished that I would request Mr. Conant to give notice from his desk. I hesitated, but finally informed Mr. Conant, and the address was appointed, and there was a considerable sensation visible. The next morning visited Mr. Glidden—found a number of the inhabitants thought there would be a riot—it was thought best to visit Mr. Storrs, and request him to pass away and prevent a riot—the Selectmen returned and said there was no prospect but that the address would be delivered.—The Selectmen then thought best to issue a warrant to prevent a mob—they thought that would be a less evil.

Cross-examined by Mr. Storrs. Q. Were all the Selectmen present? A. They were not. Two Selectmen were present; it was only general advice of a number together, a dozen or more. Q. Can you give the names of some of the principal ones? [Witness gave no name.] Q. If there were a dozen, I should suppose you could give us the name of some of them—was Judge Atkinson one? A. I could not say. Q. Was Esq. Tilton? A. I could not say. I could not say, under *oath*, that any one in particular did—I was of opinion myself that it was best to issue a warrant. Question by the Justice. Did you hear me advise, as one of the Selectmen, to make out a warrant? A. I could not say.* Q. By Judge Atkinson. From the conversation you heard was it not thought there would be a riot? A. It was. When Mr. Storrs was here last spring, there was difficulty in families; there was in *my* family—some of the *women* and *children* got to be abolitionists. The day after the address last spring, Elder Harding came to my house, left pamphlets and newspapers—they were sent back again. Q. Was you at the meeting last Monday. A. Yes. [Witness was then questioned in regard to Mr. Storrs' reading.] He read in a little book—it read different from what I have been in the habit of hearing: I do not know whether it was all scripture or not. He then prayed—invoked a blessing

* Dr. Hoyt had said, as will be seen by his testimony, that "the Selectmen [of whom only two were present] thought best to issue a warrant."

1*

on Rulers—and expressed something about *blacks*, bought and sold like cattle in the market—and that they were degraded—denied the Bible, and religious privileges.

Question by Mr. Storrs. Did I pray that the slaves might be quiet, patient, and not *avenge themselves!* A. I believe you did.

Henry Thorn—sworn. Questioned by Judge Atkinson. Do you know any thing about Mr. Storrs? A. I know only by report. Q. Have you heard him preach lately? A. Not within three or four years—had a meeting when he first came on the circuit at Mr. Merrill's— Q. What do you know about the case before us? A. *Don't know anything about it.*

Daniel Hill—sworn. Q. Was you requested to give Mr. Hoyt an invitation to circulate the appointment? A. Was not. Q. Was Mr. Storrs here when the Society was formed? A. He was. Q. Did he take an active part? A. He did. Q. Who read the Constitution? A. I cannot say. Q. How long was Mr. Storrs here? A. Cannot recollect—there was a protracted meeting at that time, and other ministers present. Q. How often does your Society meet? A. It has a yearly meeting on Thanksgiving day. Q. Did it meet? A. It did. Q. Do you know how many belong to it? A. I do not. Q. Has there been any collections made? A. I believe not. Q. Had you a Treasurer? A. I can't say. Q. Did Mr. Storrs request any collection?—A. No.

Mr. Sanborn was again called up by Judge Atkinson. Q. Have you a Treasurer? A. We have. Q. Has there been a contribution? A. None.

Question by Mr. Storrs. Have I not told you that we take up no public collections. A. You have, I believe.

Question by Judge Atkinson. No *public* collections—have there not been *private* ones? A. Not that I know of.

The Prosecution now signified, that the examination of witnesses on their part was closed. Mr. Storrs then rose and said, "I shall make no defence at *this* time. I am ready to hear the sentence of the Court."

The Justice immediately announced, "The opinion of the Court is, that the Prisoner ought to be discharged."

The public will judge for themselves, whether the evidence produced in this trial is of such a character as to justify an Hon. Judge and Justice of the Peace throughout the State, in writing such a *Complaint*, Rogers in *swearing* that in his belief it was just and true, Justice Wells in issuing a warrant and Sheriff Tilton in violating the sanctuary of God, in tearing a minister from the pulpit, while on his knees, in the most solemn act of worship, prayer to Almighty God,—and whether the people of the *State of New-Hampshire*, in the behalf of which the complaint was made, are willing to pay *cost* incurred by such prosecutions.

At the close of the Court, Mr. Storrs addressed himself to Judge Atkinson, told him he had understood the mob party had threatened to be upon him and "*black*" him if the Justice acquitted him. The Judge assured him he should have no molestation, and he had none, thus showing, it would seem, that the Judge and the Sheriff have had an *increase of influence* since the *two* "hard" days labor spoken of by the Sheriff, or else the influence they first exerted was turned in another *direction*.

After Mr. Storrs was discharged, he had no occasion to be a "beggar," to prove which Judge Atkinson labored so hard with the witnesses. His friends gathered around him, and one after another, with their free will offerings, supplied him with much more than was needful to meet all the expenses his detention and prosecution had occasioned him.

In presenting to the public this account of my arrest and trial, I wish to say a few words to my *Christian* friends in particular.

Dear Friends, I doubt not that it has been through your prayers, instrumentally, that through all the scenes I have passed in this matter, God has kept my mind in *perfect peace*. Never did I realize deeper and sweeter communion with Him, and feel more the excellency of the religion of Jesus Christ. The strengthening of my religious *principles* has, to me, been great gain. Those principles which teach us to trust in God at all times; and lead us to reject the abominable doctrine, that we are not to do *duty*, or *obey* Him through fear that some *imaginary* evil "consequences" may follow. God is true to his word. Not one jot thereof shall in anywise fail. While duty to the *oppressed* may make it necessary that we should expose the *wickedness* and *malice* of those who have outraged our rights, I beseech you pray for them, pity them, and indulge in no revengeful feelings towards them.—"They know not what they do." Let us rejoice if God shall account us worthy to suffer anything with those in bonds as bound with them. May the time soon come when oppression shall cease. Allow me to say in conclusion I was never more satisfied than now of the perfect agreement of the *principles* of *abolition* with the Bible—and never more determined that nothing but death, or the overthrow of slavery shall induce me to stop pleading in behalf of perishing slaves. GEO. STORRS.

Concord, N. H., Dec. 22, 1835.

APPENDIX.

About two hours previous to the time appointed for the sermon on Monday, at Northfield, Rev. Mr. Templeton had an interview with Judge Atkinson, in which the Judge gave him to understand that Mr. Storrs would be arrested if he attempted to lecture. Mr. Templeton said, he had given notice to the people that they should have a sermon, and if Mr. Storrs was arrested he should give them one himself. To this the Judge replied, if he did he would have his "*face blacked.*" Mr. Templeton responded, "I had rather have a black *face* than a black *conscience.*"

After Mr. Storrs' arrest, Mr. Templeton read the notice that was given of the meeting the day previous, then chose for his text, Eccl. 4th chapter, 1st and 2d verses. The Records of the Anti-Slavery Society say, that he addressed them "in an able and interesting manner."

Mr. Templeton had never made an attempt to give a sermon on slavery before; his effort, therefore, was much to the credit of his head and heart.

Let mobs force away one lecturer, the Lord can speedily raise up another to fill his place. Mr. Templeton was *cheered* a little in the course of his sermon, by the fag end of the mob, who tarried behind or returned after Mr. Storrs was taken away.

March of Mind.

The inventive and improving genius of our people is not limited to material or inanimate objects. It extends to those intellectual and spiritual agencies, known vulgarly by the name of *mobs*—the staple of the republic and its glory. Some of these precious manifestations, which are every where bidding us not to despair of the republic (or of the Granite State) have recently been elicited, which demonstrate, that there *is* a redeeming spirit in the people!—and that in our other improvements and advancements our mobocracy is not forgotten by us.

Our ingenious fellow-citizen, the honorable Judge Atkinson, got up one the other day at Sanbornton-Northfield, which promises to afford the desideratum so much desired by the higher classes—and the want of which has been such an embarrassment in our late mobs—*a mob according to law*. Our aristocracy are afraid of the mob, because it is contrary to law, and they are apprehensive it will not confine itself to anti-slavery men—but will begin by and by to bray and paw at some of their own thresholds. The law is a convenient protection, and the mob does not exactly acknowledge it. But Judge Atkinson's mob is *according to law*. Mr. Storrs intended to lecture in Northfield.—The anti-slavery people there wanted him to address them. To prevent his being mobbed *contrary* to law, the Judge got up a mob *according* to law, as they vaccinate to keep off small pox. The Judge as was understood, drew a complaint for wanton and lascivious conversation and idleness, and such other things, in the vagrancy act, as most shocked his moral sensibilities, (saying nothing of drinking) and let a poor, irresponsible "gentleman," without "property or standing," swear to it in advance, and had a warrant issued on *ante*-facts, and put on to Mr. Storrs, just as he was dissolving the Union, by a prayer that the slave might not be left to rise upon his oppressors—alamode de '76!

'Squire Tilton served it in the true spirit of *the compact*, and, except the brutality and rudeness of it, in a way to meet the wishes of our "southern brethren." The details of the Judge of Probate's invention will be found in this paper.

Another specimen of mobocracy occurred at Bradford since the above—a sort of *town* mob. It differs from the Canaan mob, which was according to vote of the town—this being by authority of the Selectmen merely, without the intervention of "town meeting"—a sort of incident to their offices, as prudential fathers of the town. The following proclamation which is inserted *verbatim, literatim et punctuatim* and *spell-atim*, is the model of this improvement. There is no limit to yankee genius—and what is peculiar, our great men are among our inventors—men high in station deign to stoop to trial of their wits, and compete for the honors of the patent office.

To Rev. George storres Sir

We had the evidince of your going to hold forth in the Meeting house of this place—the disorganizing doctrine of abolition to the utter detestation of 19/20th of the Peaceble inhabitants of this place—we therefore as Selectmen of the Town of Bradford request you to desist from the under taking. by so doing you manifest your regard for our laws and the peac of the citizen of Bradford and likewise show that you can be operated upon by some thing beside Lynch law.. by your noncomplyanc you will manifest to world that nothomg but mob. will deter you

Moses D Wadley } Select
John Harriman } Men of Bradford

Bradford Dec 21—1835

Well may our fellow-citizens Wadley and Harriman be styled "*select*" among the "men of Bradford." They are not ignorant of the name of Lynch, that sage of the law, who is to supersede in this republic the old Cokes and Hales, and the modern Marshalls.

Extract from Geo. Storrs' Journal.

1835. Dec. 19th. Came to Bradford. Received a hearty welcome by Rev. O. G. Thatcher, Congregational Minister—an unflinching abolitionist. The report of my arrest, at Northfield, had arrived at Bradford before me.

Dec. 20th. Spent the Sabbath pleasantly with Mr. Thatcher—by his request preached three times, to his congregation, during the day and evening. Mr. Thatcher made appointments for meetings on slavery to-morrow afternoon and evening.

Dec. 22. Just as I was about to go to the meeting house, in Bradford, yesterday, I received a very singular document, from two of the selectmen of that town, which may be seen in another part of this paper. We soon discovered that a *Mob* of the "PEACEABLE CITIZENS" had collected, and were nerving themselves up to keep the "*peace*" by the old and faithful *ally* of slaveholders, RUM!!

As the meeting house is owned by the town, it was thought advisable to hold our meeting in a hall near by, which was kindly offered us by the owner, a lady. Mr. Thatcher, myself and some others passed near by the mob without molestation. We entered the hall followed by those who had come to hear the lecture, and the mob party also. There was but slight disturbance in the hall. For a time it seemed probable that notwithstanding the previous threatening aspect, we might be able to hold our meeting in peace. I commenced by prayer—proceeded to make remarks in regard to the objects, views, and designs of abolitionists. I had arrived nearly to the middle of my lecture, when one after another of the mob party rose and went out. Presently the *hurrah* began. The hall was open underneath. The mob commenced with violent assaults against the floor under my feet, this was followed with violent blows against the outside of the house immediately behind me—these efforts to keep the "peace" and "preserve the constitution" were continued, with very little intermission, through the remaining part of my lecture. We had quietness, however, *within*, and I finished in peace. The mob now collected about the door, having stripped a horse of his leading lines, which, doubtless, could do much better without them than they. After waiting in the house awhile, I passed out through the mob, in company with Rev. Mr. Thatcher and his family, without any other molestation than a little of the serpentine hissing, and something said about "nigger" and "don't you come here again." Our meeting in the evening was about two miles from the place where it was held in the day time. As there was a steep hill to ascend, and the mobites had gotten their legs weakened by rum so as to make it difficult to *climb*, or had already obtained so great "*a crown of honour*"—that we held our meeting without interruption.

I learned some rather musical conversation took place at the Post Office or store near by where I lectured, in the forenoon previous. There was a *conjecturing* who this *Storrs* was. Some thought he was a "foreigner," others concluded he must be a "southerner;" his *complexion* indicated that he had "nigger blood in him"—others thought that could not be, for "his hair was *straight*." None of them, however, took me for a slaveholder, or an apologist for slavery; it is, therefore, no matter about the rest.

NARRATIVE

OF THE

LATE RIOTOUS PROCEEDINGS AGAINST

THE

LIBERTY OF THE PRESS,

IN CINCINNATI.

WITH REMARKS AND HISTORICAL NOTICES,

RELATING TO

EMANCIPATION.

Addressed to the people of Ohio, by the Executive Committee of the OHIO ANTI-SLAVERY SOCIETY.

CINCINNATI:
1836.

NARRATIVE

Of the late riotous proceedings against the Liberty of the Press, in Cincinnati.

FELLOW CITIZENS:

The Executive Committee of the Ohio Anti-Slavery Society owe, not only to themselves and those whom they represent, but also to you, generally, an impartial exposition of the late proceedings in this city, with which they have been connected, and which have ended in undisguised outrages on private property, and in a public assault on constitutional right. In order to make this statement as intelligible as possible,—to place in a clear point of view the object of our association—and to enable you to comprehend the whole extent of present danger to our free institutions, it will be necessary to recur to facts in the early history of our country:—Facts, which from their ancientness, it might, at first view, seem unnecessary to introduce, but which will be found, when well considered, to have an intimate connexion with the state of things now before us.

During our colonial dependence, the states were all slaveholding states. They did not, as colonies, possess the power of legislation independently of the control of the mother country, exerted either directly or indirectly. Had they desired, ever so much, to abolish slavery, they could not have done so, by their own independent legislative act. But, it is believed, that prior to the enlightened discussion, and the full establishment of the great principles which led to the American Revolution—principles which are embodied in the Declaration of Independence—the desire was but feeble, in most of the colonies, to see slavery extinguished. It is true, that Petitions were presented to the competent authorities of the mother country to restrain the further importation into the colonies of slaves from *Africa*—but none, to abolish, or to mitigate slavery, as it already existed among the petitioners themselves. The history of the times will show, that it was not *repugnance to slave-holding*, as a violation of the great principles of natural justice or of revealed religion, which constituted the true grounds for urging the petitions;—but, rather, that the *few*, who held in their hands the political power of the country, and who had already become possessed of a large amount of slave-labor, might secure to themselves and their families and connexions, in perpetuity, a monopoly of such labor.* The continued importation of slaves from Africa would put it in the power of such citizens as owned none, to become purchasers, and thus interfere with the present and prospective benefits of the monopoly. The criminality in a moral and religious point of view, of slave-holding, exerted but a feeble influence, a century ago, on the public mind of the civilized world. What is so often alleged now, as "fanaticism" against the abolitionists, would have been more remarkable then. The FRIENDS, were the only sect to whom the criminality of oppression, in the form of slave-holding appeared, even sixty or seventy years ago, as it is now beginning to be seen by others. By treating it as a violation of religious duty, they succeeded in banishing it entirely from their connexion.

The able moral and political discussion to which the disagreements of the colonies with the mother country gave rise, for many years previous to the declaration of independence, brought into general recognition throughout this country, the doctrines of *inalienable rights*, as they have been distinctively termed. Their influence on the most intelligent and patriotic minds, is shown in the fact, that the first Congress, held in 1774, Resolved, *That they would neither import, nor purchase any slave imported after the 1st day of the next December; after which time they would discontinue the slave trade, and neither be concerned in it themselves, nor hire their vessels, nor sell their commodities to such as should be concerned in it.*

In the Congress of 1776, the Declaration of Independence was published—commending itself to the liberal minded every where, by asserting, in opposition to the theory and practice of all existing governments, that *all men were created free, and entitled to life, liberty, and the pursuit of happiness.*

And afterwards, when forming the articles of confederation, 1778, they refused to insert any provision for protecting the power of masters over their slaves, or authorizing a master to follow a runaway slave into another state. In the debates, it was said, that "the slaves ought to be dismissed, that freemen might fill their places."

As soon as the colonies had thrown off the British yoke, their legislative assemblies began their efforts to remove this odious institution. In the northern states, general acts of emancipation were passed—in the southern, acts authorizing

*The temporary government of Texas condemns, in the most pointed terms, the immorality of the *African* slave trade. This will not prove that it is opposed to *slavery*—when it is known, that, by her Constitution, slavery is attempted to be made perpetual, and that the greatest encouragement is given to the *American* slave trade. If the principal adventurers, who control the political affairs of Texas, had as many slaves as *they* wanted, it is not at all unlikely that the *American* slave trade would be put on terms of disgraceful equality with the *African*.

individuals to manumit. Massachusetts had asserted in her declaration of rights, that, *all men were created free and equal.* This was construed by her courts as putting an end—and it did, in fact, put an immediate end to slavery within her limits. The other New England states with New York, New Jersey and Pennsylvania pursued more gradual measures for its extinction.

So strong and rapid had been the influence of the doctrine of "inalienable rights," as set forth in the Declaration of Independence, that Pennsylvania and all the states north of it—making more than half of the whole number—prior to 1787, when the present constitution was formed, had entered on measures leading to the entire extermination of slavery from among themselves. It was this state of things that (it was erroneously supposed) rendered it *expedient* to adopt the provision, that has been construed to authorize the slave-holder to recapture his slave who has escaped into a free state. Whilst this provision was admitted, shame prevented the framers of the constitution from expressing the odious grant of power in direct terms. It is conveyed under an ambiguous form of expression, whilst the word *slave*, is not to be found in that instrument. Neither is *slavery*, the subject matter of the guarantee, by which it is so often, yet so erroneously asserted, that the "system" of the south is secured to her, to be found in the constitution. No "guarantee" by the general government could have been thought necessary to the slave-holders—because the validity of the tenure by which they held their slaves had never been drawn in question, and they themselves looked on it as equally strong, and as unassailable, as the title by which they held any other property. Besides the southern politicians, who, especially, have regarded the general government as secondary to the state-governments, and derivative from them, would not, on this account, have asked from the former a guarantee which the latter were more competent to give. From these considerations, it is believed, that at the formation of the present government, no guarantee of southern 'slavery' either constitutional, or implied, was once seriously thought of—none was demanded—none was offered. And it is not at all improbable, had any such guarantee been offered, in the structure of the general government, it would have been looked upon by the south as, not only in efficacious, but insulting, and calling for the haughtiest rejection.

Soon after the adoption of the present national union, abolition societies were formed in several of the states. Their avowed object was the total extinction of slavery in the United states. The leaders in those societies were the same men whose hands had just laid the foundations of our national institutions. Their principles coincided entirely with the prin-

1*

ciples adopted by the abolitionists of the present day. They denounced slavery as an unjust and wicked system—one that all good men should endeavor to overturn. Their acts agreed with their principles. They wrote tracts against slavery—they petitioned Congress to go to the very "verge" of its constitutional powers for its final extinction. On these petitions, Congress, in the first session, held under the present constitution, acted, and a series of resolutions was adopted, in which the constitutional powers of Congress in relation to slavery were accurately, defined. The doctrines contained in these resolutions are the doctrines of the abolitionists of the present day, namely:—That until 1808, the importation of slaves could not be prohibited by Congress. That the States possess individually the sole power to emancipate their slaves—That congress possesses the authority to regulate the slave trade, and the authority to prohibit it, even prior to 1808, in regard to the supply of foreign nations;—and during the discussion of these resolutions, the right and the duty of Congress to use all means for the abolition of slavery, not expressly prohibited by the constitution, was strongly urged by the leading members of Congress, (particularly by Messrs. Madison and Gerry), who had taken part in the formation of the constitution.

Now if the institution of slavery was, by mutual compromise, to remain inviolate and immoveable, would these illustrious men, such as Jay, Franklin, Rush, Madison, and Gerry, have conducted in this manner? Could a compact like the one in question have been formed, without John Jay being informed of it? Had such been the understanding of a compromise between the different states, is it possible, that the sagacious Franklin, who assisted in making the compromise, should never have understood it? Yet, Jay and Franklin, in their day, were as undoubted abolitionists, and as active in the formation of abolition societies, as any that can be found in modern times; and it was not owing to any lack of zeal on their part, that their labors were not equally as efficacious as those of abolitionists now, in awakening public attention to this momentous subject. John Jay, during the war of the Revolution, held this memorable language—"Till America comes into this measure, (the abolition of slavery) her prayers to heaven for liberty will be impious. "When addressing the Legislature of New York, then a slave state, he told them, that the slaves, though held in bondage by the laws of man were free by the laws of God." Franklin and Jay and Rush in 1787 united in an abolition society, "to extend the blessings of freedom to every part of our race." The writings published by this society and which contain the identical doctrines of "modern abolitionism" are still circulated by the Anti-Slavery Societies, and form a prominent part of the publications now proscribed as "incendiary." Through their influence, slavery was abolished in many of the present non-slave-holding states. The foreign slave trade was prospectively abolished. Washington, previous to his manumission of his own slaves, expressed his conviction that slavery ought to be abolished by legislative power—a sentiment, the expression of which is now thought a sufficient provocation for dissolving the Union. William Pinkney of Maryland, in the House of Delegates of that State, forty-seven years ago, predicted the very crisis to which we are now arrived. If slavery was to be continued, the principles of liberty, he said, would be corrupted and undermined. "The resistance of freemen against oppression" said he "will become a struggle of pride and selfishness, not of principle."—"The stream of general liberty will have flown so long through the mire of partial bondage, that it will have become polluted." "The habit of thinking that the great *rights of human nature*, are not so sacred, but that they may with impunity be trampled upon, will have prepared men for usurpation; *and those who have been habituated to lord it over others, will become base enough to let others lord it over them.*"

From these facts, and from all the examination we have had it in our power to make, we have no hesitation in pronouncing the supposed "compact," or "compromise," to be a groundless fiction, and one, too, of no ordinary malignity. It is nothing less than a libel on the illustrious dead, invented to deprive the living of their dearest and most invaluable rights. It represents the founders of our republican empire, but recently engaged in a most severe conflict for the preservation of those rights which they claimed under the laws of God and nature, in common with all mankind, in assuming their rank among nations, forming a government for a free people, according to the principles of freedom, and for the preservation of those principles, as solemnly contracting that the institution of slavery, every where odious and detestable, should forever remain sacred and inviolable. For the honor of these great and good men—for the honor of human nature itself—we are happy in believing, that a charge, involving such gross inconsistency, is utterly groundless. On the contrary, if there is any reliance to be placed on past history, it is certain, at the commencement of our present political system, there was a general belief and expectation, that Slavery in these United States would be abolished, and that speedily.

Forbearing to advert more particularly at this time, to the opinions of many of the most distinguished and patriotic of the Fathers of our country, we will content ourselves with the general remark, that they considered slavery a great evil in our country, and that time has only added confirmation to this sentiment. Entertaining on this subject the same opinions, and adopting the same measures that they did, a number of our fellow-citizens, from various States of the Union, assembled at Philadelphia in December, 1833, and formed what is now known as the American Anti-Slavery Society. The foundation principles of this Association are—that slave-holding, as it exists among us, is a violation of the plainest dictates of right and justice—that it contradicts all our professions as a people—that it is opposed to the spirit of our government—that it is a *sin*, and ought, therefore, to be immediately and forever abandoned. In order to succeed in convincing their fellow-citizens of the justness of these views—deemed by them the only proper mode of attaining their object (emancipation), they have used, and continue to use, the natural and constitutional right, secured to every citizen, of freely discussing and exposing the false foundations on which slavery has been, heretofore, supported, and the multiplying and fast-hastening ills with which it threatens to overwhelm us as a people. Although the American Anti-Slavery Society has been in existence so short a time, and has had arrayed against its peaceful operations, a fierce and unrelenting hostility, yet there have been formed on its model, and in nearly all the instances *auxiliary* to it, between five and six hundred anti-slavery societies, pursuing the same objects, by the same means. The Ohio Anti-Slavery Society is one of them. It was organized in April, 1835, by more than one hundred delegates, assembled at the village of Putnam, from all parts of the State. The objects of the association are thus stated in the second article of the Constitution:—

"The object of this Society, shall be the entire abolition of Slavery throughout the United States, and the elevation of our colored brethren to their proper rank as men. While it admits that the several States and Congress have, by our Federal Constitution, the exclusive right to legislate for the abolition of slavery in their respective limits, it maintains that it is our imperative duty, to collect and diffuse information on the subject of Slavery, and by all lawful means to convince our fellow-citizens throughout the Union, that Slavery is, in all circumstances, a sin against God and His revealed law,—at war with the fundamental principles of our own liberty, and ruinous to our national morals and prosperity; and that, therefore, the duty, safety, and interest of all concerned, require its utter and immediate abolition."

At the time it was formed, there were in this State, it was thought, not more than fifteen or twenty minor societies. In one year afterward their number had multiplied to more than ONE HUNDRED AND TWENTY, including of our citizens not less than from TEN to TWELVE THOUSAND. The neighborhood societies continue rapidly to grow in number. The Ohio Anti-

Slavery Society conducts its business through an Executive Committee, of which, at present, the undersigned are members.

It is thought necessary to recur to circumstances, which, in the order of time, preceded our appointment as members of the Executive Committee. When the REIGN OF TERROR was introduced into the South, last summer, by the sudden and public execution, without trial, of five American citizens, charged with being "*professional*" gamblers—whilst it was kept up by the open plundering of the National Mail—by the pretence of slave-insurrections—by the most degrading inflictions—by numberless cruel and unauthorized *scourgings* of such as had either removed from the free States to the South, or were temporarily called thither on business—by the offering of REWARDS for the forcible abduction of peaceable and inoffensive citizens, with the avowed purpose of handing them over to the tender mercies of infuriated slaveholders—by the unconcealed, the open and illegal *hangings* of many of our countrymen in the South, on whom popular suspicion had fastened the obnoxious sentiment, that they were opposed to the system of slavery as it existed there;—whilst, we say, this thirst for blood, and for the demolition of every safeguard heretofore established for the protection of individual right, was raging among our Southern neighbors, the city of Cincinnati was not altogether exempt from the disgraceful infection. Our principal daily newspapers, with, it is believed, but a single exception, sympathised with the flagellators and tormenters, and murderers of the South, and by their loud shouts cheered them on to further deeds of cruelty and blood. Whilst *one* of them was bestowing unqualified applause on the public scourging of our fellow-citizen, young Mr. Dresser, although the perpetrators of the outrage themselves, acknowledged he had violated no law of the state where he suffered*—*another*, as if to render forever unnecessary any further proof of plenary consecration to the interests of slaveholders, exultingly advised, that the Reign of Terror—more technically known as "Lynch Law"—be set up here in Cincinnati.†

One of our number, who, before the explosion of Southern violence, had projected the establishment of a journal in Kentucky, his native state, to be devoted to a full and impartial discussion of the whole subject of slavery, as connected with emancipation, was thwarted in his object by the devices of the neighboring slave-holders, and ultimately compelled, by their persecutions, to remove with his family from the state. Looking at the *Constitution* of Ohio, he there saw the fullest, the most honorable, and at the same time, the most solemn condemnation that men who love liberty could pass upon slave-

* See Appendix A. † See Appendix B.

ry—and that to every one was secured the right—pronounced "*indisputable*"—of *speaking*, *writing*, or *printing on any subject*, to the investigation of which he might choose to apply the powers of his mind. With this view of *rights* intended to be secured to him, in common with every other citizen, by you, the PEOPLE OF OHIO; and this, too, by the solemn sanction of the highest, the very organic, law, which constitutes you a PEOPLE, it was not to be supposed that any one—especially such as were using the same rights in their most wanton latitude—would be found of a temper so unjust, so treasonable, as to deny him also the enjoyment of them. In this he was mistaken; for before he had himself come to the conclusion to transfer the publication of his paper to this city, the newspapers before alluded to, were roused to opposition—were encouraged in their outrageous menaces, and animated to their work of villification and abuse; and this, too, as it was said, and as subsequent events have proved, by persons who are reckoned as of "the most respectable class in society,"—owning large real estate in the city—speculators in property, stocks, &c.—merchants, who have commercial connexions with Southern slave-holders—and artizans, who are mostly employed in manufacturing household furniture, or steam boat, sugar house, or other heavy machinery, for the South. So highly excited had the several descriptions of people just mentioned become against the proposed publication, and so effectually had they plied their efforts to alarm the great mass of peaceable and law-abiding citizens, who, otherwise, would have felt but little concern on the subject; and so desirous was the intended editor to remove even the *occasion* of any disgraceful popular explosion, that he determined to commence the publication *out* of the city, and to continue it there till a fair, and impartial, and generous character could be established for the paper.

To establish such a character was considered desirable, not only because it is right in itself—but because it would tend to allay an objection often made to the discussion of the slavery question—*that it was conducted in a fierce and uncharitable spirit*. With this object in view—and further, that all occasion of exciting the disorderly of whatever standing and condition, to any illegal out-burst might be taken away, the Philanthropist (the paper alluded to) was commenced at the village of New Richmond, twenty miles above Cincinnati. But this concession, made at no small sacrifice of convenience and pecuniary means, to the spirit of misrule, was followed by but small mitigation of its fury. Although the Editor, in the temper of conciliation that he felt, and in the most respectful language he could use, offered to *slave-holders* the use of his columns for the defence of slavery, and gave, in his own manner of treating the subject, satisfactory proof of moderation and fairness—still, this did not shield him from a deliberately concerted attempt, set on foot and prosecuted chiefly by the description of persons before mentioned, to *put down his press.* On the first appearance of the Philanthropist, the editor, and those who concurred with him in sentiment, were assailed in terms signally abusive, through two of the business papers of this place, (the Republican and Whig) although they differed widely in their views as political partisans. These journals were, on that occasion, as they have been on a more recent and more remarkable one, the instruments, busily set to work by the "wealthy and respectable," to excite the ignorant and disorderly to such deeds of mischief as the supposed necessities of the case might call for.

The Philanthropist had not reached its fourth No. when more than fifty persons, answering mainly the description above given, called, through the daily papers, a meeting, on the 22d January last, of the citizens opposed to abolition, &c. The MAYOR of the city presided, assisted by four Vice Presidents—Judge Burke, a minister of the Gospel, and Postmaster of Cincinnati—Judge Burnet, late a Senator of the United States, as well as member of the Supreme Court of Ohio—Mr. Neville, Receiver of the Land Office in this District—and the Rev. Oliver M. Spencer, a wealthy minister of the Gospel residing here Several of the resolutions were intended to convince the South of the high regard in which the meeting held their peculiar "rights." One, expressed the opinion of the meeting as adverse to emancipation in the District of Columbia. But the resolution which was calculated to evince the purest devotion to the South, was that, by which, in effect, it was resolved to suppress, either *in the city* or *in the neighborhood,* any paper which might be established for the purpose of discussing the slavery question.

After this formal proclamation of fealty by the aristocracy of this city to the paramount aristocracy of slave-holders in the South,* and an assurance of no equivocal character given, that a sacrifice of the rights of freemen *here* should be made, whenever called for, to secure the perpetuation of the wrongs of slaves *there,* a delusive calm succeeded. The Philanthropist, unawed by the menaces which had been directed against it, proceeded without interruption, The character to which it aspired was thought to have been so fully earned during the first three months of its existence, and the pro-slavery fury so

* We do not call a man an Aristocrat, because he enjoys station and wealth; nor because he is accomplished and refined; nor because he is honored and esteemed. The Aristocrat is he whose "proud look is an abomination to God;" he who "reproacheth his maker" by "despising the poor."

greatly to have passed off, that it was deemed advisable, about the middle of April, to remove the office, Press, &c. to Cincinnati. This was accordingly done, and its publication was continued without concealment, and without molestation.

At the first anniversary of the Ohio Anti-Slavery Society, held near Granville, in April, it was determined that the Executive Committee should be located in Cincinnati, and that the Philanthropist, with the consent of the Editor, should be placed under their control. Its subscription list, at the commencement, did not exceed 700; at the recent destruction of the office, it amounted to about 1700, and was rapidly increasing. Testimony was given, almost daily, of the fair, and manly, and respectful conduct of it. From the time of its removal to Cincinnati, there was not the least show of molestation till the 12th of July. At midnight a band of men, amounting to thirty or forty in number, including those who stood as sentries at different points on the street, made an assault on the premises of Mr. Pugh, the printer, scaled a high wall by which the lot was enclosed, and with the aid of a ladder and plank mounted the roof of the press-office. They then made their way through a window on the roof into the room below—intimidated into silence, by threats of bodily violence, a boy who was asleep there—covered his head with the bed-clothes to prevent him from seeing who were the perpetrators—tore up the paper that was prepared for that week's No. of the Philanthropist, as well as a large part of the impression of an omitted No. that had not yet been mailed—destroyed the ink—dismantled the press, and carried away many of its principal parts. Whilst the depredation was going on within doors, a watch of the confederates was stationed in the street, near the door of Mr. Pugh's dwelling house, to prevent him from giving the alarm. A remarkable feature in the transaction is this—notwithstanding so long time (nearly or quite two hours) was occupied in doing the mischief, and that Mr. Pugh's premises lie on one of the principal streets of the city, and that the noise and confusion made by the rioters were loud enough to wake many of Mr. P's neighbors (who were mysteriously admonished to be quiet)—still, no interference was offered by the night-watch of the city, to prevent the outrage. Whilst this circumstance must strike every one as remarkable, it has been said in explanation of it, that the watchmen generally were paying particular attention to another quarter of the city where it was expected a disturbance would take place. Although the names of the actors in this scene have not been sufficiently ascertained to authorize their publication—yet, there is reason to believe, that some of the leaders were persons of wealth and reputed respectability, who would never, before this, have been suspected of having been engaged in such a transaction. The *work* was done, as it is supposed, by their dependants and hirelings. Three of the *operatives* came from Covington, on the Kentucky side of the river. Information given to Mr. Pugh by a gentleman residing in Covington, and a note written apparently with friendly intentions to one of the Executive Committee, by a person also professing to reside in that place, confirm the accuracy of the last statement.

Next morning, as soon as the damages could be repaired, the business of the office went on as usual. Various reports as to the number, character, designs, &c. &c. of the persons concerned in committing the trespass were put in circulation. In the midst of the conflicting accounts and opinions, it was not difficult to be discerned, that there was a *plan* concerted to produce *intimidation* in those concerned in the press.

What was the immediate cause—if it was *single*—that excited to the violence, it is by no means easy to fix upon. The following incident is related as probably exercising some influence. Whilst that part of the colored people of the city, who celebrate the anniversary of American Independence on the *fifth* of July, were making ready for marching in procession, one of our white citizens of "standing" approached a knot of four or five of them conversing together in the street, and commenced abusing the colored people, as a class, in terms of unmeasured severity—opposing their walking in procession—charging them with subsisting by pilfering and plundering—and with enticing away the slaves of southern visiters. It happened that among the number thus accosted, there was one whose spirit had not been subdued into full submission to insult. He retorted with a firmness and fierceness of tone and language—inspired somewhat, perhaps, by the enthusiasm of the day—altogether unexpected by the assailant. The latter retired from the spot, galled, it may well be supposed—at the insult to which his imprudence had exposed him. This incident may have been but slightly, if at all, connected with the transaction of the twelfth. It is mentioned, because of the well known hostility of the person concerned to anti-slavery measures—because of their generally received connexion with the colored people—and because of his intimacy with many other influential citizens, who sympathise with him in his sentiments and feelings on these subjects.

A more efficient cause however may be found in the presence of slave-holding visitors from the *planting* South. Many of the southern planters and merchants, for purposes of business or pleasure, and to escape the unhealthiness of their own climate, spend much of the summer and the early part of autumn in the free states. It is a fact deserving remark, in passing, that nearly all, if not all, the larger mobocratic assaults that have been made, of late, on the constitutional rights of the free states, with a view of serving and conciliating the slave-holders, have occurred during those seasons. Judging from the crowded state of our principal fashionable Hotels and boarding houses, it was supposed, that Cincinnati had received at the usual time, this summer, her usual influx of southern visiters. It will be seen, in the progress of this exposition, that too much influence in producing the recent disorders, has not been attributed to this cause, in conjunction with that exercised by requests, or rather, *orders* from the South, requiring that the Anti-Slavery discussion should receive no entertainment here. In the mass of persons who, whilst they have their citizenship in the free states, are desirous of aiding in the perpetuation of slavery in the South, there is an alacrity of subservience, that is altogether astonishing. The presence of the slave-holder—especially if he work his ONE OR TWO HUNDRED SLAVES—kindles their zeal, and animates to acts of sycophancy and servility almost incredible. In the excess of their fidelity to the interests of the *South*, they forget that there are any interests of the *North*. Thus, they are liable, not only to overstep their orders, but frequently outrun the most sanguine expectations, the warmest hopes, of the slave-holders themselves.

We shall now endeavor, as faithfully as we can, to exhibit the machinery, and the manner in which it was worked, to bring about the catastrophe which almost every one now begins to feel has injuriously affected the character of our city. We would preface it with this remark,—that from the time the *Philanthropist* was brought to Cincinnati, up to the first onset of the 12th July, there had not a single paragraph appeared against it in any of the City newspapers. Its influence as well as its list of subscribers, in the city, was small, though gradually on the advance.

The night succeeding that on which the invasion of Mr. Pugh's premises was made, the following *placard* was stuck up on the corners of the streets. It is said to have been prepared by a Mr. Graham and a Mr. Wood, (the former somewhat conspicuous in the scenes of the recent drama, the latter the Editor of the *People's Echo*,) and to have been *printed* in Covington.

ABOLITIONISTS BEWARE.

The Citizens of Cincinnati, embracing every class, interested in the prosperity of the City, satisfied that the business of the place is receiving a vital stab from the wicked and misguided operations of the abolitionists, are resolved to arrest their course. The destruction of their Press on the night of the 12th instant, may be taken as a warning. As there are some worthy citizens engaged in the unholy cause of annoying our southern neighbors, they are appealed to, to pause before they bring things to a crisis. If an attempt is made to re-establish their press, it will be viewed as an act of defiance to an already outraged community, and on their own heads be the results which follow.

Every kind of expostulation and remonstrance has been resorted to in vain—longer patience would be criminal. The plan is matured to eradicate an evil which every citizen feels is undermining his business and property.

The following prophetic comment was made on it, the next day, by the Evening Post, one of our most decided pro-slavery papers.

ABOLITIONISM.

A considerable excitement against the Abolitionists has existed in our city for some time past. Murmurs of discontent at their proceedings have been heard on all sides, and there is reason to believe that there is something like a systematized plan on foot to prevent the publication of their Journal in this city. We had entertained a hope that there would be order and quiet after the proceedings of the night of the 12—that the Abolitionists would desist from publishing their paper here, and that those who had undertaken to prevent them, would be satisfied with what had already been done, and the peace of the city be preserved. But this morning we noticed the following handbill stuck up in all directions, and there is *cause* to fear that unless the arm of the law is strong enough to protect the Abolitionists, some act disgraceful to our city will be performed, if they attempt the re-establishment of their press.

The following note was privately deposited in the scales of a respectable and industrious tradesman of Cincinnati, on the morning of the 15th inst.

"Cincinnati, July 14, 1836.

Sir,—It is said that you profess friendship to the cause of abolition. We wish you immediately upon the reception of this to put your answer in your window so that one of many may see it, and report the same. The simple word *Yes* or *No*, will suffice. Be sure you comply immediately. ANTI-ABOLITION.

Mr.——————

Present.

The next afternoon, Mr. Pugh, accompanied by two of the Executive Committee, had an interview with the Mayor. It was suggested, that for the latter, to offer in his official character a reward for the detection of the rioters—and to call on the citizens in the usual form of a Proclamation, to be vigilant in the preservation of the peace, would contribute to allay the spirit that was at work. One hundred dollars were deposited with him, next day, as the reward to be offered, and it was expected that the Proclamation would have appeared in the afternoon. It did not however—and its postponement was apologized for, on the ground of other pressing business. It did appear however, on the morning of the 16th, and here it is—an insult to those who claimed for their constitutional rights the protection of the laws, and an invitation, in effect, to those who were aiming at their overthrow, to advance to their work without fear. It need scarcely be said, that, had it been submitted before publication to Mr. Pugh, or the Executive Committee, it would have been utterly repudiated.

MAYOR'S OFFICE, CINCINNATI, July 15th.—One Hundred Dollars have been placed in my hands with a request that it may be offered as a reward for the apprehension and conviction of the person or persons who broke into the Printing Office of A. Pugh, on Walnut street, tore the press to pieces, and destroyed a quantity of ink, paper &c. in the morning of the 13th inst.

I do therefore, hereby offer the sum of ONE HUNDRED DOLLARS, for the apprehension and conviction of the person or persons concerned in the transaction described above.—And I do hereby forwarn all persons from engaging in acts of a similar nature, and call upon them as good citizens, anxious to preserve and maintain the supremacy of the laws, to prevent as far as in their power, all others from engaging therein; and it is especially enjoined upon the officers of the police to be active and vigilant in their endeavors to maintain the good order and peace of the city.

And I do earnestly entreat those persons whose proceedings, it is alledged, have prompted to the commission of the riot complained of, as they value the quiet of the city, to abstain from the further prosecution of such measures as may have a tendency to inflame the public mind, and lead to acts of violence and disorder, in contempt of the laws and disgraceful to the city.

Given under my hand, this 15th day of July, 1836.

S. W. DAVIES, Mayor.

To what extent this singular manifesto of the Mayor may have excited the disorderly elements among us to greater boldness, may be seen with tolerable clearness by recurring to the tone and spirit of the *slavery*-part of the public press in this city. Simultaneously with the issuing of the Proclamation, the Cincinnati Whig, in opposition to its usual course, published a sensible and well written communication, signed S. condemning the recent assault on the press, and insisting on the reasonableness of meeting the abolitionists with arguments, rather than with brute-force. The tenor of the communication was extolled by the gentleman, to whom, during a few days absence of the regular editor, the conduct of that paper had been entrusted. Although the slavery-press here had not rebuked, with any severity, the violence already perpetrated, yet, it is not remembered that it published any article, *stimulating* the mob to further assault, prior to the publication by the Mayor. On Sunday the 17th July the following hand-bill was posted up at the corners of the streets.

"A FUGITIVE FROM JUSTICE,"
$100 REWARD.

"The above sum will be paid for the delivery of one James G. Birney, a fugitive from justice, now abiding in the city of Cincinnati. Said Birney in all his associations and feelings is *black*; although his external appearance is white. The above reward will be paid and no questions asked by OLD KENTUCKY.

The next day the Whig contained the following editorial article,—

"PUBLIC SENTIMENT."

"We have been informed on indisputable authority that a large number of the boarders at the Franklin House in this city have left their quarters on account of the reception of Mr. Birney, editor of the Philanthropist, as a boarder.

"There is, no doubt an overwhelming majority in the city opposed to the wild schemes of the abolitionists."

The same day the Executive Committee published the following address to the people of Cincinnati.

FELLOW CITIZENS:

The undersigned beg leave to address you. The occurrences of the last week authorize them to do so, and solemnly persuade you to hear. There is no longer any reason to doubt, that there exists among us a secret confederacy, whose bond of union is a covenent to put down the liberty of the press and the freedom of speech. Those, the gifts of God to every man, no matter what his condition; at his birth—intended to be secured to him beyond the power of interruption, by the firmest and most sacred guards of Constitutional law; these, without which all abuses, and tyrannies, and usurpations, may riot without shame or restraint, and the weak continue, without hope, to be the prey of the powerful; these, which have been provided as the means of reforming every vice in our political and social organization, are the special object of assault and violence on the part of this secret association.

On Tuesday last at the hour of midnight, the premises of a peaceable and unsuspecting citizen were invaded; a guard was placed at his door, of sufficient strength to subdue all resistance, and to repress every attempt on his part to call on his neighbors or the city-watch for aid;—in this duress his office was entered, his press dismantled, and other private property connected with the press wantonly abused and destroyed.

Nor did they stop here. The next day was used to diffuse throughout the city every means of intimidation—the association was spoken of as large in number, and respectable and wealthy gentlemen were said to be associated with it.

Nor was this all. On Wednesday night, *placards* were posted up in the most public places. threatening renewed outrage—openly declaring that a *re-establishment* of the Press would be viewed as *an act of defiance*, and that a plan was matured utterly to eradicate it as an "evil."

Nor is this all. Threats of personal violence have been made against several of the undersigned, peaceable and law-abiding citi-

2*

zens, because they think, and have dared to say, that *slavery*, as it exists in our government, is an evil which is fast eating away the pure republicanism on which our institutions were intended to be based—which brings into contempt the great and everlasting truths of God's word, as set forth in our memorable *Declaration of Independence*, that *all men are created equal—entitled to their liberty, and to the pursuit of happiness;* that it tends to rear up—nay, that it has already reared up—a fierce and domineering aristocracy in this Republic, and that it will, if not early abandoned, certainly bring upon the country terror, and carnage, and consternation and disolution.

Nor is this all. A handbill has been posted up in the streets and other public places in Cincinnati, offering a reward for the abduction of one of the undersigned, because of his opposition to slavery, describing him as a fugitive from justice: thus insulting the People of Ohio, who have in their most solemn state paper—their Constitution—passed their ever memorable reprobation of the political iniquity of slavery.

The Press that was assailed, was used for printing the Philanthropist, a journal established with the view of proving, by facts and arguments, not only the practicability of abolishing slavery by peaceable measures, but the pressing necessity of doing so, if we wish to preserve our own liberties. More than one hundred of the citizens of Cincinnati, and more than one thousand of the freemen of Ohio, are subscribers to it.

The people of Ohio have said through their *Constitution*, that the Press "shall be open and free to every citizen"—"That every citizen has an indisputable right to speak, write or print upon any subject as he thinks proper, being liable for the abuse of that liberty." A band of lawless men arrray themselves against the Constitution, declaring that *their* will and not that of the *People* is paramount. What, Fellow Citizens, ought we to do in such a case? Ought we to yield to fear? Ought we basely to surrender a right pronounced by the highest law of the land to be "INDISPUTABLE," to a band of men who have entered into a treasonable combination to overthrow *all* law? No: we feel that your answer is responsive to our determination; and that we are exhorted by every man who feels the preciousness of the great principles that have been attacked, and that are still menaced, to go on, till the entire supremacy of law, and the entire contempt of its adversaries shall be fully established in this community.—We have now, in some degree, from the force of circumstances, committed to our custody, the rights of every freeman in Ohio—of their offspring—of our own. Shall we, as cravens, voluntarily offer them up, sacrifices to the spirit of misrule and oppression—or as American citizens, contend for them, till a force which we cannot withstand, shall wrest them from our hands? The latter part of the alternative we have embraced, with a full determination, by the help of God to maintain unimpaired the freedom of speech and the liberty of the press—the PALLADIUM OF OUR RIGHTS.

JAMES C. LUDLOW,
REES E. PRICE,
JAMES G. BIRNEY,
ISAAC COLBY,
WM. DONALDSON,
JOHN MELENDY,
G. BAILEY,
THOMAS MAYLIN,
C. DONALDSON.

Executive Committee of the Ohio Anti-Slavery Society.

July 18th, 1836.

This was quickly succeeded by the two following articles—the first from the Whig—the other from the Republican of July 21st.*

Mr. Editor:—Allow me to ask the people of Cincinnati (I mean those really interested in her prosperity,)—through the medium of your paper, if they do not intend at this time, now, to give so decided an expression of their sentiments as regards abolition, that those who are injuring the character and prospects of this city, may know and *feel* that this is not the place for them.

Will they permit a band of fanatics, led on by an English emissary, to make this city the theatre of their operations, from whence they may throw fire-brands in the slave States, that will kindle a fire, that will not be quenched till this glorious Union shall be dissolved, and the blood of the innocent—of women and children—cry for vengeance?

A word of advice to Messrs. Ludlow, Price, Donaldson, &c.—Publish no more cards or addresses about midnight invasions. Eschew the society of James G. Birney. Avoid him as you would a viper. Mind your affairs. Consult your own interests and the interests of the community from whom you are deriving a support, and from whom some of you have acquired fortunes. If any of you are foreigners we would advise you, most especially to be silent on the subject of slavery. A large majority of our citizens, have taken the foolish notion into their heads that they understand their own institutions and their own interest quite as well as certain foreign dictators.—*Verbum sat.*

July 19. The Whig had the following article, purporting to be an answer to the communication before mentioned, signed S. The Editor makes this remark concerning it.

"In relation to the remarks of our correspondent, Public Sentiment, we have only to reiterate, that we are alike opposed to abolitionists and mobs."

To the Editor of the Whig.

Sir:—It is in reply to a certain article under the signature of S., in your paper of this date (July 16) and which is favorably noticed by you, upon the subject of recent occurrences in this city, that I now address you. As to the general proposition therein embraced upon the subject of government and law, there is no doubt, and no one would be more unwilling to see them infringed than myself—but occasions may arise in which these principles, however correct and true, must be set aside, they must give place to higher considerations. In a country such as ours, the public good is, and must be, paramount to all else; upon this principle it was founded, in and through it can it only be sustained. Did our fathers stop to talk about subserviency to the established institutions of the land when rebellion first raised her standard against the tyranny of Great Britain? Did they thus reason when the *tories* were to be taught that there were *other powers* in existence than their *legitimate king* and his laws? I trow they did not, as the destruction of the Tea in Boston harbor, and many a tory *dangling* from a *bough*, or garnished in his *right loyal and courtly dress of tar and feathers* can attest. No Sir—they were men who revered and respected the laws so long as they were productive of the

*Both had previously published our advertisements for the sale of Anti-Slavery publications at the Depository.

public good, and in unison with the public sentiment, but they did not deem themselves the slaves of the law—they were not such worshippers of the idol, of their own or other men's creation as not to know that when through their means they were theatened with destruction they must set them aside. In the language of one of the eloquent sons of New England, they looked upon such a state of their affairs as a most serious calamity—yet when the crisis did come they felt bound to meet it like men, to summon all the energies of the soul, rise above ordinary maxims and to hold themselves responsible only to their God. Such was the reasoning of our revolutionary fathers—may we not thus reason now? Are not the lives of thousands and thousands of our citizens threatened? The Government menaced and the union, tottering upon the verge of a dissolution, through the machinations of a few individuals amongst us? And is there not reason to suppose that many of those who are engaged in this unholy warfare upon all we hold dear are in the pay, and doing the work of the Autocrats and lordlings of Europe?—The minions of power and legitimacy, who would gladly see us destroyed and the "world's last hope" go down in blood? Is not such I say, the case? And have we not come to a state and condition which no American lawgiver could have anticipated, and by consequence, which no law can meet? And are not the American people from North to South, from East to West, now acting in accordance with this emergency.

Every where the deep execration and anathema of the people havegone up against the Abolitionists. Wherever they have dared to appear, derision, and scorn, and punishment has awaited them, for in them the people beheld their enemies, and the would-be-destroyers of their country. A Garrison, the Missionary of Britain, and probably the hired stipendiary of the Autocrat himself, was led through the streets of Boston, the cradle of Liberty, with a halter about his neck, which was only not used in a more effectual manner by his promising never again to disgrace the shores of the Republic by his presence. In other places their reception has been similar to this. In Cincinnati alone have they received even the least countenance. To what this may be attributed, whether to apathy, indifference, or a mistaken magnanimity, it is unnecessary now to enquire; let it suffice to say, that here too the day is past—that the people of Cincinnati love their country and its institutions, and in the words of our present Chief Magistrate, will say of the Union, "it must be preserved." A demonstration of their feeling has already gone forth, they have shown that they were alive to their own interest, and the general welfare. To this demonstration it appears that S. objects, but let me tell him that his objections are vain. This is not the time nor the occasion for such arguments as he advanced—the times call for other principles of action, and public sentiment will not be satisfied by any thing short of submission to its just demands. In the name of that public sentiment I would say to S. to all abolitionists and amalgamationists, emancipationists, or by whatever other name they may call themselves, who are here interfering with the laws and institutions of our neighboring slaveholding states, and serving either through blind zeal and fanaticism, or as hireling tools for pay, the enemics of America, that this city is no longer an abiding place for them. And to Mr. S. in particular I would say, far better would it be for him, to counsel those who, driven out from their native homes, as outcasts, seek to make this city the den of their iniquities, to depart in peace now while they may, than attempt in any way to screen them from the just vengeance of an injured people.

PUBLIC SENTIMENT.

On the morning of the 21st this card appeared in the Cincinnati Gazette.

PUBLIC MEETING.

A meeting of the citizens is requested on Saturday evening next, at 6 o'clock, at the Lower Market House, in Cincinnati, to decide whether they will permit the publication or distribution of Abolition papers in this city. It is requested that Nicholas Longworth, Jacob Burnet, Morgan Neville, David Loring, John C. Wright, John P. Foote, Charles Tatem, Anthony Harkness, David T. Disney, Charles Ross, David Griffin, A. L. Vorheos, Wm. Phillips, Hamilton Lyon, Thomas W. Bakewell, Archibald Irwin, John H. Groesbeck, Josiah Lawrence, Robert Buchanan, Jaboz Reynolds, Sanders Hartshorne, Geo. W: Neff, William Burke, Benjamin Urner, Wm. Greene ,Samuel Perry, Geo. P. Torrence, Joseph Gest, Wright Smith, Lewis Shoveley, Joseph Talbot, Dr. Whitman, Allen Wilson, Archibald Gordon, John Leatherbury, John Wicks, James Goodloe, Willis Tatem, Jacob Strader, Sam'l Talbot, Jacob Resor, and R. F. L'Hommedieu be a committee to prepare resolutions and submit the same to the meeting, that shall fairly and decisively be a test of the people, it being alleged that there is a settled determination existing in an overwhelming majority of the citizens to put down the alleged evil by force if admonitions are found insufficient. The peace of our city requires that the voice of the community be known.

The Whig followed this on the 23d with the second No. of Public Sentiment, as follows:—

Mr. Editor: *Sir:*—I see by your paper of this morning, (July 22,) that "Hamilton" is in the field in defence of his friend S. it is well, for we know the old adage, "two heads," &c. But it appears that Hamilton's knight errantry stops not here; for, while with one hand, he flourishes his tronchant blade in behalf of S., the other is extended in defence of the city. "Brave heart and soul of chivalry!" would that some field worthy of thy prowess might present itself. But, alas! for thy renown, as "harvest knight," the "queen city will protect herself; and if in so doing, she meet not the approbation of her would-be-gallant defender, we can only say, that "such things are and will be." Ladies and their knights have, ere this, had their quarrels; and some will say, have loved the better for them—so may it be in this case. Yes, the city will protect herself; and in so doing, will sustain a nation's *first great law, self preservation.*—Her citizens have not yet attained to that elevation of reason and thought, by which it is made to appear, as Hamilton would inform us, that her character may be attacked, her commerce and business injured, the government threatened, and the domestic peace and quiet of her neighbors disturbed, by a *few hirelings of the despots of Europe*, or fanatical refugees, who have taken shelter in her bosom, and yet her citizens, her artizans, merchants, and working men, upon whom the enquiry falls, cannot and *dare* not seek a remedy. The *few* in violation of the first principles, upon which this government is founded—compromise and forbearance—setting aside the rights of the sovereign States to the regulation and adjustment of their own internal concerns, may inflict an injury which would soon blast the fair prospects of our country, and destroy the hopes of republicanism throughout the land; yet the *many* cannot, must not resist it. See other days, when America was in danger, our fathers did not thus *reason* or *practice*. *Public sentiment* then spoke a different language. It does so now. And in its name, will I say to those whom it may concern—to those enemies of the Union, who are now here, by printing and publication, whether from *treasonable* or mistaken views, doing the work of those who would destroy us and our institutions—desist.

Thus far, the peaceful and law abiding citizens of Cincinnati, have refrained from violence towards you. Heretofore, they have remonstrated—they have argued—they have represented to you that the internal laws and institutions of other States were nothing to them, that your interference with them was destructive of the best interests of their beloved and beautiful city—injurious to the reputation of her merchants and traders in the South, producing *non-intercourse*, and an alienation of feeling on the part of the slave-holding States highly prejudicial to her mechanics and artisans, and by consequence to every part of her population. They have also told you that the course you were pursuing must lead to a dissolution of the Union—to the destruction of that government which founded through the blood and toil of their fathers, it is their choice and boast to maintain. This they have done in public and in private, by speaking and writing—through the press, and public meetings, you have known that such was the *public sentiment*. Yet you have defied it, and still persist in your course. Strangers among us as most of you are, citizens of other states and governments, fugitive amalgamationists from your native homes, here you have found an asylum and protection, but *adder* like, you have turned upon your benefactors, and to gratify a blind and mistaken zeal, or a desire for gain or notoriety, are now inflicting upon them the deepest injuries. To all this they have offered nothing but expostulation, hoping that it might prevail, and the peace and quiet of the city be preserved. In this reasonable expectation they have been disappointed; and now, feeling that they have forborne till forbearance has ceased to be a virtue, they conceive themselves called upon by an imperative sense of duty to their country, their families and themselves, to ACT. What has already occurred is "*not a beginning.*" Once more then hear the warning voice of one that will not willingly injure you, but who will be obeyed—*desist*—or sure there will be a *beginning*, and when that beginning comes the *ending* is also at hand. Remember.

PUBLIC SENTIMENT.

In the same paper was the following editorial:

Far be it from us to tolerate that murderous and despicable doctrine [abolition] in the slightest degree. We loathe, we utterly abhor it. As lovers of order, however, and as enthusiastic advocates for the supremacy of the law, we feel bound to express our belief in the pernicious tendency of mobs—and it is alone this conviction that induces us to publish the remarks of "Hamilton." We nevertheless cannot but admit that there may be *ex necessitate rei* exception to every general rule. We have not now the leisure nor the space to show by arguments, in what cases these exceptions may exist. There is, however, such a thing as "self preservation," which every one admits to be paramount to all law, and which it is perfectly justifiable to adhere to at at all hazards, no matter what the consequences. If a man stand in a threatening attitude with a knife at our throat, neither the law of God nor man require us to wait patiently until the fatal stab is given, but we are perfectly justifiable in arresting the hand of the assassin even though in doing so we find it necessary to proceed to the severest extremities. If, then, the Abolitionists place themselves in the position of the assassin, what can they expect?

The Republican republished the call for a public meeting,

that had first appeared in the Gazette, and on Saturday morning, 23d, (the day the meeting was to be held) followed it with these remarks:

The foregoing call is copied from the Cincinnati Gazette. The views of the Editor of this paper upon the subject of abolition and abolitionists are too well known to require from him an expression of opinion with regard to the propriety or impropriety—the expediency or inexpediency of the call. We believe some action is required upon the subject by our citizens. We believe that the course pursued by the abolitionists very reprehensible, and we believe also that their influence has operated injuriously to the interests and character of our city. [Compare this with what the same Editor says in his paper ten days after—"The prospects of Cincinnati were never, probably, more promising than at the present time."] Cincinnati is intimately identified with the slave states, in business and social intercourse. There is no class of individuals in our community whose interests are not more or less affected by the proceedings of these misguided men. The very men who are most officious in behalf of abolition, are those who are most dependant upon the slave states for support and countenance—Men who but for the "*villainous dealers in human flesh*"! would either starve or be compelled to return to whence they came, and sink into their former insignificance. Who are the loud and noisy abolitionists in Cincinnati? Adventurers! Men who, with the exception of Mr. Birney, and a few other reckless and unprincipled fanatics, are as ignorant of the character of our slave institutions, as many who are most zealous in the cause of abolition, are ignorant of the nature of the institutions of their adopted country. We have no patience with the abolitionists. Yet we would not hang them, tar and feather them, quarter or drown them. We would put them under the ban of public sentiment. We would publish them to the world. We would say to our southern brethren—here is Mr. ——, an extensive Merchant on —— street. He is an enemy to your institutions. He would persuade your slaves to cut your throats. If you visit our city do not trade with that man. This is the only true method of of reaching these incendiaries. Touch their interest. Refuse to trade with them. Shun them as you would a rattlesnake. Leave them to their *backers*, the Birneys, the Tappans, and the Garrisons, and in a very short time there would be little left of them.

Saturday, 6 o'clock, P. M. The meeting was held in the open *Market House*, (where we believe no other meeting, for a deliberative purpose, was ever held before) on *Saturday evening*. It consisted of not more than 1000 persons—from 200 to 300 of these belonging to the mob-party. We here give the account of it as taken from the Whig.

GREAT ANTI-ABOLITION MEETING.

In accordance with previous notice, an immense meeting of the citizens of this place was held in the Lower Market House, at 6 o'clock on Saturday evening last, to take into consideration the propriety of permitting James G. Birney and his deluded associates, to publish their abolition paper in this city; and to express the feelings of the people of Cincinnati upon the course pursued by the abolitionists in this quarter. The proceedings of the meeting will be found below.

The resolutions were all adopted unanimously, and with enthusiastic acclamation. Three thousand persons are supposed to have been present.

ANTI-ABOLITION MEETING.

At a very large and respectable meeting of the citizens of Cincinnati, convened at the Lower Market House, in pursuance of a public call, on the 23d day of July, 1836, the following proceedings took place—

WILLIAM BURKE was elected President, MORGAN NEVILLE Vice President, and TIMOTHY WALKER Secretary.

The following preamble and resolutions were then unanimously adopted:

Whereas, The citizens of Cincinnati are now laboring under a serious excitement, in consequence of the existence of an Abolition Press in this city, from the influence of which, the most deplorable results may be justly apprehended. *And, whereas,* although we deprecate the existence of slavery as a great evil, yet we hold it to be one for which the present generation is not responsible; and disclaiming all right to interfere with the regulations of our sister states on this subject, we regard the conduct of the abolitionists as justly calculated to excite unfriendly dispositions on their part, and thus to effect injuriously our own business and prosperity. *And whereas,* While we recognize the constitutional right of liberty of speech and of the press, in its utmost extent; yet, being anxious to preserve the peace and tranquility of our city, and continue those amicable relations which have hitherto existed between the States, we deem it our duty to utter a warning voice to those concerned in the promulgation of abolition doctrines, through the aforesaid press, because we believe their course calculated to influence to passions of one portion of our yet happy country against the other, and to lessen that moral influence upon which the perpetuity of our Union mainly depend. Be it therefore

Resolved, That the spirit exhibited by the immediate supporters of the abolition press in this city, is entirely at variance with the feelings and opinions of the great mass of our population, is as unjust to our sister states, as it is prejudicial to our own quiet and prosperity.

Resolved, That the establishment of the said abolition press in this city is in direct violation of the solemn pledge heretofore given by its conductor at a public meeting on this subject.

Resolved, That in the opinion of this meeting nothing short of the absolute discontinuance of the publication of the said abolition paper in this city, can prevent a resort to violence, which may be as disastrous to its publisher and supporters, as it must be to the good order and fair fame of our city.

Resolved, That we will use all 'awful means to discountenance and suppress every publication in this city which advocates the modern doctrines of abolitionism.

Resolved, That a committee consisting of twelve persons be appointed by the Chair to wait upon James G. Birney and his associates in the publication of the said paper, to remonstrate with them upon the dangerous tendency of the course they are pursuing, to communicate to them the actual tone of public feeling in the city, to request them by every motive of patriotism and philanthropy to desist from the publication of their paper; and to warn them that if they persist, we cannot hold ourselves responsible for the consequences.

The Chair then appointed the following persons as the above committee, viz: Jacob Burnet, Josiah Lawrence, Robert Buchanan, Nicholas Longworth, John C. Wright, Oliver M. Spencer, David Loring, David T. Disney, Thomas W. Bakewell, Stephen Burrows, John P. Foote, and William Greene.

To whom on motion the officers of this meeting were afterwards added.

It was then resolved that the committee publish the result of their interview, and that these proceedings be published in all the papers in the city.

The following resoluion was then offered by Wilson N. Brown, and adopted.

Resolved, That we entertain the most profound respect for the memories of the venerated Patriots of more than "sixty years since" who in the harbor of Boston, *without* the sanction of law, but in the plenitude of the justness of their cause took the responsibility of re-*shipping* the Tea Cargo, and for which illegal act they were entitled to and did receive the warmest thanks and gratitude of every lover of good order and well-wisher of his country—and that we in imitation of the noble and fearless example set us by those true-hearted Americans, declare that whenever we shall find an existing evil—wicked and mischievous in its conceptions—warring against the best interests and happiness of our common country by its effects—aiming at the destruction and disunion of our happy government; and only prompted and sustained by those untiring engines of human ambition hope of gain and love of notoriety—but shielded from legal enactment according to the usual practice of our laws so as to leave us but one channel through which we can rid our fair land from its withering influence, that in seizing that one tangible point our exertions shall be firm, united, and decided.

WILLIAM BURKE, President.
MORGAN NEVILLE, Vice President.

TIMOTHY WALKER, Secretary.

From the foregoing extracts it would appear, that from the period of the first assault, when by no means *all* the mischief that was *intended* was perpetrated—there was a continued effort to excite the profligate, and to bring them into the usual mobocratic combination—and that to this purpose the *slavery* press of this city prodigally lent its aid, *after the publication by the Mayor*. If there was ever an occasion when those who are called "leading and influential" men might, with honor to themselves and signal benefit to the country, have made a stand, *on principle*, for the integrity of the laws, for the inviolableness of constitutional right, that occasion was now presented.

The fatal error was committed when *such* men consented in any way—even by silence—to participate in the acts of those who were setting the laws at open defiance. The call was for an *illegal* object; to decide whether we, as citizens, should be "*permitted*" to enjoy a right secured to us by the constitution of the state—to have it wrested from us by violence, or tamely surrender it. The object was *clearly* illegal, and the *assembling together for the prosecution of that object* constitutes

3

an offence punishable as a misdemeanor by our laws. To suppose that the many *legal* gentlemen who shared in the proceedings from the first, were ignorant of the nature of the acts they were forwarding, would be to suppose they have never read the "horn-book" of their profession.

If the persons constituting the list nominated in the *call* to act as a committee to prepare resolutions for the meeting on Saturday, had, publicly and at once, refused to have any connexion with a proceeding undisguisedly and avowedly in opposition to the laws, there would have been no *meeting*, and if there had been no meeting there would have been no *mob*; for, notwithstanding the auxiliaries of "*wealth* and *respectability*," it was, at last, a hard matter to strain it up to the point of action. For this purpose, not only the usual stimulant of ardent spirits was resorted to, but the sons of some of the committee-men entered the ranks as *operatives* in the work of demolition. But in this long list of names, the weight of whose influence we do not at all question, there was not found *one* who came out publicly as the advocate of good order, and the upholder of the laws—although, we believe many of them are truly such—notwithstanding *two whole days and more* intervened between the *call* and the *meeting*. In order that you may the better appreciate the influence which this list of names *might* have exerted had they chosen to make the effort, we subjoin a sketch of the occupations and standing of the committee-men afterwards appointed, taken from the Cincinnati Gazette of the 2d August. In addition to what the Gazette says, we add, that EIGHT of the THIRTEEN who *acted* on the committee are members of the Episcopal, Methodist Episcopal, Wesleyan Methodist, New Jerusalem, and Unitarian churches. Here is the extract:

Jacob Burnet—He is known as a man of wealth, a lawyer of the first eminence, a Supreme Judge, a Senator in Congress, a citizen of extensive influence.

Josiah Lawrence—A merchant of high character, and President of the Lafayette Bank.

Robert Buchanan—Also a merchant of high reputation—late President of the Commercial Bank of Cincinnati.

Nicholas Longworth—A lawyer, retired from practice—the most extensive property holder in the city.

Oliver M. Spencer—A Minister of the Methodist Episcopal Church, a man of wealth, and highly esteemed in the city.

David Loring—A large property holder, one of the most enterprising and active business men of the city.

David T. Disney—Has been a member of both Houses of the Ohio Legislature, and Speaker of both; an influential politician, conversant with the interests of the city, and extensively engaged in business.

Thomas W. Bakewell—A wealthy and highly respectable merchant.

John P. Foote and William Green—Gentlemen of Intelligence and wealth, and proprietors of a large stock in the Cincinnati Water Works. No men stand better in society.

William Burke—Postmaster of the city, and a Minister of the Gospel.

Morgan Neville—Known throughout the country, and esteemed wherever he is known.

Timothy Walker—A respectable lawyer; one of the law lecturers in the Cincinnati College.

The same print, in giving an account of the *getting up* of the meeting, has these remarks:

This it must be noted is rather a new mode of calling a town meeting. Here is the explanation: Nicholas Longworth, Morgan Neville, and some others of the committee named, came to a determination, that the abolition paper should be put down, *peaceably if it could, forcibly if it must.*' They devised the plan of this meeting. Without consulting them, the names of some of the most respectable men of the city were set down on the Committee. The meeting was appointed at the hour when most of those who labor in the foundries and ship-yards, and elsewhere, would be discharged from labor, for the week, and at a place convenient for their assembling. It was anticipated that most of the gentlemen named, would commit themselves to the object of the meeting by remaining silent, either from real apprehension, or from repugnance to controversy. The anticipation was verified: and thus two principal objects were attained: it was expected the array of names would weigh with the abolitionists to give up their publication: and, on the other hand, should this fail, it was conceived that the same array would operate to intimidate the citizens from the ultimate design to employ violent means if necessary to effect the object.

A set of resolutions were prepared for the meeting, by N. Longworth and M. Neville, perhaps others had an agency in them, by consultation or suggestion.

Ordinary courtesy, it seems to us, would now have demanded that—as a committee had been appointed to confer with the editor of the Philanthropist "and his associates"—open hostilities on the part of our opponents should have ceased, at least, till the negotiation had been closed. This was far from being the case. The slavery-press remitted none of its violence—every effort was put in requisition to keep the mobocratic effervescence ready for explosion, as soon as the report of the Town-Committee should publish, what before they all ought to have known, that *we would lay down our rights at the bidding of no set of men—and, least of all, when they backed their demands of* ABSOLUTE SURRENDER, *by menaces of force and extermination.*

On Monday succeeding the meeting, Judge Burnet addressed the following note to Mr. Birney.

CINCINNATI, July 25th, 1836.

J. G. BIRNEY, Esq.

SIR:—You have probably seen, in the proceedings of a meeting, held in this city, on the 23d inst., that we were appointed a Committee to confer with you, and those who may be associated with you, in the publishing of an abolition paper, in this place.

The object of this note, is, to ascertain at what time and place, it will be convenient for you, and your associates in that publication, to meet us, for the purpose of having a free conversation, on the subject matter of the resolution by which we were appointed.

We are, very respectfully,

J. BURNET.

Chairman of the Committee.

To this the following reply was made.

CINCINNATI, July 25th, 1836.

J. BURNET, Esq.

SIR:—Your note of to-day, has just been received:—and I hasten to answer it.

By 'an abolition paper,' it is presumed, the *Philanthropist* is intended. Of this Journal I am the editor. Whilst it would give me much pleasure to have 'a free conversation' with you and any other gentlemen who might think proper to call on me, on any subject in which you might feel interested, and on which I could give any information, yet, I apprehend, my want of power, *singly*, to act in reference to any matter effecting the Philanthropist—except, as to the mere conduct of the editorial department—would render such a conversation ineffectual, so far as your immediate object is concerned.

The Philanthropist is the organ of the 'Ohio Anti-Slavery Society,' which numbers at this time, perhaps, not less than twelve thousand of our citizens, in different parts of the State. The business of the Society is conducted by an *Executive Committee*, whose names you will find in a pamphlet which I do myself the pleasure to transmit to you, with this reply to your note. Any communication it may please you to make to that body, through its corresponding Secretary, will meet, I doubt not, with the earliest and most respectful attention.

Very respectfully,

JAMES G. BIRNEY.

The next day, July 26th, the following articles appeared, the first in the Whig, the last in the Republican.

Will Birney and his Abolition associates still persist in the publication of their villainously misnamed *Philanthropist*, in despite of the public voice so *significantly* expressed at the immense meeting on Saturday? If they do, they are to all "intents and purposes" *mobocrats*, and we move that they be arrested by the Police officers as rioters and disturbers of the public peace. If a mob, however, be excited by their pugnacity and violence, let them not after this have the effrontery to say that they were not the offenders and did'nt commence it. They can't expect to be permitted to turn the people of Cincinnati, and their neighbors out of their houses, destroy their trade, pull down the law and Union which protect them, and then call themselves *peaceable* citizens!

The ANTI ABOLITION MEETING which took place in this city on Saturday last, was one of the largest, most orderly, and unanimous assemblages we have ever seen in Cincinnati, notwithstanding it was held in a public market house, in a public part of the city, and in the open day. The proceedings were characterized by great moderation. There were no outbreakings; no violations of the public peace or tranquility; which, considering the vastness of the multitude, is as remarkable as it is creditable to our city.

The abolitionists and their croaking friends were industrious during the day and for several days previous, in creating the belief, that the meeting would result in disturbance and riot—that those who called it and gave it countenance, where actuated by a desire to excite a mob, and outrage upon the peace and property of our citizens. In other words, that they in calling for an expression of public sentiment on the subject of abolition, and the doings of abolitionists in our city, were invoking the spirit of licentiousness, and inciting tumult and commotion. This was done to prevent an expression of public opinion. The abolitionists knew that they had nothing to hope, and every thing to fear, from public sentiment; so they thought to prevent its expression.— Vain effort! They might as well attempt to turn the current of the Ohio, or arrest the progress of the electric bolt, as to attempt either to stifle public opinion in Cincinnati, or stem it, successfully or *with impunity*. The "raw head and bloody bone" stories of *disturbance*, *riot*, and *disgrace* were laughed at by the major portion of our citizens. The meeting was held in spite of their remonstrances. With regard to the spirit which pervaded those who participated in the proceedings of the meeting; we cannot better illustrate it than by referring to the resolutions which were adopted upon the occasion. These resolutions, though temperate, are nevertheless strong and conclusive. They speak a language that cannot be misunderstood o rmisrepresented. They declare in so many words that the doctrine of abolition as preached in this city by a few fanatics, will not receive the countenance of Cincinnatians, and that the open and unblushing advocacy of principles so repugnant to the feelings of more than nine tenths of the community, will not be tolerated. The abolitionists in Cincinnati, the Birneys, the Donaldsons, &c. have doubtless received their *last warning*. If their infatuation has not rendered them both blind and deaf, or if they are not perfectly reckless of consequences, they will now come to a halt in their mad career, adopt the advice and heed the warning which we gave them long since.

There are points beyond which public sentiment, even in a free government, may not be trifled with, with impunity. That the abolitionists have arrived at that point in this city, is plainly indicated in the proceedings of the Saturday's anti-abolition meeting. The proceedings of that meeting show a determination to prohibit—"peaceably if they can, but forcibly if they must,"—the distribution of abolition papers in this city, and if needs be, the publication of them too.

The following note, although dated 27th July was not received by Mr. Birney till late in the afternoon of the next day.

CINCINNATI; July 27th, 1836.

Dear Sir:—I have received your letter in answer to my note of the 25th inst., which was written on behalf of the Committee appointed by the citizens assembled at the Market House; on the 23d inst. I regret that the interview which was solicited, has been declined.

If you will advert to my note again, you will see that we do not ask:

3*

for a conference with yourself singly, but request the presence of those who are associated with you in supporting the publication complained of. The object at which we aim, is to convince you, and all those who are connected with you, that the course you are now pursuing, is not calculated to obtain what you professedly, and, no doubt sincerely, have in view. Such being our aim, the request was formal. The names of your associates were not mentioned, because we did not know them, but taking it for granted, that they were known to you, the request was made in the form in which you received it, under a belief that you would communicate to them the design of the committee, and inform us whether it would be conceded, or not. As you are the editor of the offensive publication, it was natural for the committee to address themselves to you, taking it for granted, that you would see your associates, or give them notice of the proposed interview. The committee yet hope it will take place, and that it may terminate auspiciously. It is in vain to disguise the fact, that nineteen twentieths of the population of this city are opposed to the cause you are pursuing, and believe it has a direct tendency to injure both its reputation and its business. It must also be apparent to the most careless observer, that a high degree of excitement exists in the minds of a large portion of our population, which the most prudent and discreet among us, find it difficult to restrain. It is to be feared, that this excitement cannot be kept down much longer, unless some arrangement be made for removing the cause which has produced it. The individuals who compose the committee entertain no other than friendly feelings towards you, and those who act in connection with you; they have reasons to believe that you and they may repose confidence in the purity of the motives by which they are governed. They will not recommend a course to you which they would not pursue, and approve, were they placed in similar circumstances. Taking it for granted, that you are open to conviction, the committee are induced to hope, that it will be in their power to convince you, that you ought to yield your opinions and preferences to the opinions of so large a majority of those with whom you are connected in society, and particularly so, as it is evident from the state of the public feeling, that no other course will be likely to pacify the minds of your fellow citizens.

The committee have no idea of engaging in a protracted correspondence in performing the duty which has been assigned them, their private business renders this mode of proceeding impracticable. They therefore renew their request, that you will confer with persons who are engaged with you, and if it be concluded to grant our request, that you inform us, when and where the interview may take place.

I am very respectfully,

J. BURNET,

Chairman of the Committee.

To J. G. BIRNEY, Esq.

The same day on which this letter was dated, the Whig published the following communication.

Mr. EDITOR,

The following resolutions, I find in the daily papers of this morning, adopted at an Anti-Abolition meeting, held in this city on Saturday last.

Resolved, That the establishment of the said abolition press, in this city, is a direct violation of the solemn pledge, heretofore given by its conductors, at a public meeting on this subject.

Now Mr. Editor, it would seem from the above, that Mr. Birney pledged himself not to publish his paper in the city. If such is the case, I would not give a straw for the cause he is advocating. It is plain to the mind of every man of sense, that he who would pledge himself to do a thing, and violate that pledge, is an enemy to his country; and instead of advocating a just and righteous cause, he is doing more injury to our beloved country, in throwing dissensions through the columns of his paper, of an inflammatory character, in the slave states, than the acts of the notorious Burr; which will, inevitably, be the means of destroying our republican institutions. The editor of the *Philanthropist*, (Birney) is doing more to overthrow our government, and cast a stain upon her character, than any abolition editor in the United States. That paper is a disgrace to Cincinnati; and I hope the meeting held on Saturday, will have a salutary effect. *The interest of Cincinnati demands that he should desist from publishing his paper.*

HAMILTON.

[It may be well to state here that no such pledge as that mentioned, was ever given. Mr. Birney has publicly denied it, and no one has yet been found on his individual responsibility, to come forward and deny his assertion.]

July 28. The following note addressed to the Corresponding Secretary was received, and submitted to the Executive Committee.

CINCINNATI, July 28, 1836.

SIR:—The Committee appointed by the citizens on the 23d inst., have directed me to request, that the Executive Committee of the Ohio Anti-Slavery Society, will have a conference with them, on the subject matter of the resolution by which they were appointed. Will you, sir, have the goodness to communicate this request to the members of the executive committee, and, if it be acceded to, to inform me when and where the interview shall take place.

The committee which I represent, will meet this afternoon at 5 o'clock, at the office of Morgan Neville, on Front street, where, if it be convenient, they will be pleased to see the executive committee.

I am, very respectfully,

J. BURNET,
Chairman of the Committee.

AUGUSTUS WATTLES, Esq. Cor. Sec'y, &c.

The note of the day before addressed to James G. Birney, was not received until an answer had been almost prepared to be sent to that addressed to the Corresponding Secretary. It was then concluded, as the time had nearly arrived, for the afternoon meeting of the Market House Committee, to send by Christian Donaldson, a message, that we would hold the desired "conference" with them that evening, at the house of Dr. Colby. At the time appointed all the members of the Executive Committee who lived in the city, with the exception of Dr. Colby who was called off by a professional emergency, met, it is believed, *twelve* out of *thirteen* who composed the Market House Committee. Judge Burnet, the chairman commenced by giving a long explanation of the manner in which he had been brought into the position he, at present occupied. This being disposed of, he spoke of the high degree of excitement which pervaded a large portion—nineteen twentieths we believe—of the inhabitants of the city. In proof of it he related a conversation he had held with a man apparently of low condition in life, who had accosted him in the street—though altogether unknown to the judge—in tone and phrase dark and mysterious. We will not undertake to give it in the graphic manner in which it was related by the chairman who seemed still to feel the impression, that the mysterious stranger had made on him. We will give only the result—which was that the stranger on parting with the judge said in reference to the destruction of the Philanthropist press, as it was understood, *make haste—(we)—or I am ready to help you.* Judge Burnet professed himself alarmed at the excitement which he believed was in the city—and we do not in the least call in question the sincerity of the declaration, for his whole manner and language gave proof of it. He further stated, that by report, the excitement pervaded not only the city, but that it had gone some distance into the neighborhood; that there were, between Cincinnati and Columbia (6 miles above on the river) 100 men who were banded together, to destroy the Philanthropist establishment—who had their officers appointed—were fully drilled, and ready, at the first signal, to make the onset. He also stated that for four or five miles the excitement had passed into Kentucky, and that the three towns (Covington, Newport, and Cincinnati) were ready, at any moment, to rise for the same purpose. He further represented, that the mob were becoming impatient,—were beginning, from what they supposed was the dilatory conduct of the Committee, to lose confidence in that body, and to suspect them, of rather a favorable leaning towards the object of their hate. Other gentlemen of the Market House Committee were called on to give their views as to the state of the public mind. There was no material difference among them. One, or more of them spoke of the excitement, already nearly irrepressible, that prevailed, among the workmen employed in the iron foundries and boat yards situated generally near the river—of one of which, with a large number of hands, he himself was the proprietor. Judge Burke said the abolitionists were beginning to be regarded as intending to effect their object by *revolution* and in no other way—all other ways being set down as utterly impracticable.—Rev. Mr. Spencer rose from his seat, when he made *his* speech—apparently a *set* one:—He commenced by saying, there were those present in whose veins flowed the blood of our revolutionary patriots, and who were as desirous *as any other men*, to see no longer in our country the track of a *slave*. He then recited a stanza of poetry condemning slavery,—winding up with taunting the abolitionists for not going to the south, and preaching their doctrines where they might have an opportunity of closing the scene with a glorious martyrdom. Much more was said, in relation to the excitement than we can take room to narrate.

The next point mooted was the *business of the city*. It was on this ground—and on this solely—that the *merits* of the question seemed to be placed. It was asked by us, if rents were not high—houses to rent scarce, real property on the advance—commercial business brisk for the season of the year, and every body—artizan or common laborer—who would work, employed at high wages? All this was admitted—and it did appear to our plain judgments to be evidence of at least as much prosperity as ought to satisfy reasonable men. But it was insisted on the other hand, that this state of things (*in which all were employed at good wages*,) was not the true criterion of prosperity. All this might be true—yet if abolitionism in Cincinnati had prevented the south from sending her orders for even more work than could be executed by the mechanics now here, it had injured the city,—because these very orders would be the means of introducing among us more artizans from other places. In the solidity of this reasoning the gentlemen on the other side, no doubt had entire confidence—but it seemed to us not more conclusive, than that of the Kentucky farmer who undertook to prove to a neighbor that he had lost a hundred calves that spring, by not having, *as he might have had*, a hundred cows to produce them.

It was asked by us, what evidence there was, that the south was withdrawing her business from us because of the existence of abolitionism here? To this it was replied, that it was to be found in various communications and letters from the south. One of the Market House Committee, (Mr Buchanan) an extensive and prosperous merchant, who has large connections, in the way of business with the south, said the subject had been frequently mentioned to him by his southern correspondents, and that they were now beginning to present the alternative to this city, either to suppress the abolition discussion, or to be content to lose their southern business. He was asked if the Philanthropist or its editor had ever been specified, as items in the complaint. Mr. B. said they had not—he did not know that either of them was particularly known at the south—but the complaint was one of general character, *that the anti-slavery discussion was entertained in Cincinnati.*

On Judge Burnet's remarking, that abolitionists were injuring the property-holders of Cincinnati, he was asked to specify how *he* was injured. He stated, in reply, that four or five years ago—[*this was between two and three years before the commencement of the abolition question in this place*] it was customary for thirty or forty families from the south, attended by their servants who were indispensable to them in their excursions, to spend a great part of the summer in Cincinnati.—That, since the abolitionists had commenced their operations, the people of color had become so bold in enticing away the servants of the southern visiters that they would no longer venture among us; [Compare this with the following from the Cincinnati Republican of August 2. "Our hotels and boarding houses are always crowded, and hundreds of southern families who contemplate a sojournment of some weeks in the queen city of the west, have been compelled to relinguish their intentions for want of accommodations,"] and that the abolitionists had contributed to make the people of color much more impudent to the *whites* than formerly. *Now*, if a man was wise, when he saw four or five of them on the pavement, he would diverge into the street to pass around them to avoid their insolence in not giving the way—and that *he* had been jostled by them on the side walks. This was the account, the chairman gave of the injury, *he* was suffering from abolitionists.

The chairman having professed satisfactory knowledge of the measures and objects of the anti-slavery societies—and stated that there was no one who was more a friend of emancipation than he was, and after alleging that African colonization was the only feasible way of accomplishing the extirpation of slavery amongst us, and having uttered sentiments in reference to the principles and results of abolitionism that seemed unusually crude for one of his station in society—and being seconded in his opinion by another of the Market House Committee,—it was remarked by one of our number, that the entertainment of *such* sentiments by *such* men convinced him more forcibly than he had yet been, of the necessity of having the whole subject *discussed*. He then proposed, that, if the members of the Market house Committee would give the influence of their recommendation to a meeting, to be held in some church of the city for that purpose, he [the member alluded to] would give an exposition of anti-slavery principles, and be willing to hear any arguments that might be offered against them. It was at once replied, that such a meeting could not be held in the city, that the people would hear no public discussion on slavery, and that the speaker would lose his life in attempting to discuss it. No change was produced on the Market House Committee by the assurance of the member that with their sanction for the call of such a meeting, he was willing to hazard all personal peril to himself.

The conversation was at length turned to the main object of the meeting—the *discontinuance of the Philanthropist.*—The first suggestions were, that it should be "postponed," or "suspended for a time." All such modified propositions, however, were at length, put aside as useless—and the demand made, of an *absolute discontinuance*, with the certain alternative in case of refusal, of a mob unusual in its numbers, determined in its purpose, and desolating in its ravages. The chairman expressed it as his opinion, that it would be one of unprecedented character—that it would consist of *four or five thousand persons*, bent on the wide destruction of property, and that *two-thirds of the property holders* of the city would join it. That it would be utterly vain for any man or set of men to attempt to restrain it—it would destroy any one who would set himself in opposition to it.

In order to ascertain, what was the temper of the Market House Committee gentlemen, themselves, they were asked, whether *if a mob could be averted* THEY *would be content that the publication of the Philanthropist should be continued?*—The question was scarcely uttered, when the chairman and several of the other members replied unhesitatingly, *they would not.* One of them qualified what he said, by saying he would be content, if he could be satisfied that it would produce *no injury to the city in any way.* It was next asked, if they had read the Philanthropist, and if they had, whether the objection to its continuance was made on the ground of there being any thing exceptionable in the *manner and spirit* of conducting it. The answer on the part of one of the Committee was, that he had read several of the latter numbers—another said that *he* had read portions of the last three or four numbers—another, that he had read a column or two, or an article or two, in some one of the first numbers. This was the whole amount of knowledge, on the part of the Committee, as to the *manner* in which the Philanthropist conducted the slavery discussion.—But it was further added on their part—that the *manner* and *spirit* of the paper had nothing to do with the question—it was the *discussion of slavery here*, that was thought to be injuring the business of the city. That the paper was believed to be a prominent instrument in carrying on this discussion.—that therefore, its *absolute discontinuance* was called for—that the public sentiment would be satisfied with nothing short of this, and that it was in such a condition that it could not be reasoned with. No definite answer from the Executive Committee was expected to be given at the conference—which was dissolved after the following resolution was adopted by the market House committee.

"Resolved, that the Executive Committee of the Ohio Anti-Slavery Society, be requested to communicate to the committee in writing, by 12 o'clock on Friday, to-morrow noon, an explicit answer to the question, whether they will discontinue or not the publication of an abolition paper in this city called the Philanthropist."

The next morning our Committee assembled, and agreed on the following reply to the request of the Market House Committee. It was handed in at the time mentioned in their resolution.

CINCINNATI, July 29, 1836.

J. BURNET, Ch. Com.

SIR:—Whilst we feel ourselves constrained altogether to decline complying with your request, as submitted last evening, *to discontinue the Philanthropist*, we think it but just to ourselves, and respectful to our fellow citizens generally, to offer a brief exposition of the reasons that persuade us to this course.

1. We decline complying—not so much from the fear that the particular cause in which our press is employed may be injured—but because compliance involves a tame surrender of the FREEDOM OF THE PRESS—THE RIGHT TO DISCUSS.

2. The Philanthropist is the acknowledged organ of some twelve thousand, or more, of our fellow citizens of Ohio, who believe that slavery, as it exists in our country, is altogether incompatible with the permanency of her institutions; who believe that the *Slavery* of the *South* or the *Liberty* of the *North* must case to exist; and who intend to do, what in them lies, to bring about a happy and a peaceful termination of the former—and this as speedily as facts, and arguments, and appeals to the consciences and understandings of the slave-holders can be made instrumental to effect it.

3. The Philanthropist is the only journal in this city or neighborhood, through which these facts, and arguments, and appeals can be fully addressed to the community. It has been conducted with fairness and moderation, as may be abundantly proved by the acknowledgements of those who are opposed to its objects. It has invited the slaveholders themselves to the use of its columns for the defence of slavery, and has given up to a republication of their arguments a large share of its space.

To discontinue such a paper under existing circumstances, would be a tacit submission to the exhorbitant demand of the South, that *Slavery* shall never more be mentioned among us.

4. We decline complying with your request—because if it has originated among our own citizens, it is an officious and unasked for intrusion on the business of others—If among the citizens of other States, it is an attempt at dictation as insolent and high-handed on their part, as a tame submission to it would be base and unmanly on ours.

5. We decline complying with your request—because we would not preclude ourselves, and others, from discussing in the most advantageous manner a subject, which, by the acknowledgement of all is of momentous consequence, and which is now occupying the minds of the whole nation.

6. We decline complying—because the demand is virtually the demand of slave-holders, who, having broken down all the safe-guards of liberty in their own States, in order that slavery may be perpetuated, are now, for the fuller attainment of the same object, making the demand of us to follow their example.

[The two remaining reasons were omitted—unintentionally, we have no doubt—in the published report of the Market House Committee. They were part of the letter sent to the Market House committee, and are here supplied.]

We decline complying—because the attempt is now first made in our case, formally and deliberately to put down the freedom of speech and of the press. *We* are, to be sure, the object of the attack—but there is not a freeman in the State whose rights are not invaded, in any assault which may be made on us, for refusing to succumb to an imperious demand to surrender our rights.

8. We believe, that a large portion of the people of Cincinnati are utterly opposed to the prostration of the liberty of the press---and that there is among us---whatever may be said to the contrary---enough of correct and sober feeling to uphold the laws, if our public officers faithfully discharge their duty.

With these reasons—to which many more might be added, did time permit—we leave the case with you:—expressing, however, our firm conviction, should any disturbance of the peace occur, that you, gentlemen, must be deeply, if not almost entirely, responsible for it, before the bar of sober and enlightened public opinion.

JAMES C. LUDLOW,
ISAAC COLBY,
WM. DONALDSON,
JAMES G. BIRNEY,
THOS. MAYLIN,
JOHN MELENDY,
C. DONALDSON,
GAMAL. BAILEY.
} *Executive Committee of the Ohio Anti-Slavery Society.*

J. BURNET, Chairman, &c. Cincinnati.

Thereupon, the following resolution was unanimously adopted by the Committee:

Resolved, That the members of this Committee reluctantly accepted the responsible trust committed to them, with no other motive than the hope of being able to allay the excitement which they believed to exist, and to prevent the violence which they feared might be its result. That, in discharging their duties, they have used all the measures of persuasion and conciliation in their power. That their exertions have not been successful, the above correspondence will show. It only remains, then, in pursuance of their instructions, to publish their proceedings and adjourn without day. But ere they do this, they owe it to themselves and those whom they represent, to express their utmost abhorrence of every thing like violence; and earnestly to implore their fellow citizens to abstain therefrom.

JACOB BURNET,	DAVID T. DISNEY,
JOSIAH LAWRENCE,	THOS. W. BAKEWELL,
ROB'T BUCHANAN.	JOHN P. FOOTE,
NICH'S LONGWORTH,	WILLIAM GREENE,
OLIVER M. SPENCER,	WILLIAM BURKE,
DAVID LORING,	MORGAN NEVILLE,

TIMOTHY WALKER.

4

Note.—John C. Wright, one of the Committee, has been absent during all its proceedings, and Stephen Burrows, another member, declined acting.

Thus terminated one of the most singular negotiations—whether we regard *the subject matter—the causes leading to it*—or *the parties*—that has yet been recorded in the annals of our country. 1. The *subject matter* was, *the right to investigate and discuss Truth*—a right bestowed by the CREATOR on Man as his intelligent creature, to use as freely as he walks the earth, or breathes the air—the exercise of which is required of him as a *duty*—a right which, as an accountable being, he has no power voluntarily to relinquish, any more than he has voluntarily to sell his liberty, or to part with his life—a right so clear that the *people* of Ohio have, in their constitution, pronounced it "INDISPUTABLE"—so inestimable, they have adopted it as one of the ELEMENTS of their government, and so liable to be invaded by *power*, that they have attempted to secure its freest exercise by the most stable, the most solemn sanctions. 2. The reasons for demanding its surrender—slave-holders called for it—*oppression* in the South having prostrated there, all legal barriers of individual right and personal safety; having overthrown within her own limits the freedom of the press and of speech—*the right to discuss*—in order that her reign might be perpetuated, demanded it; a mob of three or four hundred—a mere fragment of our population—the very feculence of the city, countenanced and encouraged to the deed by leading and influential men among us, to whom the exercise of the right of discussion was displeasing, demanded it. 3. The parties to it—on the one hand, ten thousand of our fellow-citizens, not, to be sure [with but few exceptions] *leading* and *influential*, but yet of the freemen, the plain and honest yeomanry of Ohio, who, within the limits of the Constitution are contending for its very citadel—who are fighting, only with the weapons of truth, for that liberty which becomes the more precious the more it is endangered by the assaults of its enemies. On the other—there are merchants and manufacturers, closely united with the slave-holder—lawyers and judges—officers of the government, and ministers of the Gospel—there are wealth and influence, slave-holding servility and aristocratic pride—all, marshaling into their service for the *work*, a band fearless of God and regardless of man. Surely, such an attempt to trample under foot the liberties of our people—so deliberate—so carefully matured, and backed by such an amount of moral, intellectual, and pecuniary power, has rarely been made in this country! However to resume our narrative.

The Market House Committee, on their dissolution, forthwith despatched their report, as given in a foregoing part of this statement, to the city papers for publication next morning. The Cincinnati Gazette refused to publish it till Monday, knowing that Saturday, of all the days of the week, is the most favorable for a popular disturbance. It was heralded forth in the Republican on Saturday morning. The same morning the Whig, as if a knowledge of the preliminaries to an attack had not been sufficiently disseminated, and there was need of a signal to begin, sounded the charge in the following strain:

> "Lay on M'Duff, and d——d be he
> Who first cries hold, enough!"

> The editor and publisher of the "*Philanthropist*," the abolition paper in this city, seem to have fully adopted the above aphorism, and to be determined to put the great mass of the people of this city at utter and contemptuous defiance.
>
> We observe that the offensive paper appeared yesterday, *as usual*, bearing upon its front the name of James G. Birney as editor, and *A. Pugh*, as printer. Publishing office corner of Main and Seventh streets.
>
> What has become of Pugh's recent pledge to the public to have nothing to do with the Philanthropist?
>
> Are the abolitionists in this city mad? Will they not take counsel of what has occurred! Or will they persist in contemning public sentiment until they bring upon themselves the excited vengeance of the multitude? Once more we say to them, *pause!*

Nor was even this sufficient. For at 6 o'clock in the evening a *preparatory* meeting was held at the Exchange, at which Joseph Graham presided, and J. A. D. Burrows acted as Secretary—where it was resolved, 1. That the Press should be destroyed, and the types thrown into the street; and 2. That Mr. Birney should be notified to leave the city in 24 hours. This meeting, composed mostly of well-dressed young men, having the appearance of clerks, store-boys, &c. adjourned to the Texas meeting held in the Court House, at 8 o'clock.

The following account of the subsequent disturbances is taken from the Cincinnati Gazette, and is, we believe in the main, more correct than any other we have seen.

DESTRUCTION OF PROPERTY.

On Saturday night, July 30, very soon after dark, a concourse of citizens assembled at the corner of Main and Seventh streets, in this city, and upon a short consultation, broke open the printing office of the Philanthropist, the abolition paper, scattered the type into the streets, tore down the presses, and completely dismantled the office. It was owned by A. Pugh, a peaceable and orderly printer, who published the Philanthropist for the Anti-Slavery Society of Ohio. From the printing office the crowd went to the house of A. Pugh, where they supposed there were other printing materials, but found none, nor offered any violence. Then to the Messrs. Donaldsons', where ladies only were at home. The residence of Mr. Birney, the editor, was then visited, no person was at home but a youth, upon whose explanations, the house was left undisturbed. A shout was raised for Dr. Colby's, and the concourse returned to Main street, proposing to pile up the contents of the office in the street, and make a bonfire of them. Joseph Graham mounted the pile, and advised against burning it, lest the houses near might take fire. A portion of the press was then dragged down Main street, broken up and thrown into the river. The Exchange was then visited and refreshments taken. After which the concourse again went up Main street to about opposite the Gazette Office. Some suggestions were hinted that it should be demolished, but the hint was overruled. An attack was then made on the residence of some blacks, in Church alley; two guns were fired upon the assailants, and they recoiled. It was supposed that one man was wounded, but that was not the case. It was some time before a rally could be again made, several voices declaring they did not wish to endanger themselves. A second attack was made, the houses were found empty, and their interior contents destroyed.—It was now about midnight, when the party parading down Main street, was addressed by the Mayor, who had been a silent spectator of the destruction of the printing office. He told them they might as well now disperse. A dispersion to a considerable extent followed: but various other disturbances took place through the night, of the magnitude and particulars of which we are not advised.

The following, taken down by a gentleman who was present, has been furnished as an accurate report of the Mayor's speech.

"Gentlemen.—It is now late at night, and time we were all in bed—by continuing longer, you will disturb the citizens, or deprive them of their rest, besides robbing yourselves of rest. No doubt, it is your intention to punish the guilty, and leave the innocent. But if you continue longer, you are in danger of punishing the innocent with the guilty, which I am convinced no one in Cincinnati would wish to do. *We* have done enough for one night. ["three cheers for the Mayor"] The abolitionists themselves, must be convinced themselves by this time, what public sentiment is, and that it will not do any longer to disregard, or set it at naught. [three cheers again] As you cannot punish the guilty without endangering the innocent, I advise you all to go home. [cries of home! home! from the crowd drowned the balance of his harangue.]

From the Cincinnati Gazette of August 4th.

On Sunday evening, there was another collection of our citizens on Main stteet opposite the Franklin boarding House, in search of Mr. Birney, alleging he was harbored there. The Mayor with one or two citizens, officiated as a *domiciliary committee* to examine the house, and having performed the service, reported that the object of search was not there. After this the residence of the blacks were again disturbed, but no actual violence perpetrated. Through the forepart of Monday, the city was much agitated as is evinced by the subjoined document.

PROCLAMATION.

MAYOR'S OFFICE,
City of Cincinnati.

WHEREAS, a most violent excitemen exists in every class of the inhabitants of the city, demanding every effort to prevent its breaking out in further acts of violence and disorder.

I do, therefore, call upon the citizens, disposed to aid in the preservation of the peace, and restoring the city to that state of quietness and obedience to the laws, for which it has been heretofore distinguished, and from which, it is to be regretted, it has lately departed; and request them to assemble at the Mayors Office, this evening at half past seven o'clock.

Given under my hand, this arst day of August, 1836.

SAMUEL W. DAVIES, *Mayor.*

Another of the city papers says that "on Monday several volunteer companies were organized, which, with others who came forward at the call of the Mayor, acted for the defence of the city on Monday night. Several mobs collected on Monday night, but were prevented from violence and dispersed by the volunteers acting under tbe authorities. A mob of some two hundred came down Elm street to make an attack on the negro houses, but were kept at bay by a volunteer company of *fifteen*, till an additional force of some two hundred came to their aid, when the mob dispersed. No violence was committed on Monday night."

"This state of things "says the editor of the Cincinnati Gazette, speaking of the transaction of Monday.

This state of things, being thus upon us, notwithstanding the undertakings of the Maiket House meeting to prevent it, there were some citizens, who conceived it time to look to themselves. They were sickened aud exhausted with the alarm and apprehension of two days and two nights, and the threatening aspects of the third day.—They thought enongh had been done to assure our fellow citizens of the South, that the citizens of Cincinnati were earnestly devoted to securing them the safe enjoyment of their slave property. There were some of us, who conceived we had at least, an *equal right*, to make an effort to restore the quiet of our own city. Those of our fellow-citizens, whose chief care seemed to be, securing to the slave-owner his slaevs, had spoken and acted—and we, who thought the preservation of our own peace, the execution of our own laws, the security of our own persons and property, were considerations *equal*, if not paramount, to those that looked mainly to the security of citizens of other States, in one description of property, proposed also to speak our opinions and feelings.

In order that something might be done toward the restoration of order and the reign of law, the following call for a public meeting appeared in the Gazette of Tuesday the 2nd August.

4*

'PUBLIC MEETING.'

'The friends of order, of Law, and the Constitution, having no connection with the Anti-Slavery Society, and who are opposed to the action of a mob, under any possible circumstances, are requested to meet THIS AFTERNOON, (TUESDAY,) at 3 o'clock, at the Court House..

E. Hulse, M. Lyon, E. W. Chester, James Calhoun, Thos. H. Shreve, C. P. Barnes, J. Weatherby, S. P. Chase, H. M. Beecher, A. D. Coombs, W. F. Barnes, Geo. H. King, Wm. Hart. George Guilford, James Eshelby, Osgood Fifield, R. Ayres, C. Hammond, W. G. Webster, D. L. Talbott, Jno. Garrison, J. W. Yost, R. M. Hawkins, T. Surguy, J. H. Woodruff, W. D. Gallagher, H. K. Wells, J. W. Kendall, Edmund Gage, Thos. McGechin, Joseph Claypool, J. M. McCullough, William B. Squire, B. F. Coates, Hiram P. Randall, E. Whipple, James D. Taylor, William Wood, John H. Layman, N. G. Burgess.

The editor of the Gazette, who was one that signed the call, gives this account of what was *intended* to be done:—

Preliminary to the hour of meeting, a few put their heads together, as is usual on such occasion, and prepared a declaration of views, in the usual form. We contemplated asserting the general principles upon which our institutions were founded, and avowing the sentiments, in which we had been instructed by our fathers, and which, hitherto through life, we had seen and heard received as of unquestionable truth, and undoubted obligation. In this spirit and feeling what follows was prepared.

"This meeting has witnessed, with mingled sentiments of pain, mortification and indignation, the repeated disturbances of the public peace, and the repeated aggressions upon private property, and personal security which have within a few days, tarnished the fair fame of our city, hitherto proudly distinguished as being exempt from mobs. We have deplored the efforts of a portion of fellow citizens, who have aimed to bring about a premature abolition of slavery, as calculated by their tone and spirit, to excite hostile feelings between different sections of our common country.

We regard slavery as a domestic institution of the States in which it exists, with which the other States have no right to interfere. But while we respect the rights of our fellow citizens of the slave-holding States, and would, by no means, break through, or suffer any others to break through, the sacred barriers of the law, for the purpose of invading those rights: we also respect the rights of our fellow citizens of the non-slave-holding States, and will never suffer the law and constitution to be trampled in the dust for the purpose of destroying those rights. Among these rights—and of all the dearest because it is the bulwark of all the rest—is the right of FREE DISCUSSION—the right of every citizen to write, speak, and print, upon every subject, as he may think proper, being responsible to the laws and the laws ONLY, for the abuse of that liberty. If this right shall perish through the violence of a mob, the grave that entombs it must be the sepulchre of American freedom. True-hearted Americans, therefore, must defend this right, at all times, in all places, under all circumstances, by whomsoever assailed. When this right is abused, the remedy is at hand. The Courts are open. If the existing laws do not provide an efficient remedy, let new laws, adapted to the object, be enacted. The annual sessions of our Legislature are held for that purpose. But let not the hand of violence be raised against the exercise of this precious right. However obnoxious the exercise may be, let the right itself be acknowledged and respected. Let us not, for the sake of removing some unsightly blemish, pull out the very corner-stone of the great temple of constitutional liberty.

Resolved, therefore, That it is with deep regret and shame, that we have to acknowledge that our city, heretofore so distinguished for its public order, has recently presented a scene of unlicensed violence; and that private property has been destroyed, and personal security endangered, and domestic peace invaded, by an unrestrained mob.

Resolved, That the direct tendency of resorts to violence and unlawful assemblages for the suppression of ANY public evil, is, to invite among us strangers to our laws, and dissolute persons of every description to take upon themselves the regulation of our city, and to commit every species of aggression upon the property, life, and liberty of our citizens.

Resolved, That the right of free discussion, the freedom of the press, the safety of person and property from unlawful seizure, are principles yet dear to our hearts. These rights constitute the very basis of our political institutions, AND MUST BE PRESERVED.

Resolved, That we are fully determined to observe the constitutional compact with our brethren of the slave-holding States, and so far as in us lies, by argument and all other lawful means to cause it to be repected by others; but we cannot consent to surrender any one of the blood-bought rights, which our fathers bequeathed to us, for the purpose of securing a southern trade; nor do we believe that such an offering to the spirit of gain, would be acceptable to any American freeman, whether of the South or the North.

Resolved, That we are fully of opinion, that while a considerable number of our fellow citizens have been led to approve, or acquiesce in the action of a mob, the greater majority of the voters in the city, and the almost unanimous voice of the freemen of the county, concur in the sentiment, that there are no times and no circumstances, in this land of universal suffrage, of equal right, and equal laws, which can justify or excuse a resort to the violence of mob force, or a submission to the employment of such force, while the power of resistance remains.

Resolved, That we regard the recent outrages upon our peace, and upon our laws, as another example, added to the thousands of past experience, that an attempt to conciliate a threatened mobbish violence, by concessions of any kind, is but an invitation to the completion of its purposes.

Resolved, That in a city of the extent and location of Cincinnati, it is the imperious duty of every peace officer, and of every good citizen, upon the first hint or thr at of mobbish violence, to assume a stern and undaunted front in support of a due observation of the laws, and for the maintenance of the public peace; and we take to ourselves the shame and reproach of having failed to adopt this course in the case that has just occurred.

Resolved, That we pledge ourselves, one to another, forthwith to organize an efficient Committee of safety, so to act in concert, and in sufficient numbers, to crush any future attempt by mobbish violence, in night time or in day time, to subvert the laws, and jeopardize the security of life, liberty, or property."

At the appointed hour, with the foregoing in our pockets, we repaired to the Court House, when, '*lo and behold!*' there was a meeting organized! Our friends of the Lower Market House meeting had anticipated us.—Never were men more completely discomfited than we were. Nothing remained for us, but to witness what took place, and hold our peace—or be the occasion of noise and turbulence, of anger and strife. With common consent, and without concert, those who called the meeting forbore to take any part in its proceedings. The results are before the public. The temper of those of our citizens who thus organised a meeting upon a call by others, cannot be mistaken by dispassionate men, nor can there be a doubt of the estimate most of themselves will hold of this transaction at a future day.

The "friends of the Lower Market House" had organized a meeting on the aforesaid notice—had placed in the chair judge Burke, [the same who presided at the meeting in the Market House] had appointed Judge Burnet, the chairman of the Market House Committee, and Mr. Levi James, distinguished for his uncompromising hostility to the discussion of the subject of slavery, their *Vice-Presidents*—and Joseph Graham, who presided at the *preparatory* meeting at the Exchange on Saturday evening, their *Secretary*. Tht following resolutions were passed by the meeting:—

Whereas the peace and order of the city has been lately disturbed—

Resolved, That this meeting deeply regret the cause of the recent occurrences, and entirely disapprove of Mobs or other unlawful assemblages.

Resolved, that we will cordially support the city authorities in their efforts to preserve the public peace, and will heartily co-operate with each other in all exertions to effect that object.

On motion of Joseph Graham it was then unanimously

Resolved, That this meeting are of the opinion that the establishment of the Abolition Press in this city has been the cause of all our recent difficulties.

On motion of Mr. Whitcomb, it was

Resolved, That the discretion, prudence, and energy of our worthy Mayor, and the city authorities generally, during the late excitement, are worthy of all praise.

Resolved, That the Committee appointed on the 23d ult., though unsuccessful in their efforts, justly merit the entire confidence of this community, and that they receive the thanks of this meeting.

On motion of M. N. McLean, Esq., it was

Resolved, That this meeting approve of the course of the Colonization Society, and that they are decidedly of opinion that it is the only method of getting clear of the evils of slavery.

On motion, *Resolved*, That the proceedings of this meeting be published in the different papers in this city.

Resolved, That this meeting now adjourn.

WM. BURKE, *President*.
JACOB BURNET, } *V. Pres'ts.*
LEVI JAMES, }

JOSEPH GRAHAM, *Secretary*.
Cincinnati, August 2, 1836.

A very unexpected influence was brought to bear upon us, in the proceedings of the Cincinnati Union Society of colored persons. The resolutions are said to have been prepared, if not the whole project set on foot, by one of the actors in the Court House Meeting on just mentioned. Here are the proceedings:—

UNION MEETING.

At a meeting of the Cincinnati Union Society of colored persons, held on Monday, August 1st, at 12 o'clock, at noon.

The Society having met on the call of the President, to take into consideration, the situation of the colored inhabitants of this city.

The President having taken the Chair, and called the society to order, the following preamble and resolutions were introduced, and unanimously adopted:

WHEREAS: We have, for the last ten months, witnessed the efforts making by a few misguided and fanatical men amongst us, styled abolitionists, and headed by one Birney, and whereas, we have become convinced, that the means they are using have a direct tendency to injure the interest of the colored population of the free states by exciting the passion of the white inhabitants, and we believe, to rivet more firmly, the chains of the slave.

Therefore, be it *resolved*, That we disclaim, in the most positive manner, all connection with the abolitionists, and hold in horror and contempt, their amalgamation doctrine in principle, as degrading, both to the white and colored population.

Resolved, That the publication of the Philanthropist and other abolition papers and tracts in this city, have had, and, we believe, will continue to have an injurious and prejudicial effect on the interests of the colored population.

Resolved, That if Mr. Birney and his associates have, as they pretend, the well being of the colored race at heart, they will cease their misguided efforts here, and leave us as they found us, to work out our own salvation.

Resolved, That we will consider the future publication of abolition papers in this city, as an attempt to excite against us, angry feelings and the personal violence of anti-abolitionists.

Resolved, That we have nothing to do with either colonizing or abolition societies.

Resolved, That the proceedings of this meeting be signed by the President, and Secretary, and the Members of this Society, and published in the Cincinnati Papers.

DENNIS HILL, *President.*

GEORGE TOSPOT, *Secretary.*

This is followed with thirty-five signatures of names.

A few days afterward, the following disclaimer of all participation in the foregoing, signed by twenty-eight names, was published in the Cincinnati Gazette:

"We, the undersigned, members of the Cincinnati Union Society of colored persons, having seen, with regret, our names affixed to a publication, purporting to be the proceedings of a meeting of the Union Society, held on August 1st, at 12 o'clock, in which proceedings, the motives, principles, and characters of the friends of abolition are impugned and denounced:—We do hereby declare that our names were used (by Dennis Hill, the President of our Society,) without our knowledge or consent."

In the foregoing pages we have endeavored to present to you an impartial account of an attack, the most formidable—because of the *character* of the persons concerned, and of the *deliberation* with which it was planned—that has yet been made on our common liberties. A few words more, and we have done. Notwithstanding the *right to discuss* belongs to MAN, as indisputably as the right to use his senses, or the organs of his body in their appropriate functions—and the exercise of it is, as it ought ever to be, free from all foreign control, save that which makes us responsible for the abuse of it in invading other's rights no less sacred than our own—yet have we been, again and again, held up by the slavery presses of this city as *obstinate, contumacious*, for not at once surrendering it on the demand of the Market House Committee. This charge has been so confidently preferred, and so often reiterated, that, we believe, the impression is made on many, that our conduct *has* been actuated by the spirit to which it is ascribed. They have been led to judge of our course, rather by the fury of the onset to which we have been exposed, than by the calm stedfastness with which it has been met. We ask, if *any* property can be more rightfully ours, than that which the Market House Committee demanded of us to lay down? *The right to discuss* is granted to us by God, and secured to us by the highest law of the land. Had the Market House Committee seen proper to demand, in the name of their constituents, the absolute surrender of our *houses* and our *goods*—backing their demand by the menace, that if they were not *voluntarily* yielded, they would be *forcibly* taken—would their demand have been less unreasonable? Have we any higher title to *these* subjects of property, than the gift of God and the security of the constitution? Ought we, then, to have rendered a servile compliance? Or ought we not rather (as we did) have firmly repelled the unjust demand, choosing to suffer the consequences, however disastrous to ourselves, in order that you, the proper correctors, by legal modes, of all public wrongs, might be made fully acquainted with the dishonor in which the majesty of the LAW was held, and the dangers with which our most precious rights were threatened, by a lawless and fierce aristocracy.

These same organs of the south charge the undersigned with answering the Market House Committee in terms of "*insult and defiance.*" Whilst we fully believe that no committee ever came on an errand more surcharged with wrong, and one which furnished on its very face stronger grounds of palliation for the treatment complained of, yet, are we persuaded, on a review of our communications addressed to them, that they contain nothing but a firm and respectful expression of a lawful and patriotic determination. The controversy to which we were called was too high—the principles for which we contended were of a dignity too lofty, to be stained by any resort to insult or abuse. And that our plainness of speech should be construed into "*insult and defiance*" shows that our editorial upholders of slavery begin already to demand from us that servility to their aristocratic instigators, which, as republicans yet free, we can render to no man or set of men, however influential, and which ought no where in this country to be looked for, except it be in the south, and under that "system," to the support of which they would seem so entirely to have consecrated their labors.

Notwithstanding the unusual outburst of lawless aristocratic violence to which our peaceful, yet decided support of the *freedom of the press—of liberty of speech—of the right to discuss*—has exposed us, we have lost no confidence in the rectitude of our principles, nor in the judgment which you, and those which may succeed us, will pass on our conduct. Unconvinced by the *force* with which our arguments have been replied to, we shall still continue fearlessly to maintain, and publicly to inculcate, the great principles of liberty incorporated in the constitutions of our state and general governments—believing, that if ever there was a time, it is now come, when our republic, and with her the cause of universal freedom, is in a strait, where every thing that ought to be periled by the patriot should be freely hazarded for her relief.

JAMES C. LUDLOW,
REES E. PRICE,
ISAAC COLBY,
WM. DONALDSON,
JAMES G. BIRNEY,
THOS. MAYLIN,
JOHN MELENDY,
C. DONALDSON,
GAMAL. BAILEY.
AUGUSTUS WATTLES
WM. YOLYOKE.

Executive Committee of the Ohio Anti-slavery Society.

APPENDIX.

A

From the Cincinnati Whig of August 15, 1835.

ABOLITIONISTS AND INCENDIARISM.

The account we published yesterday of a Mr. Dresser's being well *dressed* in Nashville, for his incendiary interference with the Slave population of Tennessee, has excited a good deal of attention among our citizens. The punishment he received seems to give universal satisfaction; and the injury likely to arise from the fanatical measures of the Abolition gentry, is apparent to every one with whom we converse.—The people of Cincinnati are exceedingly indignant, that Ohio should have been disgraced by having her name identified with any such contemptible enthusiasts. Our citizens, with unanimous accord, and in the strongest terms, condemn the conduct of Dresser and his miserable and misguided associates.

Many are talking of calling a public meeting for the purpose of expressing to our southern friends, the abhorrence entertained in this community towards the individuals and schemes that so manifestly tend to disturb their domestic relations, and endanger their lives.

B

From the Cincinnati Daily Evening Post.

INCENDIARY TRACTS.

Lots of the same vile incendiary publications that have been sent in such numbers to the south lately, were received here yesterday by mail, directed to many of our most respectable citizens. What ought to be done with them? We would say, send them back to the place from whence they came, and if any of their authors, or the agents of them should be found here, *Lynch* them. What is gambling in its most disgusting form, compared to the circulating of these fire-brands? Yet gambling produced the Vicksburg tragedy! What is swindling, such for instance, as gave rise to the Baltimore tragedy, the particulars of which we publish to-day, in comparison with this stirring up of a servile war? which, when fully commenced, can only terminate with the *extinction* of one or the other party! In a word, what crime is there that man can commit, that in its results is pregnant with so much ruin? None! A million of lives, and hundreds of millions of property depend upon the result!

Let the incendiaries beware; be they *located* where they may, means will be found to reach them, and bring them to the bar of public justice.

C

From the Cincinnati Republican of August 2.

OUR CITY.—The prospects of Cincinnati were never, probably, more promising, than at the present moment. It is true we don't hear of extraordinary sales of real estate, or witness vast and extensive improvements; but we see a steady, enterprising and industrious population, advancing in wealth, intelligence and refinement. We see also solid and substantial improvements going on in various parts of the city. We see property gradually but intrinsically increasing in value. We see old and unsightly buildings disappear one by one and comfortable and elegant ones rise in their place. We, cannot boast of our "five or six hundred new buildings," in progress of erection, though we believe there are not less than two hundred houses being built in the city and suburbs at this moment; but we can boast an increase of population beyond the increase of accommodations. We do not believe there is a city in the Union where the difficulty of procuring dwellings is so great. Our hotels and boarding houses are always crowded, and hundreds of southern families, who contemplated a sojournment of some weeks in the queen city of the West, have been compelled to relinquish their intentions, for want of accommodations.

ALTON TRIALS:

The Mob attacking the Warehouse of Godfrey Gilman & Co. Alton Ill. on the night of the 7th Nov. 1837.

ALTON TRIALS:

OF

WINTHROP S. GILMAN,

WHO WAS INDICTED WITH

ENOCH LONG, AMOS B. ROFF. GEORGE H. WALWORTH, GEORGE H. WHITNEY, WILLIAM HARNED, JOHN S. NOBLE, JAMES MORSS, Jr., HENRY TANNER, ROYAL WELLER, REUBEN GERRY, and THADDEUS B. HURLBUT;

FOR THE CRIME OF RIOT,

Committed on the night of the 7th of November, 1837, while engaged in defending a

PRINTING PRESS,

FROM AN ATTACK MADE ON IT AT THAT TIME, BY

AN ARMED MOB.

WRITTEN OUT FROM NOTES OF THE TRIAL, TAKEN AT THE TIME,

BY A MEMBER OF THE BAR OF THE ALTON MUNICIPAL COURT.

ALSO,

THE TRIAL OF

JOHN SOLOMON, LEVI PALMER, HORACE BEALL, JOSIAH NUTTER, JACOB SMITH, DAVID BUTLER, WILLIAM CARR, AND JAMES M. ROCK,

INDICTED WITH

JAMES JENNINGS, SOLOMAN MORGAN, AND FREDERICK BRUCHY;

FOR A RIOT COMMITTED IN ALTON,

On the night of the 7th of November, 1837, in unlawfully and forcibly entering the Warehouse of GODFREY, GILMAN & Co., and breaking up and destroying a

PRINTING PRESS.

WRITTEN OUT FROM NOTES TAKEN AT THE TIME OF TRIAL.

BY WILLIAM S. LINCOLN,

A Member of the Bar of the Alton Municipal Court.

NEW-YORK:

PUBLISHED BY JOHN F. TROW,

University Press, 36 Ann-street.

1838

Reprinted by Mnemosyne Publishing Co., Inc. Miami, Florida

First Mnemosyne reprinting 1969

Reprinted from a copy in the
Fisk University Library Negro Collection.

Library of Congress Catalog Card Number:
73-89440

Printed in the United States of America

TO THE PUBLIC.

There has rarely been an occurrence that has produced so deep and intense interest, throughout our whole country, as the disgraceful and murderous affair at Alton, Illinois, on the night of the 7th November last.

But the indictment of the *defenders*, and the trial of an *owner* of the warehouse, for the *crime of riot*, in attemping to protect his property from mob violence, together with the *singular* verdict of the Jury, in the case of those of the mob that were tried, has, if possible, increased the feeling, and created a great desire in the public mind, to know the facts in the case. The publication of these trials has been loudly called for through several public journals.

To gratify the public, and at the same time correct the contradictory reports that have been circulated, by giving the facts without comment, as they were drawn out in evidence, is deemed sufficient apology for spreading the "ALTON TRIALS" before the public.

THE PUBLISHER.

New-York, March 27, 1838.

ALTON TRIALS.

Municipal Court, City of Alton, January Term, 1838.	Hon. William Martin, Judge.
People of the State of Illinois, *vs.* Winthrop S. Gilman.	INDICTMENT FOR RIOT.

B. F. Murdock, City Sol'r. Samuel G. Bailey, U. F Linder, Att'y Gen'l.	For Gov't.	G. T. M. Davis, Esq., A. Cowles, Esq., G. W. Chickering, Esq.,	For Def'ts

AT the opening of the Court on this the 16th day of January, 1838, the above case came on for trial. The Clerk proceeded to empannel a jury. The regular pannel having been exhausted, talesmen were returned by the Sheriff, and at last, after the names of thirty-four persons had been returned, a jury was obtained, sworn to try the issue, consisting of the following named individuals :—James S. Stone, Timothy Terrel, Stephen Griggs, Effingham Cock, George Allcorn, Peter Whittaker, Horace W. Buffum, Washington Libbey, Luther Johnson, George L. Ward, Anthony Olney, Jacob Rice. In constituting this Jury the Government and accused exercised each their prerogative of peremptory challenge to its full extent, and twelve individuals called to the jury box were set aside for incompetency, by reason of their having formed or expressed an opinion as to the guilt or innocence of the accused.

Upon the first calling of the case, W. S. Gilman, by his counsel, moved for a trial separate from the other individuals included with him in the indictment, alleging that it was grounded, as well upon his right to have a separate trial, as upon the fact, that it was necessary for his complete, full, and perfect justification:

1*

that intent entered into the composition of the offence with which he was charged, and he could in no way so well as by a separate trial, show how utterly devoid he was of any criminal intent in the commissions of the acts for which he here stood indicted as a criminal. He urged, that if denied his application he might suffer injustice and wrong, inasmuch as the exercise by the individuals jointly indicted with him, of their separate rights to peremptory challenge, might conflict with the formation of a jury by which his acts were to be judged. "Having the right, I ask," said his counsel, "to be permitted its full exercise. I have the right, and I cite Dane's Abridgement to the point."

Per Curiam. The motion is granted, and thereupon a plea of Not Guilty, individually, nor jointly with the others named in the indictment, was entered.

Murdock, for Government, in opening.—The defendant is indicted for a violation of the 117th section of the criminal code of this State, which runs in these words: "If two or more persons actually do an unlawful act with force or violence against the person or property of another, with or without a common cause of quarrel, or even do a lawful act, in a violent and tumultuous manner, the persons so offending shall be deemed guilty of a Riot, and, on conviction, shall severally be fined not exceeding two hundred dollars, or imprisonment not exceeding six months."

The indictment is in these words: "Of the January Term of the Municipal Court of the City of Alton, in the year of our Lord one thousand eight hundred and thirty eight.

State of Illinois, City of Alton, ss.

The Grand Jurors chosen, selected, and sworn, in and for the body of the City of Alton, in the county of Madison, in the name and by the authority of the People of the State of Illinois, upon their oaths present, that Enoch Long, Amos B. Roff, George H. Walworth, George H. Whitney, William Harned, John S. Noble, James Morse, junior, Henry Tanner, Royal

Weller, Reuben Gerry, and Thaddeus B. Hurlburt, and Winthrop S. Gilman, all late of the City of Alton, in the county of Madison, and State of Illinois, on the seventh day of November, in the year of our Lord one thousand eight hundred thirty-seven, with force and arms, at the city of Alton aforesaid, and within the corporate limits of said city, unlawfully, riotously, and routously, and in a violent and tumultuous manner, resisted and opposed an attempt then and there being made to break up and destroy a printing press, then and there being found the goods and chattels of
contrary to the form of the statute in such cases made and provided, and against the peace and dignity of the people of the State of Illinois.

And the Jurors aforesaid, in the name and by the authority aforesaid, upon their oaths aforesaid, do further present, that Enoch Long, Amos B. Roff, George H. Walworth, George H. Whitney, William Harned, John S. Noble, James Morse, junior, Henry Tanner, Royal Weller, Reuben Gerry, Thaddeus B. Hurlburt, and Winthrop S. Gilman, all late of the city of Alton, in the county of Madison, and State of Illinois, on the seventh day of November, in the year of our Lord one thousand eight hundred and thirty-seven, with force and arms, at the city of Alton aforsesaid, and within the corporate limits of said city, unlawfully, riotously, routously, and in a violent and tumultuous manner defended and resisted an attempt then and there being made by divers persons, to the jurors aforesaid unknown, to force open and enter the store-house of Benjamin Godfrey and Winthrop S. Gilman, there situate, contrary to the form of the statute in such case made and provided, and against the peace and dignity of the People of the State of Illinois.

FRANCIS B. MURDOCK,
Prosecuting Attorney for the Municipal Court
of the City of Alton "

Endorsed upon the back 'A true bill.'
THOMAS G. HAWLEY, Foreman."

You perceive, Gentlemen of the Jury, that the indictment charges in each count a distinct offence. In the first it is alleged, that the defendant, with others, unlawfully, riotously, and in a violent and tumultuous manner, on the 7th day of November last, resisted and opposed an attempt made by divers persons to break up and destroy a printing press, then being the property of Benjamin Godfrey and Winthrop S. Gilman: and in the second count it is charged against the same individuals, that they in the same violent and tumultuous manner defended and resisted an attempt then and there being made by divers persons to break open and enter the storehouse of Godfrey & Gilman. The charge is for an unlawful defence of property—unlawful, because violently and tumultuously done. The defendants had a right to defend their property—every individual has. The offence consists in doing the act in a manner not sanctioned by law, but in direct violation of its letter and spirit. They assembled at the storehouse of Godfrey & Gilman, armed with muskets and rifles, with the acknowledged intent of using them in defence of property; and they did use them. The assembly of such a body of men armed in this manner, and for the avowed purpose of defending property from destruction, was calculated greatly to excite the feelings of the community, and to lead to a breach of the peace.

The counsel for the defence will place their justification upon the principles of the Common Law of England, which recognises the right of every individual to defend his own house from a violent intrusion, and also to assemble his friends to aid him in its defence. This rule of law was established in a barbarous age, when man fought with man, and clan was arrayed against clan. Then, every man's house was his castle and protection, and men were justified in using more violent means in defence of their homes and their firesides, than in protection of other property. But, gentlemen, I take the broad ground, that the common law of England, so far as it relates to crimes, has no force in the state of Illinois. This is the opinion of many of the ablest lawyers of the state. No one will say that an individual can be indicted at common law in our courts. We have a criminal code of our own, and unless the crime be defined and punished by statute, it is not an offence here. The first clause of the criminal code is in these words, "That the following shall, from and after the first day of July next, constitute the code of criminal jurisprudence of this State." The Legislature intended to establish a new system of criminal law. To define crimes, and fix their respective punishments. And when the Legislature said that a "violent and tumultuous" defence of property shall constitute crime, it said that the law, and the law only, shall be every man's castle and sure protection; and the section under which these defendants were indicted, was enacted for the purpose of providing for the punishment of such, who, not relying upon its power to protect their rights, endangered the peace of society by the use of violent means. The facts, gentlemen, the people expect to prove, it is unnecessary for me to detail to you. You are all familiar with the melancholy history.

Attend to the evidence.

Edward Keating, Esq. called and sworn.—On the night of the seventh of November last, I went into the storehouse of Godfrey, Gilman & Co. accompanied by Mr. Henry H. West. I saw in the store a number of people, and perhaps eight or ten of them armed. Mr. Gilman was not in the room. Mr. West inquired for him,—he was sent for, and came down from above to see us. Gilman was not armed. We went in to apprise Mr. G. and the rest, that the storehouse would be blown up or burned, if the *press* was not given up. Gilman expressed a great deal of surprise that such a proceeding should be thought of, and that the citizens of Alton would allow such a thing to take place. He said they had come to the determination to defend the property, and should do so if necessary, with their lives. This was perhaps an half hour before the mob assembled. Mr. Gilman was not armed if I recollect aright. I saw there Messrs. Gilman, Tanner, Walworth, Lovejoy, and (here witness was interrupted by counsel for defence, who admitted that all who were named in the indictment were present in the building during the attack.) All whom I saw had arms, except Gilman. I saw no guns stacked up in any part of the room. I left the building, and soon after went to my office. At the time of the attack by those outside upon the building, I heard the report of firearms. The first report I supposed to be from a pistol, and immediately after, or nearly at the same time, I heard another report, which I took to be that of a gun. My impression is, that these guns were from those outside. I judged so from the sound, or noise of the report. Almost immediately after the report of the second gun, I heard a third, and exclaimed as I sprung to my office window, *that* must be from the inside. I heard, as I raised my window, the cry that a man was shot. I soon heard the report of another gun fired from the inside, and a man immediately cried out he was wounded. I now went down stairs, and out, and met persons carrying the body of Bishop to the office of a physician (Dr. Hart.) The mob had dispersed generally. I stood a few moments, and then returned to my office. Soon I heard a rush, and upon going to my window, found the mob had again assembled. I went out and joined the Mayor, whom I found addressing the crowd. We stood a little while—a gun was fired, the shot whistled about and came close round us. Soon after I saw another gun, pointed in the direction in which I stood, flash, and I decamped. These shots I now speak of, came apparently from the corner of the warehouse next the river,—were fired in the direction of those attacking the building, and appeared to be fired at some people who were engaged in raising a ladder to the roof of the warehouse. The press was soon afterwards given up. I then went into the building, and found there Mr. Weller, one of its defenders, and the only one of them I saw there. He was wounded, and was sitting in a chair, near the stove, in the counting-room, bathing his leg. I went into the building previous to the attack upon it, and before any persons had assembled outside. I met no one on my return when I left the warehouse. I did not see Mr. Gilman when I first went in; he was sent for at the request of myself and Mr. West, and came down stairs to meet us. I did not recognise more than five or six of those in the building. All I saw, except Mr. Gilman, had arms. I saw no supernumerary arms. I don't know whether I saw any others in the building than those indicted. (By defendant's counsel objected, that the prosecution have no right to question a witness whether other individuals than those indicted were present, and objection sustained.) I did see Tanner, Lovejoy, Walworth, and Gilman. I was informed, before Gilman came down stairs, by some of those whom I saw there, that they had assembled to defend the press, but that they did not expect any attack that night. Gilman, however, not only said they had assembled to defend the press, but that they should do so, if it was necessary, with their lives. Each man whom I saw, except Gilman, had a gun. The doors were not "blockaded," and I was astonished at the little preparation for defence I saw. I was sitting in my office at the time of the first shots. I heard a pistol fired first, and then one or two guns on the outside, then heard another gun, which, from the sound, I judged to be fired from the inside. As I went to my office window, another gun was fired from the warehouse, and perhaps two; and some one screamed he was wounded. This was after Bishop was wounded, but before he was carried off. I had made up my mind an attack would be made that night, before it actually took place.

Cross-examined.—Did you not know a company had assembled that night to break open the warehouse? By walking the street that evening, I met five or six persons, and I felt confident that an attack would be made, and in the manner I have related. My object in going into the warehouse, was to let those inside know that unless the press was given up, there was danger the building would be burned or blown up. Such was the rumor. I believed it. After I left the warehouse, I went to the Mayor's office, staid there perhaps fifteen minutes, left, went into my own, and had been there about the same time when the attack first was made.

At the time the Mayor was addressing the people outside, I saw four or five guns in the hands of individuals in the crowd. This was after the guns had been fired by those inside the warehouse. The mob first armed themselves with stones. The reports of the first two guns fired were at the same time—simultaneous with the shower of stones; the smaller explosion, that which I took to be a pistol, was a moment before. At the time of the third gun, I started to my window; the mob were then in front of the warehouse, and about six or eight feet from it. The crowd were then throwing stones.

I saw the preparation to burn the building, but it was after the time I now speak of. There were cries to burn the building, and from a great many voices; they were given at the onset, after Bishop was shot.

It was about eight o'clock in the evening that I understood that the building would be burned or blown up, if the press was not given up.

Q. Did Gilman state to you, at the time you were in the warehouse, that they were there by, and acting under authority? I do not recollect; Gilman appeared to be very much astonished at the communication I made him. *Q.* Did Gilman, at the time when he said they would defend the press, if necessary, with their lives, request you and Mr. West, or either of you, to call upon the Mayor, and request him, from them, to summon the people to suppress the mob? He did ask Mr. West to do so. *Q.* Did Gilman address the people outside? I do not know, I was not there. *Q.* Did

West go to the Mayor, in pursuance of such request made him? I do not know. I left West in the warehouse, and went to the Mayor's office alone.

Q. Did others express surprise that an attack was to be made upon the building, or press, that night, besides Gilman? (Objected to, by Government, on the ground that Gilman was alone on trial, and so irrelevant, and objection sustained.)

Examined by Counsel for Government.—I saw no attempt to fire the building till Bishop was killed; nor did I see any intention to use firearms till that event. In fact, I saw no arms, till the period when the Mayor was addressing the crowd. I knew of the intention to blow up, or set fire to the building, and communicated such knowledge to Gilman before the mob assembled.

Again Examined by Counsel for Defendant.—*Q.* Did you not see persons assembled together, prior to the night of the 7th, armed with pistols, and avowing their intention to destroy the press? (Objected to by Government, but sustained.) Prior to the night of the 7th, and on that of the 6th, I was down upon the bank of the river: a number of people were there together. I talked with one who had a club; told him that his stick was not much of a weapon, or some such thing. He dropped his club, and showed me a pair of pistols in his dress, about his body. An order was soon issued by some one of them, "Forward march. Let's go up to H——, and get some drink." They marched off, but soon came back again,—had further conversation, in which they said they were waiting for the press; (here objection made by Government's Counsel, that this evidence was improper, unless connected with individuals who composed the mob, and objection sustained;) at this time, there were ten or fifteen people assembled. I had pocket pistols, I carry them always.

The Court here stopped the witness, and stated, that a petition had been presented to the Court, requesting the Government would draw to its aid the services

2

of the Attorney General of the State, U. F. Linder. Under the law, the Court has the power to appoint counsel for Government, to assign to gentlemen the duty of appearing in any cause, where, for any of the causes stated in the law, the necessity should exist for such appointment. But in the case at Bar, it seems to the Court that none of the emergencies contemplated by the law, as ground for the exercise of the power of the Court, in reality exist. The Government are represented in this cause by the City Attorney, and if he does not choose to seek aid in the services of others, it is not for the Court to interfere. While the people's. Attorney is acting in the discharge of his duty, the Court have no authority to interfere and direct him to accept the tendered services of others. The Court would say it entertained a high regard for the petitioners, but, to grant the prayer of their petition, it would arrogate to itself power not delegated to it by law. Under the law, and the facts presented, the Court has no right to appoint any Counsel in aid of the prosecuting officer; and an arrangement to secure Mr. Linder's services must be by consent and agreement of the officer, upon whom the law had imposed the duty of conducting the prosecution.

Davis, in behalf of Mr. Gilman, expressed perfect acquiescence in any arrangement which should be made. They had supposed they should find him and the Attorney General side by side with the City Attorney in the prosecution of this cause; they knew not that he was not to assist the prosecuting officer, until the very moment the trial came on,—and in behalf of his client, the defendant, he would say, that though he could not deprive the Government of the aid, if the individual tendered it; nor compel the Government to receive the services, if they were disinclined so to do; yet he hoped he might be permitted to express the perfect satisfaction the defendant would feel at finding the Attorney General supporting the laws of the land in conducting this prosecution.

By Murdock.—The gentleman's services are accepted.

Question by one of the jurors.—At the time you went to the warehouse, had there been any attack upon the building? Ans.—Not to my knowledge.

Henry W. West.—On the night of 7th of November last, about eight o'clock in the evening, I was standing in my store door. John Solomon passed, and remarked, that he believed there would be a mob that night, and that preparations were making to burn or blow up the warehouse unless the press was surrendered, and that the building would be destroyed, unless the press should be given up; said Gilman had been friendly to him, and he did not want to see him injured, or his property destroyed. He urged me to go up and tell Gilman. In company with Mr. Keating I went into the warehouse, and inquired for Gilman; he was up stairs; we sent up to him that we wanted to see him, and he came down. I then told Gilman the rumors, and the circumstances. Gilman replied to me that he had thought the matter over seriously, and said he should not give up the press, but should defend his property at the risk of his life. I returned to my store. Soon started to go to the warehouse again. Met Dr. Beall on the way, and asked him to go with me; he declined. I then asked him to use his influence to suppress the mob and to endeavor to get them to disperse; he replied he could have no influence and would have nothing to do with it. I kept on, and went up to and into the warehouse.

The mob came while I was in the warehouse—a stone was thrown against the door. I think Gilman went to the garret door, opened it, and asked them what they wanted. The mob replied, the press. Gilman said it did not belong to him, it was stored with them, and he should defend it. The mob said they would have it, and started off round the corner to the other front of the store. At this time pistols were fired, then a gun from the mob, and Mr. Gilman requested me to go and see the Mayor.

After some time I went again into the warehouse with Mr. Krum, the Mayor, and Mr. S. W. Robbins. The Mayor had some conversation with Gilman. It was about 8 o'clock when I first went to the warehouse. I saw there Walworth, Long, Morse, Tanner, Lovejoy, Gilman, and others. They were most of them armed, principally with muskets or rifles. I don't know whether the arms were loaded or not. I heard nothing said about it. I saw some guns standing in the room; appeared to be stacked supernumerary. When the firing commenced I was in the third story of the warehouse. There was firing by those inside while I was there, though not a rapid discharge. One gun only was first fired. Some individual inquired, "who fired that gun?" "I," was replied by some one, but by whom I don't know. Shortly afterwards there were two or three guns fired from another part of the warehouse than that in which I was. I now saw Gilman the second time with a gun. I am positive, though I do not recollect what he was about the first time when I observed he had a gun. When Bishop was killed I was still in the warehouse. I saw Gilman with a gun both before and after the firing commenced, but he did not fire. I think it was Gilman who asked "who fired?" and the question was asked in a remonstrating tone. I do not know who fired of those who were in the warehouse. I did not hear it spoken of at all, neither do I know what was said or done by the persons assembled out of the warehouse at the time of the firing. About the time or soon after the first gun was fired from the inside, some persons remarked they saw some person picked up.

The stones came through the windows and near me. The people inside could have sheltered themselves from the stones behind the walls of the house. The firing was from that end of the warehouse next the Penitentiary, and I understood that the person who was shot, was shot in that direction.

I did not see any person when about to fire from the windows.

Before there was any firing there was some conversation about the manner of doing it, though I do not recollect precisely what. I said, however, that if it was found necessary to fire at all, in my opinion it would be best at first to fire over the heads of the crowd. Mr. Lovejoy replied, that "they must not waste a fire." There was an attempt made by the people inside the store to effect a reconciliation so far as this, Mr. Gilman addressed the people who had collected outside. People inside among themselves seemed firm, cool, and collected. Gilman remarked that he thought he had a right to defend his property, and he should do so at all hazards or at all risks. I once attempted to prevent Gilman from firing; he was then in the garret at the door or near to it. Gilman told me I should get hurt if I staid at the door, and advised me to move away. The second time I was in the warehouse, I saw two guns which were not in any one's hands; they were standing up.

My own opinion was that the press had better be given up, and I so advised Gilman. The reply by Gilman was that they would not give it up—he said he did not believe the mob would go to such extremes when I told him that they would burn or blow up the building in order to get the press, and he seemed solicitous about it; "he seemed anxious nothing of the kind should be done." When I came out of the warehouse Bishop had been killed, and the mob then had guns. The mob first approached the warehouse on Water street. I did not see them at that time, as I was standing back from the door in the warehouse at the time. I should think there were from fifteen to twenty people in the warehouse, though I don't know with certainty how many there were. All were not armed. Mr. Noble had no gun, and he remarked that he would not shoot. When Gilman was at the window intending to fire, the stones were flying through the room. It was prior to Bishop's death. I heard Gilman say that the press was stored with them. The members of the firm

2*

are Benjamin Godfrey, and Winthrop S. Gilman. I know nothing which took place prior to the night of the 7th of November, in regard to this matter.

Cross-examined.—There was a good deal of danger to those inside from the rocks flying into and through the rooms unless they were protected behind the walls. The glass was all broken from the windows, and I think the sash also. There was no opening in the building except the skylight, that I know of, other than what was on the ends fronting the river, and Penitentiary. Some of those whom I had seen in the street threatening to blow up or fire the house, were some of those who composed the crowd attacking the building. There was a discharge from some weapon on the outside before there was any firing by those within the building. I think the weapon discharged was a pistol, and that it was fired when the crowd were passing from Water street round the building.

I was present at the time of the Mayor's address. Where the shot which reached us at that time were fired from I don't know. He was standing so that shots fired by those inside the building could have reached him. Mr. Gilman, previous to any firing from any one addressed the mob, and requested them to retire and desist from their purpose. I could not see the crowd at the time of his address to them, and I do not know whether any one of the mob presented a pistol to him or not at that time. After the Mayor had concluded his address to the mob, the firing was renewed by those on the outside and within the warehouse. I had two different interviews with Gilman. Those inside the warehouse avowed their intention of defending the press solely, and disclaimed any other object. They said they would not be the first to commence an attack. Mr. Gilman remarked, that he should be sorry that any blood should be shed, but that they would defend the building at all hazards, if need were with their lives.

Small shot were first fired; this was so when the

Mayor was addressing the mob, and I saw some holes made in hats by the fire from the building.

Re-examined by counsel for Government.—I saw Bishop after all was over, his wounds were not made with small shot, he appeared to have been shot with buckshot.

Sherman W. Robbins.—I know and can state nothing which transpired on the night of the 7th of November last, which has not been already stated, and indeed I can not state so much as Mr. West has. I knew nothing of the riot till after Bishop was killed. I went with the Mayor and Mr. West to the warehouse and we were admitted. Most of the individuals whom I saw in the building had firearms. There was no firing from the building while we were inside. We went into both buildings; there is means of communication from the one to the other inside. We went into the second story, but I think not into the third. There were persons placed in the second story, in each room of said story—they appeared to be stationed at certain places in each room. I saw Mr. Gilman there; he had a gun in his hands; he said but little in my hearing. The Mayor, Deacon Long, and Mr. Gilman, stepped aside and had some conversation. Our object in going in was to communicate the request that those outside had made of us.

I saw the doors of the warehouse, but did not notice them particularly. It was a few minutes before we could gain admittance, and I presume they were fastened. I saw a number of individuals with firearms, and two or three guns were set up against the side of the room. I did not see so many as twenty or thirty guns loaded while in the house, though I understood they had as large a number with them.

Cross-examined.—I told those inside that the persons outside *said*, "that if the press was not given up, the building would be burned or blown up." I told Mr. Lovejoy that I understood this course was to be taken from the mob outside, and distinctly said that such was the determination of the mob, as we were informed.

Samuel Avis.—I was not out till after the fire had been put out, Bishop had been killed, and the firing was over. I went inside the warehouse, saw no one there whom I thought had been in the building during the riot except Mr. Weller. I saw the body of Mr. Lovejoy. I saw firearms. I saw only one gun, however, I think, and that was in the counting-room. I remained but a few moments. I saw no ammunition, no preparation for, nor indication of war.

This witness was not cross-examined. The court here adjourned. At the afternoon session,

Anson B. Platt, a young lad was called, and by agreement of counsel for the people and accused, he was examined by the court. The indictment was first explained to him, and then in answer to the interrogatories of the court the witness testified as follows:

I know there were some guns fixed at our establishment. I run some bullets by the orders of Mr. Tanner. By our establishment, I mean Mr. Roff's establishment. I saw some guns standing in the room but did not count them to know how many there were. I don't know when they were taken away nor where they were carried to. I saw them there before "the mob took place." The guns were standing there when they were taken to be carried to the church. They were returned to the store after the night of the "church affair." I saw no one carrying away the guns. I run nearly a tumbler full of buck-shot, and some of other kinds. don't know for what purpose they were run. Mr. Tanner did not tell me why he wanted me to run them, nor what he was going to do with them. Henry and William Tanner, both of them asked me to run the balls. Mr. Gilman didn't ever ask me to run any balls. Tanner did not tell me what they were going to do with the balls. I was at the store at the time of the riot. I did not go to Mr. Gilman's store till the fuss was over. I saw one gun standing near the door, and no more than one. I did not know the gun as I know of. I did not see any of the balls or shot I run in the store. I did not see Mr. Gilman in the warehouse. I saw no one firing the guns but only standing in our store. There was one old gun among them. They were principally rifles, but there was one shot-gun. I know of no balls that were run except those I run. I run the balls at different times, and they were taken away from the store. Mr. Butcher took away the last I run. I don't know where he took them to. He went down stairs. Mr. Roff is a merchant, and he keeps guns to sell. I know he keeps guns to sell because they are offered for sale. The guns we keep in the store for sale are new. I saw only one old gun and that was a fowling-piece. I know the guns were gone. They were missing before Lovejoy was shot, how long before that I don't know. I don't know how many guns there were in the store. I should think there were a dozen in all, and all of them were gone. The balls I run were made to fit the guns I expect, but I don't know. All the guns I saw and speak of were up stairs on the second floor. They were not usually kept up there. The guns were put up there after they were brought back from the church. They were the same guns that Mr. Roff had previously in the store for sale.

John H. Watson.—I know nothing at all about Mr. Gilman. I did not see him at all that night. I was not at the warehouse till all was over. I know of no previous preparations. I went to the warehouse, but could not get in. I tried to get in after I heard Lovejoy was killed, but could not get in. I was in Mr. Keating's office when the crowd first passed by the office towards the warehouse. They had no firearms among them that I saw. They picked up some stones as they passed the office, and proceeded towards the building. The mob threw stones at the warehouse for some few moments. About the third gun Mr. Keating sprang to his office window, and remarked he thought it was fired by those inside the building. I then found out that Bishop was killed. I left Mr. Keating's office:

went into Dr. Hart's office. I soon left there and went to Hawley, Page & Dunlap's, and staid till 2 o'clock.

Cross-examined.—There was firing at the time the stones were thrown,—I saw but few thrown. I had not been in the streets at all that evening.

Joseph Greeley.—I went to my boarding-house the evening of the seventh of November last, at the usual tea hour. At the table I was told that an Independent Militia company was to be formed that evening under the laws of the State. I was told that the individuals favorable to the formation of such a company were to meet at Godfrey & Gilman's store that evening, and was urged to attend. I declined going on the ground that I feared it might be an abolition meeting, but was assured that it was no such thing. In the evening I met another individual who said he also had been requested to attend, and we went down to the warehouse together. I found an individual there with the laws of the State. They requested me to sign a paper which was drawn up and ready, and which was a set of by-rules, as I understood, and I did so. The number of people which the law requires having signed the paper, we proceeded to an election of officers and made choice of Mr. W. G. Attwood, as Captain. After we had made choice of officers we proceeded up into the second story where we found some arms. We took them and paraded and drilled for a little time, but as the guns were loaded we did not exercise much. This was between seven and eight in the evening. About eight o'clock the inquiry was made, "Who would stay and defend the building that night?" The company were at this time in a circle, and some of them stepped forward and volunteered. I was asked to stay, but declined doing so, and went home. I knew nothing else till the bells rung. I then got up and went down to the spot. There were about thirty or forty guns in the warehouse. The guns were said to be loaded. We exercised a little with them, and but little, and I supposed it was because they were loaded. I understood so. Mr. Gilman was present at the time we were drilling, but was not active. Mr. Gilman was one of the company which was formed. It was remarked that Mr. Gilman was tall, and must take the right of the company. I was informed that the company was to be formed under the provisions of the laws of the State, and there was one individual there who had the laws in his possession. I do not know that there had been any steps taken preliminary to the formation of the company except what was done that evening. When I got there I was informed that they were waiting only to get a few names to enable them to choose officers. They were soon got, and then the company proceeded to the election. Nothing was said about the object of forming the company.

Question by Counsel for Government.—What appeared to be the motive of those who volunteered to stay that night in the building?

Why, some appeared to think that they would have a good time if they stayed. They expected to have some crackers and cheese, and hear some good stories. The volunteers, when they were called, stepped forward in the circle. It was generally understood that a press was in the building, and I suppose those who volunteered to defend it expected an attack. I saw no press. I was present at its destruction—saw it knocked in pieces. The behavior of the mob engaged at the work was orderly—it was done in a quiet sort of way. They seemed to be happy while engaged in breaking it in pieces. Soon after the press was broken up I went home.

Cross-examined.—I heard something said about fire, but don't know what it was. I heard nothing said about any design of attacking the building previous to the attack. The streets were deserted at the time I went home from the warehouse. I understood the formation of the company to be under the provisions of the law. Mr. Walworth (one of the defendants) asked me to go up to the warehouse and join the company. I do not recollect seeing Mr. Murdock (City Solicitor) there. [Admitted, however, to be true that he was there.] I understood the defence of the press was an entirely distinct affair. I joined the company, understanding it was formed for the defence of the city. I cannot tell how many people were in the warehouse at the time I was there.

The People here rested their cause.

For defence. To save the trouble of examining witnesses to the point, there being no doubt as to the fact, the defendant's counsel admitted the warehouse was the property of Benjamin Godfrey and Winthrop S. Gilman.

William L. Chappell called and sworn.

Q. On the night of the 7th of November last past, previous to any attack by the mob upon the warehouse, did you go with Winthrop S. Gilman to the Mayor? If so, state what passed at the interview between the parties.

The People, by Linder, here interposed an objection to any answer being made to the question by the witness. I anticipate the object aimed at by the counsel, your honor; and I may as well state my objection here, now, and in full, to any answer which may come from the witness. For what is this witness introduced? Why is he brought here? Sir, it is to show, by hearsay, that the defendant now upon trial had a conversation with the Mayor, and also the nature of that conversation; it is to show that the defendant acted under an authority, which this witness is to swear he received from the Mayor; it is to show, so far as the declarations of this witness go, that the acts done by this defendant, on the night of the seventh, were legalized beforehand by the Mayor. Now suppose this witness should swear, that the Mayor authorized the defendant to arm himself and his friends, and assemble for the protection of that warehouse;—suppose he should swear that the Mayor gave him permission to act as he did; what then? why sir, we say that the Mayor had no right, had no business, had no power to give such authority! Sir, he had not such power. Where does he derive his power? The Mayor is invested with certain authority under the act which incorporates the City of Alton, under the by-laws,—under the rules and regulations which the City Council have ordained. But, sir, in the act of incorporation such power is no where given to the officer—you can't find it there—you can't find it in the City charter—you can't find it in the ordinances of your City Council. We contend that he did not have such power as a peace officer, for the laws have not given to peace officers such authority. Then we say that such power as would enable the Mayor to grant Winthrop S. Gilman the authority contended for is not vested in that officer by the City Charter, nor by the By-Laws of the Council. The Mayor is only a peace officer, having certain delegated powers in criminal cases, which are entrusted to all peace officers. But, sir, suppose such authority was given,—suppose the Mayor had a right to give such authority, I then object that this witness cannot be called to testify to it. If he should be permitted to do so it would be hearsay evidence. The Mayor is in Court,—he knows what authority he gave. Let them ask him. They are bound to produce the best evidence, and they cannot be permitted to give evidence of the Mayor's declarations, when he himself is in Court, ready, if called upon, to testify. A party is bound to produce the best evidence.

Cowles, for Court.—The Mayor is, ex-officio, a Justice of the Peace. The Government, in the long speech just submitted to the Court, has assumed that the Mayor had no power, had no right to grant Winthrop S. Gilman the authority which we propose to show he did grant to him. There is some difference between assumption and proof. But may it not be shown that the defendant had no criminal intent in doing the acts, in the commission of this offence, if the

3

Government will persist that it was an offence, by proving, that he asked the advice of the Mayor—that he anxiously sought his direction, by proving that he was careful to do nothing until he had first consulted that officer Suppose, sir, we show that Mr. Gilman, on that evening, consulted the Mayor of this city; and that at the close he went away actually having, or honestly supposing he had, full and complete authority from the Mayor? what then will be the consequence? what will be the effect upon this jury? what becomes of this indictment? how will you make out a crime? where then is the criminal intention, a necessary ingredient in crime? But take the question upon consideration of power, of authority in the Mayor. The criminal code of this State has the following provisions:—"If two or more persons assemble for the purpose of disturbing the public peace, or committing any unlawful act, and do not disperse on being desired or commanded so to do by a judge, justice of the peace, sheriff, coroner, constable, or *other public officer*, such persons so offending," &c.—§ 113.

Again, "Every male person above eighteen years of age who shall, by neglecting or refusing to aid and assist in preventing any breach of the peace, or the commission of any criminal offence, being thereto lawfully required by any sheriff, deputy sheriff, coroner, constable, justice of the peace, or *other officer concerned in the administration of justice*, shall, upon conviction," &c.—§ 137.

Now, sir, your Mayor is, ex-officio, a justice of the peace, and by your laws "all officers concerned in the administration of justice" are conservators of the peace, having full power to take such measures as they may deem expedient for the *prevention* of offences, as well as the punishment of offenders.

Well, here was a plan premeditated, openly and boldly promulgated, avowed with such boldness as that it reached the ears of your very *peace officers*, to destroy the press; and if it was necessary to the accomplishment of that purpose, they proclaimed their intention of burning or blowing up the warehouse. Will the Attorney General say that a peace officer could make no provision to prevent the commission of such a crime? Will he hazard the assertion, that our laws compel one who is a conservator of the peace, to stand by, and folding up his arms, await with such patience as he could, the arrival of the period when he might interfere, not for the prevention of the offence, but for the detection and arrest of the offenders? Sir, prevention is better than cure, and our laws guard as well against the commission of crime, as provide for the punishment of offenders. But your Mayor, ex-officio, is a justice of the peace, and as such, had authority to take such steps as would prevent the commission of the offence which was threatened.

But the ground upon which we contend we have a right to the testimony of this witness is, that he goes to show the absence of all criminal intention on the part of this defendant.

The Government urge, secondly, as ground of objection to the admissibility of this evidence, that it is in the nature of hearsay. But may not the declarations of an officer of the law be given in evidence? may not the official declarations of an official person be admitted? We wish, however, only to show by this witness, the absence of all criminal intention on the part of the defendant, and for that purpose offer to prove, that he went with the defendant to the Mayor, and that in the conversation that was held Mr. Gilman had, or supposed he had, received, the authority of the Mayor, to pursue the course which was taken.

Bailey for Government.—The witness is offered to prove the declarations of a third party. The fact that Mr. Gilman had, or supposed he had, authority from the Mayor, is proposed to be proved by hearsay. Such evidence is inadmissible. The person, whose declarations are sought to be proved, is present in Court. He can best tell what authority he gave. The course proposed by the Counsel is most extraordinary.

Per Curiam. It is unnecessary for the Court to give an opinion upon one branch of the subject argued. The question whether the Mayor had the authority contended for by the one and denied by the other side, is not necessarily involved in the decision of the question presented to the Court.

The only question to decide, is, as to the admissibility of the evidence proposed to be introduced. The declarations sought to be proved are inadmissible. They are in the nature of hearsay evidence. Any evidence of the declarations of a third person as a general rule would be inadmissible, and especially when the person whose declarations you seek to prove may himself be sworn to testify. It makes no difference whether such person speaks officially, or as a private individual. The evidence cannot be received.

Cowles.—I offer the witness to prove a fact. I wish to prove that Mr. Gilman, in company with the witness, went to the Mayor for the purpose of getting his permission, his authority to enter and defend the building. I do not offer the witness to prove what the declarations of the Mayor were.

But the testimony of the witness for this purpose was objected to by the Government, and the objection sustained by the Court.

The Record Book containing the Minutes of the doings of the Common Council of the City of Alton, was here introduced, and F. B. Murdock called and sworn.

Q. Are these the Records of the Common Council of this City? They are. Are you the Clerk of the Council? I am.

By Cowles.—I propose to read to the Jury an extract from this book. It is part of the Record of the doings of the Common Council on the sixth day of November last, the day preceding the commission of the act for which my client is now arraigned as a criminal. I offer it as proof of the fact, that the Mayor on that day applied to the City Council, at the instigation of Mr. Gilman, to appoint an additional police.

The evidence was objected to, and Mr. Linder, Counsel for the people, said: We make the same objections to the introduction of this book in evidence, that we have previously made to the admission of the testimony of the witness, Chappell. They propose to prove by this book, what? Why, that the Mayor stated to the Common Council, that Mr Gilman had stated to him, he apprehended danger to his property, and desired that a body of special constables should be appointed. Our objection to the testimony sought to be derived from the witness, was, that it would be in the nature of hearsay evidence. The Court so decided, and ruled it to be inadmissible. We now object to the introduction of this book, because it goes to the Jury as the hearsay of a hearsay. This case is like that which might arise in legislative proceedings. I had the honor, sir, of once introducing to the assembly of this state, for its consideration, some famous resolutions, in regard to the bank; and would your honor hold, that I could prove the contents of those resolutions by the minutes of the doings of that body? Could the proceedings of that time be proved by the Journal of the House of Assembly? The evidence offered here, is the record of a representation, made on the sixth of November, to the Common Council by the Mayor; of an application made to him by Winthrop S. Gilman, in relation to an apprehended attack upon his property. It is made competent evidence because it happens to be enrolled upon parchment, and included in doings of the Council Board!

Defendant by Cowles.—The defendant is indicted for doing a lawful act in an unlawful manner. He is charged with resisting with force and arms, in a violent and tumultuous manner, an attempt to break open his warehouse. Our object is, to show that the attack upon the building was not only premeditated, but that the Mayor was apprized of such premeditated attack beforehand,—that Mr. Gilman communicated to him his fears, his anxieties in regard to the matter, and that by rea-

3*

son of the communication made to him by Mr. Gilman, the Mayor acted, and applied to the City Council to appoint a body of special constables. If we can show the fact, we shall ask the Jury to draw certain inferences.

Sir, it is the business of your Mayor to preserve the peace of the city,—it is his duty. He has the power, upon him rests the responsibility. His acts are public acts, and when he, for the purpose of preserving the peace of the city, makes application to a co-ordinate branch of the city government, and that body act upon such application, it then becomes a public act, entitled to credit, entitled to be received as evidence in a court of law. We want to show the fact that the conservators of the peace of the city, the guardians of its welfare, those invested with power, those clothed with authority,—who were bound to suppress tumult and riot,—who were bound to preserve order and peace, whose duty it was to stretch the strong arm of the law over the humble and peaceful citizen, knew of the danger Gilman apprehended to his property. And if we can prove this knowledge; if we can bring it home to them, and also prove how, and for what purpose it was communicated to them, and prove it too by the record of their own proceedings, drawn up, and written out by their own officer, we ask the privilege, as we claim the right. The acts of the Common Council of this city are public acts—their record of those acts is a public record—and it not only is evidence, but it is the best evidence that can be produced.

People by Bailey.—The object for which this book is offered in evidence is to show the intention of the defendant; to prove to the Court, that he had no criminal design, and to clothe such evidence with peculiar sanctity, by deriving it from a public record.

But although this evidence might avail other defendants upon another trial, it will not be deemed relevant in this. Mr. Gilman is now alone upon trial, his name is not mentioned in the record, and the book cannot therefore be admitted in evidence. If admitted, it would only prove that the Mayor received the information, which he communicated to the City Council in relation to the apprehended attack, from *some* citizens, and would be no proof that the defendant was the one from whom he received the information.

Per Curiam.—What is the Issue made in this cause?

On the part of the people, that there was an unlawful assemblage on the night of the 7th of November last. On the part of the defendant, that certain facts exist which warranted that assemblage; that in the commission of the acts charged to be criminal, the defendants were justified, they having acted under the authority of the Mayor. There can be no question that if they acted under such authority, they may justify their acts. The Mayor and Common Council are the guardians of the city—they are intrusted with certain powers, among which they have the authority necessary to preserve the peace of the city;—if they have reason to fear the tranquillity of the community to be in danger—no matter from what cause—they are bound at all hazards, and at all times, to provide means to protect the persons and property of the citizens commensurate to the apprehended danger. By virtue of his office the Mayor may call out the militia and other citizens to suppress tumult and riot—all are subject to his authority—all are bound by any order he may issue on such an occasion, and the citizen who should refuse to obey, would be liable to the penalty of the law.

The defendant, for the purpose of showing the intention which actuated him in the premises, offers the records of the Common Council in evidence, to show that he communicated the danger which he apprehended to his property, to the Mayor of the city, and requested the appointment of special constables to prevent the anticipated destruction of property, and disturbance of the peace of the city. But it is objected, that the admission of the book would be permitting evidence to go to the Jury, which, on account of its character, is inadmissible. The book contains the proceedings of the Common Council. It is the record of their official acts, and, by the charter creating the city, a certified copy of their proceedings is admissible as evidence in every court of this State; therefore the record itself must be admissible. The Court can perceive no objection to the admission of the book in evidence.

The book was thereupon handed to Mr. Murdock, who was requested to read from the record of the doings of the Board, at its sitting on the 6th of November. He read as follows :—" The Mayor informed the Council that individual citizens had represented to him that they believed themselves to be insecure in their persons and property, and that he, the Mayor, from the facts in his knowledge, and from the faith reposed in the representations made him, had much reason to believe that the peace of the city would be disturbed: and he submitted to the Council the propriety of authorizing him to appoint special constables to aid in the maintenance of order."

At the request of Linder, for the People, he proceeded to read further from the records, and as follows :—

" Mr. King moved the following resolution :

" That the Mayor and Common Council address a note to Mr. Lovejoy and his friends, requesting them to relinquish the idea of establishing an abolition press at this time, in the city, and setting forth the expediency of the course."

" Not acted on."

John M. Krum, Mayor, was called to the stand, sworn, and said: With the permission and indulgence of the Court, I should be glad to avail myself of this opportunity to make a few remarks before I proceed with my testimony. Such leave having been granted, he proceeded. I profess to know the prerogatives of the Court and Jury, and the province of a witness. It is my desire to keep within the province of a witness.

There are circumstances however attending this case, so peculiar in their nature and tendency, that I feel it due to myself, due to my official station, and due to the defendants and the public, that I should ask from the Court, from Counsel, and the Jury, in giving my testimony, a somewhat wider range than is usually allowed witnesses in ordinary cases.

I am not insensible of the conspicuous position which I occupy as a witness, in this instance; nor am I destitute of the feelings and sensibilities that are natural to mankind. But from the relation I bear to the citizens of Alton—from the official station I occupy—and when the peculiar attitude in which I have been placed, from the force of circumstances, in reference to the unfortunate transactions which have led to this prosecution, are considered, I trust the Court, the Jury, the accused, and Counsel, will pardon me for asking the indulgence.

It will not I trust be considered strange that I should manifest some sensibility, when called to testify in a case attended with such unusual excitement: it will not be considered strange, that I should manifest some feeling and timidity, while the attention of this large and anxious assembly—of this community, and the public, is directed to myself, and to the evidence I shall give before the Court and Jury. And when it is considered how strangely, how wickedly and meanly, the recent. melancholy excitements in this city, and my own conduct and motives have been misrepresented, impugned and calumniated before the public, it will not be thought out of place, that I should ask of the Court, of Counsel, and the public, the most careful and scrutinizing attention to my evidence.

I have hitherto borne the injuries done to my feelings, and the imputations against my character, in silence and with regret. I have deeply regretted that the public and the press should give birth and circulation to reports, which have been without foundation;—false and libellous in their character.

Doubtless many have aided the circulation of such reports, very innocently, and with no bad or criminal intention.—I most cheerfully forgive all who ha vebeen in any way instrumental in this, when they were ignorant of the situation in which our citizens were placed.

Those who have given origin to false statements and misrepresentations, connected with the recent affairs to which I now allude, whether in reference to myself or to others, are guilty of the most heartless, reckless, and degrading meanness, and well deserve individual and public execration. I profess to know and appreciate the responsibilities and duties that rest upon me as a man and a citizen: I trust I feel and appreciate the responsibilities of my official station, and my duties to my fellow citizens.

Nor have I been insensible of the peculiar and trying situations in which I have recently been called, in discharge of my official duty. Few men, in so brief a period, have been placed in more trying or critical situations.—During the whole of the unhappy excitements that have heretofore prevailed to such an alarming extent in this city, I endeavored to act with firmness, prudence, and with moderation.

It was my firm conviction that the exigency of the times required at my hands the course of conduct, official as well as private, that I did pursue. It was my earnest desire, to heal the unhappy dissensions and avert the fatal and disastrous calamities with which we were threatened—my time, labors, and influence, have been cheerfully and zealously devoted to accomplish an object so desirable.

I leave my fellow citizens and the public to judge of the propriety and correctness of my motives and conduct. Notwithstanding the calumnies that have been heaped upon me and my official conduct—although my motives have been assailed in a manner that might well arouse my feelings, I am grateful, and feel proudly elevated in my own estimation, that I can stand before my fellow citizens, fully conscious of the rectitude of my conduct and my motives.—I have the consoling reflection, that I have at all times endeavored to discharge my duty as an officer and a citizen with unflinching firmness, to the best of my judgement and abilities. I am grateful that I have been called upon to give evidence, before this Court and Jury, under the fearful solemnity and unction of an oath, of matters that have so long been the theme of abuse and defamation, and I hope the result of this investigation will save in future, the feelings of sensibility from defamation and outrage, and serve to disabuse the public mind.

I am ready for examination as a witness.

It was proposed and agreed, that the witness, commencing at the organization of the City Government, should give a connected narrative of the facts from that time to the time of the riot, so far as they were connected with the defendants on trial.

At the time Dr. Beecher preached upon anti-slavery, I forget the day of the month, and perhaps some one will remind me, (here some one remarked it was on the 30th day of October,) as I was going to dinner, Mr. Alexander informed me that he (Beecher) was to preach that night at the Presbyterian Church. He asked me if I would not attend. I replied that I did not know—I would see. I had an appointment, which I expected would occupy a part of the afternoon, and thought would extend into the evening. In the afternoon, Mr. Gilman came into my office, and commenced a conversation with me. In the course of it, he told me that they expected another press would arrive in a few days; that they had organized themselves into a company, and that they would be ready, in case any violence should be offered, or any disturbance take place, to act in obedience to any civil authority. At the close of the conversation, he asked me to go with him into Mr. Roff's store. I went with him, and found there, Messrs. Roff, Walworth, Breath, one or both the Mr. Lovejoys, I think both, certainly Rev. E. P. Lovejoy, and I presume others. They stated to me that they expected the press would arrive soon; that it was consigned to A. B. Roff, and that they expected it would be landed at Mr. Roff's store. Some one, I do not recollect who it was, remarked that Col. Buckmaster had told them he would not have it in his store, on account of the insurance. They then remarked, they had prepared themselves with guns, in case of there being any trouble, and said they expected the press would be assaulted. I thought, and told them so, that if the press was landed in the day time, I should apprehend no danger, and could not believe that an attack would be made under such circumstances. They replied to me by saying, that in case any disturbance should take place, they would hold themselves ready to obey my orders. I thanked them for their offer, said it was all very well, and left. They had guns in the store at this time. I saw them. Some one (I think Mr. H. Tanner) proposed the plan of taking the guns to Mr. Gilman's warehouse, and asked me what I thought of it. I urged upon them the propriety, the absolute necessity of acting with moderation and prudence, and remarked to them, that it seemed to me that nothing would tend more to increase the excitement then existing upon the subject, than for them to appear in the street with arms. I did not consider that I was there, at that time, in my official capacity, as Mayor. They again repeated to me their readiness to act and obey any orders they might receive from the civil authorities. I thanked them for their readiness to do so, and begged of them, if they should deem it necessary to take the guns to Mr. Gilman's store, they would take them there in such manner as to avoid exciting any suspicion, and suggested the plan of carrying them there in a box. In the meantime, a boat, I think the ——— was coming up the river. She was in sight, and soon reached the town. As she arrived and landed Mr. Gilman and myself went on board of her, to ascertain whether the press was on board or not. I soon ascertained, from the Captain, that the press was not there, and we, or I left. When

I got to Roff's store, as I was passing to tea, J. S. Clark and Mr. Gilman were standing there, engaged apparently in conversation. Mr. Gilman asked me if I should attend the Church that evening: I replied that I had not intended to. He urged me to go; said he apprehended there might be some difficulty, and in such case my presence might be desirable. I said if my presence was necessary I would go. The conversation then turned upon the arms which were in the store, and he (Mr. Gilman) asked me what I thought of having the arms in readiness, near the Church, in case any disturbance should take place. I told him I did not apprehend there would be any necessity for having them there. Mr. Gilman replied, he hoped that no disturbance would take place, but that he feared there was more danger than was imagined. I then told him that I did not know but it would be well enough to have the arms in some convenient place here, (meaning at Roff's store,) in case they should be wanted. At the proper time I went to the Church. I found there a large congregation assembled. All was quiet and peaceable. During the services, and towards the close, a stone was thrown through the west window of the Church, but did no injury. The congregation rose immediately to their feet, and some one, I think from the gallery, cried out, "To arms." I afterwards was informed that this individual was Mr. H. Tanner. There was a rush towards the doors, but Mr. Beecher asked the audience for their attention again; order was soon restored, and the services proceeded to their close without further interruption. The congregation was soon dismissed: with the others I went out. The people were crowded together around the doors, and Mr. Mansfield, and some others, stood there with their arms. There was quite a crowd (a good many boys) around the doors in front of the Church, halloing, and calling those who had guns cowards. I immediately endeavored to get the attention of the crowd, and soon succeeded, when I commanded them, one and all, immediately to depart, and repair to their respective homes. The first intimation I had that the arms had been carried to the Church, was by observing them in the hands of those who stood at the doors. The crowd, soon after I made proclamation, dispersed, and, in company with others, I started and came down the street. At the bridge there was quite a collection of people, and I took a gun away from a man by the name, as I have since been informed, of John Adams, who stood there. Subsequently to this, I was frequently called upon by Mr. Lovejoy, (now deceased,) Mr. Tanner, Roff, and others, and my opinion asked in regard to the propriety and expediency of organizing an armed force. I remarked that at present there was no organized militia force in the city, and no force upon which I could depend in case of emergency. They stated that they thought of forming a military company, and asked me if, in case they did, I would head it. I told them I could not, that my official situation was such as would render it impossible. Mr Lovejoy, in particular, called repeatedly upon me, and said that I ought to command a military force. I told him I could not consent to do so; that I never should do so unless it became necessary for the protection of the laws. We had repeated conversations upon this subject. I repeatedly, and I believe always, told Mr. Lovejoy, that it was within the province of any citizens to organize such force, if they deemed it necessary, that they could do it, if they pleased, at any time. Mr. Lovejoy stated to me that they wished to organize their company under my sanction in an official capacity, and asked me if I would give such sanction. I told him that I could not, and explained to him the reason why I should feel bound to withhold it. I told him what the provisions of the law in regard to the formation of such companies were; explained to him the mode of proceeding necessary to be followed in the organization of their company. Subsequently to this, loaned my law books to some one, who, I understood was to join the company.

Mr. Gilman, in an interview shortly after, told me that they had organized a company, and had put themselves under the command of William Harned: he tendered me the services of the company, and said that they would at all times hold themselves in readiness to obey any commands I might issue. I replied again, thanking him for his readiness to act, so often expressed, and told him that whenever the time should come in which I should think the occasion would warrant me to call for their services, I should unhesitatingly do it.

On the night of the 6th, or rather the morning of the 7th of November last, at about 3 o'clock, Mr. Gilman and Mr. Roff came to my room and called me up. They stated that the press was coming, that the boat was in sight coming up the river, and that Mr. Moore was upon the boat and had charge of the press; that arrangements had been made to have it safely landed and stored that night, and they requested me to go down and be present at its landing, so that, in case of difficulty or disturbance I might be there to suppress it. I got up, dressed as quickly as I could, and went down to the river. I stood at Mr. Gilman's warehouse while the boat was nearing, and till she landed. I did not go on board, I think. The hands of the boat put the press on shore and removed it into the warehouse. I think I did not have conversation with any one but Mr. Gilman at this time. After the press was stored, I went up into the warehouse. I found some twenty or thirty people assembled: they were all armed, and again offered me their services in aid of the laws. I told them, as I had repeatedly before, that at the time I did not see any occasion for their services, but that if occasion should arise when their services should be needed by me, I should not only call for, but should expect to receive their assistance. On the 6th Mr. Gilman called upon me at my office,—he introduced, as matter of conversation, the subject of the rights of citizens to defend their property. We had a long conversation; I gave him my opinion upon the subject; I think I read the law, and explained to him its principles; I do not know whether he asked my advice as Mayor, as lawyer, or as a friend and citizen. I did not consider that I was then advising him as Mayor;—in the course of our conversation we spoke of our municipal regulations; I told him I thought they were exceedingly deficient, and I believe I mentioned in what particulars. He asked me if I would appoint special constables; said he apprehended danger to his property; I told him that I had no authority to make any such appointment, that I would cheerfully do all I could; that the Council would meet that day, and that at their meeting I would lay the whole matter before them. When the Council met, I did make the application, but I did not recommend in terms the appointment of such officers; I left the whole matter to the action of the Board. I was absent at the next meeting of the Council when the Records were read, or I should have noticed the mistake in the record, and had it corrected.

On the evening of the 7th of November last, Mr. Gilman and Mr. Chappell called at my office. They told me they apprehended an attack would be made upon the warehouse, as they had understood the mob were determined to destroy the press; that a number of armed men had assembled and were then in the building for the purpose of defending it, and that they had come to the resolution of remaining there, and defending it at all hazards; they asked me what I thought of their determination: they spoke of the rumors they had heard in regard to the determination of the mob to destroy the press. At that time, all was quiet in the city, so far as I know, and I had but a little while before been in the streets, and observed nothing which led me to suppose an attack was meditated. I did not believe an attack would be made. I had exerted myself that day as much as I was able, and had endeavored to get all the information which was possible. People seemed to shun me, and were very reluctant to communicate with me at all, and I could succeed in getting no information which should have induced me to believe any design to destroy the press was meditated. Mr. Gilman asked me what I thought of the armed men who were in the building, remaining there for the purpose of defending their property. I told him in my opinion they had an undoubted right to be there,—that they might rightfully remain there, and that they would be justified in defending their property; I did not understand them as making this application for advice to me, as Mayor. Mr. Gilman stated to me that they were well prepared with arms; that they should remain there during the night; that they were fully determined to defend the press and the building; and that if the attack which they apprehended was made, they wished it to be understood that their services would be ready to execute any order they might receive from any civil officer. I replied to them, that if the emergency should require the aid of armed men, I should not hesitate a moment in commanding the men who were assembled there to suppress the riot, but that I should be the sole judge of such an emergency. He repeatedly asked me what I thought of their being there. I never ordered any man to repair to the warehouse; but in every instance, I was informed that they had already repaired there. Mr. Gilman repeatedly told me, that all he desired was to act under the authority of law, and the civil officers. After Mr. Gilman left, I remained in my office till between nine and ten o'clock. I stepped in to Dr. Hart's office at that time, and while I was there I heard a number of people passing by,—there were from fifteen to twenty. I immediately came down stairs. I recognised two of the crowd; one of them had a gun. I got my overcoat, prepared myself, returned to the street, but saw no one. I came down to Mr. Robbins' office, sent for Judge Martin and other civil officers, and waited some time for them to come. Mr. Robbins and myself finally started together. As I was going down the stairs I

4*

heard two reports of firearms; from the sound I thought they were pistols; the reports seemed to be low. I soon heard another which I took to be a gun. I hastened up, and soon saw people carrying a man,—it was Bishop. I stepped up to them and asked if any one was hurt; they replied yes, one of our men was shot. I asked if he was much hurt; they said they thought not. They seemed very much excited. I endeavored to persuade them to disperse. A crowd gathered round me; I addressed them, and used all the means in my power to induce them to disperse. I asked them what they intended to do. They said they were determined to have the press. Some one proposed that I should let those inside the warehouse know that they wanted the press;—that they would have it at all events, and said they would retire while I went in and communicated their derermination. I acceded, supposing that if we could once get them scattered, the excitement would subside and we could then control them. They retired; I went to the warehouse; Mr. Gilman opened the door and let me (with Mr. Robbins and I believe Mr. West also) in. He, Mr. Gilman, asked me how many outside were injured, if any. I told him there was but one injured, so far as I knew, that there were but few outside. I then told Mr. Gilman what the mob said they wanted, and the determination they had expressed, and I also stated my impression, that when I went out we could control them. I staid in the warehouse some time purposely, longer than I otherwise should, in order that the excitement should subside, as I had no doubt it would.

While in the warehouse, I went up on to the second floor. I saw there Gilman, Lovejoy, Walworth, (I think, but am not positive,) Long, Hurlbut, and some others. I think I saw some arms about the walls. Gilman, Long, and Lovejoy, had guns in their hands. Gilman told me that two or three guns had been fired from the house. Deacon Long asked me if they were justified. I replied, most certainly; I thought they were. My impression was that we should be able to quell any further disturbance, when we went out; and I so expressed myself. I had no idea any further attack would be made.

Question by W. S. Gilman.—On the night of the 6th, when I called you up and you went down to the warehouse, did you not go into the building before the press was landed? *Ans.* Yes, I believe I did, I think I did.

Q. Did you not ask me to go out, and did I not go out, and did I not stand by your side on the wharf at the time the press was landed? *Ans.* Yes, you did.

Q. When the press was landing did I not ask you to go down and receive it, and did you not say that as I was the owner, I had better go down and receive it, and you would be by my side?

Ans. There was a proposition of that kind made, and I believe I made it; I thought as you owned it, you ought to be there to receive it when it was landed.

Q. Did you not tell us we had better not leave the warehouse, not even to go to our meals, without some being there to guard it?

Ans. I think I told you you had better keep a guard there, or something to that effect.

Q. Did I not seem anxious to know what to do?

Ans. You did; you appeared anxious that whatever was done, should be done under the sanction of the civil authority.

Q. What course did you say you should take in case the press should be attacked?

Ans. I told you that if there was any danger that the people should attack the press, I should order them to desist, and should warn them of the serious consequences which would follow any attempt on their part to disturb or destroy the press.

Q. Did you not say that if the press was attacked, you should first order the mob to desist, and that if they persisted, you should then order us to fire?

Ans. I believe I did; I said I should if it became necessary.

Q. Did you not at this time consider you appeared there as Mayor?

Ans. I did.

I once agreed in one of the interviews I had with Mr. Gilman, to appoint Capt. Harned as special constable at his (Mr. Gilman's) request; but afterwards, upon an examination, I found I had no authority to make such appointment. I did not consider the armed force at the church, or at the landing of the press, as organized under my authority.

I have lived in the city for nearly five years. Godfrey & Gilman built the warehouse which was attacked; it has been in their possession ever since I have known the place.

I heard no noise in the warehouse on the night of the 7th. I saw but few persons there; saw Mr. Gilman first on the lower floor. I saw Mr. Long, Lovejoy, and Hurlbut, and I presume others, but don't recollect who.

I know Mr. Gilman to be an orderly citizen. I gave no orders while I was in the building, either to Gilman, or any one else, restraining them from firing, or doing any thing else. I saw no occasion for doing so. I thought they had a right to do as they were doing. When I went out, I commanded the people assembled there to disperse. If I had seen any thing riotous on the part of those in the warehouse, I should have ordered them to desist; I should have commanded them to disperse. When I first went up, the front of the store had been broken in. Some shot struck my hat while I was addressing the crowd. The guns were fired on the outside of the building, and, I thought, from the southeast corner of the warehouse; there were three guns fired at the people who were raising the ladder to the warehouse. I supposed the shot which reached me, were fired at them; and I afterwards ascertained that I stood about in the direction.

The two first discharges were from the outside, and they were the first which were fired, I think.

Question by Defendant's Counsel.—From all the circumstances in the case, have you any doubt that Mr. Gilman, in what he did, supposed he had your sanction? *Ans.* From all the circumstances, I am induced to believe that Mr. Gilman supposed he was acting under my authority. While I was in the storehouse, some conversation took place about the right which a man had to defend his property. I uniformly told them, that they had a right to be there. I told them they were justified in defending their property; but I told them so as a lawyer. While I was in the warehouse, I told them, that if they were out of doors, I should command their aid in suppressing the riot; but that I could not command them while they remained there.

Cross-examined.—While I was in the building, I gave no directions to those inside, as to the mode of resistance they should adopt. I considered that they acted upon their own responsibility; but I gave them my legal opinion. I took the message which the mob requested me to take, and communicated it to those inside. I told them that the mob swore they would have the press, at all hazards.

Gilman replied, that they had resolved to defend the press at the risk of their lives, and that they could not give it up. I saw Gilman, Lovejoy, Hurlbut, and Long, and I recollect of no others now whom I saw with guns.

In my remarks to the mob, I returned the language of G.; I spoke to them of the dangers they were in, the laws they were violating, and the penalties they were incurring by the breach of those laws.

Question by Linder for Government.—Did Mr. Gilman ever tell you what principles that press was intended to advocate? *Ans.* I don't think he ever did. He once told me that it was not determined whether the press should be established here, or at some other place. I don't know that I ever heard Gilman say any thing about keeping Mr. Lovejoy here, or persuading him to go off. I never did confer upon those who were inside any authority to assemble, or give them any order to fire upon the people outside. I endeavored in the interviews I had with Mr. Gilman to explain to him the law.

Question by Linder for Government.—Did you ever state to Mr. Gilman that he could not resort to violence, unless under the direction of an officer of the law? *Ans.* I don't think I ever did. I told him that every man had a right to defend his person, and property, and to use violence if it was necessary; and that each man must judge of his extremity. I repeatedly stated to him that whenever a case presented itself, where I thought the emergency required it, I should not hesitate to call upon those men, or any other, to aid me in maintaining order; but I thought it must be an extreme case which would justify such a course. I advised Mr. Gilman, in case of any disturbance, to address the crowd in the first place; I thought he took a correct view of the matter. I told him what course I should probably take, if I was placed in a similar situation; but in all instances I advised him as a friend, and a citizen, and not as an officer. I might have been desired to remain in the building at the time I went in, I think I was, and that I replied, that I could have more influence with the crowd out of doors. At the time I addressed the crowd, after I came out of the warehouse, I think I stated to them, that unless they dispersed they would be fired upon by those in the building. If I recollect right, the mob made no reply. They advised me to get out of the way and go home.

Question by Defendant's Counsel.—At the time you stated to Mr. Gilman and others, that if they were outside you should command them to aid you, was any proposition made by any one for them to go out?

Ans.—There was no proposition made by them, or

to them, to go out of doors. They expressed their readiness to obey any orders I might give them.

Question by Linder for Government.—Did you give them any orders?

Ans.—I did not.

Samuel J. Thompson called and sworn.—I was in the warehouse on the night of the 7th of last November. Before the mob assembled Mr. Gilman spoke of sending for the Mayor. Something, I don't recollect what, prevented at the time. The mob assembled before the matter was arranged, and he was not sent for that I know of.

Cross-examined.—I was one of those inside the warehouse on that night.

Q. Was you a militia man? *Ans.* No, sir, I was in the regular service, such as I hope to be always in. I was there all the time. I do not know who shot first. I was stationed towards the river, and the stones rattled so that it was difficult for me to tell whether a gun was fired or not. The first gun I heard, was fired from the outside. I don't know whether it was the first which was fired or not. There were three or four guns fired before the cry was heard that Bishop was dead. I never saw Bishop. It was remarked inside, that they were sorry to shoot any one, and that they hoped this would put an end to the attack. Some of the guns were loaded with fine, and some with buckshot. I had a gun, but did not fire it. We had resolved to defend the press at the risk of our lives. The thought never entered our minds that the mob was as bad as it turned out to be; and therefore, we did not prepare as we ought to have done. I should myself act differently again. I remained in the warehouse till the mob left it.

Question by Linder for Government.—Whereabouts were you? *Ans.* I was all over the house, from the garret to the cellar.

Question by same. Did Mr. West find you there? *Ans.* Yes, sir.

Q. And the Mayor? *Ans.* Yes, sir.

Examined again by Defendant's Counsel.—I supposed I acted under the authority of the Mayor. When the Mayor came into the building he was asked if we had done right in firing; he replied, Yes, perfectly. The Mayor and Mr. Robbins both said that the mob were determined to go headlong and get the press at any rate. I do not use their expressions. The Mayor was asked to remain. He said, No; I can do more good on the outside, or I would. The understanding we had among ourselves was not to fire until we were fired upon. We did not fire until we were attacked, and guns were fired.

Linder for Government.—I now move, your honor, to reject this evidence. This witness, by his own showing, is equally guilty with those indicted. He is *particeps criminis;* and one standing in such situation can never testify in favor of his fellow criminals—cannot be permitted to give evidence, where such evidence goes directly to exculpate those with whom he was associated in the commission of an offence—shall not be permitted to swear away the guilt of his co-actors in crime.

Cowles for Defendant.—This seems to me a strange course to pursue, and a singular time to adopt it. The evidence has gone to the jury; it has had its effect; it has produced its impression, and if the evidence *could be* withdrawn from them, what course will the Attorney General point out, by which its effect can be withdrawn, or its influence removed? And it is too late to take the objection now. If it was to be made at all, it should have been made long ago. But the government has sat still and permitted it to go to the jury, and because the witness has disclosed some rather unpalatable facts, they now start up with this wild proposition. We had a right to presume that the evidence was given in, not much to the satisfaction, I acknowledge, but surely with the full consent of the Government. The presumption of law is, that if a party sits by, hears evidence improper in its character given to a jury, and does not object, that he has no objection; or having any waives it. It is a fair presumption that it was given in by his consent, if he do not make his objection at a proper time. It is so decided by the Supreme Court, in the case of Suyder *vs.* La Frambraise, and this is the first time it has ever been controverted. Suppose the present defendant is convicted under the indictment now pending; and suppose he discharges such penalty as may be imposed, will the Attorney General say he would be incompetent to testify upon the trial of the remaining individuals, included with him in this indictment? Surely not; and yet he would stand before the jury, not only a criminal, but a convicted one. And if Gilman would be a competent witness for individuals over whose heads this indictment still pends; whose guilt or innocence is yet to be passed upon; why is this witness to be excluded upon this trial? 'Tis true a witness cannot be compelled to criminate himself—cannot be forced to disclose facts, which if disclosed by him would enable the Government to convict him. But whose privilege is this? to whom does this right belong? To the witness introduced, and to whom the question is propounded, and from whom the evidence is sought to be obtained. But, if a party chooses to disclose facts which may be injurious to himself; if a witness voluntarily discloses his participation in an act which is criminal;—who suffers? who is injured thereby? The Government? Not so. They gain, in this way, the disclosure of the crime, and the knowledge of the criminal. The witness? Not so. He waives his privilege, throws from him the shield which the law has furnished him, and thereby braves the danger, and seeks the liability.

Per Curiam. The motion cannot be sustained. An accomplice not indicted with others who may be on trial, is a competent witness, although he cannot be compelled to give evidence against himself. The rule is, that the objection only goes to the credibility of the witness; and if such testimony is not corroborated by

5

the testimony of other credible witness or witnesses, it is not entitled to full credit. The witness is competent, and the jury must judge of the degree of credit to be placed upon the evidence.

The defendant here rested, and proposed submitting the case to the Jury without argument, but the proposition was declined by the Counsel for the People.

For the People.—Mr. Murdock rose and said: Permit me, Gentlemen of the Jury, before I proceed to the argument of the case, publicly to express the pleasure I felt while listening to the testimony of Mr. Krum. The eloquent, candid, but indignant manner with which he repelled the often repeated story of inefficiency and indecision in the discharge of his important and highly responsible duties during the trying events which have given our city such unenviable fame; and his satisfactory detail of the measures recommended and adopted, must have given gratification to all his friends. And if any thing that I may have said tended to confirm public opinion in the truth of reports so prejudicial to him, I feel called upon by every gentlemanly consideration, in this public manner to confess the charges to be unfounded, and that he stands before this community in the character of an efficient and upright Mayor.

I regret, Gentlemen of the Jury, that in the discharge of my duty to the people, I am called upon to animadvert upon the conduct of men for whom personally I entertain the highest esteem. In every relation in life the defendant possesses as high claims upon our regard as any other individual in the community. Gentlemanly in all his deportment; strictly moral in life, and enterprising in business; few men possess to a higher degree, or deserve, the respect and confidence of their acquaintance, than the defendant, Mr. Gilman. But, gentlemen, he has been charged by the Grand Jury of the city, with a violation of the laws of the State, and no matter how wealthy he may be—how useful as a citizen—how pure and unoffending in the general course of his conduct, if guilty of the offence charged, it is your duty to say, by your verdict, that neither the rich and good, or the poor and profligate shall violate the law with impunity. It is the palladium of every thing dear to freemen. It is lamentable, gentlemen, to consider the excesses to which fanaticism, in the name of our holy religion, often drives the best and most intelligent men. If the defendant had been led by the dictates of the religion he adorns, if he had consulted the precepts of that Divine Master, whose professed disciple he is, how different would have been his conduct, amidst the appalling events of the 7th of November last! Did he, who is God alone—did he, when nailed to the cross, curse his cruel persecutors, and die? Did he oppose violence to violence? And yet, gentlemen, the defendants thought themselves justified by the religion of the Saviour. It is humiliating to man, to think how weak we are,—how liable, with the best intentions, to err. The warmth of his heart, his benevolent zeal for the good of the oppressed of his fellow men, will extenuate, but cannot wipe away the guilt of the defendant.

But, gentlemen, this is a question of law;—Is the defendant guilty or not guilty? The facts no one denies—they are fully, clearly made. Do they constitute crime is the question. I will not deny that at common law every individual had the right by force to repel a forcible entry into his house, nor will I deny that he had a right to assemble his friends to aid him in so doing—but is it so in Illinois? has every one this right here? is it one of those natural rights which no law can deprive us of? If it is, gentlemen, then our statute is a dead and useless letter. It was manifestly the intent of the Legislature to change the common law, to abridge the right of defending one's domicile, to an orderly and peaceable resistance, free from violence and tumult. If the defence of property by means of firearms be not a "violent and tumultuous" defence, can any acts constitute the offence? It is the manner in which the defence is made, not the defence itself, which constitutes the crime. We must give the statute its natural and evident import. It may be that the defendant supposed he was acting under the authority of the Mayor; but is this a justification? The Mayor cannot legalize an illegal act—he cannot give a warrant to commit crime. His office is to maintain law, not to give authority to violate it.

Few states, gentlemen of the jury, have a criminal code so severe as our own. Its provisions, if carried into effect, are amply sufficient to protect the property of our citizens, or to punish the lawless destroyer; and it was the duty of the defendant, as a good citizen, to have fled to it for redress of his injuries. The Legislature intended by the severity of its enactments to manifest its design to throw around the rights and property of our citizens ample protection, or to punish rigorously its violations. To the law then the defendant should have resorted for redress: he should have reflected, that in our day and country a rabble cannot long hold the ascendancy: that soon a returning sense of propriety will come over the people: that so soon as reason has time to exercise her power, unaided by passion, that love of order, that respect for law, that regard for the rights of others which distinguish Americans, would have exerted their influence over our misguided citizens.

I need not say to you, gentlemen, how much I deplore the tragical event, the details of which you have been so long listening to. It has exerted, and will continue to exert a baleful influence upon our prosperity, and worse, upon our good name. But the evil has been committed, and gone forth to all the world, to blacken the page of our history; it is your proud duty, your high power, to do much to soften the coloring. And how, but by the fearless execution of the law? I will not, gentlemen of the jury, trespass longer upon your time, exhausted by the extended examination of testimony. I resign the case to the able counsel who aid me in the prosecution.

Remarks of George T. M. Davis, upon the defence of W. S. Gilman.

Having, for the last fortnight, gentlemen of the jury, been confined to my room with indisposition, it is with a perfect consciousness of my own inability, (increased from feebleness) to do justice to my client that I attempt to address you in his behalf; and were it not that I am to be followed by other, and far more able counsel, you might indeed charge me with arrogance and presumption in making an effort in his defence. I must consequently throw myself upon your kind indulgence for the few moments I shall occupy in taking a cursory view of the testimony in this cause. Fortunately for my client, gentlemen of the jury, we have been enabled to sever him from the other individuals who are included in the indictment with him; neither to you or to the prosecution, is it any matter what motive prompted the application; it was a right secured to him by the law; a right which was deemed valuable in its exercise, and which was properly granted us by this court; you have, therefore, only to inquire into the guilt or innocence of my client, without regard to the others who stand charged in the same indictment with him.

I know not, gentlemen, hardly why I stand here; how it is that I am called to defend Winthrop S. Gilman, upon a charge of violating the laws of his country. I can hardly reconcile to myself the fact that I am here to defend, and you there to try this individual for an alleged crime; a man who in all the relations of life is respected, beloved, and honored, who has proven the most dutiful of sons, the kindest and most affectionate of husbands and fathers, the most faithful of friends, the most valued as a neighbor and citizen, honored as a public benefactor, and whose memory will be cherished in grateful remembrance for his many acts of private and public benevolence, while that of his persecutors will have been forgotten, or only spoken of with pity and contempt. The best evidence in the power of my

5*

client to offer you of his confidence in the purity and uprightness of his motives, the innocence of his acts and the justice of his cause, and of the integrity and impartiality of those by whom he is to be tried, is that he has committed his defence to the hands of a junior counsel. In that confidence, gentlemen, I most fully participate; but it would be criminal in me were I to deny that I enter upon the discharge of my duty with the liveliest solicitude, for it is neither the evidence or the law, nor the strength of the learned and able counsel that is to enforce it, that we are to contend against. No! we have other and more formidable antagonists; it is the rumor which has floated, the prejudice which exists, and the calumny which has been so industriously circulated throughout this community previous to this trial. You will therefore pardon me when I assure you, that I am not without one lingering apprehension as to the safety of my client, and that is lest you should have unconsciously imbibed that poison which has been so widely diffused; but when I say this, let no one of you understand me as casting the least doubt upon either his integrity or his judgment; in both I have the most unlimited confidence, for I know you to be upright, intelligent, and honest; but you were created men before you were appointed to be jurors, and we tremble lest in your hearts you entertained prejudices which may have been imbibed in ignorance, but now cherished almost as virtues. I ask you, therefore, gentlemen, to make a strong effort to rise above all extraneous considerations, and divesting yourselves of every thing like prejudice or partiality, to give to the testimony and the law, applicable to this cause, a fair and candid review, and see if you will not be warranted by both in arriving to the same conclusion that we have; that the defendant acted under a fair and honest conviction that he was doing right; that he was in the discharge of his duty to himself in defending his property, and his duty to his country in maintaining her laws. Let me then call your attention in the first place to the indictment, which contains two counts. In the first you will perceive that the defendant, with others who are therein named, is charged with having "*resisted* and *opposed* with force and arms, violently, tumultuously, and unlawfully, an attempt of certain persons unknown, to break up and destroy a printing press, *the property of the said defendant*, and one Benjamin Godfrey." By the second count, the offence is somewhat varied, and the prosecution have charged that he, with certain other individuals, with force, unlawfully, and in a violent and tumultuous manner, "*defended and resisted*" an attempt then and there being made by divers persons unknown, to break open and enter a storehouse of *the said defendant*, and Benjamin Godfrey. Thus you will perceive that the government have alleged that the property was in us, and that the defence was made for the protection of our own rightful property; and all the offence for which my client is here arraigned, and for the trial of which you are there empannelled, consists in the fact that he found it necessary to use force and arms in his own defence, and that defence was made in a violent and tumultuous manner. All, therefore, gentlemen, that you have to inquire into is, the *manner* in which this defence was made; this is the true issue before you, and upon it the acquittal or conviction of my client must rest. The people have charged us with making this defence in a violent and tumultuous, and therefore in an unlawful manner; we reply, and we ask you from the testimony to believe, that there was no tumult on our part—that the violence we made use of, was but proportionate to the attack we were compelled to resist, and necessary to our protection, and therefore justified; but before I proceed to consider the grounds of our defence, let me say to you what in my opinion it is necessary for the prosecution to show, before they can ask you to convict this defendant—they must prove to you the time when, the place where the act was committed, and that the manner in which the act was done was tumultuous. Have they done so? Have they shown *this defence and resistance* of which they complain to have been made at the time and in the place alleged? Who has sworn to it? Who has told you when? Who has told you where? What witness has proven to you that this transaction took place within the Corporate Limits of the City of Alton? I call upon the two learned gentlemen who are to reply to me, to answer; and to name if they can that individual who stated in his testimony before you, that the offence charged was committed in the City of Alton. If each and every one of these facts are not distinctly and unequivocally proven, the foundation of this prosecution fails and the whole superstructure must tumble to the ground; for unless this offence was committed within the Corporate Limits of this City, neither this Court or the Grand Jury who have presented this bill have any jurisdiction of the matter. Remember you are sitting in judgment upon the liberty and reputation of a fellow man, and the law requires you in the discharge of your duty, either to acquit or convict from the testimony that is adduced before you; you are not to arrive at any fact by deduction, and because the government prove to you one circumstance you are not therefore to presume another; it therefore lies with the prosecution to show you that each allegation in their bill is true, and if they have failed so to do, you, from any knowledge you or either of you may possess separate and distinct from the testimony, cannot supply it; you are there as judges of crime from the facts proved; as jurors, you can nothing of yourselves, for you are not brought here as witnesses, but as impartial men selected to stand between my client and the prosecution, and sworn to try the issue upon the law and the facts as submitted to you. If therefore in your opinion the people have failed in proving any material allegations in their indictment, no matter how unnecessary it was that they should have made them; I claim the benefit to be derived from such omission. I waive no right, I release no error, I admit nothing that is not proved; standing upon all my rights.

I ask at your hands an acquittal of my client, not indeed through the imperfection of the testimony upon the part of the people, but upon the merits; admitting them to have proven all they were bound to before you could convict; but, gentlemen, whatever your verdict may be, the defendant will go hence as he came here, with a pure conscience. Yes, in the sight of God, in the sight of the world, he can lay his hand upon his heart and fearlessly avow his innocence. Your verdict may indeed stamp upon him the semblance of guilt, you may declare that his name shall be enrolled upon the records of this court as a felon, you may doom him to unmerited punishment and consign his person to a dungeon within the walls of your prison. These things in the exercise of our power you may do, but you cannot take from him an unsullied reputation, a high and unimpeachable character for honor and integrity; you cannot disturb him in the possession of a conscience free from stain, from pollution, from guilt, a conscience void of offence towards all mankind.

In the further remarks which I shall make to you, (for I already perceive that my strength fails me,) I shall scrupulously abstain from allusion to the events of the exciting past. I shall not recite to you the dreadful, yes! the fearful scenes of the memorable night of the 7th November—memorable to all after time as a period when men could be found to throw away life in an attack upon another's property—and when your streets were crimsoned with the blood of those gallant and undaunted few who had rallied for its defence; nor shall I ask you to travel with me in imagination onward to the future and conjecture the consequences of your verdict—the good or the evil to this community and to posterity, as you may uphold law or sanction licentiousness; far be it from me unnecessarily to recur to an event which has made us as a people a bye-word and a reproach to the whole Union; but on the contrary, would to God that by any act of mine I could pour upon the troubled waters of this excitement the oil of reconciliation—and could restore to this once happy and united people that peace and unity of action with which but a few months since they were blessed; but I cannot do it; the seeds of discord are too deeply sown to be uprooted by human effort, and time can alone allay the raging of those worst passions of the human heart which to us has been attended with such lamentable consequences. I stand here, gentlemen, solely for the purpose of interposing the shield of the law as a protection to a man innocent of the crime alleged against him—not to screen the guilty. I have shut no fact from this jury—have objected to none of the disclosures which have been made—resolved from the beginning the whole facts should appear in this investigation whether it made for us or against us; to you they have been given fully, clearly, and I have no doubt impartially; and I am perfectly willing that my client should be judged by you and by the world—by the development that the witnesses have made; and I commit into your hands his case with entire confidence in the issue. But the prosecuting Attorney has read to you a section of the criminal code of this State which he contends regulates the *only manner* in which a citizen shall defend his property; and one would almost think he had worked himself into the belief that the inalienable right of defending one's person and property was not a natural right founded in nature and sanctioned by law; but that in compassion to human frailty the law had kindly permitted its occasional exercise, provided that when exercised due regard was paid to all the forms and ceremonies prescribed in your statute; but I care not what the criminal code of Illinois may be; I care not what is contained therein, provided it is in violation of the Constitution of this State or of the United States. Such, gentlemen, I contend is the fact in this case; I aver before you, fearless of contradiction, that the extraordinary section of the criminal code under which the City Attorney seeks to convict my client is in direct violation of the Constitutions both of the

United States and of the State of Illinois; and as you are in criminal matters the sole judges, both of the law and the facts, and by your verdict must determine the correctness or fallacy of my position, I will call your attention to the 5th Article of the Amendment to the Constitution of the United States, which declares that "no person shall be deprived of life, liberty, or property, without due process of law." I turn then to your own Constitution, which in the 1st section of the 8th Article declares, that "all men have certain inherent and indefensible rights; among which are those of enjoying and defending life and liberty, and of acquiring, possessing, and *protecting* property and reputation;" and in the 8th section, same article, that "no freeman shall in any manner be deprived of his life, liberty, or property, but by the judgment of his peers or the laws of the land." I call your attention gentlemen to these sections of the two Constitutions, and leave them for your consideration without further comment, satisfied that with me you will agree that the Legislature of our State in the enactment of this law have violated (unintentionally) the Constitution both of this State and the United States. Having in my humble opinion disposed of the law satisfactorily to you, to which the prosecuting Attorney has called your attention, and upon which he relies to sustain this indictment, the only question, gentlemen, now left for you to determine is, whether Mr. Gilman on the night of the 7th November last, was or was not employed in the exercise of his constitutional right in resisting an unlawful attack upon his property and an attempt to take his life. The indictment charges the fact that he was engaged in defending a certain printing press then being in his warehouse; and the prosecuting Attorney since the commencement of this trial has seen fit to insert in the indictment that the said printing press was the property of my client and one Benjamin Godfrey; to accommodate him, therefore, and in order that he may sustain this *inserted allegation*, we admit the ownership and claim the allegation as a true one. Let me now for a single moment recur to the testimony, and see if it does not clearly and unequivocally show that Mr. Gilman in every instance on the night of the 7th acted only on the defensive, and that too after he had used every persuasive means in his power to induce the belligerents to retire. Mr. Keating, the first witness introduced by the prosecution, swears that he heard of the intended attack upon the warehouse of Godfrey & Gilman, and that the rumor was, that the same was to be blown up or burned, provided the press stored in it could not be obtained by other means—that in the forepart of the evening, about a half or three-quarters of an hour before any attack was made upon the building, he and Mr. West went to the warehouse of Mr. Gilman with a view of informing him of the attack and the consequences that would result from it—that they did communicate to him the intelligence, and that he expressed great astonishment—that he was unprepared and did not expect an attack that night—that he replied he could not believe the citizens of Alton would stand by and see such a thing done—and that he requested Mr. West to proceed to the Mayor's office and request him to rally the law-abiding portion of the community in order to suppress the riot. He further states to you, that shortly after he left the building the mob assembled and made the attack by dashing in the windows with stones, and that before any gun was fired from within, a gun and a pistol had been discharged on the outside by the mob, and that not until the assailants had twice fired did those within resort to their arms for the protection of their lives. Mr. West, who was the next witness on behalf of the people, also fully and in every respect corroborates the testimony of Mr. Keating, and tells you further, that John Solomon called upon him early in the evening and told him he (Solomon) *knew* that Mr. Gilman's building was to be blown up or burnt up that night if the press could not be had, and urged Mr. West to inform Mr. Gilman of the same.

Thus you will perceive, gentlemen, that the property (valued at thousands of dollars) and the life of my client was coolly and deliberately determined upon by the mob some two or three hours at least before their attack upon the warehouse of this defendant. Can you then doubt, if the witnesses for the prosecution have testified to the truth, who were the assailants? Can you for a moment doubt but that the firing commenced first with the mob; and that it was their fixed and matured determination not only to destroy the property but the life of my client and his associates? If then the attack was first made from without both with stones and firearms, and the assailants had coolly determined upon blowing up the warehouse and its eighteen inmates, do you believe the defence that was made by my client was disproportionate to the attack? do you believe that it was greater than any man in the exercise of his reasoning faculties would have adopted? If you do not, I then in behalf of this defendant place myself upon my reserved rights—I plant myself upon the rock of the Constitution—I interpose before my client that instrument as his shield; and protected by its letter, guarded by its spirit, I bid defiance to the statute the prosecutor has produced, and laugh to scorn the indictment he has read to you.

But if, gentlemen, I have failed to satisfy you upon this point, I ask you to grant me your indulgence a moment longer, while I take another view of this case. It is in evidence before you that Mr. Gilman repeatedly sought, from the Mayor of our City, authority to act as he was at last compelled to—that frequent and long were the interviews had with the Mayor upon that sub ject—and that he had stated to Mr. Krum, that he was anxious that whatever act was done in the protection of the press, should be done under the sanction of the law, and by virtue of authority derived from an officer of the law; that on the night of the 6th, just preceding that of the riot, the Mayor was present in his official capacity at the warehouse of my client, and that,

6

upon the question being asked him what course he intended to pursue if the attack should be made while landing the press, he replied, he should order the mob to disperse, and warn them of the consequences if they did not; and that, if they then still persisted, and his injunctions were disregarded, he should peremptorily give Mr. Gilman and his associates orders *to fire upon the assailants*. But again, we have further shown to you, that on that night after the press was landed and placed in the warehouse, the Mayor advised, or assented, to an arrangement, by virtue of which that warehouse and that printing press was to be guarded by those whom he knew had assembled for the avowed and isolated purpose of protecting it. We have also shown to you, that on the night of the 7th, which resulted in the loss of two lives, when the Mayor went into the building, at the solicitation of the mob, to endeavor to persuade those within to give up the press, and after the death of Bishop had occurred, he was then and there again interrogated by Mr. Gilman, whether he had acted under the authority of the law, and was justified in what had been done, and that to such inquiry Mr. Krum replied in the affirmative; and although the Mayor unqualifiedly testified that such advice was given Mr. Gilman as a citizen and a friend, and as one, who, from his profession, was conversant with the law and the rights of my client under it, and not in his official capacity as Mayor, he has, nevertheless, also stated to you, that from the knowledge he possessed of all the facts, he did believe that Mr. Gilman *supposed* he was acting under his official authority. And is it not natural, gentlemen, that he should have so supposed? In all these interviews had by him with Mr. Krum, the uniform advice given him was, that defence might lawfully be made, and that if requisite for completing that defence, firearms might legally be resorted to, and even life taken, and that the act would be justified by the law. Why, let me ask you, should Mr. Gilman, Lovejoy, and others, hold these *repeated interviews* with Mr. Krum? If they sought his advice merely as a lawyer, or a friend, or a citizen, would it not have proven sufficient for them that he had given it to them, clearly and unequivocally, during the first interview? Why these constant applications to him at every step they took, and why this great solicitude on their part to have their every act sanctioned with his approbation? The reason is a most obvious and irresistible one: it was because he was the highest civil officer within their reach; clothed, as they believed, with full power to grant them the authority subsequently exercised by them, and because they were anxious and determined that nothing should be done on their part, in the way of resistance or defence, unless under his authority and with his consent. And then, too, (that this matter may be placed beyond any doubt as to the firm belief of my client that he was acting only the part of a subordinate to the Mayor,) let me recur to the conversation in the store, after Bishop's death. When an application was made to him to remain on the inside with them, what was his reply? "I would if I did not think I could do more good out of doors." Did he then disclaim all connection with them in his official capacity, and give them to understand that they were acting without his authority, and upon their own responsibility; or was his reply such as to leave them under the conviction that they were acting under the authority of the law? To my mind this combination of facts is proof most conclusive, that this defendant, naturally, fairly and honestly supposed he had the authority of that officer for his every act; and if you, gentlemen, should so also believe, even though you wholly disregarded his constitutional rights, you are then bound to acquit him, for it negatives most fully every idea of a *criminal intent*, and without which no man can be convicted of crime. *Never* was there a man arraigned before a jury of his country who more conclusively showed his innocence, not only in acts, but in word and thought, than has my client, and he stands before his God and the world, if the testimony in this cause can have any weight, purged of even the shadow of guilt, and with a reputation rendered, if possible, more bright and enviable than he possessed before this indictment was preferred against him. But I fear, gentlemen, I am tasking your patience beyond endurance, and exhaustion on my part admonishes me that I must draw to a close, notwithstanding there are several points to which it was my intention to have invited your notice. I am fully sensible that I have done the cause of my client but little justice, but am consoled by the reflection that the injury I have done him will be more than repaired by the talents, the experience, and the eloquence of my associate, who will close the argument in his behalf. All that is left me to say is, that I would be doing the most gross injustice to my feelings, did I not return you, gentlemen, my most sincere acknowledgements for the patience with which you have listened to, and the attention you have given my unconnected remarks. I fear that in the course of them I may have displayed an overheated zeal and a warmth of feeling that, in your opinion, was unjustifiable ; if so, do not, I beseech you, gentlemen, let it prejudice the rights of my client. I could not avoid it. It is not by mere professional ties that I am connected with him ; I am bound to him by the strongest and most enduring ties of friendship ; a friendship which may have had its foundation in repeated and unsolicited acts of kindness, bestowed upon me when I most needed them, but which, I am proud to declare, has been matured and strengthened by a subsequent knowledge of his virtues ; and never can I bring my mind to believe that, possessed as he is of all those ennobling qualities which have rendered him a model of social and domestic virtue, he could so far have forgotten himself as to have committed the crime with which he stands charged by this indictment.

By request of Mr. Bailey, who appeared in the trial of this cause as one of the counsel for the Government, and who followed Mr. Davis in an address to the jury, his remarks are not included in this report of the trial.

Remarks of Alfred Cowles, Esq. for defendant.

Gentlemen of the Jury: the case which you are empannelled to try, is one of no common occurrence, whether it be considered in respect to its effect upon each of us, upon individual security, property, liberty and life; upon the right of free discussion, upon the question whether the law and constitution shall be the par amount rule of action; or whether misrule and the un licensed will of an irresponsible multitude shall henceforth be our governing authority.

The issue of this trial is to write the character of this community in no illegible impress, but in one that will be known, understood and appreciated of all men; it will be either of a returning sense of justice, a respect to law and the obligations of civilized society; or a closing over of our sky with a dark and portentous cloud pregnant with future ill.

In approaching the defence of the very respectable gentleman, who stands at the bar as a prisoner and a culprit, the question of his guilt in itself considered, in comparison of other and more important results, shrinks into insignificance. In conducting his defence I feel that I am defending the supremacy of law and constitution, the sacred right of individual opinion, of free discussion, and of self defence, against unbridled lawless violence: I then, after hearing the evidence, am affected with the same surprise as was expressed by one of your fellow jurors, who on his being examined touching his qualification to sit on the traverse, remarked that he did not understand how a man could be indicted for defending his own property; nor could I conceive how any man in the warehouse could be indicted, much less that the defendant, the builder and owner of the warehouse, and who in the legal defence of that warehouse and the property within it, in which he had a general or special ownership, could be subjected to penal consequences—but this strange attitude is exhibited in the person of the defendant—standing in defence of property, liberty and life—in which defence

6*

the blood of an innocent victim had been shed to satisfy the insatiable passion of a lawless multitude, unparalleled in atrocity.

The very act of indicting this individual and his associates, supposes that their acting upon the defensive was criminal.

This right of self-defence addresses itself to this jury, and if by your verdict you pronounce him guilty, you deny it to the defendant, and in effect say that the armed, excited, ruthless multitude without, had the right to judge upon the individual rights of the prisoner—and to carry out that judgment to a forcible, unrestricted execution.

It is then to you that we appeal, as the barrier and rampart, behind which liberty and law may intrench itself—and against which the waves of misrule and disorder may beat in vain. In protecting this defendant you are defending yourselves, you are restoring peace and security to this much injured community.

By what tenure do we hold our property and lives, if not by the organization of society? Are we to go back to an unorganized condition and be subjected to brute force and unprincipled will? or shall we throw around us the shield of the constitution? You will answer by your verdict.

By an amendment to the Constitution of the United States, the right of every citizen to keep and bear arms is secured; the fact then that the prisoner and his associates had arms within the warehouse was in no sense criminal; especially when it appears from the testimony that they were advertised of meditated and threatened violence from without; and when the same force had distinguished itself by its triumphs over the *freedom of speech and of the press* in the destruction of other printing presses.

By the Constitution of this State, p. 45, §   it is provided, "that no person shall be deprived of his life, liberty, or property, but by the judgment of his peers, or the law of the land." The violation of this provision of the Constitution in the attack upon the life and property of the prisoner is manifest; so much so, that he that runs may read; unless it be assumed that the violators of law and order were his constitutional peers!

It is proved that Mr. Gilman and his partner owned the warehouse, and received the Observer press for safe keeping on storage, and being responsible to the actual owner, had such a property in it as justified him in resisting force by force. The law knows no difference whether the property be general or special in regard to the right of defending it, or in regard to criminal liability for invading it.—*Archbold.*

But it may be argued by the Attorney General that the press, which was the object of attack and defence, was intended to promulgate principles, and discuss subjects, which many citizens repudiated; and therefore the right to destroy the press was complete! and that any means might be used to accomplish that end.

We again recur to our Constitution, at § , which provides "that no law shall ever be passed to impair the freedom of speech or the liberty of the press, and that every citizen may freely speak, write, and print, being responsible for the abuse thereof." Is this a responsibility to a mob! or to the judicial tribunals of the country, the peers of the person charged with abuse?

In this land of constitutional *immunity*, freedom of speech and the press, it is reserved for those living under that immunity, to supervise the press, and prescribe what shall, and what shall not be printed; and even whether the press in a given place shall exist! Thus arrogating to themselves a power, which only exists in acknowledged arbitrary governments! The exercise of which power is the most effective instrument of despotism; and this power is assumed by some that call themselves the democracy of the country dyed in the wool.

What but the exercise of this power in France and Germany is it, that has stifled the spirit of liberty in those countries, and perpetuated the arm of tyranny?

This interference with the liberty of the press is one that American citizens will not brook or give place to; nor will they yield that to an irresponsible multitude, of which their Legislature could not deprive them! This is their political ægis.

Are these reservations in behalf of the people, preserved in an American Constitution to be an idle and unmeaning principle? And shall it be in vain that our sires poured out their blood like water, and left their whiting bones scattered in many a glorious, well fought field, to secure them?

And shall their recreant sons yield up tamely this best of political gifts? It is impossible, if any drop of the blood of their ancestors yet animates them, and unless "judgment is fled to brutish beasts, and men have lost their reason."

An examination of the proofs will justify most fully the accused, before this jury and all who understand the condition of those defending the property. It was a case verily of self-defence, upon the most valid and unquestionable grounds.

The arrival of the press was notorious; in anticipation of its arrival, the prowling conspirators against the Constitution were on the alert; and after its arrival, when the Mayor had been desired to be present at its arrival to take measures for its security, and had actually superintended its landing and deposit at Godfrey & Gilman's warehouse, at a late hour of the night a few of their dark forms were seen hovering about at a distance, and the next day developed fully the avowal of their heartless and atrocious design, which was to blow up or burn the building where the press was deposited, if necessary to destroy it. Not unapprised of such an intention from the conspirators, but being wholly incredulous as to its truth, that band assembled in the warehouse on the fatal night of the 7th, to repel if necessary any attack upon the house and property of the accused; they were fired upon from without by at least two guns or pistols; and showers of stones were thrown into and against the building before any defensive act was done by those within; and as is proved to you, such was their design, as avowed and agreed among themselves. Now can it enter into the mind of any human being, that these persons in their act of self-defence, were guilty of a riot? Every ingredient of crime is wanting. It is apparent that no criminal intent existed in their minds. By our criminal code, there must exist a joint operation of act and intention, to constitute crime; every act of the accused exhibited a want of criminal intention. It is true the first blood was shed by those in the defensive; but it is equally true that it was a legitimate and justifiable consequence of their exercise of the right of self-defence. After Bishop, one of the assailants, had been shot, and those without had been stimulated and infuriated by the use of intoxicating drink, freely administered at certain houses miscalled "coffee houses," a second attack was made upon the building, and the cry was raised to fire the building. You have seen that Mr. Gilman in the most kind and conciliating terms remonstrated with those without, and avowed the determination of himself and friends to defend the property and possession at the risk of their lives, but that they had no desire to injure any one without. This reasonable intimation served no other purpose but to produce a reiteration of the design of the mob.

The Mayor with other civil officers appeared, and ordered the rioters to disperse; this was disregarded; and the Mayor was desired to enter the building and propose a capitulation, and authorized to stipulate for those without, that those within should depart unharmed; and while this very negociation was carrying on, fire was communicated to the warehouse, and those within urged to depart to save their lives and prevent the warehouse from conflagration. Mr. Gilman was incredulous, as was the Mayor; they had no conception of the dark malignity which actuated those without. The thing threatened was incredible! against whom? and for what?

Winthrop S. Gilman had been the first man to vest his capital in Alton and give it importance; his patronage had given bread to many of the inhabitants of that town; he had been with the town in its struggling infancy, and its palmy state of manhood; when it had been visited by the "pestilence that walketh in darkness," before which the forms of men were shrinking and withering, he stood by a ministering angel; and now this population were turning against him "like dogs upon the hand that fed them, to bite and devour." The dark characters of such deeds can only find a parallel in the regions below.

And for what was all this? Merely because a disposition had been expressed to sustain and protect the freedom of speech and of the press.

The accused and his associates were among those most deeply interested in the prosperity of Alton, entire strangers to riot and to that society in which its elements consisted. There was a pledge in their character which would and ought to weigh deeply with the jury. But they had entered upon the subject after cool reflection, and their determination was not the result of a sudden ebullition of passion—but one to which their consciences pointed in fortifying approbation. They knew they were in the exercise of a constitutional right, and they felt that in that respect they would be justified. The public authorities had been previously consulted as to their right of self-defence, and had approved of the assertion of that right, in repelling force by force. But what did all this avail against a mob!—there they stood, that little band; within that building there was no riot, no tumult; but that deep silence which precedes great actions!—without all was tumult, uproar and violence; upon those without the nerveless arm of the law had been exerted in vain—within, the same arm had approved and justified. Matters now arrived at a crisis; the building was fired over their heads and they were besought by some benevolent individuals to yield to that lawless force, which they were forced to do, to save their lives, and prevent the total destruction of the building and one hundred thousand dollars in value of property within. And yet these individuals were fired upon as they fled from the horrors of that night. And the assailants entered the citadel, and destroyed that press. Here was a consummation of all that was vile and atrocious, all that tyranny could inflict, upon the rights and liberties of a free people. The arm of the law was broken, the sword of justice trampled on, and treason was perpetrated in its fullest form. "Then you and I, and all of us fell down, whilst bloody treason flourished o'er us."

A calm review of this transaction cannot but justify the defendants—on the ground of a want of criminal intention as a legal justification. It is laid down in authors of the highest authority in criminal law, that a man may assemble his friends in his own house to prevent an unlawful entry, or to protect his property therein. 1 Russel on Crimes, vol. 1, p. 254. Hawkins' Pleas of the Crown Book, v. 1, ch. 65, p. 158. This right is by the law of nature, aside from constitutional right; wherever, as here, the civil authority is inadequate, we are remitted to our original rights. The law of civil society only regulates the mode of self-defence; when organized society fails to afford protection, we are then thrown back upon our original rights, with power to defend them, either in regard to person or property, as we best may. Gilman applied to the civil authorities for protection--it was not given. Where was the city authority in that dark hour of violence and misrule? As though it had not been. Mr. Gilman stands therefore before you, gentlemen, justified in the sight of men and of God; by all the principles that are in the human heart; by the wisdom of ages; and if you, gentlemen, can say he is guilty, pronounce such a verdict, and add to the dishonor of the country, that what a lawless mob executed, twelve men were found to justify and approve.

Linder, for the people.

I feel, gentlemen of the jury, that I have to contend against fearful odds, when I have the conviction pressed home upon me, by the argument of the gentleman that, as citizens you probably were influenced by the excitement occasioned by the fearful tragedy which has been acted in this city; and am reminded that, as jurors, you may not have forgotten the prejudices which you imbibed before you were sworn to try this issue. I feel that the odds against me are greatly increased, when I recollect the threats made use of to frighten you from returning a verdict of guilty, and when I remember that, in anticipation of such a verdict of guilty, you were denounced by the venerable Counsel who has preceded me, as participators in the crime for which this defendant is now on trial; as coadjutors in the treason, which was committed by those who destroyed the press. But, gentlemen, if you have feeling upon this subject you may control it: all may divest themselves of prejudice, if they are determined to do so.

You must have observed how hampered the defence has been; how the Counsel, in their remarks, crippled along. All their remarks showed that they thought they were prosecuting the outside, instead of defending those who were guilty of a riot in the inside of the warehouse. I ask you to travel along with me as I relate to you the facts in this case. Last August, the first press was destroyed: the "boys" broke it to pieces and threw it into the river. Another was brought here, and after repeated failures to establish a press by which they could disseminate their fiendish doctrines, another course was adopted. A convention was called at Upper Alton. Alton was chosen as the scene of their operations. Alton was to be made the theatre of their preachings—and all their presses, and all their preachings, and all their conventions, were to be held in the poor, devoted city of Alton. Dr. Beecher was warned to attend, and these people thought they were going to have it all their own way. But it happened that these Western boys knew a thing or two: knew a trick worth two of that; and so they got together and out-voted them, and the convention blew up in smoke. It was a farce. Not satisfied with this; not satisfied with the blowing up of this farce; not satisfied with the result of this convention, headed by interlopers from other states, headed by an alien to our laws and our country, they issued their handbills, they made proclamation in the streets, of their intention to preach their doctrines in the Church. They posted up placards, notifying the world that Dr. Beecher would preach upon this damning doctrine of abolition. Now mark the course of these people; these advocates of good order; these lovers of religion. These men, these peace-loving men, who profess to be the followers of the meek and lowly Jesus, mark how they besiege the Mayor, how they importune him to go to the Church; how they beseech him to attend their meeting; how they notify him that arms, yes, arms, are provided in case of disturbance. And here let us pause. Is this the age when virtue, religion and morals are to be forced upon us by the strong arm of power? when, if we will not hear, the sword shall compel us to do so? when, by muskets and bayonets, we are to be compelled to swallow, whether we will or not, any doctrine which this set of people may tell us is good for instruction, or profitable for salvation? And these men, who assemble with arms, who run bullets by the tumbler full, who parade their armed men within the walls of a Church, are they to claim exemption from crime under the plea that they are followers of a heavenly master? Save one solitary instance, where do we find the Apostles, the original Christians, with arms in their hands? and in the only solitary instance in which they resorted to the strong arm of power, how quick, how decided the rebuke which their peaceful Master gave them!

But here these men, these peace-loving men, as they call themselves; these advocates of law; these friends of good order; these professed disciples of him who came to bring peace and good will to all men, don't find such a peaceful course answer their purposes quite so well. So they resort to arms for protection; and

7

they pollute the worship of their peaceful Master by a martial array around the altar dedicated to his service. Mark how peaceful their course runs! In this instance, there were first, prayers! then a sermon! then a stone!—and then, "To arms, boys."

But let us go to the 7th, memorable as the closing scene in this comic tragedy. And, to proceed in regular order:—the arms, the next we hear from them, were brought from the church; "fixed," as the witness says, and Tanner calls upon boys to run him a tumbler full of bullets; and people are called to array themselves upon the one side or the other of this vexed question. Forty-two men are found willing to form themselves into a military company; men are drafted from among you; enrolled in the service; officers are elected, and the post of honor, the title of Captain of a squad of these men, is conferred upon my corpulent friend, William Harned. There is marching and countermarching; drilling and exercising; file movements, and movements in echellon, up in the garret of a warehouse, at dead of night. I can't imagine how they managed to do all this in a place where I should hardly have expected my friend the Captain would have found room to have squeezed himself in half-file, much less, to have managed to drill and manœuvre a whole company of men. So that you see, gentlemen, when all other sources fail; when they find the conventions won't do, and armed men at churches won't answer their ends; the doctrines of abolition are to be forced down our throats, by means of the formation of an independent, peace-loving, military company, with my friend and brother counsellor Mr. Chickering as clerk, and my honored friend, Mr. Harned, as Captain. And was not all this calculated to disturb the peace? was not this calculated to excite terror? to stir up the feelings? to rouse the passions, and to provoke an attack? Precisely what we should have expected, exactly what these peace-loving men should have anticipated, did result.

Gentlemen, a man who is conscious that he is acting from right impulses, wants no advice; he acts from his own honest convictions. But Mr. Gilman was always seeking advice; always asking counsel and direction; always proffering his services; always stating his readiness to act; always declaring his willingness to be employed, and asking orders; always seeking, in every way, in every manner, and at all times, to gain the arm of civil authority. Here was a party for war in times of unalloyed peace, and, for aught we know, "a party for peace in times of war."

My aged friend has read to you law, under which he asks you to acquit this defendant. He has resorted to the books, and read authority to prove to you that a man's house is his castle; and that force may lawfully be used by the owner to defend it against the entry of those who would trespass. But the law speaks of a man's house; of his domicil; of the place where he lives; of the place which he has provided for his family, and not of one's store; not of a warehouse which is erected for the storage or sale of articles of merchandise. Who had threatened to attack these men in their domicils? Who had threatened to destroy their houses? or even to break open and enter them to destroy any article of property kept therein?

But the press came at last: the press which was intended to preach insurrection, and to disseminate the doctrines which must tend to disorganization and disunion. With what delight they caught the first glimpse of their new-born child; with what joy they hugged it to their hearts! It was consigned to the tender care, to the fatherly protection of Mr. Roff; but by mutual agreement, from some cause or other, perhaps from fear that it would be taken from the arms of Mr. Roff, and like its predecessors, be consigned to the bosom of the father of rivers, its destination was altered, and it was received by Mr. Gilman. And a noble thing they thought this was: a fine arrangement they thought this would be, I doubt not.

Mr. Gilman was popular; he was loved; he was

respected and honored; he was wealthy; and doubtless, gentlemen, they supposed that if it was once under his charge, all would be well; that the press would be safe, and the flag of abolition would wave in triumph over the prostrate City of Alton. These men sought the battle; they volunteered for the warfare; they acted before the necessity called for it; they waited not for the call of the law, but madly and rashly rushed to the contest, and the blood of the unfortunate Bishop, and the infatuated Lovejoy, flowed in consequence. They had no direction from your civil officers; they had no authority: and they must suffer the consequences. It probably is true, as a witness has told you, that they determined not to fire till they were fired upon. They did not want to strike the first blow. And, gentlemen, their conduct puts me in mind of the manner in which we used to act as long ago as when we went to school. We felt cross; we wanted to fight; but like these grown up boys, we did not care about striking first. So one would put a chip on his head, and then tell another to knock it off, if he dared: and another would draw a line on the ground, and planting himself behind that, would dare his adversary to cross it; or bid him keep off, if he knew what was good for himself.

Admit that it is lawful for a man to assemble his friends for the forcible protection of his domicil; is it therefore lawful for him to assemble them in a warehouse, and importune the officers of the law for authority, and under cover of advice given as a friend, provoke a fight? Suppose this press had not been guarded; suppose that, taking advantage of the absence of those who had assembled for its protection, the mob had destroyed it. Had these people no remedy? Is there no law which would have given them redress? They talk of being friends to good order; lovers of law!! Have they not taken the law into their own hands, and violated the laws of man and of God in depriving man of life? And for what? For a press! a printing press! A press brought here to teach rebellion and insurrection to the slave; to excite servile war; to preach murder in the name of religion; to strike dismay to the hearts of the people, and spread desolation over the face of this land. Society esteems good order more than such a press: sets higher value upon the lives of its citizens than upon a thousand such presses. I might depict to you the African, his passions excited by the doctrines intended to have been propagated by that press. As well might you find yourself in the fangs of a wild beast. I might portray to you the scenes which would exist in our neighbor states from the influence of that press: the father aroused to see the last gasp of his dying child, as it lays in its cradle, weltering in its blood; and the husband awakened from his last sleep by the shrieks of his wife as she is brained to the earth. I might paint to you a picture which would cause a demon to start back with affright, and still fall short of the awful reality which would be caused by the promulgation of the doctrines which this press was intended to disseminate. Bear with me while I turn your attention to a law of this State.

Be it enacted by the people of the State of Illinois, &c., "That the judges of the Supreme Court, throughout the State, the judges of the Circuit Courts throughout their circuits, and justices of the peace in their respective counties, shall, jointly and severally, be conservators of the peace, within their respective jurisdictions," &c. "And shall have power to cause to come before them, or any of them, all persons who shall threaten to break the peace, or shall use threats against any person within this State, concerning his or her body, *or threaten to injure his or her property, or the property of any person whatever;* and also, all such persons as are not of good fame, and the said judge or justice of the peace, being satisfied by the oath of one or more witnesses of his or her bad character, or that he or she had used threats as aforesaid,

7*

shall cause such person or persons, to give good security for the peace, or for their good behavior towards all the people of this State, and particularly towards the individual threatened." Here there is law to suit the case of these individuals. Why did they not resort to it? They were threatened; their property was threatened: why not take the redress pointed out and given them by the law? They knew the individuals who threatened; why not go to a Justice of the Peace, enter their complaints, and bind the boys over to keep the peace and be of good behavior? Why not do this, instead of assembling their friends who would make law for themselves, and prostrate that enacted by competent authority? No, gentlemen, these men did not want to take the course of the law; their whole course was a crusade upon law; a crusade against your Constitution, a war against right; a war against peace; a war against liberty and good order.

But, gentlemen, I regret that in the execution of my duty, I am obliged to prosecute this defendant. I respect him as a man and a citizen. I regret that he suffered himself to be drawn into this excitement. His honesty and ingenuousness have been taken advantage of, and he made the dupe of others more artful and designing than himself. I cannot believe that this defendant, of his own accord, would ever have placed himself in a situation, where, by any possibility, criminal intention could have been manifested, or criminal act committed. But, like poor Tray, who you know was a very honest dog, this man must suffer, because he was caught in the company of Tiger. These abolitionists have got the smell of this man's money, and they have hung round him; they have dogged his pathway through your streets, they have besieged him in his place of business, they have fastened their fangs upon him, and they will not leave him till they have drawn the last drop of blood from the quivering fibres of his flesh; I mean the last dollar from his purse.

You are urged to acquit this man; to say that his

acts are justified because the attack upon his property was of that nature that he could not repel it, and unless he had assembled his friends, armed them and resorted to the strong arm of force. Can one wrong be justified because another wrong was committed? There is no set-off in crime. The prayer sometimes made in other places, "excuse me because Bill has done worse," is not good authority here. You are sworn men; sworn not to say who was most riotous, which party had the most law; but sworn to try the guilt or innocence of this defendant, by the law and the evidence. This meeting was dangerous, doubly dangerous, because it had the outside appearance of law about it.

The fact that these people assembled together, that they, when so assembled, protected or endeavored to protect their property, is not in itself criminal; but it is the manner in which such assemblage and such defence was made, that we charge as unlawful. It is the manner in which such defence was made, that has brought this man to your bar, to answer to his country for the offence he committed.

The purpose of petitioning is lawful, and men may assemble and do assemble for the exercise of their rights in the fulfilment of that purpose almost daily. The purpose of mustering the militia is lawful, though these meetings are getting to be quite rare, but yet, if a large number of men should assemble with arms in their hands, even if for the purpose of consulting about matters of common grievance, or with the design of petitioning to your legislature, I hardly think my venerable friend upon this defence would pronounce such assemblage lawful. It would be calculated to excite terror and distrust; it would be calculated to disturb the good order of the community, and lead to a breach of the peace, and therefore it would be unlawful. It is the wisdom of law to prevent crime, rather than to punish criminals. The knowledge of its provisions is within the reach of all men, and if men may know their rights and liabilities, and will not, or, if knowing the law, they wilfully violate its principles, let them feel the power have despised it, let them suffer from the vengeance they have braved.

If Mr. Gilman is indicted for acts done in defence of his natural rights, if he is to suffer for his prosecution of a good cause, let such considerations be addressed to the court, in mitigation of punishment; they should not be urged to you, in justification.

Who questions the lawfulness of the act done, by these defendants? Who doubts the unlawfulness of the manner in which those acts were done?

Some forty individuals assembled in the first instance, some fifteen or twenty remained, with firearms in their hands, well provided with ammunition, with tumult, with disorder, or, as the gentleman told you, with the stillness of the calm which precedes the storm; but the stillness made not the thunder and lightning of that storm less fierce, or less fearful when it burst.

It was unnecessary that Gilman should have fired a gun; the laws, as I have shown you, are broad enough to have ensured his safety, amply sufficient to have afforded protection to his property. If he chose to strike a blow for his own rights, let him suffer the consequences.

And the address to the mob, "we will not give up the press," but have resolved to lose our lives, if necessary, in its defence, affords conclusive proof, bears ample testimony to the intent, by which this defendant was actuated. And that other remark, proceeding from him who was the first victim to its truth, "we must not lose a fire;" how prophetic the exclamation!!

Go then, gentlemen, if you can, and say upon your oaths this defendant is not guilty; regard the purity, the honor, and integrity of his character; value the kind feelings, the expanded benevolence, the generous spirit, the warm heart of this man as highly as you choose; but in paying a just tribute to these feelings and qualities of the man, forget not the calls of your country, the demands of the law.

I will not threaten you, I will not warn you of your

danger in returning a verdict of "not guilty," by way of intimidation. I will not say, you will not be safe in returning such a verdict. I believe there is no danger; I will guarantee your safety; I will underwrite for the City of Alton.

No, gentlemen, you need no such protection, you are safe in returning any verdict; safe in your own high characters as men; safe in your sacred characters as jurors. Neither are you to be affected by calumny; such weapon would fall harmless at your feet.

But remember, that when men like Mr. Gilman are convicted; when they are held amenable to the laws for their acts, and the natural consequences of those acts; a salutary chastisement is inflicted upon the individual, and a useful lesson taught to others, who are humbler in life than the accused.

Go then to your retirement, act independently, without fear or prejudice, honestly, without favor or affection. I put the cause into your hands; weigh well the evidence, examine carefully the law, and pronounce fearlessly your verdict.

The jury retired, and after an absence of about fifteen minutes, came into court and declared a verdict of "Not Guilty."

January 17th, 1838.

At the opening of the Court this morning, U. F. Linder stated to the Court, that upon consultation with the Prosecuting Attorney for the City, they both had come to the conclusion, that the trial of the individuals included with Mr. Gilman in the indictment, would result in the return of a similar verdict as the one given in the case of Mr. Gilman, and he therefore would enter with permission from the Court a nolle prosequi against Enoch Long, Amos B. Roff, George H. Walworth, George H. Whitney, William Harned, John S. Noble, James Morse, jr., Henry Tanner, Royal Weller, Reuben Gerry, and Thaddeus B. Hurlbut; and upon proclamation the aforenamed individuals were discharged without day.

ALTON TRIALS.

In the Municipal Court, of the City of Alton, at its January Term, in the year A. D. 1838, and on the nineteenth day of said month, came on for trial the following case, before Hon. William Martin, Judge.

The People of the State of Illinois,

vs.

John Solomon, Solomon Morgan, Levi Palmer, Horace Beal, Josiah Nutter, James Jennings, Jacob Smith, David Butler, William Carr, James M. Rock, and Frederick Brucky, indicted for a Riot, committed on the night of the 7th November last, within the limits of the City of Alton, in entering the storehouse of Benjamin Godfrey, and Winthrop S. Gilman, and breaking up and destroying one printing press, then and there found, the property of the said Benjamin Godfrey, and Winthrop S. Gilman.

For the People,
Francis B. Murdock, City Att'y.
Alfred Cowles, Esq.,

For Def'ts. on trial,
U. F. Linder, Esq.,
S. T. Sawyer, Esq.,
Junius Hall, Esq.

Morgan Jennings, and Bruchy, not having been arrested, the trial proceeded against the remainder.

And at the calling of the case, the defendants presented the following Demurrer:

John Solomon,
Levi Palmer,
Horace Beal,
Josiah Nutter,
Jacob Smith,
David Butler,
William Carr, and
James M. Rock,
Impleaded with James Jennings, Solomon Morgan, and Frederick Bruchy,

alt.
The People of the State of Illinois.

In the Municipal Court of the City of Alton, January Term, 1838. In an indictment for Riot.

And the said Solomon, et. al. who are impleaded with the said James Jennings, et. al. in their own proper persons, come into Court here, and having heard the said indictment read, say that the said indictment, and the matters therein contained, in manner and form as the same are above stated and set forth, are not sufficient in law, and that they the said Solomon, &c., are not bound by the laws of the land to answer the same; and this they are ready to verify. Wherefore, for want of a sufficient indictment in this behalf, they pray judgment, and that by the court here they may be dismissed, and discharged from the said premises, in the said indictment specified.

Linder and Sawyer for Defendants Solomon and others.

And Linder in support of the motion.

This demurrer has been drawn up, and I now present it for the purpose of saving the time of the court; and also saving the jury from any trouble in the case, if the indictment is defective. It is not presented from any fear I have as to the result of this trial; nor from any apprehension I feel as to the fate of the defendants. I know how useless it would be to consume time in the investigation of the facts of this case; if, after a verdict, a motion in arrest of judgment could be sustained, upon the ground, that the charge as set out in this instrument, is not properly made. And I have a disposition too, to allay any heart-burnings which may be felt in this community. I have made up my mind that this indictment is defective, that the offences with which the prosecuting attorney has charged us, are not properly alleged. and I ask the attention of the court, to sections 113, 115, 116, 117, of the criminal code.

Sec. 113. "If two or more persons assemble together for the purpose of disturbing the public peace, or committing any unlawful act, and do not disperse," &c.

Sec. 115. "If two or more persons shall assemble together to do an unlawful act," &c.

Sec. 116. "If two or more persons shall meet to do an unlawful act, upon a common cause of quarrel, and make advances towards it," &c.

Sec. 117. "If two or more persons actually do an unlawful act, with force or violence, against the person or property of another, with or without a common cause of quarrel, or even do a lawful act, in a violent and tumultuous manner, the persons so offending shall be deemed guilty of a Riot," &c.

Now it will be seen that all these sections contemplate an assemblage; a meeting together of two or more persons for an unlawful purpose. But it will be seen, that this indictment is framed under the 117th section; and I ask of the court, a close examination of that section, and I expect that the court will give a rigid construction to it. Criminal laws are always construed more rigidly than any others, and I ask your honor to construe this law strictly. I will not trouble the court with the first principles of law. I will not repeat the general rules. Every one knows, that if an indictment is framed so as to cover an offence specially described by statute, that the letter of the statute must be followed. That if the offence charged in the indictment differs from that specifically pointed out, and defined by the statute, that it is a fatal variance, and may be taken advantage of by demurrer. Every one knows that more strictness is required in drawing an indictment under a statute than by common law.

Now for the Indictment. The Grand Jurors, &c., present, that James M. Rock, &c. on, &c. at, &c. "with force and arms unlawfully, and with force and violence, did enter into the storehouse of Benjamin Godfrey and Winthrop S. Gilman, there situate; and one printing press, the property, goods and chattels of the said Benjamin Godfrey and Winthrop S. Gilman, then and there being found, did unlawfully, riotously, and routously, and with force and violence break and destroy." Now sir, in the 117th section of the criminal code under which this indictment is framed, there are two distinct offences; and the wording of the statute requires that each of these offences should be charged in a particular manner. Now in an indictment under the 116th section, if there was an omission, in stating that the act alleged to have been committed was done with a common cause of quarrel, such omission would be fatal.

If this indictment is framed under the second clause of the 117th section, it should set forth the offence in the words of the statute, and these individuals should have been charged with doing a lawful act in a violent and tumultuous manner. But it is not so, and therefore it is under the first part of that section, that this indictment was framed. And let us see if these two apparently independent and distinct offences, specified in the 117th section, are not so closely, so directly and intimately con-

8

nected in their character and nature, that an allegation of a violent and tumultuous manner, is not necessary in charging both offences.

If two or more do an unlawful act, with force and violence, or even do a lawful act in a violent and tumultuous manner, *which manner attaches to both offences*, they shall be guilty of riot. The two clauses of the section being connected by the nature of the language employed to define the offences, the violent and tumultuous manner is necessary to the completion of both offences. There is no period, no punctuation of any kind, nothing which separates the two clauses of the section, unless it be the words with or without a common cause of quarrel, and do these words, slipt in as they are in the middle of a sentence, sever the offences? Do they make the clauses and offences so distinct, as that what is necessary to one, is unnecessary to the other? If we can judge by force of language what necessarily attaches to an offence; if we can judge by the nature of the language, employed to define what constitutes crime, a violent and tumultuous manner must be alleged in an indictment under either of the clauses of this section. A tumultuous manner should be attached to both;—it is required by the language of the statute, and if it is dispensed with in practice, the omission can be taken advantage of, and the indictment be quashed, or the judgment be arrested.

Per Curiam. No objection need be made to the demurrer: the argument would be applicable, and entitled to consideration if the words in a violent and tumultuous manner were not omitted in the first clause of the 117th section. Two distinct offences are there defined; one, the doing an unlawful act; the other a lawful one. A lawful act may be done with force and violence, and still the individual be guilty of violating no law. An unlawful act is criminal in its very nature, and the manner in which it is done, determines the nature of the crime, whether it shall be of a higher, or lower denomination.

The Demurrer is overruled.

Linder. I don't myself see any great force in the demurrer: it was drawn up by my brother Sawyer, and at first did not I know but I might make something of it.

A plea of "Not Guilty" was entered.

Linder. I know the opinion of the Court upon the point, but I conceive that each of the defendants is entitled to a peremptory challenge of his full number.

Per Curiam. I think not.

Linder. I cite——

Per Curiam. The Court is willing that each of the individuals indicted for this offence may have a separate trial, if he requires it; inasmuch as the rule was adopted in the indictment against Gilman and others. But for the purpose of saving time, the Court is willing to order a nolle prosequi to be entered in favor of any of the defendants, against whom the People shall fail to produce any evidence of guilt, that such acquitted persons may subsequently testify for the other defendants.

The following individuals were then called as Jurors and sworn on the "voir dire."

George Carlton. Challenged by People.

Timothy Terrell. Sworn.

John P. Ash. Sworn.

James Mansfield. Rejected as incompetent, having formed or expressed an opinion as to the guilt or innocence of the defendants.

William Lewis. Rejected as Incompetent for reason as above.

Aaron Corey. Rejected as incompetent, for reasons as above.

Jas. Wellington. Challenged by people.

Peter Whittaker. Rejected as incompetent, for reasons as above.

Mahlon Weber. Rejected as incompetent, for reasons as above.

William S. Gaskins. Sworn.

Richard P. Todd. Objected to by Government as not being on the regular panel.

Per Curiam. The Court has no objection that the regular pannel should be first called. Mr. Todd, however, was returned as a juror in place of one of the regular panel, who was excused.

Murdock. Stand aside, Mr. Todd.

George Allcorn. Linder for defence. We take the juror.

Cowles for people. We take him.

Juror to the Court. I have formed and expressed an opinion as to the guilt or innocence of the defendants.

Per Curiam. The juror is incompetent.

Linder. What? if both parties agree to take him?

George Allcorn. Sworn.

Stephen Griggs. Challenged by defendants.

Jas. Stuart. Had been excused.

Luther Johnson. Rejected as incompetent, for reasons as above.

Horace W. Buffum. I was excused on Wednesday morning from any further attendance, on account of sickness. I am better now than I was.

Murdock for people. We want the regular panel.

Juror. I have both formed and expressed an opinion as to the guilt or innocence of all the individuals.

Horace W. Buffum, rejected as incompetent, for reasons as above.

Effingham Cocke—had formed an opinion as to the guilt or innocence of some who were indicted.

Per Curiam. The juror is incompetent.

Chauncey Underwood—had been previously excused.

John Clark. Sworn.

Robert M'Farland. Challenged by the people.

William T. Hankinson. Sworn.

Richard P. Todd. Sworn.

William P. Little. Rejected as incompetent.

James E. Starr.

Q. By Linder. How old are you? over twenty-one? *Ans.* I am.

Q. By same. Do you pay taxes? *Ans.*—I do. Challenged by defendants.

R. K. Wheeler. Rejected as incompetent.

Alexander Botkin—had formed no opinion as to the guilt or innocence of the defendants in entering the store.

Cowles, for people. The charge of riot; have you formed or expressed an opinion as to the guilt or innocence of any of the individuals, upon that charge?

Linder. No riot is charged in the indictment.

Juror. I saw some of the individuals indicted, in the street that evening, but I did not see them beyond State-street: and I have formed no opinion as to their guilt or innocence under the indictment.

Cowles. It matters not whether the juror had formed an opinion as to the existence or truth of certain facts. If he has formed an opinion that certain facts, if proved, will not constitute a riot, then he is incompetent.

Linder. My position is this; that the People can only convict these defendants upon the charge alleged against them in this indictment.

Cowles. The jurors are judges of both law and fact; if they have formed an opinion upon the law, provided the facts are proved, then they are not, and cannot be impartial jurors. The question which should be propounded to this individual is, whether, supposing certain facts are proved, he has formed an opinion.

Per Curiam. Two essential things are necessary to sustain an indictment. First, that certain facts should be proved to have existed; and secondly, that those facts should be such as to constitute an offence. The juror should not be asked whether he has formed an opinion as to the existence of certain facts, but whether he has formed an opinion as to facts constituting guilt. The indictment is under the 117th section.

8*

Certain facts are set forth, but the charge is riot. If any juror has formed an opinion as to the innocence or guilt of the charge, then he is incompetent.

Linder. My question was whether the juror had formed an opinion of the guilt or innocence of the individuals as to the charge in the indictment.

Per Curiam. The individuals on trial are charged with having committed a riot. Have you, Mr. Juror, formed an opinion of their guilt or innocence upon that charge?

Juror. I have not. I know nothing of the facts.

Q. By Juror. Does not the fact of having been elected justice of the peace excuse me from serving?

Linder. No!

Cowles. Has not a justice of the peace a right, by common law, to act as coroner, so is he not incompetent?

Per Curiam. That is a personal privilege which the individual may or may not claim.

Q. By Linder. Have you been commissioned as a Justice of the Peace? *Ans.* No.

Sworn as Juror.

E. Breath.

Q. By Linder Are you a tax-payer? *Ans.* I am not; I have got nothing to be taxed.

Per Curiam No matter whether he pays taxes or not. The law includes all free taxable persons.

Q. By Cowles. Do you pay highway taxes? *Ans.* I do.

Q. By Linder Rejected as incompetent by reason of having formed an opinion.

Treadway—never had expressed an opinion, although he had formed one. Rejected as incompetent.

Rice. John Solomon has related to me some facts. I have formed an opinion as to him, but not as to the others. Rejected as incompetent.

Evans. Rejected as incompetent.

Wheeler. I don't know who the defendants are. Have formed no opinion. Sworn.

Walter Lachelle.

Q. By Linder. Have you been naturalized? *Ans.* I have. Sworn.

Job Lawrence. Challenged by defendants.

Daniel Carter. Sworn.

Samuel W. Hamilton—had formed an opinion, but the counsel agreed to take him, and he was sworn.

A jury having been obtained, Murdock for the People in the opening of the case, said: So much of the time of the court has been occupied in the trial growing out of the same tragedy, for a participation in which these individuals have been indicted, and so much of your own time has been consumed in the preliminary steps of this trial, that I am warned to be as brief as possible. It is unnecessary to tell you that these individuals are indicted for a Riot; that the Grand Jurors have found that these individuals, with divers others, assembled on the night of the 7th of November last, with a determination to attack the storehouse of Godfrey & Gilman, and of breaking up and destroying a printing press stored therein.

The indictment is in these words.

"Of the January Term of the Municipal Court of the City of Alton, in the year of our Lord one thousand eight hundred and thirty-eight."

State of Illinois, }
City of Alton, ss. }

The Grand Jurors, chosen, selected and sworn, in and for the body of the City of Alton, in the county of Madison, in the name, and by the authority of the people of the State of Illinois, upon their oaths, present that John Solomon, Solomon Morgan, Levi Palmer, Horace Beal, Josiah Nutter, James Jennings, Jacob Smith, David Butler, William Carr, and James M. Rock, and Frederick Bruchy, all late of the City of Alton, in the County of Madison, and State of Illinois, on the 7th day of November, in the year of our Lord one thousand eight hundred and thirty-seven, with force and arms, at the City of Alton aforesaid, and within the corporate limits of said City, unlawfully and with force and violence, did enter the storehouse of Benjamin Godfrey and Winthrop S. Gilman, there situate, and one printing press, the property, goods, and chattels of the said Benjamin Godfrey and Winthrop S. Gilman, then and there being found, did, unlawfully, riotously, and with force and violence, break and destroy, contrary to the form of the statute in such cases made and provided, and against the peace and dignity of the people of the State of Illinois.

Francis B. Murdock, Prosecuting Attorney,
for the Municipal Court of the City of Alton

Endorsed 'a true bill.'

Thomas G. Hawley, Foreman."

For the purpose of sustaining the indictment, gentlemen, of the jury, it is necessary that the government should show, that two or more persons assembled, for an unlawful purpose; that they entered the storehouse of Godfrey & Gilman, with force and violence, and that they broke up and destroyed the printing press, then and there found, as is charged in the indictment. It is necessary that the people should show that Godfrey & Gilman were in the possession of the property destroyed. They need not have been the actual owners of the property; it is sufficient if they were in the possession of the property, at the time it was broken up and destroyed. If they had a special property, as for instance, if they were *bailers* of the property, it is enough.

The indictment is framed under the 117th section of the criminal code, and charges the defendants with having committed a riot.

Linder for Defendants. This case, gentlemen, is the last trial, the closing scene in the comic tragedy which has been played off in your city. You are to determine the guilt or innocence of the individuals now on trial, by the law and the evidence which shall be given you, and you will have to believe three things before you can find these defendants guilty: first, that two or more entered the storehouse with *force and violence*, because that is the charge contained in the indictment: and here let me say to you, that you are the judges both of the law and the fact; the government are bound to satisfy you of the truth of every allegation they have charged against my clients: they are bound to satisfy you that certain facts existed; that these persons entered the storehouse of Godfrey & Gilman with force and violence; that they unlawfully, riotously, and with force and violence, broke and destroyed the press; and that that press was the property of the individuals whom they have alleged were the owners of it.

Here is the section under which the indictment is framed: "If two or more persons actually do an unlawful act, with force or violence, against the person or *property of another*," &c.

Now the prosecutors are bound to prove all their allegations; they are bound to prove that the building was the property of Gilman & Godfrey; that the press was the property, the bona fide property, of Gilman & Godfrey; that two or more persons, unlawfully and with *force and violence, entered the building*; that when they had so entered, they broke up and destroyed the press, with force and violence; and, further, that they had no right to do so: and if they fail in proving, in satisfying you of the truth of any one of these allegations, you will be bound to return a verdict of "not guilty."

Murdock. I now propose to enter a "noll. pros. against those individuals included in the present indictment, who have not come in."

Broughton called and sworn. I know nothing of what took place on the night of the 7th of Nov. last. I was not present at the time of the riot; have had conversation with some of the defendants; no particular recollection of what passed; it was a general conversation, in regard to the riot; every body was talking about it; have heard it spoken of by a great many individuals. I was on the ground after the battle was fought; did not see the press broke up; did not see it that night, as I recollect; saw a part of it next morning; no persons ever told me that they broke it up, and I never made but little inquiry about it. No proposition was ever made to me, that I should be the captain of the mob. There was a great crowd, when I got to the warehouse, that night. I don't know that I saw any of the defendants in it. I went into the warehouse, to look at the corpse; some one asked me to do so, and I did.

Henry H. West. On the afternoon of the 7th, I was standing at the store door, and I saw John Solomon coming along the street. This was perhaps an hour or an hour and a half before the mob. Solomon stopped, and told me that a mob was gathering; that preparations were making to burn or blow up the warehouse, unless the press was given up; said Gilman had been a friend to him, and he did not want to see him or his property injured; and he requested me to go and tell Mr. Gilman what was going to be done. Soon afterwards I saw him again. I went up to my counting room, found Mr. Keating, and in company with him went up to see Gilman. I told him what Solomon had told me. I soon returned from the warehouse, came down street to the counting room, and staid a little while. I soon started up, and as I came into the street, I saw squads of men gathering about the street, principally in and before the coffee houses. I don't know that I recognised any of the defendants at that time in the street. I started to go up to the warehouse again, and on the way, met Dr. Horace Beal. I asked him if he would not go up with me. He said no. I then asked him if he would not use his influence to induce the mob to desist and disperse. He replied, he could have no influence with them, and would do nothing about it. I went up and into the warehouse; had been there but a little while before the mob came; they came on the side of the store next the river. I knew only one of them. I started to find the Mayor, Mr. Krum. I met him on the street, talking to a crowd of people. Among the crowd I saw Rock and Bruchy. I saw Morgan some where round at that time, but do not recollect exactly where. I saw Nutter early in the evening; heard him say he was sorry to do any thing criminal. While I stood there, an arrangement was made, by which Mr. Krum was to go into the warehouse, and let them in the house know what the mob wanted. I went into the warehouse again with Krum and Mr. Robbins. We came out soon, and Mr. Krum addressed the crowd that was collected. At that time I saw Rock and Beal in the crowd. I soon saw the fire applied to the building, and ran down to put it out. I started to go up the ladder; but desisted, as I found guns were aimed at me, and saw them flash. At the time I ran down, I saw Rock; he was standing near the ladder. I saw another man standing about there at the same time, whom I noticed. I did not know him at that time. I see him now; it was Palmer; he had no gun then. I saw Frederick Bruchy there at that time; he was swearing a good deal. Soon after this I went up and stood at the corner of the Penitentiary wall. I saw Beal there; he had a gun. It was soon said that the people inside would give up. I went again into the crowd, and run round the warehouse to help them get away if I could. I went up the river a little way, thinking that would be the best direction for them to run when they left the building. Some one called out to me, and told me to "*stand*" or they would shoot. I turned round—saw Gilman and the others at the door, and requested them to wait a few minutes. I turned and assured the crowd that Lovejoy was dead, and told Mr. Gilman and others to run then. They did so. I then run round the building and up the ladder to put out the fire on the roof of the building, and called to them below to help put out the fire. Dr. Beal run down to the river, and soon came back and said he could find nothing to bring any water in. I took off my hat and threw it down to them. Dr. Hope picked it up, filled it with water, brought it to me, and I put out the fire. I came down the ladder and went into the warehouse. I saw Lovejoy laying there. I went up into the garret; as I came down I saw Gerry, (one of those who had been in the warehouse,) and secreted him. I watched for an opportunity, (as he was rather disinclined to remain there,) took him down stairs with me, saw the way was clear, and told him to run. He did so. I saw Beal again then, and Jacob Smith. This was the only time I saw Smith that evening. At this time I recognised Butler's voice. I saw Palmer too, I think. About the time the fire was set to the buildings he was near the ladder. I don't think I saw Solomon.

I went into the warehouse with the crowd. I went in before the press was thrown out—at that time I went into the counting-room. When I went out, I saw some one breaking up the press, I don't know who; I did not notice, as I was anxious about Gerry. I made some remark to divert the attention of the mob from him, and told him to run. I don't know what Palmer did. I don't think I saw Palmer on the ground. I saw him early in the evening in the coffee-house—he was talking loud, but I don't know what he said. When I saw Beal he had a gun, and was standing next the penitentiary wall.

I was the first who went into the warehouse after Gilman and the others left it. I saw Rock at the foot of the stairs. I saw Dr. Beal up stairs. We went towards where Lovejoy laid, nearly together. I saw a good many of our citizens in the warehouse soon afterwards. I saw Rock and Beal there early, before the press was thrown out of the house. Dr. Beal went with me into the counting-room—think Beal had no arms by him at that time. When I saw Rock at the time the fire was set to the warehouse, he was standing some distance this side of the ladder—he had a gun. Dr. James Jennings had a gun. I believe he has taken French leave. I saw Solomon Morgan some time during the evening, on the street—he *seemed crazy*—was rallying the boys as he called them—he had no gun, I think. I did not see the commencement of the attack upon the warehouse. I was in the building at that time. I understood the attack was made entirely upon the side of the house next the penitentiary wall.

The guns were first fired by those outside; the windows were all broken while I was in the building; at the time I was conversing with Mr. Gilman, I was a good deal exposed by the attack made from without.

The mob poured into the warehouse soon after Mr. Gilman and the rest left it—soon after the fire was put out. I went into the warehouse on the front side; and don't know how the mob got in. I went in because I was anxious that no property should be injured or destroyed; there were a good many candles burning about in the store, and I thought there was danger of injury to the property. When I saw Dr. Beal at the penitentiary wall, it was about the time the fire was first set to the building. I do not know whether any guns were fired from that quarter at that time or not. I heard guns fired at that time; and saw the flash, but don't know whether it was in the place where Dr. Beal was standing or not. I recognised Morgan encouraging the "boys;" he said, "go and finish your work," and a good many other expressions. When I saw Rock he had a gun; and Beal had a gun when he stood up by the penitentiary wall; he stood behind or close by some salt barrels which laid there; I saw both Beal and Rock inside the warehouse before the press was thrown out—as soon as it was found, I left and went down stairs—they were moving it when I turned away—I don't know who the persons were who moved it. I thought I heard Butler's voice under the bluff as I was told to "stand" when I was going up the river—I was on the ground when the ladder was brought—I don't know who brought it there—I saw it laying on the ground; when it was put up to the building I was standing some distance off; it was up when I saw Rock standing there with

9

his gun; the fire had been put on the roof at that time. When I was running round the warehouse, Rock told me I had better keep away. I did not hear Beal call the boys to rally after the press was destroyed. I did not hear any thing said about preventing any arrest; when John Solomon told me that preparations were making to burn or blow up the warehouse, if the press could not be got without, I do not recollect whether he used the word "We" or "They." Godfrey & Gilman were in the occupancy and possession of the building; the press was in the warehouse; Solomon appeared to be anxious about the safety of Mr. Gilman; said he had been a friend to him. I do not recollect what day of the month the riot was, it was in November last, the first part of the month, in the corporate limits of the City of Alton.

Cross-examined. The warehouse is built of stone, was occupied by Godfrey & Gilman for selling goods; their house is a commission and storage and forwarding house.

Q. By Linder. Do you know whether they keep printing presses for sale by wholesale or retail? *Ans.* I do not.

Q. By same. Do you know who that press belonged to? *Ans.* I do not: I understood that it either belonged to Lovejoy or was under his control.

Q. By same. Did you hear any thing said while you were in the warehouse that night about the ownership of the press? *Ans.* I did not.

John M. Krum. The riot was on the night of the 7th of November last; at the time I first had information, I went to the spot with Mr. Robbins. I first met, if I recollect rightly, those who were carrying Bishop. Bruchy, Solomon, Morgan, Butler, Carr, Palmer, were among them. I went up to them as they were carrying Bishop to Dr. Hart's office. I inquired of them if any one was hurt; was told some one of "our" or "their" company was shot. I asked if he was hurt badly; was told they thought not. I endeavored to persuade them to disperse. Carr, Palmer, and Morgan, conversed with me; soon Bruchy came up again, and some others I did not know. All seemed a good deal excited. I asked them what they wanted; Carr, I think it was, answered me that all they wanted was the press; that they did not want to injure any one or any one's property, but that they wanted the press, and would have it. I used all the means in my power to induce them to disperse. I told them of the penalties and liabilities they were incurring; quite a crowd had gathered round me by this time.

Some one, I don't know who, first proposed, and afterwards Carr repeated the proposition, that I should go into the warehouse and let the people who were inside know what they wanted. I think Palmer urged the proposition. This is all which I recollect of it at that time. When I first went up, the crowd were doing nothing, they seemed a good deal excited, and were talking loud and angrily. I saw Dr. Beal that evening; I saw him for the first time standing before me when I addressed the crowd after I came out of the warehouse. I think he spoke to me. At this time the mob were some distance from the warehouse. Beal said something about the conduct of those who had shot Bishop. This was after I had come out of the building. I next saw Dr. Beal, in State-street, as I was standing by the corner of Mr. Marsh's building; he, Dr. Beal, came down State-street, passed by where I stood, and went down towards the river; he had a gun by his side at that time; the first time I saw him he had no gun; at the time I saw him with a gun he was going towards the river; he came down State-street; he was alone. A person might go down State-street and so up Front-street to Godfrey & Gilman's warehouse; I say he might do so, he could if the river was not too high. I do not know how high the river was that night; neither do I know that he went to Front-street. I noticed him a moment or so as he was passing along in State-street. I was not at the warehouse immediately at the destruction of the press; it was broken up when I got there. I saw Solomon Morgan at that time; I mean when I got to the warehouse after it was given up. I saw Mr. Nutter there, but I do not know his christian name; he keeps a livery stable in Upper Alton; I see him now, he is the same person. I think I saw Bruchy; there was such a crowd and the candle light struck me in such a direction, that it partially blinded me; I could not see faces distinctly. When I saw the men I have mentioned, I stood by the side of Mr. Greeley. I noticed Solomon Morgan; he was making a good deal of noise. Bruchy and Beal, were there, standing near; they were doing nothing. I don't think I saw Rock at the south end of the building (side where the press was broken) at all. I did see him that night; the first time was when Bishop was carried to Dr. Hart's office. I did not speak to him, nor did I hear him speak at that time as I recollect. As I went towards the warehouse, when I was going in I saw him; he was standing a little distance off, and as I came out I also saw him again; I saw him again after I had addressed the crowd; the next time I saw him was in State-street; my attention was called to him by a reply he made to young Pinchard. I spoke to him, stopped him, and he walked off; he had a gun in his hand at the time.

When I saw Dr. Beal at the time they were breaking up the press, he made a remark like this, "Now boys we must stick together; and if any one is arrested we must come to the rescue." This was when the press was broken up and nearly all thrown into the river. I don't recollect that I saw Carr at that time. I was standing at the corner of State-street, near Marsh's store, at the time the warehouse was entered. After I went into the building I saw Drs. Beal and Jennings in the building. These are the only ones of the defendants I recollect to have seen in the building. I was there but a few moments. At the time I commanded the crowd to disperse, Solomon and Palmer stood near me. I don't recollect that I saw Smith at all. Butler I saw in Second-street when I first went along. I did not see him again that night. He had a gun at that time. When Dr. Beal said, "Now boys, we must stick together," &c., Bruchy stood in front of him; and I think Butler also, although I am not positive about Butler. At the time Dr. Beal made the remark, there were but two or three persons very near him. I think Butler was one of them, though, as I said before, I am not positive. One of those who stood near him was a stranger to me. Beal had a gun in his hand at the time. I could not see unless I stood upon something. One of them had arms. I think it was Butler. While standing there I was several times crowded off the box I was standing on. I heard no guns fired while I stood there. Hammers were flying pretty busily, and it was somewhat dangerous standing there.

Cross-examined. I am not positive whether Dr Beal said "Now boys *we*" must stick, or "*you*" must stick together, &c. I think he used the word "*we*." I saw Bruchy and Morgan use the hammer in breaking up the press. I saw Nutter throw pieces into the river. I think I saw some of the present defendants breaking up the press. The press had been thrown out before I got to the building. Lovejoy had been killed when Beal made the remark I have repeated. I don't know what Dr. Beal alluded to. I think I have given his remark *verbatim*. All the persons whom I have said I saw were out of the house. They stood a little east of the store door. The press was broken up about where this and another warehouse join together. I heard the crowd say, all they wanted was the press. I heard Beal, when I closed my remarks to the crowd, address some words to me, but what they were I can't swear. It was about the time I received a shot. There were a great many people standing round during the greater part of the riot; and I heard others besides those who were armed say, that they wanted the press. At

9*

one time I should think there were 200 people in State and Second streets.

I don't know who the press belonged to. I don't know whether Mr. Lovejoy claimed it or not. I heard Lovejoy speak of the press, but I don't know whether he said any thing about the ownership of it. I don't know who went into the house and threw the press out.

Q. By Linder. The press was broken on the wharf, was it not? *Ans.* It was.

Q. By same. Was it broken near the river? *Ans.* Not very near.

Q. By same. If the pieces had not been thrown into the river, would they not have been in the way of drays? *Ans.* They might.

Examined again by people's Counsel. I never saw the press. I saw some boxes in which I was told the press was.

Sherman W. Robbins was now called, but stood aside at the request of defendant's Counsel, who said that Mr. W. S. Gilman had been summoned as a witness, and was in court; and that he was anxious to be released from attendance as soon as was possible.

They, therefore, proposed that he should be examined at the present time, and after his examination was concluded, the remaining witnesses for the people could be called.

Consent having been given by the Counsel for the People to this arrangement,

Winthrop S. Gilman, was called by the defendants' Counsel, and sworn, and testified as follows:—The press which was destroyed on the night of the 7th of November last, was received by us on storage, at the request of Mr. Roff. It was not owned by us.

Cross-examined by Counsel for Government.—The press was in the possession of Benjamin Godfrey and Winthrop S. Gilman; I did not know how the last press came to be sent, nor who sent it. Godfrey & Gilman own the store; it has been built since 1833 or 1834. We have title deeds to the property. Linder objects to evidence of this kind as to the ownership of the building. "Title deeds are the best evidence of property, let them be produced." Objection sustained.

I was one of those who were in the building on the night of the riot. We were forced to leave the building by the mob: the first attack was made by stones, which were thrown against the building; a gun and a pistol, as I thought, were then fired by those on the outside; there was firing then from both parties; after this there was a short intermission; firing soon was again resorted to, and in a little while the fire was put to the roof of the store. Mr. West gave us this information. We soon left. We left the store to prevent its being burnt up. We received the communication from West that the fire was actually kindled; the press was in a box; there was a cast-iron roller, however, which composed a part of it, that was not in a box; the boxes which were taken out of the store, and which contained the press that was destroyed, were the same that were received on the 6th of November, when Mr. Krum was present.

I don't know that I recognised any one of the mob, unless it was Carr. When the mob first came up to the building, and after I had addressed them, I think it was Carr who answered me. I judged it to be him from the voice and appearance. He said they would have the press at the risk of their lives. I saw no one else whom I recognised. We left the building, persuaded that our lives would have been sacrificed if we had remained. The building was occupied by Godfrey, Gilman & Co., Mr. Benjamin Godfrey and myself. After we left the store several guns were fired at us; no one was wounded that I know of. None of the shot took effect upon my clothes. I understood that they did upon some of the others: these guns were fired by the mob outside.

Q. By Cowles for Government. If you receive goods for storage, are you or are you not liable?

Linder. You need not answer the question, witness.

I regret, your honor, that I feel called upon by a sense of duty, to interpose objections so often, to the different questions which are propounded by the Counsel for the People. It is matter of regret to me, and I fear that I may fall under the displeasure of the Court by so doing. But I cannot sit still and permit questions to be asked of the witness, so plainly, so positively, and so absolutely improper as this. When the witness is asked whether he is not liable for the loss of goods in his hands on storage, what is it but asking the witness to be a judge? The question of liability is a pure question of law; one which the witness is presumed not to know; which he is to be presumed to be incompetent to decide, and one which, whether he knows or not, he will not, I trust, be permitted to answer. If witnesses are to be allowed to testify as to points of law, why do you sit on that bench?—or why has our statute declared that the Jury shall be the judges of both law and fact? If there has been any contract of responsibility entered into, by which this witness is liable for this property, let the witness be inquired of concerning such contract; let him give us the facts of the case, and we will take care of the law.

But suppose he is responsible: does that fact make him the owner of the press? does that fact vest the property in him? It puts a special property in him I admit, but I wish to lay down the doctrine here, as I shall lay it down, by and by, to the jury; that it is not sufficient to sustain the allegation in this indictment, that Godfrey & Gilman should have had a bare special property in this press. When a man is indicted for stealing property, it is not competent, it is not sufficient to prove a special property barely, in the individual whose property is alleged to have been stolen.

The property must be proved to belong to him, in whom it is alleged to have been, at the time it was stolen. It is useless to travel back to the "Form Books," to prove the truth of this doctrine. Our statute lays down the law—prescribes the rules—and it is there positively and expressly declared that the property must be alleged and proved to be the property of another individual.

I care not what the English law says, when our statute declares that the property must belong to another individual.

And now an attempt is made to show a special property in the men in whom the actual, the general property is laid! How are statutes to be construed? how is the criminal code to be construed? Is it to be done in such a way as, if possible, tc make it reach a man? in such a way as to make it cover a case? is it to be stretched? is it to be strained till it fits? If so, America, like England, may boast of having a Jeffries.

But our code is by itself; it has no reference to common law; it is a code of enacted offences. Crimes under our laws are specially defined. Certain acts, or certain acts done in a particular manner, have been laid down as criminal; and where, as in our state, statutes define what shall, or what shall not constitute crime, the common law definition is dispensed with. When statutes have altered an offence, enlarged or limited the boundary of crime, it is for the Court to give such construction to those statutes as it may deem proper: it is for the Court to say whether it will give such a broad construction to the statute as will cover this case. What the statute means when it speaks of persons, it means when it speaks of property. When it speaks of persons, it means natural persons; and so when it speaks of property, it means general property: when it speaks of ownership, it means general ownership. This witness proves that the press was not owned by Godfrey & Gilman, that they had no property in it. Is not that falsifying the indictment? that alleges that the press was the property of Godfrey & Gilman; this man disproves it.

Suppose these individuals were indicted for having destroyed this press, the prosecution alleging it to be the property of Lovejoy? would an acquittal, under such an indictment, bar another one which should charge the property in the actual owner? If the Court should so construe the statute as to refine and whittle away the law, I put confidence in the jury; I know an honest jury will always rally to the rescue.

Cowles in reply. Per curiam. It is unnecessary to proceed. The Court is called upon to put a construction upon the statute. If examined, it will be seen that our lawgivers did not intend to modify any general principles of the common law. Our science of jurisprudence is derived from the English common law.

The Court will hazard the general remark, that no decision can be found where, in ordinary cases, although it is necessary that property in some one should be charged and proven, any distinction is made between a general and special property. I defy gentlemen to produce such an authority. What the statute intends when it speaks of property, is simply that the property alleged to have been destroyed should be charged as the property of another, which may be either a general or special property.

The jury are the judges of the law and the fact; and if the persons in whom the property is laid have either a general or special property, it is sufficient for the jury to consider whether the law arising on such facts is sufficient to satisfy the allegation in the indictment as to ownership.

The objection is therefore overruled.

By the Witness. When we receive property on storage we consider ourselves responsible to the owner for any loss or damage while it is in our hands. We had a case a short time ago where we had to pay the damage which the property sustained while in our possession. We have been engaged somewhat extensively as forwarding merchants. We now turn over such business to another house, although we do receive and forward some goods for some few friends.

Q. By Cowles for people. Are you responsible to any one for this press?

Q. Objected to by defendants' counsel, but objection overruled, and a bill of exceptions tendered.

Ans. We paid the charges upon it.

Q. By same. Have you paid or do you expect to pay any thing for this press?

Ans. I will state the facts. When the press was sent for, the one that was taken from Gerry & Weller's store, and destroyed, I had an interest in it, to the amount of $100. The press was destroyed, but not the types, and this last press came on to supply the place of that one.

Q. By Linder for defendants. Who contributed to that first press you speak of?

Ans. Deacon Long of Upper Alton, and I think a number of gentlemen at Quincy, but I don't know who they were. I subscribed first, I think, and I believe I did not see the paper after I set my name down.

Q. By same. Did Mr. Godfrey subscribe any thing towards that press? *Ans.* He did not.

Q. By Sawyer for defendants. Who compose the firm of Godfrey, Gilman, & Co.? *Ans.* Benjamin Godfrey, and myself.

Q. By same. Is there no one else interested in it? *Ans.* Not at present. Originally my brother, Arthur, was interested with us, but his death dissolved the firm.

Q. By same. Are not your brother Arthur's heirs interested? *Ans.* They are not.

Sherman W. Robbins, was now recalled by the Government and sworn. My testimony would corroborate that of Mr. Krum's up to the time he addressed the crowd; soon after that we parted. I went into the warehouse at the time Mr. West went in. I only went into the cellar room. I recognised but one of the defendants in the building; that one was Rock. I did not go up stairs; I was satisfied they would do no injury to any of the property in the building, except the press, and turned round and came out. I understood the object the mob had was to obtain the press;

I understood this from Carr, and Palmer, and I think Bruchy, but as to him I am not very positive, nor am I certain as to Palmer; there were two or three who made the declaration; they said they would have the press at all hazards. I understood from the mob that they would have the press, if they had to burn the building to get it. I would not swear positively who made the remark. I understood so from Carr; and I think Palmer also, but as I said before, I would not swear positively.

By Cowles for people. State if you commanded Carr and Palmer to disperse, and if so, state whether any resistance was made, and by whom. Objection raised by counsel for defendants, because the individual has been already tried and acquitted for the offence. But per Curiam. The fact is proper to go to the jury as showing the intention of the parties. To this the defendants' counsel tendered exceptions. I don't know that I saw Palmer after the fire was kindled, in the street; I did see him before and desired him to go home. Palmer took hold of me and said, "I must," or I had better go away, that he did not want to injure me; but he said the press would be had at all events. I can't swear whether he said "*he*" or "*they*" would have it; but he did use one or the other of the expressions. I saw Solomon early on the ground, in Short-street; I saw him in no other place; he was doing nothing; he took no part as I saw; he was running about; I don't know that I heard him say any thing till I heard him say he was wounded. I saw Morgan all about; he was crazy or drunk; I thought he could not have superintended any thing; he made a great noise; I did not see him do any thing. I saw Dr. Beal, but I don't know where or at what time; I think it was when the press was first thrown down; he had no arms as I recollect. I saw Jennings; he had a gun; it is reported that he has gone to "parts unknown." I did not see Jacob Smith, nor Butler, through the evening to recognise them. I saw Carr, when I first went up to the place, and afterwards two or three times; he requested me to go in the warehouse and see if the people there would give up the press. I understood from him that they had determined to have the press. I don't know that I saw him after that time. I recognised Rock but once, and that was when I went into the building after the press was given up. The press was pitched out from the upper story on the ground, it fell on a stone I think. I saw Bruchy, but don't recollect where. I don't know who broke up the press; when I left no blow had been struck upon it. When I left I went into the counting-room and staid till morning. I think the people inside were compelled to leave. If they had remained they would have been burned up. I know of their having been shot at as they were leaving the building, only from report.

Cross-examined. At the time I met Palmer he was doing nothing; he was someway from the warehouse in the street, probably walking this way; I did not see him doing any thing that night; I saw him three or four times between the time Bishop was shot and the time the building was fired; he was doing nothing; he was anxious I should go into the warehouse and see if the press could not be given up; he appeared anxious that nothing should be injured unless it was the press; he said the building would be destroyed if the press was not given up; he wished me to go in and see if I could not persuade them to give up the press; he seemed to think that if it could be given up it would save burning the building; I do not know that he spoke of himself. I don't know who threw the press out nor who broke it up. I don't know whether Rock was where the press was or not; I saw him on the floor of the first story; I can't say whether he went farther up or not.

The court at this time twenty minutes past 1 o'clock, adjourned till 2 P. M.

At the opening of the Court in the afternoon Samuel L. Miller was called by the government and sworn.

On the night of the 7th of November last, shortly

10

after sunset, I noticed people gathering in Second-street. I saw John Solomon. He told me that they were about to attack the warehouse and break up the press—that if they could not get it by fair means, he was afraid they would have it by foul means. He went on to tell me that he should be sorry—that Mr. Gilman was a friend of his—that he did not want to see him injured—that Mr. G. had helped him a good deal, &c. I went immediately to the mayor, and communicated to him what I had heard. He said he could not believe it, but he asked me to remain in town and be ready in case the disturbance should take place. I did so; and about 10 o'clock I saw the crowd collected, and followed them up to the warehouse. I did not see Solomon among them. When the mob was addressed by Mr. Gilman, some one replied to him. Judging from the voice I should think it was Carr. I can't tell what words he used. Gilman stated to them that he was sorry they had come at such an unusual hour to create a disturbance—that he felt it his duty to defend his property—that he should do so, and should do so at the risk of life. The reply was: We don't come to injure you or your property—but as you say you will defend your property at the risk of life, so we say we will have the press at the risk of our lives. There were a good many round in every direction. I can't identify any of those whom I saw except Butler, Carr, and Rock. They went down in the crowd. I would not be certain but I also saw Bruchy. At the time Gilman addressed the crowd they were standing in a line on the bank of the river. I don't know where Butler and Rock were when Carr replied to Gilman. I went into the warehouse with the crowd. West and Robbins went in about the same time—after a little time I saw the house full of people. I saw Palmer in the warehouse about fifteen minutes after I went in. I did not see the press thrown out. I heard it fall; I saw part of it next morning. I saw Dr. Beal around the building on the Levee on the back side of the building. He was forbidding the boys touching some arms standing there. I was there as a peace officer. I had no orders to be there. I repeatedly commanded the crowd to disperse. I spoke to no one in particular at such times. I was not present when the ladder was raised to the building. At that time I was guarding the door to Dr. Hart's office to keep the crowd from rushing up there where Bishop was. I saw Gilman and the others run across the foot of State-street. I heard guns fired at that time. I did not see where they were fired. I did not see Nutter till all was over. I saw Rock and Beal, but can't say what any one was doing. Stones were thrown by the crowd at first. I saw some people throwing stones who were not indicted; but none of those who are indicted.

Cross-examined. When Gilman and others run across State-street they run quite fast. Some one of them fell down. They had no arms at the time. Beal forbid the boys taking any thing away. He said he did not want any property injured, nor any thing taken away. I saw Palmer but twice, once with the Mayor and Mr. Robbins, and again after the affray was over. Palmer asked Weller (one of those inside, and who had been wounded) how he felt. When I saw him he was not disorderly. I saw no one in the warehouse who was disorderly. There was not much riot by the crowd in entering the building. Mr. West led the crowd in.

Q. By Linder. Was you standing by when Beal said, now boys we must hang together? *Ans.* I heard nothing of the kind.

Anson B. Platt called by government, but set aside.

Aaron Corey. I know but little that happened on the night of the 7th. I was on the ground. Shortly before the building was fired I saw there several of those indicted. I don't know who first said "fire the building." I don't know who brought the fire. I saw the man go up the ladder. I can't swear positively who it was. I heard a gun—then a cry of fire the building. I don't know who cried out to fire the building. I did not see Carr. I saw Dr. Beal; he had arms by his side. I saw Rock; he had on different clothes than I ever saw him wear before or since. I don't know about his hat. I was there till all was over. I saw a great many in the building. West asked me to go in with him. I did so. We went in on the north side. The crowd came up the stairs from the basement story. I inferred from that that they came in on the south side. I saw Beal inside, and Rock and Palmer about the building somewhere. I saw Solomon that evening. I saw him opposite Marsh's building, in the street. He told me he had three shot, and I think he said in his back. Butler I don't recollect, nor Bruchy. I did not see the press thrown out. I went to the back side of the building soon afterwards; there was a great crowd there; stood there but a few moments. I did not recognise Carr, nor Beal, nor Butler, nor Morgan, nor Nutter, among the crowd. I did not see the press broken up nor thrown into the river.

Cross-examined. There were a great many people in the building; when I first went into the building I went in on the north side with West; the second time I went in on the south side; there was quite a rush at that time, should think fifty people; there were a good many people there who had not been engaged in the crowd; I saw Judge Martin in the 2d story of the building.

Joseph Greeley called and sworn. I did not see Solomon nor Palmer; I don't know Morgan; I saw Dr. Beal; I don't know whether he had a gun or not; I saw Jennings, he had a gun on his shoulder; I saw Nutter when the press was broken up; Butler I saw in the early part of the evening at the Tontine Coffee House; he was excited, was swearing about Abolition and the press; he said he would have the press any how. I did not see Carr, I don't know at all, nor Rock; Bruchy I saw when the press was broken up. After the fire was put out I went down to the bank of the river; when I got there Bruchy was staving up the press. Some one said, Fred, you have done enough; I went up into the counting-room. Mr. Lovejoy lay there dead. I don't know that I heard Dr. Beal speak during the evening; I did not go to the place till the bells rang for fire. At the time they were breaking up the press I saw Dr. Beal looking on, but I did not hear him say any thing.

Cross-examined. Mr. Krum stood by my side a part of the time while they were breaking up the press. I spoke to him. I think that I stood there when Mr. Krum came up. I don't know which of us left first.

Samuel Avis called and sworn. I know but little about the matter. I was not there till the bells rung. I recognised a number of people. I did not see Solomon nor Morgan; I did see Dr. Beal and Palmer; I did not see Nutter. I saw Jennings with a gun. Jacob Smith I don't know, nor Bruchy, nor Butler. I saw Carr, I thought I saw Rock; I saw a man whom I took to be Rock, although he was differently dressed than Rock usually is. Dr. Beal was armed, was exulting, said he would kill, or would like to kill every damned abolitionist in town. He did not say he had killed any. I thought he said it in joke. I was not afraid of him, although he said I was an abolitionist. The press had been thrown out. I saw him on the upper side of the building. Dr. Beal was in pretty good spirits. I saw no one engaged in breaking up the press; the crowd was so great I could not get near enough to see who was busy. I don't know that I saw any of the defendants in the building. I was not there when the crowd entered the building. I presume I was in the street before the press was thrown out. I saw none of those who are indicted enter the building, or have any share in breaking up the press.

Edmund Beal called and sworn. On the night of the 7th of November last, John Solomon was the first man I saw on the docket, and soon afterwards Butler. I think about the time Bishop was shot, I heard the

10*

voices of different persons, some cried, there goes an abolitionist broke out of the house; some said shoot him, some stone him, some throw him into the river. I saw somebody pick up a stone at the time. Solomon came along up where I was standing; that is all I know of him; didn't know Morgan, nor Beal, nor Nutter; I saw Smith; he appeared to be quite cool; exhorted the "boys" not to be intimidated because Bishop was shot; told them they had better go up and make a finish of it. Butler I did not know, Carr I did not see; James M. Rock; that is the man I did see; I saw him with twenty or thirty persons when they were marching up to the warehouse; Rock came to me and asked what I wanted; I told him I came after my boy; he pointed him out to me, and told me to take him and be off; said I had better go home, and I did so, according to his orders. However, I soon returned; came down and stood near the post at Mr. Marsh's store. I saw the flash of the gun when Bishop was shot; they brought him up by where I stood to the Doctor's office. Soon after that I saw Rock pass by with a ball, or bunch of fire in his hand, swearing that he would burn down the building, and all in it. I don't recollect of seeing any others of the defendants; I don't recollect seeing Frederick Bruchy. I did not go but little further than the corner of Dr. Marsh's drug store, during all the time.

Cross-examined. It was between 11 and 12 o'clock when I saw Rock pass by with the fire, I think. I saw no one else carrying fire. I stood in the same place most of the time. I went home once or twice during the riot; once soon after Rock passed with fire, and staid a few minutes; I saw fire kindled in the street soon after Rock carried it by, and soon after that I saw a ladder raised to the building. It was perhaps 20 minutes after Rock passed with the fire, before I saw fire put to the building: I went home between and staid a few minutes; I was a good deal concerned about the matter, and watched the man who had the fire pretty closely; I had as much anxiety as any good citizen would have had, I think.

John H. Watson called and sworn.

My history will be short: I only saw two of the persons indicted, John Solomon and James M. Rock; I saw Rock at the corner, near Dr. Marsh's store, and Solomon in Dr. Hart's office; Solomon came in and said he was shot; upon examination, one or two shot were found in him; in his arm, I think; as I came down from the Doctor's office, I saw Rock; he was doing nothing; I left, and came down to Hawley, Page & Dunlap's till all was over; it was about two o'clock; I then went up; all was still.

Webb C. Quigley. On the night of the 7th of November last, I went into the Tontine. There were a number there; they went out into the street, formed a line, and marched up to Mr. Gilman's warehouse; I followed, and went into one of the unfinished buildings. The mob drew up on the side next the river; Gilman addressed them; some one replied to him; I supposed from the voice it was Carr; the mob soon started to go up to the north end of the building; I started to go up to the corner of the penitentiary wall; some one cried out, there goes an abolitionist; some one cried out "shoot him," some "throw him into the river," some "stone him." Morgan run up to me, and swore if I did not fall into the ranks he would kill me. Bruchy came up, made some remarks, and they passed on. Beal came up to the penitentiary wall where I was, and staid there a little while; he had no gun with him; I saw Rock coming down the hill in State-street with Dr. Jennings; he had a keg in his arms; looked about the size of a keg of gunpowder; he passed me; I did not ask him what it was. I saw Morgan; he was running from home in his shirt sleeves and bare-footed, told some one after his gun. The Mayor stopped him; Morgan asked the Mayor how he would like to have a damned nigger going home with his daughter. The Mayor said, not very well. At last he said, well, Morgan, all I have to say is, don't let them hurt you. I went up to the penitentiary wall; was at the corner of the wall when Bishop was shot. Dr. Beal went down and came back, and said he thought he was not hurt much. I was there when the press was thrown out; saw a man beating upon it; could not see his face; from the dress and size I took it to be Nutter; he had a great-coat on. The people, when they left the Tontine, formed in line; I did not see Solomon, nor Beal, nor Jennings there. I did not notice Palmer; they were ranged round the walls in the Tontine; Carr was carrying round liquor to them. I saw Butler, Rock, and Bruchy there; I did not hear them say what they were going to do. I did not see Carr, that I know of, after the mob left the Tontine. I was standing at the corner of the penitentiary wall when Bishop was shot. I heard the crowd say that Bishop was standing at the corner of the warehouse when he was shot. When Bishop was shot Dr. Beal went down that way, and came back and said that he did not believe he was much hurt. Beal had no gun that I saw. I went into the warehouse; saw none of the defendants in there, that I recollect. When I was in the warehouse, Smith came down and cried out, "Solomon, where have you been?" "I have been up there and thrown some stones." He, Smith, told how many stones he had thrown, but I don't recollect the number. I don't know what reply Solomon made: Morgan was drunk at the time I saw him.

Q. By Linder. Were there not a great many people there? *Ans.* Yes.

Q. By same. Did you see Mr. Murdock there? *Ans.* No.

Q. By Murdock. Did you see Mr. Linder there? *Ans.* No.

Solomon Woolters called and sworn. I was in the city on the night of the 7th, but not at the warehouse. I was sleeping soundly at home when the tragedy took place. I know of no previous preparations having been made. I expect the "boys" were afraid to let me know any thing about their arrangements. I went through Second-street between nine and ten o'clock that evening. I saw no one passing; and there were but *three* lights burning in the whole square. I expected likely something was brewing, and came down to see if there were any preparations for the attack, or any interruption in the peace likely to take place. I went home believing no attack would be made that night.

The people here rested their case; and in behalf of the defendants Seth T. Sawyer, Esq., was called and sworn.

I know but little about the matter. The Mayor called upon me that night (the night of the 7th) among others. I had been in his office a little while before, and had been in my office but a few minutes when the Mayor came in and informed me of the disturbance. He requested me to go and get Judge Martin. I went as soon as I could. When I came back and got on the ground Bishop had been shot, and a great many people had collected. I was there near the Mayor when he received the shot. We both took to our legs. I came into Second-street. There I saw Nutter; and I was with him a long while. I saw some persons carry a ladder along; but I don't know who they were. Saw the man pass with the fire in his hand. Don't know who it was. Don't know whether it was Rock or not. I saw the ladder raised to the building. Nutter had been with me all this while. I came away about that time; was not there when the mob broke into the house, nor when the press was broken up. I went back again to the ground before a great while, and went into the counting-room of the warehouse. Nutter did not appear to take any active part while I saw him. I had no idea that he had, or intended to have, any part in the affair. I don't know that I know any thing else about it.

Cross-examined. I saw, I should think, 150 people when I first got on to the ground. I recognised Solomon, Morgan, Beal. I saw Beal when the Mayor made his address to the crowd. At that time he stood nearly opposite the Mayor. I saw Solomon in Dr. Hart's office. He had some shot in his right side; they were in his right leg, arm, and side, I think. He was tolerably well peppered. The shot were only skin deep.

Alexander Botkin, one of the Jurors, sworn. I saw a man carrying fire through the street. He passed near the post at the corner of Marsh's store. It was a short time after Bishop was shot. The last time I saw the fire, was when it was kindling in the street. I know the man who carried the fire. I know him well. *It was not Rock.* I should not think it was so late as eleven o'clock when the fire was carried along.

Cross-examined. I had no conversation with Rock, nor with any one in particular. At one time I saw Smith, and I had a conversation with him. Exchanged a few words only. The person whom I saw carry fire was about Mr. Linder's size, (though it was not him.) "He was thinner and more stoop shouldered than Rock." I did not see the building fired. I knew after wards that preparations were made to burn or blow up the building, if it was necessary to do so, to get the press. I did not know this till the next day. I did not see the ladder carried along. The man who carried the fire along, as he went down the street was running. I asked him where he was going. He said it was none of my business. As he came back with the fire he was coaxing it. It was not a large bunch or ball of fire.

Judge William Martin was called upon to state what he knew, and said that he did not arrive at the scene of action until late. He saw the person go up the ladder, and put fire to the house. Didn't know who the individual was. Didn't know whether it was any of those named in the indictment; that the distance was so great from where he stood that he could not recognise the person; that the ladder was rather short; and he thinks the man who went up the ladder had to reach up over the end to put the fire on the building; that he saw Rock but twice that night; that when he first came to the scene of the riot he went into Dr. Hart's office, and examined the man who had been shot; that he soon came down, and then saw Rock on the corner of State and Second streets—who had a gun—and was in an altercation with young Princhard concerning abolitionism; that he interposed and stopped it; that he returned to Dr. Hart's office; remained but a few moments; came down; passed up Second-street; that the mob were then attempting to raise the ladder to the building; they were fired upon from the corner of the warehouse; that the firing dispersed the multitude, and the ladder was dropped.

That he next saw Rock running down State-street, with a gun in one hand and a large bucket in the other, which he professed to have procured for the purpose of putting out the fire. That he saw some one with fire in his hand; that the fire which was put to the house was taken from the street; that he saw a person going through State-street with fire; that it was not a *large* ball of fire; that the man who had it was going deliberately; that he walked in the centre of the street; that he did not observe him particularly till he had got to the west line of State-street; that he spoke to Rock, but not in regard to the riot; that there were 100 people standing as spectators, all, or most of whom being owners of property, had a deep interest in the preservation of good order; that he applied to many people to aid him, but that he found no one who was willing to assist in the suppression of the mob; that he did not use his authority as a peace officer, because he was satisfied it would do no good.

That he saw Solomon that night, but did not see him doing any thing; and he was standing, when he was shot, somewhere near the Penitentiary wall; that Mr. Krum (Mayor) and himself were together part of the evening, though he did not hear the Mayor's address; that he saw Solomon a moment, who told him (Martin) that he had been shot; that he himself went no nearer the scene of riot than the north side of Second-street; that the fire was communicated to the roof of the building on the end farthest from the river.

That he saw Palmer, but none of the others named in the indictment, except as before stated; that it was dangerous to have gone very near the assailants; that at one time he asked Smith, one of the defendants, if something could not be done to suppress the riot, and that Smith replied that he would help if any one else would; that he saw Beal—passed him and spoke to him—but what was said he can't tell—does not recollect.

Shemwell called and sworn. I saw Nutter the evening of the 7th. Was with him in a private house in the city when the riot commenced. We went out when we heard the noise. The crowd had marched up to the building then. We went to the corner of Marsh's store, and stood there; I don't know how long. I was with Nutter during that night. I saw him make no attempt to do any thing I thought wrong. He said nothing. We walked about. I was standing near when the people went out of the house. We were on Water-street when the press was thrown out of the building. Nutter said then, "Let us go home." We went in to see Lovejoy. I was with Nutter all the evening, and could have seen him if he had done any thing. Nutter picked up a piece of the press after it had been broken up, and said it would make a good thing for painters to rub paints on, or with, and he dropped it again on the ground. Nutter had on a blanket coat.

Cross-examined. I did not know any one who was engaged in breaking up the press. I left soon after the press was broken. Nutter and myself were together all night. I don't know whether Nutter threw the piece of the press which he picked up into the river or not. I did not see him throw any stones at the building. He had no gun. Nutter and myself came down that evening from the upper town, after we had our supper. I had business in the city to do. I asked Nutter if he would come down. He said he had heard that the press had arrived, and asked if I supposed it would be broken up that evening. I told him I thought not. We each had business in the city. We went to Mr. Mooney's house. I live in Upper Alton. Have lived here three years. Am but little acquainted in the town (city). I did not hear that there was to be any row. I heard the press had arrived. I don't know of any one's coming up to our village to let us know that the press had come. I don't know how I heard it had come. I was not invited to come down and assist in breaking it up. I heard about the arrival of the press late in the afternoon. I knew I had business to do in the city before that time. Nutter asked me if the press had come. I don't know why he inquired. I heard of no preparations going on to break it up. Nutter asked me if the press had come, and if there was going to be a mob that night. I told him not that I knew of. I did not get through with my business that night. Had business with Mr. Mooney. Mooney formerly lived in Upper Alton, and he has got two or three pretty daughters. I am a single man. Nutter staid with me—in my company. My object in coming down was to do some business with the lady. I agreed to do some business with her for another lady. I don't know what Mr. Nutter's intentions were in coming down that evening. I know he had no hand in breaking up the press.

The evidence here rested.

Murdock in opening.

I shall not occupy much of your time, gentlemen of the jury, in opening this case to you, on the part of the prosecution, but shall leave the burthen of the argument to my able associate, who will conclude. Indeed there is but little room for argument. The indictment in all its parts is fully and clearly proved; and if it were not for the lawless spirit which has long pervaded our land

11

and swept over and desolated our city and rested here; if I did not feel that it was my duty to impress upon your minds the necessity of vindicating the law in its majesty, I would say less. The offence charged on the defendants and so fully proved, is one that strikes at the existence of social peace and security, and tears away the barriers which the law has thrown around the citizen, his life and property. It aims at government itself, for a time prostrates its power, and rears up anarchy to run lawless over our dearest privileges. What is government worth unless it affords protection to property? What are laws worth unless they bring punishment upon the head of offenders? What are governments and laws worth unless the jurors of the country give full efficacy to their provisions? Is government valuable? Shall the laws which the people, through the proper authority, have passed, intended for the protection of the citizen, and the punishment of offenders, be of any practical operation? It is for you to say, for through you only can they be made operative. If the facts of any offence present a case deserving of punishment, then do these call upon you, most imperatively, for a verdict of guilty. Gentlemen, reflect upon the terrible malignity of the facts disclosed. The defendants assemble on the night charged in the indictment, for the purpose of committing an act long deliberately formed, enter one of the groceries, (those sinks of curruption which so much disgrace our city,) then range themselves in order around the walls of the house, drink down a glass of maddening alcohol, and from thence, infuriated, proceed to the storehouse of Godfrey & Gilman, with design of forcibly entering it, and destroying a printing press, and complete their purpose. Gentlemen, shall the perpetrators of an act so lawless, so diabolical, go unpunished? shall they be permitted to live among us unbranded by a verdict of guilty? Shall it be said that you permitted such an outrage, scarcely denied, to go unredressed? Shall it go forth to the world that property is unsafe in Alton; that law is powerless; that juries are the shields of crime? I will not, gentlemen, suffer myself to believe, that you will permit your prejudices to influence your verdict. You will regard the solemn oath you have taken. What has the private opinion of any individual to do with the question of guilt or innocence? What has the exciting subject of abolition to do with the issue formed between the people and the defendants? Are the defendants guilty as charged? is the only question you are sworn to try.

But, gentlemen, anti-slavery with all its horrors will be glowingly portrayed. You will be told that a verdict of guilty will be an approval of its principles, and the triumph of a party whose object is to sever the Union, to rob our citizens of their property, to excite the slave to murder his master, wife, and children, and to plunge our common country into the horrors of an exterminating civil war. I have too much respect for you, gentlemen, to believe that you will be driven from the line of your duty by such considerations. If there is one privilege more dear to us than another, it is the right of free discussion; the liberty of the press; the freedom of conscience. These have civilized and elevated a world; and better, far better, that all the evils which it is predicted abolition will bring on the country, should be actually fulfilled, than that these dearest rights of freemen should be surrendered, and the Constitution of your country, bought with the blood of freemen, and sanctified by the memory of our fathers, should be nugatory. Then, indeed, will we be slaves. Yes, gentlemen, the liberty of the press is inseparably connected with our freedom, and the day that high prerogative of a free people is given up, will be the birthday of a nation of slaves.

Gentlemen, in this offence, there are no accessaries, all are principals. The act of one is the act of all who participated in the commission of the common design. I leave the case with you, confiding in the ability of my friend, Mr. Cowles, to strip it of the difficulties and doubt the ingenious counsel for the defence will endeavor to cloud it with.

Hall. In the few remarks which I shall make to you, gentlemen, I shall aim to be as brief as possible. I appear before you as the Counsel for Josiah Nutter solely. I appear before you, no less from a conviction that he is unjustly charged of being concerned in the commission of this offence, (a conviction which is forced upon me by my whole acquaintance with him,) than from a feeling of entire satisfaction, that the evidence is not such as to warrant you in returning against him a verdict of guilty. The indictment charges my client, jointly with others, with having on the night of the 7th of November last, with force and arms, entered the storehouse of Godfrey & Gilman, and with force and violence broke and destroyed a printing press, then and there found, and being the property of the said Godfrey & Gilman. The question presented for your consideration here, is a bare question of fact. Did Nutter enter? Did he break up, or was he concerned in destroying the press? Gentlemen, you hear nothing of Nutter till the press was thrown out from the building, as having been concerned in any acts of violence. No one sees him; none of the civil officers, who, if they were unable to suppress the mob, were at least active in discovering the leaders of it, swears to his presence on the ground; none of the whole array of witnesses drawn here by the people testify to any act of violence done by his hand. He was not seen in the streets; he was not in the coffee houses; he was not recognised as having been engaged in the attack upon the building—and it was not till the affray was over, till hundreds of your citizens were also attracted to the spot where the act of violence was committed, that he was discovered among the crowd. But other individuals were called, by whom we are enabled to prove to you where he was, and the sort of feeling he had in relation to this matter.

Mr. Sawyer says that he was with him a good part

of that evening; and that in conversation with him Nutter expressed his disapprobation of the proceedings of the mob.

Fortunately, however, gentlemen, we have been enabled to show to you by one witness how this individual spent that evening. Mr. Shemwell says that he came from Upper Alton with Nutter that afternoon; that they came to visit at the house of a friend; that while employed in making that visit, the disturbance commenced; that they had a curiosity to see what would be done, and went up towards the warehouse. But, gentlemen, no one will pretend before you that all who were present, idle spectators of that affray, were guilty of the crime actually committed. If such is the doctrine, heaven save the Court, this Jury, this Bar, and, I doubt not, two-thirds of those now within the walls of this room. This witness states to you that after the affray was all over, Nutter was finally persuaded to go to the building, and here it is that the witness for the people first spied him. Here is the first evidence of his being upon the ground at all, and you will judge how far this goes to his conviction.

I do not deny that Nutter picked up a piece of the press; but I ask you to say, under the evidence you have as to his declarations at the time, that it was at most but a careless act. This would be a good thing for painters to rub paint with, was the remark made by him, as, after having finished his examination of the piece of the press he had picked up, he let it fall to the ground. Why, gentlemen, what stronger evidence could you have of this man's intention? what more conclusive proof could be given that this man was drawn there by mere motives of curiosity? Why is it that you hear no such remark from the mouths of other individuals? Would it be likely, gentlemen, that this man would have made a remark like that, if he had just come in, heated by the struggle, and glorying in the triumph which he might have achieved? No, gentlemen, no such thing! The remark itself, unconnected

11*

with any other fact, would be proof positive that his intentions were not criminal in being there that evening.

Besides, if his intentions had been criminal; if his object had been the destruction of the press, think you he would have kept aloof till that late hour? think you he would not have been seen and identified, as active in the perpetration of the crime? think you he would not have been recognised and sworn to as present, aiding and abetting, before the press was actually destroyed?

Gentlemen, his remark at the time he picked up the piece of the press is no more inconsistent with guilt than all his actions.

Why should he have come forward at that late hour, when the battle had been fought—the victory won—when the house had been taken—the press captured and destroyed? What object could he have had in making himself so active—so conspicuous after the affray was all over?

No! no! the proof, if the evidence proves any thing, shows fully and conclusively his entire innocence of the crime alleged against him. With a simple remark as to one other fact, I will leave the case. The Government will ask you to believe this man guilty, because one witness has sworn that Nutter threw the piece of press which he picked up into the river. But, gentlemen, may not this witness have been mistaken? Is it not just as likely that the piece rolled into the river, as it fell from the hands of Mr. Nutter, as that he threw it there? Is it natural that directly after a remark which denoted entire innocence of criminal intention and design, he should have committed an act which would at once fix guilt upon him.

Gentlemen, to constitute crime, there must be not only an act done, but done from a bad motive, from a bad design. There must be a criminal intention, or the charge alleged against Nutter fails entirely. I leave the fate of this defendant in your hands, confident that you value too highly the rights and liberties of a citizen, to sacrifice them to the prejudices of an excited community; trusting that you will jealously guard his interests; knowing that you will require a strong array of facts—proof strong as that from holy writ—before you will deprive him of his good name, and doom him to a felon's punishment.

Sawyer for Prisoners.

The duty of opening the case in behalf of the defendants has devolved upon me, and I will promise you that I will consume no more of your time than is absolutely necessary to enable me to do justice to the case. The trial is of vital importance to the defendants, inasmuch as it is with you to say whether they shall go hence free, or with the judgment of the Court pronounced against them, for a violation of the laws of the land. It is of deep interest to the community too, inasmuch as this is the last of all the indictments presented by the Grand Jury, and which grew out of the Riot which took place in this city on the night of the 7th of last Nov. The testimony is so insufficient to warrant a conviction, that I would not address you at all, if, provided I said nothing, it would not seem that I was negligent of the duty of my profession.

In the first place, is there any testimony that these individuals did enter the storehouse of Godfrey and Gilman and break and destroy the press? for that is the charge brought against them. You are not to try the question whether or not any of the citizens of Alton, on the night of the 7th of Nov. last collected in a riotous and tumultuous manner; and therefore you have nothing to do with a greater part of the testimony. Then what is the evidence? Mr. Broughton was first called, but he knew nothing about it. Next Mr. West came, and what says he? Why he told you what information he received from Solomon. But is that any evidence that Solomon was concerned in the breaking up of the press? Where then is the evidence that Solomon was concerned? Did his meeting with West prove it? I think that upon your oaths you will say it did not. Then he speaks to you of stones thrown and guns fired—and then of the fire being set to the house—then he comes to the entering into the warehouse, and he tells you that the crowd rushed in—but does he tell you there was any violence used to break in to the warehouse? There is as yet no evidence that any person used any. But West did not see the press broken up. He tells you that he saw Palmer, Butler and Carr, but that he did not see them do any act of violence—he did not see them do any thing. There is no question, gentlemen, but a number of persons assembled at that time and place; and that acts of violence were done, but these acts are not brought home to the defendants. Then comes Mr. Krum; and his testimony is but a reiteration of what West swore to. Where is the evidence which shows that any of these persons were guilty of breaking the house or press? Krum swears to no such thing. All he testifies to is that he saw Beal at the back part of the house and that Beal said something about the boys hanging together; but does that prove that the defendants were guilty of the charge brought against them? But may not Mr. Krum be mistaken? Why should not Mr. Greeley have heard this declaration? from Mr. Krum's own showing he was by his side. There is no evidence then from Mr. Krum of the guilt of the defendants; not the least particle. There is no question but that these persons assembled before the warehouse; no question but that they were noisy; perhaps a little riotous; but that is not the charge. If the indictment is not sustained by the testimony, it is not the fault of the defendants. The prosecuting attorney cut the garment, and if he could not make it fit, he can't expect us to. Sawyer proceeded to state that all those who were spectators, and who did not assist to suppress the riot might have been indicted as well as the present defendants.

Per Curiam. I wish to state that though the citizens did not aid me, I was satisfied it was on account of the great excitement which existed; and from a consciousness that it would require a strong and well organized force to quell the Mob. We had no such force in the city, and the acts of those outside passed in such quick succession that the citizens had no time to adopt any efficient means of resistance. I make this remark, that it may not be supposed I thought the citizens would not have aided in suppressing the mob, had they been properly organized.

Sawyer in continuation.

It is in evidence that the Mayor addressed the crowd. Now, by the 113th section of the criminal code it is enacted, "That if two or more persons assemble for the purpose of disturbing the public peace, or committing any unlawful act, and do not disperse on being desired or commanded so to do by a judge, sheriff, coroner, constable, or other public officer, persons so offending shall, on conviction, be severely fined in any sum not exceeding fifty dollars, and imprisoned not exceeding one month."

Now that is the law for the prosecution to have indicted these persons for violating; but they have chosen to take a different ground; they have chosen to charge us with destroying this press, and I suspect they will think, as the devil did when he heard the pig squeal, that there is a great cry and little fleece.

But this press is the firebrand which has produced all the excitement and disturbance out of doors; this press is the thing kept constantly in mind—its destruction is what is so horrible; and I suppose that these friends of the press thought if they could only convict these few poor men of having destroyed it, that it would be a crown of glory on their heads. The prosecutors have therefore brought their indictment for the destruction of this press, and they must abide it. If, however, in trying to prove that these persons destroyed the press, they should prove that they committed any other offences, you are not to try them for it, at least not now.

Then Mr. Robbins was called, but he knew nothing more than Krum. He knew of no riotous conduct; he saw no force or violence used in the house. Does his testimony prove any thing? I contend not.

Aaron Corey was called next. He knew nothing, except that he heard a great noise; and how far does his testimony go? Mr. Miller came next, and he says he saw no man engaged in a violent manner in the house.

Mr. Quigley was called next, and he swore that he saw people at the Tontine; that he heard Gilman address the crowd, and heard a man reply to him—he thought the man was Carr; that he stood in the door of the warehouse, and heard Smith say that he had been throwing stones, and that is all he knows. He also says that he saw Nutter with a great-coat on. But does all this prove the allegations in the indictment. He also tells you that he saw Beal at the Penitentiary wall, and that he had no gun; and I presume Quigley must know about this fact better than any one else, as he had better opportunities for knowing; and I ask you to presume that Beal had no gun until he picked up one of those which were left by the foe in their retreat.

Quigley saw none of the defendants in the house.

Samuel Avis came next, and he knows no more than the others. He saw Beal, and heard him say that he would kill, or he would like to kill all the damned abolitionists in town; but the witness says that he thought the remark was spoken in jest; and a pretty good reason I think you will say he had for his supposition, since, being an abolitionist, he is here to tell you what he saw and heard that night. Apply this evidence to the indictment and does it prove any thing? I think not.

The next witness is old man Beal, and he swears to nothing at all. All you can get from him is, that he was afraid; that he dare not move from the post up by Marsh's store.

This is all the testimony, and these are all the witnesses on behalf of the prosecution.

And now let us recur to that on the defendants' part.

The first one introduced was Mr. Gilman, whose name figures in this matter with considerable ——, any thing you have a mind to call it, gentlemen, and he swears that he did not own the press. Then, if you find the defendants guilty of the charge in the indictment, will you not find contrary to Gilman's testimony. The people must prove what they charge; and it turns out that this Mr. Gilman was not even the special owner of that press; that he was not the bailer of it. He swears that the press was consigned to Mr. Roff. Admitting, then, that the prosecution may travel out of the indictment, and prove that he was the special owner of the press. Have they proved it? A bailer is one who keeps property for hire or gain. It is the reward which he receives for keeping the property, which attaches responsibility to him in case of loss or danger. If one of you keep a trunk for me—but without any reward for it—and the trunk is lost, are you responsible? Do the prosecution show that Gilman was the keeper of this press for hire or reward? No, but the contrary, and by their own showing; by the testimony of this very Mr. Gilman, if this press was in any one's possession, it was in Mr. Roff's.

The rule I have laid down is the *law*, and I challenge the production of any other from my aged friend. Gentlemen, there is no further testimony to be commented upon, except that of Shemwell, in regard to Mr. Nutter. He swears to you that he and Nutter came down to the city to do business; that that business was with the ladies; and as he was a single man I shall leave it to you to imagine what that business was. I do not believe Nutter is guilty, because of my own knowledge I tell you that he expressed disapprobation of the doings of that night. Although he might have picked up a part of the press, it is no evidence of his guilt. If it were, you might be called upon to convict one half the community.

With these remarks I submit the case to your consideration with perfect confidence in the result, knowing you cannot doubt the innocence of these individuals.

Linder for Defendants, in conclusion.

It is now, gentlemen, near six o'clock, and I do not doubt that you are somewhat wearied after the long examination to which you have listened. After a long struggle, I am enabled to have a cheerful prospect before me. Recognising the clear heads and the strong minds of those who sit upon that jury, I feel like a sailor, when, after a long voyage, he catches the first glimpse of land. I have been out at sea for the last three weeks, and, fore God, gentlemen, this is the first sight of land I have had during that period; and it is with great pleasure that I find I am to appear before a jury capable of appreciating the questions to be submitted to them in the further progress of this cause.

The trial by Jury is the greatest blessing we enjoy—it is the greatest boon we have received. It is the shield of the citizen, which is to protect him from the attacks of prejudice and power. It is truly the pillar of fire by night, and the pillar of cloud by day. The citizen may stand upon this prop, and defy the attacks of arbitrary power; and these individuals, hunted as they have been; pursued with all the bitterness and malignity which wealth and talents can command; protected under that shield, and guarded by that prop, may stand erect, and bid defiance to the storm which howls around their heads.

A strong and well organized effort will be made to secure the conviction of these defendants. I am willing to make issue with the prosecution. This occasion will be seized, by the venerable gentleman who is to follow me, as a favourable opportunity to pour out some portion of that invective for which he is so admirably qualified. My remarks will undergo a severe scrutiny. You will be addressed in the cold and chilling expression of puritanical feeling, and the severe language of the law; and while I was anticipating the remarks to which you will be called to listen, as I came down to this court-room from dinner, and looking upon the broad current of the mighty river which floats by these walls, I could not help drawing a comparison between the fate of his address in the hands of this jury, and that of the ice which is borne along upon the bosom of the water; and I could not help feeling, that his address would meet with the same fate in the warm hearts of this honest jury, that the ice finds when it is borne by the current within the influence of a warmer atmosphere.

I know no greater gratification than to appeal to a jury whose hearts are warmed by "sympathy for others' wo."

It will be unnecessary for me to awaken or disturb the feelings which, in time that is past, have distracted this community. I have no object to obtain in so doing. My simple desire, my plain purpose is, to submit to you the facts which have been testified to, and the law which must govern you, and then leave *you* to determine whether these defendants are guilty or not of the charge preferred against them. This is my duty. Your duty is also plain and easy. You are sworn to try the issue made up. What is that issue? What is the allegation upon the one side, and the denial by the other? I will present it to you, as it is contained in the indictment, and I ask your careful attention to the charge there made.

The Grand Jurors chosen, &c., upon their oaths present, that John Solomon, and others, now upon their trial, on the night of the 7th of November, A. D. 1837, with force and violence, entered the warehouse of Godfrey & Gilman, and unlawfully, and with force and violence, a printing press, then and there found, the property of said Godfrey & Gilman, did break and destroy.

To this charge the defendants have plead that they are Not Guilty—as charged in the indictment.

12

Recollect, gentlemen, that that press is charged to have been the property of Godfrey & Gilman, the latter of whom cuts so conspicuous a figure in this whole affair. And when my brother Sawyer was trying to tell you what he thought of the man Gilman's conduct; was hunting for some word which would convey to you his idea of his actions, I was forcibly reminded of a publication which I once saw, and which was made for the purpose of giving to the world the writer's opinion of the character of some individual or other. After the writer had exhausted every abusive word which he could think of, for fear he had not conveyed his meaning strong enough, he proceeded thus: In conclusion, if there is any epithet in the vocabulary of the English language more abusive than any other, the reader will please to consider it applied.

Then, gentlemen, the charge made against these defendants is, that they entered the house with force and violence. What evidence is there? whose testimony proves to you that they unlawfully or violently entered the house? Who entered first? Why, West led the way. Was there any door broke? Did any individual swear to you that these persons made use of any violence, more than all of the crowd who rushed into the house, impelled by natural curiosity? If, from the circumstance of entering alone, you are to suppose that the entry was forcible and violent, then there are an hundred individuals as guilty as these. In the decision of this case you are to inquire about nothing, except the entering the house and breaking the press. You have no concern with the throwing of stones, or firing of guns, in the early part of the riot.

The proof must not exceed the allegation; one is not the ceasing of the other; and under this charge you cannot convict these persons of being guilty of another crime. Now Rock and others have been indicted for burglary, and a noll. pros. entered, and under this indictment, you cannot convict them of any other offence, than that of forcibly and unlawfully entering the house, and breaking up the press.

But it will be said by the counsel for the prosecution, that they do not ask you to convict these people of burglary; but that they have introduced evidence to you to show that high misdemeanors were committed on that night, by way of aggravation.

Is it, however, gentlemen, a necessary consequence, that because these men were upon the spot armed, that they entered the house in a violent manner? is it a consequence, that any door was broken? that any tumult was committed? that there was any violence used after the entry was made? A violent and forcible entry is not proved, from the fact, that there was a rush, when it was known that the house was abandoned; but the jury are bound to presume that the rush was made by men innocent of crime; yet who, from the knowlege of Bishop's and Lovejoy's death, and Roff's and Weller's wounds, were eager to enter the house, that they might early see all the consequences which had resulted from the engagement. West led the way. Corey went in with all the others who were anxious to gratify their curiosity. And these men were as guilty of a violent entry as any others, although they were entirely unconnected with the mob in the other acts of violence and riot. Where is the witness who swears to any act of violence committed in entering the house, by any of those indicted? There is none, and therefore the first charge falls to the ground; there is no pillar to support it; it exists only upon paper, without the least shadow of proof to sustain it.

We then come to the second charge made against these persons, that of breaking up and destroying the press. Where is the evidence to convict them upon this charge? for if you are called upon to convict them, from the mere fact that they stood by and witnessed its destruction, then farewell to the innocence of your Judge, your Mayor, your peace officers, and all those citizens who, from curiosity, attracted by the thrilling interest of the scene, had assembled to witness the proceedings of that night. All who were there, friends as well as foes, are, upon that principle, guilty of this crime. One man only is proved to have been guilty of breaking the press, and he is not upon trial; no one swears that he saw any of these persons throw out the press; no one tells you that he saw any of them assisting in the act, but, on the contrary, all swear that they first saw the press on the ground, between the warehouse and the river; and Frederick Bruchy hammering upon it, as he had been accustomed, I believe, to do upon other presses.

Nutter only, besides Bruchy, is connected with this press, and what did he do? Why, merely this; he found a piece laying on the ground, picked it up, remarked that it would do for painters to rub paint with, and threw it down again.

This, gentlemen, is all the testimony which bears upon the point in issue. This is all the evidence that has been offered to your consideration, to prove these persons guilty of breaking up and destroying that press.

And, gentlemen, upon the strength of this testimony you will be asked whether you will let these individuals go unpunished? Loud declamation, horrific appeals will be addressed to you, based upon the criminality of the acts done at the first commencement of the riot.

But it is not our fault that we are not indicted for those acts; it is not our fault that the bill of pains and penalties is not broad enough to cover all the offences committed that night. If they were so strongly bent upon proving us guilty of criminal acts; if they expected to convict us of participation in the riot, it was the duty of the prosecuting attorney to have laid his indictment broad enough to have included all the facts in the case. But as it is, the course the counsel have taken puts me in mind of a story once told by Mr. Clay: A fellow wanted a search warrant, to enable him to hunt for a turkey, which had been stolen from him. The magistrate, to whom he applied for the warrant, after examining all his form books, said, that he could find no form for a turkey. But said he, I find one for a cow, and I will give you that, and while you are looking for your cow, "perhaps you may find your turkey." Now we stand in just such a situation. The government are attempting to convict us of a riot; of criminal acts done out of doors, done too previously to the commission of the offence for which these persons are on trial, under an indictment for an unlawful and violent entering of a house; and the only way in which they endeavor to prove guilt, is by showing you that certain acts were done, and then asking you to draw a presumption that other acts were done.

They ask you to return a verdict of guilty upon presumption alone. Now I put the question to you, whether if these persons did enter that building with force and violence, from the crowd of people who stood around, from the cloud of witnesses they have arranged upon that stand, the prosecution could not have found some one, some little boy, at least, who saw the offence committed?

They have failed to produce any witness to prove such fact, and that is an incontestable rebutter to any such presumption as the one they will ask you to draw. The same remark will apply to the breaking up of the press.

But it is not worth while to say any thing else about the riot; or about the breaking up of the press. At times, in the investigation of some crimes, it may be more safe to rely upon circumstantial evidence to prove guilt, than upon a connected story. As for instance, in the case of murder. The person who sets himself about the commission of such a crime works in the dark; he selects his time and opportunity so that no one can observe his actions, or defeat his plan; and, from the necessity of the case, we rely upon circumstantial evidence to bring the person to justice.

But this act was not done in a corner: it was not

12*

an outbreak of popular violence, such as is seen in times of revolution; but it was done at a time when all could see the persons of those so engaged, and was the result of long premeditation. Neither was there any attempt at concealment on the part of those engaged. All openly carried their guns by their side; all who said any thing on the subject, said boldly, and this too, to your civil officers, as well as others; that they would have the press at all risks. All the witnesses called, swear that Bruchy was the man who destroyed the press. If any one else assisted, where is the evidence of it? Now let me ask you one question. You must recollect that where there is a rational doubt of the guilt of a person on trial, the jury are bound to acquit: and can you swear that any of these persons broke that press? or can you say that any one of them authorized its destruction? You, as jurors, will not volunteer for the prosecution; if the people have failed to show the guilt of these persons, you will not lend them your aid; you will not convict them of this crime upon a presumption that they are guilty. Suppose Dr. Beal was guilty of this crime; it might have been him, and suppose you say so; suppose you start with that *presumption*, there is no *evidence* as to his guilt; and without such evidence, in what situation are you left? Why, in *doubt;* and if you are once in that situation, you are bound to acquit.

The law sets too high a value upon the rights of individuals, to permit a conviction upon any other than positive evidence. I regret that the prosecution are in this dilemma. If they had laid their indictment broader, I really think that the "boys" would have stood a bad chance. But the good stars of these men so provided that the indictment should specify but two distinct allegations; and those of acts done in the house. But the circumstances! the circumstances! cry the gentlemen; the keg of powder! the stones that were thrown! the guns that were fired! the voice from the crowd addressing Gilman! the fire at the building! the battle cry! the shouts of victory!! Well, what of them? They don't prove the fact that these people were actually guilty of violently entering the house; or of breaking up and destroying the press. They only prove the commission of a distinct and different offence. The indictment might have been formed so as to have included these facts; but the Grand Jury neglected so to do, and we claim the advantage.

I have got the Government upon an island, and I intend to keep them there; and unless the Government can satisfy you that these individuals are guilty of the crime alleged against them, you are bound to acquit them. Are you to select these eight out of the hundred men who entered that building with them, and say that these, and these only, are guilty? Are you sworn jurors? or do you set there as sworn guessers? You can't say one is guilty and another is innocent. You can't make this selection: you can't be permitted to guess in this way.

But it is a waste of words and of time to comment upon the danger of trusting to circumstantial evidence. Monuments still stand to attest to the fatality occasioned by credulous juries in trusting to such evidence. The books are full of cases to the point. You undoubtedly have heard of the case where an individual was arrested, tried, and executed, for taking the life of his bed-fellow; the jury having been satisfied from the facts which were testified to, of his guilt. It appeared in evidence, upon trial, that they were both put into the same bed at night; that in the morning, but one of them made his appearance; that search being made, blood was found upon the sheets, which was traced from the bed, down stairs, out of the house, by a back way, to the banks of the river, where all further trace was lost. The man's companion was arrested; the jury convicted him upon this evidence, and he was executed, notwithstanding his denial of guilt. It turned out some time after, that the man who was supposed to have been murdered, made his appearance again in the coun try: and his story was, that he had been bled some short time before; that he awoke in the night, found the bandage had slipped from his arm, and that the wound was bleeding afresh; that he got up, went down stairs, and out of doors to the river, and that while he was there, washing his arm, a press-gang came along and carried him on board of a vessel; which set sail without his having an opportunity of afterwards going on shore. And this is but one of a thousand instances with which our books of reported cases are filled. Gentlemen, circumstantial evidence *is* always, *must* always be fallacious; it is an unsafe basis for a jury to rely upon. *You* are not safe in so doing. All history attests the danger of founding verdicts upon it; and the darkest spot upon the pages of English history, upon the records of her jurisprudence, is that which attests the credulity of her juries.

And what is the character, what the complexion of this evidence? It is all circumstantial; and it seems like occupying and reoccupying the same ground to comment upon it.

I will submit two plain points to your consideration, and leave the case.

And first, has the prosecution shown that the press was the property of any one at all? They have shown it to be Roff's, if they have proved it to be the property of any one. It was consigned to Roff, and because it was considered more safe at Godfrey & Gilman's than at Roff's, because it was landed there, because it was stored there, it does not follow that it thereby became the property of these men.

I recognise the doctrine, that if I store property with you, and it is taken from your possession, you have the right of action for its recovery. But I do not recognise it when applied to criminal cases.

Have the government shown that any one had property in this press? Where is the witness who has sworn to the ownership of it? Gilman tells you it is not his; but he tells you a long story about it. and leaves it to you, to draw your own conclusions. Whose was it? not Gilman's, for he swears it was not his:—not Godfrey's, for Gilman swears he did not subscribe to the other press. Whose was it then? Gentlemen, do you believe Lovejoy would have offered himself as a victim for a press, in which he had no interest?

In what light shall we regard this testimony, as to the ownership of that press? Lovejoy was to have been the editor of the paper, which was to have been published from that press; then Lovejoy and not Gilman was the owner of it.

Roff was the consignee, and went to defend it: then Roff was the owner, and neither Lovejoy nor Gilman.

And if it was not the property of Roff, then it must have been the property of those who bought it, and sent it here, and should have been so alleged and proved.

And as to the ownership of the warehouse—the only proof introduced before you, is that Godfrey & Gilman have title deeds to it. It is proved that Godfrey & Gilman were in possession of the building, at the time of the riot, and possession is evidence of title, only in case of the non-existence of title papers. Where there are title papers, the rule applies that the best evidence should be produced—and in the absence of these deeds there is no legal evidence that this firm owned the property.

Then the prosecution have not proved that this building, or this press was the property of Godfrey & Gilman, and all their allegations have failed. The people have proved nothing—just nothing at all—and this day has been consumed in the enactment of another farce.

But one word as to Nutter. The purpose for which he came down to the city, on the night of the riot, cut a considerable figure in the cross-examination of the witness Shemwell. The young man very frankly stated to you, that he came down to do some business for one lady, with another; and I thought, that when that fact was disclosed, common decorum would have prevented the prosecuting attorney from pressing the point any farther. But nothing would satisfy the prying curiosity of the gentlemen, till they had ascertained that the young men actually, and bona fide, "came a courting." Nutter is the only one of the eight persons on trial who is proved, by the evidence, to have had any thing to do with the destruction of that press. And I will leave to you to say, whether his act was more than the careless act of a curious person. It was inconsiderate perhaps, but I think you will hardly say it was criminal.

The witness Shemwell tells you, that Nutter engaged in none of the acts of violence, which were committed that night; that he and Nutter kept together all the time, and it was natural that they should have done so. It seems that all who had much to do at that time kept together, as much as circumstances would allow them. When you hear of Rock, the rest of these persons who are on trial were near him. Those in the warehouse kept together so long as they remained in the building, and when they abandoned it, they still kept as close together as the speed of the different individuals would allow. And there was old Morgan, running about like a dog in high rye, crazy, as one of the witnesses said. He always takes care to be on the strongest side, and if the defenders of the warehouse had been successful, no doubt he would have exhorted them, "to go up and finish their work," as it is proved he did in this case.

Gentlemen, it is not on suspicion that you will say that these men clubbed together—congregated into a body, and violently entered the building, and destroyed the press. It is not on suspicion, that you will convict these men, even though they are of what the gentleman calls the "genuine democracy." I expect that the democracy will be cut up by the venerable counsel, with all the superciliousness belonging to the well born and well bred. I have yet, however, to learn that an honest jury, will convict a man for the "cut of his coat," or because he is seen in a coffee-house, or because he happens to fall into what the gentleman may call bad company.

I have said all. And in conclusion, I ask at the hands of this jury, that indulgence which my situation demands. I know abuse will be, and has already been heaped upon all of us. Scarce one has escaped it. I know that this community—that the community beyond our own vicinity, are anxiously waiting the issue of this trial. I am aware, that for the exercise of your good sense, of your reason, in the question of the guilt or innocence of these men, your motives will be assailed, your characters attacked, and the basest and vilest imputations cast upon you. But I rely confidently upon this jury, well knowing that against an independent, honest, high-minded jury, the torrent of abuse will be harmless; that like the rock of Gibraltar, which withstands the fury of the tempest, and the waves of the sea, as they beat against its base, so this jury will stand, proudly erect, high above the storm, while the waves of invective are dashing themselves to pieces at their feet.

Cowles for the People.

Gentlemen of the Jury,—It has become my duty, in closing the argument in behalf of the people, to bring to your minds considerations of duty, and not to distract your attention from the points in issue, or obscure the exercise of sound legal discretion. You have been chosen to stand between the people and the defendants, and while you are vigilantly to guard the rights of persons, you are also religiously to protect and preserve the interests of the government. Your verdict is to determine, whether law or licentiousness is to prevail; whether we are to live under the rule of law, or the "reign of terror." Your duty is one of great responsibility; for your verdict is to decide, whether the enactments of your Legislature, or the law of the lawless, is of greater authority. Your position is one which requires great firmness. You may be infected with that spirit, which has wrought deeds of dishonor, and violation to your laws and constitution; you may be infected with that spirit, which has caused a stain upon the character of this city, which the whole current of the mighty Mississippi cannot wash away; which has cast a blot upon the escutcheon of our State, that ages cannot efface. You may be infected with that spirit, which by the sanction it has given to the violent, illegal, and murderous acts, of the 7th of November last, has made the name of this city a by-word of reproach to all coming generations. Your verdict may legalize riot, may legalize arson, may legalize murder. If your verdict sanctions those acts, it will sanction any and every dishonor, which can disgrace civilized society

I trust, however, that almost in the words of one, whom many have delighted to honor, you, by your verdict, will say, that the government must be preserved; that you will prove true to your country, its laws and institutions; that you will prove true to your constitution, and that you will say, that whenever the evil passions of men burst out in crime, you will apply to them the corrective of the law. I trust that a jury of my citizens cannot be found, who are prepared to sanction these outrages; those acts of licentiousness, which have struck a vital blow to the best interests of this city, and defamed and disgraced the character of both its rulers and ruled.

But let us turn from considerations like these. And in the first place, permit me to remark, that you are not bound to return a verdict of guilty against all, if you find satisfactory evidence of the guilt of a part only, of those included in this indictment. If you come to the conclusion, that one or more of these individuals, are unjustly charged with the commission of this crime, and still find that any two or more of them are guilty, you can so return your verdict.

And what is the evidence? Some of the facts testified of before you, are not disguised. The sophistry, and shuffling of the counsel for the accused, could not avail in disguising them. They stand out in too strong relief to be disguised; as they were proved too plainly and distinctly to be denied.

Was the warehouse of Godfrey & Gilman entered with force and violence? Was the press of Godfrey & Gilman violently destroyed? And were such acts lawful? Because, gentlemen, it is no matter what principles that press was intended to promulgate. They will not entice the jury, although they inflamed an armed multitude. You, gentlemen, stand between the living and the dead. The voice of him, who would have spoken through that press, is hushed in the sleep of death; he cannot speak to you from the cold and silent tomb; he cannot speak to you of injured faith, of broken laws, of a violated constitution; he cannot speak to this community, of rights which have been trampled upon, or privileges which have been denied to him; he cannot speak to these men of laws which have been violated, and to those who were his fellow citizens, of duties which they may have disregarded. But by your voice, that press, and those lips may speak trumpet-tongued. It may be a voice which will calm excitement—call back tranquillity—restore confidence—uphold law—and invite population.

I trust that you all approach this case, conscious of the responsibility which rests upon each one of you; that you have banished prejudice from your hearts; that you feel a high resolve, to render life safe and property secure; and a noble determination to rally around the institutions of your country, and preserve inviolate your laws and your constitution. You have been told that the institution of a jury, is a noble institution; that it is the shield which protects and guards the rights of the humblest of us all; that it is the rampart behind which the citizen may defy the attacks of arbitrary power, and the barrier raised to protect him, from the assault of lawless force. Could the gentleman have forgotten, that these individuals, whose guilt you are now called to pass upon, broke down that bulwark, and overthrew that barrier? Could he have for-

13

gotten that these men usurped the authority of this tribunal, and overthrew the institutions, they themselves had aided to erect, when they said that that press should be destroyed?

Was that act lawful? Have the people of any village or city, have the people of any precinct or county, have the people of your whole State, a right to say what shall and what shall not be printed? because this is the question you are to decide. You must decide it; because, if you acquit these individuals, you admit that they were justified in the commission of this crime; and you say that a portion of the people may declare and determine what principles may be promulgated through the press, and what shall not.

Let me turn you to your Constitution, and in the 8th article of that instrument, I find that "the free communication of thoughts and opinions is one of the invaluable rights of man, and every citizen may freely speak, write, and print on any subject, being responsible for the abuse of that liberty." Responsible to whom? That same instrument also tells us that "no freeman shall be imprisoned, or deprived of his freehold, liberties or privileges, or outlawed, or exiled, or in any manner deprived of his life, liberty, or property, except by the judgment of his peers, or the laws of the land."

Who are a man's peers? You, as jurors! and only by you, as jurors, can a man's life, his liberty, his privileges, or property be taken away. If there are any who have constituted a different tribunal; who have established an arbitrary power; who have organized a different body, and, by force, have taken away the liberty, privilege, the property or life, of any other individual of the community, have they not usurped the province of your body, assumed the prerogative of law, and invaded the spirit and trampled upon the letter of your Constituiton? You must be jealous of any invasion of your province as a jury: you must be jealous of your prerogatives; you must be jealous of any violation of your Constitution: because, if you will not, if you do not preserve that instrument unharmed, where are your own rights? either of life, liberty or property? If you prove recreant to your duty; *if* you are false to the trust reposed in you, where is your redress when your own rights are violated? If you will not maintain the laws of your country, the case of Gilman yesterday, may be yours to-morrow; and like the murdered Lovejoy, when the authorized officers of the law are unable or unwilling to protect, you may be called upon to stand up, alone and unaided, and strike one blow for the defence of your own property and rights, against the lawless attack of an armed and infuriated rabble. And the press has been destroyed, because, in the exercise of a freeman's spirit, he who was to have given energy to its powers refused to surrender any of his rights to the dictation of a band of bravos. Take care, gentlemen, lest you so act that the same body, when offended to-day by the sound of a freeman's voice, by the feelings of a freeman's heart, by the expression of a freeman's thoughts, may strike the knife to his heart, and plead your special license for riot and pillage, for arson and murder, as their best excuse and sole justification. Europe has its nominal liberty of thought and speech, without the shadow of its reality. Germany, land hallowed by the memory of her literati of former days, has given to her princes dominion over the exercise of this invaluable right. France is once more under the rule of the Goths and Vandals; for her Council of Supervision, with their arbitrary power, not only suppress the expression of principles, in nonaccordance with their creed, when found in articles designed for instruction, but also when they appertain to those lighter works intended only for the amusement of an idle hour. The governments of these countries are arbitrary; they have established a supervision of the press, an inquisition of the mind. Tyranny suppresses all sentiments of liberty; and the land groans, and the peoole turn pale under such iron despotism. But in this government, your Constitution has made provision that the press should be free and uncontrolled, has said that the free communication of thought was an invaluable right of man, and that mind should be free as the mountain breeze. Your Legislature could not restrain the operation of that instrument; could not alter or take away the rights there guarantied. Yet a mob, an armed band of ruffians, have usurped that authority, and have said that a free communication of thought should not be allowed; that men's minds should be trammelled, if not by constitutional enactments, then by the strong arm of brute force; have said that the press should be destroyed, and that too, before it uttered one word by which its principles could have been ascertained.

The word of a mob has been almost undenied and undeniable law. With profane oaths they swore they would destroy that press; and amidst the cries of the battle field, with the shrieks of the wounded, and groans of the dying, by the light of the incendiary's torch, and over the dead bodies of their fellow citizens, they accomplished their purpose. By the blow which finished the destruction of that press did your own rights receive no wound? *The arm that was uplifted to break that press in pieces was raised to violate your Constitution.* Can you, gentlemen, as you are asked to do, sanction by your verdict the acts and the actors of that night, and to say God speed to the next violation of your rights and privileges?

Now who were concerned in these outrages? I admit that you must be satisfied, beyond a doubt, that the defendants are guilty, before you can convict them.

We have proved that the plan of destroying that press was not only long premeditated, but openly avowed.

Do you doubt the formation of such a resolution? It is written in characters no man can mistake; it is proved by evidence as plain as the existence of a noonday sun. Bear with me while I turn your attention to that point; while I show you that the individuals named in the indictment avowed their determination to do the act they afterwards accomplished.

The first witness to the point is West. He swears that he had a conversation with Solomon, that Solomon communicated to him the plan which had been determined upon; that he saw Beal, and had a conversation with him, in the course of which, and in reply to a request which he made, that Beal would use his influence to induce the "boys" to abandon their project, Beal said he could have no influence and would do nothing about it.

Now recollect the testimony of Mr. Krum, who tells you that Beal, while the mob were breaking up the press, said, Now boys we must stick together, and it any one is arrested we must come to his rescue. Beal had firearms by his side, and made this declaration, after the mob had accomplished the purpose for which they assembled, and which they had sworn they would do. Butler and Rock, too, stood by his side; they too were armed; and can you doubt that these persons were guilty?

Again, a company of fifteen or twenty armed men marched through your streets to Gilman's warehouse. Who were among them? Carr and Palmer addressed the Mayor when Bishop was shot. Rock, Butler, and Beal stood near, and Solomon was round, as is plainly proved by the testimony of the Mayor, Messrs. Robbins and West. Admit it is not proven that Nutter was among this company when their resolution of destroying the press was formed, or avowed. It is proved that he was apprised of the act that was to be done that night; that he left his home; that he travelled miles till he reached this city; that he was at the place of attack; and, finally, that he joined in the work of destruction. Why was he here at all? His presence is attempted to be accounted for by a story of an affair of gallantry, but the proof in the case affecting him is too strong to be overthrown by such slight pretext. If he was honest in his intentions, he, like honest old

13*

Tray, (spoken of by the Counsel for the accused the other day, when pressing the guilt of another person,) must suffer for associating with Tiger. Whether Nutter wanted the excitement which so powerfully influenced the others, and so kept back till he thought he could safely come forward, I know not. Certain it is, however, that he participated in the work of destruction which was going on.

Then in regard to Carr, Palmer, Rock, Butler, Beal, Solomon and Nutter, is there any doubt? They declared the press should be destroyed; they attacked the building in which it was; they entered that building; the press was destroyed; and one of them is proved to have assisted in its destruction; and is it not an irresistible inference that those who swore they would, actually did destroy it? Suppose a man's life is threatened, and lost? and you know that an enemy had threatened to take it away? are you not forced to the conclusion that the man who threatened he would, in reality did take his life? Miller swears to you that Carr, surrounded by his confederates, backed up by the presence of Rock, Bruchy, Butler, Palmer, and others, told Mr. Gilman that they would have the press at the risk of their lives; and will you doubt, after this avowal of their determination, upon the very spot of the violence, who destroyed the press? or will you doubt who entered the building? or will you doubt that both acts were done with force and violence?

Gilman swears that the defenders of that property abandoned the building for fear of their lives; and yet the Attorney General has told you that there was no force used in entering the building. But suppose a man comes to my house, presents firearms to my breast, demands my property, and, to preserve my life, I retire from it; abandon its defence. Is there no force in such case? Will the gentleman say that I surrendered my property of my own free will? Gentlemen, let us turn to the testimony of Mr. Krum; and what is it? He tells you that when he first reached the ground, he met a crowd carrying Bishop in their arms; that he asked what was the matter: that he was told one of their company was shot; that he asked their object; and that Carr said all they wanted was the press. Is there any doubt about their object? He proceeds, and says that he saw the mob breaking up the press; that he saw it thrown into the river; that Rock stood by with arms; that Beal said, "Now boys we must stick together, and if any of us are arrested we must come to the rescue."

And so with Mr. Robbins, who swears to you that these men avowed their detemination to have the press at all hazards; that they had arms in their hands at the time; and that he saw some of those within the walls of the building where the press was stored.

And as it regards Solomon, although he is not proved as having been conspicuous in the attack, still he was shot; and that I hold conclusive proof that he was engaged; because, with the exception of the men who, after their capitulation, were shot at while retreating, no one was shot unless he was engaged. The evidence, gentlemen, proves conclusively, that Butler, Carr, Jennings, Beal, Rock, Palmer, Morgan, Bruchy, Solomon, Nutter and Smith, were engaged in the commission of the offences for which they have been indicted.

Now, are the jury so incredulous as to believe that unless all went in—all threw out—and all broke up the press, none are guilty? Suppose some entered the building and threw out the press; others broke it up; and others stood by, encouraging and approving the doing and the violence, are they not all guilty? Suppose one man assaults another in the street, and a third person stands by refusing to aid, preventing others from assisting the man who is assaulted; would you say that they were not *both guilty* of the offence committed?

Then when we prove to you that these individuals swore that this act should be done—and also prove that the act was done, in the presence of these persons, some standing by encouraging those who were engaged in the work of violence, how can you help believing that all were guilty? how can you avoid returning a verdict of guilty against all?

The gentleman tells you of the danger of relying upon circumstantial evidence; and he has arrayed before you all the bugbears which he could conjure from a fertile imagination, to endeavor to deter you from relying upon the evidence which the people have brought against these men.

But we ask you to make no violent presumptions. We prove to you that these men determined this act should be done; that in pursuance of this determination they assembled together; that in the execution of their plan they assaulted the warehouse; that they forced its defenders to capitulate and fly for their lives; that these people entered the warehouse; that the press was seized by some one, and thrown out of the warehouse; that these persons destroyed it; and the gentlemen calls this evidence, such evidence as a jury cannot safely rely upon. Each fact by itself, it is true, is not sufficient to warrant you in convicting these men; but when the links are all united they form a chain of irresistible force; and all together form a conclusive whole.

You have been also informed by the Attorney General that there was no violence used, in entering this building; and because no doors were broken, you are asked to say that the first charge in the indictment falls to the ground. But I call to your recollection the declaration made by Mr. Gilman, that he left that building from fear that his life would be lost, if he remained longer. Suppose this declaration had not been made? We have proved that the windows were broken out; that the building was set on fire, and were those acts done without the application of actual force? Suppose Rock did not bring the fire which was applied to that building; some one else did; Rock stood by, saw it put to the building; encouraged the act, and was guilty of the violence used.

But it is not necessary that we should prove any actual violence; it is sufficient if we prove a constructive force. A constructive breaking is where by fraud, by trick of any kind, any entrance into a building is effected.

A constructive breaking, is where an entrance is obtained into another's building by threats or violence to the owner's person or property; *even though the owner should open the door, with his own hands, and let the individuals in; provided he did so from fear of actual violence.*

I will refer you to Archibald for the law which I have now given you, p. 258; and Starkie, 2d, p. 320.

Now, gentlemen, apply to this law Mr. Gilman's evidence. He swears to you, that he, and those that were with him, left that building from actual fear that their lives would be destroyed if they remained; and I ask you, whether if we have failed to prove an actual entering with force, we have not succeeded in proving a *constructive breaking, from the effect of threats and violence to this man's person or property.*

But the counsel for the accused have also said, that we have introduced no evidence that Gilman & Godfrey were the owners of the building, or the press.

It was testified to you, however, by Mr. Gilman, that he and his partner built the warehouse; and that they still had the possession and occupancy of it, and the Court ruled that proof of possession was sufficient to support the allegation of ownership, made in the indictment.

And as to the press, the jury will recollect, that when we asked of Mr. Gilman, whether he was not liable for that press, as a bailee, the attorney general objected to the question, and argued the point, but the Court would hear no reply from the counsel for the people, holding the law to be undeniable, that where property is alleged to be in any individual, and proof of a special property existing in the individual is offered, such proof shall be admitted, and shall be deemed sufficient evidence of the charge, which the indictment makes.

The attorney general, in his argument in defence of these men, admitted the correctness of this rule in civil cases, but denied its application to criminal charges.

You will find the law, as it is laid down in the books, in Archibald, pp. 32, and 176, which you will take with you in your retirement.

Mr. Gilman has sworn to you that Godfrey & Gilman took this property on storage; that they paid the charges upon it; that it was landed at, and stored in their warehouse. True it was consigned to Roff, but it never reached him; he had neither actual nor constructive possession of it, and therefore, it could not be considered, nor have been charged as his property. Godfrey & Gilman, however, had both actual and constructive possession, and the indictment charging the press as their property is well laid. There is no denying the law I have produced; there are no exceptions to the rules I have read; the whole current of authority supports the position I have laid down to you. We have, therefore, proved to you that there was an unlawful and violent act done; that these persons swore that they would do that act; and that they assembled for the purpose of carrying their threats into execution.

With proof of these facts, do I, speaking in the name of the people, ask you to do too much, when I ask you to observe the oaths you have taken; to regard the law and the evidence you have heard, and return a verdict of guilty? No force in entering that building! There was all the force which lawless violence, in the exercise of unregulated authority, under the excitement of unbridled passion could make; there was that force which compelled the owner of that property to abandon his castle and flee, for his life, from the hot pursuit of bravos bent upon murder. If the fire, or the powder, had actually burnt up or blown up that building, would there have been force? and was there none because the fire which was applied did not actually consume it to ashes?

No, gentlemen! the people have proved all they are bound to do; they have sustained all the allegations they have made, and having discharged the duty incumbent upon them, the counsel for the people now ask you fearlessly to perform that which is incumbent upon you. They ask you to stand up for your laws, and constitution, and put your frown upon this attempt to drown the voice of the law, by the louder uproar of an excited mob.

They ask you to believe these men guilty upon the evidence you have heard; upon the proof before you, that a plan to destroy that press was formed; that the place where it was stored was besieged, and attacked; that the windows were broken; that the building was fired; that from fear their lives would be sacrificed, the defenders abandoned the building; and that the press was destroyed, and destroyed by a portion of these very men; the remainder standing by with arms in their hands, ready to assist in the work of destruction, or resist any interference, or interruption, which might be offered to the full accomplishment of their purposes. Like the bundle of twigs which, separated from each other, a child might break; yet which when bound together, would resist a giant's strength; so is this evidence; separate the facts, and the proof they offer is weak and inconclusive; unite them, and they form irresistible proof of the guilt of these individuals. Thousands of cases are found in the books, where convictions have been had upon less conclusive, less satisfactory evidence.

Why the remark, we must stick together, and, if any one is arrested, all must rally for his rescue? What does the language mean? Why should it have been used? Why should the tongue of any man give utterance to such thoughts, unless he was conscious of guilt? What danger was there that these men would be arrested, unless they had committed an unlawful act? Why must they stick together, unless they were then casting about for some means of preventing the law from reaching its victims?

These are not the expressions of men conscious of innocence! No! they proceeded from one who knew he had violated the laws of his country. The conclu sion to which a candid, an honest and impartial jury must irresistibly be led, is, that these misguided men, who had worked themselves up to the belief that they were about to do a meritorious act; who falsely imagined, that when this deed was done, they should have suppressed abolition, and thereby rendered good service to their country; when the whirlwind of passion had passed, when the hour for reflection had come, realized the enormity of their guilt, and resolved to trample upon other laws than those they had already violated.

I am no abolitionist. I have no sympathy for the party; no communion with their creed. But I am a friend to law; an enemy to mobs; and an advocate for good order. I am opposed to the lawless acts of an unprincipled, an infuriated, a licentious mob. I am opposed to any resort to brute force, much more when it is resorted to to break down the barriers which the constitution has thrown around us all. Put down the freedom of thought! suppress the freedom of speech! restrain the freedom of the press! Lawless force cannot do it. The effort will be useless; the trial will be as idle, as was that when Canute the Dane planted his chair upon the sea shore, and commanded the waves to roll back from their appointed place. That effort was idle; but not more so than this one. The press still speaks out in tones of thunder, and it will speak out in tones that cannot be resisted, and in a language which cannot be misunderstood or disregarded. You cannot put down the press by force. I warn you; I warn all against such inconsiderate acts. Let abolitionists think if they please; let them speak if they choose; let them print if they will. Freedom of thought is the birthright, and freedom of speech the charter of every American citizen. Let him use his privileges, let him exercise his rights, "responsible to his peers and the law of the land."

This verdict will determine, for weal or for wo, the fate of this community. If lawless violence can be restrained; if it is ascertained that mobs shall not rule over us; if it is determined that licentiousness shall not prevail; that crime shall not be legalized among us, then all will be well; but, if the verdict of this jury is to sanction the deeds of violence and murder which have disgraced this city, then who will stay, or who come among us?

Remember that the eyes of this community, of the whole country are upon you; that the record of this trial will go to the world, and that upon yourselves it depends whether you are honored through coming ages as men, who, in an hour not without its danger, fearlessly asserted the prerogatives of law, or whether your names shall go down to all after time, as fixed figures for the hand of scorn to point his unerring finger at. I have an unyielding hope, an unshaken confidence that this jury will apply the law and the evidence as it should be applied. I have a firm belief that you will act well your duty to yourselves, your country, and your God; and that you will, so far as in you lies, remove the stain which now rests upon this community.

I throw the responsibility upon you; I have faithfully laid before you the law and the testimony; I have discharged with what ability I ought, the duty which devolved upon me; I wash my hands of the consequences; I throw from my shoulders the weight of responsibility which has rested till now upon them, and I lay it where the law has placed it, upon your heads. In your hands is the fate of the accused; the cause of

14

good order; the interests of society; and the mainten ance of the laws.

The Jury retired, and after waiting about an hour, the court adjourned; previously instructing the officer not to permit the jurors to separate unless they should agree upon a verdict. If they should agree during the evening, the verdict was to be sealed and placed in the hands of the clerk.

January 20th.

The Court met pursuant to adjournment, at 9 o'clock this morning. The jurors answered to their names as they were called.

The verdict of the jury (which had been given to the clerk the night before sealed) was declared to be, "Not Guilty," by Alexander Botkin, Foreman.

NOW IN PREPARATION,

AND WILL SHORTLY BE PUT TO PRESS,

TWELVE MONTHS IN ALTON,

Including a brief history of the City; the establishment of the Alton Observer; the first, second, third and fourth destruction of the Press by a Mob; and the death of the Rev. E. P. Lovejoy; with Views of the City, *and the position of the Warehouse of Messrs. Godfrey, Gilman & Co., from which the Press was taken.*

BY JOHN S. CLARK.

A

LEGAL ARGUMENT

BEFORE THE

SUPREME COURT OF THE STATE OF NEW JERSEY,

At the May Term, 1845, at Trenton,

FOR THE DELIVERANCE OF

4,000

PERSONS FROM BONDAGE.

BY ALVAN STEWART, Esq.,
COUNSELLOR AT LAW.

NEW YORK:
FINCH & WEED, 118 NASSAU STREET.

1845.

S. W. BENEDICT,
Stereotyper and Printer 16 Spruce Street.

PREFACE.

The public will not expect a preface to a disquisition on Constitutional Law, which can go far to encourage them, in the perusal of a legal argument; but when that public are informed that the argument was not to change the title to a farm, or test the Constitutionality of a bank charter, but that it was made for the deliverance of four thousand human beings from bondage, and to overthrow the Institution of Slavery in the State of New Jersey, further attempts at apology or to propitiate their kind perusal, would seem unnecessary.

Several distinguished gentlemen of the bar have been so kind as to wish to see this argument in a more perfect form than could be expected from the desultory notes of a reporter, which only glanced at some of the most important topics which formed the basis of discussion; to meet which desire, and contribute a single mite to the deliverance of my countrymen from Slavery, it is hoped, will insure the reading of the following pages.

A. S.

New York, June, 1845.

SLAVERY IN NEW JERSEY.

SUPREME COURT OF NEW JERSEY

THE STATE,
vs.
EDWARD VAN BUREN. } *Writ of Habeas Corpus.*

THE STATE,
vs.
JOHN A. POST. } *Writ of Habeas Corpus.*

Before the Justices of the Supreme Court of New Jersey,

THE HONORABLE CHIEF JUSTICE HORNBLOWER,

And Judges Associated, NEVIUS, CARPENTER and RANDOLPH.

E. P. PALMER, Esq., Petitioner for the Slave and Apprentice.

ALVAN STEWART, Esq., of the State of New York, Counsellor and Advocate for the slave and apprentice, admitted to argue these causes by the courtesy of the Court.

A. O. ZABRISKIE, Esq., of New Jersey, Counsel for VAN BUREN.

JOSEPH P. BRADLEY, of Newark, Counsel for JOHN A. POST.

These causes were argued before the Hon. Justices of the Supreme Court, at the Capitol in Trenton, on the 21st and 22d day of May, 1845. MR. STEWART occupied about eleven hours, and the defendant's counsel five hours, during two days and an evening.

The argument in these two causes, in behalf of *Mary Tebout*, held, in the first case, as property, until twenty-one years of age, her mother being a slave, and she being 19 years of age; and in the second case, *William*, a colored man, claimed by JOHN A. POST as a slave for life, being about sixty years of age. Returns to the Writs of Habeas Corpus were duly made on Wednesday, the 21st of May, 1845, in these causes respectively, before the Justices aforesaid. These writs had been granted on a previous day, on motion of ALVAN STEWART, Esq., in open Court.

The object of those writs was to test the institution of slavery in the State of New Jersey, which the Counsel for the slave and apprentice contended was abolished, by the first section of the Bill of Rights, in the new Constitution of this State, which went into operation the 2d September, 1844. The defendant VAN BUREN, by his Counsel, returned to said writ, that he held the said Mary Tebout, by means of several intermediate conveyances, from a person who owned the mother of said Mary; the said mother being a slave for life, and that the said Edward claimed to hold the said Mary, as his property, until she was twenty-one years of age, she now being nineteen years old, by virtue of a Statute, passed for the gradual abolition of slavery, in February, 1820, by which all slaves born previous to the fourth July, 1804, were slaves for life, and all children born of said slaves after 1804, were declared free, but to be held by the owners of their mothers as apprentices were; who were bound out by the overseers of the poor, males till twenty-five years of age, and females until twenty-one. The said male until twenty-five, and female until twenty-one, were held by the owners, their administrators and assigns, as property, or as other slaves are, until their time was out.

The return in the case of JOHN A. POST was the same in substance, that he held the said William, a colored man, as a slave by virtue of the law aforesaid, being born before 1804. To these returns general demurrers were put in, alleging the institution of slavery was abolished, and that the returns did not state sufficient authority to authorize the defendants to hold said persons To which there was a joinder in demurrer.

Both of these causes were argued together, depending on the same laws for their support, and for the purpose of obtaining a judicial decision, overthrowing the system of slavery in New Jersey, in all its parts. The following pages are intended to be the substance of the argument and reply of ALVAN STEWART, Esq., of New York, who appeared for the slave and servant, as their Counsel.

The first article of the new Constitution of New Jersey, of September, 1844, is entitled "RIGHTS AND PRIVILEGES."

"All men are by nature free and independent, and have certain natural and unalienable rights, among which are those of enjoying and defending life and liberty, acquiring, possessing and protecting property, and of pursuing and obtaining safety and happiness."

It was supposed there were from seven hundred to one thousand slaves, and from twenty-five hundred to three thousand servants or more, whose liberties were involved in the argument and decision of these causes, as well as the institution itself.

ALVAN STEWART, Esq., arose and invoked, as he said, the kind consideration of this Court, while he endeavored to break into a new, and almost uncultivated region, to explore and investigate the long neglected rights of man to his own body and soul. The Courts of our country had sounded the depths of human learning, and all the vast stores of history, and the remains of antiquity had been overhauled, sifted and analyzed, with metaphysical sagacity, to determine with judicial accuracy, all the rights which men had to property, lands and tenements, corporeal and incorporeal. Everything in the shape of human acquisition had been again and again labored and belabored by the highest talents of the land, until learning and genius could do no more, to add to man's possessions; while the great right of *man to himself*, while innocent *self-ownership*, under all circumstances, is a great question, which has rather been *grazed* than lifted up, shunned than embraced, or duly considered, in all its mighty amplitude, and its solemn importance; and then only at distant periods of time, and under the greatest disadvantage in point of time, place, position and circumstance. The controversies about lands and estates, and the personal rights of *freemen*, with all the subtle ramifications of the schoolmen, of various legal questions of our age, have been pressing the highest judicial forums of our land for decision, and constitute much of the drudgery of counsel, and labor of the judges. A modern legal opinion of counsel or judge is, that it is *his opinion* that he has clearly discovered what was the *opinion* of Chief Justice Mansfield, or Lord Thurlow, on this question, when Lord M., or Lord T. saw fit to express an *opinion* on this subject.

Considering the mighty questions of human liberty placed under the control of twenty-seven State Constitutions, their laws, and the Federal Constitution and acts of Congress, and the ten thousand forms in which human liberty may be abused, from the most horrible slavery, to the slightest invasion of a trespass; it seems passing belief, to be told, there is not one volume of reports, arguments and decisions, touching the great inalienable rights of man, invaded as they are, by communities, states and individuals, as a regular commerce carried on in crushed and violated human rights, assaulted in every direction, overthrown, trodden under foot as they are, at every step and angle of passing life. The attention of our countrymen seems to have been turned to the contingencies and appurtenances of our race, rather than to man, and the elevation of the race itself. Congress has shown more anxiety to protect the hats, the boots, and the coats which men wear, than the heads they cover, the bodies they surround, and the feet they enclose. That grave assembly can dispute from Christmas to dog-days, about the Tariff, Protection, Free Trade and Revenue, while a petition to abolish slavery in the District of Columbia, to give a man to himself, a wife to a husband, and children to their parents, is received with profound astonishment as a moral anomaly, and when the house has recovered from its surprise, the petition being so completely at right angles with the course of a republican Congress, that unread, unprinted, undebated, and undecided, it is ordered to lie upon the table, until the clerk removes it to its sepulchral silence in one corner of the Capitol, to rest with the other entombed memorials of a nation's dishonored humanity.

Nothing has been held so cheap as our common humanity, on a national average. If every man had his aliquot proportion of the injustice done in this land, by law and violence, the present freemen of the northern section would many of them commit suicide in self-defence, and would court the liberties awarded by Ali Pasha of Egypt to his subjects. Long ere this, we should have tested, in behalf of our bleeding and crushed American brothers of every hue and complexion, every new Constitution, custom, or practice, by which inhumanity was supposed to be upheld, the injustice and cruelty they contained, emblazoned before the great tribunal of mankind for condemnation; and the good and available power they possessed, for the relief, deliverance and elevation of oppressed men, permitted to shine forth from under the cloud, for the refreshment of the human race.

Yet these laws and constitutions should have long ere this felt the weight of judicial pressure, and their good or evil been made prominent to the men of America, and the breadth and depth of the stream of national justice ascertained, so that we might know the exact distance between our self-glorifications, or our pompous anniversaries, and the pretended magnitude of our personal liberties, as compared with the stern and inexorable mandates of judicial decrees; or what was the difference between an abstract dogma of liberty, and a practical decision of tyranny.

Alas! said Mr. S., how vast the distance between an abstraction and a practicality! Oh! when, said Mr. S., shall we see that glorious day, when the lion and the lamb shall lie down together? that day when the law, with its mercy, shall be extended to all, when none shall be so powerful as to override its injunctions, none so *low* as to fall beneath its merciful protection, defending all in their possessions; the rich man in his castle, the poor man in his liberty, and the value of his labor, whether in the wilderness, or the city, on the highway or in the closet; let this law of liberty brace the strong man on his journey, and its precious breathings fill the lungs of the infant in the cradle.

Oh! for the glorious day when we shall have freedom for all, wages for labor, education for all, mercy to all, justice for all, and God's religion in all!. Mr. S. said it was a horrid thought, that in the 19th century, there should be found educated men, who were so weak, or so ignorant, as to suppose the title to the great inalienable God-given rights of life, liberty, and the pursuit of happiness, depended upon the complexion of a human being, whether white, black, brown, red, or in combinations of these, with curled or long hair, thick or thin lips; the body is the casket, the soul, the immortal mind is the jewel. The jewels are homogeneous, the caskets may be infinitely diversified. To deny the existence of the jewel, from the caskets being more or less plain than some other we have seen (when we know the jewel is within), is not more absurd than to make a man's right to liberty depend upon the color of his skin. But, said Mr. S., such are the raw material of apologies for gross wickedness, and the vileness of the material is never improved by its manufacture. The raw material, its manufacture, the manufacturer, and the consumer of such strange productions, ought to be bottled and hermetically sealed, where they might be seen through a glass case as *certain lusus naturæ*, or as a calf with two tails and no head are seen in some of our museums.

In order, said Mr. S., to understand the blessings which the new constitution of this State confers on the subject of liberty, it may not be amiss to look, for a few moments, at the past ages of the world, on the subject of slavery, and see how the men of antiquity saw and treated this terrible perversion of human rights. The ancient world, before the advent of our blessed Saviour, was filled with this awful crime. All pagan lands abounded with idolatry and slavery. But the glorious new religion, wherever it made a lodgment, amidst cruel scourgings, the faggot and the flame, the block and the cross, the dungeon and the gibbet, obtained the ascendency; and this dreadful institution fell before the mercy of the cross. From the conversion of Constantine in the 4th Century, until the 12th, Christianity fought her victorious battle with slavery, and came off conqueror and drove it from the entire regions of continental Europe, or wherever Christianity obtained a foot-hold throughout Christendom. To be sure, said Mr. S., there existed, owing to the Feudal Law, a sort of serfdom, in some countries, which was different in appellation and character from the chattel-hood of slavery. Time fails, said Mr. S., to tell how the various devices of Pope, Pontiff, Bishops, ecclesiastical councils, decrees of councils, of kings, diets and parliaments, accomplished during what is called the dark ages—this most glorious work.

Said Mr. S., but the ever-memorable year of 1492 came for ever to be reckoned the most wonderful in the history of our race since our Saviour was born,—a new world was discovered by Christopher Columbus, the grandest man of his race.

The human passions burst into a mighty flame, fed by the accursed thirst of gold, discovery, and conquest. The peaceable and inoffensive red man of the islands of the Antilles was forced as slaves to do work in the fields and in the mines; and that age of innocent red men, a whole generation of which found that mercy in death, which their Spanish conquerors denied them. The good *Las Casas*, moved by a considerate sympathy for the red man, absurdly recommended to his prince and country, to repeal slavery as to the red man who could not endure its cruelty, and in lieu, *abduct and kidnap* laborers from the burning tropics of Africa; and from 1520 this dreadful wound was opened in the side of Africa, which has continued from year to year, and from century to century, to flow on without intermission, until this very hour. For more than 300 years has Africa been despoiled of her people by the kidnappers from the nations of Christendom, until Christendom in three centuries had made it the law of nations to rob the men of Africa of life, liberty, and the pursuit of happiness, and made and revived the extinct law of slavery, and with armed bands marched into defenceless villages on the Senegal and Gambia, set their habitations at midnight on fire, and with pistols, swords, fetters, and ropes, pursued and overtook the distracted people and bound and sent them to this continent amidst hunger, thirst, contagion, disease, and death, the survivors in the pirate's ship, and in a land of strangers, they were sold to drag out life on the plantation of the haughty, the thankless, and the cruel. By such deplorable means has this continent fought against her own prosperity.

Mr. Stewart then said he had two cases in his mind, which illustrated what all knew respecting slavery, and few whose opinions were entitled to respect would dare deny them.

Said Mr. S., lifting his head and turning to the north-east, directing all to look, and see what they could behold on the last day of November, 1620, on the confines of the Grand Banks of Newfoundland, Lo, I behold one little solitary tempest-tost and weather-beaten ship, it is all that can be seen on the length and breadth of the vast intervening solitudes, from the melancholy wilds of Labrador and New England's iron-bound shores, to the western coasts of Ireland and the rock-defended Hebrides, but one lonely ship greets the eye of angels or of men, on this great thoroughfare of nations in our age. Next in moral grandeur, was this ship, to the great discoverer's; Columbus found a Continent; the May-flower brought the seed-wheat of states and Empire. That is the May-flower, with its servants of the Living God, their wives and little ones, hastening to lay the foundations of nations in the occidental lands of the setting sun. Hear, the voice of prayer to God, for his protection, and the glorious music of praise, as it breaks into the wild tempest of the mighty deep, upon the ear of God. Here in this ship are great and good men. Justice, mercy, humanity, respect for the rights of all; each man honored, as he was useful to himself and others; labor respected, law-abiding men, constitution-making and respecting-men; men, whom no tyrant could conquer, or hardship overcome, with the high commission sealed by a spirit Divine, to establish religious and political liberty for all. This ship had the embryo-elements of all that is useful, great and grand in Northern institutions; it was the great type of goodness and wisdom, illustrated in two and a quarter centuries gone bye; it was the good genius of America.

But, look far in the south-east, and you behold on the same day in 1620, a low rakish ship hastening from the tropics, solitary and alone, to the New World, what is she? She is freighted with the elements of unmixed evil, hark! hear those rattling chains, hear that cry of despair and wail of anguish as they die away in the unpitying distance. Listen to those shocking oaths, the crack of that flesh-cutting whip. Ah! it is the first cargo of slaves on their way to Jamestown, Virginia. Behold the May-flower anchored at Plymouth rock, the slave ship in James river. Each a Parent, one of the prosperous labor-honoring, law-sustaining institutions of the North; the other the Mother of slavery, idleness, lynch-law, ignorance, unpaid labor, poverty, and duelling, despotism, the ceaseless swing of the whip, and the peculiar institutions of the South. These ships are the representation of good and evil in the New World, even to our day. When shall one of those parallel lines come to an end?

Mr. Stewart then proceeded to the definition and origin of the word slave. He cited the encyclopedia under title, slave, as authority. The word, according to Vossius, is derived from *sclavus*, the name of a Scythian people, called the Sclavoni. The Romans called slaves *servi*, from *servare*, to *keep* or *save*, being such as were not killed in battle, but were saved, to work or yield money. A slave bred in a family was called *verna*, hence our word *vernacular*, or the slave's tongue.

A Roman slave being set free, took the cognomen of his master for his sur or sir-name, and his slave name for his Christian—hence, our sur-name means the name of the lord or sir. So curiously has slavery interwoven itself in the affairs of men, that all men are made most singularly to feel the disgrace of the institution in their paternal name. The Romans had those called *mercenarii*, who had been rich, but having become poor, sold themselves for a time.

The Greeks had those called Prodigals, who, having lost their estates by their extravagance, were sold to discharge their debts by law, for a longer or shorter time. Delinquents to the revenue, or unfaithful subtreasurers of the Roman Empire, were sent to the oar as slaves. But Tacitus describes the most remarkable slaves, De Moribus Germanorum, called enthusiasts, who were gamblers, who having staked and lost their money, goods and lands, finally staked their own bodies, and if they lost, the strong and the young lifted up their hands and received the fetters thereon, from the aged and weak, and were marched off forthwith to the slave market and sold by the winner as slaves for life. This was done under the code of a gambler's honor.

Those are the two kinds, among the ancients, of slavery, voluntary and involuntary. Some think slavery did not exist before the Flood. But Alexander Pope thinks differently, and says:

> "Proud Nimrod first the bloody chase began,
> A mighty hunter, and his prey was man."

A man has no right to sell himself, and if he had, he could not bind his posterity. A man is not allowed to kill himself.—*Blac. Book* 1, C. 14. *Montesquieu Spirit Laws*, B. 15, C. 2, and 6.—Both say, if a man might be taken in war and made a slave, this war-right of the captor could not extend to the captive's posterity. This alone would abolish slavery. The Romans exercised the power of life and death over a slave. So do slaveholders in the United States under certain circumstances; if the slave refuse to work, he, the master, may, by slave law, whip and beat him until he is dead, unless he submits to go to work; or if a slave attempt to run away, and the master commands him to stop, and he refuses, the master may shoot him down, and the slave laws of more than ten States say, *amen*. The Romans were very cruel, and had an Island in the Tiber, where by law, they might send *old, useless and sick* slaves to starve to death or die. It is said as an evidence of slavery's hardening of the heart to human suffering, that the elder Cato sold his superannuated slaves for any price rather than maintain them. The Romans had slave dungeons under ground, called "ergastula," where the slaves were worked in chains. The same in Sicily, which country was cultivated by slaves in chains. Eunus and Athenio excited an insurrection of 60,000 slaves and broke up the dungeons.

But we are more immediately interested in the light in which our English ancestors viewed these great questions of human rights, and we have derived most of our ideas of law and liberty from that interesting source. The case of Somerset, to be found in the 20th Vol. of British State Trials, also in Long's Reports and Burrows', is one of manifold interest. It was justly said by that great lawyer and civilian, Mr. Hargrave, the counsel of the slave Somerset, though greatly aided in his brief by that eminent philanthropist, Granville Sharp, "that slavery corrupts the morals of the master by freeing him from those restraints so necessary for the control of the human passions, so beneficial in promoting the practice and confirming the habit of virtue." It is often dangerous to the master, as exciting implacable resentments on the part of the slave.

Said Mr. Stewart, slavery communicates all the afflictions of life to its victim without leaving scarce any of the pleasures; it depresses the excellence of the slave's nature, by denying to the slave the ordinary means of improvement and elevation in the social scale of existence; it brings forth the gross, malignant, cruel, mean, deceitful and hypocritical portions of human nature, without a counterpoise or a power of suppression. The slave is always the natural and implacable enemy of the State, he owes it nothing but deadly hate.

Said Mr. S., instead of the Constitution and the laws being his shield and his inheritance, they are employed to strip him of his natural rights, of life, liberty and the pursuit of happiness, existing antecedent to all human compacts; and what should be employed for his protection and defence in the shape of law, is used for his prostration and destruction. It is the element of constant fear to the family and the State, and is therefore real weakness to the State from the constant apprehension from insurrection at home, or invasion from abroad, when it is always expected the slave will range himself in the ranks of the invader of the land. The slave has no country, no real home for which he will fight. Judge of the surprise of General La Fayette, said Mr. S., when on the first day of being introduced to the American Congress in Philadelphia, in the summer of 1777, he listened to the extraordinary request of South Carolina to be released from raising and equipping the quota of troops designed by Congress to be raised by that State as her proportion in the eventful struggle of the Revolution, on the ground if she spared that number of troops from the State, it was feared that there might be a servile insurrection, that it was necessary the troops should remain at home to restrain a domestic enemy in her own bosom. If all the States had been under the weight of slavery like South Carolina, our Independence could never have been achieved. Such States as South Carolina may bluster and threaten their brethren in time of peace with nullification and revolution, but when war comes, her power to act out of her own territory will be in the inverse ratio of the noise and threats she made in time of peace. The enemy of her own household will furnish a good market, not only for her capabilities but her courage. If the home market is the best one, she will find one at her own door, as ample as her productions may be abundant.

In the late war, about midsummer of 1814, this nation, said Mr. S., was overwhelmed with shame, grief and astonishment, at the capture and sack of the city of Washington, by a body of British troops, soldiers, sailors and marines.

The public authorities had sufficient notice of the enemy's intention, the militia of the three cities of the District, and of the surrounding counties in the adjacent portions of the old States of Virginia and Maryland, could have driven the British force into the sea, had not a report been universally circulated on the morning of the battle, and on the battle-ground at Bladensburgh, that the slaves of the District and of the adjacent counties, from which the militia were drawn for the defence of Washington, were to rise that day in insurrection during the absence of their masters. The moment the British approached our troops, President Madison, with the Secretaries of the Departments, fled from position to position, abandoning, as all who know the ground, one favorable place after another, and finally retreated eight miles from Bladensburgh to

Washington, and at last the retreat became a general rout; each man having his mind on the danger he feared in his own house or plantation from the insurrection of his slaves, rather than the immediate work of defending the Capitol of the nation. This, said MR. S., is a perfect solution of that disgraceful affair. It was the natural consequence which the weakness of a servile population creates, and the fear in a day of adversity which it will inspire.

MR. S., said he learned the cause of our disaster in 1818, while going over the ground of this disgraceful retreat, with a General, who was a Brigadier on that mortifying day, who assigned the above reasons to MR. S., as the cause of this most shameful result.

MR. S. said, John Locke declared a right to preserve life is inalienable, that freedom from the exercise of arbitrary power is essential for the exercise of this right.

Said MR. S., in the sixth year of the reign of Edward III., 1334, a law was enacted declaring that all idle vagabonds should be made slaves, fed on bread and water or small drink, and *refuse meat*, and should wear an iron-ring around their necks and legs, and should be compelled by beating, chaining and otherwise, to perform the work assigned, were it never so vile; the spirit of the English nation could not brook this, as applied to the most abandoned rogues, and repealed the law in two years after its enactment. But nothing places the judiciary of England on higher ground, than its patient work in extirpating villeinage from England. It was an institution connected with the feudal system, and the Norman Conquest of 1060, and the other conquests obtained in previous ages, and was nearly allied to slavery, in everything but the name, so that it is supposed at one period, there was not less than three quarters of the population of the kingdom, who were either villeins regardant, or villeins in gross. The dishonor of such a state of things has been so deeply felt by thousands, who are descendants of these bondmen in England, and who now rank high in the scale of society, that there is rather a desire to conceal than reveal the odious state in which our ancestors existed; therefore, David Hume and Sir William Blackstone are very niggardly in dealing out information on an infamous and obsolete institution, so humiliating to our ancestors, and humbling to their descendants.

But, said MR. S., to understand the terrible hardships endured and suffered by our ancestors, for many generations, and the glorious way of their deliverance by the judges of England, may furnish us with valuable deductions, which may be applied to solve any difficulty growing out of the causes under consideration, by learning what use a court may make of *law* to establish justice.

A villein in blood and by tenure was one whom the lord might whip and imprison. The villein could acquire no property except for the lord. "*Quidquid acquiritur servo, acquiritur domino.*" A villein regardant passed with the land of his lord, on which he lived as a kind of property like the trees, but might be severed and sold when the lord pleased.—*Co. Littleton* 117 *a.* If he was a villein in gross, he was an hereditament, or chattel real, according to the lord's interest, being descendable to the heir, when the lord was absolute owner of the soil, and to the executor, when the lord was possessor for only a term of years. The common law held if both parents were villeins, or the father only, the issue were villeins. The child at common law followed the condition of the father, *Partus sequitur patrem;* while the civil law held, *Partus sequitur ventrem.* Therefore, it was a departure from all principle, for the slaveholders of the United States, who if they inherited anything from England it was the common law, to substitute the principle of the civil law, because they could make more money by it, and say the child in slavery should follow the condition of the mother, when the common law said it should follow the father! But why reason on a subject, when brute force and selfishness stand in the place of right reason and truth? Had, said Mr. S., the doctrine of the common law been followed, slavery from its *mulattoism* a significancy of the times, would have been in its *last quarter*. The object, said Mr. S., of drawing this all but obsolete learning from past centuries, was not to make a public parade for the sake of its strangeness; but to show in the great struggle, in past ages, between slavery and liberty, how the judiciary of England conducted itself in those encounters between the powers of light and darkness.

The Courts of Law in the British Isles, from the Conquest down, employed every intendment of humanity, every device, every fiction, in behalf of the unfortunate serf. One rule was for the court always to presume in favor of liberty; but in some thirteen States of our Union, if a man is of African descent, he is presumed a slave, until the victim proves a negative. In England the *onus probandi* lay on him who asserted slavery or villeinage to prove it. If a villein prosecuted a writ of *Homine Replegiando* against his lord, on the trial the lord had to prove affirmatively the plaintiff was his villein, and the villein, though the plaintiff, might stand still in court till that was done by the defendant. The lord's remedy for a fugitive villein was the writ *Nativo Habendo*, or *Neifty*. If the lord seized the villein by his writ of *Nativo Habendo*, the villein procured the writ of *Homine Replegiando*, or *Libertate Probanda*.

By the writ of *Nativo Habendo*, the master asserted slavery, and if the master was *once nonsuited*, he could never sue the serf again, and the villein might plead the record of nonsuit as a perpetual bar. Not so, if the poor villein was nonsuited on the writ of *Homine Replegiando*, or *Libertate Probanda*. He might sue again for his liberty, and the record of nonsuit, if made ten times or more against him, could never be pleaded or used against him. The slightest mistake on the part of the lord, or accident, was laid hold of by the court to defeat the recovery of the lord.—*Somerset's Case*, 20th vol. of Haswell's State Trials. So this honorable court of New Jersey should do, said Mr. S., under the new constitution of this State—the constitution adopted by the people in 1844. This court, in accordance with the noble example of England's judiciary, should make every intendment in behalf of your bondmen, as between the selfish and cruel demand of slavery and the ceaseless cry of liberty. Give the slave the benefit of every sensible doubt, which may cloud the mind of this Honorable court.

Sueing, or being sued by a villein, freed him. The lord's granting him an imparlance, manumitted him, or asking an imparlance of the villein did the same. Almost, said Mr. S., the last case of villeinage reported, was near the year 1600, on the accession of James I. Crouch's case is reported in Dyer. All of these obstructions thrown in the way of this sort of slavery, are most interesting legal relics of servitude, showing the metaphysical dress in which it was clothed by our subtle and ingenious ancestors. These were patterns of extinct fashions of opinions, now only to be found in the ponderous tomes of antiquity, garnered up in the library of the legal antiquarian; as the visors, steel and brass armor, of the 10th century, disclose to us the mode and appearance of the knights on the field of battle in the days of chivalry.

To establish villeinage, the villein must be proved such by two other male villeins, *ex eodem stirpe*, from the same stock, or the villein might confess in open court, being a court of record, that he was one. The female villein was not allowed her testimony to prove a man a villein. A villein was called *nativus*, as well as *villanus*, from the lord's villa, *nativus* from being found on the soil—a native. The lord, on declaring on a writ *nativo habendo*, had to bring his two witnesses with him at the same instant he declared, and if he did not, the villein went for ever free. A man might plead bastardy, in himself, father, grandfather, or ancestor, and if the plea be true, that alone manumitted the villein, for the *filius nullius est filius populi.* For if there was a link of illegitimacy, it set the line of descendants from the bastard free, because the lord could not show that he was the son of his bondmen in particular.

Another plea of the villein was called *adventiff* by the Norman French Law, showing that a person was born off from the *manor*, and if true, it set the man and his descendants free.

Said Mr. S., Sir Thomas Grantham, about the year 1684, bought a monster in the East Indies, and brought him to England as a show. The monster had growing on his breast, the entire parts of a child, except its head. The monster being carried through the kingdom as a show, was baptized, and he brought a writ of *Homine Replegiando* against his master, and was set free.

Said Mr. S., I have done with villeinage in England,—such in a dark age was the view which learned jurists and judges took of this important matter. The judiciary in many countries have been, at different periods of civilisation, the last branch of human government, to feel the force of popular opinion, in behalf of liberty, or employ its power in accelerating the march of freedom, or the overthrow of strongholds of fortified oppression. It is not, said Mr. S., a matter of complaint that the judiciary is the *hold-back power* of the State, or conservative in its character, but with all that, it has a high mission to discharge on the part of liberty. And the English judiciary have shown the world during those dark ages what they understood to be contained in their commissions, touching England's bondmen, even, under the iron rule of the haughty Norman and his imperious descendants, who, by rights of conquest, and by the subserviency of supple parliaments connected with the agency of the Feudal System, had reduced four-fifths of the inhabitants of England to the condition of villeins regardant, and villeins in gross, attached to the soil, or the person of some grandee of the realm, as slaves, whom their lord might scourge, sell, or transfer with the soil, or at will.

The judiciary of England became the Temple of Mercy to which these unfortunate bondmen cast their imploring eyes for relief through a succession of five cruel centuries, during eighteen generations of men The courts of English law during this long period, employed all the subtleties, fictions, and presumptions, in which the English Law abounds, in behalf of the liberty of these grossly injured men, so that at last, the sublime moral spectacle was presented to this world, of many unrepealed statutes, and the common law still in full force in favor of villeinage, while the bloody useless fetters hung on the tyrant's dungeon walls, but the last bondman of the three-fourths of the population of a mighty kingdom was enfranchised from captivity by force of England's glorious judiciary alone. The king, and iron-mailed barons, the land owners, and man-holders, were foiled, and their prey taken from their power by the resolution of the judges, who, being determined, did administer *justice through the law.*

Montesquieu says that Aristotle, in reasoning to sustain slavery as derived from war, cites authorities from barbarous ages, and appears in this matter as unphilosophical as he does in the nature of the thing. The war-power to be the source of a right, when the war is prosecuted for no other motive except the value of the captive, is as rational as to give the robber title to his spoil, because he had the courage to take it—making a crime the most bold and daring, the parent of a civil right. Behold bleeding Africa, for three hundred years her bleeding side has flowed, and yet flows on, unstaunched by the humanity of the Nations. Behold this accursed crime which has crawled up with beastly impudence, and enthroned itself as one amongst the laws of Nations. *Laws of Nations!* What was this law of Nations? That Christendom had a common right to plunder, burn, murder, enslave irredeemably, and make property of the inhabitants of that ill-fated continent, in and through all coming generations of their posterity. A *law* of *Nations!* that all law, justice, mercy, humanity, should be suspended, as to one quarter of the globe; a *law* of *Nations*, that piracy, murder, fraud, arson, kidnapping, ravishment and stealing, should be considered lawful as an injunction of the law of Nations, to be honored and obeyed. A law of Nations directly at war with every other law constituting that code; a law of Nations, striking justice down, and sending it into eternal banishment from the world, subverting the decalogue of God, blaspheming Omnipotence, brandishing the powers of perdition in the face of the Allseeing, calling this bold defiance of the Almighty, the law of Nations! Out upon such infinite perversion, such inexpressible criminality. Russia, Prussia, Holland, Austria, England, France, Sardinia and the United States, in the last forty years, as it regards themselves, by treaty and legislation; have abolished their respective portions in this frightful law of Nations, while Spain, Portugal and Brazil, three of the basest kingdoms of earth, are now retrograding into the darkness of barbarism and infamy, and without competition are now almost the exclusive proprietors of this law of Nations and its abounding criminality. Look at Spain three hundred and fifty-three years ago, as she stood on the day of Columbus' discovery, head and shoulders above the powers of Europe. Conquest, avarice, slavery and idleness, which she introduced to the New World, re-acted on her, and in our day, she has been stripped of her mines, her provinces, viceroyalties, kingdoms and one half of a continent, and is now reduced to the Island of Cuba, with its crimes of flowing blood, slavery, idleness and avarice; these relatives have been punished in so signal a manner, in the case of Spain, by Him who rules the destinies of Nations, that to deny it, is a proof that our ignorance is only surpassed by our infidelity.

The Court will pardon me in these remarks, which in the first instance may appear remote from this question, yet when we consider the character of the human mind, they will all be found to bear on the great question in the Constitution of this State. What do we mean by liberty and independence? Infinitely absurd to say, a man has power even in himself, by contract, to dispose of his own liberty and all the rights he possesses. Society has claims on him, his wife, his children, and his God, which he cannot cancel by selling himself to another. Yes, coming generations have a voice in the question. He has no more right to sell his body than he has to commit suicide, for, by so doing, he passes from manhood to thing, or chattel-hood, and becomes a piece of breathing property. The great rights of manhood are not given to us by our Creator, to give, sell, and barter away. The powers of life, liberty, and the pursuit of happiness, cannot be resigned to a power inferior, to that of the one, from *whom* they have been received.

As to consideration that might be given for those God-inherited rights, described in your Constitution, said Mr. S., as unalienable, who is rich enough to buy them, who is able to make title to them? Suppose that some Crœsus owned this continent, and the mines of Golconda, and should offer them to me to become his slave, according to the laws of South Carolina and Louisiana; at the same instant, he executes for the consideration of my person, a deed of the continent and mines to me, and I execute to him a deed of my body. The purchaser of me, by the operation of the slave laws, instantly becomes repossessed of what passed to me by grant, under the maxim that the slave and all he hath, or may find or acquire, belongeth to the master, therefore, I the slave would say the consideration having failed, and by operation of law, my master having become re-seized of his continent and mines, I am free again. Thus, it would be found impossible to make a bargain resting upon equity, for the sale of one's person, as the whole subject revolves in a circle of never-ending absurdities, justice leaving the parties where it found them: man with equal success having attempted to quadrate the circle, create perpetual motion, and make a contract for the sale of a man, by his own agreement, on consideration of value for value received by the slave upon the principles of slaveholding law! If a man could not perform the act of making himself a slave, how could another do it for him, or a state or a government, without doing an act repugnant to that law of nature spoken of in the first article of your new Constitution? When, said Mr. S., I applied for these writs of *Habeas Corpus* some days since, to one branch of this court, it was remarked by one member of the court, that this case would require great consideration from its effect on the towns of this State, as it might subject said towns to the maintenance of worn-out, aged and infirm slaves, in the shape of paupers. That contingency is possible, said Mr. S., but forms no ground against awarding to the bondmen, that constitutional justice, so long withheld by the consent of these towns, as well as the avaricious masters. It was argued in the Somerset case by Mr. Dunning, the Counsel of the claimant of Somerset, that if this slave was set free by the judgment of the court, there were then at large fourteen thousand slaves in England, belonging to gentlemen in the West Indies, who, for their own convenience, had brought them to England, and valuing them at £50 per head, they would amount to £700,000, or $3,500,000. What was the memorable reply of Lord Mansfield? It was, "that a man's natural relations go with him *everywhere*, his municipal to the bounds of the country of his *abode*." And in answer to the suggestion of a loss by the proprietors of the 14,000 negro slaves in England, said Lord Mansfield, "*we have no authority to regulate the conditions on which law shall operate.*" We cannot direct the law, the law must direct us."

So, said Mr. Stewart, the *argumentum ab inconvenienti* should not apply in this case. If these slaves have been worn out by the consent of the public, if that public have folded their arms in silence, and witnessed the robbery of these men, from year to year, of their earnings (which might have supported them in the evening of life), it is right they should support them when they can toil no more in the enjoyment of their just liberty. For it is always dangerous for men to see liberty struck down in others, and because they do not taste its bitterness personally, passively to look on without resistance. It will sooner or later strike back on themselves. That man is not worthy of liberty, who will not fly to the rescue of his brother when he sees his freedom struck down or assailed. Our liberties are always invaded when the humblest individual is deprived of his, without our making all the resistance within our power. At the time of the argument of the Somerset case, in 1771, the world was full of slavery, especially the West Indies, and the colonies of this continent—it was tolerated in all. But behold what may be done by the indomitable perseverance of one man, if that man be Granville Sharpe. He was a gentleman of small means, but of a great heart, and had for some time made the study of human rights a subject of great consideration. He had read, thought, and written in their behalf, and was the prosecutor who interested himself for Somerset, the slave of one William Stuart, a West India planter, and prepared much of the brief of Mr. Hargrave, and obtained the writ of *Habeas Corpus*, returnable in the court of King's Bench, at his own expense. The court heard the argument patiently the live-long day, and decided against the slave, on the authority of a case in 1749, in Lord Hardwick's and Lord Talbot's time. Nothing discouraged Granville Sharpe; at the next term he brought up Somerset a second time, and the question was so important, the court heard the argument a second time, and decided as before against the slave. Poor Granville Sharpe still contended that a slave "could not breathe in England," and having spent months in deep study, upon the law of England, though a layman, he brought up Somerset for the third time before the court of King's Bench which had Lord Mansfield for its chief, who did not meet poor Sharpe and his counsel with a rebuke for his unconquerable fanaticism and obstinacy, nor did the court throw down the common impediment to the march of mind and further consideration, by saying "*res adjudicata*," "*res adjudicata!*" No! where human liberty was concerned, or the great rights of self-ownership staked upon human reasoning and judicial determination, Lord Mansfield was not in haste to say "we have decided against human nature." The cause was argued a third time for a day in Westminster Hall, and Granville Sharpe had, since the last argument, descended into the deepest wells of English liberty and brought up a draught of the waters of life, liberty, mercy, and law, so pure, that when it was commended to the lips of the judges, they were made wise, the scales fell from their eyes, and they saw in its length and breadth the mighty truth beaming on the forehead of justice herself,—"that slaves cannot breathe in England," and the light of that day has shone on with increasing strength and beauty, until we can now say, that the sun which never sets upon the realms of the British Empire, beholds in his circuit through the heavens, no slave to crouch beneath her vast illimitable power.

But oh! what shall we say of the sublime humanity of Lord Mansfield and his compeers, who were not afraid to confess they had been wrong, and had the magnanimity to say it before a slaveholding age? This day saw the longest stride which British greatness ever took on the highway of human glory.

Would to Heaven, said MR. S., that all courts might imitate the illustrious example in administering justice in the sublime humility, which dignified the court and exalted our kind, as in the case of Somerset! The great principles established in the Somerset case awakened the philanthropy of England, and put forth its strength in 1783, '88, '92, '96, '97, and finally, in 1806, was successful in the abolition of the African slave trade by Parliament. Wilberforce, Pitt, and Fox were foiled again and again, in Parliament, the theatre of their eloquence, and seat of their power, but justice finally prevailed. This was the first great blow struck for the man of Africa, in three hundred years from the beginning of his American and West Indian enslavement. But from that day, the vindication of his rights has been *onward*. Congress, in 1774, recommended the *ceasing* of the African slave-trade in December, 1775, but it was not abolished until Jan., 1808, by a law passed the March before, in 1807. Three acts of Congress were passed in 1814, 1820, and in 1824, increasing the penalties against transgressors, until it finally declared all who were engaged therein, were pirates, and subject to the pirate's doom. An act of Congress passed in 1787, declared involuntary servitude, or slavery, should never exist in the North Western Territory, comprising the present States of Ohio, Indiana, Illinois, Michigan, and the Territories of Wisconsin and Iowa. These early acts of national legislation show which way the mind of the nation pointed at *this* time.

A slave is a rational human being, endowed with volition and understanding, like the rest of mankind, and whatever he lawfully acquires

2

and gains possession of, by finding or otherwise, is the acquirement and possession of his master.—4 *Dessaus.*, 266. 1 *Stewart Rep.*, 320—*s. p.* A slave cannot contract matrimony; their earnings and their children belong to the master.—*Slave-Law.* Indians are held as slaves in New Jersey.—*Halstead's Rep.*, 374.

Behold the shameful injustice of the Law of Slavery.

If it be found by a jury on inspection, that the person claimed to be a slave is white, the claimant must prove him a slave or he will go free; but if the jury find the person to be of African descent, the law of slavery presumes the person a slave, by whomsoever he may be claimed, and the burden is thrown on the alleged slave to prove a negative, that he is *not* a slave.—*Wheeler's Law of Slavery*, 22. The owner of a female slave may give her to one person, and the children she may thereafter have to another!—*Law of Slavery*, 2. A slave cannot be a witness before any Court or Jury against a free white in the land for the greatest injustice. This is one of its most horrible features.

Look, said Mr. S., to the case of an alien-white-child. Suppose her to be the daughter of parents of the lowest class of those who migrate from Ireland to America, and that these parents should die on their passage over the Atlantic, leaving to the mercy of New Jersey Laws, and the good people of Perth Amboy, their daughter, twelve years old, who cannot read or write, barefooted, destitute and friendless. Under your laws, the Overseers of the poor bind her out, to the Mayor of Trenton; she has lived with this rich, popular and influential citizen but one little month; when by violence she is dishonored, by her master, the Mayor. Is he safe from the retributions of justice? Is she deprived of her oath? No. She comes friendless and lonely, and knocks at the door of your Grand-Jury-room. Humble and feeble as is that knock, it is quickly heard by the acuteness of humanity's ear. She enters the vestibule of the great temple of justice, and immediately the majesty of the entire law of the land, not only of New Jersey but of this vast Empire, stands in its mighty invisibility around for her protection, ready to be revealed in its power. She is invited, on oath, to tell the story of her wrongs, the indignant Grand-Jurors listen and believe, and find a bill against the Mayor; she goes and comes under the law's broad shield. This haughty man is found by the officers of the law, is arrested by its power, and brought before a Court to plead to this indictment. He is tried; a second time, she, the friendless, comes and tells the tale of her dishonor; confiding justice, humanity, loving and honoring men believe her story; he is convicted and attempts to fly the power of the State and Union, which is by that child's oath already set in motion, and will prevail against money and mobs of rescue, all of these cannot save the big criminal from the vengeance of the law; to the Penitentiary, for ten long years, he must and does go; yes, the merciful majesty of the law shines gloriously on the head of the friendless foreigner. This is being born free and independent by the law of nature, under your Constitution.

But not so of the poor injured slave, man or woman, native born though they be, however cruel or terrible the wrong inflicted on them, by their owner or other free man, the slave is not to be heard to tell his or her story, however true, before any human tribunal in the land against a free white person. Is this being free and independent by the law of nature? Is this possessing the safety and happiness described in the first Article of the New Constitution, which your organic law declares to be the portion of all, of woman born? Slavery imports perpetual obligation to serve another! Does that look like being free and independent?

Slavery, said Mr. S., is so abhorrent to all justice and mercy, that all the intendments of law and justice are opposed to it; so that the legal writers of slave countries say that it can only exist by force of positive law. The *lex scripta* must be its foundation, and that I think you no longer have. The *lex scripta* must be the source of all of its mischievous power, which one human being can exercise over another, by making a fellow-being his slave, his chattel. The foundation of slavery which sprang up in our colonies, had, as a general rule, nothing but the barbarous custom of a few inhuman planters, in its origin, which custom was one within legal memory, and ran not back to that unsurveyed point of antiquity, transcending all human memory, where its source was hidden in the night of byegone ages. It has not that common law authority for its support, which was supposed to be handed down from generation to generation, in the libraries of judges and lawyers, as copies, as some conjecture, of obsolete, worn-out and extinct statutes. As the soul survives the body, so it is supposed these customs called common law, are the souls or spirits of departed statutes, the tomb-stones and graves of which can no longer be found. *Cineres perierunt.* But their imperishable souls still remain to guide and direct us on the journey of life, and as far as they speak in the language of authority over this land, they forbid in trumpet-tongues, the existence of this vile institution of slavery

Institution of slavery! Institution of horse-stealing, institution of gambling, and the institutions of highwaymen, sound equally sensible, to a just and philosophical thinker. But slavery is within the memory of men, so far as its advent to the New World is concerned. We track it from the middle passage to this hour, from its first unholy foot-print at Jamestown to the last ones made this day by those now held in New Jersey; and if the Court finds a well-grounded doubt as to the authority for this institution existing, which is trying to nestle down on our soil, and taking rank with your scientific, religious and agricultural institutions, then give humanity the advantage of that doubt, and put it to death. As between strength and weakness, power and imbecility, if a strong doubt arise in the minds of the judges, the mercy of the law says, decide in favor of imbecility and weakness, "those who are ready to perish," let their blessing come upon you. Every intendment is in favor of natural rights, until the contrary doth most manifestly appear. If the new Constitution has seriously drawn in question the villainies and crimes of this complicated institution of wrong, then this Court, acting within the spirit and scope of American institutions, are bound to give the slave the benefit of that doubt and set him free. A solid doubt should secure emancipation. But thanks to the freemen of New Jersey, the court is not obliged to look through clouds to see the clear sky of Liberty beyond, for its Constitution, in its first section, asserts in the strongest form of the English language, the explicit principles put forth in the Declaration of Independence, when our country was introduced into the family of nations, by which we declared the great self-evident truth to be, that all men were created free and equal, and possessed of certain inalienable rights, among which are life, liberty, and the pursuit of happiness, which is the proposition of the Constitution of New Jersey, expressed so distinctly, that *cavil* itself looks on in humble silence, and hangs his head in mute despair. For these great man-rights, said Mr. S., as I have said, there is no buyer, no seller, no market. They are a trust confided to man, by his Maker, in order to place him at the head of the created life, and give him dominion over it; and his rank he can never sell, lose, or forfeit, so as to take his station as property among the quadrupeds and animals. In the fall of Adam man never fell so low, as the slaveholder would have wished; for, according to the law of slavery, the poor slave in the disastrous fall of the first transgression "which brought death into the world, and with it all our woes," the slave fell out of his manhood into chattel-hood, and fell on till he lost his wife, his children, and in the amazing descent as he further fell, he lost all his property, and all he should thereafter acquire; and as he further fell, he himself became property, and brought not up on solid ground, until he could say to the neighing horse, on the one hand, "thou art, as property, my brother," and to the lowing ox, on the other, "thou art my equal, my peer." Such is the slaveholder's fall, but this is one of man's pit-falls, and not one of his Maker's. Said MR. S., he had an argument, which the Court might regard as novel, which he wished to urge—that each and every branch of our government, state or national, were under a most solemn covenant with one of the great nations of the earth, to use our best endeavors to abolish slavery, in every part of our country; and we have been living under the weight of that solemn and disregarded undertaking for the last thirty years. Said MR. S., I understand a treaty made by the treaty-making power to be the solemn and paramount law of this land, and if I am right in its construction, the duty is imposed upon our nation, as I may well urge it even upon the judiciary of this State, as a co-ordinate branch of the government, to employ all the power it constitutionally may possess by its decision, to fulfil this engagement of the nation.

The article, said MR. S., to which I refer, is the 10th article of the treaty of Ghent, of the 24th December, 1814, made by the United States of America on the one side, and his Britannic Majesty on the other. Lest there should be some attempt to cavil, and pretend this article of the treaty had reference to the African slave-trade, I may be allowed to say there is not one word in the treaty, except in the 10th article, which touches or relates to the subject of slavery, and it is an engagment relating to slavery as to the traffic generally in the two countries, for each had abolished the African slave-trade under the most tremendous penalties long before 1814; therefore the treaty referred to slavery generally in the two countries. The words of the 10th section of the treaty of Ghent are as follows:

"10th Article, Whereas the *traffic* in slaves is irreconcilable with the principles of humanity and justice, and whereas both his Majesty, and the United States are desirous of contributing their efforts to promote its entire abolition, it is hereby agreed that both the contracting parties shall use their best endeavors to accomplish so desirable an object."

Signed 24th December, 1814.

("Done in triplicate.")

"GAMBIER,
HENRY GOULBURN,
WILLIAM ADAMS,
JOHN QUINCY ADAMS,
J. A. BAYARD,
H. CLAY,
JONATHAN RUSSEL,
ALBERT GALLATIN."

United States Laws, 1st vol., 699.

This treaty, so long dishonored on our part, has been most faithfully respected and obeyed on the part of Great Britain. They immediately began to adopt means for the subversion of slavery as a system in the West Indies. To be sure the violence, disorder, and Lynch-law of the slaveholders of the West Indies defeated the kindness, and deferred the approaching justice of the English nation for some years. It was astonishing to see the impudence of the West India planters, threatening dismemberment of the empire, revolution, and treason, as often as the mother country originated a measure in any degree preparatory to emancipation. These contumacious slaveholders did all in their power to frighten

England from her high purposes, 1st, by asserting that the slaves would cut their masters' throats if emancipated; 2d, that the slaves were so brutified, they would all starve to death, and die from laziness, and could not take care of themselves; that the slaves were thieves and drunkards; that the whites would have to abandon the Island if they were set free, and lose their estates; in fact that slaves were not men, and had no souls. Amalgamation, house-burning, and universal desolation would be the first fruits of such procedure.

The Moravian, Baptist and Methodist ministers exposed themselves to great rage from the slaveholders in attempting, as Christian ministers and good subjects, to preach the Gospel to the slaves, and aid them in information in furthering the objects of the mother country. Baptist and Methodist meeting-houses or churches were torn down and burnt, and these blessed ministers were in constant peril of losing their lives, and were occasionally imprisoned and banished from their homes and families. In fact, everything, which is said against emancipation and abolitionists in Mississippi, Georgia, and South Carolina, was said in the British West-Indies thousands and thousands of times by the press, resolutions of public meetings, the Island Legislatures, and the voice of man, against emancipation and British abolitionists; but on the passage of the great Reform Bill of England in 1833, about 500,000 new law-makers or voters were added to the old Parliamentary constituency of England, and when this fresh stream of popular power flowed, it rose so high, that on the bosom of its flood it carried into the New Parliament men deeply sympathizing with the great principles of justice, and one of their first acts of legislation was to declare slavery abolished in the West Indies, paying £20,000,000 sterling to the slaveholders, and giving them, the masters, six years more of the services of the slaves, so that emancipation would not take place until the first of August, 1840. This apprenticeship-system, regulated by a most complicated law, with especial justices to stand between master and apprentice, proved, if possible, more bitter than slavery itself. Nothing could have been more unfortunate, or fraught with greater injustice to the colored people.

The master's avarice and cruelty arose in proportion to the shortness of the time he could exercise his despotism. The special justices intended for the slave-apprentice's friend, eat sumptuous dinners with the planter, and decided controversies in his favor. The humanity of the government in the apprenticeship was entirely defeated by the greediness, cruelty, and avarice of masters. The horrid flogging, the treadmills, and other instruments of slaveholding vengeance and torture were in full play during the probationary state. The mother country had been overreached in paying twenty millions of pounds sterling to see the objects of their solicitude so shamefully treated. The mistake of the home government was in supposing it possible to engraft a system of apprenticeship, education, and a preparation for freedom, on the old tree of slavery, and in having confidence in those brutal, cruel, and avaricious slaveholders, who, with their twenty millions of pounds, and six years of labor, only hated the poor slave the more as his liberty advanced day by day in his chains. Finally in January or February, 1838, the British minister wrote to the Governors of these Islands, requesting them in the coming spring and summer to convoke those insular legislatures and ask them forthwith to abolish the remaining two years of the apprenticeship system, if the islands wished for the future good will of the slaves, or in fact, the protection of the parent country, in case of insurrection. This stringent measure brought the obstinate slaveholders to their senses. The West India Island Parliaments were convoked, and the final acts of emancipation passed, to take effect simultaneously on the 1st August, 1838, except the

Island of Antigua, whose Parliament, with great good sense, abolished slavery and apprenticeship both, in 1834, in an island of 30,000 blacks, and 5,000 whites—six to one. Great kindness, love, education, and prosperity followed this island. However, the eventful first of August, 1838, at last came, and instead of blood and insurrection, as prophesied by the selfish and cowardly, the blacks throughout the British West Indies, to the number of 800,000 human beings, who had been slaves, met in the evening of the 31st of July, 1838, and there continued in a solemn and quiet manner until the moment of midnight came, when the bells of the churches of the British West Indies struck and played from island to island, while cannons were roaring throughout the Great Antilles—they were the glorious peals of freedom, the joyful freedmen raising notes of thanksgiving and praise to Heaven from bended knees, falling with hysteric transports of wild and delirious joy, into each other's arms. No mortal tongue or pen can describe the overflowing ecstasies of these naked and scourged bondmen, now standing up as British freemen—slaves no more. They sung, they cried, they danced, and thus in wild and rapturous joy they passed the terrific bourne so long wished for by them—so long feared and dreaded by the guilty white man. But the first drop of the white man's blood has not yet been shed, by these deeply abused and emancipated people. Many thousands of these long-injured people are now proprietors of two, four, eight, ten, and fifteen acres of land. Their wives and children stay at home and cultivate and raise enough for the family's food and clothing; the father works, or some older sons, on some neighboring plantation,—the money he or they earn pays for land:—his wife and children create subsistence from his own fields. Hundreds of schools, and many colored churches, have sprung up for the adults and colored children. Once the planters raised nothing but sugar, molasses, rum, and coffee, and bought all their provisions from abroad; now the laborers' families raise their provisions on the island. Less sugar, to be sure, is raised, but two-thirds of the sugar goes, as a money question, farther now than all did in slavery, as more than one-third, sometimes one half, was spent for provisions which are now raised at home. So they have gone on with remarkable prosperity, both master and freedmen. The plantations have arisen, some twenty, thirty, and others forty and fifty, and many sixty and sixty-five per cent. above their slave value. In fact, the English government now feel that they acted unwisely in giving the twenty-millions of pounds, for the lands alone of those slave islands are now worth more than slaves and land both were in 1830. In fact, that is a matter of regret now, that the slave had not received what England had to give. On the same day, the fetters fell from the slaves of South Africa; from the Cape of Good Hope, six-hundred miles north, inland, the institution expired on the last acre of British supremacy—from ocean to ocean. On the 1st of April, 1844, England, through her East India Company's mighty powers, struck slavery dead through her Oriental Regions—twelve millions of slaves, serfs, and caste—crushed beings, lifted their unfettered hands to God to bless his power, and that of England's, which, amidst a population of one hundred millions of Eastern Indies, left them in chains to pine no more. Has not England most gloriously, in thirty years, from 1814 to 1844, performed her high and glorious undertaking with these United States in the treaty of Ghent? Has she not blotted out that great dishonor of our race from her vast dominions? What have we done to fulfil our part of this great national covenant? When the abolitionists presented from year to year, petitions clothed in dignified and respectful language, praying Congress to abolish the internal slave trade between the States, in the Territory of Florida, and in the District of Columbia, signed by tens of thousands of names, unread, undebated, unprinted, and unconsidered, they were laid upon the table. This being esteemed too great a privilege for humanity, during three years, these petitions, by a rule of the House of Representatives, were forbidden a reception by the House. The abolitionists, for endeavoring to fulfil the paramount law of the land, the 10th Article of the treaty, were defamed in Congress and out, their names cast out as fanatical and incendiary, they were mobbed by the countenance of men in high places, their churches destroyed, their halls burnt, and their people imprisoned and murdered! If slavery not only forbids and restrains a nation from performing its most solemn treaties, but violates them, and thus endangers the peace, prosperity, and happiness of the whole people, can it be doubted that it contravenes the 1st Article of your Constitution, which assures us that man has the right of "acquiring, possessing, and protecting property, and of pursuing, and of obtaining *safety and happiness*."

Can *safety, property* and happiness be maintained by men or nations who violate faith, who are truce breakers? Is not that *slavery* which hazards the peace of a Nation by refusing obedience to the highest law of individual and national preservation, something that is contrary to the great law of *nature?* Every branch of our government—legislative, judicial or Executive—should have lent every encouragement and aid in their power to the removal of this cancer, battening with its roots in the jugulars of the Republic. But instead of Presidential and gubernatorial messages urging Congress and the State Legislatures, under this standing paramount treaty-law, to do all in their power within their respective jurisdictions to abolish slavery, slavery has mounted the highest places of power, and has rescinded and annulled the treaty, and compelled Presidents and Governors by messages and inaugurals to forewarn the Legislative Assemblies and the people to violate this treaty, and turn their entire power and legislative action against those who had petitioned for the abolition of slavery. Is not this high treason against the State and man's best interests? Has not slavery caused these high dignitaries to commit official perjury? And is not such a terrible institution hostile to man, his safety and happiness as a man and as a citizen, and is it not within the inhibition of the first section of your Constitution, and does it not violate that freedom and independence conferred upon him by the law of nature, and does it not stand between you and the enjoyment of the first article?

What is that law of nature, by which all men are made free and independent? Allow me to define it as I understand it, said Mr. S. The law of nature is that great Omnipotent law of God, ever in full force amidst the busy hum of thousands in your emporium, or in the solitudes of the wilderness, on the sea, or on the land; it follows man down into the mines of the earth, it ascends with him to the Chimborazo's top; it has no latitude, no longitude, no length, no breadth; it is truth, and is as earnest in its pleadings, amidst the inhospitalities of polar cold, as in the boundless prodigalities of the burning tropics; it is the everlasting justice and mercy of the Eternal; it is the great imprint of God upon man, which can never be counterfeited, erased, or repealed; it is so immutable that it never changes, *man cannot* repeal it; it is a part of each human being's inheritance, which without crime he can never spend or squander; it abides with him, though unhonored, under all circumstances of bereavement, and guarantees man's right to life, liberty and the pursuit of happiness as inalienable.

The law of nature is taken up and recognized by the good people of New Jersey, in the most solemn form as a rule of action, in her organic law. This first section declares that amongst man's unalienable rights are life, liberty, and the right of acquiring property. What, can a slave have safety, or acquire property? he who is nothing but a chattel, a piece of property himself, can he acquire safety? No; of all the innumerable murders committed by white men and women upon the slaves of the south (and there is no day goes by in which there is not more than one murder in each slave State, on an average), not a single white person has yet been executed for the murder of the colored man. The white is frequently hung in the slave States for stealing slaves, but not for killing them. Oh, sum of all human villanies, let the curse of God rest upon it, let every wind of Heaven be charged with its destruction, every rising sun be its destroyer, the rolling seasons its executioner!!

Said MR. S., slavery is the exact converse of every proposition contained in the first article of your new Constitution.

Slavery throws down every human right in the market to the highest bidder. If slavery or semi-slavery, in the shape of children of slaves in this State continuing to be slaves, males until twenty-five, and females until twenty-one years of age, and this operation is to pass under the name of being born free, and persons forty-one years old and upwards to be retained as slaves for life, and slaveholders are to stand asserting their wicked power, then the first great section of your Constitution is converted into a vapid and senseless abstraction. Shall your Constitution be withered by the power of slavery? Shall this Constitution stand gilt with the gold of high pretension, while within it is full of ravening and dead men's bones? Shall this slave institution continue to exist in hostility to so plain a provision? This frightful institution claims to exist by the apology of some since the 2d of last September, even since this Constitution went into operation, without a platform on which to place its accursed feet. Said MR. S., the best foundation I can see for slavery in this State, at this time, and the length of time it should continue, should be the amount of time it would take the people of this State to recover from their astonishment at its inexpressible *impudence*.

The institution of slavery is the converse proposition of the Ten Commandments, the essence of injustice and meanness in its most compact form; and it would seem that no nation not struck down by a mortal paralysis, would wait a moment before rising and striking down the monster, the first instant they discovered his seven heads and ten horns emerging from the forlorn regions of "Eldest Hell."

Said MR. S., which shall stand—the great written, organic law of liberty, or the unwritten and inexpressible villany of slavery? Which shall stand—the natural God-inherited rights of life, liberty, property, safety and happiness for each human being in New Jersey, or that of an institution which subverts every object for which a good Constitution was ever made?

A Constitution *ex vi termini* imports a covenant made by the whole people, with each person, and each person with the whole people, to protect and defend their God-inherited rights of life, liberty, property and safety from violence and invasion. A Constitution is made for the defence of human rights and not for the destruction; a Constitution is the highest evidence of man's weakness; and to combine society's strength, for the defence of each individual. How is it possible that a Constitution, whether of this State, or of the United States, which were created on purpose for the protection of life, liberty, property and Safety, can exist and be entitled to the name, without overthrowing every institution villany or stratagem created or made, intending to cheat man out of life, liberty, property, safety and happiness?

The men who framed the old State Constitution of New Jersey in the year 1776 were not such hypocrites as to stamp that Constitution with the protection of human rights. No, they said nothing on that subject, for they knew there were no inconsiderable class of the population of this State, who were wedded to the insatiable desire of appropriating the labor of others, without compensation, by compelling negroes, mulattoes, mestees and Indians, to work for them for nothing, and make chattels or property of their persons, their wives and children,—yes, of those human sinews as a marketable commodity, men were to be degraded and forbidden, under penalties of thirty-nine lashes, from wandering from their masters' homes on Sunday, for the infliction of which stripes, by the order of a justice of the peace, a constable did and yet does receive from the master the sum of $1 for performing the brutish service. To add to all other ignoble acts on the part of the State, was a provision forbidding emancipation of the slave, if forty years old or more, for fear of the distant contingency, that this freedman might become a public burthen to the township, by being a pauper in his old age, and rather than subject the towns to that they preferred to let the man and his posterity remain in slavery. Such was the gross inhumanity of the age; thus cheap were human rights held by the people of this State at large. Gross inhumanity to the master himself; it took away his *locus penitentiæ*, his space of repentance. And if slavery is not abolished, this infamous provision is still in full force. The reason, said Mr. S., why slavery was not abolished by name in Massachusetts and New Jersey is to be found in this, that the conscious shame of the fact restrained the framers of those Constitutions from immortalising their own disgrace by admitting slavery's previous existence, in and by its distinct abolition. They therefore put it to death by suffocation by the hands of liberty, without a name, hoping the judiciaries would attend its funeral and burial, and for ever remove its unsightly corpse from the sight and smell of men with as little parade as possible; and further hoping a generous posterity would disbelieve their early public history, and consider it as apocryphal and slanderous of their illustrious ancestors, as the Constitutions of these States do not so much as name so great a moral blemish on their historical fame.

Said Mr. S., by the statute of this State (which he contended was repealed by the 1st section of the new Constitution) passed February, 1820, all children born of slaves after 1804 were to be free, but belong as servants, and be held as apprentices, who are bound out by the overseers of the poor to the owners of their mothers, their administrators, executors and assigns, males till 25, and females until 21. These persons were property in every sense of the word, until their time expired; they are purchased and sold in private and at public auction, pass under the insolvent acts and bankrupt acts, the same as oxen and horses. What is the difference between this Mary Tebout and her mother? Nothing, until Mary has passed 21 years of unrewarded toil. She is called a servant, she is said to be born free, now but 19, and has been sold three times. The Southern States call slavery involuntary servitude, or persons bound to service by the laws of the States. The domestic institutions of the South, the patriarchial institutions and the peculiar institutions of the South—by such soft hypocritical use of words, do they mean to make the English language a partner in their guilt, by using it as a cloak to conceal the hideous visage of that frightful monster, whose mouth is filled with spikes, and cover her face with iron wrinkles, with burning balls of fire for eyes, whose every hair is a hissing serpent, whose fetid breath would kill the Bahon Upas, whose touch is ruin, whose embrace is destruction, who is fed on blood, tears and sweat, whip-extracted, from unpaid toil—her music is unpitied groans of broken hearts, of ruined hopes, and blasted expectations.

Away, said Mr. S., with such artifice to shield deformity, by those cruel and wicked States, boasting of their republicanism, and rights of man. Even New York and Pennsylvania once held persons born free, whose mothers were slaves, the males till 28, and females till 25, as slaves. Terrible nick-naming of human rights, as in bold derision of them. These New Jersey servants are property, in its base sense, slaves for years, the parents deprived of all jurisdiction of their offspring, all direction of their education, and paternal tenderness; the law confining these poor servants, and obliging them to live with those who have owned and abused the mother who bore them, and are still continuing to hold their parents until death as slaves. The master can sell this servant and horse together. This servant-woman at 15, and the male-servant at 18, contract marriage, and when the woman is 19, and man 22 years of age, having three little children, the father is sold to one end of the State, and the mother to the other; their little children left in the street, the marriage relation broken, the paternal and maternal relation dissolved; these little ones not to see their parents for two years or more; the husband cannot see his wife or little ones, nor the wife her husband or babies for two years to come. Call you this being born *free?* The man is deprived of his wife, and the wife becomes a widow, and children orphans, according to law, to satisfy the claims of certain old slaveholders in this State! Is this being born free? This sort of being born free, "is keeping the word of promise to the ear to break it to the hope." This looks none like respect for the law of nature, by which we are born free and independent. We can never honor or respect the new Constitution, till we feel there is meaning, power, vitality, in those blessed words of justice, truth, mercy, freedom, safety; and further, feel that there are no birth-impediments, or interest of others in the use of our bodies, inconsistent with our own happiness. Each individual should be left to fulfil the object of his mission to this world in the best way he may; society should not load him with burdens for the benefit of others, but should give him every facility to run his race of existence, with dignity to himself, and thus truly serve the ends of society and his own creation, in passing from the great eternity of the past into the illimitable future. Here, Mr. S. said, we are not left in the dark, as to the meaning of the words of the New Jersey new Constitution, for it is almost an exact copy of the first section of the Massachusetts Constitution of 1780. Here Mr. S. read the first section of the Massachusetts Constitution in these words.

"Article 1st. All men are born free and equal, and have certain natural, essential, and inalienable rights, among which may be reckoned the right of enjoying and defending their lives and liberties; that of acquiring, possessing, and protecting property; in fine, that of seeking and obtaining their safety and happiness."

Here Mr. S. asked Mr. Zabriskie, counsel for the claimant of Mary Tebout, if he contended there was any difference between the two sections of these Constitutions? Mr. Zabriskie replied, he did not.

The New Jersey Constitution has in the 10th Article these words, "The common law and statute laws now in full force, *not repugnant* to this Constitution, shall remain in force until they expire by their own limitation, or be altered or repealed by the Legislature."

Further, Mr. S. said that he relied on a portion of the Constitution of the United States for emancipation, by this Honorable Court, to wit, the Magna Charta portion, where it asserts "that no person shall be deprived of life, liberty or property, without due process of law."

Mr. S. said that the case of *Winchendon* v. *Hatfield*, *4th Mass. Rep.*, 123, is the case of one Edoin Landon, in relation to the question as to which of the towns should support him, he having been a slave in Massachusetts, and sold eleven times, enlisted twice in the Revolutionary army, the second time for three years, his master receiving his bounty and his wages, —also, *4th Mass.*, 539. Chief Justice Parsons decided in this cause that slavery had been abolished by the first section of the Massachusetts Constitution, as had been decided in formerly unreported cases. This is legal authority, in effect, on the very words of the New Jersey Constitution, 1st article; Massachusetts being the same in substance, as admitted. Need I say Massachusetts has shed from the lamp of her Judiciary as pure, bright and steady a light as any Court in the new world, and has done her fair share in elevating the science of the law. I repose with great confidence upon this authority; it covers the whole controversy.

The case of the slave—*Med. 18th Pickering*, 193, known under the name of *Commonwealth* vs. *Thomas Aves*, presented within the last half dozen years this same great question collaterally. The argument was elaborate, and opinion of Chief Justice Shaw luminous.

The Chief Justice Shaw says, Massachusets in 1641 abolished slavery, except of *captives taken in lawful war* or guilty of crime. But slavery grew up in Massachusetts, and in 1703 an act was passed in that colony, imposing restrictions on the transmission of aged and infirm slaves; and by an act of 1705, a duty was levied on the importation of slaves, showing slavery in full force until abolished by their Constitution of 1780. The Chief Justice, in this case, says it is now well established law that slavery was abolished by the Constitution of 1780, and before the adoption of the Constitution of the United States, slavery being *repugnant* to the principles of justice, of nature, and the declaration of rights, which are a component part of the Constitution of Massachusetts. Slavery, said he, crept into Massachusetts by force of custom existing in the West Indies and in several other States, encouraged by the mother country (miserable apology better than none, even in Massachusetts).

Chief Justice Shaw says, "Slavery is a relation founded in force and not in right; existing where it does by force of positive law, and not recognized and founded in natural rights." Slavery, he says, "is contrary to natural rights, to the principles of justice and humanity." He then says, "Bond slavery cannot exist in this Commonwealth, because it is contrary to natural right, *repugnant* to the Constitution and law, designed to secure the liberty and rights of all persons who come within the limits of this State, as entitled to the protection of law."

But what case can I have stronger than the opinion of Chief Justice Marshall, himself a slaveholder? Borne down by slaveholding construction as he was, still his innate integrity triumphed over cultivated wrong, and compelled him to define slavery as contrary to the law of nature, for the definition of slavery by the civil law, showed it an institution contrary to the law of nature, which law of nature New Jersey has adopted. In case of the *Antelope, 10th Wheaton*, 120, the Chief Justice Marshall says, "That slavery is contrary to the law of nature will scarcely be denied; that every man has a natural right to the fruits of his own labor is generally admitted, and that no other person can rightfully deprive him of those fruits and appropriate them against his will, seems the necessary result of that admission" Chief Justice Marshall quotes the definition of slavery in the Latin from the civil law, which, with his own opinion, would seem to put the question in this cause for ever to rest. It is this, "*Servitus est constitutio juris gentium qua quis Domino alieno* CONTRA NATURAM *subjicitur*." Slavery is an institution by the laws of Nations, by which one is subjected to another man, as master, *contrary to nature*. Slavery strikes down and repeals, if it could, the law of nature referred to in the 1st article of your Constitution; what can be stronger and more complete? said

Mr. S. Here Mr. Stewart gave way for an adjournment until 3 P. M. for dining.

The court being present at 3 o'clock, P. M., Mr. Stewart resumed by saying, Has any lawyer the courage to say that the legislature of New Jersey could create the institution of slavery to day in defiance of the new constitution? Perhaps most, if not all, would say No. Why could not the legislature enact such a law so as to create the relation of slave and master? It would be correctly answered, and would be by all, it would be *repugnant* to the new Constitution and its first section. Do not we discover that a law sustaining slavery is equally repugnant to the new Constitution, whether passed ten years before it, or ten years after it? and that the repugnance is not a question of past or present time? If it is repugnant, it is equally so in the one case as the other,—" it is so odious nothing but positive law can sustain it," says Lord Mansfield.

Mr. S. said that he confessed himself to have much respect for a *being* so highly honored as man by his Maker, a being created in the image of God, who showed at all times the grandeur of his descent, and the illustriousness of his lineage by that great unimpeachable record written upon his countenance sublime, by the finger of God, which no poverty, sorrow, or crime, could erase: its marks of origin were open to all, read of all, and should be comprehended by all. In the first place we must look at the immense natural wealth, or God-given possessions, which belong to the meanest man, who prints the green earth, with his foot, or drinks from its waters, and renews life every moment from the unbought atmosphere—is fanned by the wings of the wind, cheered with the eye-possession of the universe; yes, his every-day existence could not be sustained, at a less expense than the fitting up of two worlds, for his accommodation, the earth and sun; the bread he eats, the wool, the flax, and cotton he wears, is warmed into life by rays of light from the sun, sent over ninety millions of miles in profusion, without stint, each ray having its definite office and distinct commission to aid to life, strength and joy, a single human being. If there were but one man on this globe, these vast structures of two worlds must be reared in all their architectural grandeur and fitness. This globe must revolve around on its own axis every twenty-four hours, and shoot along upon the vast plane of the ecliptic, at the inconceivable rate of sixty-eight thousand miles per hour. Man perishes, if the globe were to revolve around the sun at the rate of thirty-four thousand miles per hour; man could not live in these regions with a year of seven hundred and thirty days, with the unbroken severities of a double winter, or the scorching heat of a protracted summer.

The outlay of Almighty power, which sends this noble earth careering round the sun with such prodigious force, and brings it back to the same point, in absolute space with infinite precision, with the punctuality of God, is a portion of each man's inheritance; and all the powers ever displayed by man, exerted by beasts, felt from winds, or overwhelmed by tornadoes, or moved in tempests, or lifted or sunk by earthquakes, swept by tides, or driven by inundations, put forth since the morning of creation, would not furnish a sufficient force, to propel our globe on its everlasting journey, a single day. Yet for man these high demonstrations are made, to fit him up an abode with the finish of Omnipotence, commensurate with his every want, it is his God-inherited estate; and were the poorest man on earth to exchange that estate, for the power of Bonaparte, when all Europe shook beneath his tread, and trembled at his power, this poor man would be undone, by the exchange; the property is too great for any one to buy it, of another; this is the benevolence of Heaven to his honored creature, man. When each man's God-inherited estate is reckoned and computed, though possessing nothing else, and compared with that of any other man's God-inherited estate, they are equal; and if one possess a million of pounds, and the other no money, still when their whole possessions are considered, one has one hundred and the other but one hundred and one. This proposition or statement will for ever vindicate the goodness of Heaven, and show the absolute equality of all men, if considered possession-wise.

Therefore it seems to me, said Mr. S., the Declaration of Independence, in asserting, that all men are created free and equal, istrue as a proposition, and is not a rhetorical flourish, but a sublime estimate, no less grand than true, when we refer to the vast possessions of each human being; and that any accidental variance by the acquisitions of one, of more wealth than another, does not disturb the great result any more than the dust which may fall upon one of the scales shall change their general equipoise.

All men are created equal, and shall a being of such amazing dignity and immense possessions, of such grand lineage, be made a slave? God forbid. Equality, life, liberty of locomotion, the rights of acquiring happiness in every way we see fit, not violating the rights of our brother man, or the edicts of Heaven, with the God-inherited estate, constitute what your constitution and that of Massachusetts and the Declaration of Independence, describe as rights *inalienable*. Is it not so? What kind of a deed, said Mr. S., must that be which should attempt to convey my right and title in the wind, atmosphere, earth, and my share in the power that propels this ponderous globe around the sun?—my title to the exhaustless fires and light of that great luminary, and of those rays which might fall on me or on the earth and produce my raiment and food? Is there not deep and philosophical truth in asserting the *inalienability* of rights like these, so essential to man's existence, and his everlasting accountability, to the Father of all, for his abounding munificence, with which man can invest no other being, or divest himself. Can it not truly be said that a being who is born to such great possessions, is born free and *independent?* The greatest blot on American character is, to have been deluded by slaveholders into a belief that those great words expressed by the men, who wrote and adopted the Declaration of our Independence, were mere abstractions and the flourish of oratory, where they declared the great self-evident truth "that all men are created free and equal, and are possessed of certain inalienable rights, among which are life, liberty, and the pursuit of happiness," and that the same were meaningless. These truths are self-evident, and why? said Mr. S. They are evident in every breath of air we respire through our lungs, every step we take, in every object we behold printed on every tree, written on every cloud, bursting forth in every falling drop of rain, reflected in every ray of light, by which the universe is warmed, and in glory lit up, and by the succession of day and night, summer and winter, seed-time and harvest, in fact, its self-evidence is stereotyped in eternal beauty upon the earth, the sea, the mountain, the valley, upon the moon, the sun, and stars of heaven. This constitutes the great record of ever-during *self-evidence*, that all men are created free and equal, and are possessed of certain inalienable rights, &c.

Said Mr. S, this rises to a moral, if not a mathematical demonstration, and that a great nation should, so far as individuals, forget the dignity of their origin, the vastness of their inalienable possessions, and should hunt for arguments to force their debasement and search for reasons to *undervalue* such a being as man, especially in a great *selfocracy*, where each man is a sovereign, is among all strange things, one which would exceed belief were we not met by the strange phenomenon at every turn of human affairs. Had we incorporated the Divine sentiments of our great Declaration into our minds, as an everlasting first-principle, and lived under the sway of its glorious dominion, no slavery would then have disgraced our magnificent country; no half cultivated, forlorn and deserted sections of Slave States, would have told the world their melancholy tale. No *coffled* gang of slaves would have dishonored our nation, driven from State to State, for sale. No, our prosperity, riches, glory and moral elevation, would have presented so imposing an example of man's capabilities for his own advancement, that king-craft aristocracies and all of that coarse mode of working, taxing and governing men, as family-jobs, would, long ere this, have been thrown into the rear of the camp of human progress, and new forms of self-government would have succeeded, in which the governed should have been the governors, and the interest of the governed would have prevailed, in the true advancement of the human race.

We, said MR. S., have terrible penalties to pay, for abandoning principles so glorious, so wise, of which we had a full view, and by saying, most shamefully, the Declaration of Independence is a formula and not serious, it is the poetry of excited minds. By thus forsaking these great truths, certain and as practical as the Decalogue, we fell back into the arms of a low, base expediency, and *relived* the forms of crimes and follies of former ages, holding these sublime truths as abstractions, fitted only for the meridian of Heaven, with angels for their operatives, to carry them out, while we fed ourselves upon the husks of former absurdities, rejecting truth, holding it too beautiful for practical use.

Said MR. S., will not this Court set the nation the shining example of doing right, on this question, by acting up to the full measure of their judicial and moral power?

Said MR. S., a nation may lose its liberty in a day, and not miss it in an hundred years; this nation lost its true liberty, the clear light, the first moment the great words of the Declaration of Independence ceased to be honored and respected as household, every-day truth, the fundamental rules of action, as the political and moral mathematics of the nation.

Although we make several hundred volumes of fourth of July orations, poetical self-glorifications and boasting eulogiums for the home-market yearly, in which the most beautiful descriptions are given of the dress and form of liberty, as a wonderful unknown goddess, and amuse ourselves in describing her altar, the costliness of her sacrifices, and the riches of her perfume, and the curling smoke of her incense; if in the everyday intercourse of man with man, of courts of justice with causes, in expounding the doctrines of the great declaration and of legislation, in framing new rules of action, we should with one consent, have asserted that in the Declaration of Independence and other national and State Constitutions containing the same thoughts, that liberty was sincere, in declaring the freedom and equality of all men, and the inalienability of the rights, of life, liberty and the pursuit of happiness; for not so doing, we have lost liberty, though we do not miss it; we have only liberty's casket, but the jewel is gone; we are playing and satisfying ourselves with forms when the substance has departed. We make the loud acclaim, we fire the cannon of salutation, crackers burst under our feet, our toasts may be drank in three times three, in the wildest uproar of animal excitement; still these demonstrations are worse than senseless, because they make us think we are true believers in liberty and the divine dignity of man, while we are only high-heeled hypocrites and fanatics, spinning in concentric circles, like brain-turned dervishes around an abstraction of liberty, being neither flesh nor spirit, being the great *indefinable*, our adoration increasing with our ignorance, until the beatitude of our worship is made complete in the perfect *idealess*. Still for a pretence we make long speeches about Republicanism and Democracy, while we have nailed and crucified, in and through our colored brother, Liberty on the cross. We have so long been absent from *true* liberty, that we should require a formal introduction before we should dare address her, for she is not that tawdry dressed cyprian bearing her name, who had sold her charms to demagogues, pimps, panders, pirates, buccaneers and slaveholders, whip in hand, who have declared that slavery is the chief corner-stone of our republican institutions: while the clergy of the south have most impiously averred slavery to be a Bible, God-honored, Christian institution to be kept. Shameful impiety and desecration of the fountain of Eternal truth!

Said Mr. S., the Court will pardon me while we look for a moment at the sublime teaching of that wonderful and holy book the Bible, so often lugged in to uphold piracy at the expense of the Eternal's justice and man's happiness. The Almighty has done a thousand-fold more, to express his infinite abhorrence of slavery, than of all other crimes and offences against his law. He has suspended the laws of nature and in one instance of time, smote two and a half millions of people with death, and caused the sea itself to retreat before the fugitive slave, and made, as predicated on these amazing exercises of power, a direct revelation of himself, and immediately caused our revealed religion to be produced, to express his everlasting detestation of a crime which would unthrone Him, and crush his creature man, and place him beside the beast of the field. Said Mr. S., our Maker destroyed the first edition of mankind. In the second emission and publication of our race Egypt became the school-master-nation of the human race, and the great instructor of mankind. The nations of the earth, on camels and dromedaries, came, in the infancy of antiquity, to Egypt, to exchange their rude materials and ignorance for the Egyptian works of art and knowledge. In fact, no opinion was considered worthy of general acceptance, by the surrounding barbarians, unless it had an Egyptian endorsement, and their wise men's stamp and mark upon it.

It appeared the Israelites in near 400 years had increased to two and a half millions of people, as would seem from the number of men spoken of in their Exodus. The Pharaohs had a slave market for centuries. The poor Jews had become slaves of the most distressing type. They had their overseers, their distinct tasks; they were scourged, and had every mark of human debasement and slavery inflicted. The day of their deliverance was in an age, in which the passion for public structures, imposing in their magnitude, wonderful in their display of high-wrought efforts of genius, constituted the chief employment of their kings, and great men, for centuries. The poor Hebrews had often laid their petitions before Pharaoh through Moses and Aaron, asking to be permitted to go into the wilderness, and worship their God. But Pharaoh, as a slaveholder, stood between this people and their conscience, and refused to let them go. Slavery strikes down the rights of conscience always, for there is not a slave in the United States, who is informed in any reasonable degree in the Christian religion, who does not remain in slavery, contrary to the plainest teachings of his own conscience. The Almighty having warned the Egyptian government of the great crime of holding men in bondage, was determined, in the early ages of mankind, to settle the question of his infinite abhorrence of slavery, in a manner so elementary and signal, that the stamp of His finger-marks should remain unerasable through all coming ages. For slavery overthrows the *will* of the victim, and the claim of the Almighty to the adoration of his creatures; and no power can get in between God and man, and interfere on this subject, unless it is slavery. Slavery breaks down the will, volition, and choice of its victim; the slaveholder steps in between the slave and his Maker, and says, Oh, slave, talk not of conscience, your religion, or your God; do my will, or die; my will is your law, and not your God's; my will you must obey, or die. Slavery always disputes our Maker's supremacy; warning after warning, miracle after miracle, had been lost upon the obduracy of Egypt's king. One morning, as the population of that kingdom of 15 millions of people arose and looked at their beloved Nile, lo! and behold, it was one vast river of blood, from the cataracts where its tumbling torments of blood fell in mighty roar, and pursued its sweeping course for 600 miles to its seven mouths, where the Mediterranean, receiving its tribute from this ancient servant, *blushed* for twenty leagues around, at Pharaoh's impudence. The stranger from afar, the traders, seekers of knowledge, and the citizens, stood that livelong day, and wondered at the bloody Nile; and as reasons were asked and given, I think I hear them say, the reason why the Nile runs blood is that Pharaoh holds the Hebrews as slaves, and the Hebrews' God demands their release, and shows his anger and his power at Pharaoh's refusal. The stranger would carry this news to the utmost bounds of living man, saying, one entire day I saw the Nile run blood, to express the abhorrence of the Hebrews' God against the crime of slavery. Again, the heavens were darkened at noon by the gyrations of armies of locusts, which shut out the sun, and they consumed the vegetation of this fertile land; men cried for mercy, and in a few hours this army of destructive locusts was carried on the wings of a strong west wind into the depths of the Red Sea, not one left. The Egyptian and the stranger knew that the Hebrews' God had done this, to cause these poor slaves to be delivered from the mighty monarch's cruel power. On a certain other day the obstinate Pharaoh refused, after many promises, to let the poor Hebrew slaves go free. It is noon; the burning power of a June sun strikes the land; anon, all eyes in Egypt are turned to a black cloud rising out of the west, over the Lybian desert.

Said Mr. S., this was the first thunder-storm in Egypt, and the last, for it neither rains nor hails in Egypt, owing to the great Lybian desert of sand on the west, and the Arabian desert on the east, as philosophers suppose. It skirts the western heavens, and the terrific clouds raise themselves higher and higher; men turn pale; anon the low and solemn tones of thunder are heard; men tremble, and say it is the voice of the slaves' God,—in a moment the flashes of forked lightning play with infinite quickness, men fall on their knees and declare it is the flashing of the angry eyes of the Hebrews' God at the Egyptians' cruelties. The clouds rise to the high altitude of noon; the lightning, the winds, and roaring thunder send consternation into the hearts of affrighted men. It appears like night, nature in agony, men fear to speak, and believe they are on the eve of doom; men and beasts hide themselves in extreme terror; the thunder makes the earth tremble from pole to pole; the pyramids rock from their deep foundations, the rains descend, the hail beats the earth, fire and ice leap from the clouds, while the lightning strikes down the trees, plays round the pyramid tops, smites the sphinx, and runs along upon the ground, men in agony praying for deliverance; Pharaoh and his court lie prostrate in the palace, the earth seems shaken out of its place, and all nature in convulsions. The king implores mercy, and the Father of all hears, pities and delivers, the faithless king and people, and ere the sun went down, that storm and desolation had for ever gone by, and the last cloud sunk below the horizon, in the Red Sea, while the beautiful sun rolls down the western heavens, smiling in mercy from and beyond the dark solitudes of the interminable Lybian sands. This storm, all men knew, was an evidence of God's displeasure at slavery. But Pharaoh would not let the people go.

It is in Egypt, and is midnight, when the young wife, but two years married, awoke and placed her hand on the shoulder of her youthful husband; he was as cold as marble, he would not awake at her mournful cry—he was dead, he was the first born of his parents. She arose in wild despair, she lit a flambeau, and looked at her little babe on the mattress; the fixed smile was there, rigid in death, never to be relaxed; *he* was the *first* born of his parents; she flies to her father's and mother's bed in the next room, she awakes her father, but none but the archangel can arouse her mother from death's sleep, most profound; she was the first born of her parents. She sends her man-servant to her neighbor for help in this awful hour; the servant enters the neighbor's, a light is there, wailing and horror meet him. The aged father of the second house was the first born of his parents, and is dead, and the infant first born is also. No contortion, no groan was ever heard of all who fell in a single instant, on that dreadful night; they lay with all the peace of eternal sleep upon them. The servant finds another servant in this second house of death, they go out, they hear the survivors' wail, and see the baleful torch lit up in every house around; they ascend a tower on the banks of the Nile, high above and all around as in a moment for forty miles, as far as eye can measure light upon the earth's dark face, the beams of the death torch of that direful hour from all directions strike their wretched eyes. The lamentations were loud and long; and when the morning sun arose, the angel of death for long hours had been gone from the abodes of man and beast, and there was not one house in all the land of Egypt in which there was not one dead, or about two and half millions, or one sixth of the people, or a life of one of Egypt's slaveholders had been taken, for each Hebrew slave *detained*. No mistaking the power and will of the God of the bondmen longer, and the affrighted Pharaoh and his court cry to these slaves, " up and be gone, or we are all dead men." The funeral, the most terrible in time, then followed. Nothing like these deaths or funerals, in the history of our race. The fugitive slaves had marched to the north-east and reached the Red Sea, and were in great fear, reposing on its banks between two mountains, the one on their right, and the other on their left. Solemn hours! As they rested we may feign that young Hebrews climb to the mountain tops, and saw the rising clouds of dust on the south-western edge of the heavens. That army is led on by Pharaoh's generals, of chariots and cavalry, the notes of trumpets fell upon their ears, and the young men cry to their friends below, " They come! they come! we hear their trumpets on the plain!"

Then the desponding fugitives cried, " Were there no graves in Egypt?" The night came, portentous; a mighty cloud rested between the slaveholders and the trembling fugitives. On the side next to the poor slaves, the cloud beamed as from a pillar of fire, all light, the smile of heaven. On the other side of the cloud the pursuing slaveholders saw it all dark, lugubrious, presaging to them the horrors of their last day. This was another finger-mark of Divine power. The morning lowered, and in clouds, to these sad and impious slaveholders heavily brought on that day whose end they would never see. The trembling fugitives stood looking nine miles across the intervening Red Sea, whose waves broke in melancholy murmurs at their feet. Despair was on every face. When Moses spoke, " stand still and see the salvation of the Lord," another finger-mark of Omnipotence was made, and Moses stretched out his rod over the Red Sea, and anon a long line of subsidence of the waters appears. Every fugitive eye saw it. Then the re-flowing of waters from that central line, the piling of waters follow; the waters ascend and pile, ascend and pile, until the naked bottom across appears with perpendicular water walls of great height, by Omnipotence held up, and probably one mile wide is left like a clean beach. The fugitives pass down on this untraveled road, and finally division after division rose upon the further side. At length the weak passed up, the cripple climb the bank, and lo! there see those little orphans pull themselves up by twigs, and that poor old man on his crutches, they help pull him up—they are all up and over. Now rises the wildest, grandest, and most sublime music which ever burst from human lips—the fugitives' song! The headlong vindictive slaveholders, burning with rage, thirsting for revenge, follow on the fugitives' track into the sea; and as they were at the central depths of the Red Sea, gravitation was permitted to re-assert her ancient law, when down came these mighty mountains of waters to their ancient bed. Pharaoh and his haughty hosts expired in the centre of a miracle. For forty years the Almighty fed these poor fugitive slaves directly from His own table.

Said Mr. S., the God of Heaven, as in mercy to man, that he might never again commit the atrocious crime involved in slavery, caused Mount Sinai to quake from its deep foundations, and amidst the thunders and the lightnings the Almighty, with his own finger, wrote the tables of the law, his ten eternal orders, which is most eminently anti-slavery in character, that the crime which had shook Egypt to its foundations might never occur again for want of a Divine prohibition. This was the decalogue, "Love the Lord thy God with all thy heart, mind, and strength, and thy neighbor as thyself." This command obeyed, destroys all the slavery in the world. What slaveholder can kindly love his slave unless he manumits him?

The preface to these commands, in the sixth verse of the fifth chapter of Deuteronomy, "I am the Lord thy God, which brought thee out of the land of Egypt, and from the house *of bondage*."

"Honor thy father and mother." No, says the slaveholder, I will sell your father and mother, you must obey your master.

"Thou shalt not kill." I will kill, says the slaveholder, if it is necessary, by flogging to obtain submission; or if the slave will run from me when I tell him to stop, I will shoot and kill him, and Southern law says, amen.

"Thou shalt not commit adultery." I will commit adultery, and break the marriage covenant between my slaves, and compel them to marry over when my interest will be promoted, or separate man and wife by sale, or purchase and make them marry again.

"Thou shalt not steal." I will steal, and appropriate, says the slaveholder, all the man hath, all he can earn, and the *man himself*, when *my* interest can be promoted thereby.

"Thou shalt not covet." I will covet that man's or that woman's body, and I will possess myself of them, and appropriate them to my own use, says the slaveholder."

Said Mr. S., look at the condescension of the Almighty. He made these poor fugitive slaves, the Librarians and Custodians of the revelation of his will to mankind. Slavery treads this revelation under foot, and quotes the Bible to prove slavery, when there is the most incontestable evidence that there never would have been a revelation in the decalogue, but a the finishing stroke of those awful wonders and miracles, on the faith of which our religion rests, all originating, converging and terminating in that great fundamental proposition, that God infinitely abhors slavery, because it supplants his direct authority over the will of His child, and throws His child, with an immortal mind, made in his own image, into the category of brute-beasts, thus for ever overthrowing the fundamental relation of God to man, of man to his neighbor, and of man to himself. To vindicate the character, power, and justice of the Supreme, and bring man home again to his true relations, was well worthy of a display of such awful power, introducing Himself as God to the ancient world.

Mr. S. said there was another proposition which he wished to glance at in passing. That was the Constitution of the United States, for he contended, were he before the King's Bench, in Westminster Hall, he would there insist, and he believed with entire success, that there was not a slave in New Jersey, or in any slave State, who had been deprived of his liberty according to law. I mean slaves as they are generally and at large, and not those who have been convicted of crimes; and therefore there is not a slave, if you admit him a person, as slaveholders contend, but must be discharged by a judge or a court, on being brought before said court on the ground that he has never been deprived of his liberty by due process of law, according to the Constitution of the United States. That record must be produced, originating in a decision or an indictment of a grand jury, and the finding of a petit jury, and the pronouncing of judgment thereon, by a court of competent jurisdiction. This, Sir Edward Coke, and Judge Story on Sir Edward's authority, in his Commentaries, 440, says is the meaning of due process of law at common law, as used in *Magna Charta*. But I, said MR. S., am willing to reduce the character of the court, and even strike out the petit and grand jury from the instrumentality—and then I say that "due process of law" means a court or some judicial personage, one or more making a court, who have adjudicated the man to be a slave; and if that record cannot be found, the man must go free, or the individual must not lose his liberty without due process of law. That record cannot be found in this land. Will any man pretend that plantation and cart-whip discipline is due process of law? Will any pretend that being deprived of the right to learn to read, or write, as in some of our States, under the penalty of twenty-five lashes on the naked back of the teacher and the taught, is due process of law? Yes, for the mother to teach her child to spell the name of the Saviour, for the second attempt, mother and child are to be whipped one hundred lashes; for the third offence, the punishment is death. Is this the due process of law, named in the Constitution of the United States? The pursuing of fugitives with blood-hounds, cannot be the due process of law of the Constitution?

The separation by sale of husband from wife, and wife from husband, and children from both, to suit the convenience of the master, cannot be due process of law? The being born of slave mother, on a slaveholder's plantation, cannot be due process of law? The being torn away from home, kindred and friends, and sent by the middle passage to a slave auction in South Carolina, and sold on the boards into hopeless bondage, cannot be due process of law?

Is not slavery a punishment or an infliction on men beyond the track of the common misfortunes of mankind, of sufficient magnitude to have it left to the adjudication of some mortal man, in the shape of a justice or judge, adjudicating a man into the great drag-net of slavery? For, we find it takes the strongest judicial power in the land to get him out. Slaveholders claim him under the word "person" in the Constitution, because they say, there is no other word by which they can denote slavery. The word person, I have, in this argument in relation to due process of law used in the slaveholding sense, which is, after all, downright perversion.

The word person, in the Constitution of the United States, means a human being possessed of natural rights of life, liberty, and the pursuit of happiness. The word person means a human being in the fullness of his natural rights, and nothing more. The Greeks, Romans, and English, whether using the word in law or in common parlance, mean this, and nothing more; and you can legally no more express the idea of a slave by it than you can that of a King. A man who is a slave according to slave law, has lost his *personage*, if I may so speak, and has passed into chattelhood, or thinghood, and all the rights of person are annihilated, or in a state of suspended animation, until the pure air of Liberty inflates his lungs again. The Constitution of the United States is an Anti-slavery document, in its general spirit and tendencies; and under other auspices and circumstances would have been called a great act of universal emancipation, and have set every slave free in the land, being paramount law, without doing the thousandth part of violence in construction which has been done by a slaveholding interpretation, by which it has been made into a slaveholding document, to create the horrid institution by re-enacting the slave laws of the two States of Virginia and Maryland, thereby covering the two sections of the District of Columbia, in creating and regulating by territorial laws, slavery in eight of the new States, five of which, Florida, Louisiana, Mississippi, Arkansas and Missouri, were not a portion of the United States or its territories at the adoption of the Constitution of the United States. The Congress of the United States under slaveholding dictation created slavery, therefore, in Kentucky, Tennessee and Alabama, a portion of our territory at the adoption of the Constitution; and in the other five States the nation purchased the territory and created the institution in them, as territories, and the Congress then brought these five slave States into the sisterhood of the republic. And now we are told slavery is a State-institution and is beyond the reach of any power of Congress, for its extermination; that is, that Congress has power to create and fasten this infernal institution on a territory, but has no power to abolish it anywhere, after it has enacted it once into existence, either in its territorial or State character; it has no power to lop, restrain or eradicate slavery from a State or territory, but is bound to foster and nurture it with parental care, as one of the *patriarchal, domestic* and *peculiar institutions* of the south. Permit me to assert, as it regards these States, that Congress had no more power to create slavery there in the beginning, than it had to create an autocrat in either of those States or territories, in whose hand and his heirs, all power, legislative, judicial and executive, should be centred for ever with full power to sell or dispose of the bodies of all the people or inhabitants who should or might come within the bounds of his territory or State. For the power exercised in the case of slavery by one half of the inhabitants, over the other, is precisely the same in degree and kind as that described, only the number of the autocrats is increased. Each autocrat has a less number of subjects, but the power exercised is precisely the same in extent, and in relation to those on whom it operates, is the same precise autocratism, as though there was but one despot. Now I deny that Congress has lawful power to do any such thing.

Many persons run to the Madison papers published in the last few years, to ascertain the meaning of the framers of the Constitution, who met in Philadelphia in 1787, as a mere committee of the nation, sent out to report to the people the form of a Constitution for their adoption in the summer of 1788. I deny in any event, the right to resort to this mode of interpretation, to contradict the noble and glorious text of that document; but supposing this a correct mode of getting darkness into the room to show the light, still it is not applied at the right point. Thirteen State conventions were held in the year 1788, by the authority of their respective legislatures, to adopt or reject what had been framed, by a committee-convention of the nation, as a body of draughters of the form of the Constitution, who had been sent to Philadelphia, during the summer of 1787, to do that very work; not to adopt that Constitution, but to report the form of one, to the people of the States.

In the summer of 1788, the people, in their thirteen State Conventions, by the constitutional number of nine, adopted this Constitution; and if this rule of interpretation now sought to be adopted, could be made applicable anywhere, we should have to go to the *adopters*, and not the framers. What, and how did the *adopters*, the people, understand this instrument when they adopted it? Did they understand it in any sense different from what it imports on its face? Where are the secret intentions, private understandings, those implied guarantees and curious fanciful compromises of those thirteen Conventions of *adopters?* Have they ever come to light except in some long speech of some Southern slaveholding orator? How come the descendants of those slaveholders of 1788 to be made the special depositees of all those secret guarantees, compromises, and implied understandings, in behalf of slavery, now spoken of with a confidence as startling as the information communicated is important, novel, and false. This was not so. These are mere after-thoughts of despotism. No man has ever shown one word from the adopters, conflicting with the text. Shall a committee sent out by the nation, affix to well understood language of the common law, and of every day use, some secret cabalistic meaning in hostility to the text; and then get the people, through their Conventions, to adopt the Constitution for the beautiful principles it expressed on its face, and after that was accomplished, to wait till the framers and adopters are dead, and then to come out and say, ah, the people have adopted this Constitution, for what it purported on its face, but we, the sons and grandsons of the Southern framers, have a cabalistic key left by our grandfathers in the South, by which, when the word justice appears, our grandfathers meant *slavery* or *injustice;* when we used the word *persons* we meant *slaves* sometimes, and sometimes *free persons;* when we said "no person shall be deprived of life, liberty, or property without due process of law," we *there* understood a slave *to be* a chattel or a piece of property, and not *a person;* we had a sliding-scale by which we used the word person for slave when the interest of the slaveholder is to be promoted, but when the language can be applied to him as a person in another part of the instrument, and thereby set him free, the intendment is to be against liberty, and that we did not mean that he should have any of the blessings of the Constitution, but only its curses and its cruelty. When the word person means *bitter*, it is the slave's portion; when the word person means *sweet*, he has no lot or part in that matter. Although the word person never meant slave in any written document before we affixed, it among ourselves, or our grandfathers did, in this *peculiar* sense, and refused to use the word slave. This was the secret opinion of the drafters, who supposed they could thus *deceive* the adopters into adoption. When we enacted that Article by which we said "The United States shall guarantee a republican form of government to each of the States," we knew the old and true meaning of a republican government to be one in which the government was made by and for the benefit of the governed, and that each person in a republican form of government was born free and equal, and entitled to life, liberty, and the pursuit of happiness. This, we knew, would, by force of this provision in the Constitution of the United States, if faithfully honored, blot out slavery from every State Constitution, and every State upholding a proposition of slavery by State legislation, it being diametrically opposite to a republican form of government; therefore, it was agreed secretly, as a compromise, by the framers of the Constitution, as one of the secret compromises or implied guarantees, against liberty, that this should be an *unexercised article*, or an *unused function* of the Federal Constitution, as a sort of fifth wheel to a coach; because, if carried out, it would cut up slavery, root and branch, in the old States then made, and in the new *to be made*. Therefore, says this secret compromise-keeper, we, at the session of Congress in 1845, in pursuance of our secret compromise of interpretation of language, with its *use* and *disuse*, and under the suspension of that article of the Federal Constitution guaranteeing a republican form of government, we admitted Florida as a State, as we had several slave States before, in which we permitted this Article of the Constitution, guaranteeing a republican form of government to each State, to be overridden and totally disregarded, as though it did not exist; and in the Florida Constitution Slavery is held such a sacred and central right among her Institutions, that it is placed out of reach and beyond the control of her own legislature, and that colored freemen coming into that State from Maine, Massachusetts, or other free States, may be sold as slaves: and the right the Constitution guarantees to each citizen of one State in enjoying all the privileges of citizenship in another State, says our secret compromise-keeper, means, as it was understood by the framers in the cabalistic catalogue, that this part of the Constitution should never apply to a Massachusetts or Rhode Island citizen, if his great grandmother had a drop of African blood in her veins; and that although the Constitution of the United States had abolished attainders in this country, still, so far as free colored citizens were concerned in coming from free to slave States, they were to be regarded, in defiance of the Constitution of the United States, as attainted,—yes, the victims of a *colored attainder*, and subject to the awful judgment of perpetual slavery for showing their colored heads with no helmet but the Federal Constitution for their protection in a slave State. And if the old State of New Jersey had had the benefit of the Federal Constitution before the adoption of your new Constitution of 1844, and if Congress had given this State the practical benefit of a Republican form of Government, by abolishing in Congress your State slave laws, as contrary to a Republican form of Government, it would not have been necessary for me to have troubled your Honors, the legislation of Congress being paramount to all State Constitutions and State legislation on all points within its Constitutional jurisdiction. And although the Constitution of a State may be silent on the subject of slavery, still, if slaveholding legislation dishonor the State statute book, then Congress has jurisdiction to abolish such State law, as renders the form of that State Government hostile to a Republican form of Government. The form of a State Government may be Republican in its Constitution, but legislatiom may spring up in that State, by which one half of the people may assume to own the other half, in direct hostility to a Republican form of Government, and the United States, said Mr. S., is then bound, by some exercise of sovereign power, to restore to the people of New Jersey, a Republican form of Government, either by legislation in Congress or by the exercise of judicial power through the Federal or State judiciaries; and if through the latter, then I am in my proper place to contend here this day that this old law of slavery was unconstitutional ever since the adoption of the Constitution of the United States, as being contrary to the fundamental guarantee of the Republic, and all State laws conflicting with said guarantee of a Republican form of Government are null and void, as much as a State law violating the liberty of conscience secured by the Constitution; and if this ground be a sound position, the slave laws have been void from the adoption of the Constitution, as being in direct hostility to the solemn guarantee in the Constitution in favor of a Republican form of Government. Give me, said Mr. S., a Republican form of Government in the Constitution and the legislation of a State, and I defy any man to hold a human being in that State as a slave, according to the law of that country, until the meaning of language is revolutionized.

Said Mr. S., the very idea of a Constitution of the United States in an enlarged view, if he were able to take one, would be replete with consequences full of glorious import to the bondmen of this land. As has been said by me before in the course of this argument, a Constitution springs from our weakness and need of protection, and is a covenant of the whole people with each *person*, and of each *person* with the whole people, for the protection and defence of our natural rights, of life, liberty, and the pursuit of happiness. Is it possible to conceive that a people meeting from their mutual weakness, and after coming together, conclude to make a charter party of piracy? That, although they agree to protect and defend five-sixths of the people in their natural rights, yet, as it regards the other sixth, they solemnly covenant and guarantee, to give them no protection or advantage therefrom, but covenant to strip said one-sixth of their natural rights of life, liberty, and the pursuit of happiness; and reduce them to chattels, men-breathing-property, so that they would be infinite losers by forming a Constitution. Instead of having their natural rights protected, they are stript of the right to themselves, and delivered over to masters, who, drunk or sober, reasonable or unreasonable, sensible or foolish, are to make for them Constitutions and laws, in the height of passion, prompted by lust, avarice or meanness, from hour to hour, and day to day, until life's end. The slaveholders contend the Constitution of the United States secured them these terrible advantages. If it did, and the adopters had so understood it, I do not believe a single State would have seriously entertained an idea for its adoption for a single moment, north of the State of Delaware.

To be sure, said Mr. S., we have lived under an invisible Constitution of slaveholding construction for fifty-five years, which we have never seen, but have often bitterly felt—the good honest anti-slavery Constitution which should have gone into operation on the fourth of March, 1789, as it was honestly adopted, and if carried out, in the integrity of its high and glorious purpose, would, long ere this, have extirpated slavery from this guilty land, and made it the paradise of the New World. But the government, from its adoption, has been under, as a general proposition, the control of slaveholding Presidents, Vice Presidents, Speakers of the House of Representatives, who organized the legislative power with five millions of whites at the south, and ten millions of whites in the north. The south should have had three of the nine judges of the Supreme Court of the United States, but they have five and the north four; they have two-thirds of the foreign ministers, the principal officers on the sea and on the land. The south have furnished the spiracles through which the government has breathed, yes, and the eyes with which it saw, the ears with which it heard, and the tongues and pens by which it spoke and wrote. It is no wonder the ship lost the track of its contemplated voyage, and became the abused organ of a section of the land whose supposed interests prosecuted an implacable war upon human rights, or in other words the basis and prosperity of whose peculiar institutions were quickened into life by tears and blood, and found their proper aliment in crushing and prostituting the rights of one half of their own population, and holding human labor in contempt, by which three millions of their own population being white men, could not labor by the side of the slave without disgrace; and they, the whites, having no capital but their labor, sunk down to a point of degradation but little above the slaves, no schools, they became the *lazaroni* of this continent, while some forty thousand oligarchists, owning most of the land and the slaves, and being prompted by ambition and money, moved by the common spirit of slavery, the true bond of connection and source of their political power; these men have snatched this Constitution from the nation, and have given us by the force of suppression, violation, construction and interpretation, commingled with their fanciful guarantees and compromises, a Constitution as by them administered, bearing a faint resemblance to the one given us by the fathers of the Revolution, with their wounds yet unhealed from the battle-fields of freedom. The preamble of the Constitution of the United States must have been adopted after the whole document had been prepared by the framers, as the grand exponent of intention; and as so much is said by slaveholding casuistry, that I have often thought the framers of that instrument had a melancholy foreboding, that attempts might be made by the crafty and designing of an after age, to pervert that document so plain and so full of good sense and virtuous principle to some sinister purpose; therefore, as an everlasting finger-board pointing to the straight road of intent, they virtually said,—"Here we unlock our hearts, as to object and design, and we say, trust not those who tell you this is not the truth. This is our design: We, the people of the United States, in order to form a more perfect union, establish justice, secure domestic tranquillity, provide for the common defence and promote the general welfare, and secure the blessings of Liberty, for us and our posterity, do establish and ordain this Constitution for the United States of America."

What purity and nobility of object! How much have we had practically of this Constitution, by slaveholding construction? said Mr. S. Let us see how it would read if made for the object contended by slaveholders and their apologists, and as we practically see it administered. "We, five-sixths of the people of the United States, in order to secure a union among ourselves, which shall make the other sixth curse the union, and to establish justice for five-sixths by the most cruel injustice to the other sixth; to provide for the common defence of five-sixths, by taking away all public and private defence from the other sixth; to promote the particular welfare of five-sixths by destroying the entire welfare of the other sixth; to secure the blessings of liberty to five-sixths, and the curses of never-ending slavery to the other sixth, we do ordain this Constitution for the United States of America."

What would the adopters in the thirteen States have said to such a draft of a Constitution? Most of the thirteen States, on organizing the conventions of 1788, for rejection or adoption, would have resolved to have let the common hangman hang this Constitution on the gallows, with caricatures of the leaders in the convention of 1787, and closed the scene by burning it up, and have adjourned *sine die*. Another Convention of the United States would have been called by an indignant people, and the first article would have abolished slavery, by name, in the United States, as an everlasting disturbing cause, no longer to be trusted to disgrace our soil. Many seem to think, we derive our natural, as well as citizen, rights, from a Constitution. That, said Mr. S., cannot be so. Our natural rights are derived from our Maker, and the Constitution is like a fence around them to protect them from the invasion of others. Men derive title by letters-patent from the Supreme power of the State, to their land, and the fence is placed around it to protect it from the wandering herd. Constitutions may also be said, said Mr. S., to be of American origin, and it is not possible we were so corrupt in the morning of the science. To be sure England talks of her Constitution; she speaks of *Magna Charta* obtained by fierce and ignorant barons, in the year 1215, with sword in hand from feeble John; also the introduction of the Protestant religion, by Henry VIII., and the Revolution of 1688, and some other important epochs like the Reform Bill, which added to the current stream of imperial Legislation, all considered, being "*moles indigesta*," make the sum and substance of what an Englishman means by the Constitution of his country. France made several Constitutions during the political paroxysms and revolutions of that curious people, during the latter end of the eighteenth and the beginning of the nineteenth centuries, but at last this gallant people revolved in a circle of elementary expedients, from

1789 to the war of the Barricades in 1830, making organic experiments, to collect the true sense of the nation respecting the safest place or hands in which to lodge power, from which the greatest amount of protection might be expected with the least burden to the people. Different forms of primal law were submitted to the people for adoption or rejection.

But, look at Russian, Prussian, German, and Italian States; here each person is looking to imperial, royal, or ducal prerogatives, for that security of life, liberty, and property, which should never have been absorbed by the Crown, but should always have constituted a fundamental *layer* of human rights, coming from, and adopted by the people, as their wall of defence.

Our Colonies were in the habit of receiving gifts of a political character, carefully sent over the Atlantic after them, in grants, patents, bills of rights, and charters; the very rights which they could not have left behind them, and *been men*. These Constitutions, anywhere and everywhere, as a general rule, are made to defend human rights and not to crush them. The very idea of a Constitution is like a life-preserver, made to save men in their danger in the water, and is not to be loaded with lead to sink them. There are innumerable modes by which human rights have been crushed, without calling in the very thing which should protect them, with which to accomplish so diabolical a purpose. To suppose ships made on purpose to preserve five-sixths, and expressly to drown the other sixth who sailed in them; the bridge to precipitate its sixth passenger over it into the river; is not more absurd in supposition, than to suppose a United States Constitution an instrument of ruin and destruction to every sixth man who sought its protection. Instead of an asylum he finds it to be a dungeon with fetters; that he is to be bereaved, and his posterity in all coming generations, of all capacity to have natural rights; the forlorn victims of avarice, lust, cruelty, and contempt; *himself*, property owned, and in the most abject form, shorn of the power to assert the strength Heaven gave him to protect his most valuable rights. Rights! Amazing! he has no rights but the right to be abused, to be whipped, to starve, to suffer, and to die!! This idea of a Constitution being used as a death-warrant to execute human rights, is a horrid solecism! incomprehensible, yea, a sublime absurdity; the greatest insult ever offered to the human understanding; and certain men pretend such is the Constitution of the United States. If the Constitution was an animated being, with reason and a voice, said Mr. S., and were you to ask her to speak and say, was she made to uphold slavery, and destroy human rights, she would answer, "As to slavery I know not what you mean by the word, I never used it in my life; I was born and brought into this world for the single purpose of protecting the rights of persons, defending men from the violations of their human rights, from invasion from abroad, or forceful wrong on the soil. I know no one, except as a *person* possessing the rights of life, liberty, and the pursuit of happiness, and for their protection I put forth my power. When the free men and women of this country are counted as a basis of representation in Congress and for Presidential Electors (Indians not taxed excepted), and three-fifths of all other persons are to be counted, and if States or individuals call those three-fifths slaves, serfs, or connecting links between men and monkeys, and even treat them as such, I only know them as I do the rest of mankind, as persons; my eyes can only see men as persons, my ears can only hear the cry of men as persons, possessed of natural rights. I cannot be used to destroy the liberties of any innocent man. It is not within the range of my power, unless I am perverted to purposes contrary to my instincts." Who dare affirm, says she, that I guarantee slavery and make compromises for its support. Oh! says she, it is all false, it is directly the reverse; I guarantee to each State a republican form of government, which confers the equal right of life, liberty, and property to each innocent human being in each of the twenty-seven States; that is my right, my power, my nature, prerogative, scope, end, and object of my existence; and slavery exists in this country to my unutterable confusion, by my violation direct, and by reason of the people of this land having refused to allow me to prostrate slavery through the judiciary or Congress, under my guarantee of a republican form of government to the States. *Persons* bound to service or labor by laws of one State, I say, shall not be withheld, but shall be delivered up on claim of him to whom such service or labor is due. Here I deal with persons again. If the wife, the son, the daughter, the apprentice, the prisoner from his bail, escape into other States, I order all of these persons to be delivered to the husband, or the father, or the master, or their bail, to whom such labor and service is due, and for this purpose I am a perpetual treaty between the States, to accomplish these just objects, and save the effusion of blood. If, says the Constitution, a slave is not a person within the protection which I afford to all persons where I say "no person shall be deprived of life, liberty, or property, without due process of law," then he is a being I have no right to touch and deliver up, for I can only deliver up persons bound to, or who owe service or labor as persons and not as slaves; and if these persons are slaves, then I am under the most solemn promise and obligation not to explain away, but to see that slave-persons, if you please, are not deprived of life or liberty, without due process of law, which must have been some distinct adjudication that the being was a slave by a court, acting on the principles of the common law. No such court has been organized in this land, no such judgments have been rendered. If he is within the protection of the *magna charta* part of my character, then I will not deliver the man to his master, as you are pleased to call him, until a judgment of some kind, showing that the man owes service to another, and has been deprived of his liberty by due process of law. Some record of that kind must be shown, or I cannot deliver him up.

Said Mr. S., I demand that these persons be delivered up to enjoy their liberty, on the ground of the declaration in the Constitution of the United States declaring that "no person shall be deprived of life, liberty, or property, without due process of law." There is not a slave or servant, so held, of the four thousand of both sorts in New Jersey, but what are entitled to their liberty by the Constitution of the United States.

Said Mr. S., it is a curious and a ridiculous idea of some, that our fathers had secret thoughts of crime against man, which they had not the courage to express, under the name of intentions, when they drafted the Constitution of the United States; and that we, out of respect to the unrecorded, unwritten, villanous intentions, and wicked wishes of our venerable ancestors, should take those wicked thoughts and unrecorded intentions of crime against the rights of man, as our Contsitution, under the idea of intention, rather than the beautiful text itself, so full of life, liberty, and justice. Said Mr. S., the Constitution of the United States, on its own face, is safe, and more to be relied on to explain its own meaning with justice to the framers, adopters, and us, their posterity, than all we could learn from each drafter and each adopter, could we summon them before a court of justice to explain it as they understood it, on the 4th of March, 1789, the day it went into operation. To be sure, if the adopters ever thought of slavery, they did not think to name it, and must have supposed it near its end, and they did not wish to disgrace the nation by the admission that so foul and base a thing ever existed. This is truly lamentable, to think the human mind is yet in such a low state of civilization, that from this point to enter goose-hood, would be elevation, and that men should delight to lay hold of absurd views, as the one exposed, to justify themselves in the perversion of that glorious instrument, to some low and grovelling purpose, pecuniary or political.

Mr. S. said that he felt mortified to think it should be necessary for him, in the 19th century, to stand in Republican America, the live-long day, before one of the highest courts in intellect, learning, and station, to prove a human being a man, and not a thing. The proposition that the colored people of this State held in bondage, are men, born free and independent, by the law of nature, is one above all demonstration, outstrips all logical deductions, and addresses itself to our every perception, for its truth, which can gain nothing from analogy, and borrow nothing from illustration, comparison cannot aid in its development, and similes cannot make it more clear to the human mind. Antiquity and to-day utter the same response. It is the same yesterday, to-day and for ever. Every degree of latitude and longitude renders the same verdict, whether at Timbuctoo or at Trenton; whether in mind, or in body, for time or eternity, they are men and women, creatures of hope, gazing on the same bright, strong, beautiful and ancient Heavens, on which Adam and Solomon, Daniel and Paul, Copernicus and Columbus, turned their admiring eyes; the frames of colored men, their human countenance divine, containing the same unerased lineaments, vindicating in celestial heraldry the grandeur of their descent, the greatness of their origin—showing that God is their Father, that all men are brethren of one blood, that the sweets of life, the joy of liberty, the hope and pursuit of happiness, are the gifts of the Great Father, to all, and each of his children, with a power and privilege for ever to climb the ascending heights of eternity, through the merits of His Son, increasing in happiness and knowledge, through the endless day of Heaven.

Said Mr. S., the greatest announcement affecting the interests of man ever made since the advent of the Redeemer, was the synopsis of the rights of man, made by the immortal signers of the Declaration of Independence, on the 4th day of July, 1776.

The announcement was antagonistic to the opinions of all former ages, and the then existing powers of this world. Russel, Sidney, Milton, Cromwell, and Locke, were permitted to ascend the mount of discovery, and behold, as by prophetic sight, in the land of the setting sun, beyond the vast Atlantic, a people asserting what these philosophers believed; that all men were created free and equal, and possessed of certain inalienable rights, amongst which were life, liberty, and the pursuit of happiness. What they hoped for man, we have seen and heard. When this sublime declaration was made on the 4th of July, 1776, it was high treason, and political atheism, in every other Government on earth.

To all other governments with birth-born kings, birth-born legislators, birth-born judges, this declaration of the American revolutionists was a thousand times more formidable, said Mr. S., than war or revolution itself. This was a great fundamental proposition, placing all men on a level, and as equals, in the start of the journey of existence; stating the value, the riches of their elemental capital, which no insolvency could divest, no bankruptcy carry away. Slavery, or the inheritable dominion of man over man, with its complicated train of truckling dependencies, artificial distinctions, the iron-railing of caste, were in one day, by the great proposition of the 4th of July, struck down as false in principle. This was the sentiment of a New World, and the signers of the great human being *postulatum*, spoke for themselves, and the unborn nations of this great continent, representing this great Americanism of the new hemisphere. The glorious sound went careering through the world, that all men are created free and equal. The Massachusetts slave heard its music, and joined in the chorus, and his freedom was confessed. The slaves of New York and Pennsylvania listened to the joyful acclaim; the man-chattel of New Hampshire caught the still-small voice, and joined in thanks to Heaven, that all were free. Congress caught the sound, and said, the African slave-trade should cease on our part for ever, and that no slave should tread the States of Ohio, Illinois, Indiana, Michigan, and the territories of Wisconsin and Iowa. The angel of deliverance flew with the mighty scroll in her right hand over valley and mountain to the vast lands of Mexico, and proclaimed from the summit of her smoking volcanos, that all men were born free and equal; and in one day, 50,000 black slaves, and two millions of enslaved indians, in their *repartimentos*, in the mountains, in the mines, in the workshops, and on the roads, in their chains, heard the glorious decree, and they all in chorus joined, and sung, "that all men are created free and equal," and in that instant they stood up free. The angel cried again in Guatimala and Peru, from the depth of the blue heavens, "that all men were created free." The black and red slave heard his voice, from the mountain and the mine, the hill and the hollow, that all men were created free and equal, and their fetters fell from their delivered hands as they lifted them to Heaven; and then they sung, "all men are created free and equal," for they were free.

Along upon the mighty Andes the angel flew, and from Chimborazo's icy top, she cried again so loud and long, that the tens of thousands of poor bondsmen of Chili heard, some in those unvisited regions, subterranean, damp, dreary, digging gold ore and veins of silver, far under the floor of the roaring Pacific, who never saw light; while others were delving in the depths and bowels of the Andes, to satisfy the accursed thirst of gold; others in smelting-houses loaded with chains; others driving, as serfs, their master's flocks of goats and sheep on the mountain's side, and the loaded mule along; others with loads upon their heads, in the rounds of common life, who wore out their being for thankless masters; others to galleys chained; others bound to posts, whose backs were being scourged; others in a deferential form were listening to the raging words of graceless masters. All heard the long, the loud trumpet sound, "that all men were created free and equal." All around the whips and fetters fell, and in one joyful hour, in time, up went the glorious chorus of response from men who were slaves no more, who said and sung "*all men are created free and equal.*" The joyful proclamation, by the angel made, and the sublime chorus, and humanity's reply, rolled over the great mountain, and down its eastern slant, and the slaves of Guayaquil, Columbia, Venezuela, and Bolivia, learnt to sing the holy notes, "that all men are created free and equal;" and in one day deliverance came to all these sons of sorrow and of toil. The angel then to the West Indies flew, and the men of Hayti said, throughout that Island, all men are free, and one million stood up enfranchised; the anthem of deliverance was sung in each British Isle on the 1st of August, 1838, and 800,000 slaves in one moment became 800,000 British Freemen. The angel flew to the Cape of Good Hope, and sung her celestial song, and in one day, 100,000 bondmen cried from the Cape inland 600 miles East and West, from sea to sea, "we all are free." The angel balanced on his pinions, flew and cried in the ears of the Bey of Tunis, and in the Egyptian Ali Pasha's, "that all men are created free and equal." These sons of Mahomet heard, and the Heaven-made-decree obeyed, and in those lands of darkness and of death, in one day each slave cried out, "I am free! I am free!" On the 1st of April, 1844, the angel of peace and good will towards men, blew a louder and longer blast than he ever yet had done; it was heard over the hundred millions of the East Indies, saying "all men were created free and equal." In a moment the hereditary serf, the caste-marked million, and slaves by descent, for ages, in all 12,000,000 told, started into life and joy, amidst rattling chains and broken fetters falling from them, their eyes streaming with tears, grateful to Heaven as they flowed, and they all joined in the glorious song which they now sung, "that all men are created free," and "that they were slaves no more!"

Said MR. S, we live in an abolition age, when the dungeons which have incarcerated suffering humanity, are being broken in, and unlocked in every corner of our benighted world, and the captive bid come forth; and may I entreat this Honorable Court to share in the unfading glory of opening this castle of slavery, New Jersey, with the key of the new Constitution, and the other keys he had the honor to submit to this Court, by which to let oppressed men go free.

Here MR. S. closed his opening argument, having spoken until six o'clock P. M.

The Court adjourned until Thursday morning, at ten o'clock, A. M. The Court met at ten o'clock A. M., on the 22d of May, and Chief Justice HORNBLOWER made a very able, eloquent, and affecting address, to two fine looking young men, who were sentenced to be executed in August next, for the murder of Parke and Rasner.

At eleven o'clock A. M., MR. ZABRISKIE opened his argument for the defence of the Claimants of these persons, and spoke till half after one, with a good deal of talent and power. The Court adjourned until three o'clock P. M. MR. ZABRISKIE resumed, and concluded at half after three, P. M.

MR. BRADLEY, as Counsel for the Claimants, spoke with much energy and ingenuity until five o'clock P. M., when he closed.

MR. STEWART replied from five o'clock P. M. to six. The Court adjourned until seven, P. M., and MR. STEWART spoke from seven P. M., until half after ten, and closed.

It is regretted that the arguments of Messrs. ZABRISKIE and BRADLEY, could not have been given at length, but many of the points which they made will appear in MR. STEWART'S reply. It is not expected we should report all MR. S. said, first and last, in eleven hours of delivery.

MR. STEWART said in reply, that he must express his gratitude to the learned Counsel, for the kind compliments paid to his intellect, by one who had given us so strong evidence, that he himself enjoyed the singular fortune of a fine mind, embellished with the advantages of a polished education, and what he could not command from research, he might still enjoy by the power of reflection.

MR. S. said the learned Counsel had alluded to the fact, that the first person they had seen alive, who was an abolitionist, in the county of Bergen, was the person, who served these writs of *Habeas Corpus*, MR. PALMER, and the Counsel gravely informs us, that the people did not *tar* and *feather* him. Said MR. S., I suppose this statement is made as a distinguished compliment to his neighbors in that county, and as the highest proof they have ever given of their civilisation; and it is to be hoped they may never, in an evil hour, fall below this high water mark of their advancing elevation. MR. ZABRISKIE has told us, to frighten and almost alarm us out of this effort in behalf of crushed men, and to make us leave these slaves in the great man-trap, that if your Honors let those slaves go free under your new Constitution, the Courts will be compelled to hear arguments by wives and children, to be set free from the dominion of their husbands and parents. The bare statement of so strange a proposition relieves me from a reply to it. The gentleman has endeavored to alarm the sensibilities of the Court, by a parade of several distinct orders of modern philosophers, known under the name of Fouriers, Anti-Renters, Socialists, Owenites, Fanny Wrighters, Non-Resistants, and No-Human-Government-men, Dissolvers of the Union, Nullifiers, and Infidels. And he would wish to fasten the opinion upon the Court, that there is some sort of relation between these philosophers' views and this dry law question, which is, whether slavery in the State of New Jersey, is a *legal* and *lawful* institution or not. I confess I cannot discover any more relation between the philosophical dogmas of these different philosophers, than there is propriety in the following question: "If it is two hundred miles from this place to Boston, what is the amount of the first quarter's salary of the Lord Mayor of London?" I think when the pertinency of one of these propositions is made manifest, the other will then appear.

But, said MR. S., as there have been several attempts to lock and hook together during the gentleman's reply, things the most dissimilar and uncongenial, I will take, if the Court permit, the present opportunity to define the liberty party abolitionists' creed, a body of men who, at the late election, appeared to number about 62,500 voting men, of which body the speaker was an humble member. The liberty party abolitionists, in the United States, had been a political party, with its candidates, ever since April, 1840; and was formed from necessity, to overthrow slavery, after having tried both of the old parties in vain, each of the old parties having a slave end to it, so it was impossible to get either to undertake this work. The liberty party hold the Constitution of the United States to be, when properly interpreted, an anti-slavery document, replete with tendencies in favor of freedom; but that the slaveholding portion of this country have seized upon the reins of government, and perverted the Constitution's high intent, to the base purposes of sustaining, and increasing the power of slaveholders in every possible way, and have violated the Constitution by employing it to sanction slavery in many ways, and in the overthrow of the right of petition. The liberty party abolitionists mean to employ the Constitution, and in pursuance of its authority, and not contrary thereto, to overthrow slavery in every way, and by all lawful means. We mean as a body, and it is a part of our creed, to cling to the Union or Confederacy under all circumstances, and never give it up; slavery in, or slavery out, Texas in or Texas out: we hold on to the Union and every acre of its soil, whether it be the sands of Georgia or the mountains of Vermont, for the exaltation, purification, and enfranchisement of this land from slavery, root and branch. It is a cardinal principle from the beginning, never to vote for a slaveholder, or an apologist of slavery, but hold it our duty to vote at every election for men for town, county, State, and national officers, who will employ all lawful power to banish slavery from the nation, for the sake of three millions of slaves compelled to work without wages, as well as three millions of ignorant, poor, and *unschooled* whites in the South, the lazaroni of this continent, who are ruined by the most abject poverty, it being disgraceful, for them to labor for wages by the side of the slave. To save six millions of human beings from ruin or desolation, or one-third of our countrymen, is the exact object of the liberty party abolitionists, let it take ever so long to accomplish it. We have no motive for advancing the one, or retarding the other of the great parties, as we mean, in the end, to overthrow them both as soon as we can get our countrymen to adopt our belief; we are law-abiding and law-sustaining men, and there is no more connection between the liberty party abolitionists, and the list of philosophers just enumerated, than there is between the Chinese wall and the Erie canal. We believe in short, a man has a better right to his own wife and children, than any other man, and we suppose the curse of slavery has, as a mass, nearly ruined the men of the South, as well as the land of the slave States, and we wish to improve and save our country and our people, by our party organization. And my apology to the Court for this statement, defining our position, is, said MR. S., the attempt to injure and dishonor as high-minded and pure body of men as breathes, by making them keep company with those philosophers, however respectable they may be; yet we have not chosen their society, or opinions, in the prosecution of our enterprise. The counsel of defendant, said MR. S., has attacked New York for calling a State Convention,—I can see nothing ULTRA or radical, once in a quarter of a century, in a State's reviewing the ground it has passed over, and thus lay hold of the improvements time suggests, or brings to light, for perfecting her great social edifice. The old way to amend the fabric of government in Europe, was on the battle-field, amidst the clangor of arms and roar of artillery, with bullets for *yeas*, and cannon balls for *nays.* Mr. S. confessed he much preferred the mode adopted by the State of New York. The learned counsel, to get rid of the force of the first Article of the new Constitution of this State, says it is a mere abstraction, a rhetorical flourish, and is not a *part* of the Constitution, in reality, not binding us to do anything. Said MR. S., I should like to know where I am to begin to read the new Constitution, and how much of it is to be rejected as surplussage?

The other counsel, MR. BRADLEY, says this section of the Constitution is a mere braggadocio, a mere telling England that all men are free and independent by nature, and it is *so* said, to let England know that our people *know* that we are as good as her Lords and Commons, Kings and Queens, and that it grew out of our revolutionary jealousy, of our own importance, when we first inserted it, in the Declaration of Independence. Said MR. S., this is queer indeed! New Jersey, in her old Constitution, made two days before the Declaration of Independence, was perfectly silent then; when the reason for bragging might have operated, she is very meek *then;* not one word is said about human rights; but 68 years afterwards in September, 1844, when all danger is for ever passed, according to the gentleman, New Jersey sticks up her bristles, and says, "I would have you know, old England, yes, old John Bull, and you Miss Victoria Guelph, and Mr. Albert Coburg, that we are as good by nature, and as independent as any of you, *yes, that we be.*" But the sober-minded, brave, and considerate Jerseyman never had such a thought pass through his mind, at the time he voted for its adoption. He had too much regard for his own dignity, and too much respect for England, to employ himself in such a miserable small game of swelling and surf-making, to elevate the character of his country. The noble-minded Jerseyman is willing that other countries should amuse themselves with the baubles of kings, queens, and lords, as national dolls and play-things, without considering himself undervalued in the least by not being used for the same puerile and harmless purpose by his own countrymen; and the last place in the world he would seek to curl the lip of scorn, would be in his own great fundamental and organic law, asserting his own freedom, dignity, and independence. Said MR. S., MR. B. contends that Moses' law sanctioned slavery, and the buying the heathen around about for money. Yes, there was a kind of servitude which looks like the buying the heathen by those ancient Jews for money. But, said MR. S., the Jewish government was a theocracy, and everyl aw, decree, or order of government, began with "Thus saith the Lord," as a standing formula; whether the document, law, or proclamation, came from the elders, a king, a general, or a high-priest, from a good man, or bad one, whoever had occasion to employ the character of the government, as that was a theocracy, and these rulers always used "Thus saith the Lord," as a universal preface to the law. All of Moses' laws were not from God; but Moses' system was a code of particulars, some from God, and others from man. The Saviour settles this question in the case of that law of Moses, by which a man might live with his wife, a month after marriage and if he did not like her, then gave her a bill of divorcement, and sent her away, however virtuous and he worthy. The Saviour says, "Moses suffered it from the hardness of your hearts, it was not so in the beginning," &c. Now, said MR. S., this month divorce; the case of a Jew being permitted to take a cow, or an ox, which had suddenly died, to the gates of the city, and there sell it to the heathen and strangers to eat (forbidding the Jews to eat it), also the case of taking interest of the heathen, and none of a Jew. Polygamy is a fourth case, and the fifth is a man's making his captive into a wife, living with her as long as he pleased, and then setting her adrift, as in the 21st chapter of Deuteronomy, all of these cases have thus "Saith the Lord," as much as good laws. These laws Moses suffered this ignorant people to adopt as a matter of expediency, but they were not the laws of God, but are properly recorded, as our laws formerly in New York were, in favor of lotteries, and regulating Long Island horse-races. But the terrible injustice of these laws, proves that man was their author, and not God; but they are recorded under the general appellation of "thus saith the Lord," because the Government was a Theocracy. This view, MR. S. believed necessary, to vindicate the purity and glory of God. There was a law of Heavenly origin which said, "whoso stealeth a man shall surely die or be put to death," which form he did not recollect, and is found in these same chapters. He, MR S., did not see how that law of God could be reconciled with American slavery; for every man and woman, or his or her ancestor, had been stolen in this country. Again, if slavery is a Bible and Heavenly institution, we should not be *opposed to it in the abstract*, as the defendant's counsel are, but everything should be done to foster and encourage it, and their honors should resign their seats rather than decide in MR. S's favor, however plain the new Constitution or other thing might be for the slave; for if the Bible countenances slavery, it is abstractly right, and the plaintiff's counsel commits a great sin in opposing slavery in the abstract, which they intend to atone for by going with all their might for it practically, and thus purge themselves for opposing what the Bible sustains in the abstract and concrete. If it is a Bible institution, which we have been abolishing in New England, New York, and Pennsylvania, let us repent in dust and ashes, and run down all the colored, the weak, the young, the Irish, the English, and the strangers on their first arrival; and catch our few suffering Indians, who are still straggling as wanderers among their fathers' graves, and make them all into slaves, and their posterity in the free States; and thus secure the blessings of Heaven, that are poured out so bountifully on Virginia, Maryland and the Carolinas.

Mr. S. said that of all remarkable arguments for ingenuity, he had heard one urged by both of his learned and ingenious adversaries, and, in fact, the main one, on which they sought to continue the institution of slavery, in this State, which surprised, yes, astonished him, by its subtlety and cruelty. In the 1st section of the 10th Article of the new Constitution of New Jersey, among other things, it says, "The common law and statute laws now in force, and not *repugnant* to this Constitution, shall remain in force until they expire by their own limitation, or be altered or repealed by the legislature; and all writs, actions, causes of action, prosecutions, contracts, claims, and rights of individuals, and of bodies corporate, and of the State, and all charters of incorporation, shall continue, and all indictments which shall have been found, or may hereafter be found for any crime or offence committed before the adoption of this Constitution, may be proceeded upon, as though no change had taken place."

The point the defendant's counsel would raise, is this; admitting that the new Constitution has abolished the old slave laws, root and branch, as being "repugnant" to the new Constitution; still under the name of "claims and rights of individuals" which "should continue," the rights of master and slave are both preserved in the 1st section of the 10th Article of the new Constitution under the head of "rights *preserved*," as defendant's counsel contend. The counsel further contend for defendants, that it is good law without such saving clause in the Constitution; and that all rights are preserved, notwithstanding a constitution, hostile to them on its face, has abolished the laws which created the rights, in so many words, *totidem verbis.*

Said Mr. S., I deny these propositions *in toto*, as applied to a case of slavery. *Reserved rights!* said Mr. S., they would be *reserved wrongs!* and upon that principle a State could not abolish slavery, as for instance, suppose South Carolina makes a new Constitution, and abolishes slavery, and with, or without a reservation of the *rights* of the citizens; according to the argument we hear, the rights of the master are all taken up and preserved in the new Constitution, to the services of the slaves; the rights of sale of labor, or sale of the slaves, or their offspring, are the same as before. They alter this Constitution again, and re-assert, ten years afterwards, that slavery shall never exist in South Carolina; but the planter smiles at the imbecility of the Convention, and says, although they have for the second time abolished slavery by the Constitution, and all laws which maintain it, yet according to the arguments of the defendant's counsel, in New Jersey, my rights are all preserved to the slaves, and that is all I ask; and furthermore, says he, it is curious to see how the body of this glorious institution of slavery survives its own decapitation. They cannot, says he, abolish slavery, even in a Constitution made on purpose, but the Divine rights of slavery will survive, and ride carcering over all human attempts at their annihilation; and what, says the South Carolina planter, is the peculiar beauty of this proposition, is, that by the universal admission of all jurists, slavery can only exist by positive law, for its support; but, says he, I have now discovered how it may exist without positive law for its support, but in deadly opposition to the most stringent organic Constitutional Law, for its entire abolition and express destruction. Once in a nation, and adopted by law, no form of law can banish it, as it lives under the name of a "right preserved;" yes, it lives and flourishes with an endless life. It is the real "live-for-ever." Yes, if this argument is sound, the most monstrous wrong in the universe, for whose destruction a new Constitution was expressly made, flourishes and prevails; yes, lo! the melancholy spectacle is presented to the astonished world, that although the laws sustaining slavery are all abolished, yet slavery has a more solemn and formidable protection, as a reserved right, than it ever had before, and that too in the bosom of its own executioner. The counsel, I have no doubt, hopes the shrewdness of this argument will be its apology for want of solidity. The master never had a single just right to the slave, and the Constitution no more preserves any for him, than it does the turnpike for highwaymen, the treasure in my house for a thief, or the thoughtless young heir, for a prey to black-legs and sharpers.

Mr. S. said, after this view of this question had been taken, he should consider the concession virtually made, that slavery was repugnant to the new Constitution; that the Massachusetts decision ended this cause, if good authority. But slavery had been spoken of by the defendant's counsel with great respect. Said Mr. S., I regard it as the curse of the Nation. Virginia, at the time of the first census, in 1790, had more than double the inhabitants of the State of New York: now it is sadly reversed, New York has about double that of Virginia. Virginia, with nearly double the territory of New York, and more good land than New York, situated in the most benignant climate, to be found under the bright Heavens, penetrated

4

with large bays, and beautiful, noble, and navigable rivers, stretching to the metropolis of our land, washed by the Ohio; no land whose mountains are more ready to burst with their mineral wealth than her's; whose lead, iron, coal, and copper, lie hoarded in those beautiful mountains, in value beyond the computations of numbers, or the dreams of avarice. But that wealth shall never be explored, raised, or enjoyed by the palsied arm of slavery. No, it is reserved for the vigor of the freeman's strength; not dishonored by the blight of unpaid labor: those treasures will only come at the call of honored and free labor.

Look at hundreds of thousands of acres of fair and valuable land in Western Virginia, which would make beautiful farms, when free labor shall be honored, now sold at six cents, ten cents, and twenty-five cents an acre. Look at hundreds of old farms within forty and fifty miles of Washington, to be sold from $4 to $10 per acre, with their dilapidated buildings, covered with mortgages and trust deeds; the same land, slavery abolished, and freemen to cultivate, would be worth from $30 to $80 per acre. Look at whole regions and portions of counties abandoned, as commons, in old Eastern Virginia, where you may ride for hours, without meeting an inhabitant in the lower counties of this State,—land yet beautiful, if its powers of fecundity were truly developed by freemen, once the seats of joyful hospitality of the last century, now as silent as the ruins of Palmyra and Babylon. The young growth of timber coming up, the wild animals resuming their ancient dominion, the traveller from the old world, as he measured his lonely steps over these forsaken abodes of men, would inquire what desolating wars have consumed the sons and daughters of this fair land? in what Chronicles shall it be found, or what more than Egyptian plague has been and bereaved these uncultivated lands of their proprietors, and has left the fox to come in at the window, and the owl to hoot at noon, and appointed the stork, the raven, the cormorant and bittern, to perform the hospitalities of these dilapidated homes of departed men? Alas! the curse of the slave's foot-print has been *here*, unrewarded toil has been *here*, inalienable rights have been cloven down *here*, man has ranked with the ox, in the market, *here;* marriage-rights were trodden under foot *here;* the father who begot, and the mother who bore the son and the daughter, had no rights in their children *here;* men had no right to cultivate their immortal minds *here;* justice and mercy had no abode *here;* free labor was dishonored *here;* the lash, the fetter and the chain, ruled *here;* and at last, hunger expelled the oppressor from his home *here*.

Said Mr. S., the splendid and princely plantation of George Washington, the Father of his country, presents in forty-five years one of the most melancholy and remarkable instances of that ceaseless vigilance of Providence which pursues injustice with unerring certainty, from year to year, and at last overtakes and awards the punishment affixed to fundamental violations of the great rights, which the Father of all has in the welfare of his abused children.

Thousands of acres, and money in vast amount, united in the official station of President, this plantation lying within some ten or twelve miles from the three beautiful cities of Georgetown, Washington and Alexandria, partly surrounded by the majestic Potomac river, bearing on its commercial bosom ships from the ends of the world, freighted with every human want, this plantation was ready to ship at its own door, every redundancy it bore at remunerating prices. The ambition of General Washington during the last years of his retirement was to make this favored place, with his hundred slaves, his abounding wealth, the great pattern plantation of this continent. Having done much to see his high purpose accomplished, in December, 1799, he died, having emancipated his slaves by his will. Judge Bushrod Washington, his nephew, with a large family of slaves, with a salary of $4500 from the United States as Judge for life, succeeded his illustrious uncle; and in 1819 or thereabouts, made a large sale of some thirty to fifty slaves, being near one-half. The nation was incensed at the act; his public apology was, that he was compelled to sell part to support the rest, and thus the process of *anthropophagi*, or man eating man, indirectly commenced; the cultivation was miserable and the bushes encroached; some fields by 1828 or 1829 at the time of the Judge's death began to be given up. John A. Washington, the nephew of the Judge, succeeds, the woods still gained, field after field, under slave and master's cultivation, went back to primeval forest. And about 1839 or '40 Colonel Washington died, and in the month of April or May, 1842, the widow and her children were like Adam and Eve from Paradise driven out. "Great Burnam Wood had come to Dunsinane" as in Macbeth; the door was locked, the gate was shut, slavery's curse and the wilderness had expelled them from this ancient home of America's great man. This is slavery, sooner or later, everywhere; the curse of Heaven is upon it.

Mr. S. said, it would be a fraud on the people of New Jersey, so to construe their new Constitution, as the defendant's counsel had contended. There was not one in fifteen of the seventy-thousand who voted for its adoption, who would not glory and feel elevated by the act. To see these poor bondmen and their children free, must be matter of joy to all. The argument they would not be so well off, is too stale to be used in 1845 in New Jersey. For if the argument proves anything it proves too much, and that it would be better for the great mass of mankind to be slaves, and that it is a desirable institution. On that point I have no more to say except that those who believe such doctrines can easily put themselves and families in possession of its blessings, as several of the slave States are so kind as not to refuse to those of Anglo-Saxon descent the *peculiar privileges of that pleasant-spoken institution.*

To illustrate one of the abhorrent features of the institution in the slave States, Mr. Stewart, adverting to one of the positions of the opposite counsel, supposed the following case. An old man, said he, whom we will call Tinkem, lived in Trenton, once upon a time, and not being long for this world, called his ten sons around him and told them, My sons, I have but little to give you of worldly property, and, therefore, in order to start the five oldest of you comfortably in this life, I give each of them one of their five younger brothers, to be his property,—in other words, his slave for life, and his posterity after him. And you, the five youngest of my sons, must be the slaves of your elder brothers. I do this in conformity with the usage of the citizens of a large number of the States of this Union! But the eldest son says, "Father, what are the rights and prerogatives which we shall, in that case, possess over our our slave brothers?"

"Oh," said the old man, "you will reduce them to chattels, or cattle,—living, breathing property,—that is all. It is perfectly legal, and you will be protected in the enjoyment of your property; you are no longer to regard them as sentient beings; you are to deprive them of all education, except the cart-whip instruction; you are to make them know and feel that their every moment is to be regulated by your wish and will, and that they are subject to be sold, and worked, husband apart from wife, and wife from husband; and their children from both. So, now, my sons, take your slaves, and begone!" Now (continued Mr. Stewart), the story of this horrible deed reached the ears of the citizens of Trenton, and the sanctums of its editors. A burst of indignation is the consequence. Everybody and every press exclaims "monster! monster! monster!" with one voice. It is taken up by the people, and the press of Philadelphia and New York, and language grows weak, and imagination weary, in searching for fitting epithets in which to condemn the foul and damning act of this heartless old villain, Tinkem of Trenton! Men come from a prodigious distance to get a sight of so much moral deformity, existing in a single man. The phrenologists come to examine his craniological developments, wondering what manner of man-monster he can be; and the whole nation rings with the story, and but one opinion is expressed, everywhere, in public and in private,—and that of horror and astonishment. But, your honors, pause in your honest outburst of indignation. Old Tinkem stands excused, in view of the fact that not a week comes and goes in the regions of the sunny south, that does not furnish a parallel to his conduct. A slaveholding father there gives the children of his own body, by his bond-woman, to be slaves for life, to his children by his free-woman,—I mean, his wife! It is done in twelve States out of the seven and twenty of which this Union is composed, whenever the father wishes to endow his heir out of his possessions. And this I hold to be slavery in the length and breadth of its flagitiousness; it is yet but one phase of its abounding villany. The picture is startling, frightful, revolting; but it is neither overdrawn, nor too highly colored.

Mr. S. replied to several subordinate points made, and authorities cited by the counsel of the defendants, which it is not supposed would materially improve the report of the argument. What is further said is a part of a report made of what Mr. S. said, by Mr. Otis, reporter of the New York Evening Express, and what followed Mr. Stewart's close is the report of Mr. Otis also.

Mr. Stewart drew his remarks to a close by appealing to the Court very earnestly as to the high and solemn duty left to them to perform. It is yours, may it please your honors (he said), to put the last, the finishing stroke upon slavery, in one of the noblest old States of this glorious confederation. It is an honor which you should covet. Let no man take it from you. Leave it not to other hands to finish so noble a work. What would the world say, to see a case like this, argued as it has been before this Court for two days, with the full light of this blessed and glorious Constitution shedding its rays upon it, turned off and decided against liberty, upon the worse than doubtful authority of a few extinct and exploded statutes, which stand repealed in your code by the voice of the people speaking through a Convention of their choice,—the acts of which they have also confirmed by their solemn votes? May it please your honors, I cannot believe that such will be your decision. I have too much faith in my kind for this. I feel that New Jersey will hold up the hands of this Court in coming to the support of freedom and of free institutions in her borders.

Never can the act be regretted. Conscience will approve it. Time will approve it. Death-bed reflection will approve it. Eternity and heaven will approve it. It has been long, too long postponed. But it is not too late to come up, manlike, statesmanlike, patriotlike, godlike, and declare that it is indeed true, in the language of your now organic law, that within all your pleasant borders, at least, all mankind are, by nature, entitled to perfect freedom in the possession of life, liberty, and the pursuit of happiness!

After Mr. Stewart resumed his seat, there was a pause of some duration. The scene was quite impressive. The auditory was numerous and highly respectable, and such was the impressiveness with which the closing appeal of the advocate for freedom was delivered, that no one seemed to like to be the first to break the spell his eloquence had cast upon the assembly. At length, the Bench arose, the Chief Justice adjourned the Court until to-morrow morning, and the hearing of the cases which have occupied our attention for these two days past was terminated.

The decisions therein will probably be given some time during the next term of the Court.

ARGUMENT

OF

CHARLES SUMNER, ESQ.

AGAINST THE

CONSTITUTIONALITY OF SEPARATE COLORED SCHOOLS,

IN THE CASE OF

SARAH C. ROBERTS *vs.* THE CITY OF BOSTON.

Before the Supreme Court of Mass., Dec 4, 1849.

BOSTON:
PUBLISHED BY B. F. ROBERTS,
1849.

PRINTED AT NO. 3 CORNHILL.

ARGUMENT.

May it please your Honors: —

Can any discrimination, on account of color or race, be made, under the Constitution and Laws of Massachusetts, among the children entitled to the benefit of our public schools? This is the question which the Court is now to hear, to consider, and to decide.

Or, stating the question with more detail, and with a more particular application to the facts of the present case, are the Committee, having the superintendence of the public schools of Boston, entrusted with the *power*, under the constitution and laws of Massachusetts, to exclude colored children from these schools, and to compel them to resort for their education to separate schools, set apart for colored children only, at distances from their homes less convenient than those open to white children?

This important question arises in an action by a colored child, only five years old, who, by her next friend, sues the city of Boston for damages, on account of a refusal to receive her into one of the public schools.

It would be difficult to imagine any case which could appeal more strongly to your best judgment, whether you regard the parties or the subject. On the one side is the city of Boston, strong in its wealth, in its influence, in its character; on the other side is a little child, of a degraded color, of humble parents, still within the period of natural infancy, but strong from her very weakness, and from the irrepressible sympathies of good men, which, by a divine compensation, come to succor the weak. This little child asks at your hands her *personal rights*. So doing, she calls upon you to decide a question which concerns the personal rights of other colored children; which concerns the constitution and laws of the Commonwealth; which concerns that peculiar institution of New England, the common schools; which concerns the fundamental principles of human rights; which concerns the Christian character of this community. Such parties, and such interests, so grand and various, may justly challenge your most earnest attention.

Though this discussion is now for the first time brought before a judicial tribunal, it is no stranger to the public. For five years it has been an occasion of discord to the School Committee. No less than four different reports — two majority reports, and two minority reports — forming pamphlets of solid dimensions—devoted to this question, have been made to this Committee, and afterwards published. The opinions of learned counsel have been enlisted in the cause. The controversy, leaving these regular channels, has overflowed the newspaper press, and numerous articles have appeared, espousing opposite sides. At last it has reached this tribunal. It is in your power to cause it to subside for ever.

Forgetting many of the topics, and all of the heats which have heretofore mingled with the controversy, I shall strive to present the question in its juridical light, as becomes the habits of this tribunal. It is a question of jurisprudence on which you are to give judgment. But I cannot forget that the principles of morals and of natural justice lie at the foundation of all jurisprudence. Nor can any reference to these be inappropriate in a discussion before this Court.

The great principle which is involved in this case, I shall first exhibit in the Constitution of Massachusetts, next in the legislation, and then in the judicial decisions. I shall then consider the special circumstances of this case, and show the violation of the Constitution and laws, by the School Committee of Boston, answering, before I close, some of the grounds on which their conduct has been vindicated.

I. I begin with the principle, that, according to the spirit of American institutions, and especially of the Constitution of Massachusetts, *all men, without distinction of color or race, are equal before the law.*

I might, perhaps, leave this proposition without one word of comment. The equality of men will not be directly denied on this occasion, and yet it has been so often assailed of late, that I trust I shall not seem to occupy your time superfluously in endeavoring to show what is understood by this term, when used in laws, or constitutions, or other political instruments. Mr. Calhoun, in the Senate of the United States, and Lord Brougham, in his recent work on *Political Philosophy*, (Part 2. cap. 4.) have characterized equality as impossible and absurd. If they had chosen to comprehend the true extent and application of the term, as employed on such occasions, something, if not all of the force of their objections, would have been removed. That we may better appreciate its character and its limitations, let me develop with some care the origin and growth of this sentiment, until it finally ripened into a formula of civil and political right.

The *sentiment* of equality among men was early cherished by generous souls. It showed itself in the dreams of ancient philosophy. It was declared by Seneca; when writing to a friend a letter of consolation on death, he said, *Prima enim pars Equitatis est Equalitas.* (Epist. 30.) The first part of Equity is Equality. But it was enunciated with persuasive force in the truths of the Christian religion. Here we learn that God is no respecter of persons; that he is the father of all; and that we are all his children, and brethren to each other. When the Saviour taught the Lord's prayer, he taught the sublime doctrine of the Brotherhood of mankind, enfolding the Equality of men.

Slowly did this sentiment enter the *State.* The whole constitution of government in modern times was inconsistent with it. An hereditary monarchy, an order of nobility, and the complex ranks of superiors and inferiors established by the feudal system, all declared, not the equality, but the inequality of men, and they all conspired to perpetuate this inequality. Every infant of royal blood, every noble, every vassal, was a present example, that, whatever might be the truths of religion, or the sentiments of the heart, men living under these institutions were not born equal.

The boldest political reformers of early times did not venture to proclaim this truth; nor did they truly perceive it. Cromwell beheaded his king, but caused the supreme power to be secured in hereditary succession to his eldest son. It was left to John Milton, in poetic vision, to be entranced —

With fair Equality, fraternal state.

Sidney, who perished a martyr to liberal sentiments, drew his inspiration from the classic, and not from the Christian fountains. The examples of Greece and Rome fed his soul. The Revolution of 1688, partly by force, and partly by the popular voice, brought a foreigner to the crown of Great Britain, and the establishment, according to the boast of loyal Englishmen, of the freedom of the land. But the Bill of Rights did not declare, nor did the genius of Somers or Maynard conceive the political axiom, that all men are born equal. It may find acceptance in our day from individuals in England, but it is disowned by English institutions.

It is to France that we must pass for the earliest development of this idea, for its amplest illustration, and for its most complete, accurate, and logical expression. In the middle of the last century appeared the renowned *Encyclopedie*, edited by D'Alembert and Diderot. This remarkable production, where science, religion and government were all discussed with a revolutionary freedom, contains an article on Equality, which was published in 1755. Here we find the boldest expression which had then been given to this sentiment. "Natural Equality," says the Encyclopedia, "is that which exists between all men by the constitution of their nature only. This Equality is the principle and the foundation of liberty. Natural or moral equality is then founded upon the constitution of human nature, common to all men, who are born, grow, subsist, and die in the same manner. Since human nature finds itself the same in all men, it is clear, that according to nature's law, each ought to esteem and treat the others as beings who are naturally equal to himself; that is to say, who are men as well as himself." It is then remarked, that political and civil slavery is in violation of this equality: and yet there is a recognition of the inequalities of nobility in the state. Alluding to these, it is simply said, that those who are most elevated above others, ought to treat their inferiors as beings naturally their equals, shunning all outrage, and demanding nothing beyond what is due, and demanding with humanity that which is most incontestably their due.

When we consider the period at which this article was written, we shall be astonished less at its incompleteness and vagueness, than by its bravery and generosity. The dissolute despotism of Louis XV. overshadowed France. Selfish nobles and fawning courtiers filled the royal antechambers. The councils of Government were controlled by royal mistresses. Only a few years before, in 1751, the

King had founded, in defiance of the principles of equality — but in entire harmony with the conduct of the School Committee in Boston — a military school, *for nobles only*, carrying into education the distinction of Caste. At such a period the Encyclopedia did well in uttering such important and effective truth. The *sentiment* of equality was here fully declared. Nor could it be expected at that early day that it should adequately perceive, or if it perceived, that it should dare to utter, our axiom of liberty, that all men are born equal in civil and political rights.

It is thus with the history of all moral and political ideas. First appearing merely as a sentiment, they animate those who receive them with a noble impulse, filling them with generous sympathies, and encouraging them to congenial efforts. Slowly recognized, they finally pass into a formula to be acted upon, to be applied, to be defended in the concerns of life.

Almost contemporaneously with this article in the Encyclopedia, our attention is arrested by a solitary person, poor, of humble extraction, born in Geneva, in Switzerland, of irregular education and life, a wanderer from his birth-place, enjoying a temporary home in France, — a man of audacious genius, who set at nought the received opinions of mankind, Jean Jacques Rousseau. His earliest appearance before the public, was by an eccentric *Essay on the Origin of Inequality among Men*, in which he sustained the irrational paradox, that men are happier in a state of nature than under the laws of civilization. This was followed by a later work, the *Contrat Social*. In both of these productions, the sentiment of Equality was invoked against many of the abuses of society, and language was employed going far beyond equality in civil and political rights. The conspicuous position that has been awarded to the speculations of Rousseau, and the influence which they have exerted in diffusing this sentiment, make it proper to refer to them on this occason; but the absence of precision in his propositions renders him an uncertain guide.

The French Revolution was now at hand. This great movement for enfranchisement was the expression of this sentiment. Here it received a distinct and authoritative enunciation. In the constitutions of government which were successively adopted, amidst the throes of bloody struggles, the equality of men was constantly proclaimed. King, nobles, and all distinctions of birth, passed away before this mighty and triumphant truth.

Look at these Constitutions, and see at once the grandeur of the principle, and the manner in which it was explained and illustrated. The Constitution of 1791 declares in its first article as follows: "Men are born and continue free and *equal in their rights.*" In its sixth article it says: "The law is the expression of the general will. It ought to be the same for all, whether it protects or punishes. *All citizens being equal in its eyes, are equally admissible to all dignities, places, and public employments, according to their capacity, and without other distinction than their virtues and talents.*" At the close of the Declaration of Rights there is this further explanation of it: "The National Assembly, wishing to establish the French Constitution on principles which it has just acknowledged and declared, *abolishes irrevocably the institutions which bounded liberty and equality of rights.* There is no longer, neither nobility, nor peerage, nor hereditary distinctions, nor distinction of order, nor feudal rule, nor patrimonial justices, nor any titles, denominations and prerogatives, which were thence derived, nor any order of chivalry, nor any corporations or decorations, for which proofs of nobility are required, or which supposed distinctions of birth, nor any other superiority than that of public functionaries in the discharge of their functions. * * * *There is no longer, for any part of the nation, nor for any individual, any privilege or exception to the law, common to all Frenchmen.*"—*Moniteur*, 1791, *No.* 259.

In fitful mood another Declaration of Rights was brought forward by Condorcet, Feb. 15, 1793. Here also are fresh inculcations of the equality of men. Article 1st, places Equality among the natural, civil and political rights of man. Article 7th declares: "*Equality consists in this, that each can enjoy the same rights.*" Article 8th: "*The law ought to be equal for all*, whether it recompense, or punish, or repress." Article 9th: "All citizens are admissible to all public places, employments, and functions. *Free people cannot know other motives of preference than talents and virtues.*" Article 23d: "Instruction is the need of all, and society owes it equally to all its members." Article 32d: "There is oppression when the law violates the natural, civil, and political rights which it ought to guarantee. There is oppression when a law is violated by public functionaries in its application to individual facts." — *Moniteur*, 1793, *No.* 49.

Next came the Constitution of June, 1793. This announces in its second article, that the natural and imprescriptible rights of men are "*Equality*, liberty, safety, property." And in the next article it shows what is meant by Equality. It says, "All men are equal by nature, *and before the law.*" (*Moniteur*, 1793, *No.* 178.) Here we first meet this form of definition. At a later day, after France had passed through an unprecedented series of political vicissitudes, in some of which the rights of Equality had been trampled under foot, when, at the revolution of 1830, Louis Philippe was called to a "throne surrounded by republican institutions," the charter which was then promulgated repeated this phrase. In its first article, it declared, that "Frenchmen are *equal before the law*, whatever may be their titles or ranks."

While recognizing this peculiar enunciation of the equality of men as more specific and satisfactory than the naked statement that all men are born equal, it is impossible not to be reminded that this form of speech finds its prototype in the ancient Greek language. In the history of Herodotus, we are told that "the government of the many has the most beautiful name of *isonomia*" — or *equality before the law.* (Book 3, § 80.) Thus this remarkable language, by its comprehensiveness and flexibility, in an age when equality before the law was practically unknown, nevertheless supplied a single word, which is not to be found in modern tongues, to express an idea which has been practically recognized only in modern times. Such a word in our own language, as a substitute for Equality, might have superseded some of the criticism to which this political doctrine has been exposed.

After this review, the way is now prepared to consider the nature of Equality, as secured by the Constitution of Massachussetts. The Declaration of Independence, which was put forth after the French Encyclopedia, and the political writings of Rousseau, places among self-evident truths this proposition, — "*that all men are created equal*, and that they are endowed by the Creator with certain unalienable rights; that among these are life, liberty, and the pursuit of happiness." The Constitution of Massachussetts repeats the same idea in a different form. In the first article it says: "*All men are born free and equal*, and have certain natural, essential and unalienable rights, among which may be reckoned the right of enjoying and defending their lives and liberties." The sixth section further explains the doctrine of Equality. It says: — "*No man, nor corporation, or association of men, have any other title to obtain advantages, or particular and exclusive privileges, distinct from those of the community, than what arises from the consideration of services rendered to the public;* and this title being in nature neither hereditary, nor transmissible to children, or descendants, or relations by blood, the idea of a man being born a magistrate, law-giver, or judge, is absurd and unnatural." The language here employed, in its natural signification, condemns every form of inequality, in civil and political institutions.

Though these declarations preceded, in point of time, the ampler declarations of France, they may, if necessary, be construed in the light of the latter. It is evident that they aim to declare substantially the same things. They are declarations of *Rights*, and the language employed, though general in its character, is obviously to be restrained to those matters which are within the design and sphere of a declaration of *Rights*. It is a childish sophism to adduce in argument against them the physical or mental inequalities by which men are characterized.

It is a palpable truth that men are not born equal in physical strength, or in mental capacities; in beauty of form or health of body. Diversity or inequality, in these respects, is the law of creation. From this difference springs divine harmony. But this inequality is in no particular inconsistent with a complete civil and political equality.

The equality which was declared by our fathers in 1776, and which was made the fundamental law of Massachussets in 1780, was *equality before the law*. Its object was to efface all political or civil distinctions, and to abolish all institutions founded upon *birth*. "All men are *created* equal," says the Declaration of Independence. "All men are *born* free and equal," says the Massachussets Bill of Rights. These are not vain words. Within the sphere of their influence no person can be *created*, no person can be *born*, with civil or political privileges, not enjoyed equally by all his fellow-citizens, nor can any institution be established recognizing any distinctions of birth. This is the Great Charter of every person who draws his vital breath upon this soil, whatever may be his condition, and whoever may be his parents. He may be poor, weak, humble, black — he may be of Caucasian, of Jewish, of Indian, or of Ethiopian race — he may be of French, of German, of English, of Irish extraction —

but before the Constitution of Massachussets all these distinctions disappear. He is not poor, or weak, or humble, or black — nor Caucasian, nor Jew, nor Indian, nor Ethiopian — nor French, nor German, nor English, nor Irish; he is a MAN, — the equal of all his fellow-men. He is one of the children of the State, which, like an impartial parent, regards all its offspring with an equal care. To some it may justly allot higher duties, according to their higher capacities, but it welcomes all to its equal, hospitable board. The State, imitating the divine justice, is no respecter of persons.

Here nobility cannot exist, because it is a privilege from birth. But the same anathema which smites and banishes nobility, must also smite and banish every form of discrimination founded on birth.

Quamvis ille niger, quamvis tu candidus esses.

II. I now pass to the second stage of this argument, and ask attention to this proposition. The legislature of Massachussets, in entire harmony with the Constitution, has made no discrimination of color or race, in the establishment of Public Schools.

If such discrimination were made by the laws, they would be unconstitutional and void. But the legislature of Massachussets has been too just and generous, too mindful of the Bill of Rights, to establish any such privilege of *birth*. The language of the statutes is general, and applies equally to all children, of whatever color or race.

The provisions of the law regulating this subject are entitled, *Of the Public Schools*. (Revised Statutes, chap. 23.) It is to these that we must look in order to ascertain what constitutes a Public School. None can be legally such which are not established in conformity with the law. They may, in point of fact, be more or less public: yet, if they do not come within the terms of the law, they do not form a part of the beautiful system of our public schools — they are not public schools.

It is important then to examine these terms. The first section provides that in "every town containing fifty families, or householders, there shall be kept in each year, at the charge of the town, by a teacher or teachers of competent ability and good morals, *one school* for the instruction of *children* in Orthography, Reading, Writing, English Grammar, Geography, Arithmetic and Good Behavior, for the term of six months, or two or more such schools for terms of time that shall together be equivalent to six months." The 2d, 3d, and 4th sections provide for the number of *such* schools to be kept in other towns having more than five hundred inhabitants. The language here employed does not recognize any discrimination of color or race. Thus in every town, whether there be one or more schools, they are all to be "schools for the instruction of *children*" generally — not children of any particular class, or color, or race, but children, — meaning the children of the town where the schools are.

The 5th and 6th sections provide for the establishment, in certain cases, of a school, in which additional studies are to be pursued, "which shall be kept *for the benefit of all the inhabitants* of the town." Here the language not only does not recognize any discrimination among the children, but seems directly to exclude it.

In conformity with these sections is the peculiar phraseology of the memorable law of the Colonies in 1647, founding public schools, "to the end that learning be not buried in the graves of our forefathers." This law obliged towns having fifty families "forthwith to appoint one" within their limits "to teach *all such children as shall resort to him*, to write and read." (Ancient charters, 186.)

It is on this legislation that the public schools of Massachusetts have been reared. The clause of the Revised Statutes (chap. 23) and the statute (1838, chap. 154) appropriating small sums, in the nature of a contribution, out of the school fund for the support of common schools among the Indians, do not interfere with this system. These partake of the anomalous character of all the legislation with regard to the Indians in this Commonwealth. It does not appear, however, that any separate schools are established by law among the Indians, nor that the Indians are in any way excluded from the public schools in their neighborhood.

I conclude from this examination, that there is but one kind of public school established by the laws of Massachusetts. This is the general Public School, free to all the inhabitants. There is nothing in these laws establishing any exclusive or separate school for any particular class, whether rich or poor, whether Catholic or Protestant, whether white or black. In the eye of the law there is but *one class*, in which all interests, opinions, conditions and colors commingle in harmony — excluding none, comprehending all.

From the legislation of the Commonwealth, I pass to the adjudication of the Courts.

III. The Courts of Massachusetts have never recognized any discrimination, founded on color or race, in the administration of the Public Schools, but have recognized the equal rights of all the inhabitants.

There are a few decisions only of our Court bearing on this subject, but they all breathe one spirit. The sentiment of equality animates them. In the case of *Commonwealth* vs. *Davis*, 6 Mass. R. 146, while declaring the equal rights of all the inhabitants, both in the grammar and district schools, the Court said: "The schools required by the statute are to be maintained for the benefit of the whole town, *as it is the wise policy of the law to give all the inhabitants equal privileges for the education of their children in the public schools.* Nor is it in the power of the majority to deprive the minority of this *privilege.* * * * * Every inhabitant of the town has a right to participate in the benefits of both descriptions of schools, and it is not competent for a town to establish a grammar school for the benefit of one part of the town to the exclusion of the other, although the money raised for the support of schools may be in other respects fairly apportioned."

In the case of *Withington* vs. *Eveleth*, 7 Pick. 106, the Court said, they "were all satisfied that the power given to towns to determine and define the limits of school districts, can be executed only by a geographical division of the town for that purpose." A limitation of the district, which was merely *personal*, was held invalid. This same principle was again recognized in *Perry* vs. *Dove*, 12 Pick. R. 213, where the Court say, "Towns, in executing the power to form school districts, are bound so to do it as to include *every inhabitant* in some of the districts. They cannot lawfully omit any, and thus deprive them of *the benefits of our invaluable system of free schools.*"

The Constitution, the legislation, and the judicial decisions of Massachusetts, have now been passed in review. We have seen what is contemplated by the Equality secured by the Constitution. We have seen also what is contemplated by the system of Public Schools, as established by the laws of the Commonwealth, and illustrated by the decisions of the Supreme Court. The way is now prepared to consider the peculiarities in the present case, and to apply the principle which we have thus recognized in the Constitution, in the laws and judicial decisions.

2

IV. The exclusion of colored children from the Public Schools, open to white children, is a source of practical inconvenience to them and their parents, to which white persons are not exposed, and is, therefore, a violation of Equality. The black and the white are not equal before the law.

It appears from the statement of facts, that among the rules of the Primary School Committee, is one to this effect: "*Scholars to go to the school nearest their residence.* Applicants for admission to our schools (with the exception and provision referred to in the preceding rule) are especially entitled to enter the schools nearest to their places of residence." The exception here is "of those for whom special provision has been made" in separate schools; that is, colored children.

In this rule — without the exception — is seen a part of the beauty of our Public School system. It is the boast of England, that justice, through the multitude of courts, is brought to every man's door. It may also be the boast of our Public School system, that education in Boston, through the multitude of schools, is brought to every *white* man's door. But it is not brought to every black man's door. He is obliged to go for it — to travel for it — often a great distance. The facts in the present case are not so strong as those of other cases which have come to my knowledge. But here, the little child, only five years old, was compelled, if she went to the nearest African School, to go a distance of 2100 feet from her dwelling, while the nearest Primary School was only 900 feet, and, in doing this, she would pass near no less than five different Primary Schools, forming part of our Public Schools, and open to white children, all of which were closed to her. Surely this is not equality before the law.

This simple fact is sufficient to determine this case. If it be met by the suggestion, that the inconvenience is trivial, and such as the law will not notice, I reply, that it is precisely of that character which reveals distinctly an existing inequality, and, therefore, the law cannot fail to notice it. There is a maxim of the civilian, Dumoulin, which teaches that even a trivial fact may give occasion to an important application of the law. *Modica enim circumstantia facti inducit magnam juris diversitatem.* Also from the best examples of our history, we learn that the insignificance of a fact cannot obscure the grandeur of the principle at stake. It was a paltry tax on tea, laid by a Parliament in which they were not represented that aroused our fathers to the struggles of the Revolution. They did not feel the inconvenience of the tax, but they felt its oppression. They went to war for a principle. Let it not be said, then, that the inconvenience is so slight in the present case as not to justify the appeal I now make, in behalf of the colored children, for Equality before the law.

I may go, however, beyond the facts of this case, and show that the inconvenience arising from the exclusion of colored children, is of such a character as seriously to affect the comfort and condition of the African race in Boston. The two primary schools open to these children are in Belknap street and in Sun court. I need not add that the whole city is dotted with schools open to white children. The colored parents, anxious that their children should have the benefit of education, are compelled to live in the neighborhood of the schools, to gather about them, as in the East people come from a distance to rest near a fountain or a well. They have not, practically, the same liberty of choosing their homes, which belongs to the white man. Inclination, or business, or economy, may call them to another part of the city; but they are restrained on account of their children. There is no such restraint upon the white man, for he knows that wherever in the city inclination, or business, or economy, may call him, he will find a school open to his children near his door. Surely this is not equality before the law.

Or if a colored person, yielding to the necessities of his position, removes to a distant part of the city, his children may be compelled, at an inconvenience which will not be called trivial, to walk a long distance in order to enjoy the advantages of the school. In our severe winters, this cannot be disregarded by children so tender in years as those of the primary schools. There is a respectable colored person, I am told, who became some time since a resident at East Boston, separated by the water from the main land. There are, of course, proper public schools at East Boston, but none that were then open to colored children. This person, therefore, was obliged to send his children, three in number, daily, across the ferry to the distant African school. The tolls for these children amounted to a sum which formed a severe tax upon a poor man.

This is the conduct of a colored parent. He is well deserving of honor for his generous efforts for his children. As they grow in knowledge, they will rise and call him blessed; but at the same time they will brand as accursed the arbitrary discrimination of color, in the public schools of Boston, which rendered it necessary for their father, out of his small means, to make such sacrifices for their education.

Such a greivance, even independent of any stigma from color, calls for redress. It is an inequality which the Constitution and laws of Massachusetts repudiate. But it is not on the ground of inconvenience only that it is odious. And this brings me to the next point.

V. The separation of children in the Public Schools of Boston, on account of color or race, is in the nature of *Caste*, and is a violation of Equality.

The facts in this case show expressly that the child was excluded from the school nearest to her dwelling, the number in the school at the time warranting her admission, "on the sole ground of color." The first Majority Report presented to the School Committee, to which reference is made in the statement of facts, gives, with more fulness, the grounds of this discrimination, saying, "It is one of *races*, not of *color*, merely. The distinction is one which the Almighty has seen fit to establish, and it is founded deep in the physical, mental, and moral natures of the two races. No legislation, no social customs, can efface this distinction." Words more apt than these to describe the heathenish relation of Caste, could not be chosen.

This will be apparent from the very definition of Caste. This term is borrowed from the Portuguese word *casta*, which signifies family, breed, race. It has become generally used to designate any hereditary distinction, particularly of race. It is in India that it is most often applied; it is there that we must go in order to understand its full force. A recent English writer on the subject, says, that it is "not only a distinction by birth, but is founded on the doctrine of an essentially distinct origin of the different races, which are thus unalterably separated." (Roberts on Caste, p. 134.) This is the very ground of the Boston School Committee.

But this word is not now applied for the first time to the distinction between the white and black races. Alexander Humboldt, in speaking of the negroes in Mexico, has characterized them as a Caste, and a recent political and juridical writer of France, has used the same term to denote, not only the distinctions in India, but those of our own country. (Charles Comte, *Traite de Legislation*, tom. 4, p. 445, 129.) In the course of his remarks he refers to the exclusion of colored children from the public schools, as among "the humiliating and brutal distinctions" by which their caste is characterized. It is, then, on authority and reason, that we apply this term to the hereditary distinction on account of color, which is established in the Public Schools of Boston.

It is when we see this discrimination in this light, that we learn to appreciate its true character. The Brahmins and the Sudras, in India, from generation to generation, were kept apart. If a Sudra presumed to sit upon a Brahmin's carpet, he was punished with banishment. It is with a similar inhumanity, that the black child who goes to sit on the same benches at school with the white child, is banished, not from the country, but from the school. In both cases it is the triumph of Caste. But the offence is greater with us, because, unlike the Hindoos, we acknowledge that men are born equal.

So strong is my desire that the Court should feel the enormity of this system, thus legalized, not by the legislature, but by an inferior local board, that I shall here introduce an array of witnesses to the unchristian character of Caste, as it appears in India, where it has been most studied and discussed. As you join in detestation of this foul institution, you will learn, perhaps, to condemn its establishment among children in our Public Schools.

I borrow these authorities from the work to which I have already referred, of Mr. Roberts, *Caste opposed to Christianity*, published in London, 1847.

Bishop Heber, of Calcutta, characterizes Caste as follows:

"*It is a system which tends, more than any else the devil has yet invented, to destroy the feelings of general benevolence, and to make nine tenths of mankind the hopeless slaves of the remainder.*"

Bishop Wilson, also of Calcutta, the successor of Heber, says:

"The Gospel recognizes no such distinctions as those of castes, imposed by a heathen usage, bearing in some respects a supposed religious obligation, condemning those in the lower ranks to perpetual abasement, placing an immovable barrier against all general advance and improvement in society, cutting asunder the bonds of human fellowship on the one hand, and preventing those of Christian love on the other. Such distinctions, I say, the Gospel does not recognize. On the contrary, it teaches us that God 'hath made of one blood all the nations of men.'"

Bishop Corrie, of Madras, says:

"Thus Caste sets itself up as a judge of our Saviour himself. His

2*

command is, 'condescend to men of low estate. Esteem others better than yourself.' 'No,' says Caste, 'do not commune with low men; consider yourself of high estimation. Touch not, taste not, handle not.' Thus Caste condemns the Saviour."

Rev. Mr. Rhenius, a zealous and successful Missionary, says:

"I have found *Caste*, both in theory and practice, to be diametrically opposed to the Gospel, which inculcates love, humility, and union; whereas Caste teaches the contrary. It is a fact, in those entire congregations where Caste is allowed, the spirit of the Gospel does not enter; whereas in those from which it is excluded, we see the fruits of the Gospel spirit."

The Rev. C. Mault, also a Missionary, says:

"*Caste* must be entirely renounced; for it is a noxious plant, by the side of which the graces cannot grow; for facts demonstrate that where it has been allowed, Christianity has never flourished."

The Rev. John McKenny, a Wesleyan Missionary, says:

"I have been upwards of twelve years in India, and have directed much of my attention to the subject of *Caste*, and am fully of opinion that it is altogether contrary to the nature and principles of the Gospel of Christ, and therefore ought not to be admitted into the Christian Church."

The Rev. R. S. Hardy, a Wesleyan Missionary, and author of "Notices of the Holy Land," says:

"The principle of *Caste* I consider so much at variance with the spirit of the Gospel, as to render impossible, where its authority is acknowledged, the exercise of many of the most beautiful virtues of our holy religion."

Rev. D. J. Gogerly, of the same Society, says:

"I regard the distinction of *Caste*, both in its principles and operations, as directly opposed to vital godliness, and consequently inadmissible into the Church of Christ."

The Rev. W. Bridgnall, also of the same Society, says:

"I perfectly agree with a writer of respectable authority, in considering the institution of *Caste* as the most formidable engine that was ever invented for perpetuating the subjugation of men; so that, as a friend of humanity only, I should feel myself bound to protest against and oppose it; but in particular as a Christian, I deem it my obvious and imperative duty wholly to discountenance it, conceiving it to be utterly repugnant to all the principles and the whole spirit of Christianity. He who is prepared to support the system of Caste, is, in my judgment, neither a true friend of man, nor a consistent follower of Christ."

The Rev. S. Allen, of the same Society, says:

"During a residence of more than nine years in Ceylon, I have had many opportunities of witnessing the influence of *Caste* on the minds of the natives; and I firmly believe it is altogether opposed to the spirit of Christianity; and it appears to me that its utter and speedy extinction cannot but be desired by every minister of Christ."

The Rev. R. Stoup, of the same Society, says:

"From my own personal observation, during a four years' residence in Ceylon, I am decidedly of opinion that *Caste* is directly opposed to the spirit of Christianity, and, consequently, ought to be discouraged in every possible way."

The Rev. Joseph Roberts, author of the work on Caste, says:

"*We must, in every place, witness against it, and show that even government itself is nurturing a tremendous evil, that through its Heathen managers it is beguiled into a course which obstructs the progress of civilization*, which keeps in repulsion our kindlier feelings, which creates and nurses distinctions the most alien to all the cordialities of life; and which, more than any other thing, makes the distance so immense betwixt the governed and governors."

This is the testimony of a native of Hindostan, converted to Christianity:

"Caste is the stronghold of that principle of pride which makes a man think of himself more highly than he ought to think. Caste infuses itself into, and forms the very essence of pride itself."

Another native speaks as follows:

"I therefore regard Caste as opposed to the main scope, principles, and doctrines of Christianity; for, either Caste must be admitted to be true and of divine authority, or Christianity must be so admitted. If you admit Caste to be true, the whole fabric of Christianity must come down; for the nature of Caste and its associations destroy the first principles of Christianity. Caste makes distinctions among creatures where God has made none."

Another native expresses himself as follows:

"When God made man, his intention was not that they should be divided, and hate one another, and show contempt, and think more highly of themselves than others. Caste makes a man think that he is holier than another, and that he has some inherent virtue which another has not. It makes him despise all those that are lower than himself, in regard to Caste, which is not the design of God."

Another native uses this language:

"Yes, we regard Caste as part and parcel of idolatry, and of all heathen abominations, because it is in many ways contrary to God's word, and directly contrary to God himself."

In the words of these competent witnesses may be read, as in a mirror, the true character of the discrimination of color, which I now arraign before this Court.

It will be vain to say that this distinction, though seeming to be founded on color, is in reality founded on natural and physical peculiarities, which are independent of color. These peculiarities, whatever they may be, are peculiarities of race, and any discrimination on account of them constitutes the relation of Caste. Disguise it as you will, it is this hateful institution. But the words Caste and Equality are contradictory. They mutually exclude each other. Where Caste is, there cannot be Equality. Where Equality is, there cannot be Caste.

It is unquestionably true that there is a distinction between the Ethiopian and Caucasian races. Each has received from the hand of God certain characteristics of color and form. The two may not readily intermingle, although we are told by Homer that Jupiter

> —— "did not disdain to grace
> The feast of Ethiopia's blameless race."

One may be uninteresting or offensive to the other, precisely as different individuals of the same race and color may be uninteresting or offensive to each other. *But this distinction can furnish no ground for any discrimination before the law.*

We abjure nobility of all kinds ; but here is a nobility of the skin. We abjure all hereditary distinctions; but here is an hereditary distinction, founded not on the merit of the ancestor, but on his color. We abjure all privileges derived from birth ; but here is a privilege which depends solely on the accident, whether an ancestor is black or white. We abjure all inequality before the law; but here is an inequality which touches not an individual, but a race. We revolt at the relation of caste ; but here is a caste which is established under a Constitution, declaring that all men are born equal.

Condemning caste and inequality before the law, let us now consider more particularly the powers of the School Committee. Here it will be necessary to enter into some details.

VI. The Committee of Boston, charged with the superintendence of the Public Schools, have no *power* under the Constitution and laws of Massachusetts, to make any discrimination on account of color or race, among children in the Public Schools.

It has been already seen that this power is inconsistent with the Constitution and laws of Massachusetts, and with the adjudications of the Supreme Court. The stream cannot rise higher than the fountain-head, and if there be nothing in these elevated sources, from which this power can draw its sanction, it must be considered a nullity. Having already seen that there is nothing, I might here stop. But I wish to show the shallow origin to which this power has been traced.

Its advocates, unable to find it among the express powers conferred upon the School Committee, and forgetful of the Constitution, where "either it must live, or bear no life," place it among the implied or incidental powers. Let us consider this. The Revised Statutes (cap. 23, § 10) provide for the appointment of a School Committee "who shall have a *general charge and superintendence* of all the Public Schools" in their respective towns. Another section (§ 15) provides that the "Committee shall determine the number and qualifications of the scholars to be admitted into the school kept for the use of the whole town." These are all the clauses conferring powers on the Committee.

Surely from these no person will be so rash as to imply a power to defeat a cardinal principle of the Constitution. It is absurd to suppose that the Committee, in their general charge and superintendence of the schools, and in determining the number and qualifications of the scholars, may ingraft upon the schools a principle of inequality, unknown to the Constitution and laws, and in defiance of their spirit and letter. In the exercise of the general charge and superintendence, they cannot put colored children to personal inconvenience in attending school, greater than that of white children. Still further, they cannot brand a whole race with the stigma of inferiority and degradation, constituting them into a *caste*. They cannot in any way violate that fundamental right of all citizens, Equality before the law. To suppose that they can do this, would place the Committee above the Constitution. It would enable them, in the exercise of a brief and local authority, to draw a fatal circle, within which the Constitution cannot enter; nay, where the very Bill of Rights shall become a dead letter.

But the law, in entire harmony with the Constitution, says expressly what the Committee shall do. Besides having the general charge and superintendence, they shall "determine the *number* and the *qualifications* of the scholars to be admitted into the school;" thus, according to a familiar rule of interpretation, excluding other powers. *Mentio unius est exclusio alterius.* The power to determine the *number* is easily executed, and admits of no question. The power to determine the *qualifications*, though less simple, must be restrained to the qualifications of age, sex, and moral and intellectual fitness. The fact that a child is black, or that he is white, cannot of itself be considered a qualification, or a disqualification. It is not to the skin that we can look for the criterion of fitness for our Public Schools.

But it is said that the Committee are intrusted with a discretion, in the exercise of their power, and that, in this discretion, they may distribute, assign, and classify all children belonging to the schools of the city, *according to their best judgment*, making, if they think proper, a discrimination of color or race. Without questioning that they are intrusted with a discretion, it is outrageous to suppose that it can go to this extent. The Committee can have no discretion which is not in harmony with the Constitution and laws. Surely, they cannot, in their mere discretion, nullify a sacred and dear-bought principle of Human Rights, which is expressly guaranteed by the Constitution.

Still further, — and here I approach a more technical view of the subject, — it is an admitted principle, that the regulations and by-laws of municipal corporations must be *reasonable*, or they are inoperative and void. This has been recognized by this court in *Commonwealth* vs. *Worcester*, (4 Pick. R. 462,) and in *Vardine's Case*, (6 Pick. 187.) And in the *City of Boston* vs. *Jesse Shaw*, (1 Met. 130,) it was decided that a by-law of the city of Boston, prescribing a particular form of contribution towards the expenses of making the common sewers, was void for inequality and unreasonableness.

Assuming that this principle is applicable to the School Committee, their regulations and by-laws must be *reasonable*. Their discretion must be exercised in a reasonable manner. And this is not what the Committee, or any other body of men, may think reasonable, but what shall be reasonable in the eye of the law. It must be *legally reasonable*. It must be approved by the *reason* of the law.

And here we are brought once more, in another form, to the question of the validity of the discrimination on account of color by the School Committee of Boston. Is this *legally reasonable?* Is it reasonable, in the exercise of their discretion, to separate the descendants of the African race from the white children, in consequence of their descent merely? Passing over now those principles of the Constitution, and those provisions of the law, which of themselves would decide the question, constituting as they do *the highest reason*, but which have been already amply considered, look for a moment at the Educational system of Massachusetts, and it will be seen that practically no discrimination of color is made by law in any part of it. A descendant of the African race may be Governor of the Commonwealth, and as such, with the advice and consent of the Council, may select the *Board of Education*. As Lieutenant Governor, he may be, *ex officio*, a member of the Board. He may be the *Secretary* of the Board, with the duty imposed on him by law of seeing "that *all* children in this Commonwealth, who depend upon common schools for instruction, may have the best education which those schools can be made to impart." He may be a member of any School Committee, or a teacher in any public school of the State. As a legal voter, he can vote in the selection of any School Committee.

Thus, in every department connected with our Public Schools, throughout the whole hierarchy of their government, from the very head of the system down to the humblest usher in the humblest primary school, and, to the humblest voter, there is no distinction of color known to the law. It is when we reach the last stage of all, the children themselves, that the beautiful character of the system is changed to the deformity of Caste; as, in the picture of the ancient poet, what was a lovely woman above terminated in a vile, unsightly fish below. And all this is done by the Committee, with more than necromantic power, in the exercise of their mere discretion.

It is clear that the Committee may classify scholars, according to their age and sex; for the obvious reasons that these distinctions are inoffensive, and especially recognized as *legal* in the law relating to schools. (Revised Statutes, c. 23, § 63.) They may also classify scholars according to their moral aud intellectual qualifications, because such a power is necessary to the government of schools. But the Committee cannot assume, *a priori*, and without individual examination, that an *entire race* possess certain moral or intellectual qualities, which shall render it proper to place them all in a class by themselves. Such an exercise of the discretion with which the Committee are intrusted, must be unreasonable, and therefore illegal.

But it is said that the Committee, in thus classifying the children, have not violated any principle of Equality, inasmuch as they have provided a school with competent instructors for the colored children, where they have equal advantages of instruction with those enjoyed by the white children. It is said that in excluding the colored children from the Public Schools open to white children, they furnish them an equivalent.

To this there are several answers. I shall touch upon them only briefly, as the discussion, through which we have now travelled, substantially covers the whole ground.

1st. The separate school for colored children is not one of the schools established by the law relating to Public Schools. (Revised Statutes, chap. 23.) It is not a Public School. As such, it has no legal existence, and, therefore cannot be a legal equivalent. In addition to what has already been said bearing on this head, I will call the attention to one other aspect of it. We have already seen that it has been decided, that a town can execute its power to form a School District only by a geographical division of its territory—that there cannot be, what the Court have called a *personal* limitation of the District, and that *certain individuals* cannot be selected and set off by *themselves* into a District. (*Perry* v. *Dover*, 12 Pick. 213.) The admitted effect of these decisions is to render a separate school for colored children illegal and impossible in towns that have been divided into Districts. They are so regarded in Salem, Nantucket, New Bedford, and in other towns of this Commonwealth. The careful opinion of a member of this Court, who is not sitting in this case, given while at the bar, (Hon. Richard Fletcher,) and extensively published, has been considered as practically settling this point.

But there cannot be one law for the country, and one for Boston. It is true that Boston is not divided strictly into geographical districts. In this respect its position is anomalous. But if separate colored shools are illegal and impossible in the country, they must be illegal and impossible in Boston. It is absurd to suppose that this city, by failing to establish school Districts, and by regarding all its territory as a single district, should be able legally to establish a *Caste* school, which it otherwise could not do. Boston cannot do indirectly what the other towns cannot do directly.

This is the first answer to the suggestion of equivalents.

2d. The second is, that, in point of fact, it is not an equivalent. We have already seen that it is the occasion of inconveniences to the colored children and their parents, to which they would not be exposed, if they had access to the nearest public schools, besides inflicting upon them the stigma of Caste. Still further, and this consideration cannot be neglected, the matters taught in the two schools may be precisely the same; but a school, exclusively devoted to one class, must differ essentially, in its spirit and character, from that public school known to the law, where all classes meet together in equality. It is a mockery to call it an equivalent.

3d. But there is yet another answer. Admitting that it is an equivalent, still the colored children cannot be compelled to take it. Their rights are Equality before the law; nor can they be called upon to renounce one jot of this. They have an equal right with white children to the general public schools. A separate school, though well endowed, would not secure to them that precise Equality, which they would enjoy in the general public schools. The Jews in Rome are confined to a particular district, called the Ghetto. In Frankfort they are condemned to a separate quarter, known as the Jewish quarter. It is possible that the accommodations allotted to them are as good as they would be able to occupy, if left free to choose throughout Rome and Frankfort; but this compulsory segregation from the mass of citizens is of itself an *inequality* which we condemn with our whole souls. It is a vestige of ancient intolerance directed against a despised people. It is of the same character with the separate schools in Boston.

Thus much for the doctrine of equivalents, as a substitute for equality.

In determining that the Committee have no *power* to make a discrimination of color or race, we are strengthened by yet another consideration. If the power exists in the present case, it must exist in many others. It cannot be restrained to this alone. The Committee may distribute all the children into classes — merely according to their discretion. They may establish a separate school for the Irish or the Germans, where each may nurse an exclusive spirit of nationality alien to our institutions. They may separate Catholics from Protestants, or, pursuing their discretion still further, they may separate the different sects of Protestants, and establish one school for Unitarians, another for Presbyterians, another for Baptists, and another for Methodists. They may establish a separate school for the rich, that the delicate taste of this favored class may not be offended by the humble garments of the poor. They may exclude the children of mechanics from the Public Schools, and send them to separate schools by themselves. All this, and much more, can be

3

done by the exercise of the high-handed power which can make a discrimination on account of color or race. The grand fabric of our Public Schools, the pride of Massachusetts — where, at the feet of the teacher, innocent childhood should meet, unconscious of all distinctions of birth — where the Equality of the Constitution and of Christianity should be inculcated by constant precept and example — may be converted into a heathen system of proscription and Caste. We may then have many different schools, the representatives of as many different classes, opinions, and prejudices; but we shall look in vain for the true Public School of Massachusetts. Let it not be said that there is little danger that any Committee will exercise their discretion to this extent. They must not be entrusted with the power. In this is the only safety worthy of a free people.

VII. The Court will declare the by-law of the School Committee of Boston, making a discrimination of color among children of the Public Schools, to be unconstitutional and illegal, although there are no express words of prohibition in the constitution and laws.

It is hardly necessary to say any thing in support of this proposition. Slavery was abolished in Massachusetts, by virtue of the declaration of rights in our constitution, without any specific words of abolition in that instrument, or in any subsequent legislation. (*Commonwealth* vs. *Aves*, 18 Pick. R. 210.) The same words which are potent to destroy slavery, must be equally potent against any institution founded on inequality or *caste*. The case of *Boston* vs. *Shaw*, (1 Metcalf 130,) to which reference has been already made, where a by-law of the city was set aside as unequal and unreasonable, and therefore void, affords another example of the power which I now invoke the Court to exercise. But authorites are not needed. The words of the Constitution are plain, and it will be the duty of the Court to see that these are applied to the discrimination of color now in question.

In doing this, the Court might justly feel great delicacy, if they were called upon to revise a *law* of the legislature. But it is simply the action of a local committee that they are to overrule. They may also be encouraged by the fact, that it is only to the Schools of Boston that their decision can be applicable. The other towns throughout the Commonwealth have already voluntarily banished Caste. In removing it from the schools of Boston, the Court will bring them into much-desired harmony with the schools of other towns, and with the whole system of Public Schools in Massachusetts. I am unwilling to suppose that there can be any hesitation or doubt in coming to this conclusion. But if any should arise, there is a rule of interpretation which may be our guide. It is according to familiar practice that every interpretation is made always in favor of life or liberty. So here, the Court should incline in favor of Equality, that sacred right which is the companion of these other rights. In proportion to the importance of this right will the Court be solicitous to vindicate it and uphold it. And in proportion to the opposition which it encounters from the prejudices of society, will the Court brace themselves to this task. It has been pointedly remarked by Rousseau that "it is precisely because the force of things tends always to destroy Equality, that the force of legislation ought always to tend to maintain it." (*Contrat Social, liv.* 2, *chap.* 11.) In a similar spirit, and for the same reason, the Court should always tend to maintain it.

There are some other matters not strictly belonging to the juridical aspect of the case, and yet of importance to its clear comprehension, upon which I shall touch briefly before I close.

It is sometimes said in extenuation of the present system in Boston, that the separation of the white and black children was originally made at the request of the colored parents. This is substantially true. It appears from the interesting letter of Dr. Belknap, in reply to Judge Tucker's queries respecting slavery in Massachusetts, written at the close of the last century, (4 Mass. Hist. Coll. 207,) that at that time no discrimination on account of color was made in the public schools of Boston. "The same provision," he says, "is made by the public for the education of the children of the blacks, as for those of the whites. In this town, the Committee who superintend the free schools, have given in charge to the schoolmasters to receive and instruct black children as well as white." Dr. Belknap adds, however, that he has not heard of more than three or four who have taken advantage of this privilege, though the number of blacks in Boston probably exceeded one thousand. It is to be feared that the inhuman bigotry of Caste — sad relic of the servitude from which they had just escaped! — was at this time too strong to allow colored children a kindly welcome in the free schools, and that from timidity and ignorance, they shrank from taking their places on the same benches with the white children. Perhaps the prejudice against them was so inveterate that they could not venture to assert their rights. It appears that in 1800, a petition was presented to the School Committee from sixty-six colored persons, praying for the establishment of a school for their benefit. Private munificence came to the aid of the city, and the present system of separate schools was brought into being.

These facts are interesting in the history of the Boston Schools, but they cannot in any way affect the rights of the colored people, or the powers of the Committee. These rights and these powers stand on the Constitution and laws of the Commonwealth. Without adopting the suggestion of Jefferson, that one generation cannot by legislation bind its successors, all must agree that the assent of a few persons, nearly half a century ago — at a time when their rights were imperfectly understood — to an unconstitutional and illegal course, cannot alter the Constitution and the laws, and bind their descendants forever in the thrall of Caste. Nor can the Committee derive from this assent, or from any lapse of time, powers in derogation of the Constitution and of the Rights of Man.

It is clear that the sentiments of the colored people have now changed. The present case, and the deep interest which they manifest in it, thronging the court to hang on this discussion, attest the change. With increasing knowledge, they have learned to know their rights, and to feel the degradation to which they have been doomed. Their present effort is the token of a manly character which this court will cherish and respect. The spirit of Paul now revives in them, even as when he said, "I am a Roman citizen."

But it is said that these separate schools are for the mutual benefit of children of both colors, and of the Public Schools. In similar spirit, slavery is sometimes said to be for the mutual benefit of master and slave, and of the country where it exists. In one case there is a mistake as great as in the other. This is clear. Nothing unjust, nothing ungenerous can be for the benefit of any person, or any thing. Shortsighted mortals may hope to draw from some seeming selfish superiority, or from a gratified vanity of class, a permanent good; but even-handed justice rebukes these efforts, and with certain power redresses the wrong. The whites themselves are injured by the separation. Who can doubt this? With the law as their monitor, they are taught to regard a portion of the human family, children of God, created in his image, co-equals in his love, as a separate and degraded class — they are taught practically to deny that grand revelation of Christianity — the Brotherhood of Mankind. Their hearts, while yet tender with childhood, are necessarily hardened by this conduct, and their subsequent lives, perhaps, bear enduring testimony to this legalized uncharitableness. Nursed in the sentiment of Caste, receiving it with the earliest food of knowledge, they are unable to eradicate it from their natures, and then weakly and impiously charge upon their Heavenly Father the prejudice which they have derived from an unchristian school, and which they continue to embody and perpetuate in their institutions. Their characters are debased, and they become less fit for the magnanimous duties of a good citizen.

The Helots of Sparta were obliged to intoxicate themselves, that they might teach to the children of their masters the deformity of intemperance. In thus sacrificing one class to the other, both were degraded — the imperious Spartan and the abased Helot. But it is with a similar double-edged injustice that the School Committee of Boston have acted, in sacrificing the colored children to the prejudice or fancied advantage of the white.

It is fit that a child should be taught to shun wickedness, and, as he is yet plastic to receive impressions, to shun wicked men. Horace was right, when, speaking of a person morally wrong, false and unjust, he called him black, saying,

> —— hic niger est, hunc tu, Romane, caveto.

The Boston Committee adopt the warning, but apply it, not to those black in heart, but only black in skin. They forget the admonition addressed to the prophet: "But the Lord said unto Samuel, *look not on his countenance*, for the Lord seeth not as man seeth: for man looketh at the outward appearance, *but the Lord looketh at the heart.*" (1 Samuel, chap 16, v. 7.)

Who can say, that this does not injure the blacks? Theirs, in its best estate, is an unhappy lot. Shut out by a still lingering prejudice from many social advantages, a despised class, they feel this proscription from the Public Schools as a peculiar brand. Beyond this, it deprives them of those healthful animating influences which would come from a participation in the studies of their white brethren. It adds to their discouragements. It widens their separation from the rest of the community, and postpones that great day of reconciliation which is sure to come.

The whole system of public schools suffers also. It is a narrow perception of their high aim which teaches that they are merely to furnish to all the scholars an equal amount in knowledge, and that, therefore, provided all be taught, it is of little consequence where, and in what company it be done. The law contemplates not only that they shall all be taught, but that they shall be taught *all together*. They are not only to receive equal quantities of knowledge, but all are to receive it in the same way. All are to approach together the same common fountain ; nor can there be any exclusive source for any individual or any class. The school is the little world in which the child is trained for the larger world of life. It must, therefore, cherish and develop the virtues and the sympathies which are employed in the larger world. And since, according to our institutions, all classes meet, without distinction of color, in the performance of civil duties, so should they all meet, without distinction of color, in the school, beginning there those relations of equality which our Constitution and laws promise to all.

As the State receives strength from the unity and solidarity of its citizens, without distinction of class, so the school receives new strength from the unity and solidarity of all classes beneath its roof. In this way, the poor, the humble, and the neglected, share not only the companionship of their more favored brethren, but enjoy also the protection of their presence, in drawing towards the school a more watchful superintendence. A degraded or neglected class, if left to themselves, will become more degraded or neglected. To him that hath shall be given ; and the world, true to these words, turns from the poor and outcast to the rich and fortunate. It is the aim of our system of Public Schools, by the blending of all classes, to draw upon the whole school the attention which is too apt to be given only to the favored few, and thus secure to the poor their portion of the fruitful sunshine. But the colored children, placed apart by themselves, are deprived of this blessing.

Nothing is more clear than that the welfare of classes, as well as of individuals, is promoted by mutual acquaintance. The French and English, for a long time regarded as natural enemies, have at last, from a more intimate communion, found themselves to be natural friends. Prejudice is the child of ignorance. It is sure to prevail where people do not know each other. Society and intercourse are means established by Providence for human improvement. They remove antipathies, promote mutual adaptation and conciliation, and establish relations of reciprocal regard. Whoso sets up barriers to these, thwarts the ways of Providence, crosses the tendencies of human nature, and directly interferes with the laws of God.

May it please your Honors: Such are some of the things which it has occurred to me to say in this important cause. I have occupied much of your time, but I have not yet exhausted the topics. Still, which way soever we turn, we are brought back to one single proposition —*the equality of men before the law*. This stands as the mighty guardian of the rights of the colored children in this case. It is the constant, ever-present, tutelary genius of this Commonwealth, frowning upon every privilege of birth, upon every distinction of race, upon every institution of Caste. You cannot slight it, or avoid it. You cannot restrain it. It remains that you should welcome it. Do this, and your words will be a "charter and freehold of rejoicing" to a race which has earned by much suffering a title to much regard. Your judgment will become a sacred landmark, not in jurisprudence only, but in the history of Freedom, giving precious encouragement to all the weary and heavy-laden wayfarers in this great cause. Massachusetts will then, through you, have a fresh title to regard, and be once more, as in times past, an example to the whole land.

You have already banished slavery from this Commonwealth. I call upon you now to obliterate the last of its footprints, and to banish the last of the hateful spirits in its train, that can be reached by this Court. The law interfering to prohibit marriages between blacks and whites, has been abolished by the Legislature. The railroads, which, imitating the Boston schools, placed colored people in a car by themselves, have been compelled, under the influence of an awakened pnblic sentiment, to abandon this regulation, and to allow them to mingle with other travellers. It is only recently that I have read that his Excellency the present Governor of Massachusetts, took his seat in a car by the side of a negro. It is in the Caste schools of Boston that the prejudice of color has sought its final legal refuge. It is for you to drive it forth. You do well when you rebuke and correct individual offences; but it is a higher office far to rebuke and correct a vicious institution. Each individual is limited in his influence; but an institution has the influence of numbers organized by law. The charity of one man may counteract or remedy the uncharitableness of another, but no individual can counteract or remedy the uncharitableness of an established institution. Against it private benevolence is powerless. It is a monster which must be hunted down by the public, and by its constituted authorities. And such is the institution of Caste in the Public Schools of Boston, which now awaits its just condemnation from a just Court.

The civilization of the age joins in this appeal. It is well known that this prejudice of color is peculiar to our country. You have not forgotten that two youths of African blood only recently gained the highest honors in the college at Paris, and dined on the same day with the king of France, the descendant of St. Louis, at the palace of the Tuileries. And let me add, if I may refer to my own experience, that in Paris, I have sat for weeks, at the School of Law, on the same benches with colored persons, listening, like myself, to the learned lectures of Degerando and of Rossi — the last is the eminent minister who has unhappily fallen beneath the dagger of a Roman assassin; nor do I remember observing in the throng of sensitive young men by whom they were surrounded, any feeling towards them except of companionship and respect. In Italy, at the Convent of Pallazuola, on the shores of the Alban Lake, and on the site of the ancient Alba Longa, I have seen, for several days, a native of Abyssinia, only recently conducted from his torrid home, and ignorant of the language that was spoken about him, yet mingling with the Franciscan friars, whose guest and scholar he was, in delightful and affectionate familiarity. In these examples may be discerned the Christian spirit.

And, finally, it is this spirit that I invoke. Where this prevails, there is neither Jew nor Gentile, Greek nor barbarian, bond nor free; but all are alike. It is from this that we derive new and solemn assurances of the equality of mankind, as an ordinance of God. The bodies of men may be unequal in beauty or strength; these mortal cloaks of flesh may differ, as do these worldly garments; these intellectual faculties may vary, as do the opportunities of action and the advantages of position; but amidst all unessential differences there is an essential agreement and equality. Dives and Lazarus were equal in the sight of God. They must be equal in the sight of all just institutions.

But this is not all. The vaunted superiority of the white race imposes npon it corresponding duties. The faculties with which they are endowed, and the advantages which they possess, are to be exercised for the good of all. If the colored people are ignorant, degraded, and unhappy, then should they be the especial objects of your care. From the abundance of your possessions you must seek to remedy their lot. And this Court, which is as a parent to all the unfortunate children of the Commonwealth, will show itself most truly parental, when it reaches down, and, with the strong arm of the law, elevates, encourages, and protects its colored fellow-citizens.

www.ingramcontent.com/pod-product-compliance
Lightning Source LLC
LaVergne TN
LVHW091522200926
848483LV00002B/279

* 9 7 8 1 5 8 4 7 7 7 3 9 7 *